Linux

Programming

Kurt Wall, Mark Watson, and Mark Whitis

SAMS

201 West 103rd Street, Indianapolis, Indiana 46290

Unleashed

Linux Programming Unleashed

Copyright © 1999 by Sams

International Standard Book Number: 0-672-31607-2

Library of Congress Catalog Card Number: 98-89984

Printed in the United States of America

First Printing: August 1999

01   00   99   4   3   2   1

Trademarks

Warning and Disclaimer

EXECUTIVE EDITORS
Rosemarie Graham
Don Roche

ACQUISITIONS EDITOR
Angela Kozlowski

DEVELOPMENT EDITORS
Scott Warner
Heather Goodell

MANAGING EDITOR
Charlotte Clapp

PROJECT EDITOR
Carol Bowers

COPY EDITOR
Kim Cofer

INDEXER
Erika Millen

PROOFREADER
Cindy Fields

TECHNICAL EDITORS
Richard Blum
Michael Hamilton
Jason R. Wright

SOFTWARE DEVELOPMENT SPECIALIST
Dan Scherf

INTERIOR DESIGN
Gary Adair

COVER DESIGN
Aren Howell

LAYOUT TECHNICIANS
Brandon Allen
Tim Osborn
Staci Somers

ASSOCIATE PUBLISHER
Michael Stephens

Overview

Contents

PART II SYSTEM PROGRAMMING 135

9 I/O Routines 137

About the Authors

Kurt Wall

Kurt Wall is a Linux author, consultant, and enthusiast in Salt Lake City, Utah. He has used Linux since 1993. In addition to avoiding real work by writing books, he is Vice President of the Salt Lake Linux Users Group and President of the International Informix Users Group Linux SIG. When not sitting in front of a computer screen, he plays with his children, Ashleigh Rae, 10, and Zane Thomas, 8, drinks gourmet coffee, and takes afternoon naps everyday.

Mark Watson

Mark Watson is the author of 12 books on artificial intelligence, Java, and C++. He is a senior AI software engineer at Intelligenesis. Mr. Watson lives in Sedona, Arizona with his wife Carol and enjoys hiking with his dog, music, cooking, and playing chess and Go.

Mark Whitis

Mark Whitis is a self-educated consulting computer engineer. He has his own company, Free Electron Labs, and works for Digital By Design. He has worked at various research and development labs in the academic, corporate, and military sectors doing hardware and software development and has also done software development for the financial sector. He has been developing software for UNIX-compatible operating systems for more than ten years, including about four years with Linux. He does not do Windows. His work includes security consulting, system and network administration, and developing scientific applications, device drivers, client/server applications, simulations, diagnostic software, and online Web-based financial transaction systems. He is the author of a number of publicly available software packages. He currently lives in Charlottesville, VA. His Web site is at `http://www.freelabs.com/~whitis/unleashed/`.

Dedication

Kurt Wall

To Ashleigh Rae and Zane Thomas.

Mark Watson

For Julie, Josh, and Calvin.

Mark Whitis

To Troy Sorbello (1963-1998)

Acknowledgments

Kurt Wall

Now I get to blame all of the people responsible for this book. Thanks to Nick Wells, who got me involved in this through a seemingly innocuous post to a Caldera users' mailing list. I appreciate the folks on `comp.os.linux.development.*`, `comp.lang.c`, and `comp.unix.programmer` who answered an endless stream of questions. Thomas Dickey graciously reviewed the chapter on ncurses, catching silly errors.

My family, Dad, Rick, Amy, Morgan, Jennifer, Candy, Cindy, Chris, Marty, Ashleigh, Zane, and Patsy, were terrifically supportive when my life flew apart while writing this book. For continued cheerleading and moral support, I deeply appreciate Tricia, Joan, Steve, Allen, Tineke, Renee, and Lora. I now understand why authors always thank their editors (I never knew how many editors could be involved in a book!).

The folks at Macmillan made this thing succeed: Brian Gill and Ron Gallagher got me off to a great start. Scott Warner kept me busy adding material and helped me write my first book. Angela Kozlowski picked up a project in mid-stream and watched it age prematurely, so she deserves a special award for her patience in the face of perpetually slipping deadlines—thanks, Angela! I owe Gretchen Ganser dinner. Kim Cofer, Kelli Brooks, Katie Robinson, Jeff Riley, Heather Goodell, and Carol Bowers made sure it all looked nice and gently reminded me to get my artwork submitted. My technical editor, Robert Blum, caught many blunders; the rest of the warts and mistakes are mine alone.

This wouldn't have happened without Linus Torvalds and all of the other kernel hackers and the unknown bazillions of people who contribute to Linux in one way or another.

Thanks, finally, to God and all of the friends of Bill Wilson.

If I've left anyone out, drop me a line at `kwall@xmission.com` and I'll rectify the oversight.

Mark Whitis

Thanks to Keith Pomroy for proofreading one of the chapters.

Tell Us What You Think!

As the reader of this book, *you* are our most important critic and commentator. We value your opinion and want to know what we're doing right, what we could do better, what areas you'd like to see us publish in, and any other words of wisdom you're willing to pass our way.

As a Publisher for Sams, I welcome your comments. You can fax, email, or write me directly to let me know what you did or didn't like about this book—as well as what we can do to make our books stronger.

Please note that I cannot help you with technical problems related to the topic of this book, and that due to the high volume of mail I receive, I might not be able to reply to every message.

When you write, please be sure to include this book's title and author as well as your name and phone or fax number. I will carefully review your comments and share them with the author and editors who worked on the book.

Fax: (317) 581-4770
Email: mstephens@mcp.com
Mail: Michael Stephens
        Associate Publisher
        Sams
        201 West 103rd Street
        Indianapolis, IN 46290 USA

Introduction

Linux has always provided a rich programming environment, and it has only grown richer. Two new compilers, egcs and pgcs, joined the GNU project's gcc, the original Linux compiler. In fact, as this book went to press, the Free Software Foundation, custodians of the GNU project, announced that gcc would be maintained by the creators and maintainers of egcs. A huge variety of editors stand alongside the spartan and much-maligned vi and emacs' marvelous complexity. Driven largely by the Linux kernel, GNU's C library has evolved so dramatically that a new version, glibc (also known as libc6) has emerged as the standard C library. Linux hackers have honed the GNU project's always serviceable development suite into powerful tools. New widget sets have taken their place beside the old UNIX standbys. Lesstif is a free, source-compatible implementation of Motif 1.2; KDE, the K Desktop Environment based on the Qt class libraries from TrollTech, answers the desktop challenge posed by the X Consortium's CDE (Common Desktop Environment).

What This Book Will Do for You

In this book, we propose to show you how to program in, on, and for Linux. We'll focus almost exclusively on the C language because C is still Linux's lingua franca. After introducing you to some essential development tools, we dive right in to system programming, followed by a section on interprocess communication and network programming.

After a section devoted to programming Linux's user interface with both text-based and graphical tools (the X Window system), a section on specialized topics, including shell programming, security considerations, and using the GNU project's gdb debugger, rounds out the technical discussion. We close the book with three chapters on a topic normally disregarded in programming books: delivering your application to users. These final chapters show you how to use package management tools such as RPM, how to create useful documentation, and discuss licensing issues and options. If we've done our job correctly, you should be well prepared to participate in the great sociological and technological phenomenon called "Linux."

Intended Audience

Programmers familiar with other operating systems but new to Linux get a solid introduction to programming under Linux. We cover both the tools you will use and the environment in which you will be working.

Experienced UNIX programmers will find Linux's programming idioms very familiar. What we hope to accomplish for this group is to highlight the differences you will encounter. Maximum portability will be an important topic because Linux runs on an ever-growing variety of platforms: Intel i386, Sun Sparcs, Digital Alphas, MIPS processors, Power PCs, and Motorola 68000-based Macintosh computers.

Intermediate C programmers will also gain a lot from this book. In general, programming Linux is similar to programming any other UNIX-like system, so we start you on the path toward becoming an effective UNIX programmer and introduce you to the peculiarities of Linux/UNIX hacking.

Linux Programming Unleashed, Chapter by Chapter

This is not a C tutorial, but you will get a very quick refresher. You will need to be able to read and understand C code and understand common C idioms. Our selection of tools rarely strays from the toolbox available from the GNU project. The reason for this is simple: GNU software is standard equipment in every Linux distribution.

The first seven chapters cover setting up a development system and using the standard Linux development tools:

- gcc
- make
- autoconf
- diff
- patch
- RCS
- emacs

The next section introduces system programming topics. If you are a little rusty on the standard C library, Chapter 9 will clear the cobwebs. Chapter 10 covers Linux's file manipulation routines. Chapter 11 answers the question, "What is a process?" and shows you the system calls associated with processes and job control. We teach you how to get system information in Chapter 12, and then get on our editorial soapbox in Chapter 13 and lecture you about why error-checking is A Good Thing. Of course, we'll show you how to do it, too. Chapter 14 is devoted to the vagaries of memory management under Linux.

We spend four chapters on various approaches to interprocess communication using pipes, message queues, shared memory, and semaphores. Four more chapters show you how to write programs based on the TCP/IP network protocol. After a general introduction to creating and using programming libraries in Chapter 24 (including the transition from libc5 to libc6), we cover writing device drivers and kernel modules in Chapter 25, because considerable programming energy is spent providing kernel support for the latest whiz-bang hardware device or system services.

User interface programming takes up the next eight chapters. Two chapters cover character-mode programming; first the hard way with termcap and termios, and then the easier way using ncurses. After a quick introduction to X in Chapter 28, Chapter 29 focuses on using the Motif and Athena widget sets. Programming X using the GTK library is Chapter 30's subject, followed by Qt (the foundation of KDE) in Chapter 31, and Java programming in Chapter 32. For good measure, we also cover 3D graphics programming using OpenGL.

The next section of the book covers three special-purpose topics. Chapter 34 examines bash shell programming. We deal with security-related programming issues in Chapter 35, and devote Chapter 36 to debugging with gdb.

The book ends by showing you the final steps for turning your programming project over to the world. Chapter 37 introduces you to tar and the RPM package management tool. Documentation is essential, so we teach you how to write man pages and how to use some SGML-based documentation tools in Chapter 38. Chapter 39, finally, looks at the vital issue of software licensing.

4

The Linux
Programming Toolkit

PART

I

IN THIS PART

Overview

by Kurt Wall

CHAPTER 1

Linux has arrived, an astonishing feat accomplished in just over eight years! 1998 was the year Linux finally appeared on corporate America's radar screens.

The Little OS That Did

It began in March 1998, when Netscape announced that they would release the source code to their Communicator Internet suite under a modified version of the GNU project's General Public License (GPL). In July, two of the world's largest relational database vendors, Informix and Oracle, announced native Linux ports of their database products. In August, Intel and Netscape took minority stakes in Red Hat, makers of the market-leading Linux distribution. IBM, meanwhile, began beta testing a Linux port of DB/2. Corel Corporation finally ported their entire office suite to Linux and introduced a line of desktop computers based on Intel's StrongARM processor and a custom port of Linux. These developments only scratch the surface of the major commercial interest in Linux.

> **Note**
>
> As this book went to press, Red Hat filed for an initial public offering (IPO) of their stock. It is a delicious irony that a company that makes money on a free operating system is going to become a member of corporate America.

I would be remiss if I failed to mention Microsoft's famous (or infamous) Halloween documents. These were leaked internal memos that detailed Microsoft's analysis of the threat Linux posed to their market hegemony, particularly their server operating system, Windows NT, and discussed options for meeting the challenge Linux poses.

The Little OS That Will

As a server operating system, Linux has matured. It can be found running Web servers all over the world and provides file and print services in an increasing number of businesses. An independent think tank, IDG, reported that Linux installations grew at a rate of 212 percent during 1998, the highest growth rate of all server operating systems including Windows NT. Enterprise-level features, such as support for multi-processing and large file-system support, continue to mature, too. The 2.2 kernel now supports up to sixteen processors (up from four in the 2.0 series kernels). Clustering technology, known as Beowulf, enables Linux users to create systems of dozens or hundreds of inexpensive, commodity personal computers that, combined, crank out supercomputer level processing speed very inexpensively compared to the cost of, say, a Cray, an SGI, or a Sun.

On the desktop, too, Linux continues to mature. The KDE desktop provides a GUI that rivals Microsoft Windows for ease of use and configurability. Unlike Windows, however, KDE is a thin layer of eye candy on top of the operating system. The powerful command-line interface is never more than one click away. Indeed, as this book went to press, Caldera Systems released version 2.2 of OpenLinux, which contained a graphical, Windows-based installation procedure! No less than four office productivity suites exist or will soon be released: Applixware, Star Office, and Koffice, part of the KDE project, are in active use. Corel is finishing up work on their office suite, although WordPerfect 8 for Linux is already available. On top of the huge array of applications and utilities available for Linux, the emergence of office applications every bit as complete as Microsoft Office establishes Linux as a viable competitor to Windows on the desktop.

A Brief History of Linux

Linux began with this post to the Usenet newsgroup `comp.os.minix`, in August, 1991, written by a Finnish college student:

```
Hello everybody out there using minix-
I'm doing a (free) operating system (just a hobby, won't be
big and professional like gnu) for 386(486) AT clones.
```

That student, of course, was Linus Torvalds and the "hobby" of which he wrote grew to what is known today as Linux. Version 1.0 of the kernel was released on March 14, 1994. Version 2.2, the current stable kernel release, was officially released on January 25, 1999. Torvalds wrote Linux because he wanted a UNIX-like operating system that would run on his 386. Working from MINIX, Linux was born.

Linux and UNIX

Officially and strictly speaking, Linux is not UNIX. UNIX is a registered trademark, and using the term involves meeting a long list of requirements and paying a sizable amount of money to be certified. Linux is a UNIX clone, a work-alike. All of the kernel code was written from scratch by Linus Torvalds and other kernel hackers. Many programs that run under Linux were also written from scratch, but many, many more are simply ports of software from other operating systems, especially UNIX and UNIX-like operating systems.

More than anything else, Linux is a POSIX operating system. POSIX is a family of standards developed by the Institute of Electrical and Electronic Engineers (IEEE) that define a portable operating system interface. Indeed, what makes Linux such a high quality UNIX clone is Linux's adherence to POSIX standards.

Programming Linux

As Linux continues to mature, the need for people who can program for it will grow. Whether you are a just learning to program or are an experienced programmer new to Linux, the array of tools and techniques can be overwhelming. Just deciding where to begin can be difficult. This book is designed for you. It introduces you to the tools and techniques commonly used in Linux programming. We sincerely hope that what this book contains gives you a solid foundation in the practical matters of programming. By the time you finish this book, you should be thoroughly prepared to hack Linux.

Why Linux Programming?

Why do people program on and for Linux? The number of answers to that question is probably as high as the number of people programming on and for Linux. I think, though, that these answers fall into several general categories.

First, it is fun—this is why I do it. Second, it is free (think beer *and* speech). Third, it is open. There are no hidden interfaces, no undocumented functions or APIs (application programming interfaces), and if you do not like the way something works, you have access to the source code to fix it.

Finally, and I consider this the most important reason, Linux programmers are part of a special community. At one level, everyone needs to belong to something, to identify with something. This is as true of Windows programmers as it is of Linux programmers, or people who join churches, clubs, and athletic teams. At another, more fundamental level, the barriers to entry in this community are based on ability, skill, and talent, not money, looks, or who you know. Linus Torvalds, for example, is rarely persuaded to change the kernel based on rational arguments. Rather, working code persuades him (he often says "Show me the code.").

I am not supposing or proposing that Linux is a meritocracy. Rather, one's standing in the community is based on meeting a communal need, whether it is hacking code, writing documentation, or helping newcomers. It just so happens, though, that doing any of these things requires skill and ability, as well as the desire to do them. As you participate in and become a member of Linux's programming community, we hope, too, that you will discover that it is fun and meaningful as well. I think it is. In the final analysis, Linux is about community and sharing as much as it is about making computers do what you want.

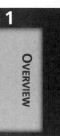

Summary

This chapter briefly recounted Linux's history, took a whirlwind tour of the state of Linux and Linux programming today, and made some reasonable predictions about the future of Linux. In addition, it examined Linux's relationship to UNIX and took a brief, philosophical look at why you might find Linux programming appealing.

Setting Up a Development System

by Mark Whitis

CHAPTER 2

Hardware Selection

This section is, of necessity, somewhat subjective. Choice of a system depends largely on the developer's individual needs and preferences. This section should be used in conjunction with the Hardware Compatibility HOWTO, as well as the more specialized HOWTO documents. The latest version is online at `http://metalab.unc.edu/LDP/HOWTO/Hardware-HOWTO.html`; if you do not have Net access, you will find a copy on the accompanying CD-ROM or in `/usr/doc/HOWTO` on most Linux systems (if you have one available). The Hardware HOWTO often lists specific devices that are, or are not, supported, or refers you to documents that do list them. This section will not try to list specific supported devices (the list would be way too long and would go out of date very rapidly) except where I want to share specific observations about a certain device based on my own research or experience.

Internet access is strongly recommended as a prerequisite to buying and installing a Linux system. The latest versions of the HOWTO documents can be found on the Net at Linux Online (`http://www.linux.org/`) in the Support section. The Projects section has many useful links to major development projects, including projects to support various classes of hardware devices. If you do not have Net access, the HOWTO documents are on the accompanying Red Hat Linux CDs (Disc 1 of 2) in the `/doc/HOWTO` directory.

Considerations for Selecting Hardware

I will try to give you an idea of what is really needed and how to get a good bang for your buck rather than how to get the most supercharged system available. You may have economic constraints or you may prefer to have two or more inexpensive systems instead of one expensive unit. There are many reasons for having two systems, some of which include the following:

- To have a separate router/firewall
- To have a separate "crash and burn" system
- To have a system that boots one or more other operating systems
- To have a separate, clean system to test installation programs or packages (RPM or Debian) if you are preparing a package for distribution
- To have a separate untrusted system for guests if you are doing sensitive work
- To have at least one Linux box to act as a server that runs Linux 24 hours a day

Most of the millions of lines of Linux code were probably largely developed on systems that are slower than the economy systems being sold today. Excessive CPU power can be detrimental on a development station because it may exacerbate the tendency of some developers to write inefficient code. If, however, you have the need and economic resources to purchase a system more powerful than I suggest here, more power to you (please pardon the pun). A good developer's time is very valuable, and the extra power can pay for itself if it saves even a small percentage of your time. The suggestions in this chapter will be oriented toward a low- to mid-range development workstation. You can adjust them upward or downward as appropriate. I do not want you to be discouraged from supporting the Linux platform, in addition to any others you may currently support, by economic considerations.

Basic development activities, using the tools described in this book, are not likely to demand really fast CPUs; however, other applications the developer may be using, or even developing, may put additional demands on the CPU and memory. Editing and compiling C programs does not require much computing horsepower, particularly since make normally limits the amount of code that has to be recompiled at any given time. Compiling C++ programs, particularly huge ones, can consume large amounts of computing horsepower. Multimedia applications demand more computing power than edit and compile cycles. The commercial Office suites also tend to require large amounts of memory. If you like to use tracepoints to monitor variables by continuous single stepping, that could heavily consume CPU cycles.

Some people will recommend that you choose a system that will meet your needs for the next two or three years. This may not be a wise idea. The cost of the computing power and features you will need a year from now will probably drop to the point where it may be more cost effective for you to buy what you need today, and wait until next year to buy what you need then. If you do not replace your system outright, you may want to upgrade it piecemeal as time passes; if that is the case, you don't want to buy a system with proprietary components.

Processor/Motherboard

One of the most important features of a motherboard is its physical form factor, or its size and shape and the locations of key features. Many manufacturers, particularly major brands, use proprietary form factors, which should be avoided. If you buy a machine that has a proprietary motherboard and you need to replace it due to a repair or upgrade, you will find your selection limited (or non-existent) and overpriced. Some manufacturers undoubtedly use these proprietary designs to lower their manufacturing cost by eliminating cables for serial, parallel, and other I/O ports; others may have more sinister motives.

The older AT (or baby AT) form factor motherboards are interchangeable, but have very little printed circuit board real estate along the back edge of the machine on which to mount connectors. The case only has holes to accommodate the keyboard and maybe a mouse connector. The newer ATX standard has many advantages. Although an ATX motherboard is approximately the same size and shape as a baby AT motherboard (both are about the same size as a sheet of 8-1/2"×11" writing paper), the ATX design rotates the dimensions so the long edge is against the back of the machine. An ATX case has a standard rectangular cutout that accommodates metal inserts, which have cutouts that match the connectors on a particular motherboard. The large cutout is large enough to easily accommodate the following using stacked connectors:

- 2 serial ports
- 1 parallel port
- keyboard port
- mouse port
- 2 USB ports
- VGA connector
- audio connectors

Also, ATX moves the CPU and memory where they will not interfere with full-length I/O cards, although some manufacturers still mount some internal connectors where they will interfere. Many case manufacturers have retooled. More information about the ATX form factor can be found at `http://www.teleport.com/~atx/`. Figure 2.1 illustrates the physical difference between AT and ATX form factors.

FIGURE 2.1
AT versus ATX motherboard form factors.

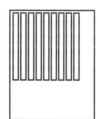
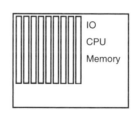

AT   ATX

Onboard I/O

A typical Pentium or higher motherboard will have two serial, one parallel, one keyboard, one mouse, IDE, and floppy ports onboard; all of which are likely to work fine with Linux. It may have additional ports onboard that will have to be evaluated for compatibility, including USB, SCSI, Ethernet, Audio, or Video.

Processor

For the purposes of this section, I will assume you are using an Intel or compatible processor. The use of such commodity hardware is likely to result in a lower-cost system with a wider range of software available. There are a number of other options available, including Alpha and Sparc architectures. Visit http://www.linux.org/ if you are interested in support for other processor architectures.

Cyrix and AMD make Pentium compatible processors. There have been some compatibility problems with Cyrix and AMD processors, but these have been resolved. I favor Socket 7 motherboards, which allow you use Intel, Cyrix, and AMD processors interchangeably. There are also some other companies that make Pentium compatible processors that will probably work with Linux but have been less thoroughly tested. IDT markets the Centaur C6, a Pentium compatible processor, under the unfortunate name "Winchip," which apparently will run Linux, but I don't see the Linux community lining up to buy these chips. IBM used to make and sell the Cyrix chips under its own name in exchange for the use of IBM's fabrication plant; these may be regarded simply as Cyrix chips for compatibility purposes. Future IBM x86 processors will apparently be based on a different core. The Pentium II, Pentium III, Xeon, and Celeron chips will simply be regarded as Pentium compatible CPUs.

There have been some very inexpensive systems made recently that use the Cyrix MediaGX processor. These systems integrate the CPU, cache, Video, Audio, motherboard chipset, and I/O onto two chips. The downside is that you cannot replace the MediaGX with another brand of processor and that the video system uses system memory for video. This practice slightly reduces the available system memory and uses processor/memory bandwidth for screen refresh, which results in a system that is about a third slower than you would expect based on the processor speed. The advantages are the lower cost and the fact that all Media GX systems are basically the same from a software point of view. Therefore, if you can get one Media GX system to work, all others should work. Video support for the Media GX is provided by SuSE (go to http://www.suse.de/XSuSE/XSuSE_E.html for more info) and there is a MediaGX video driver in the KGI. Audio support has not been developed at the time of this writing, although it may be available by the time this book is published.

My primary development machines have been running Linux for a couple years on Cyrix P150+ processors (equivalent to a 150MHz Pentium) and upgrading the processor is still among the least of my priorities. Given current processor prices, you will probably want to shoot for about twice that speed, adjusting up or down based on your budget and availability.

The Linux community seems to be waiting with interest to see the processor being developed by Transmeta, the company that hired Linus Torvalds and some other Linux gurus (including my friend, Jeff Uphoff). The speculation, which is at least partially corroborated by the text of a patent issued to the company, is that this processor will have an architecture that is optimized for emulating other processors by using software translators and a hardware translation cache. It is suspected that this chip may be a very good platform for running Linux. Linux might even be the native OS supported on this chip under which other operating systems and processor architectures are emulated.

BIOS

For a basic workstation, any of the major BIOS brands (AWARD, AMIBIOS, or Phoenix) may suffice. The AMI BIOS has some problems that complicate the use of I/O cards that have a PCI-to-PCI bridge such as the Adaptec Quartet 4 port ethernet cards. The AWARD BIOS gives the user more control than does AMIBIOS or Phoenix. A flash BIOS, which allows the user to download BIOS upgrades, is desirable and is standard on most modern systems. Older 386 and 486 systems tend not to have a flash BIOS and may also have the following problems:

- An older BIOS that may not be Y2K compliant
- May not support larger disk drives
- May not support booting off of removable media

Memory

64MB is reasonable for a typical development system. If you are not trying to run X windows, you may be able to get by with only 8MB for a special purpose machine (such as a crash and burn system for debugging device drivers). Kernel compile times are about the same (less than 1.5 minutes) with 32MB or 64MB (although they can be much longer on a system with 8MB). If you want to run multimedia applications (such as a Web browser), particularly at the same time you are compiling, expect the performance to suffer a bit if you only have 32MB. Likewise, if you are developing applications that consume lots of memory, you may need more RAM. This page was written on a system with 32MB of RAM but one of the other authors' primary development system has ten times that amount of memory to support Artificial Intelligence work.

Enclosure and Power Supply

Select an enclosure that matches your motherboard form factor and has sufficient drive bays and wattage to accommodate your needs. Many case manufacturers have retooled their AT form factor cases to accommodate the ATX motherboard; if you order an AT case, you may receive a newer ATX design with an I/O shield that has cutouts for AT keyboard and mouse ports. For most applications, Mini-Tower, Mid-Tower, or Full-Tower cases are likely to be the preferred choices. For some applications you may want server or rack mount designs.

> **NOTE**
>
> The power supply connectors are different for AT and ATX power supplies.

If you are building a mission-critical system, be aware that some power supplies will not restore power to the system after a power outage. You may also be interested in a mini-redundant power supply; these are slightly larger than a normal ATX or PS/2 power supply but some high end cases, particularly rack mount and server cases, are designed to accommodate either a mini-redundant or a regular ATX or PS/2 supply.

User Interaction Hardware: Video, Sound, Keyboard, and Mouse

The devices described in this section are the primary means of interacting with the user. Support for video cards and monitors is largely a function of adequate information being available from the manufacturer or other sources. Monitors usually require only a handful of specifications to be entered in response to the Xconfigurator program, but support for a video card often requires detailed programming information and for someone to write a new driver or modify an existing one. Sound cards require documentation and programming support, like video cards, but speakers need only be suitable for use with the sound card itself.

Video Card

If you only need a text mode console, most VGA video adapters will work fine. If you need graphics support, you will need a VGA adapter that is supported by Xfree86, SVGAlib, vesafb, and/or KGI.

Xfree86 is a free open-source implementation of the X Windowing System, which is an open-standard-based windowing system that provides display access to graphical applications running on the same machine or over a network. Xfree86 support is generally

necessary and sufficient for a development workstation. For more information, visit
http://www.xfree86.org/. For drivers for certain new devices, check out XFcom
(formerly XSuSE) at http://www.suse.de/XSuSE/.

SVGAlib is a library for displaying full screen graphics on the console. It is primarily
used for a few games and image viewing applications, most of which have X Windowing
System versions or equivalents. Unfortunately, SVGAlib applications need root privileges to access the video hardware so they are normally installed suid, which creates
security problems.

GGI, which stands for Generic Graphics Interface, tries to solve the problems of needing
root access, resolve conflicts between concurrent SVGAlib and X servers, and provide a
common API for writing applications to run under both X and SVGAlib. A part of GGI,
called KGI, provides low-level access to the framebuffer. GGI has also been ported to a
variety of other platforms so it provides a way of writing portable graphics applications,
although these applications are apparently limited to a single window paradigm.
Documentation is very sparse. This package shows future promise as the common low-
level interface for X servers and SVGAlib and a programming interface for real-time
action games.

OpenGL (and its predecessor GL) has long been the de facto standard for 3D modeling.
OpenGL provides an open API but not an open reference implementation. Mesa provides
an open source (GPL) implementation of an API very similar to OpenGL that runs under
Linux and many other platforms. Hardware acceleration is available for 3Dfx
Voodoo–based cards. For more information on Mesa, visit http://www.mesa3d.org/.
Metrolink provides a licensed OpenGL implementation as a commercial product; visit
http://www.metrolink.com/opengl/ for more information. Frame buffer devices pro-
vide an abstraction for access to the video buffer across different processor architectures.
The Framebuffer HOWTO, at http://www.tahallah.demon.co.uk/programming/
HOWTO-framebuffer-1.0pre3.html, provides more information. Vesafb provides frame
buffer device support for VESA 2.0 video cards on Intel platforms. Unfortunately, the
VESA specification appears to be a broken specification that only works when the CPU
is in real mode instead of protected mode, so switching video modes requires switching
the CPU out of protected mode to run the real mode VESA VGA BIOS code. Such
shenanigans may be common in the MS Windows world and may contribute to the insta-
bility for which that operating system is famous. KGIcon allows the use of KGI supported devices as framebuffer devices.

> **Tip**
>
> Some companies offer commercial X servers for Linux and other UNIX-compatible operating systems. Among them are Accelerated-X (http://www.xigraphics.com/) and Metro-X (http://www.mctrolink.com/).

AGP (*Accelerated Graphics Port*) provides the processor with a connection to video memory that is about four times the speed of the PCI bus and provides the video accelerator with faster access to texture maps stored in system memory. Some AGP graphics cards are supported under Linux.

> **Tip**
>
> To determine which video cards and monitors are supported under Red Hat run /usr/X11/bin/Xconfigurator --help as root on an existing system.

You will probably want at least 4MB of video memory to support 1280×1024 at 16bpp (2.6MB). You will need 8MB to support 1600×1200 at 32bpp. Some 3D games might benefit from extra memory for texture maps or other features if they are able to use the extra memory. The X server will use some extra memory for a font cache and to expand bitmap. If you want to configure a virtual screen that is larger than the physical screen (the physical screen can scroll around the virtual screen when you move the cursor to the edge) be sure to get enough memory to support the desired virtual screen size. The FVWM window manager will create a virtual desktop that is by default four times the virtual screen size, and will switch screens if you move the cursor to the edge of the screen and leave it there momentarily; instead of using extra video memory, this feature is implemented by redrawing the whole screen. The X server may use system memory (not video memory) for "backing store" to allow it to redraw partially hidden windows faster when they are revealed. If you use high resolution or pixel depth (16bpp or 32bpp) screens, be aware that backing store will place additional demands on system memory.

There are some distinct advantages to installing a video card that supports large resolution and pixel depth in your Linux system. If you intend to make good use of the X server, this can be invaluable. Since Linux can easily handle many different processes at once, you will want to have enough screen real estate to view multiple windows. A video card that can support 1280×1024 resolution will satisfy this nicely. The other advantage to a good video card is the pixel depth. Not only do the newer window managers run more smoothly with the better pixel depth, it is also very useful if you want to use your system for graphics work. Your monitor also has to be able to support the resolution of your video card—otherwise you could not take full advantage of the capabilities your system offers. (The following section discusses monitor selection in more detail.) It is very important that you check the specifications of your hardware when deciding which video card/monitor combination to use so that the two will work well together. Also, it is always important to check out the hardware compatibility lists for Linux.

Monitor

Almost any monitor that is compatible with your video card will work under Linux if you can obtain the specifications, particularly the vertical and horizontal refresh rates or ranges supported and the video bandwidth. Note that bigger is not always better. What matters is how many pixels you can put on the screen without sacrificing quality. I prefer the 17″ monitor I have on my development machine at one office to the very expensive 20″ workstation monitor that sits next to it. I prefer many 15″ monitors to their 17″ counterparts. If you have trouble focusing up close or want to sit very far away from your monitor, you may need a large monitor, but otherwise a quality smaller monitor closer to your head may give you equal or better quality at a lower price.

As discussed in the preceding section, the monitor and video card selections are very closely related. It is good to test your monitor selection for clarity. One of the main contributing factors to the clarity of a monitor is the dot pitch—the smaller the spacing between pixels, the better. However, this can boost the price of a monitor. The other issue here, again, is related to the video card. One monitor tested with different video cards can have quite different results. A video card aimed more for business use (such as a Matrox Millenium G200) will often produce a crisper image than a video card that is intended for game use (such as Diamond V550). This is because some cards are optimized for good 2D, 3D, or crisp text, but are not optimized for all three.

I recommend running your monitor at as close to 60Hz as you can even if it can run at 70Hz or higher. In some cases a monitor may look better at 70Hz, particularly if you are hyped up on massive doses of caffeine and your monitor has short persistence phosphors, but I find that usually it looks better at 60Hz. The reason for this is the ubiquitous 60Hz interference from power lines, transformers, and other sources. Not only can this interference be picked up in the cables and video circuitry but it also affects the electron beams in the monitor's cathode ray tube (CRT) directly. Shielding is possible but expensive and is not likely to be found in computer video monitors. If your image is visibly waving back and forth, this is likely to be your problem. If the beat frequency (the difference between the two frequencies) between the 60hz interference and the refresh rate is close to zero, the effect will slow and become imperceptible. But if the beat frequency is larger you will have instabilities that will be either very perceptible or more subtle but irritating. So a beat frequency of 0.1Hz (60Hz versus 60.1Hz) is likely to be fine but a beat frequency of 10Hz (60Hz versus 70Hz) is likely to be very annoying.

Some countries use a frequency other than 60Hz for their power grid; in those countries, you would need to match the refresh rate to the local power line frequency to avoid beat frequency problems. Incidentally, some monitors deliberately make the image wander around the screen slightly at a very slow rate to prevent burn-in; as long as this is very slow, it is imperceptible (your own head movements are likely to be far greater).

The video configuration in Linux gives you much latitude in how you want to set up your hardware. It is important to remember to have your settings within the specified ranges for your hardware. Pushing the limits can result in poor performance or even the destruction of your hardware.

Sound Cards

Linux supports a variety of sound cards, particularly Sound Blaster compatible (but not all sound cards that claim to be compatible are—some use software assisted emulation), older ESS chip-based cards (688 and 1688), Microsoft Sound System– based cards, and many Crystal (Cirrus Logic) based cards. Consult the Hardware Compatibility HOWTO document, Four Front Technologies Web site (at `http://www.4front-tech.com/`), or the Linux kernel sources (browsable on the Net at `http://metalab.unc.edu/linux-source/`) for more information. Four Front Technologies sells a package that includes sound drivers for many cards that are not supported by the drivers shipped with the kernel. Most newer sound cards seem to be PnP devices. Support for PnP cards is available using the ISAPnP utilities mentioned above or the Four Front drivers.

Keyboard and Mouse

USB keyboards and mice are not recommended at this time; see "USB and Firewire (IEEE 1394)," later in this chapter for more details. Normal keyboards that connect to a standard AT or PS/2 style keyboard port should work fine, although the unusual extra features on some keyboards may not work. Trackball, Glidepoint, and Trackpad pointing devices that are built in to the keyboard normally have a separate connection to a serial or PS/2 mouse port and may be regarded as separate mouse devices when considering software support issues. Normal PS/2 and serial mice are supported, including those that speak Microsoft, Mouse Systems, or Logitech protocols. Mouse support is provided by the gpm program and/or the X server. Many other pointing devices, including trackballs, Glidepoints, and Trackpads will work if they emulate a normal mouse by speaking the same communications protocol; some special features of newer trackpads, such as pen input and special handling of boarder areas, may not work. Many X applications require a three-button mouse, but gpm and the X server can be configured to emulate the extra middle button by chording both buttons on a two-button mouse.

Communication Devices, Ports, and Buses

This section contains information on various devices that provide communications channels. These channels can be used to communicate with other computers and with internal or external peripherals.

The high-speed buses that connect expansion cards to the processor are included here. Neither the ISA bus nor the PCI bus will be covered in detail, although ISA Plug and Play devices and PCMCIA cards will have their own subsection since there are some special considerations. Plain ISA and PCI cards should work fine as long as there is a driver that supports that specific card. Most IDE controllers will work; for other IDE devices, see "Storage Devices," later in this chapter. Devices that connect to a parallel (printer) port are discussed in their separate categories.

Modems

Most modems, with the exception of brain-dead winmodem types, modems that use the proprietary Rockwell Protocol Interface (RPI), or modems that depend on a software component for their functionality will work fine with Linux. Be aware, however, that there is a real difference between the more expensive professional models and the cheaper consumer grade models. Almost any modem will perform well on good quality phone lines, but on poor quality lines the distinction will become significant. That is why you will see people on the Net who are both pleased and extremely dissatisfied with the same inexpensive modems. It requires much more sophisticated firmware and several times as much processing power to resurrect data from a poor quality connection as it does to recover data from a good connection.

Serious developers are likely to want a dedicated Internet connection to their small office or to their home. Some more expensive modems can operate in leased line mode. This allows you to create a dedicated (permanent) 33.6Kbps leased line Internet connection over a unconditioned 2 wire (1 pair) dry loop. This can be handy if ISDN and xDSL are not available in your area. A *dry loop* is a leased telephone line with no line voltage, ringing signal, or dial tone that permanently connects two locations. It is sometimes referred to as a "burglar alarm pair." These lines are very inexpensive for short distances. The average person working in a telco business office has no clue what these terms mean. Expect to pay $200 or more for a modem that supports this feature.

Your chances of finding a pair of leased line modems that will work at 56K are not very good since only modems with a digital phone line interface are likely to have the software to handle 56K answer mode. I used a pair of leased line capable modems for a couple years over a wire distance of two or three miles, at a cost of about $15 per month; more information on how to set this up is available on my Web site (`http://www.freelabs.com/~whitis/unleashed/`). It is also possible to run xDSL over a relatively short distance dry loop (I now use MVL, a variant of DSL which works better on longer lines and provides 768Kbps, on the same dry loop) even though xDSL is intended to be used with one of the modems located in the central office; this costs about $13,000 for 16 lines and the equipment is not, as far as I know, readily available in configurations that are economically viable for a small number of lines. If you can spread the capital cost over many lines, xDSL can be very economical compared to ISDN or T1 lines. In my example, a dry loop costs $15 per month and provides a 768K connection versus $75 per month for an ISDN line or $400 per month for a T1 line (these charges are for local loop only and do not include IP access).

If you want to support incoming (dial-in or answer mode) 56K connections, you will need a modem with a digital phone line interface. Normally, ISPs use expensive modem racks that have a T1 line interface for this purpose, which is only economically viable if you are supporting dozens of lines. You might be able to find a modem that functions both as an ordinary modem and as an ISDN terminal adapter and can produce 56K answer mode modulation over an ISDN line.

If you want to set up a voice mail or interactive voice response (IVR) system, you will probably want a modem that is capable of voice operation and is compatible with the vgetty software. Check the Mgetty+Sendfax with Vgetty Extensions (FAQ) document for voice modem recommendations.

For fax operation, your software choices include HylaFAX, mgetty+sendfax, and efax. A modem that supports Class 2.0 FAX operation is preferred over one that can only do Class 1 fax. Class 1 modems require the host computer to handle part of the real time fax protocol processing and will malfunction if your host is too busy to respond quickly. Class 2.0 modems do their own dirty work. Class 2 modems conform to an earlier version of the Class 2.0 specification, which was never actually released as a standard.

The mgetty+sendfax and efax packages come with Red Hat 5.2. HylaFAX comes on the Red Hat Powertools CD. All three packages can be downloaded off the Internet. HylaFAX is more complicated to set up but is better for an enterprise fax server since it is server based and there are clients available for Linux, Microsoft Windows, MacOS, and other platforms. Table 2.1 summarizes fax capabilities.

TABLE 2.1   FAX SUPPORT

	Class 1	*Class 2*	*Class 2.0*
HylaFax	Yes	Yes	Yes
Sendfax	No	Yes	Yes
Efax	Yes	Yes	Support untested

Network Interface Cards

The Tulip chips are considered by many to be the best choice for a PCI-based ethernet card on a Linux system. They are fairly inexpensive, fast, reliable, and documented. There have been some problems lately, however. There have been frequent, often slightly incompatible, revisions to newer chips. The older chips, which were a safer choice, were discontinued (this is being reversed) and the line was sold to competitor Intel, and there was a shortage of cards. Many of these problems may be corrected by the time this book is released, however; check the Tulip mailing list archives for more details. If you need multiple ethernet interfaces in a single machine, Adaptec Quartet cards provide four Tulip-based ethernet ports on a single machine. One of my Web pages gives more information on using the Quartets under Linux.

For an inexpensive ISA 10MB/s card, the cheap NE2000 clones usually work well. These cards tic up the CPU a bit more than more sophisticated designs when transferring data, but are capable of operating at full wire speed. (Don't expect full wire speed on a single TCP connection such as an FTP transfer, however—you will need several simultaneous connections to get that bandwidth.)

3Com supports their ethernet boards under Linux, and Crystal (Cirrus Logic) offers Linux drivers for their ethernet controller chips. Most WAN card manufacturers also seem to provide Linux Drivers. SDL, Emerging Technologies, and Sangoma provide Linux drivers.

SCSI

Linux supports most SCSI controllers, including many RAID controllers, host adapters, almost all SCSI disks, most SCSI tape drives, and many SCSI scanners. Some parallel port–based host adapters are notable exceptions. Advansys supports their SCSI adapters under Linux; the drivers that ship with the kernel were provided by Advansys. The Iomega Jaz Jet PCI SCSI controller, which may be available at local retailers, is actually an Advansys controller and is a good value. It is a good idea not to mix disk drives and slow devices such as tape drives or scanners on the same SCSI bus unless the controller (and its driver) and all of the slow devices on the bus support a feature known as "disconnect-reconnect"; it is rather annoying to have your entire system hang up for 30 seconds or more while the tape rewinds or the scanner carriage returns. The SCSI HOWTO has more information on disconnect-reconnect.

> **Warning**
>
> Beware of cheap SCSI controllers, particularly those that do not use interrupts. In my limited experience with boards of this type, they often did not work at all or would cause the system to hang for several seconds at a time. This may be due to bugs in the driver for the generic NCR5380/NCR53c400 driver although in at least on case the card was defective. The SCSI controllers I had trouble with came bundled with scanners or were built-in on certain sound boards.

USB and Firewire (IEEE 1394)

USB and Firewire support are being developed. USB support is provided by a package called UUSBD. It is apparently possible to use a USB mouse if you have a supported USB controller (although you will need to download and install the code before you can run X) but keyboards don't work at the time of this writing. It is probably too early to plan on using either of these on a development system except for tinkering. Links to these projects are on `linux.org` under projects.

Serial Cards (Including Multiport)

Standard PC serial ports are supported, on or off the motherboard. Very old designs that do not have a 16550A or compatible UART are not recommended but those are likely to be pretty scarce these days.

Most intelligent multiport serial cards are supported, often with direct support from the manufacturer. Cyclades, Equinox, Digi, and GTEK are some of the companies that support their multiport boards under Linux. Equinox also makes an interesting variation on a serial port multiplexor that supports 16 ISA Modems (or cards that look exactly like modems to the computer) in an external chassis.

Most dumb multiport serial cards also work, but beware of trying to put too many dumb ports in a system unless the system and/or the ports are lightly loaded. Byterunner (http://www.byterunner.com) supports their inexpensive 2/4/8 port cards under Linux; unlike many dumb multiport boards, these are highly configurable, can optionally share interrupts, and support all the usual handshaking signals.

IRDA

Linux support for IRDA (Infrared Data Association) devices is fairly new, so be prepared for some rough edges. The Linux 2.2 Kernel is supposed to have included IRDA support, but you will still need the irda-utils even after you upgrade to 2.2. The IRDA project's home page is at http://www.cs.uit.no/linux-irda/. I suspect that most laptops that support 115Kbps SIR IRDA may emulate a serial port and won't be too hard to get working.

PCMCIA Cards

Linux PCMCIA support has been around for a while and is pretty stable. A driver will need to exist for the particular device being used. If a device you need to use is not listed in the /etc/pcmcia/config file supplied on the install disks for your Linux distribution, installation could be difficult.

ISA Plug and Play

Although some kernel patches exist for Plug and Play, support for PnP under Linux is usually provided using the ISAPnP utilities. These utilities do not operate automatically, as you might expect for plug and play support. The good news is that this eliminates the unpredictable, varying behavior of what is often referred to more accurately as "Plug and Pray." You run one utility, pnpdump, to create a sample configuration file with the various configurations possible for each piece of PnP hardware, and then you manually edit that file to select a particular configuration. Red Hat also ships a utility called sndconfig, which is used to interactively configure some PnP sound cards. Avoid PnP for devices that are needed to boot the system, such as disk controllers and network cards (for machines that boot off the network).

Storage Devices

Linux supports various storage devices commonly used throughout the consumer computer market. These include most hard disk drives and removable media such as Zip, CD-ROM/DVD, and tape drives.

Hard Disk

Virtually all IDE and SCSI disk drives are supported under Linux. Linux even supports some older ST506 and ESDI controllers. PCMCIA drives are supported. Many software and hardware RAID (Reliable Array of Independent Disks) configurations are supported to provide speed, fault tolerance, and/or very large amounts of disk storage. A full Red Hat 5.2 with Powertools and Gnome sampler installation and all source RPMs installed, but not unpacked, will take about 2.5GB of disk space.

Removable Disks

More recent versions of the Linux kernel support removable media including Jaz, LS120, Zip, and other drives. Using these drives as boot devices can be somewhat problematic. My attempts to use a Jaz disk as a boot device were thwarted by the fact that the drive apparently destroyed the boot disk about once a month; this may have just been a defective drive. Problems with the LS120 included being unable to use an LS120 disk as a swap device because of incompatible sector sizes. Also be warned that there are software problems in writing a boot disk on removable media on one computer and using it to boot another living at a separate device address (for example, an LS120 might be the third IDE device on your development system but the first on the system to be booted).

CD-ROM/DVD

Almost all CD-ROM drives will work for data, including IDE, SCSI, and even many older proprietary interface drives. Some parallel port drives also work, particularly the Microsolutions Backpack drives (which can be used to install more recent versions of Red Hat). Some drives will have trouble being used as an audio CD player due to a lack of standardization of those functions; even fewer will be able to retrieve "red book" audio (reading the digital audio data directly off of an audio CD into the computer for duplication, processing, or transmission).

Linux has support for many CD changers. The eject command has an option to select individual disks from a changer. I found that this worked fine on a NEC 4x4 changer. Recording of CD-R and CD-RW disks is done using the cdrecord program. The UNIX

CD-Writer compatibility list at `http://www.guug.de:8080/cgi-bin/winni/lsc.pl` gives more information on which devices are compatible. Be warned that due to limitations of the CD-R drives, writing CDs is best done on very lightly loaded or dedicated machines; even a brief interruption in the data stream will destroy data, and deleting a very large file will cause even fast machines to hiccup momentarily. There are GUI front ends for burning CD's available, including BurnIT and X-CD-Roast.

Tape Backup

A wide variety of tape backup devices are supported under Linux, as well as various other types of removable media. Linux has drivers for SCSI, ATAPI (IDE), QIC, floppy, and some parallel port interfaces. I prefer to use SCSI DAT (Digital Audio Tape) drives exclusively even though they can cost as much as a cheap PC. I have used Conner Autochanger DAT drives, and although I could not randomly select a tape in the changer under Linux, each time I ejected a tape the next tape would automatically be loaded. Other autochangers might perform differently.

> **Warning**
>
> I caution against the use of compression on any tape device; read errors are common and a single error will cause the entire remaining portion of the tape to be unreadable.

External Peripherals

The devices in this section are optional peripherals that are normally installed outside the system unit. From a software perspective, the drivers for these devices usually run in user space instead of kernel space.

Printer

Printer support under Linux is primarily provided by the Ghostscript package (`http://www.ghostscript.com/`). Support for Canon printers is poor, probably due to Canon's failure to make technical documentation available. Canon has refused to make documentation available for the BJC-5000 and BJC-7000 lines (which are their only inkjet printers that support resolutions suitable for good quality photographic printing). Most HP printers (and printers that emulate HP printers) are supported, due to HP making documentation available, except for their PPA-based inkjet printers, for which they will not release the documentation.

The Canon BJC-5000, Canon BJC-7000, and HP PPA based printers are all partially brain dead printers that apparently do not have any onboard fonts and rely on the host computer to do all rasterization. This would not be a problem for Linux systems (except for the unusual case of a real time system log printer) since Ghostscript is normally used as a rasterizer and the onboard fonts and other features are not used. Some printers may be truly brain dead and not have any onboard CPU; these might use the parallel port in a very nonstandard manner to implement low level control over the printer hardware. The HP720, HP820Cse, and HP1000 are PPA based printers. Partial support, in the form of a ppmtopba conversion utility, is available for some PPA printers based on reverse engineering. Some Lexmark inkjet printers might be supported, but many others are Windows-only printers. I have used a Lexmark Optra R+ laser printer with an Ethernet interface with Linux. It supports the LPD protocol so it is simply set up as a remote LPD device.

A Linux box can act as a print server for Windows clients or act as a client for a Windows printer by using the Samba package. A Linux box can act as a print server for MacOS clients by using the Netatalk package. A Linux box running the ncpfs package can apparently serve as a print server for NetWare 2.x, 3.x, or 4.x clients with bindery access enabled, or print to a remote Netware printer. HP printers with JetDirect ethernet interfaces support LPD and will work as remote printers under Linux.

Ghostscript can run on almost every operating system that runs on hardware with enough resources to function as a rasterizer. A single ghostscript driver (or PBM translator) is sufficient to support a printer on virtually every computer, including those running every UNIX-compatible operating system, MacOS, OS/2, and Windows 3.1, Windows 95, Windows 98, Windows NT, and many others. Ghostscript can coexist with, replace, or already is the native printing rasterizer (if any) on these operating systems and can integrate with the queuing system on almost all of these. Ghostscript can produce PBM (Portable BitMap) files. The use of a PBM translator can avoid various copyright issues since it does not have to be linked into a GPLed program. Therefore, the failure of printer manufacturers to provide Ghostscript drivers or PBM translators is reprehensible.

> **TIP**
>
> More detailed information on printing under Linux can be found in the Linux Printing HOWTO.

Scanners

Support for scanners is a bit sparse, although close to 100 different models from a couple dozen manufacturers are supported by the SANE package; manufacturers who not only fail to provide drivers themselves but also withhold documentation are culpable for this state of affairs.

There have been various projects to support individual or multiple scanners under Linux. These have been eclipsed by the SANE package(http://www.mostang.com/sane/) which, no doubt, benefited from its predecessors. The name is a play on, and a potshot at, TWAIN, which passes for a standard in the Microsoft world. In TWAIN, the driver itself paints the dialog box that appears when you request a scan. This is not a "sane" way of doing things. It interferes with non-interactive scanning (such as from a command line, Web cgi, or production scanning applications), interferes with network sharing of a device, and interferes with making drivers that are portable across many platforms. SANE is able to do all of these things.

In SANE, the driver has a list of attributes that can be controlled, and the application sets those attributes (painting a dialog box or parsing arguments as necessary). SANE has been ported to a variety of platforms including about 18 different flavors of UNIX and OS/2. SANE provides a level of abstraction for the low level SCSI interfaces, and abstractions are being worked on for a few other OS specific features (such as fork()) which interfere with portability to some platforms. SANE has not been ported to the Windows and MAC platforms, although there is no reason this can't be done. Some have questioned the need to do this because the manufacturers ship drivers for these operating systems with most scanners. However, once SANE has been ported to these operating systems and a TWAIN to SANE shim has been written, there will be no legitimate reason for anyone to ever write another TWAIN driver again as long as the port and shim are distributed under license agreements that allow scanner manufacturers to distribute the software with their products.

Digital Cameras

There are programs to handle many hand-held digital cameras which will run Linux. Cameras that support compact flash or floppy disk storage of standard JPEG images should also work using those media to transfer the image data. A new application called gPhoto (http://gphoto.fix.no/gphoto/) supports about ten different brands of digital cameras. Some digital cameras may also be supported under the SANE library.

There are software drivers for a variety of Frame Grabbers, TV tuners, and the popular Quickcam cameras available on the Net. Consult the relevant section of the Hardware Compatibility HOWTO for links to these resources.

Home Automation

I will give brief mention to a few gadgets that can be used to control the real world. There are a couple of programs to control the X10 CM11A (usually sold as part of the CK11A kit) computer interface module. The X10 system sends carrier current signals over your household or office power lines to control plug in, wall switch, or outlet modules that switch individual devices on or off. The X10 carrier current protocol is patented but well documented; the documentation for the computer interface is available on the Net. The CM11A may be superseded by the CM14A by the time this gets into print.

Nirvis systems makes a product called the Slink-e, which is an RS-232 device used to control stereo and video gear using infrared, Control-S, S-link/Control-A1, and Control-A protocols. It can also receive signals from infrared remotes; this would allow you to write applications that record and replay remote control signals or respond to remote controls (handy for presentations). There is no Linux driver available yet, as far as I know, but the documentation is available from their Web site at `http://www.nirvis.com/`. Among other things, this unit can control a Sony 200 disk CD changer and not just queue up CD's, but actually poll the track position and the disk serial number (other brands of CD players apparently cannot do this); the company supplies a Windows based CD player application that works with the Internet CD Database. The folks at Nirvus have already done the reverse engineering on some of the protocols.

Complete Systems

A number of companies specialize in preinstalled Linux systems. VA Research and Linux Hardware Solutions are two popular examples; consult the hardware section at `Linux.org` for a much more complete list of these vendors.

Corel Computer Corp has versions of their Netwinder systems (which use StrongARM CPUs) with Linux preinstalled. These are fairly inexpensive systems aimed at the thin client and Web server market. Cobalt Networks offers the Qube, a Linux-based server appliance in a compact package that uses a MIPS processor. It appears that SGI will be supporting Linux on some of their MIPS based workstations.

A few of the major PC brands have recently announced that they will be shipping some of their servers or workstations reconfigured with Linux, including Dell and Hewlett Packard. Compaq is now marketing a number of their systems to the Linux community, although apparently they are not available with Linux preinstalled. IBM has announced that they will be supporting Linux but it will apparently be up to the authorized reseller to preinstall it. Rumor has it that many other PC brands will announce preinstalled Linux systems by the time this book is printed.

Laptops

Support for laptops is a bit tricky because laptops have short development cycles, often use very new semiconductors, and the manufacturers rarely provide technical documentation. In spite of this, there is information on the Net concerning using Linux on approximately 300 laptop models. Consult the Hardware Compatibility HOWTO document for links to pages that have the latest information on support for specific laptop models and features.

Note

Linux supports a number of electronic pocket organizers. 3Com's PalmPilot is the most popular and best supported.

Linux supports Automatic Power Management (APM). There can be problems with suspend/resume features not working correctly; there can be problems with the graphics modes being restored properly for X (you may have better luck if you switch to a text console before suspending) and you may need a DOS partition for the suspend to disk feature to work. Some laptops do not allow you to have the floppy and the CD-ROM present simultaneously, which can make installation tricky (although most newer models probably support booting off of CD-ROM).

Installation

Installation of Red Hat Linux, which is included on 2 CD's in the back of this book, is covered in The Official Red Hat Linux Installation Guide, which is available in HTML on the Net at `ftp://ftp.reddat.com/reddat/reddat-5.2/i386/doc/rhmanual/` or on the enclosed Red Hat Linux CD-ROM in the directory `/doc/rhmanual/`. If you wish to use a different distribution, consult the documentation that came with that distribution.

I recommend making a complete log of the machine configuration, the choices made during the installation, and all commands needed to install any packages you may have installed later. This is a nuisance at first but becomes very valuable when you want to install a second system, upgrade, or reinstall a system after a crash or a security compromise. Copy this log file offline and/or offsite or make printouts periodically. I normally log this information in a file called `/root/captains-log` as executable shell commands, as shown in Listing 2.1. If I edit a file, I record the diffs as a "here document" (see the bash man page) piped into "patch." One very important thing to log is where you down-loaded code from; I do this as an ncftp or lynx -source command.

LISTING 2.1 SAMPLE CAPTAINS LOG

```
# First, lets introduce some of the commands we will
# be using.  The commands marked with "***" will be
# covered in detail in later chapters.  Refer to the
# bash man page or the man page
#
# cat           - copies its input to its output
# diff          - compares two files   ***
# patch         - applies the changes in a diff ***
# ncftp         - ftp client program
# lynx          - text mode web broswer
# tar           - pack and unpack tar archives
# cd            - change current directory
# make          - drives the compilation process ***
# echo          - display its arguments
# echo hello, world      - says "hello world"
#
# These are some examples of shell magic, see the bash
# man page for more details:
# #             - marks a comment line
# foo=bar       - set variable foo equal to bar
# export FOO=bar  - similar, but subprocesses will inherit value
# echo $(foo)   - substitute $(foo) into
# xxx ¦ yyy     - pipe output of command xxx into command yyy
# xxx >yyy      - redirect the output of command xxx to file yyy
# xxx >>yyy     - same, but append to file yyy
# xxx <yyy      - redirect input of command xxx from file yyy
# xxx\          - Line continuation character "\"
# yyy           - .. continuation of above line, i.e  xxxyyy
# xxx <<\...EOF...     - "here document" - runs the program xxx
# line1               - .. taking input from the following
# line2               - .. lines in the script up to the line
# ...EOF...           - .. which begins with "...EOF...";



###
### Gnozzle
###
# This is a sample captains-log entry to install
# a ficticious package called gnozzle

# datestamp produced using "date" command:
# Mon Feb 22 21:39:26 EST 1999
```

continues

LISTING 2.1 CONTINUED

```
# download it
cd /dist
ncftp -r -D ftp://ftp.gnozzle.com/pub/gnozzle-0.63.tar.gz
# or...
#lynx -source http://www.gnozzle.com/gnozzle-0.63.tar.gz \
   >gnozzle-0.63.tar.gz

# Here we unpack the tarball, after first checking
# the directory structure
cd /usr/local/src
tar ztvf gnozzle-0.63.tar.gz
tar zxvf gnozzle-0.63.tar.gz
cd gnozzle-0.63/

# Here we create a permanent record of changes we
# made using a text editor as a patch command.  In this
# case, we changed the values of CC and PREFIX in the
# file Makefile.  The patch has one hunk which spans
# lines 1 through 7.
#
# the following patch was made like this:
#    cp Makefile Makefile.orig
#    emacs Makefile
#    diff -u Makefile.orig Makefile
# beware of mangled whitespace (especially tabs) when
# cutting and pasting.
patch Makefile <<\...END.OF.PATCH...
--- Makefile.orig      Mon Feb 22 21:12:41 1999
+++ Makefile     Mon Feb 22 21:13:14 1999
@@ -1,7 +1,7 @@
 VERSION=0.63
-CC=pcc
+CC=gcc
 CFLAGS=-g
-PREFIX=/usr
+PREFIX=/usr/local
 BIN=$(PREFIX)/bin
 LIB=$(PREFIX)/bin
 MAN=$(PREFIX)/man/man1
...END.OF.PATCH...

# Here we build the program and install it
make clean
make
make -n install          # see what it would do first
make install

# Here we create a new file with a couple lines of text
cat >/etc/gnozzle.conf <<\...EOF...
```

```
gnozzlelib=/usr/local/lib/gnozzle
allow
...EOF...

# Here, we append a couple lines to the magic file,
# which is used by the some commands to
# guess the type of a file, to add the characteristic
# signature of a gnozzle data file.
cat >>/usr/share/magic <<\...EOF...
# gnozzle
0       long        FEDCBA98          Gnozzle data file
...EOF...


###
### Here are some more commands which are useful to create
### a logfile of everything which was done, from which you
### can extract pertinent details for the captains log.
### Their effect may not be apparent unless you have a
### Linux box up and running and try them.
# # the script command runs another shell with all output
# # redirected to a file.  Not to be confused with a
# # "shell script" which is a sequence of commands
# to be executed by the shell.  Do not include "script"
# commands in a "shell script".
# script install_101.log
# PS4=+++
# set -v -x
# ...
# # do diffs so they can easily be extracted from log:
# diff -u Makefile.orig Makefile ¦ sed -e "s/^/+++ /"
# ...
# ^D          (control-D - end script, and shell )
# fgrep +++ install_101.log ¦ sed -e s/^+++//
```

If you purchased a machine that has Windows 98 preinstalled, you will want to boot Windows and examine the resource settings (IO, IRQ, and DMA) for all installed hardware. This information can be very valuable during the Linux installation. Doing so may, however, prevent you from refusing the terms of the Windows 98 License Agreement and returning it for a refund.

After you have completed the installation program, you may need to do some other things that are outlined in the Post Installation section of the Red Hat Manual. There are two steps that I normally do first, however. First, I reorganize the disk layout to undo the concessions I made to accommodate the limitations of the Red Hat install program. You may or may not wish to do this; there are problems with the install program during upgrades as well. Second, I use a script to disable all unwanted daemons (I tell the install program to enable all daemons to preserve the information about the starting sequence). Disabling unnecessary services is one of the most important and simplest things you can do to secure your computer from attack. The scripts to accomplish both of these tasks are available on my Linux Web pages.

After installation, you may wish to upgrade or install software packages that Red Hat does not include because of export controls or licensing reasons. You may wish to upgrade Netscape to a version that supports 128-bit encryption. You may want to install Adobe Acrobat Reader software to handle PDF files. You may wish to install SSH to permit secure, encrypted remote logins, file transfers, and remote program execution; use of SSH may require a license fee for some commercial uses. You may wish to upgrade the Web server to support SSL. And you probably will want to download any upgrades, particularly security related ones, from the Red Hat FTP site.

Next, you may wish to install any additional applications you know you will need. To locate RPM versions of these applications, consult the RPM database at `http://rufus.w3.org/`. If you are concerned about security, you may not want to install any binary packages except from a few well trusted sources; instead, inspect and then install from source RPM's or the original source tarballs (archives created with the `tar` program).

Summary

Careful selection of hardware will simplify installation. As more manufacturers are forced by the marketplace to act more responsibly by releasing documentation for their products or, better yet, direct support for Linux, this will be less of an issue. Also, as the distributions become more robust the support for more types and makes of hardware are being supported. As a general rule of thumb it is always a good practice to confirm support for your hardware using the sources available on the Internet, the HOWTO's, and the SuSE's hardware database. This can save you many headaches and frustrations during your install. When installing your development system, it is your turn to further document your system, lest you find yourself reinventing the wheel. Once you have one system up and running, you may wish to experiment with hardware that has less stable support.

Using GNU cc

by Kurt Wall

GNU cc (gcc) is the GNU project's compiler suite. It compiles programs written in C, C++, or Objective C. gcc also compiles Fortran (under the auspices of g77). Front-ends for Pascal, Modula-3, Ada 9X, and other languages are in various stages of development. Because gcc is the cornerstone of almost all Linux development, I will discuss it in some depth. The examples in this chapter (indeed, throughout the book unless noted otherwise), are based on gcc version 2.7.2.3.

Features of GNU cc

gcc gives the programmer extensive control over the compilation process. The compilation process includes up to four stages:

- Preprocessing
- Compilation Proper
- Assembly
- Linking

You can stop the process after any of these stages to examine the compiler's output at that stage. gcc can also handle the various C dialects, such as ANSI C or traditional (Kernighan and Ritchie) C. As noted above, gcc happily compiles C++ and Objective C. You can control the amount and type of debugging information, if any, to embed in the resulting binary and, like most compilers, gcc can also perform code optimization. gcc allows you to mix debugging information and optimization. I strongly discourage doing so, however, because optimized code is hard to debug: Static variables may vanish or loops may be unrolled, so that the optimized program does not correspond line-for-line with the original source code.

gcc includes over 30 individual warnings and three "catch-all" warning levels. gcc is also a cross-compiler, so you can develop code on one processor architecture that will be run on another. Finally, gcc sports a long list of extensions to C and C++. Most of these extensions enhance performance, assist the compiler's efforts at code optimization, or make your job as a programmer easier. The price is portability, however. I will mention some of the most common extensions because you will encounter them in the kernel header files, but I suggest you avoid them in your own code.

A Short Tutorial

Before beginning an in-depth look at gcc, a short example will help you start using gcc productively right away. For the purposes of this example, we will use the program in Listing 3.1.

Listing 3.1   Canonical Program to Demonstrate gcc Usage

```
1   /*
2    * Listing 3.1
3    * hello.c - Canonical "Hello, world!" program 4   4   */
5   #include <stdio.h>
6
7   int main(void)
8   {
9       fprintf(stdout, "Hello, Linux programming world!\n");
10      return 0;
11  }
```

To compile and run this program, type

```
$ gcc hello.c -o hello
$ ./hello
Hello, Linux programming world!
```

The first command tells gcc to compile and link the source file hello.c, creating an executable, specified using the -o argument, hello. The second command executes the program, resulting in the output on the third line.

A lot took place under the hood that you did not see. gcc first ran hello.c through the preprocessor, cpp, to expand any macros and insert the contents of #included files. Next, it compiled the preprocessed source code to object code. Finally, the linker, ld, created the hello binary.

You can re-create these steps manually, stepping through the compilation process. To tell gcc to stop compilation after preprocessing, use gcc's -E option:

```
$ gcc -E hello.c -o hello.cpp
```

Examine hello.cpp and you can see the contents of stdio.h have indeed been inserted into the file, along with other preprocessing tokens. The next step is to compile hello.cpp to object code. Use gcc's -c option to accomplish this:

```
$ gcc -x cpp-output -c hello.cpp -o hello.o
```

In this case, you do not need to specify the name of the output file because the compiler creates an object filename by replacing .c with .o. The -x option tells gcc to begin compilation at the indicated step, in this case, with preprocessed source code.

How does gcc know how to deal with a particular kind of file? It relies upon file extensions to determine how to process a file correctly. The most common extensions and their interpretation are listed in Table 3.1.

TABLE 3.1   HOW gcc INTERPRETS FILENAME EXTENSIONS

Extension	Type
.c	C language source code
.C, .cc	C++ language source code
.i	Preprocessed C source code
.ii	Preprocessed C++ source code
.S, .s	Assembly language source code
.o	Compiled object code
.a, .so	Compiled library code

Linking the object file, finally, creates a binary:

```
$ gcc hello.o -o hello
```

Hopefully, you will see that it is far simpler to use the "abbreviated" syntax we used above, gcc hello.c -o hello. I illustrated the step-by-step example to demonstrate that you can stop and start compilation at any step, should the need arise. One situation in which you would want to step through compilation is when you are creating libraries. In this case, you only want to create object files, so the final link step is unnecessary. Another circumstance in which you would want to walk through the compilation process is when an #included file introduces conflicts with your own code or perhaps with another #included file. Being able to step through the process will make it clearer which file is introducing the conflict.

Most C programs consist of multiple source files, so each source file must be compiled to object code before the final link step. This requirement is easily met. Suppose, for example, you are working on killerapp.c, which uses code from helper.c. To compile killerapp.c, use the following command:

```
$ gcc killerapp.c helper.c -o killerapp
```

gcc goes through the same preprocess-compile-link steps as before, this time creating object files for each source file before creating the binary, killerapp. Typing long commands like this does become tedious. In Chapter 4, "Project Management Using GNU make," we will see how to solve this problem. The next section will begin introducing you to the multitude of gcc's command-line options.

Common Command-line Options

The list of command-line options gcc accepts runs to several pages, so we will only look at the most common ones in Table 3.2.

TABLE 3.2   gcc COMMAND-LINE OPTIONS

Option	Description
-o FILE	Specify the output filename; not necessary when compiling to object code. If FILE is not specified, the default name is a.out.
-c	Compile without linking.
-DFOO=BAR	Define a preprocessor macro named FOO with a value of BAR on the command-line.
-IDIRNAME	Prepend DIRNAME to the list of directories searched for include files.
-LDIRNAME	Prepend DIRNAME to the list of directories searched for library files. By default, gcc links against shared libraries.
-static	Link against static libraries.
-lFOO	Link against libFOO.
-g	Include standard debugging information in the binary.
-ggdb	Include lots of debugging information in the binary that only the GNU debugger, gdb, can understand.
-O	Optimize the compiled code.
-ON	Specify an optimization level N, 0<=N<= 3.
-ansi	Support the ANSI/ISO C standard, turning off GNU extensions that conflict with the standard (this option does not guarantee ANSI-compliant code).
-pedantic	Emit all warnings required by the ANSI/ISO C standard.
-pedantic-errors	Emit all errors required by the ANSI/ISO C standard.
-traditional	Support the Kernighan and Ritchie C language syntax (such as the old-style function definition syntax). If you don't understand what this means, don't worry about it.
-w	Suppress all warning messages. In my opinion, using this switch is a very bad idea!

continues

3

USING GNU CC

TABLE 3.2   CONTINUED

Option	Description
-Wall	Emit all generally useful warnings that gcc can provide. Specific warnings can also be flagged using -W{warning}.
-werror	Convert all warnings into errors, which will stop the compilation.
-MM	Output a make-compatible dependency list.
-v	Show the commands used in each step of compilation.

We have already seen how -c works, but -o needs a bit more discussion. -o FILE tells gcc to place output in the file FILE regardless of the output being produced. If you do not specify -o, the defaults for an input file named FILE.SUFFIX are to put an executable in a.out, object code in FILE.o, and assembler code in FILE.s. Preprocessor output goes to standard output.

Library and Include Files

If you have library or include files in non-standard locations, the -L{DIRNAME} and -I{DIRNAME} options allow you to specify these locations and to insure that they are searched before the standard locations. For example, if you store custom include files in /usr/local/include/killerapp, then in order for gcc to find them, your gcc invocation would be something like

```
$ gcc someapp.c -I/usr/local/include/killerapp
```

Similarly, suppose you are testing a new programming library, libnew.so (.so is the normal extension for shared libraries— more on this subject in Chapter 24, "Using Libraries") currently stored in /home/fred/lib, before installing it as a standard system library. Suppose also that the header files are stored in /home/fred/include. Accordingly, to link against libnew.so and to help gcc find the header files, your gcc command line should resemble the following:

```
$gcc myapp.c -L/home/fred/lib -I/home/fred/include -lnew
```

The -l option tells the linker to pull in object code from the specified library. In this example, I wanted to link against libnew.so. A long-standing UNIX convention is that libraries are named lib{something}, and gcc, like most compilers, relies on this convention. If you fail to use the -l option when linking against libraries, the link step will fail and gcc will complain about undefined references to "function_name."

By default, gcc uses shared libraries, so if you must link against static libraries, you have to use the -static option. This means that only static libraries will be used. The following example creates an executable linked against the static ncurses. Chapter 27, "Screen Manipulation with ncurses," discusses user interface programming with ncurses:

```
$ gcc cursesapp.c -lncurses -static
```

When you link against static libraries, the resulting binary is much larger than using shared libraries. Why use a static library, then? One common reason is to guarantee that users can run your program—in the case of shared libraries, the code your program needs to run is linked dynamically at runtime, rather than statically at compile time. If the shared library your program requires is not installed on the user's system, she will get errors and not be able to run your program.

The Netscape browser is a perfect example of this. Netscape relies heavily on Motif, an expensive X programming toolkit. Most Linux users cannot afford to install Motif on their system, so Netscape actually installs two versions of their browser on your system; one that is linked against shared libraries, netscape-dynMotif, and one that is statically linked, netscape-statMotif. The netscape "executable" itself is actually a shell script that checks to see if you have the Motif shared library installed and launches one or the other of the binaries as necessary.

Error Checking and Warnings

gcc boasts a whole class of error-checking, warning-generating, command-line options. These include -ansi, -pedantic, -pedantic- errors, and -Wall. To begin with, -pedantic tells gcc to issue all warnings demanded by strict ANSI/ISO standard C. Any program using forbidden extensions, such as those supported by gcc, will be rejected. -pedantic-errors behaves similarly, except that it emits errors rather than warnings. -ansi, finally, turns off GNU extensions that do not comply with the standard. None of these options, however, guarantee that your code, when compiled without error using any or all of these options, is 100 percent ANSI/ISO-compliant.

Consider Listing 3.2, an example of very bad programming form. It declares main() as returning void, when in fact main() returns int, and it uses the GNU extension long long to declare a 64-bit integer.

LISTING 3.2 NON-ANSI/ISO SOURCE CODE

```
1   /*
2    * Listing 3.2
3    * pedant.c - use -ansi, -pedantic or -pedantic-errors
```

continues

LISTING 3.2   CONTINUED

```
4   */
5   #include <stdio.h>
6
7   void main(void)
8   {
9       long long int i =  01;
10      fprintf(stdout, "This is a non-conforming C program\n");
11  }
```

Using gcc `pedant.c -o pedant`, this code compiles without complaint. First, try to compile it using -ansi:

```
$ gcc -ansi pedant.c -o pedant
```

Again, no complaint. The lesson here is that -ansi forces gcc to emit the diagnostic messages required by the standard. It does not insure that your code is ANSI C[nd]compliant. The program compiled despite the deliberately incorrect declaration of main(). Now, -pedantic:

```
$ gcc -pedantic pedant.c -o pedant
pedant.c: In function `main':
pedant.c:9: warning: ANSI C does not support `long long'
```

The code compiles, despite the emitted warning. With -pedantic- errors, however, it does not compile. gcc stops after emitting the error diagnostic:

```
$ gcc -pedantic-errors pedant.c -o pedant
pedant.c: In function `main':
pedant.c:9: ANSI C does not support `long long'
$ ls
a.out*      hello.c      helper.h      killerapp.c
hello*      helper.c     killerapp*    pedant.c
```

To reiterate, the -ansi, -pedantic, and -pedantic-errors compiler options do not insure ANSI/ISO-compliant code. They merely help you along the road. It is instructive to point out the remark in the info file for gcc on the use of -pedantic:

"This option is not intended to be useful; it exists only to satisfy pedants who would otherwise claim that GNU CC fails to support the ANSI standard. Some users try to use `-pedantic' to check programs for strict ANSI C conformance. They soon find that it does not do quite what they want: it finds some non-ANSI practices, but not all—only those for which ANSI C *requires* a diagnostic."

Optimization Options

Code optimization is an attempt to improve performance. The trade-off is lengthened compile times and increased memory usage during compilation.

The bare -O option tells gcc to reduce both code size and execution time. It is equivalent to -O1. The types of optimization performed at this level depend on the target processor, but always include at least thread jumps and deferred stack pops. Thread jump optimizations attempt to reduce the number of jump operations; deferred stack pops occur when the compiler lets arguments accumulate on the stack as functions return and then pops them simultaneously, rather than popping the arguments piecemeal as each called function returns.

O2 level optimizations include all first-level optimization plus additional tweaks that involve processor instruction scheduling. At this level, the compiler takes care to make sure the processor has instructions to execute while waiting for the results of other instructions or data latency from cache or main memory. The implementation is highly processor-specific. -O3 options include all O2 optimizations, loop unrolling, and other processor-specific features.

Depending on the amount of low-level knowledge you have about a given CPU family, you can use the –f{flag} option to request specific optimizations you want performed. Three of these flags bear consideration: -ffastmath, -finline-functions, and –funroll-loops. –ffastmath generates floating-point math optimizations that increase speed, but violate IEEE and/or ANSI standards. –finline-functions expands all "simple" functions in place, much like preprocessor macro replacements. Of course, the compiler decides what constitutes a simple function. –funroll-loops instructs gcc to unroll all loops that have a fixed number of iterations that can be determined at compile time. Inlining and loop unrolling can greatly improve a program's execution speed because they avoid the overhead of function calls and variable lookups, but the cost is usually a large increase in the size of the binary or object files. You will have to experiment to see if the increased speed is worth the increased file size. See the gcc info pages for more details on processor flags.

3

> **NOTE**
>
> For general usage, using -O2 optimization is sufficient. Even on small programs, like the hello.c program introduced at the beginning of this chapter, you will see small reductions in code size and small increases in performance time.

Debugging Options

Bugs are as inevitable as death and taxes. To accommodate this sad reality, use gcc's -g and -ggdb options to insert debugging information into your compiled programs to facilitate debugging sessions.

The -g option can be qualified with a 1, 2, or 3 to specify how much debugging information to include. The default level is 2 (-g2), which includes extensive symbol tables, line numbers, and information about local and external variables. Level 3 debugging information includes all of the level 2 information and all of the macro definitions present. Level 1 generates just enough information to create backtracks and stack dumps. It does not generate debugging information for local variables or line numbers.

If you intend to use the GNU Debugger, gdb (covered in Chapter 36, "Debugging: GNU gdb"), using the -ggdb option creates extra information that eases the debugging chore under gdb. However, this will also likely make the program impossible to debug using other debuggers, such as the DBX debugger common on the Solaris operating system. -ggdb accepts the same level specifications as -g, and they have the same effects on the debugging output. Using either of the two debug-enabling options will, however, dramatically increase the size of your binary. Simply compiling and linking the simple hello.c program I used earlier in this chapter resulted in a binary of 4089 bytes on my system. The resulting sizes when I compiled it with the -g and -ggdb options may surprise you:

```
$ gcc -g hello.c -o hello_g
$ ls -l hello_g
-rwxr-xr-x   1 kwall     users           6809 Jan 12 15:09 hello_g*

$ gcc -ggdb hello.c -o hello_ggdb
$ ls -l hello_ggdb
-rwxr-xr-x   1 kwall     users         354867 Jan 12 15:09
hello_ggdb*
```

As you can see, the -g option increased the binary's size by half, while the -ggdb option bloated the binary nearly 900 percent! Despite the size increase, I recommend shipping binaries with standard debugging symbols (created using –g) in them in case someone encounters a problem and wants to try to debug your code for you.

Additional debugging options include the -p and -pg options, which embed profiling information into the binary. This information is useful for tracking down performance bottlenecks in your code. –p adds profiling symbols that the prof program can read, and –pg adds symbols that the GNU project's prof incarnation, gprof, can interpret. The -a option generates counts of how many times blocks of code (such as functions) are entered. -save-temps saves the intermediate files, such as the object and assembler files, generated during compilation.

Finally, as I mentioned at the beginning of this chapter, gcc allows you simultaneously to optimize your code and insert debugging information. Optimized code presents a debugging challenge, however, because variables you declare and use may not be used in the optimized program, flow control may branch to unexpected places, statements that compute constant values may not execute, and statements inside loops will execute elsewhere because the loop was unrolled. My personal preference, though, is to debug a program thoroughly before worrying about optimization. Your mileage may vary.

> **NOTE**
>
> Do not, however, take "optimize later" to mean "ignore efficiency during the design process." Optimization, in the context of this chapter, refers to the compiler magic I have discussed in this section. Good design and efficient algorithms have a far greater impact on overall performance than any compiler optimization ever will. Indeed, if you take the time up front to create a clean design and use fast algorithms, you may not need to optimize, although it never hurts to try.

GNU C Extensions

GNU C extends the ANSI standard in a variety of ways. If you don't mind writing blatantly non-standard code, some of these extensions can be very useful. For all of the gory details, I will direct the curious reader to gcc's info pages. The extensions covered in this section are the ones frequently seen in Linux's system headers and source code.

To provide 64-bit storage units, for example, gcc offers the "long long" type:

```
long long long_int_var;
```

> **NOTE**
>
> The "long long" type exists in the new draft ISO C standard.

On the x86 platform, this definition results in a 64-bit memory location named `long_int_var`. Another gcc-ism you will encounter in Linux header files is the use of inline functions. Provided it is short enough, an inline function expands in your code much as a macro does, thus eliminating the cost of a function call. Inline functions are better than macros, however, because the compiler type-checks them at compile time. To use the inline functions, you have to compile with at least -0 optimization.

The attribute keyword tells gcc more about your code and aids the code optimizer. Standard library functions, such as exit() and abort(), never return so the compiler can generate slightly more efficient code if it knows that the function does not return. Of course, userland programs may also define functions that do not return. gcc allows you to specify the noreturn attribute for such functions, which acts as a hint to the compiler to optimize the function.

Suppose, for example, you have a function named die_on_error() that never returns. To use a function attribute, append __attribute__ ((attribute_name)) after the closing parenthesis of the function declaration. Thus, the declaration of die_on_error() would look like:

```
void die_on_error(void) __attribute__ ((noreturn));
```

The function would be defined normally:

```
void die_on_error(void)
{
    /* your code here */
    exit(1);
}
```

You can also apply attributes to variables. The aligned attribute instructs the compiler to align the variable's memory location on a specified byte boundary.

```
int int_var __attribute__ ((aligned 16)) = 0;
```

will cause gcc to align int_var on a 16-byte boundary. The packed attribute tells gcc to use the minimum amount of space required for variables or structs. Used with structs, packed will remove any padding that gcc would ordinarily insert for alignment purposes.

A terrifically useful extension is case ranges. The syntax looks like:

```
case LOWVAL ... HIVAL:
```

Note that the spaces preceding and following the ellipsis are required. Case ranges are used in switch() statements to specify values that fall between LOWVAL and HIVAL:

```
switch(int_var) {
    case 0 ... 2:
        /* your code here */
        break;
    case 3 ... 5:
        /* more code here */
        break;
    default:
        /* default code here */
}
```

The preceding fragment is equivalent to:

```
switch(int_var) {
    case 1:
    case 2:
        /* your code here */
        break;
    case 3:
    case 4:
    case 5:
        /* more code here */
        break;
    default:
        /* default code here */
}
```

Case ranges are just a shorthand notation for the traditional `switch()` statement syntax.

Summary

In this chapter, I have introduced you to gcc, the GNU compiler suite. In reality, I have only scratched the surface, though; gcc's own documentation runs to several hundred pages. What I have done is show you enough of its features and capabilities to enable you to start using it in your own development projects.

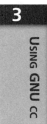

3

USING GNU CC

Project Management Using GNU make

by Kurt Wall

IN THIS CHAPTER

CHAPTER 4

In this chapter, we take a long look at make, a tool to control the process of building (or rebuilding) software. make automates what software gets built, how it gets built, and when it gets built, freeing the programmer to concentrate on writing code.

Why make?

For all but the simplest software projects, make is essential. In the first place, projects composed of multiple source files typically require long, complex compiler invocations. make simplifies this by storing these difficult command lines in the makefile, which the next section discusses.

make also minimizes rebuild times because it is smart enough to determine which files have changed, and thus only rebuilds files whose components have changed. Finally, make maintains a database of dependency information for your projects and so can verify that all of the files necessary for building a program are available each time you start a build.

Writing Makefiles

So, how does make accomplish these magical feats? By using a makefile. A makefile is a text file database containing rules that tell make what to build and how to build it. A rule consists of the following:

- A *target*, the "thing" make ultimately tries to create
- A list of one or more *dependencies*, usually files, required to build the target
- A list of *commands* to execute in order to create the target from the specified dependencies

When invoked, GNU make looks for a file named GNUmakefile, makefile, or Makefile, in that order. For some reason, most Linux programmers use the last form, Makefile.

Makefile rules have the general form

```
target : dependency dependency [...]
        command
        command
        [...]
```

target is generally the file, such as a binary or object file, that you want created. dependency is a list of one or more files required as input in order to create target. The commands are the steps, such as compiler invocations, necessary to create target. Unless specified otherwise, make does all of its work in the current working directory.

If this is all too abstract for you, I will use Listing 4.1 as an example. It is the makefile for building a text editor imaginatively named editor.

LISTING 4.1 SIMPLE MAKEFILE ILLUSTRATING TARGETS, DEPENDENCIES, AND COMMANDS

```
1     editor : editor.o screen.o keyboard.o
2             gcc -o editor editor.o screen.o keyboard.o
3
4     editor.o : editor.c editor.h keyboard.h screen.h
5             gcc -c editor.c
6
7     screen.o : screen.c screen.h
8             gcc -c screen.c
9
10    keyboard.o : keyboard.c keyboard.h
11             gcc -c keyboard.c
12
13    clean :
14             rm editor *.o
```

To compile editor, you would simply type make in the directory where the makefile exists. It's that simple.

This makefile has five rules. The first target, editor, is called the *default* target—this is the file that make tries to create. editor has three dependencies, editor.o, screen.o, and keyboard.o; these three files must exist in order to build editor. Line 2 (the line numbers do not appear in the actual makefile; they are merely pedagogic tools) is the command that make will execute to create editor. As you recall from Chapter 3, "Using GNU cc," this command builds an executable named editor from the three object files. The next three rules (lines 4–11) tell make how to build the individual object files.

Here is where make's value becomes evident: ordinarily, if you tried to build editor using the command from line 2, gcc would complain loudly and ceremoniously quit if the dependencies did not exist. make, on the other hand, after seeing that editor requires these other files, verifies that they exist and, if they don't, executes the commands on lines 5, 8, and 11 first, then returns to line 2 to create the editor executable. Of course, if the dependencies for the components, such as keyboard.c or screen.h don't exist, make will also give up, because it lacks targets named, in this case, keyboard.c and screen.h.

"All well and good," you're probably thinking, "but how does make know when to rebuild a file?" The answer is stunningly simple: If a specified target does not exist in a place where make can find it, make (re)builds it. If the target does exist, make compares the timestamp on the target to the timestamp of the dependencies. If one or more of the dependencies is newer than the target, make rebuilds the target, assuming that the newer dependency implies some code change that must be incorporated into the target.

More About Rules

In this section, I will go into more detail about writing makefile rules. In particular, I cover creating and using phony targets, makefile variables, using environment variables and make's predefined variables, implicit rules, and pattern rules.

Phony Targets

In addition to the normal file targets, make allows you to specify *phony* targets. Phony targets are so named because they do not correspond to actual files. The final target in Listing 4.1, clean, is a phony target. Phony targets exist to specify commands that make should execute. However, because clean does not have dependencies, its commands are not automatically executed. This follows from the explanation of how make works: upon encountering the clean target, make sees if the dependencies exist and, because clean has no dependencies, make assumes the target is up to date. In order to build this target, you have to type **make clean**. In our case, clean removes the editor executable and its constituent object files. You might create such a target if you wanted to create and distribute a source-code tarball to your users or to start a build with a clean build tree.

If, however, a file named clean happened to exist, make would see it. Again, because it has no dependencies, make would assume that it is up to date and not execute the commands listed on line 14. To deal with this situation, use the special make target .PHONY.

Any dependencies of the .PHONY target will be evaluated as usual, but make will disregard the presence of a file whose name matches one of .PHONY's dependencies and execute the corresponding commands anyway. Using .PHONY, our sample makefile would look like:

```
 1  editor : editor.o screen.o keyboard.o
 2          gcc -o editor editor.o screen.o keyboard.o
 3
 4  editor.o : editor.c editor.h keyboard.h screen.h
 5          gcc -c editor.c
 6
 7  screen.o : screen.c screen.h
 8          gcc -c screen.c
 9
10  keyboard.o : keyboard.c keyboard.h
11          gcc -c keyboard.c
12
13 .PHONY : clean
14
15  clean :
16          rm editor *.o
```

Variables

To simplify editing and maintaining makefiles, make allows you to create and use variables. A variable is simply a name defined in a makefile that represents a string of text; this text is called the variable's *value*. Define variables using the general form:

```
VARNAME = some_text [...]
```

To obtain VARNAME's value, enclose it in parentheses and prefix it with a $:

```
$(VARNAME)
```

VARNAME expands to the text on the right-hand side of the equation. Variables are usually defined at the top of a makefile. By convention, makefile variables are all uppercase, although this is not required. If the value changes, you only need to make one change instead of many, simplifying makefile maintenance. So, after modifying Listing 4.1 to use two variables, it looks like the following:

LISTING 4.2   USING VARIABLES IN MAKEFILES

```
 1  OBJS = editor.o screen.o keyboard.o
 2  HDRS = editor.h screen.h keyboard.h
 3  editor : $(OBJS)
```

continues

4

USING GNU MAKE

LISTING 4.2   CONTINUED

```
 4       gcc -o editor $(OBJS)
 5
 6   editor.o : editor.c $(HDRS)
 7       gcc -c editor.c
 8
 9   screen.o : screen.c screen.h
10       gcc -c screen.c
11
12   keyboard.o : keyboard.c keyboard.h
13       gcc -c keyboard.c
14
15   .PHONY : clean
16
17   clean :
18       rm editor $(OBJS)
```

OBJS and HDRS will expand to their value each time they are referenced. make actually uses two kinds of variables—recursively-expanded and simply expanded. *Recursively-expanded* variables are expanded verbatim as they are referenced; if the expansion contains another variable reference, it is also expanded. The expansion continues until no further variables exist to expand, hence the name, "recursively-expanded." An example will make this clear.

Consider the variables TOPDIR and SRCDIR defined as follows:

```
TOPDIR = /home/kwall/myproject
SRCDIR = $(TOPDIR)/src
```

Thus, SRCDIR will have the value /home/kwall/myproject/src. This works as expected and desired. However, consider the next variable definition:

```
CC = gcc
CC = $(CC) -o
```

Clearly, what you want, ultimately, is "CC = gcc -o." That is not what you will get, however. $(CC) is recursively-expanded when it is referenced, so you wind up with an infinite loop: $(CC) will keep expanding to $(CC), and you never pick up the -o option. Fortunately, make detects this and reports an error:

```
*** Recursive variable `CC' references itself (eventually).  Stop.
```

To avoid this difficulty, make uses simply expanded variables. Rather than being expanded when they are referenced, *simply expanded* variables are scanned once and for all when they are defined; all embedded variable references are resolved. The definition syntax is slightly different:

```
CC := gcc -o
CC += -O2
```

The first definition uses := to set CC equal to gcc -o and the second definition uses += to append -02 to the first definition, so that CC's final value is gcc -o -02. If you run into trouble when using make variables or get the "VARNAME references itself" error message, it's time to use the simply expanded variables. Some programmers use only simply expanded variables to avoid unanticipated problems. Since this is Linux, you are free to choose for yourself!

Environment, Automatic, and Predefined Variables

In addition to user-defined variables, make allows the use of environment variables and also provides "automatic" variables and predefined variables. Using environment variables is ridiculously simple. When it starts, make reads every variable defined in its environment and creates variables with the same name and value. However, similarly named variables in the makefile override the environment variables, so beware. make provides a long list of predefined and automatic variables, too. They are pretty cryptic looking, though. See Table 4.1 for a partial list of automatic variables.

TABLE 4.1 AUTOMATIC VARIABLES

Variable	Description
$@	The filename of a rule's target
$<	The name of the first dependency in a rule
$^	Space-delimited list of all the dependencies in a rule
$?	Space-delimited list of all the dependencies in a rule that are newer than the target
$(@D)	The directory part of a target filename, if the target is in a subdirectory
$(@F)	The filename part of a target filename, if the target is in a subdirectory

In addition to the automatic variables listed in Table 4.1, make predefines a number of other variables that are used either as names of programs or to pass flags and arguments to these programs. See Table 4.2.

TABLE 4.2 PREDEFINED VARIABLES FOR PROGRAM NAMES AND FLAGS

Variable	Description
AR	Archive-maintenance programs; default value = ar
AS	Program to do assembly; default value = as

continues

4

USING GNU MAKE

TABLE 4.2   CONTINUED

Variable	Description
CC	Program for compiling C programs; default value = cc
CPP	C Preprocessor program; default value = cpp
RM	Program to remove files; default value = "rm -f"
ARFLAGS	Flags for the archive-maintenance program; default = rv
ASFLAGS	Flags for the assembler program; no default
CFLAGS	Flags for the C compiler; no default
CPPFLAGS	Flags for the C preprocessor; no default
LDFLAGS	Flags for the linker (ld); no default

If you want, you can redefine these variables in the makefile. In most cases, their default values are reasonable.

Implicit Rules

In addition to the rules that you explicitly specify in a makefile, which are called *explicit* rules, make comes with a comprehensive set of *implicit*, or predefined, rules. Many of these are special-purpose and of limited usage, so we will only cover a few of the most commonly used implicit rules. Implicit rules simplify makefile maintenance.

Suppose you have a makefile that looks like the following:

```
1   OBJS = editor.o screen.o keyboard.o
2   editor : $(OBJS)
3       cc -o editor $(OBJS)
4
5   .PHONY : clean
6
7   clean :
8       rm editor $(OBJS)
```

The command for the default target, editor, mentions editor.o, screen.o, and key-board.o, but the makefile lacks rules for building those targets. As a result, make will use an implicit rule that says, in essence, for each object file somefile.o, look for a corresponding source file somefile.c and build the object file with the command gcc -c somefile.c -o somefile.o. So, make will look for C source files named editor.c, screen.c, and keyboard.c, compile them to object files (editor.o, screen.o, and key-board.o), and finally, build the default editor target.

The mechanism is actually more general than what I described. Object (.o) files can be created from C source, Pascal source, Fortran source, and so forth. make looks for the dependency that can actually be satisfied. So, if you have files editor.p, screen.p, and keyboard.p, the Pascal compiler will be invoked rather than the C compiler (.p is the assumed extension of Pascal source files). The lesson here is that if, for some perverse reason, your project uses multiple languages, don't rely on the implicit rules because the results may not be what you expected.

Pattern Rules

Pattern rules provide a way around the limitations of make's implicit rules by allowing you to define your own implicit rules. Pattern rules look like normal rules, except that the target contains exactly one character (%) that matches any nonempty string. The dependencies of such a rule also use % in order to match the target. So, for example, the rule

```
%.o : %.c
```

tells make to build any object file somename.o from a source file somename.c.

Like implicit rules, make uses several predefined pattern rules:

```
%.o : %.c
        $(CC) -c $(CFLAGS) $(CPPFLAGS) $< -o $@
```

This is the same as the example. It defines a rule that makes any file x.o from x.c. This rule uses the automatic variables $< and $@ to substitute the names of the first dependency and the target each time the rule is applied. The variables $(CC), $(CFLAGS), and $(CPPFLAGS) have the default values listed in Table 4.2.

Comments

You can insert comments in a makefile by preceding the comment with the hash sign (#). When make encounters a comment, it ignores the hash symbol and the rest of the line following it. Comments can be placed anywhere in a makefile. Special consideration must be given to comments that appear in commands, because most shells treat # as a metacharacter (usually as a comment delimiter). As far as make is concerned, a line that contains only a comment is, for all practical purposes, blank.

Additional make Command-line Options

Like most GNU programs, make accepts a cornucopia of command-line options. The most common ones are listed in Table 4.3.

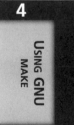

TABLE 4.3   COMMON make COMMAND-LINE OPTIONS

Option	Description
-f file	Specify an alternatively-named makefile file.
-n	Print the commands that would be executed, but don't actually execute them.
-Idirname	Specify dirname as a directory in which make should search for included makefiles.
-s	Don't print the commands as they are executed.
-w	If make changes directories while executing, print the current directory names.
-Wfile	Act as if file has been modified; use with -n to see how make would behave if file had been changed.
-r	Disable all of make's built-in rules.
-d	Print lots of debugging information.
-i	Ignore non-zero error codes returned by commands in a makefile rule. make will continue executing even if a command returns a non-zero exit status.
-k	If one target fails to build, continue to build other targets. Normally, make terminates if a target fails to build successfully.
-jN	Run N commands at once, where N is a non-zero integer.

Debugging make

If you have trouble using make, the -d option tells make to print lots of extra debugging information in addition to the commands it is executing. The output can be overwhelming because the debugging dump will display what make does internally and why. This includes the following:

- Which files make evaluates for rebuilding
- Which files are being compared and what the comparison results are
- Which files actually need to bc remade
- Which implicit rules make thinks it will use
- Which implicit rules make decides to use and the commands it actually executes

Common make Error Messages

This section lists the most common error messages you will encounter while using make. For complete documentation, refer to the make manual or info pages.

- `No rule to make target 'target'. Stop` The makefile does not contain a rule telling make how to construct the named target and no default rules apply.

- `'target' is up to date` The dependencies for the named target have not changed.

- `Target 'target' not remade because of errors` An error occurred while building the named target. This message only appears when using make's -k option.

- `command: Command not found` make could not find command. This usually occurs because command has been misspelled or is not in $PATH.s

- `Illegal option - option` The invocation of make included an option that it does not recognize.

Useful Makefile Targets

In addition to the clean target I mentioned previously, several other targets typically inhabit makefiles. A target named install moves the final binary, any supporting libraries or shell scripts, and documentation to their final homes in the filesystem and sets file permissions and ownership appropriately. An install target typically also compiles the program and may also run a simple test to verify that the program compiled correctly. An uninstall target would delete the files installed by an install target.

A dist target is a convenient way to prepare a distribution package. At the very least, the dist target will remove old binary and object files from the build directory and create an archive file, such as a gzipped tarball, ready for uploading to World Wide Web pages and FTP sites.

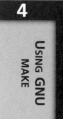

For the convenience of other developers, you might want to create a tags target that creates or updates a program's tags table. If the procedure for verifying a program is complex, you will definitely want to create a separate target, named test or check that executes this procedure and emits the appropriate diagnostic messages. A similar target, named installtest or installcheck, would be used to validate an installation. Of course the install target must have successfully built and installed the program first.

Summary

This chapter covered the make command, explaining why it is useful and showing you how to write simple but useful makefiles. It also discussed some of the subtleties of make rules and listed some of make's helpful command-line options. With this foundation, you should know enough to use make to manage the process of building and maintaining your software projects.

Creating Self-Configuring Software with autoconf

by Kurt Wall

IN THIS CHAPTER

CHAPTER 5

Linux's mixed origins and the variety of Linux distributions available demand a flexible and adaptable configuration and build environment. This chapter looks at GNU autoconf, a tool that enables you to configure your software to adapt to the wide assortment of system configurations in which it may be built, including many non-Linux systems.

Understanding `autoconf`

Developing software that runs on a number of different UNIX and UNIX-like systems requires considerable effort. First, the code itself must be portable. Portable code makes few assumptions about the hardware on which it may be run or the software libraries available to it. In addition, if it's C code, to ensure maximum portability, the code has to stick to strict ISO/ANSI C, or isolate non-standard C to as few modules as possible.

Second, you need to know a lot about the compile and runtime environments of many different systems and, possibly, hardware architectures. GNU software, while ubiquitous on Linux systems and available for a mind-boggling array of other operating systems and hardware platforms, may not always be available on those systems. In addition, the following conditions may exist:

- The C compiler may be pre-ISO
- Libraries may be missing key features
- System services may function differently
- Filesystem conventions will certainly be different

On the hardware side, you may have to deal with big-endian, little-endian, or hybrid data representation mechanisms. When you get away from Intel's x86 processors, you have to deal with, for example, PA-RISC, several varieties of Sparcs, the Motorola chips (in several generations) that drive Macintosh and Apple computers, MIPS, Amiga, and, coming soon to a computer near you, Intel's Merced or IA64 chip. Finally, you have to write a generic makefile and provide instructions to your users on how to edit the makefile to fit local circumstances.

autoconf addresses many of these problems. It generates shell scripts that automatically configure source code packages to adapt to many different brands of UNIX and UNIX-like systems. These scripts, usually named configure, test for the presence or absence of certain features a program needs or can use, and build makefiles based on the results of these tests. The scripts autoconf generates are self-contained, so users do not need to have autoconf installed on their own systems in order to build software. All they have to do is type ./configure in the source distribution directory.

To build a configure script, you create a file named configure.in in the root directory of your source code tree. configure.in contains a series of calls to autoconf macros that test for the presence or behavior of features your program can utilize or that it requires. autoconf contains many predefined macros that test for commonly required features. A second set of macros allows you to build your own custom tests if none of autoconf's built-in macros meet your needs. If need be, configure.in can also contain shell scripts that evaluate unusual or specialized characteristics. Besides the autoconf package itself (we cover version 2.12), you will need at least version 1.1 of GNU's m4, a macro processor that copies its input to output, expanding macros as it goes (autoconf's author, David MacKenzie, recommends version 1.3 or better for speed reasons). The latest versions of both packages can be obtained from the GNU Web site, www.gnu.org, their FTP site, ftp.gnu.org, or from many other locations around the Web. Most Linux distributions contain them, too.

Building configure.in

Each configure.in file must invoke AC_INIT before any test and AC_OUTPUT after all the tests. These are the only two required macros. The following is the syntax for AC_INIT:

```
AC_INIT(unique_file_in_source_dir)
```

unique_file_in_source_dir is a file present in the source code directory. The call to AC_INIT creates shell code in the generated configure script that looks for unique_file_in_source_dir to make sure that it is in the correct directory.

AC_OUTPUT creates the output files, such as Makefiles and other (optional) output files. Its syntax is as follows:

```
AC_OUTPUT([file...[,extra_cmds[,init_cmds]]])
```

file is a space separated list of output files. Each file is created by copying file.in to file. extra_cmds is a list of commands appended to config.status, which can be used to regenerate the configure script. init_cmds will be inserted into config.status immediately before extra_cmds.

5

CREATING SELF-
CONFIGURING
SOFTWARE WITH
autoconf

Structuring the File

With few exceptions, the order in which you call autoconf macros does not matter (we note the exceptions as they occur). That said, the following is the recommended order:

AC_INIT

> Tests for programs
> Tests for libraries
> Tests for header files
> Tests for typedefs
> Tests for structures
> Tests for compiler behavior
> Tests for library functions
> Tests for system services

AC_OUTPUT

The suggested ordering reflects the fact that, for example, the presence or absence of libraries has consequences for the inclusion of header files, so header files should be checked after libraries. Similarly, some system services depend on the existence of particular library functions, which may only be callcd if they are prototyped in header files. You cannot call a function prototyped in a header file if the required library does not exist. The moral is stick with the recommended order unless you know exactly what you are doing and have a compelling reason to deviate.

A few words on the layout of configure.in may prove helpful. Use only one macro call per line, because most of autoconf's macros rely on a newline to terminate commands. In situations where macros read or set environment variables, the variables may be set on the same line as a macro call.

A single macro call that takes several arguments may exceed the one-call-per-line rule; use \ to continue the argument list to the next line and enclose the argument list in the m4 quote characters, [and]. The following two macro calls are equivalent:

```
AC_CHECK_HEADERS([unistd.h termios.h termio.h sgtty.h alloca.h \
sys/itimer.h])
```

```
AC_CHECK_HEADERS(unistd.h termios.h termio.h sgtty.h alloca.h sys/timer.h)
```

The first example wraps the arguments in [and] and uses \ (which is interpreted by the shell, not by m4 or autoconf) to indicate line continuation. The second example is simply a single long line.

Finally, to insert comments into configure.in, use m4's comment delimiter, dnl. For example,

```
dnl
dnl This is an utterly gratuitous comment
dnl
AC_INIT(some_darn_file)
```

Helpful autoconf Utilities

In addition to autoconf's built-in macros, covered in some detail in the next section, the autoconf package contains several helpful scripts to assist in creating and maintaining configure.in. To kick start the process, the Perl script autoscan extracts information from your source files about function calls and included header files, outputting configure.scan. Before renaming or copying this to configure.in, however, manually examine it to identify features it overlooked. ifnames functions similarly, looking for the preprocessor directives #if, #elif, #ifdef and #ifndef in your source files. Use it to augment autoscan's output.

Built-In Macros

In many cases, autoconf's built-in macros will be all that you require. Each set of built-in tests may be further subdivided into macros that test specific features and more general tests. This section lists and briefly describes most of the built-in tests. For a complete list and description of autoconf's predefined tests, see the autoconf info page.

Tests for Alternative Programs

Table 5.1 describes a group of tests that check for the presence or behavior of particular programs in situations where you want or need to be able to choose between several alternative programs. The compilation process is complex, so these macros give you flexibility by confirming the existence of necessary programs or making sure, if they *do* exist, that they are properly invoked.

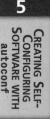

TABLE 5.1 ALTERNATIVE PROGRAM TESTS

Test	Description
AC_PROG_AWK	Checks, in order, for mawk, gawk, nawk, and awk, sets output variable AWK to the first one it finds
AC_PROG_CC	Decides which C compiler to use, sets output variable CC
AC_PROG_CC_C_O	Determines whether or not the compiler accepts the -c and -o switches; if not, defines NO_MINUS_C_MINUS_O
AC_PROG_CPP	Sets output variable CPP to the command that executes the C preprocessor
AC_PROG_INSTALL	Sets output variable INSTALL to a BSD-compatible install program or to install-sh
AC_PROG_LEX	Looks for flex or lex, setting output variable LEX to the result
AC_PROG_LN_S	Sets variable LN_S to ln -s if system supports symbolic links or to ln otherwise
AC_PROG_RANLIB	Set output variable RANLIB to ranlib if ranlib exists, to : otherwise
AC_PROG_YACC	Checks, in order, for bison, byacc, and yacc, setting output variable YACC to bison -y, byacc, or yacc, respectively, depending on which it finds

Generally, the macros in Table 5.1 establish the paths to or confirm the calling conventions of the programs with which they are concerned. In the case of AC PROG_CC, for example, you would not want to hard code gcc if it is not available on the target system. AC_PROG_CC_C_O exists because older compilers (or, at least, non-GNU compilers) do not necessarily accept –c and –o or use them the same way gcc does. A similar situation obtains with AC_PROG_LN_S because many filesystem implementations do not support creating symbolic links.

Tests for Library Functions

Table 5.2 describes tests that look for particular libraries, first to see if they exist, second to determine any differences in arguments passed to functions in those libraries. Despite the best laid plans, programming libraries eventually change in such a way that later versions become incompatible, sometimes dramatically so, with earlier versions. The macros in Table 5.2 enable you to adjust the build process to accommodate this unfortunate reality. In extreme cases, you can simply throw up your hands in despair and refuse to build until the target system is upgraded.

TABLE 5.2 LIBRARY FUNCTION TESTS

Test	*Description*
AC_CHECK_LIB (lib, function [, action_if_found [, action_if_not_found, [, other_libs]]])	Determines if function exists in library lib by attempting to link a C program with lib. Executes shell commands action_if_found if the test succeeds or adds -llib to the output variable LIB if action_if_found is empty. action_if_not found adds -lother_libs to the link command
AC_FUNC_GETLOADAVG	If the system has the getloadavg() function, add the libraries necessary to get the function to LIBS
AC_FUNC_GETPGRP	Tests whether or not getprgrp() takes no argument, in which case it defines GETPGRP_VOID. Otherwise, getpgrp requires a process ID argument.
AC_FUNC_MEMCMP	If memcmp() isn't available, add memcmp.o to LIBOBJS
AC_FUNC_MMAP	Set HAVE_MMAP if mmap() is present
AC_FUNC_SETPGRP	Tests whether or not setprgrp() takes no argument, in which case it defines SETPGRP_VOID. Otherwise, setpgrp requires two process ID arguments.
AC_FUNC_UTIME_NULL	If utime(file, NULL) sets file's timestamp to the present, define HAVE_UTIME_NULL
AC_FUNC_VFORK	If vfork.h isn't present, define vfork() to be fork()
AC_FUNC_VRPINTF	Defines HAVE_VPRINTF if vprintf() exists

AC_CHECK_LIB is arguably the most useful macro in this group, because it gives you the option to say, "This program won't work unless you have the required library." The other macros exist to accommodate the divergence between BSD and AT&T UNIX. One branch had functions or function arguments that differed sharply from the other. Because Linux has a mixed BSD and AT&T heritage, these macros help you properly configure your software.

Tests for Header Files

Header tests check for the presence and location of C-style header files. As with the macros in Table 5.2, these macros exist to allow you to take into account differences between UNIX and C implementations across systems. Believe it or not, many odd or old UNIX and UNIX-like systems lack an ANSI-compliant C compiler. Other systems may lack POSIX-compliant system calls. Table 5.3 describes these tests.

TABLE 5.3   HEADER FILE TESTS

Test	Description
AC_DECL_SYS_SIGLIST	If signal.h or unistd.h defines sys_syglist, define SYS_SIGLIST_DECLARED
AC_HEADER_DIRENT	Checks for the following header files in order, dirent.h, sysdir/ndir.h, sys/dir.h, ndir.h, and defines HAVE_DIRENT_H, HAVE_SYS_NDIR_H, HAVE_SYS_DIR_H or HAVE_NDIR_H, respectively, depending on which header defines DIR
AC_HEADER_STDC	Defines STDC_HEADERS if the system has ANSI/ISO C header files
AC_HEADER_SYS_WAIT	If the system has a POSIX compatible sys/wait.h, define output variable HAVE_SYS_WAIT

AC_HEADER_DIRENT attempts to account for the wide variety of filesystems in use on UNIX and UNIX-like systems. Since most programs rely heavily on filesystem services, it is useful to know where their header files live and what functions they make available. AC_HEADER_STDC determines whether ANSI/ISO-compatible header files are available, not necessarily whether an compliant compiler is present.

Tests for Structures

The structure tests look for certain structure definitions or for the existence and type of structure members in header files. Reflecting, again, the UNIX family split, different implementations provide different data structures. The macros Table 5.4 describes give you an opportunity to adjust your code accordingly.

TABLE 5.4   STRUCTURE TESTS

Test	Description
AC_HEADER_TIME	Set output variable TIME_WITH_SYS_TIME if both time.h and sys/time.h can be included in a program
AC_STRUCT_ST_BLKSIZE	Defines output variable HAVE_ST_BLKSIZE if struct stat has a st_blksize member
AC_STRUCT_ST_BLOCKS	Defines output variable HAVE_ST_BLOCKS if struct stat has a member st_blocks

Test	Description
AC_STRUCT_TIMEZONE	Figures out how to get the timezone. Defines HAVE_TM_ZONE if struct tm has a tm_zone member or HAVE_TZNAME if an array tzname is found

Tests for typedefs

Table 5.5 describes macros that look for typedefs in the header files sys/types.h and stdlib.h. These macros enable you to adjust your code for the presence or absence of certain typedefs that might be present on one system but absent on another.

TABLE 5.5 TYPEDEF TESTS

Test	Description
AC_TYPE_GETGROUPS	Sets GETGROUPS_T to the gid_t or int, whichever is the base type of the array passed to getgroups()
AC_TYPE_MODE_T	Define mode_t as int if mode_t is undefined
AC_TYPE_PID_T	Define pid_t as int if pid_t is undefined
AC_TYPE_SIGNAL	Define RETSIGTYPE as int if signal.h does not define signal as (void*)()
AC_TYPE_SIZE_T	Define size_t as unsigned if size_t is undefined
AC_TYPE_UID_T	Define uid_t and gid_t as int if uid_t is undefined

Tests of Compiler Behavior

Table 5.6 describes macros that evaluate compiler behavior or peculiarities of particular host architectures. Given the array of available compilers and the CPUs on which they run, these macros allow you to adjust your program to reflect these differences and take advantage of them.

TABLE 5.6 COMPILER BEHAVIOR TESTS

Test	Description
AC_C_BIGENDIAN	If words are stored with the most significant bit first, define WORDS_BIGENDIAN
AC_C_CONST	If the compiler does not fully support the const declaration, define const to be empty

continues

TABLE 5.6   CONTINUED

Test	Description
AC_C_INLINE	If the compiler does not support the keywords inline, __inline__, or __inline, define inline to be empty
AC_C_CHAR_UNSIGNED	Define CHAR_UNSIGNED if char is unsigned
AC_C_LONG_DOUBLE	Define HAVE_LONG_DOUBLE if the host compiler supports the long double type.
AC_C_CHECK_SIZEOF(type [,cross-size])	Defines output variable SIZEOF_UCtype to be the size of the C or C++ built in type type

Tests for System Services

Table 5.7 describes macros that determine the presence and behavior of operating system services and abilities. The services and capabilities that host operating systems provide varies widely, so your code needs to be able to accommodate the variety gracefully, if possible.

TABLE 5.7   SYSTEM SERVICES TESTS

Test	Description
AC_SYS_INTERPRETER	Set shell variable ac_cv_sys_interpreter to yes or no, depending on whether scripts start with #! /bin/sh
AC_PATH_X	Try to find the path to X Window include and library files, setting the shell variables x_includes and x_libraries to the correct paths, or set no_x if the paths could not be found
AC_SYS_LONG_FILE_NAMES	Define HAVE_LONG_FILE_NAMES if the system supports filenames longer than 14 characters
AC_SYS_RESTARTABLE_SYSCALLS	On systems that support system call restarts of signal interruptions, define HAVE_RESTARTABLE_SYSCALLS

Strange as it may seem, there are still filesystems, even UNIX filesystems, that limit filenames to 14 characters, so AC_SYS_LONG_FILE_NAMES allows you to detect such a barbarian filesystem. AC_PATH_X acknowledges that some operating systems do not support the X Window system.

Tests for UNIX Variants

Tests in this class address vagaries and idiosyncrasies of specific UNIX and UNIX-like operating systems. As the autoconf author states, "These macros are warts; they will be replaced by a more systematic approach, based on the functions they make available or the environments they provide (34). Table 5.8 describes these tests.

TABLE 5.8   UNIX VARIANT TESTS

Test	Description
AC_AIX	Define _ALL_SOURCE if the host system is AIX
AC_DYNIX_SEQ	Obsolete—use AC_FUNC_GETMNTENT instead
AC_IRIX_SUN	Obsolete—use AC_FUNC_GETMNTENT instead
AC_ISC_POSIX	Defines _POSIX_SOURCE to allow use of POSIX features
AC_MINIX	Defines _MINIX and _POSIX_SOURCE on MINIX systems to allow use of POSIX features
AC_SCO_INTL	Obsolete—use AC_FUNC_STRFTIME instead
AC_XENIX_DIR	Obsolete—use AC_HEADER_DIRENT instead

"Why," you might be asking yourself, "should I concern myself with obsolete macros?" There are two related reasons. First, you may run across configure.in files that contain the macros. If you do, you can replace them with the proper macros. Second, they are obsolete because better, more general macros have been created. That is, their existence reflects the fact that a large body of extant code exists that still relies upon the peculiarities of operating system implementations and the difference between UNIX implementations.

> **TIP**
>
> The easiest way to stay up-to-date on macros that have become obsolete is to monitor the ChangeLog file in the autoconf distribution, available at the GNU FTP site and many other locations all over the Internet.

Generic Macros

The autoconf manual describes the following macros as the building blocks for new tests. In most cases, they test compiler behavior and so require a test program that can be preprocessed, compiled, and linked (and optionally executed), so that compiler output and error messages can be examined to determine the success or failure of the test.

AC_TRY_CPP(includes [,action_if_true [,action_if_false]])

> This macro passes includes through the preprocessor, running shell commands action_if_true if the preprocessor returns no errors, or shell commands action_if_false otherwise.

AC_EGREP_HEADER(pattern, header, action_if_found [,action_if_not_found])

> Use this macro to search for the egrep expression pattern in the file header. Execute shell commands action_if_found if pattern is found, or action_if_not_found otherwise.

AC_EGREP_CPP(pattern, program, [action_if_found [,action_if_not_found]])

> Run the C program text program through the preprocessor, looking for the egrep expression pattern. Execute shell commands action_if_found if pattern is found, or action_if_not_found otherwise.

AC_TRY_COMPILE(includes, function_body, [action_if_found \
[,action_if_not_found]])

> This macro looks for a syntax feature of the C or C++ compiler. Compile a test program that includes files in includes and uses the function defined in function_body. Execute shell commands action_if_found if compilation succeeds, or action_if_not_found if compilation fails. This macro does not link. Use AC_TRY_LINK to test linking.

AC_TRY_LINK(includes, function_body, [action_if_found \
[,action_if_not_found]])

> This macro adds a link test to AC_TRY_COMPILE. Compile and link a test program that includes files in includes and uses the function defined in function_body. Execute shell commands action_if_found if linking succeeds, or action_if_not_found if linking fails.

AC_TRY_RUN(program, [action_if_true [, action_if_false \
[, action_if_cross_compiling]]])

> This macro tests the runtime behavior of the host system. Compile, link, and execute the text of the C program program. If program returns 0, run shell commands action_if_true, otherwise, run action_if_false. action_if_cross_compiling

is executed instead of `action_if_found` if a program is being built to run another system type.

AC_CHECK_PROG

Checks whether a program exists in the current path.

AC_CHECK_FUNC

Checks whether a function with C linkage exists.

AC_CHECK_HEADER

Tests the existence of a header file.

AC_CHECK_TYPE

If a typedef does not exist, set a default value.

An Annotated autoconf Script

In this section, we create a sample `configure.in` file. It does not configure an actually useful piece of software, but merely illustrates many of the macros we discussed in the preceding sections, some we did not, and some of `autoconf`'s other features.

The following is the beginning of a listing, which is shown in pieces throughout this section. A discussion appears after each listing to discuss what is happening.

```
1    dnl Autoconfigure script for bogusapp
2    dnl Kurt Wall <kwall@xmission.com>
3    dnl
4 dnl Process this file with `autoconf' to produce a `configure'
  ➥script
```

Lines 1–4 are a standard header that indicates the package to which `configure.in` corresponds, contact information, and instructions for regenerating the configure script.

```
5    AC_INIT(bogusapp.c)
6    AC_CONFIG_HEADER(config.h)
```

Line 6 creates a header file named `config.h` in the root directory of your source tree that contains nothing but preprocessor symbols extracted from your header files. By including this file in your source code and using the symbols it contains, your program should compile smoothly and seamlessly on every system on which it might land. `autoconf` creates `config.h` from an input file named `config.h.in` that contains all the #defines you'll need. Fortunately, `autoconf` ships with an ever-so-handy shell script named `autoheader` that generates `config.h.in`. `autoheader` generates `config.h.in` by reading `config-ure.in`, a file named `acconfig.h` that is part of the `autoconf` distribution, and a

./acconfig.h in your source tree for preprocessor symbols. The good news, before you start complaining about having to create another file, is that ./acconfig.h only needs to contain preprocessor symbols that aren't defined anywhere else. Better still, they can have dummy values. The file simply needs to contain legitimately defined C-style preprocessor symbols that autoheader and autoconf can read and utilize. See the file acconfig.h on the CD-ROM for an illustration.

```
7
8     test -z "$LDFLAGS" && LDFLAGS="-I/usr/include" AC_SUBST(CFLAGS)
9
10    dnl Tests for UNIX variants
11    dnl
12    AC_CANONICAL_HOST
```

AC_CANONICAL_HOST reports GNU's idea of the host system. It spits out a name of the form *cpu-company-system*. On one of my systems, for example, AC_CANONICAL_HOST reports the box as *i586-unknown-linux*.

```
13
14    dnl Tests for programs
15    dnl
16    AC_PROG_CC
17    AC_PROG_LEX
18    AC_PROG_AWK
19    AC_PROG_YACC
20    AC_CHECK_PROG(SHELL, bash, /bin/bash, /bin/sh)
21
22    dnl Tests for libraries
23    dnl
24    AC_CHECK_LIB(socket, socket)
25    AC_CHECK_LIB(resolv, res_init, [echo "res_init() not in
      ➥libresolv"],
26    [echo "res_init() found in libresolv"])
```

Line 25 demonstrates how to write custom commands for the autoconf macros. The third and fourth arguments are the shell commands corresponding to action_if_found and action_if_not_found. Because of m4's quoting and delimiting peculiarities, it is generally advisable to delimit commands that use " or ' with m4's quote characters ([and]) to protect them from shell expansion.

```
27
28    dnl Tests for header files
29    dnl
30    AC_CHECK_HEADER(killer.h)
31    AC_CHECK_HEADERS([resolv.h termio.h curses.h sys/time.h fcntl.h \
32    sys/fcntl.h memory.h])
```

Lines 31 and 32 illustrate the correct way to continue multiple line arguments. Use the \
character to inform m4 and the shell of a line continuation, and surround the entire argument list with m4's quote delimiters.

```
33      AC_DECL_SYS_SIGLIST
34      AC_HEADER_STDC
35
36      dnl Tests for typedefs
37      dnl
38      AC_TYPE_GETGROUPS
39      AC_TYPE_SIZE_T
40      AC_TYPE_PID_T
41
42      dnl Tests for structures
43      AC_HEADER_TIME
44      AC_STRUCT_TIMEZONE
45
46      dnl Tests of compiler behavior
47      dnl
48      AC_C_BIGENDIAN
49      AC_C_INLINE
50      AC_CHECK_SIZEOF(int, 32)
```

Line 48 will generate a warning that AC_TRY_RUN was called without a default value to
allow cross-compiling. You may ignore this warning.

```
51
52      dnl Tests for library functions
53      dnl
54      AC_FUNC_GETLOADAVG
55      AC_FUNC_MMAP
56      AC_FUNC_UTIME_NULL
57      AC_FUNC_VFORK
58
59      dnl Tests of system services
60      dnl
61      AC_SYS_INTERPRETER
62      AC_PATH_X
63      AC_SYS_RESTARTABLE_SYSCALLS
```

Line 63 will generate a warning that AC_TRY_RUN was called without a default value to
allow cross-compiling. You may ignore this warning.

```
64
65      dnl Tests in this section exercise a few of `autoconf's
        ➥generic macros
66      dnl
67      dnl First, let's see if we have a usable void pointer type
68      dnl
69      AC_MSG_CHECKING(for a usable void pointer type)
```

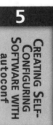

AC_MSG_CHECKING prints "checking" to the screen, followed by a space and the argument passed, in this case, "for a usable void pointer type." This macro allows you to mimic the way autoconf reports its activity to the user, and to let the user know what configure is doing. It is preferable to an apparent screen lockup.

```
70    AC_TRY_COMPILE([],
71        [char *ptr;
72         void *xmalloc();
73         ptr = (char *) xmalloc(1);
74        ],
75        [AC_DEFINE(HAVE_VOID_POINTER)
          ➥AC_MSG_RESULT(usable void pointer)],
76        AC_MSG_RESULT(no usable void pointer type))
```

Lines 70–76 deserve considerable explanation. autoconf will embed the actual C code (71–73) inside a skeletal C program, write the resulting program to the generated configure script, which will compile it when configure runs. configure catches the compiler output and looks for errors (you can track this down yourself by looking for xmalloc in the configure script). Line 75 creates a preprocessor symbol HAVE_VOID_POINTER (that you would have to put into ./acconfig.h, since it doesn't exist anywhere else except your code). If the compilation succeeds, configure will output #define HAVE_VOID_POINTER 1 to config.h and print the message "usable void pointer" to the screen; if compilation fails, configure outputs /*#undef HAVE_VOID_POINTER */ to config.h and displays "no usable void pointer" to the screen. In your source files, then, you simply test this preprocessor symbol like so:

```
#ifdef HAVE_VOID_POINTER
/* do something */
#else
 /* do something else */
#endif
```

```
77    dnl
78    dnl Now, let's exercise the preprocessor
79    dnl
80    AC_TRY_CPP(math.h, echo 'found math.h', echo 'no math.h?
      ➥- deep doo doo!')
```

On line 80, if configure finds the header file math.h, it will write "found math.h" to the screen; otherwise, it informs you that you have a problem.

```
81
82    dnl
83    dnl Next, we test the linker
84    dnl
85    AC_TRY_LINK([#ifndef HAVE_UNISTD_H
86                 #include <signal.h>
87                 #endif],
```

```
88        [char *ret = *(sys_siglist + 1);],
89        [AC_DEFINE(HAVE_SYS_SIGLIST), AC_MSG_RESULT(got sys_siglist)],
90        [AC_MSG_RESULT(no sys_siglist)])
```

We perform the same sort of test in lines 85–90 that we performed on lines 70–75. Again, because HAVE_SYS_SIGLIST is not a standard preprocessor symbol, you have to declare it in ./acconfig.h.

```
91    dnl
92    dnl Finally, set a default value for a ridiculous type
93    dnl
94    AC_CHECK_TYPE(short_short_t, unsigned short)
```

Line 94 simply checks for a (hopefully) non-existent C data type. If it does not exist, we define short_short_t to be unsigned short. You can confirm this by looking in config.h for a #define of short_short_t.

```
95
96    dnl Okay, we're done.  Create the output files and get out of here
97    dnl
98    AC_OUTPUT(Makefile)
```

Having completed all of our tests, we are ready to create our Makefile. AC_OUTPUT's job is to convert all of the tests we perform into information the compiler can understand so that when your happy end user types make, it builds your program, taking into account the peculiarities of the host system. To do its job, AC_OUTPUT needs a source file named, in this case, Makefile.in.

Hopefully, you will recall that in the descriptions of autoconf's macros, I frequently used the phrase "sets output variable FOO". autoconf uses those output variables to set values in the Makefile and in config.h. For example, AC_STRUCT_TIMEZONE defines HAVE_TZNAME if an array tzname is found. In the config.h that configure creates, you will find #define HAVE_TZNAME 1. In your source code, then, you could wrap code that uses the tzname array in a conditional statement such as:

```
if(HAVE_TZNAME)
    /* do something */
else
    /* do something else */
```

Similarly, Makefile.in contains a number of expressions such as "CFLAGS = @CFLAGS@". configure replaces each token of the form @output_variable@ in the Makefile with the correct value, as determined by the tests performed. In this case, @CFLAGS@ holds the debugging and optimization options, which, by default, are -g -O2.

With the template created, type `autoconf` in the directory where you created `config-ure.in`, which should be the root of your source tree. You will see two warnings (on lines 48 and 63), and wind up with a shell script named `configure` in your current working directory. To test it, type `./configure`. Figure 5.1 shows `configure` while it is executing.

FIGURE 5.1

`configure` *while running.*

If all went as designed, `configure` creates `Makefile`, `config.h`, and logs all of its activity to `config.log`. You can test the generated Makefile by typing `make`. The log file is especially useful if `configure` does not behave as expected, because you can see exactly what `configure` was trying to do at a given point. For example, the log file snippet below shows the steps `configure` took while looking for the `socket()` function (see line 24 of `configure.in`).

```
configure:979: checking for socket in -lsocket
configure:998: gcc -o conftest -g -O2  -I/usr/include conftest.c -lsocket
1>&5
/usr/bin/ld: cannot open -lsocket: No such file or directory
collect2: ld returned 1 exit status
configure: failed program was:
#line 987 "configure"
#include "confdefs.h"
/* Override any gcc2 internal prototype to avoid an error.  */
/* We use char because int might match the return type of a gcc2
    builtin and then its argument prototype would still apply.  */
char socket();

int main() {
socket()
; return 0; }
```

You can see that linker, ld, failed because it could not find the socket library, libsocket. The line numbers in the snippet refer to the configure script line numbers being executed.

Although it is a bit involved and tedious to set up, using autoconf provides many advantages for software developers, particularly in terms of code portability among different operating systems and hardware platforms and in allowing users to customize software to the idiosyncrasies of their local systems. You only have to perform autoconf's set up steps once—thereafter, minor tweaks are all you need to create and maintain self-configuring software.

Summary

This chapter took a detailed look at autoconf. After a high level overview of autoconf's use, you learned about many built-in macros that autoconf uses to configure software to a target platform. In passing, you also learned a bit about the wide variety of systems that, while all basically the same, vary just enough to make programming for them a potential nightmare. Finally, you walked step-by-step through creating a template file, generating a configure script, and using it to generate a makefile, the ultimate goal of autoconf.

CHAPTER 6

Comparing and Merging Source Files

by Kurt Wall

IN THIS CHAPTER

Programmers often need to quickly identify differences between two files, or to merge two files together. The GNU project's diff and patch programs provide these facilities. The first part of this chapter shows you how to create *diffs*, files that express the differences between two source code files. The second part illustrates using diffs to create source code patches in an automatic fashion.

Comparing Files

The diff command is one of a suite of commands that compares files. It is the one on which we will focus, but first we briefly introduce the cmp command. Then, we cover the other two commands, diff3 and sdiff, in the following sections.

Understanding the cmp Command

The cmp command compares two files, showing the offset and line numbers where they differ. Optionally, cmp displays differing characters side-by-side. Invoke cmp as follows:

```
$ cmp [options] file1 [file2]
```

A hyphen (-) may be substituted for file1 or file2, so cmp may be used in a pipeline. If one filename is omitted, cmp assumes standard input. The options include the following:

- -c¦--print-chars   Print the first characters encountered that differ
- -I N¦--ignore-initial=N   Ignore any difference encountered in the first N bytes
- -l¦--verbose   Print the offsets of differing characters in decimal format and the their values in octal format
- -s¦--silent¦--quiet   Suppress all output, returning only an exit code. 0 means no difference, 1 means one or more differences, 2 means an error occurred.
- -v¦--version   Print cmp's version information

From a programmer's perspective, cmp is not terribly useful. Listings 6.1 and 6.2 show two versions of Proverbs 3, verses 5 and 6. The acronyms JPS and NIV stand for Jewish Publication Society and New International Version, respectively.

LISTING 6.1   JPS VERSION OF PROVERBS 3:5-6

```
Trust in the Lord with all your heart,
And do not rely on your own understanding.
In all your ways acknowledge Him,
And He will make your paths smooth.
```

LISTING 6.2   NIV VERSION OF PROVERBS 3:5-6

```
Trust in the Lord with all your heart
and lean not on your own understanding;
in all your ways acknowledge him,
and he will make your paths straight.
```

A bare `cmp` produces the following:

```
$ cmp jps niv
jps niv differ: char 38, line 1
```

Helpful, yes? We see that the first difference occurs at byte 38 one line 1. Adding the `-c` option, `cmp` reports:

```
$ cmp -c jps niv
jps niv differ: char 38, line 1 is  54 ,  12 ^J
```

Now we know that the differing character is decimal 52, a control character, in this case. Replacing `-c` with `-l` produces the following:

```
$ cmp -l jps niv
    38  54   12
    39  12  141
    40 101  156
    41 156  144
    42 144   40
    43  40  154
...
   148 157  164
   149 164   56
   150 150   12
   151  56   12
cmp: EOF on niv
```

The first column of the preceding listing shows the character number where `cmp` finds a difference, the second column lists the character from the first file, and the third column the character from the second file. Note that the second to last line of the output (151 56 12) may not appear on some Red Hat systems. Character 38, for example, is octal 54, a comma (,) in the file `jps`, while it is octal 12, a newline, in the file `niv`. Only part of the output is shown to save space. Finally, combining `-c` and `-l` yields the following:

```
$ cmp -cl jps niv
    38  54 ,      12 ^J
    39  12 ^J    141 a
    40 101 A     156 n
    41 156 n     144 d
    42 144 d      40
```

```
    43  40        154 l
...
   148 157 o      164 t
   149 164 t       56 .
   150 150 h       12 ^J
   151  56 .       12 ^J
cmp: EOF on niv
```

Using `-cl` results in more immediately readable output, in that you can see both the encoded characters and their human-readable translations for each character that differs.

Understanding the `diff` Command

The `diff` command shows the differences between two files, or between two identically named files in separate directories. You can direct `diff`, using command line options, to format its output in any of several formats. The `patch` program, discussed in the section "Preparing Source Code Patches" later in this chapter, reads this output and uses it to re-create one of the files used to create the diff. As the authors of the `diff` manual say, "If you think of `diff` as subtracting one file from another to produce their difference, you can think of `patch` as adding the difference to one file to reproduce the other."

Because this book attempts to be practical, I will focus on `diff`'s usage from a programmer's perspective, ignoring many of its options and capabilities. While comparing files may seem an uninteresting subject, the technical literature devoted to the subject is extensive. For a complete listing of `diff`'s options and some of the theory behind file comparisons, see the `diff` info page (`info diff`).

The general syntax of the `diff` command is

```
diff [options] file1 file2
```

`diff` operates by attempting to find large sequences of lines common to `file1` and `file2`, interrupted by groups of differing lines, called *hunks*. Two identical files, therefore, will have no hunks and two complete different files result in one hunk consisting of all the lines from both files. Also bear in mind that `diff` performs a line-by-line comparison of two files, as opposed to `cmp`, which performs a character-by-character comparison. `diff` produces several different output formats. I will discuss each them in the following sections.

The Normal Output Format

If we `diff` Listings 6.1 and 6.2 (`jps` and `niv`, respectively, on the CD-ROM), the output is as follows:

```
$ diff jps niv
1,4c1,4
```

```
< Trust in the Lord with all your heart,
< And do not rely on your own understanding.
< In all your ways acknowledge Him,
< And He will make your paths smooth.
---
> Trust in the Lord with all your heart
> and lean not on your own understanding;
> in all your ways acknowledge him,
> and he will make your paths straight.
```

The output is in normal format, showing only the lines that differ, uncluttered by context. This output is the default in order to comply with Posix standards. Normal format is rarely used for distributing software patches; nevertheless, here is a brief description of the output, or hunk format. The general normal hunk format is as follows:

```
change_command
< file1 line
< file1 line...
---
> file2 line
> file2 line...
```

`change_command` takes the form of a line number or a comma- separated range of lines from `file1`, a one character command, and a line number or comma-separated range of lines from `file2`. The character will be one of the following:

- a—add
- d—delete
- c—change

The change command is actually the `ed` command to execute to transform `file1` into `file2`. Looking at the hunk above, to convert `jps` to `niv`, we would have to change lines 1–4 of `jps` to lines 1–4 of `niv`.

The Context Output Format

As noted in the preceding section, normal hunk format is rarely used to distribute software patches. Rather, the "context" or "unified" hunk formats `diff` produces are the preferred formats to patches. To generate context diffs, use the `-c`, `−context=[NUM]`, or `-C NUM` options to `diff`. So-called "context diffs" show differing lines surrounded by NUM lines of context, so you can more clearly understand the changes between files. Listings 6.3 and 6.4 illustrate the context `diff` format using a simple `bash` shell script that changes the signature files appended to the bottom of email and Usenet posts. (No line numbers were inserted into these listings in order to prevent confusion with the line numbers that `diff` produces.)

LISTING 6.3   sigrot.1

```
#!/usr/local/bin/bash
# sigrot.sh
# Version 1.0
# Rotate signatures
# Suitable to be run via cron
#############################

sigfile=signature

old=$(cat num)
let new=$(expr $old+1)

if [ -f $sigfile.$new ]; then
    cp $sigfile.$new .$sigfile
    echo $new > num
else
    cp $sigfile.1 .$sigfile
    echo 1 > num
fi
```

LISTING 6.4   sigrot.2

```
#!/usr/local/bin/bash
# sigrot.sh
# Version 2.0
# Rotate signatures
# Suitable to be run via cron
#############################

sigfile=signature
srcdir=$HOME/doc/signatures
srcfile=$srcdir/$sigfile

old=$(cat $srcdir/num)
let new=$(expr $old+1)

if [ -f $srcfile.$new ]; then
    cp $srcfile.$new $HOME/.$sigfile
    echo $new > $srcdir/num
else
    cp $srcfile.1 $HOME/.$sigfile
    echo 1 > $srcdir/num
fi
```

Context hunk format takes the following form:

```
*** file1 file1_timestamp
--- file2 file2_timestamp
```

```
***************
*** file1_line_range ****
  file1 line
  file1 line...
--- file2_line_range
  file2 line
  file2 line...
```

The first three lines identify the files compared and separate this information from the rest of the output, which is one or more hunks of differences. Each hunk shows one area where the files differ, surrounded (by default) by two line of context (where the files are the same). Context lines begin with two spaces and differing lines begin with a !, +, or -, followed by one space, illustrating the difference between the files. A + indicates a line in the file2 that does not exist in file1, so in a sense, a + line was added to file1 to create file2. A - marks a line in file1 that does not appear in file2, suggesting a subtraction operation. A ! indicates a line that was changed between file1 and file2; for each line or group of lines from file1 marked with !, a corresponding line or group of lines from file2 is also marked with a !.

To generate a context diff, execute a command similar to the following:

```
$ diff -C 1 sigrot.1 sigrot.2
```

The hunks look like the following:

```
*** sigrot.1    Sun Mar 14 22:41:34 1999
--- sigrot.2    Mon Mar 15 00:17:40 1999
**** 2,4 ****
  # sigrot.sh
! # Version 1.0
  # Rotate signatures
--- 2,4 ----
  # sigrot.sh
! # Version 2.0
  # Rotate signatures
***************
*** 8,19 ****
  sigfile=signature

! old=$(cat num)
  let new=$(expr $old+1)

! if [ -f $sigfile.$new ]; then
!     cp $sigfile.$new .$sigfile
!     echo $new > num
  else
!     cp $sigfile.1 .$sigfile
!     echo 1 > num
```

```
  fi
--- 8,21 ----
  sigfile=signature
+ srcdir=$HOME/doc/signatures
+ srcfile=$srcdir/$sigfile

! old=$(cat $srcdir/num)
  let new=$(expr $old+1)

! if [ -f $srcfile.$new ]; then
!     cp $srcfile.$new $HOME/.$sigfile
!     echo $new > $srcdir/num
  else
!     cp $srcfile.1 $HOME/.$sigfile
!     echo 1 > $srcdir/num
  fi**************
```

> **NOTE**
>
> To shorten the display, -C 1 was used to indicate that only a single line of context should be displayed. The patch command requires at least two lines of context to function properly. So when you generate context diffs to distribute as software patches, request at least two lines of context.

The output shows two hunks, one covering lines 2–4 in both files, the other covering lines 8–19 in sigrot.1 and lines 8–21 in sigrot.2. In the first hunk, the differing lines are marked with a ! in the first column. The change is minimal, as you can see, merely an incremented version number. In the second hunk, there are many more changes, and two lines were added to sigrot.2, indicated by the +. Each change and addition in both hunks is surrounded by a single line of context.

The Unified Output Format

Unified format is a modified version of context format that suppresses the display of repeated context lines and compacts the output in other ways as well. Unified format begins with a header identifying the files compared

```
--- file1 file1_timestamp
+++ file2 file2_timestamp
```

followed by one or more hunks in the form

```
@@ file1_range file2_range @@
 line_from_either_file
 line_from_either_file...
```

Context lines begin with a single space and differing lines begin with a + or a -, indicating that a line was added or removed at this location with respect to file1. The following listing was generated with the command diff –U 1 sigrot.1 sigrot.2.

```
--- sigrot.1      Sun Mar 14 2:41:34 1999
+++ sigrot.2      Mon Mar 15 00:17:40 1999
@@ -2,3 +2,3 @@
 # sigrot.sh
-# Version 1.0
+# Version 2.0
 # Rotate signatures
@@ -8,12 +8,14 @@
 sigfile=signature
+srcdir=$HOME/doc/signatures
+srcfile=$srcdir/$sigfile

-old=$(cat num)
+old=$(cat $srcdir/num)
 let new=$(expr $old+1)

-if [ -f $sigfile.$new ]; then
-    cp $sigfile.$new .$sigfile
-    echo $new > num
+if [ -f $srcfile.$new ]; then
+    cp $srcfile.$new $HOME/.$sigfile
+    echo $new > $srcdir/num
 else
-    cp $sigfile.1 .$sigfile
-    echo 1 > num
+    cp $srcfile.1 $HOME/.$sigfile
+    echo 1 > $srcdir/num
 fi
```

As you can see, the unified format's output is much more compact, but just as easy to understand without repeated context lines cluttering the display. Again, we have two hunks. The first hunk consists of lines 2–3 in both files, the second lines 8–12 in sigrot.1 and lines 8–14 of sigrot.2. The first hunk says "delete '# Version 1.0' from file1 and add '# Version 2.0' to file1 to create file2." The second hunk has three similar sets of additions and deletions, plus a simple addition of two lines at the top of the hunk.

As useful and compact as the unified format is, however, there is a catch: only GNU diff generates unified diffs and only GNU patch understands the unified format. So, if you are distributing software patches to systems that do not or may not use GNU diff and GNU patch, don't use unified format. Use the standard context format.

Additional `diff` Features

In addition to the normal, context, and unified formats we have discussed, `diff` can also produce side-by-side comparisons, `ed` scripts for modifying or converting files, and an RCS-compatible output format, and it contains a sophisticated ability to merge files using an if-then-else format. To generate side-by-side output, use `diff`'s `-y` or `--side-by-side` options. Note, however, that the output will be wider than usual and long lines will be truncated. To generate `ed` scripts, use the `-e` or `--ed` options. For information about `diff`'s RCS and if-then-else capabilities, see the documentation—they are not discussed in this book because they are esoteric and not widely used.

`diff` Command-Line Options

Like most GNU programs, `diff` sports a bewildering array of options to fine tune its behavior. Table 6.1 summarizes some of these options. For a complete list of all options, use the command `diff --help`.

TABLE 6.1   SELECTED `diff` OPTIONS

Option	Meaning
`--binary`	Read and write data in binary mode
`-c¦-C NUM¦--context=NUM`	Produce context format output, displaying NUM lines of context
`-t¦--expand-tabs`	Expand tabs to spaces in the output
`-i¦--ignore-case`	Ignore case changes, treating upper- and lowercase letters the same
`-H¦--speed-large-files`	Modify `diff`'s handling of large files
`-w¦--ignore-all-space`	Ignore whitespace when comparing lines
`-I REGEXP¦ ignore-matching-lines=REGEXP`	Ignore lines that insert or delete lines that match the regular expression REGEXP
`-B¦--ignore-blank-lines`	Ignore changes that insert or delete blank lines
`-b¦--ignore-space-change`	Ignore changes in the amount of whitespace
`-l¦--paginate`	Paginate the output by passing it through `pr`
`-p¦--show-c-function`	Show the C function in which a change occurs
`-q¦--brief`	Only report if files differ, do not output the differences
`-a¦--text`	Treat all files as text, even if they appear to be binary, and perform a line-by-line comparison

Option	Meaning
-u¦-U NUM¦--unified=NUM	Produce unified format output, displaying NUM lines of context
-v¦--version	Print diff's version number
-y¦--side-by-side	Produce side-by-side format output

Understanding the `diff3` Command

diff3 shows its usefulness when two people change a common file. It compares the two sets of changes, creates a third file containing the merged output, and indicates conflicts between the changes. diff3's syntax is:

```
diff3 [options] myfile oldfile yourfile
```

oldfile is the common ancestor from which myfile and yourfile were derived. Listing 6.5 introduces sigrot.3. It is the same as sigrot.1, except that we added a return statement at the end of the script.

LISTING 6.5   sigrot.3

```
#!/usr/local/bin/bash
# sigrot.sh
# Version 3.0
# Rotate signatures
# Suitable to be run via cron
#############################

sigfile=signature

old=$(cat num)
let new=$(expr $old+1)

if [ -f $sigfile.$new ]; then
    cp $sigfile.$new .$sigfile
    echo $new > num
else
    cp $sigfile.1 .$sigfile
    echo 1 > num
fi

return 0
```

Predictably, diff3's output is more complex because it must juggle three input files. diff3 only displays lines that vary between the files. Hunks in which all three input files are different are called three-way hunks; two-way hunks occur when only two of the three files differ. Three-way hunks are indicated with ====, while two-way hunks add a 1, 2, or 3 at the end to indicate which of the files is different. After this header, diff3 displays one or more commands (again, in ed style), that indicate how to produce the hunk, followed by the hunk itself. The command will be one of the following:

> file:1a—The hunk appears after line 1, but does not exist in file, so it must be appended after line 1 to produce the other files.

> file:rc—The hunk consists of range *r* lines from file and one of the indicated changes must be made in order to produce the other files.

To distinguish hunks from commands, diff3 hunks begin with two spaces. For example,

```
$ diff3 sigrot.2 sigrot.1 sigrot.3
```

yields (output truncated to conserve space):

```
====
1:3c
  # Version 2.0
2:3c
  # Version 1.0
3:3c
  # Version 3.0
====1
1:9,10c
  srcdir=$HOME/doc/signatures
  srcfile=$srcdir/$sigfile
2:8a
3:8a
====1
1:12c
  old=$(cat $srcdir/num)
2:10c
3:10c
  old=$(cat num)
...
```

The first hunk is a three-way hunk. The other hunks are two-way hunks. To obtain sigrot.2 from sigrot.1 or sigrot.3, the lines

```
srcdir=$HOME/doc/signatures
srcfile=$srcdir/$sigfile
```

from sigrot.2 must be appended after line 8 of sigrot.1 and sigrot.3. Similarly, to obtain sigrot.1 from sigrot.2, line 10 from sigrot.1 must be changed to line 12 from sigrot.1.

As previously mentioned, the output is complex. Rather than deal with this, you can use the `-m` or `--merge` to instruct `diff3` to merge the files together, and then sort out the changes manually.

```
$ diff3 -m sigrot.2 sigrot.1 sigrot.3 > sigrot.merged
```

merges the files, marks conflicting text, and saves the output to `sigrot.merged`. The merged file is much simpler to deal with because you only have to pay attention to conflicting output, which, as shown in Listing 6.6, is clearly marked with <<<<<<<, |||||||, or >>>>>>>.

LISTING 6.6   OUTPUT OF `diff3`'S MERGE OPTION

```
#!/usr/local/bin/bash
# sigrot.sh
<<<<<<< sigrot.2
# Version 2.0
||||||| sigrot.1
# Version 1.0
=======
# Version 3.0
>>>>>>> sigrot.3
# Rotate signatures
# Suitable to be run via cron
#############################

sigfile=signature
srcdir=$HOME/doc/signatures
srcfile=$srcdir/$sigfile

old=$(cat $srcdir/num)
let new=$(expr $old+1)

if [ -f $srcfile.$new ]; then
    cp $srcfile.$new $HOME/.$sigfile
    echo $new > $srcdir/num
else
    cp $srcfile.1 $HOME/.$sigfile
    echo 1 > $srcdir/num
fi

return 0
```

<<<<<<< marks conflicts from `myfile`, >>>>>>> marks conflicts from `yourfile`, and ||||||| marks conflicts with `oldfile`. In this case, we probably want the most recent version number, so we would delete the marker lines and the lines indicating the 1.0 and 2.0 versions.

Understanding the `sdiff` Command

`sdiff` enables you to interactively merge two files together. It displays the files in side-by-side format. To use the interactive feature, specify the `-o file` or `--output file` to indicate the filename to which output should be saved. `sdiff` will display each hunk, followed by a `%` prompt, at which you type one of these commands, followed by Enter:

- `l`—Copy the left-hand column to the output file
- `r`—Copy the right-hand column to the output file
- `el`—Edit the left-hand column, then copy the edited text to the output file
- `er`—Edit the right-hand column, then copy the edited text to the output file
- `e`—Discard both versions, enter new text, then copy the new text to the output file
- `eb`—Concatenate the two versions, edit the concatenated text, then copy it to the output file
- `q`—Quit

Editing `sdiff` is left as an exercise for you.

Preparing Source Code Patches

Within the Linux community, most software is distributed either in binary (ready to run) format, or in source format. Source distributions, in turn, are available either as complete source packages, or as `diff`-generated patches. `patch` is the GNU project's tool for merging `diff` files into existing source code trees. The following sections discuss `patch`'s command-line options, how to create a patch using `diff`, and how to apply a patch using `patch`.

Like most of the GNU project's tools, `patch` is a robust, versatile, and powerful tool. It can read the standard normal and context format diffs, as well as the more compact unified format. `patch` also strips header and trailer lines from patches, enabling you to apply a patch straight from an email message or Usenet posting without performing any preparatory editing.

`patch` Command-Line Options

Table 6.2 lists commonly used `patch` options. For complete details, try `patch --help` or the `patch` info pages.

TABLE 6.2 patch OPTIONS

Option	*Meaning*
-c¦--context	Interpret the patch file as a context diff
-e¦--ed	Interpret the patch file as an ed script
-n¦--normal	Interpret the patch file as a normal diff
-u¦--unified	Interpret the patch file as a unified diff
-d DIR¦--directory=DIR	Make DIR the current directory for interpreting filenames in the patch file
-F NUM¦--fuzz=NUM	Set the fuzz factor to NUM lines when resolving inexact matches
-l¦--ignore-white-space	Consider any sequence of whitespace equivalent to any other sequence of whitespace
-pNUM¦--strip=NUM	Strip NUM filename components from filenames in the patch file
-s¦--quiet	Work silently unless errors occur
-R¦--reverse	Assume the patch file was created with the old and new files swapped
-t¦--batch	Do not ask any questions
--version	Display patch's version information and exit

In most cases, patch can determine the format of a patch file. If it gets confused, however, use the -c, -e, -n, or -u options to tell patch how to treat the input patch file. As previously noted , only GNU diff and GNU patch can create and read, respectively, the unified format, so unless you are certain that only users with access to these GNU utilities will receive your patch, use the context diff format for creating patches. Also recall that patch requires at least two lines of context correctly to apply patches.

The fuzz factor (-F NUM or --fuzz=NUM) sets the maximum number of lines patch will ignore when trying to locate the correct place to apply a patch. It defaults to 2, and cannot be more than the number of context lines provided with the diff. Similarly, if you are applying a patch pulled from an email message or a Usenet post, the mail or news client may change spaces into tabs or tabs into spaces. If so, and you are having trouble applying the patch, use patch's -l or --ignore-white-space option.

Sometimes, programmers reverse the order of the filenames when creating a diff. The correct order should be old-file new-file. If the patch encounters a diff that appears to have been created in `new-file old-file` order, it will consider the patch file a "reverse patch." To apply a reverse patch in normal order, specify `-R` or `--reverse` to patch. You can also use `-R` to back out a previously applied `patch`.

As it works, `patch` makes a backup copy of each source file it is going to change, appending `.orig` to the end of the file. If `patch` fails to apply a hunk, it saves the hunk using the filename stored in the patch file and adding `.rej` (for reject) to it.

Creating a Patch

To create a patch, use `diff` to create a context or unified diff, place the name of the older file before the newer file on the `diff` command line, and name your patch file by appending `.diff` or `.patch` to the filename. For example, to create a patch based on `sigrot.1` and `sigrot.2`, the appropriate command line would be

```
$ diff -c sigrot.1 sigrot.2 > sigrot.patch
```

to create a context diff, or

```
$ diff -u sigrot.1 sigrot.2 > sigrot.patch
```

to create a unified diff. If you have a complicated source tree, one with several subdirectories, use `diff`'s `-r` (`--recursive`) option to tell `diff` to recurse into each subdirectory when creating the patch file.

Applying a Patch

To apply the patch, the command would be

```
$ patch -p0 < sigrot.patch
```

The `-pNUM` option tells patch how many "`/`"s and intervening filename components to strip off the filename in the patch file before applying the patch. Suppose, for instance, the filename in the patch is `/home/kwall/src/sigrot/sigrot.1`. `-p1` would result in `home/kwall/src/sigrot/sigrot.1`; `-p4` would result in `sigrot/sigrot.1`; `-p` strips off every part but the final filename, or `sigrot.1`.

If, after applying a patch, you decide it was mistake, simply add `-R` to the command line you used to install the patch, and you will get your original, unpatched file back:

```
$ patch -p0 -R < sigrot.patch
```

See, using `diff` and `patch` is not hard! Admittedly, there is a lot to know about the various file formats and how the commands work, but actually applying them is very simple and straightforward. As with most Linux commands, there is much more you *can* learn, but it isn't necessary to know everything in order to be able to use these utilities effectively.

Summary

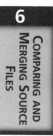

In this chapter, you learned about the `cmp`, `diff`, `diff3`, `sdiff`, and `patch` commands. Of these, `diff` and `patch` are the most commonly used for creating and applying source code patches. You have also learned about `diff`'s various output formats. The standard format is the context format, because most `patch` programs can understand it. What you have learned in this chapter will prove to be an essential part of your Linux software development toolkit.

Version Control with RCS

by Kurt Wall

IN THIS CHAPTER

Version control is an automated process for keeping track of and managing changes made to source code files. Why bother? Because one day you will make that one fatal edit to a source file, delete its predecessor and forget exactly which line or lines of code you "fixed"; because simultaneously keeping track of the current release, the next release, and eight bug fixes manually will become too tedious and confusing; because frantically searching for the backup tape because one of your colleagues overwrote a source file for the fifth time will drive you over the edge; because, one day, over your morning cappuccino, you will say to yourself, "Version control, it's the Right Thing to Do." In this chapter, we will examine RCS, the Revision Control System, a common solution to the version control problem.

RCS is a common solution because it is available on almost all UNIX systems, not just on Linux. Indeed, RCS was first developed on real, that is, proprietary, UNIX systems, although it is not, itself, proprietary. Two alternatives to RCS, which is maintained by the GNU project, are SCCS, the Source Code Control System, a proprietary product, and CVS, the Concurrent Version System, which is also maintained by the GNU project.

CVS is built on top of RCS and adds two features to it. First, it is better suited to managing multi-directory projects than RCS because it handles hierarchical directory structures more simply and its notion of a project is more complete. Whereas RCS is file-oriented, as you will see in this chapter, CVS is project-oriented. CVS' second advantage is that it supports distributed projects, those where multiple developers in separate locations, both geographically and in terms of the Internet, access and manipulate a single source repository. The KDE project and the Debian Linux distribution are two examples of large projects using CVS' distributed capabilities.

Note, however, that because CVS is built on top of RCS, you will not be able to master CVS without some knowledge of RCS. This chapter introduces you to RCS because it is a simpler system to learn. I will not discuss CVS.

Terminology

Before proceeding, however, Table 7.1 lists a few terms that will be used throughout the chapter. Because they are so frequently used, I want to make sure you understand their meaning as far as RCS and version control in general are concerned.

TABLE 7.1 VERSION CONTROL TERMS

Term	Description
RCS File	Any file located in an RCS directory, controlled by RCS and accessed using RCS commands. An RCS file contains all versions of a particular file. Normally, an RCS file has a ".v" extension.

Term	Description
Working File	One or more files retrieved from the RCS source code repository (the RCS directory) into the current working directory and available for editing.
Lock	A working file retrieved for editing such that no one else can edit it simultaneously. A working file is "locked" by the first user against edits by other users.
Revision	A specific, numbered version of a source file. Revisions begin with 1.1 and increase incrementally, unless forced to use a specific revision number.

The Revision Control System manages multiple versions of files, usually but not necessarily source code files (I used RCS to maintain the various revisions of this book). RCS automates file version storage and retrieval, change logging, access control, release management, and revision identification and merging. As an added bonus, RCS minimizes disk space requirements because it tracks only file changes.

> **NOTE**
>
> The examples used in this chapter assume you are using RCS version 5.7. To determine the version of RCS you are using, type **rcs -V**.

Basic RCS Usage

One of RCS's attractions is its simplicity. With only a few commands, you can accomplish a great deal. This section discusses the `ci`, `co`, and `ident` commands as well as RCS keywords.

ci and co

You can accomplish a lot with RCS using only two commands, `ci` and `co`, and a directory named RCS. `ci` stands for "check in," which means storing a working file in the RCS directory; `co` means "check out," and refers to retrieving an RCS file from the RCS repository. To get started, create an RCS directory:

```
$ mkdir RCS
```

All RCS commands will use this directory, if it is present in your current working directory. The RCS directory is also called the repository. Next, create the source file shown in Listing 7.1, `howdy.c`, in the same directory in which you created the RCS directory.

LISTING 7.1 howdy.c—BASIC RCS USAGE

```
/* $Id$
 * howdy.c
 * Sample code to demonstrate RCS Usage
 * Kurt Wall
 */
#include <stdio.h>
#include <stdlib.h>

int main(void)
{
    fprintf(stdout,  Howdy, Linux programmer!");
    return EXIT_SUCCESS;
}
```

Execute the command ci howdy.c. RCS asks for a description of the file, copies it to the RCS directory, and deletes the original. "Deletes the original?" Ack! Don't worry, you can retrieve it with the command co howdy.c. Voilá! You have a working file. Note that the working file is read-only; if you want to edit it, you have to lock it. To do this, use the -l option with co (co -l howdy.c). -l means lock, as explained in Table 7.1.

```
$ ci howdy.c
RCS/howdy.c,v  <--  howdy.c
enter description, terminated with single '.' or end of file:
NOTE: This is NOT the log message!
>> Simple program to illustrate RCS usage
>> .
initial revision: 1.1
done
$ co -l howdy.c
RCS/howdy.c,v  -->  howdy.c
revision 1.1 (locked)
done
```

To see version control in action, make a change to the working file. If you haven't already done so, check out and lock the file (co -l howdy.c). Change anything you want, but I recommend adding "\n" to the end of fprintf()'s string argument because Linux (and UNIX in general), unlike DOS and Windows, do not automatically add a newline to the end of console output.

```
fprintf(stdout, "Howdy, Linux programmer!\n");
```

Next, check the file back in and RCS will increment the revision number to 1.2, ask for a description of the change you made, incorporate the changes you made into the RCS file, and (annoyingly) delete the original. To prevent deletion of your working files during check-in operations, use the -l or -u option with ci.

```
$ ci -l howdy.c
RCS/howdy.c,v  <-- howdy.c
new revision: 1.2; previous revision: 1.1
enter log message, terminated with single '.' or end of file:
>> Added newline
>> .
done
```

When used with `ci`, both the `-l` and `-u` options cause an implied check out of the file after the check in procedure completes. `-l` locks the file so you can continue to edit it, while `-u` checks out an unlocked or read-only working file.

In addition to `-l` and `-u`, `ci` and `co` accept two other very useful options: `-r` (for "revision") and `-f` ("force"). Use `-r` to tell RCS which file revision you want to manipulate. RCS assumes you want to work with the most recent revision; `-r` overrides this default. `ci -r2 howdy.c` (this is equivalent to `ci -r2.1 howdy.c`), for example, creates revision 2.1 of `howdy.c`; `co -r1.7 howdy.c` checks out revision 1.7 of `howdy.c`, disregarding the presence of higher-numbered revisions in your working directory.

The `-f` option forces RCS to overwrite the current working file. By default, RCS aborts a check-out operation if a working file of the same name already exists in your working directory. So, if you really botch up your working file, `co -l -f howdy.c` is a handy way to discard all of the changes you've made and start with a known good source file. When used with `ci`, `-f` forces RCS to check in a file even if it has not changed.

RCS's command-line options are cumulative, as you might expect, and it does a good job of disallowing incompatible options. To check out and lock a specific revision of `howdy.c`, you would use a command like `co -l -r2.1 howdy.c`. Similarly, `ci -u -r3 howdy.c` checks in `howdy.c`, assigns it revision number 3.1, and deposits a read-only revision 3.1 working file back into your current working directory.

RCS Keywords

RCS keywords are special, macro-like tokens used to insert and maintain identifying information in source, object, and binary files. These tokens take the form `$KEYWORD$`. When a file containing RCS keywords is checked out, RCS expands `$KEYWORD$` to `$KEYWORD: VALUE $`.

Id

For example, that peculiar string at the top of Listing 7.1, `$Id$`, is an RCS keyword. The first time you checked out `howdy.c`, RCS expanded it to something like

```
$Id: howdy.c,v 1.1 1998/12/07 22:39:01  kwall Exp $
```

The format of the Id string is

```
$KEYWORD: FILENAME REV_NUM DATE TIME AUTHOR STATE LOCKER $"
```

On your system, most of these fields will have different values. If you checked out the file with a lock, you will also see your login name after the Exp entry.

Log

RCS replaces the Log keyword with the log message you supplied during check in. Rather than replacing the previous log entry, though, RCS inserts the new log message above the last log entry. Listing 7.2 gives an example of how the Log keyword is expanded after several check ins:

LISTING 7.2   THE Log KEYWORD AFTER A FEW CHECK INS

```c
/* $Id: howdy.c,v 1.5 1999/01/04 23:07:35 kwall Exp kwall $
 * howdy.c
 * Sample code to demonstrate RCS usage
 * Kurt Wall
 * Listing 7.1
 *
 * ******************** Revision History ********************
 * $Log: howdy.c,v $
 * Revision 1.5  1999/01/04 23:07:35  kwall
 * Added pretty box for the revision history
 *
 * Revision 1.4  1999/01/04 14:41:55  kwall
 * Add args to main for processing command line
 *
 * Revision 1.3  1999/01/04 14:40:15  kwall
 * Added the Log keyword.
 * ********************************************************
 */
#include <stdio.h>
#include <stdlib.h>

int main(int argc, char **argv)
{
        fprintf(stdout, "Howdy, Linux programmer!\n");
        return EXIT_SUCCESS;
}
```

The Log keyword makes it convenient to see the changes made to a given file while working within that file. Read from top to bottom, the change history lists the most recent changes first.

Other RCS Keywords

Table 7.2 lists other RCS keywords and how RCS expands each of them.

TABLE 7.2 RCS KEYWORDS

Keyword	Description
$Author$	Login name of user who checked in the revision
$Date$	Date and time revision was checked, in UTC format
$Header$	Full pathname of the RCS file, the revision number, date, time, author, state, locker (if locked)
$Locker$	Login name of the user who locked the revision (if not locked, field is empty)
$Name$	Symbolic name, if any, used to check out the revision
$RCSfile$	Name of the RCS file without a path
$Revision$	Revision number assigned to the revision
$Source$	Full pathname to the RCS file
$State$	The state of the revision: Exp (experimental), the default; Stab (stable); Rel (released)

The `ident` Command

The `ident` command locates RCS keywords in files of all types. This feature lets you find out which revisions of which modules are used in a given program release. To illustrate, create the source file shown in Listing 7.3.

LISTING 7.3 THE `ident` COMMAND

```
/* $Id$
 * prn_env.c
 * Display values of environment variables.
 * Kurt Wall
 * Listing 7.3
 */
#include <stdio.h>
#include <stdlib.h>
#include <unistd.h>

static char rcsid[] = "$Id$\n";

int main(void)
```

continues

LISTING 7.3 CONTINUED

```
{
    extern char **environ;
    char **my_env = environ;

    while(*my_env) {
        fprintf(stdout, "%s\n", *my_env);
        my_env++;
    }
    return EXIT_SUCCESS;
}
```

The program, prn_env.c, loops through the environ array declared in the header file unistd.h to print out the values of all your environment variables (see man(3) environ for more details). The statement static char rcsid[] = "Id\n"; takes advantage of RCS's keyword expansion to create a static text buffer holding the value of the Id keyword in the compiled program that ident can extract. Check prn_env.c in using the -u option (ci -u prn_env.c), and then compile and link the program (gcc prn_env.c -o prn_env). Ignore the warning you may get that rcsid is defined but not used. Run the program if you want, but also execute the command ident prn_env. If everything worked correctly, you should get output resembling the following:

```
$ ident prn_env
prn_env:
     $Id: prn_env.c,v 1.1 1999/01/06 03:04:40 kwall Exp $
```

The Id keyword expanded as previously described and gcc compiled this into the binary. To confirm this, page through the source code file and compare the Id string in the source code to ident's output. The two strings will match exactly.

ident works by extracting strings of the form $KEYWORD: VALUE $ from source, object, and binary files. It even works on raw binary data files and core dumps. In fact, because ident looks for all instances of the $ KEYWORD: VALUE $ pattern, you can also use words that are not RCS keywords. This enables you to embed additional information into programs, for example, a company name. Embedded information can be a valuable tool for isolating problems to a specific code module. The slick part of this feature is that RCS updates the identification strings automatically—a real bonus for programmers and project managers.

rcsdiff

If you need to see the differences between one of your working files and its corresponding RCS file, use the rcsdiff command. rcsdiff uses the diff(1) command (discussed in Chapter 6, "Comparing and Merging Source Files") to compare file revisions. In its simplest form, rcsdiff filename, rcsdiff compares the latest revision of filename in the repository with the working copy of filename. You can also compare specific revisions using the -r option.

Consider the sample program prn_env.c. Check out a locked version of it and remove the static char buffer. The result should look like the following:

```c
#include <stdio.h>
#include <stdlib.h>
#include <unistd.h>


int main(void)
{
    extern char **environ;
    char **my_env = environ;

    while(*my_env) {
        fprintf(stdout, "%s\n", *my_env);
        my_env++;
    }
    return EXIT_SUCCESS;
}
```

Now, execute the command rcsdiff prn_env.c. RCS complies and displays the following:

```
$ rcsdiff prn_env.c
===================================================================
RCS file: RCS/prn_env.c,v
retrieving revision 1.1
diff -r1.1 prn_env.c
11d10
< static char rcsid[] =
➥"$Id: prn_env.c,v 1.1 1999/01/06 03:04:40 kwall Exp kwall $\n";
```

As we learned in the Chapter 6, this diff output means that line 11 in revision 1.1 would have appeared on line 10 of prn_env.c if it had not been deleted. To look at examining specific revisions using the -r option, check prn_env.c into the repository, check it right back out with a lock, add a sleep(5) statement immediately above the return statement, and, finally, check this third revision back in with the -u option. You should now have three revisions of prn_env.c in the repository.

The general format for comparing specific file revisions using rcsdiff is

```
rcsdiff [ -rFILE1 [ -rFILE2 ] ] FILENAME
```

7

VERSION CONTROL WITH RCS

First, compare revision 1.1 to the working file:

```
$ rcsdiff -r1.1 prn_env.c
===================================================================
RCS file: RCS/prn_env.c,v
retrieving revision 1.1
diff -r1.1 prn_env.c
1c1
< /* $Id: prn_env.c,v 1.1 1999/01/06 03:10:17 kwall Exp $
---
> /* $Id: prn_env.c,v 1.3 1999/01/06 03:12:22 kwall Exp $
11d10
< static char rcsid[] =
➥"$Id:  prn_env.c,v 1.1 1999/01/06 03:04:40 Exp kwall $\n";
21a21
>         sleep(5);
```

Next, compare 1.2 to 1.3:

```
$ rcsdiff -r1.2 -r1.3 prn_env.c
===================================================================
RCS file: RCS/prn_env.c,v
retrieving revision 1.2
retrieving revision 1.3
diff -r1.2 -r1.3
1c1
< /* $Id: prn_env.c,v 1.1 1999/01/06 03:10:17 kwall Exp $
---
> /* $Id: prn_env.c,v 1.3 1999/01/06 03:12:22 kwall Exp $
20a21
>         sleep(5);
```

rcsdiff is a useful utility for viewing changes to RCS files or preparing to merge multiple revisions into a single revision.

For you GNU Emacs aficionados, Emacs boasts an advanced version control mode, VC, that supports RCS, CVS, and SCCS. For example, to check the current file in or out of an RCS repository, type **C-x v v** or **C-x C-q** and follow the prompts. If you want to place the file you are currently editing into the repository for the first time (called "registering" a file with RCS), you would type **C-x v i**. All of Emacs' version control commands are prefixed with C-x v. Figure 7.1 illustrates registering a file in an Emacs session with RCS.

Emacs' RCS mode greatly enhances RCS' basic capabilities. If you are a fan of Emacs, I encourage you to explore Emacs' VC mode.

Figure 7.1

Registering a file with RCS in Emacs.

Other RCS Commands

Besides `ci`, `co`, `ident`, and `rcsdiff`, the RCS suite includes `rlog`, `rcsclean`, `rcsmerge`, and, of course, `rcs`. These additional commands extend your control of your source code, allowing you to merge or delete RCS files, review log entries, and perform other administrative functions.

rcsclean

`rcsclean` does what its name suggests: it cleans up RCS working files. The basic syntax is `rcsclean [options] [file ... ]`. A bare `rcsclean` command will delete all working files unchanged since they were checked out. The `-u` option tells `rcsclean` to unlock any locked files and removes unchanged working files. You can specify a revision to delete using the `-rM.N` format.

```
$ rcsclean -r2.3 foobar.c
```

removes the 2.3 revision of `foobar.c`.

rlog

`rlog` prints the log messages and other information about files stored in the RCS repository. For example, `rlog prn_env.c` will display all of the log information for all revisions of `prn_env.c`. The `-R` option tells `rlog` to display only filenames. To see a list of all the files in the repository, for example, `rlog -R RCS/*` is the proper command (of course, you could always type `ls -l RCS`, too). If you only want to see a list of all locked files, use the `-L` option, as in `rlog -R -L RCS/*`. To see the log information on all files locked by the user named gomer, use the `-l` option:

```
$ rlog -lgomer RCS/*
```

rcs

The rcs command is primarily an administrative command. In normal usage, though, it is useful in two ways. If you checked out a file read-only, then made changes you can't bear to lose, rcs -l filename will check out filename with a lock without simultaneously overwriting the working file. If you need to break a lock on a file checked out by someone else, rcs -u filename is the command to use. The file will be unlocked, and a message sent to the original locker, with an explanation from you about why you broke the lock. As you will recall, each time you check a file in, you can type a check in message explaining what has changed or what you did. If you make a typographical error or some other mistake in the check in message, or would simply like to add additional information to it, you can use the following rcs command:

```
$ rcs -mrev:msg
```

rev is the revision whose message you want to correct or modify and msg is the corrected or additional information you want to add.

rcsmerge

rcsmerge attempts to merge multiple revisions into a single working file. The general syntax is

```
rcsmerge -rAncestor -rDescendant Working_file -p > Merged_file
```

Both Descendant and Working_file must be descended from Ancestor. The -p option tells rcsmerge to send its output to stdout, rather than overwriting Working_file. By redirecting the output to Merged_file, you can examine the results of the merge. While rcsmerge does the best it can merging files, the results can be unpredictable. The -p option protects you from this unpredictability.

For more information on RCS, see these man pages: rcs(1), ci(1), co(1), rcsintro(1), rcsdiff(1), rcsclean(1), rcsmerge(1), rlog(1), rcsfile(1), and ident(1).

Summary

In this chapter, you learned about RCS, the Revision Control System. ci and co, with their various options and arguments, are RCS's fundamental commands. RCS keywords enable you to embed identifying strings in your code and in compiled programs that can later be extracted with the ident command. You also learned other helpful but less frequently used RCS commands, including rcsdiff, rcsclean, rcsmerge, and rlog.

Creating Programs in Emacs

by Kurt Wall and Mark Watson

IN THIS CHAPTER

Emacs provides a rich, highly configurable programming environment. In fact, you can start Emacs in the morning, and, while you are compiling your code, you can catch up on last night's posts to alt.vampire.flonk.flonk.flonk, email a software patch, get caring professional counseling, and write your documentation, all without leaving Emacs. This chapter gets you started with Emacs, focusing on Emacs' features for programmers.

Introduction to Emacs

Emacs has a long history, as one might expect of software currently shipping version 20.3 (the version used for this chapter), but we won't recite it. The name Emacs derives from the "editing macros" that Richard Stallman originally wrote for the TECO editor. Stallman has written his own account of Emacs' history, which can be viewed online at `http://www.gnu.org/philosophy/stallman-kth.html` (you will also get a good look at GNU's philosophical underpinnings).

> **NOTE**
>
> The world is divided into three types of people—those who use Emacs, those who prefer vi, and everyone else. Many flame wars have erupted over the Emacs versus vi issue.
>
> Commenting on Emacs' enormous feature set, one wag said: "Emacs is a great operating system, but UNIX has more programs." I'm always interested in Emacs humor. Send your Emacs related wit to `kwall@xmission.com` with "Emacs Humor" somewhere in the subject line.

What is true of any programmer's editor is especially true of Emacs: Time invested in learning Emacs repays itself many times over during the development process. This chapter presents enough information about Emacs to get you started using it and also introduces many features that enhance its usage as a C development environment. However, Emacs is too huge a topic to cover in one chapter. A complete tutorial is *Sams Teach Yourself Emacs in 24 Hours*. For more detailed information, see the *GNU Emacs Manual* and the *GNU Emacs Lisp Reference Manual*, published by the Free Software Foundation, Inc., and *Learning GNU Emacs* and *Writing GNU Emacs Extensions*, published by O'Reilly.

Starting and Stopping Emacs

To start Emacs, type **emacs** or **emacs filename**. If you have X configured and running on your system, try **xemacs** to start XEmacs, a graphical version of Emacs, formerly known as Lucid Emacs. If Emacs was built with Athena widget set support, Emacs will have mouse support and a pull-down menu. Depending on which command you type, you should get a screen that looks like Figure 8.1, Figure 8.2, or Figure 8.3.

FIGURE 8.1

Emacs on a text mode console.

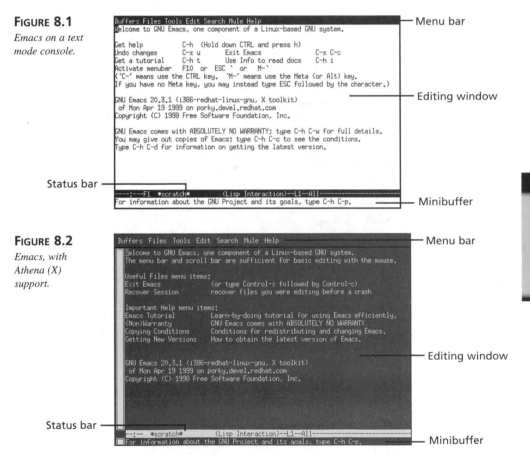

Menu bar

Editing window

Status bar

Minibuffer

FIGURE 8.2

Emacs, with Athena (X) support.

Menu bar

Editing window

Status bar

Minibuffer

8

CREATING PROGRAMS IN EMACS

FIGURE 8.3

XEmacs has an attractive graphical interface.

Menu bar

Toolbar

Editing window

Status bar

Minibuffer

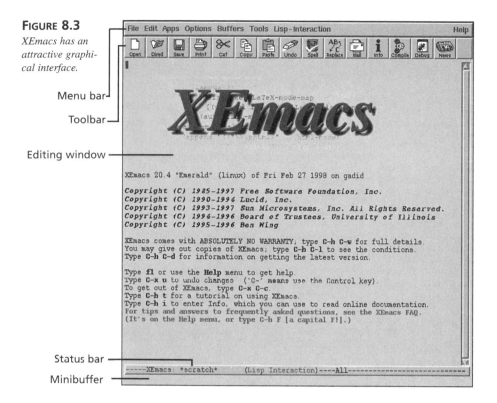

If you take a notion to, type **C-h t** to go through the interactive tutorial. It is instructive and only takes about thirty minutes to complete. We will not cover it here because we do not want to spoil the fun. The following list explains the notation used in this chapter:

- **C-x** means press and hold the Ctrl key and press letter **x**
- **C x** means press and release the Ctrl key, and then press letter **x**
- **M-x** means press and hold the Alt key and press letter **x** (if **M-x** does not work as expected, try **Esc x**)
- **M x** means press and release the Alt key, and then press letter **x**

Due to peculiarities in terminal configuration, the Alt key may not work with all terminal types or keyboards. If a command preceded with the Alt key fails to work as expected, try using the Esc key instead. On the so-called "Windows keyboards," try pressing the Window key between Alt and Ctrl.

> **TIP**
>
> To exit any version of Emacs, type **C-x C-c**.

Moving Around

Although Emacs usually responds appropriately if you use the arrow keys, we recommend you learn the "Emacs way." At first, it will seem awkward, but as you become more comfortable with Emacs, you will find that you work faster because you don't have to move your fingers off the keyboard. The following list describes how to move around in Emacs:

- **M-b**—Moves the cursor to the beginning of the word left of the cursor
- **M-f**—Moves the cursor to the end of word to the right of the cursor
- **M-a**—Moves to the beginning of the current sentence
- **M-e**—Moves to the end of the current sentence
- **C-n**—Moves the cursor to the next line
- **C-p**—Moves the cursor to the previous line
- **C-a**—Moves the cursor to the beginning of the line
- **C-e**—Moves the cursor the end of the line
- **C-v**—Moves display down one screen full
- **M-v**—Moves display up one screen full
- **M->**—Moves the cursor to the end of the file
- **M-<**—Moves the cursor to the beginning of the file

If you open a file ending in .c, Emacs automatically starts in C mode, which has features that the default mode, Lisp Interaction, lacks. **M-C-a**, for example, moves the cursor to the beginning of the current function, and **M-C-e** moves the cursor to the end of the current function. In addition to new commands, C mode modifies the behavior of other Emacs commands. In C mode, for instance, **M-a** moves the cursor to the beginning of the innermost C statement, and **M-e** moves the cursor to the end of the innermost C statement.

You can also apply a "multiplier" to almost any Emacs command by typing **C-u [N]**, where **N** is any integer. **C-u** by itself has a default multiplier value of 4. So, **C-u 10 C-n** will move the cursor down ten lines. **C-u C-n** moves the cursor down the default four lines. If your Alt key works like the Meta (**M-**) key, **M-n**, where **n** is some digit, works as a multiplier, too.

Inserting Text

Emacs editing is simple: just start typing. Each character you type is inserted at the "point," which, in most cases, is the cursor. In classic GNU style, however, Emacs' documentation muddles what should be a clear, simple concept making an almost pointless distinction between the point and the cursor. "While the cursor appears to point *at* a particular character, you should think of point as *between* two characters; it points before the character that appears under the cursor (*GNU Emacs Manual*, 15)." Why the distinction? The word "point" referred to "." in the TECO language in which Emacs was originally developed. "." was the command for obtaining the value at what is now called the point. In practice, you can generally use the word "cursor" anywhere the GNU documentation uses "point."

To insert a blank line after the cursor, type **C-x o**. **C-o** inserts a blank line above the current line and positions the cursor at the beginning of the line. **C-x C-o** deletes all but one of multiple consecutive blank lines.

Deleting Text

Del and, on most PC systems, Backspace, erases the character to the left of the cursor. **C-d** deletes the character under the cursor. **C-k** deletes from the current cursor location to the end of the line, but, annoyingly, doesn't delete the terminating newline (it does delete the newline if you use the multiplier; that is, **C-u 1 C-k** deletes the line, newline and all). To delete all the text between the cursor and the beginning of a line, use **C-x Del**.

To delete a whole region of text, follow these steps:

1. Move the cursor to the first character of the region.
2. Type **C-@** (**C-SPACE**) to "set the mark."
3. Move the cursor to the first character past the end of the region.
4. Type **C-w** to delete, or "wipe," the region.

If you want to make a copy of a region, type **M-w** instead of **C-w**. If you lose track of where the region starts, **C-x C-x** swaps the location of the cursor and the mark. In C mode, **M-C-h** combines moving and marking: It moves the cursor to the beginning of the current function and sets a mark at the end of the function.

If you delete too much text, use **C-x u** to "undo" the last batch of changes, which is usually just your last edit. The default undo buffer size is 20,000 bytes, so you can continue the undo operation. To undo an undo, type **M-C-x u**. To cut and paste, use **M-w** to copy a region of text, move to the location in the buffer where you want to insert the text, and perform a "yank" by typing **C-y**.

To facilitate yanking and undoing, Emacs maintains a kill ring of your last 30 deletions. To see this in action, first delete some text, move elsewhere, and then type **C-y** to yank the most recently deleted text. Follow that with **M-y**, which replaces the text yanked with the next most recently deleted text. To cycle further back in the kill ring, continue typing **M-y**.

Search and Replace

Emacs' default search routine is a non–case-sensitive incremental search, invoked with **C-s**. When you type **C-s**, the minibuffer prompts for a search string, as shown in Figure 8.4.

FIGURE 8.4

Minibuffer prompt for an incremental search.

Prompt ———

8

CREATING PROGRAMS IN EMACS

In most cases, a non–case-sensitive search will be sufficient, but, when writing C code, which is case sensitive, it may not have the desired result. To make case-sensitive searches the default, add the following line to the Emacs initialization file, ~/.emacs:

```
(setq case-fold-search nil)
```

As you type the string, Emacs moves the cursor to the next occurrence of that string. To advance to the next occurrence, type **C-s** again. **Esc** cancels the search, leaving the cursor at its current location. **C-g** cancels the search and returns the cursor to its original location. While in a search, **Del** erases the last character in the search string and backs the cursor up to its previous location. A failed search beeps at you annoyingly and writes "Failed I-search" in the minibuffer.

Incremental searches can wrap to the top of the buffer. After an incremental search fails, another **C-s** forces the search to wrap to the top of the buffer. If you want to search backwards through a buffer, use **C-r**.

Emacs also has regular expression searches, simple (non-incremental) searches, searches that match entire phrases, and, of course, two search-and-replace functions. The safest search-and-replace operation is **M-%**, which performs an interactive search and replace. Complete the following steps to use **M-%**:

1. Type **M-%**.
2. Type the search string and press Enter.
3. Type the replacement string and press Enter.
4. At the next prompt, use one of the following:

SPACE or **y**	Make the substitution and move to the next occurrence of search string
Del or **n**	Skip to the next occurrence of search string
!	Perform global replacement without further prompts
.	Make the substitution at current location, and then exit the search-and-replace operation
M- or **q**	Exit the search and replace, and place cursor at its original location
^	Backtrack to the previous match
C-x r	Start a recursive edit

Figure 8.5 shows the results of these steps.

Recursive edits allow you to make more extensive edits at the current cursor location. Type **M-C-c** to exit the recursive editing session and return to your regularly scheduled search and replace.

Other search and replace variants include **M-x query-replace-regexp**, which executes an interactive search and replace using regular expressions. For the very stout of heart or those confident of their regular expression knowledge, consider **M-x replace-regexp**, which performs a global, unconditional (*sans* prompts) search and replace using regular expressions.

FIGURE 8.5
Search and replace minibuffer prompt.

Minibuffer after Step 1

Minibuffer after Step 2

Minibuffer after Step 4

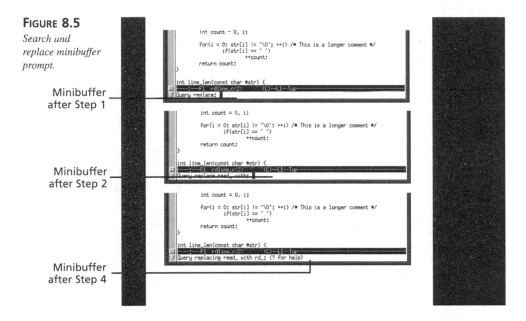

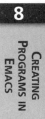

Saving and Opening Files

To save a file, use **C-x C-s**. Use **C-x C-w** to save the file using a new name. To open a file into the current buffer, type **C-x C-f** to "visit" the file, type the filename in the minibuffer, and press Enter, which opens it in the current buffer. If you only want to browse a file without editing it, you can open it in read-only mode using **C-x C-r**, typing the filename in the minibuffer, and pressing Enter.

Having opened a file in read-only mode, it is still possible to edit the buffer. Like most editors, Emacs opens a new buffer for each file visited and keeps the buffer contents separate from the disk file until explicitly told to write the buffer to disk using **C-x C-f** or **C-x C-w**. So, you can edit a read-only buffer by typing **C-x C-q**, but you won't be able to save it to disk unless you change its name.

Emacs makes two kinds of backups of files you edit. The first time you save a file, Emacs creates a backup of the original file in the current directory by appending a ~ to the filename. The other kind of backup is made for crash recovery. Every 300 keystrokes (a default you can change), Emacs creates an auto-save file. If your system crashes and you later revisit the file you were editing, Emacs will prompt you to do a file recovery, as shown in Figure 8.6.

Figure 8.6

*Recovering a file
after a crash.*

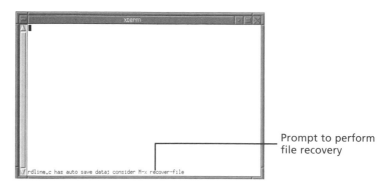

Prompt to perform
file recovery

Multiple Windows

Emacs uses the word "frame" to refer to separate Emacs windows because it uses "window" to refer to a screen that has been divided into multiple sections with independently controlled displays. This distinction dates back to Emacs' origins, which predate the existence of GUIs capable of displaying multiple screens. To display two windows, Emacs divides the screen into two sections, as illustrated in Figure 8.7.

Figure 8.7

Emacs windows.

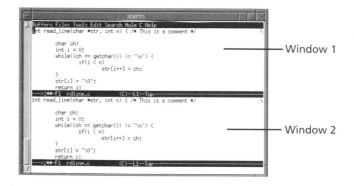

Window 1

Window 2

To create a new window, type **C-x 2**, which splits the current window into two windows. The cursor remains in the "active" or current window. The following is a list of commands for moving among and manipulating various windows:

- **C-x o**—Move to the other window
- **C-M-v**—Scroll the other window
- **C-x 0**—Delete the current window
- **C-x 1**—Delete all windows except the current one

- **C-x 2**—Split screen into two windows
- **C-x 3**—Split the screen horizontally, rather than vertically
- **C-x 4 C-f**—"Visit" a file into the other window

Note that deleted buffers are hidden, not closed, or "killed" in Emacs' parlance. To close a buffer, switch to that buffer and type **C-x k** and press Enter. If the buffer has not been saved, Emacs prompts you to save it.

Under the X Window system, you can also create new frames, windows that are separate from the current window, using the following commands:

- **C-x 5 2**—Create a new frame of the same buffer
- **C-x 5 f**—Create a new frame and open a new file into it
- **C-x 5 0**—Close the current frame

When using framed windows, be careful not to use **C-x C-c** to close a frame, because it will close all frames, not just the current one, thus terminating your Emacs session.

Features Supporting Programming

Emacs has modes for a wide variety of programming languages. These modes customize Emacs' behavior to fit the syntax and indentation requirements of the language. Supported languages include several varieties of Lisp, C, C++, Fortran, Awk, Icon, Java, Objective-C, Pascal, Perl, and Tcl. To switch to one of the language modes, type **M-x [language]-mode**, replacing **[language]** with the mode you want. So, to switch to Java mode, type **M-x java-mode**.

Indenting Conveniences

Emacs automatically indents your code while you type it. In fact, it can enforce quite a few indentation styles. The default style is gnu, a style conforming to GNU's coding standards. Other supported indentation styles include k&r, bsd, stroustrup, linux, python, java, whitesmith, ellemtel, and cc.

To use one of the supported indentation styles, type the command **M-x c-set-style** followed by Enter, enter the indentation style you want to use, and press Enter again. Note that this will only affect newly visited buffers; existing buffers will be unaffected.

Each line that begins with a Tab will force subsequent lines to indent correctly, depending on the coding style used. When you are using one of Emacs' programming modes, pressing Tab in the middle of a line automatically indents it correctly.

Syntax Highlighting

Emacs' font-lock mode turns on a basic form of syntax highlighting. It uses different colors to mark syntax elements. To turn on font-lock mode, type **M-x font-lock-mode** and press Enter. Figure 8.8 illustrates font-lock mode in the C major mode.

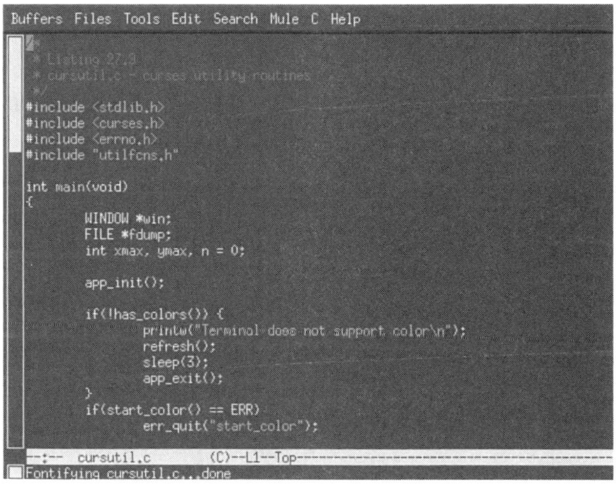

FIGURE 8.8

The effect of font-lock mode on C code.

Using Comments

M-; inserts comment delimiters (/* */) on the current line and helpfully positions the cursor between them. The comment will be placed (by default) at column 32. If the current line is longer than 32 characters, Emacs places the comment just past the end of the line, as illustrated in Figure 8.9.

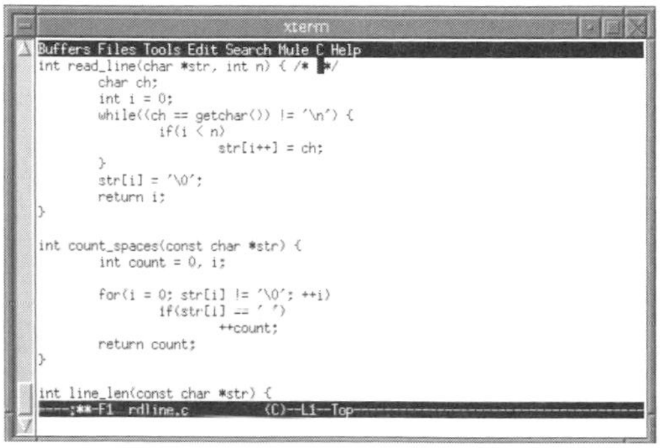

FIGURE 8.9

Inserting comments.

If you are creating a multi-line comment, an Emacs minor mode, `auto-fill`, will indent and line wrap comment lines intelligently. To set this minor mode, use the **M-x auto-fill-mode** command. In the middle of an existing comment, **M-;** aligns the comment appropriately. If you have a whole region that you want to convert to comments, select the region and type **M-x comment-region**.

Although not strictly related to comments, Emacs helps you make or maintain a change log for the file you're editing. To create or add an entry to a change log in the current directory, type **C-x 4 a**. The default filename is `ChangeLog`.

Compilation Using Emacs

The command **M-x compile** compiles code using, by default, `make -k`. Ordinarily, this would require the presence of a Makefile in the current directory. If you are using GNU `make`, however, you can take advantage of a shortcut. For example, if you are working on a file named `rdline.c` and want to compile it, type **M-x compile**. Then, when the buffer prompts for a filename, type **rdline.o**, as illustrated in Figure 8.10. GNU `make` has an internal suffix rule that says, in effect, for a given file FILE.o, create it with the `make` command "cc -c FILE.c -o FILE.o".

FIGURE 8.10

Compiling a program within Emacs.

```
                                    xterm
A Buffers Files Tools Edit Search Mule Minibuf Help
qint read_line(char *str, int n){
        char ch;
        int i = 0;
        while((ch == getchar()) != '\n') {
                if(i < n)
                        str[i++] = ch;
        }
        str[i] = '\0';
        return i;
}

int count_spaces(const char *str)
{
        int count = 0, i;

        for(i = 0; str[i] != '\0'; ++i)
                if(str[i] == ' ')
                        ++count;
        return count;

--=:**-F1  rdline.c        (C)--L1--Top--
Compile command: make -k rdline.o
```

The first time you issue the `compile` command, Emacs sets the default compile command for the rest of the session to the `make` command you enter. If you have not yet saved the buffer, Emacs asks if you want to. When you compile from within Emacs, it creates a scratch buffer called the compilation buffer, which lists the `make` commands executed, any errors that occur, and the compilation results.

If any error occurs, Emacs includes an error-browsing feature that takes you to the location of each error. In Figure 8.11, an error occurred while compiling `rdline.c`.

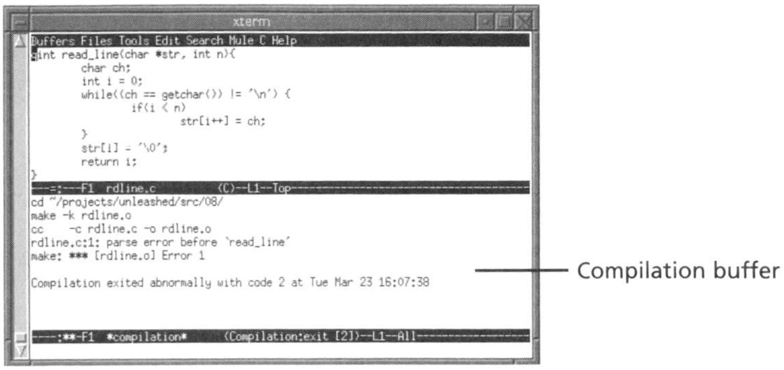

FIGURE 8.11

The compilation buffer lists compilation messages, including errors.

Compilation buffer

To go to the line where the error occurred, type **C-x `** (back quote); Emacs positions the cursor at the beginning of the line containing the error, as illustrated in Figure 8.12.

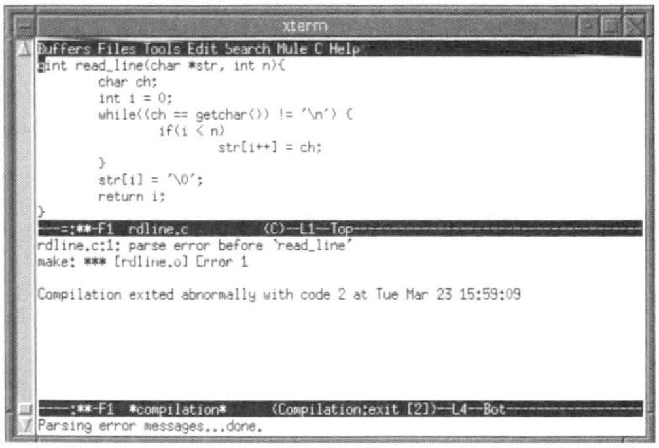

FIGURE 8.12

C-x ` positions the cursor on the line containing the error.

If there are other errors, **C-x `** will take you to each error in the source file. Unfortunately, the progression is only one way; you cannot backtrack the error list. This shortcoming aside, Emacs' error browsing feature is very handy. To close the compilation buffer, use the command **C-x 1** to delete all buffers except the current one.

Tag support is another handy Emacs programming feature. Tags are a type of database that enables easy source code navigation by cross-referencing function names and, optionally, typedefs, to the files in which they appear and are defined. Tags are especially useful for locating the definitions of function names or typedefs. The etags program creates tag files that Emacs understands. To create an Emacs tag file, execute the following command:

```
$ etags -t <list of files>
```

This command creates the tags database, TAGS by default, in the current directory. <list of files> is the files for which you want tags created. The -t option will include type-defs in the tag file. So, to create a tag file of all the C source and header files in the current directory, the command is:

```
$ etags -f *.[ch]
```

Once you've created the tag file, use the following commands to take advantage of it:

- **M-. tagname**—Finds the file containing the definition of tagname and opens it in a new buffer, replacing the previous buffer
- **C-x 4 . tagname**—Functions like **M-.**, but visits the file into another window
- **C-x 5 . tagname**—Functions like **C-x 4.**, but visits the file into another frame

Emacs' tags facility makes it very easy to view a function's definition while editing another file. You can also perform search-and-replace operations using tag files. To perform an interactive search and replace:

1. Type **M-x tags-query-replace** and press Enter.
2. Type the search string and press Enter.
3. Type the replacement string and press Enter.
4. Press Enter to accept the default tags table, TAGS, or type another name and press Enter.
5. Use the commands described for the query-replace operation.

Another help feature allows you to run a region of text through the C preprocessor, so you can see how it expands. The command to accomplish this feat is **C-c C-e**. Figure 8.13 illustrates how it works.

FIGURE 8.13

Running a text region through the C preprocessor.

In the top window, we define a preprocessor macro named `square(x)`. After marking the region, type **C-c C-e**. The bottom window, named *Macroexpansion*, shows how the preprocessor expanded the function. Pretty neat, huh?

Customization in Brief

In this section, we list a few commands you can use to customize Emacs' behavior. We can only scratch the surface, however, so we will forgo long explanations of why the customizations we offer work and ask, instead, that you simply trust us that they do work.

Using the ~/.emacs File

Table 8.1 lists the commands and variables that you will find useful for customizing Emacs. They control various elements of Emacs' default behavior.

Table 8.1 EMACS COMMANDS AND VARIABLES

Name	Type	Description
inhibit-default-init	Command	Disables any site-wide customizations
case-fold-search	Command	Sets case sensitivity of searches
user-mail-address	Variable	Contains user's mail address

The file `~/.emacs` (`$HOME/.emacs`) contains Lisp code that is loaded and executed each time Emacs starts. To execute a Lisp command, use the syntax

```
(setq lisp-command-name [arg])
```

For example, `(setq inhibit-default-init t)` executes the Emacs Lisp command `inhibit-default-init` with a value of "t" (for true). arg may be either Boolean (t = true, nil = false), a positive or negative digit, or a double quote delimited string.

To set a variable value, the syntax is

```
(set-variable varname value)
```

This initializes varname to value. So, `(set-variable user-mail-address some_guy@call_me_now.com)` sets the variable `user-mail-address` to `some_guy@call_me_now.com`.

You can also set variables and execute commands on-the-fly within Emacs. First, type **C-x b** to switch to another buffer. Press Tab to view a list of the available buffers in the echo area. Figure 8.14 shows what the buffer list might look like.

FIGURE 8.14
Sample buffer list.

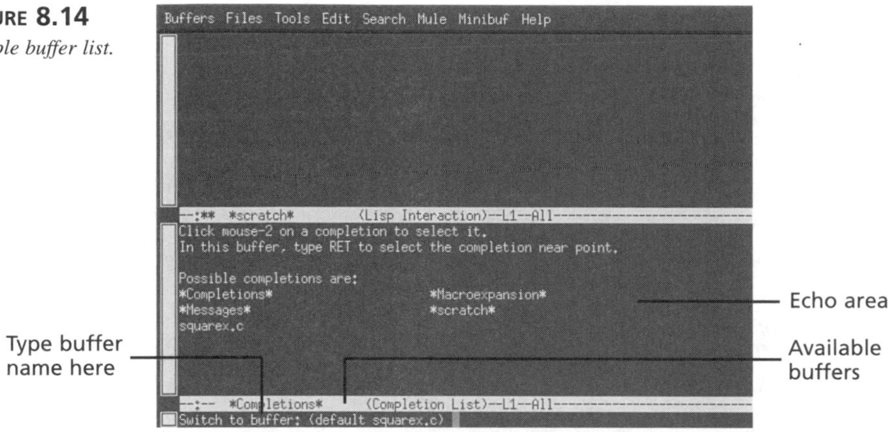

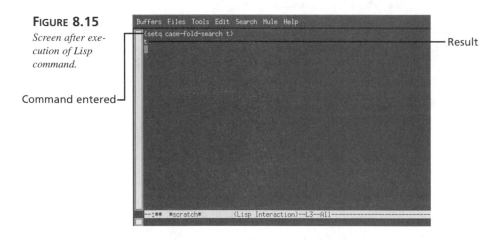

Now, type ***scratch*** and press Enter. Finally, to execute a Lisp command, type, for example, **(setq case-fold-search t)**, and press **C-j**. Lisp evaluates the statement between parentheses, displaying the result on the line below the command, as illustrated in Figure 8.15.

FIGURE 8.15
Screen after execution of Lisp command.

Follow a similar procedure to set a variable value. The syntax takes the general form

```
(setq set-variable varname value)
```

The behavior is exactly the same as executing a command. For example, to set user-mail-address on-the-fly, the command to type in the scratch buffer is **(setq set-variable user-mail-address "someone@somewhere.com")** followed by **C-j**.

Creating and Using Keyboard Macros

This section will briefly describe how to create and execute keyboard macros within Emacs. Keyboard macros are user-defined commands that represent a whole sequence of keystrokes. They are a quick, easy way to speed up your work.

For example, the section on deleting text pointed out that the command **C-k** at the beginning of a line would delete all the text on the line, but not the newline. In order to delete the newline, too, you have to either type **C-k** twice or use the multiplier with an argument of 1, that is, **C-u 1 C-k**. In order to make this more convenient, you can define a keyboard macro to do this for you.

To start, type **C-x (**, followed by the commands you want in the macro. To end the definition, type **C-x)**. Now, to execute the macro you've just defined, type **C-x e**, which stands for the command **call-last-kbd-macro**. Actually, the macro was executed the first time while you defined it, allowing you to see what it was doing as you were defining it.

If you would like to see the actual commands, type **C-x C-k**, which will start a special mode for editing macros, followed by **C-x e** to execute the macro. This will format the command in a special buffer. The command **C-h m** will show you instructions for editing the macro. **C-c C-c** ends the macro editing session.

The material in this section should give you a good start to creating a highly personal and convenient Emacs customization. For all of the gory details, see Emacs' extensive info (help) file. The next section introduces you to enough Emacs Lisp to enable you to further customize your Emacs development environment.

Automating Emacs with Emacs Lisp

Emacs can be customized by writing functions in Elisp (or Emacs Lisp). You have already seen how to customize Emacs by using the file ~/.emacs. It is assumed that you have some knowledge of Lisp programming. The full reference to Emacs Lisp, *GNU Emacs Lisp Reference Manual* (written by Bill Lewis, Dan Laliberte, and Richard Stallman), can be found on the Web at http://www.gnu.org/manual/elisp-manual-20-2.5/elisp.html. In this section, you will see how to write a simple Emacs Lisp function that modifies text in the current text buffer.

Emacs Lisp is a complete programming environment, capable of doing file I/O, building user interfaces (using Emacs), doing network programming for retrieving email, Usenet news, and so on. However, most Emacs Lisp programming involves manipulating the text in Emacs edit buffers.

Listing 8.1 shows a very simple example that replaces the digits "0", "1", and so on with the strings "ZERO", "ONE", and so on.

Listing 8.1 sample.el

```
(defun sample ()
  (let* ((txt (buffer-string))
         (len (length txt))
         (x nil))
    (goto-char 0)
    (dotimes (n len)
      ;; see if the next character is a number 0, 1, .. 9
      (setq x (char-after))
      (if x
          (let ()
            (setq x (char-to-string (char-after)))
            (if x
                (let ()
                  (if (equal x "0") (replace-char "ZERO"))
                  (if (equal x "1") (replace-char "ONE"))
                  (if (equal x "2") (replace-char "TWO"))
                  (if (equal x "3") (replace-char "THREE"))
                  (if (equal x "4") (replace-char "FOUR"))
                  (if (equal x "5") (replace-char "FIVE"))
                  (if (equal x "6") (replace-char "SIX"))
                  (if (equal x "7") (replace-char "SEVEN"))
                  (if (equal x "8") (replace-char "EIGHT"))
                  (if (equal x "9") (replace-char "NINE"))))))
      ;; move the text pointer forward
      (forward-char))))

(defun replace-char (s)
  (delete-char 1)
  (insert s))
```

The example in Listing 8.1 defines two functions: `sample` and `replace-char`. `replace-char` is a helper function that only serves to make the `sample` function shorter. This example uses several text-handling utility functions that are built in to Emacs Lisp:

- `buffer-string`—Returns as a string the contents of the current Emacs text buffer
- `length`—Returns the number of characters in a string
- `char-after`—Returns the character after the Emacs edit buffer insert point
- `char-to-string`—Converts a character to a string
- `forward-char`—Moves the Emacs edit buffer insert point forward by one character position

8

CREATING PROGRAMS IN EMACS

- `delete-char`—Deletes the character immediately following the Emacs edit buffer insert point
- `insert`—Inserts a string at the current Emacs edit buffer insert point

You can try running this example by either copying the `sample.el` file into your `~/.emacs` file or using **M-x load-file** to load `sample.el`. You run the program by typing **M-: (sample)**. Typing **M-:** should give you a prompt `Eval:`.

Much of the functionality of Emacs comes from Emacs Lisp files that are auto-loaded into the Emacs environment. When you install Emacs in your Linux distribution, one of the options is to install the Emacs Lisp source files (the compiled Emacs Lisp files are installed by default). Installing the Emacs Lisp source files provides many sample programs for doing network programming, adding menus to Emacs, and so on.

Summary

Emacs is a rich, deep programming environment. This chapter introduced you to the basics of editing and writing programs with GNU Emacs. It covered starting and stopping Emacs, cursor movement, basic editing functions, and search-and-replace operations. In addition, you learned how to use Emacs features that support programming, such as using tags tables, special formatting, syntax highlighting, and running sections of code through the C preprocessor. The chapter also showed you how to perform basic Emacs customization using the `~/.emacs` initialization file, keyboard macros, and Emacs Lisp.

System Programming

PART

II

IN THIS PART

I/O Routines

by Mark Whitis

IN THIS CHAPTER

This chapter covers file descriptor–based I/O. This type of file I/O is UNIX specific, although C development environments on many other platforms may include some support. The use of file pointer (`stdio`) based I/O is more portable and will be covered in the next chapter, "File Manipulation." In some cases, such as tape I/O, you will need to use file descriptor–based I/O. The BSD socket programming interface for TCP/IP (see Chapter 19, "TCP/IP and Socket Programming") also uses file descriptor–based I/O, once a TCP session has been established.

One of the nice things about Linux, and other UNIX compatible operating systems, is that the file interface also works for many other types of devices. Tape drives, the console, serial ports, pseudoterminals, printer ports, sound cards, and mice are handled as character special devices which look, more or less, like ordinary files to application programs. TCP/IP and UNIX domain sockets, once the connection has been established, are handled using file descriptors as if they were standard files. Pipes also look similar to standard files.

File Descriptors

A file descriptor is simply an integer that is used as an index into a table of open files associated with each process. The values 0, 1, and 2 are special and refer to the `stdin`, `stdout`, and `stderr` streams; these three streams normally connect to the user's terminal but can be redirected.

There are many security implications to using file descriptor I/O and file pointer I/O (which is built on top of file descriptor I/O); these are covered in Chapter 35, "Secure Programming." The workarounds actually rely heavily on careful use of file descriptor I/O for both file descriptor and file pointer I/O.

Calls That Use File Descriptors

A number of system calls use file descriptors. This section includes brief descriptions of each of those calls, including the function prototypes from the man pages and/or header files.

Most of these calls return a value of -1 in the event of error and set the variable `errno` to the error code. Error codes are documented in the man pages for the individual system calls and in the man page for `errno`. The `perror()` function can be used to print an error message based on the error code. Virtually every call in this chapter is mentioned in Chapter 35. Some calls are vulnerable, others are used to fix vulnerabilities, and many wear both hats. The calls that take file descriptors are much safer than those that take filenames.

Each section contains a code fragment that shows the necessary include files and the pro-totype for the function(s) described in that section, copied from the man pages for that function.

The open() Call

The open() call is used to open a file. The prototype for this function and descriptions for its variables and flags follow.

```
#include <sys/types.h>
#include <sys/stat.h>
#include <fcntl.h>
int open(const char *pathname, int flags).
int open(const char *pathname, int flags, mode_t mode);
```

The pathname argument is simply a string with the full or relative pathname to the file to be opened. The third parameter specifies the UNIX file mode (permissions bits) to be used when creating a file and should be present if a file may be created. The second parameter, flags, is one of O_RDONLY, O_WRONLY, or O_RDWR, optionally OR-ed with addi-tional flags; Table 9.1 lists the flag values.

TABLE 9.1   FLAGS FOR THE open() CALL

Flag	Description
O_RDONLY	Open file for read-only access.
O_WRONLY	Open file for write-only access.
O_RDWR	Open file for read and write access.
O_CREAT	Create the file if it does not exist.
O_EXCL	Fail if the file already exists.
O_NOCTTY	Don't become controlling tty if opening tty and the process had no control-ling tty.
O_TRUNC	Truncate the file to length 0 if it exists.
O_APPEND	Append file pointer will be positioned at end of file.
O_NONBLOCK	If an operation cannot complete without delay, return before completing the operation. (See Chapter 22, "Non-blocking Socket I/O.")
O_NODELAY	Same as O_NONBLOCK.
O_SYNC	Operations will not return until the data has been physically written to the disk or other device.

9

I/O ROUTINES

open() returns a file descriptor unless an error occurred. In the event of an error, it will return -1 and set the variable errno.

> **NOTE**
>
> The creat() call is the same as open() with O_CREAT¦O_WRONLY¦O_TRUNC.

The close() Call

You should close a file descriptor when you are done with it. The single argument is the file descriptor number returned by open(). The prototype for close() is as follows.

```
#include <unistd.h>

int close(int fd);
```

Any locks held by the process on the file are released, even if they were placed using a different file descriptor. If closing the file causes the link count to reach zero, the file will be deleted. If this is the last (or only) file descriptor associated with an open file, the entry in the open file table will be freed.

If the file is not an ordinary file, other side effects are possible. The last close on one end of a pipe may affect the other end. The handshake lines on a serial port might be affected. A tape might rewind.

The read() Call

The read() system call is used to read data from the file corresponding to a file descriptor.

```
#include <unistd.h>

ssize_t read(int fd, void *buf, size_t count);
```

The first argument is the file descriptor that was returned from a previous open() call. The second argument is a pointer to a buffer to copy the data from, and the third argument gives the number of bytes to read. Read() returns the number of bytes read or a value of –1 if an error occurs (check errno).

The write() Call

The write() system call is used to write data to the file corresponding to a file descriptor.

```
#include <unistd.h>

ssize_t write(int fd, const void *buf, size_t count);
```

The first argument is the file descriptor which was returned from a previous open() call. The second argument is a pointer to a buffer to copy the data to (which must be large enough to hold the data) and the third argument gives the number of bytes to write. write() returns the number of bytes read or a value of -1 if an error occurs (check errno).

The `ioctl()` Call

The ioctl() system call is a catchall for setting or retrieving various parameters associated with a file or to perform other operations on the file. The ioctls available, and the arguments to ioctl(), vary depending on the underlying device.

```
#include <sys/ioctl.h>

int ioctl(int d, int request, ...)
```

The argument d must be an open file descriptor.

The `fcntl()` Call

The fcntl() call is similar to ioctl() but it sets or retrieves a different set of parameters.

```
#include <unistd.h>
#include <fcntl.h>

int fcntl(int fd, int cmd);
int fcntl(int fd, int cmd, long arg);
```

Unlike ioctl(), these parameters are generally not controlled by the low-level device driver. The first argument is the file descriptor, the second is the command, and the third is usually an argument specific to the particular command. Table 9.2 lists the various command values that can be used for the second argument of the fcntl() call.

TABLE 9.2   COMMANDS FOR fcntl()

Command	Description
F_DUPFD	Duplicates file descriptors. Use dup2() instead.
F_GETFD	Gets close-on-exec flag. The file will remain open across exec() family calls if the low order bit is 0.
F_SETFD	Sets close-on-exec flag.
F_GETFL	Gets the flags set by open.
F_SETFL	Changes the flags set by open.

continues

9

I/O ROUTINES

TABLE 9.2 CONTINUED

Command	Description
F_GETLK	Gets discretionary file locks (see `flock()`.)
F_SETLK	Sets discretionary lock, no wait.
F_SETLKW	Sets discretionary lock, wait if necessary.
F_GETOWN	Retrieves the process id or process group number that will receive the SIGIO and SIGURG signals.
F_SETOWN	Sets the process id or process group number.

Since there are other ways to do most of these operations, you may have little need to use fcntl().

The `fsync()` Call

The fsync() system call flushes all of the data written to file descriptor fd to disk or other underlying device.

```
#include <unistd.h>

int fsync(int fd);
#ifdef _POSIX_SYNCHRONIZED_IO
   int fdatasync(int fd);
#endif
```

The Linux filesystem may keep the data in memory for several seconds before writing it to disk in order to more efficiently handle disk I/O. A zero is returned if successful; otherwise -1 will be returned and errno will be set.

The fdatasync() call is similar to fsync() but does not write the metadata (inode information, particularly modification time).

The `ftruncate()` Call

The ftruncate() system call truncates the file referenced by file descriptor fd to the length specified by length.

```
#include <unistd.h>

int ftruncate(int fd, size_t length);
```

Return values are zero for success and -1 for an error (check errno).

The `lseek()` Call

The `lseek()` function sets the current position of reads and writes in the file referenced by file descriptor `files` to position `offset`.

```
#include <sys/types.h>
#include <unistd.h>

off_t lseek(int fildes, off_t offset, int whence);
```

Depending on the value of `whence`, the `offset` is relative to the beginning (`SEEK_SET`), current position (`SEEK_CUR`), or end of file (`SEEK_END`). The return value is the resulting offset (relative to the beginning of the file) or a value of (`off_t`) -1 in the case of error (`errno` will be set).

The `dup()` and `dup2()` Calls

The system calls `dup()` and `dup2()` duplicate file descriptors. `dup()` returns a new descriptor (the lowest numbered unused descriptor). `dup2()` lets you specify the value of the descriptor that will be returned, closing `newfd` first, if necessary; this is commonly used to reopen or redirect a file descriptor.

```
#include <unistd.h>

int dup(int oldfd);
int dup2(int oldfd, int newfd);
```

Listing 9.1 illustrates using `dup2()` to redirect standard output (file descriptor 1) to a file. The function `print_line()` formats a message using `snprintf()`, a safer version of `sprintf()`. We don't use `printf()` because that uses file pointer I/O, although the next chapter and Chapter 35 will show how to open a file pointer stream over a file descriptor stream. The results of running the program are shown in Listing 9.2.

`dup()` and `dup2()` return the new descriptor or return -1 and set `errno`. The new and old descriptors share file offsets (positions), flags, and locks but not the `close-on-exec` flag.

LISTING 9.1   `dup.c`—REDIRECTING STANDARD OUTPUT WITH `dup2()`

```
#include <sys/types.h>
#include <sys/stat.h>
#include <fcntl.h>
#include <unistd.h>
#include <assert.h>
```

continues

9

I/O ROUTINES

LISTING 9.1   CONTINUED

```c
print_line(int n)
{
   char buf[32];
   snprintf(buf,sizeof(buf), "Line #%d\n",n);
   write(1,buf, strlen(buf));
}

main()
{
   int fd;

   print_line(1);
   print_line(2);
   print_line(3);

   /* redirect stdout to file junk.out */
   fd=open("junk.out", O_WRONLY|O_CREAT,0666);
   assert(fd>=0);
   dup2(fd,1);

   print_line(4);
   print_line(5);
   print_line(6);

   close(fd);
   close(1);
}
```

LISTING 9.2   SAMPLE RUN OF dup.c

```
$ ./dup
Line #1
Line #2
Line #3
$ cat junk.out
Line #4
Line #5
Line #6
$
```

The `select()` Call

The `select()` function call allows a process to wait on multiple file descriptors simultaneously with an optional timeout. The `select()` call will return as soon as it is possible to perform operations on any of the indicated file descriptors. This allows a process to perform some basic multitasking without forking another process or starting another thread. The prototype for this function and its macros is listed below.

```
#include <sys/time.h>
#include <sys/types.h>
#include <unistd.h>

int select(int  n,  fd_set  *readfds,  fd_set  *writefds,
fd_set *exceptfds, struct timeval *timeout);

FD_CLR(int fd, fd_set *set);
FD_ISSET(int fd, fd_set *set);
FD_SET(int fd, fd_set *set);
FD_ZERO(fd_set *set);
```

select() is one of the more complicated system calls available. You probably won't need to use it very often but when you do, you really need it. You could issue a bunch of non-blocking reads or writes on the various file descriptors, but that kind of programming is one of the reasons why DOS and Windows applications multitask so poorly; the task keeps running and chewing up CPU cycles even though it has no useful work to do.

The first parameter is the number of file descriptors in the file descriptor sets (so the kernel doesn't have to waste time checking a bunch of unused bits). The second, third, and fourth parameters are pointers to file descriptor sets (one bit per possible file descriptor) that indicate which file descriptors you would like to be able to read, write, or receive exception notifications on, respectively. The last parameter is a timeout value. All but the first parameter may be null. On return the file descriptor sets will be modified to indicate which descriptors are ready for immediate I/O operations. The timeout will also be modified on return, although that is not the case on most systems other than Linux. The return value itself will indicate a count of how many descriptors are included in the descriptor sets. If it is zero, that indicates a timeout. If the return value is -1, errno will be set to indicate the error (which may include EINTR if a signal was caught).

The macros FD_ZERO(), FD_SET(), FD_CLEAR, and FD_ISSET() help manipulate file descriptor sets by erasing the whole set, setting the bit corresponding to a file descriptor, clearing the bit, or querying the bit. All but FD_ZERO() take a file descriptor as the first parameter. The remaining parameter for each is a pointer to a file descriptor set.

Listing 9.3 has a crude terminal program that illustrates the use of select(). The program doesn't disable local echo or line buffering on the keyboard, set the baud rate on the serial port, lock the serial line, or do much of anything but move characters between the two devices. If compiled with BADCODE defined, it will spin on the input and output operations tying up CPU. Otherwise, the program will use select() to sleep until it is possible to do some I/O. It will wake up every ten seconds, for no good reason. It is limited to single character buffers so it will make a system call for every character in or out instead of doing multiple characters at a time when possible. My manyterm program also illustrates the use of select().

LISTING 9.3 select BASED TERMINAL PROGRAM

```c
#include <sys/time.h>
#include <sys/types.h>
#include <sys/stat.h>
#include <fcntl.h>
#include <unistd.h>
#include <assert.h>
#include <stdio.h>    /* for fprintf(stderr,... */
#include <termios.h>

/* crude terminal program */
/* - does not lock modem */
/* - does not disable echo on users terminal */
/* - does not put terminal in raw mode */
/* - control-c will abort */

int debug = 0;

void dump_fds(char *name, fd_set *set, int max_fd)
{
   int i;

   if(!debug) return;

   fprintf(stderr, "%s:", name);
   for(i=0; i<max_fd; i++) {
      if(FD_ISSET(i, set)) {
          fprintf(stderr, "%d,", i);
      }
   }
   fprintf(stderr, "\n");

}

main()
{
   int keyboard;
   int screen;
   int serial;
   char c;
   int rc;
   struct termios tio;

   #ifndef BADCODE
```

```
        fd_set readfds;
        fd_set writefds;
        fd_set exceptfds;
        struct timeval tv;
        int max_fd;

        /* inbound and outbound keep track of */
        /* whether we have a character */
        /* already read which needs to be sent in that direction */
        /* the _char variables are the data buffer */
        int outbound;
        char outbound_char;
        int inbound;
        char inbound_char;
#endif

keyboard = open("/dev/tty",O_RDONLY¦ O_NONBLOCK);
assert(keyboard>=0);
screen   = open("/dev/tty",O_WRONLY¦ O_NONBLOCK);
assert(screen>=0);
serial   = open("/dev/modem", O_RDWR¦ O_NONBLOCK);
assert(serial>=0);


if(debug) {
  fprintf(stderr, "keyboard=%d\n",keyboard);
  fprintf(stderr, "screen=%d\n",screen);
  fprintf(stderr, "serial=%d\n",serial);
}

#ifdef BADCODE
    while(1) {
        rc=read(keyboard,&c,1);
        if(rc==1) {
            while(write(serial,&c,1) != 1)
                ;
        }
        rc=read(serial,&c,1);
        if(rc==1) {
            while(write(screen,&c,1) != 1)
                ;
        }
    }
#else
    outbound = inbound = 0;

    while(1) {
        FD_ZERO(&writefds);
        if(inbound) FD_SET(screen, &writefds);
```

9

I/O ROUTINES

continues

LISTING 9.3 CONTINUED

```
      if(outbound) FD_SET(serial, &writefds);

      FD_ZERO(&readfds);
      if(!outbound) FD_SET(keyboard, &readfds);
      if(!inbound) FD_SET(serial, &readfds);

      max_fd = 0;
      if(screen > max_fd)     max_fd=screen;
      if(keyboard > max_fd)   max_fd=keyboard;
      if(serial > max_fd)     max_fd=serial;
      max_fd++;
      if(debug) fprintf(stderr, "max_fd=%d\n",max_fd);

      tv.tv_sec = 10;
      tv.tv_usec = 0;

      dump_fds("read in", &readfds, max_fd);
      dump_fds("write in", &writefds, max_fd);

      rc= select(max_fd, &readfds, &writefds, NULL, &tv);

      dump_fds("read out", &readfds, max_fd);
      dump_fds("write out", &writefds, max_fd);


      if(FD_ISSET(keyboard, &readfds)) {
          if(debug) fprintf(stderr, "\nreading outbound\n");
          rc=read(keyboard,&outbound_char,1);
          if(rc==1) outbound=1;
          if(outbound == 3) exit(0);
      }

      if(FD_ISSET(serial, &readfds)) {
          if(debug) fprintf(stderr, "\nreading inbound\n");
          rc=read(serial,&inbound_char,1);
          if(rc==1) inbound=1;
      }

      if(FD_ISSET(screen, &writefds)) {
          if(debug) fprintf(stderr, "\nwriting inbound\n");
          rc=write(screen,&inbound_char,1);
          if(rc==1) inbound=0;
      }

      if(FD_ISSET(serial, &writefds)) {
          if(debug) fprintf(stderr, "\nwriting outbound\n");
          rc=write(serial,&outbound_char,1);
          if(rc==1) outbound=0;
```

```
            }

        }
    #endif

}
```

The `fstat()` Call

The `fstat()` system call returns information about the file referred to by the file descriptor `files`, placing the result in the `struct stat` pointed to by `buf()`. A return value of zero is success and -1 is failure (check `errno`).

```
#include <sys/stat.h>
#include <unistd.h>

int fstat(int filedes, struct stat *buf);
```

Here is the definition of `struct stat`, borrowed from the man page:

```
struct stat
{
    dev_t          st_dev;      /* device */
    ino_t          st_ino;      /* inode */
    mode_t         st_mode;     /* protection */
    nlink_t        st_nlink;    /* number of hard links */
    uid_t          st_uid;      /* user ID of owner */
    gid_t          st_gid;      /* group ID of owner */
    dev_t          st_rdev;     /* device type (if inode device) */
    off_t          st_size;     /* total size, in bytes */
    unsigned long st_blksize; /* blocksize for filesystem I/O */
    unsigned long st_blocks;  /* number of blocks allocated */
    time_t         st_atime;    /* time of last access */
    time_t         st_mtime;    /* time of last modification */
    time_t         st_ctime;    /* time of last change */
};
```

This call is safer than its cousins `stat()` and even `lstat()`.

The `fchown()` Call

The `fchown()` system call lets you change the owner and group associated with an open file.

```
#include <sys/types.h>
#include <unistd.h>

int fchown(int fd, uid_t owner, gid_t group);
```

The first parameter is the file descriptor, the second the numerical user id, and the third the numerical group id. A value of -1 for either owner or group will leave that value unchanged. Return values are zero for success and -1 for failure (check errno).

> **Note**
>
> An ordinary user may change the file's group to any group they belong to. Only root may change the owner to any group.

The fchown() call is safer than its cousin chown(), which takes a pathname instead of a file descriptor.

The fchmod() Call

The fchmod() call changes the mode (permission bits) of the file referenced by fildes to mode.

```
#include <sys/types.h>
#include <sys/stat.h>

int fchmod(int fildes, mode_t mode);
```

Modes are frequently referred to in octal, a horrid base 8 numbering system that was used to describe groups of 3 bits when some systems could not print the letters A–F required for hexadecimal notation. Remember that one of the C language's unpleasant idiosyncrasies is that any numeric constant that begins with a leading zero will be interpreted as octal. Return values are zero for success and -1 for error (check errno).

Table 9.3 shows the file mode bits that may be OR-ed together to make the file mode.

TABLE 9.3 FILE MODES

Octal	Symbolic	Description
04000	S_ISUID	Set user id (setuid)
02000	S_ISGID	Set group id (setgid)
01000	S_SVTX	Sticky bit
00400	S_IRUSR	User (owner) may read
00200	S_IWUSR	User (owner) may write
00100	S_IXUSR	User (owner) may execute/search

Octal	Symbolic	Description
00040	S_IRGRP	Group may read
00020	S_IWGRP	Group may write
00010	S_IXGRP	Group may execute/search
00004	S_IROTH	All others may read
00002	S_IWOTH	All others may write
00001	S_IXOTH	All others may execute

The kernel may modify these bits silently while executing this call or when the file is later modified in certain circumstances to prevent security breaches; in particular the setuid and setgid bits will be reset when the file is written to.

The fchmod() call is safer than its cousin chmod().

The fchdir() Call

The fchdir() call changes to the directory referred to by the open file descriptor fd. A return value of zero means success and -1 means failure (check errno).

```
#include <unistd.h>

int fchdir(int fd);
```

The fchdir() call is safer than its cousin chdir().

The flock() Call

The system call flock() requests or removes an advisory lock on the file referred to by file descriptor fd.

```
#include <sys/file.h>

int flock(int fd, int operation)
```

The second parameter, operation, will be LOCK_SH for a shared lock, LOCK_EX for an exclusive lock, or LOCK_UN to unlock; the value LOCK_NB can be OR-ed with any of the other options to prevent blocking. At any particular time, only one process can have an exclusive lock on a particular file, but more than one can have shared locks. Locks are only enforced when a program tries to place its own lock; programs that do not attempt to lock a file may still access it. Locks, therefore, only work between cooperating programs. Return values are zero for success and -1 for error.

9

I/O ROUTINES

On Linux, and many other UNIX-type systems, there are many types of locks that may or may not interoperate with each other. Locks placed with `flock()` do not communicate with locks placed using `fcntl()` or `lockf()`, or with UUCP lock files in /var/lock. Linux also implements mandatory locks, if they are enabled on your kernel, for specific files that have the setgid bit set and the group execute bit clear; in this case, locks placed with `fcntl()` or `lockf()` will be mandatory.

The `pipe()` Call

The `pipe()` system call creates a pipe and returns two file descriptors in the two integer arrays pointed to by `filedes`. These file descriptors may be used like any file descriptors returned by `open()`. The return value is 0 for success and -1 for error (check `errno`).

```
#include <unistd.h>

int pipe(int filedes[2]);
```

`pipe()` can be used in conjunction with `fork()`, `dup2()`, and `execve()` to create pipes to other programs with redirected input and/or output. Beware of deadlock conditions if you redirect both input and output back to the parent process; it is not difficult to find yourself in a situation where both the parent and child are waiting on each other. You can also create pipes between two or more child processes in this manner.

Types of Files

A variety of types of files are manipulated using file descriptor I/O or by file pointer I/O (`stdio`), which is implemented on top of file descriptor I/O. This section mentions some of the idiosyncrasies of several different types of files.

Regular Files

All of the system calls described in the previous sections, except for `ioctl()` and `fchdir()` (which applies to directories) apply to ordinary files. The program `filedes_io.c`, shown in listing 9.4, shows most of the system calls described in this chapter applied to an ordinary file.

LISTING 9.4   `filedes_io.c`

```
/* filedes_io.c */
#include <sys/types.h>
#include <sys/stat.h>
#include <sys/file.h>
#include <fcntl.h>
```

```
#include <unistd.h>

#include <assert.h>
#include <errno.h>
#include <string.h>
#include <stdio.h>  /* for printf */

char sample1[] = "This is sample data 1\n";
char sample2[] = "This is sample data 2\n";
char data[16];

main()
{
   int fd;
   int rc;
   struct stat statbuf;

   /* Create the file */
   printf("Creating file\n");
   fd=open("junk.out",O_WRONLY¦O_CREAT¦O_TRUNC,0666);
   assert(fd>=0);

   rc=write(fd,sample1,strlen(sample1));
   assert(rc==strlen(sample1));

   close(fd);

   /* Append to the file */
   printf("Appending to file\n");
   fd=open("junk.out",O_WRONLY¦O_APPEND);
   assert(fd>=0);

   printf("   locking file\n");
   rc=flock(fd, LOCK_EX);
   assert(rc==0);

   /* sleep so you can try running two copies at one time */
   printf("   sleeping for 10 seconds\n");
   sleep(10);

   printf("   writing data\n");
   rc=write(fd,sample2,strlen(sample2));
   assert(rc==strlen(sample2));

   printf("   unlocking file\n");
   rc=flock(fd, LOCK_UN);
   assert(rc==0);

   close(fd);
```

9

I/O ROUTINES

continues

LISTING 9.4   CONTINUED

```c
/* read the file */
printf("Reading file\n");
fd=open("junk.out",O_RDONLY);
assert(fd>=0);

while(1) {
    rc=read(fd,data,sizeof(data));
    if(rc>0) {
        data[rc]=0;  /* terminate string */
        printf("Data read (rc=%d): <%s>\n",rc,data);
    } else if (rc==0) {
        printf("End of file read\n");
        break;
    } else {
        perror("read error");
        break;
    }
}
close(fd);


/* Fiddle with inode */
printf("Fiddling with inode\n");
fd=open("junk.out",O_RDONLY);
assert(fd>=0);

printf("changing file mode\n");
rc=fchmod(fd, 0600);
assert(rc==0);
if(getuid()==0) {
    printf("changing file owner\n");
    /* If we are root, change file to owner nobody, */
    /* group nobody (assuming nobody==99 */
    rc=fchown(fd, 99, 99);
    assert(rc==0);
} else {
    printf("not changing file owner\n");
}

fstat(fd, &statbuf);
printf("file mode=%o (octal)\n",statbuf.st_mode);
printf("Owner uid=%d\n",statbuf.st_uid);
printf("Owner gid=%d\n",statbuf.st_uid);

close(fd);
}
```

Tape I/O

Tape drives normally support sequential access to one or more unnamed files separated by end of file markers. Some tape drives support variable block sizes but others use a fixed block size or block sizes that are a multiple of some size. Most, perhaps all, tape drives have some maximum block size. Nine-track (open reel) tape drives support variable block sizes with a minimum block size of something like 16 bytes. Quarter Inch Cartridge (QIC) drives require block sizes to be a multiples of 512 bytes. DAT drives support variable length block sizes. If you want to preserve filename information, use an archive program such as `tar`, which will write a single file containing an archive of many files with filename, ownership, and permission information.

ANSI standard nine-track tapes do appear to have filenames. What is really happening is that two files are written to tape for every data file; the first file contains a header and the second contains the data. There is a package that handles ANSI tapes at `ftp://garbo.uwasa.fi/unix/ansiutil/ansitape.tar.Z`.

The Linux tape drive interface is pretty straightforward. You simply open the tape device (`/dev/nst0`) and perform `read()` and `write()` calls. Each `write()` writes a single block to tape; you control the block size by simply controlling how many bytes you write at a time. To read variable length blocks, and learn what block size was read, simply issue a `read()` with a size large enough to hold the largest block expected; the read will only read the data in the current block and the return value will indicate the block size. End of file markers are placed on tape by writing a block size of zero (most tape devices do not allow zero length blocks); by convention, two consecutive end of file markers mark the end of tape. If a zero length block is read, this should be treated as an end of file. Some UNIX systems require you to close and reopen the file to get past the end of file marker; Linux does not have this idiosyncrasy. If you are not concerned about block sizes, you can even use file pointer I/O on a tape drive; it is possible that selecting unbuffered input and output using `setbuf()` might even allow control over block variable sizes.

> **NOTE**
>
> The `lseek()` call does not work for tape devices, although you can accomplish this using the `MTSEEK` ioctl on those tape drives (such as DAT drives) that support this.

There are a wide variety of ioctls defined in /usr/include/sys/mtio.h that pertain to tape devices. The man page for st, the SCSI tape device, describes these in more detail. The mt program can issue many of these. Some of the things you can do with ioctls are rewind, retension tape, set tape position, eject tape, erase tape, retrieve status, set block sizes, set recording density, turn compression on and off, and initiate a drive self-test. Not all tape drives support all functions.

tapecopy.c, shown in Listing 9.5, copies all files from one tape drive to another, preserving block sizes. Remember to use the no-rewind tape device (/dev/nst0 instead of /dev/st0); the rewind device rewinds the tape every time the file is closed. You will probably want to rewind each tape with a command like mt -f /dev/nst0 rewind. If you only have one tape drive or just want to see the block sizes on an existing tape, you can use /dev/null as the output devices. The program takes three parameters, the input tape device, the output tape device, and the level of verbosity (1=verbose, 0=quiet).

LISTING 9.5   tapecopy.c

```
/* tapecopy.c - copy from one tape to another */
/*              preserving block size */
/* Copyright 1999 by Mark Whitis.  All rights reserved */

#include <sys/time.h>
#include <sys/types.h>
#include <sys/stat.h>
#include <fcntl.h>
#include <unistd.h>
#include <assert.h>
#include <stdio.h>
#include <sys/mtio.h>

int verbose=1;

main(int argc, char *argv[])
{
    int in;
    int out;
    int rc;
    int size;
    char buffer[65536];
    int lasteof;
    int filesize;
    int nfiles;
    int totalsize;
    int blocknum;

    if(argc != 4) {
        fprintf(stderr, "Usage:\n");
```

```c
        fprintf(stderr, "    tapecopy in out verbosity\n");
}

verbose = atoi(argv[3]);

in=open(argv[1],O_RDONLY);
assert(in);
out=open(argv[2],O_WRONLY|O_CREAT,0666);
assert(out);

/* set to variable block size (0) */
/* oddly, this returns EINVAL even though it works */
/* expect an ENOTTY on /dev/null or plain file */
rc=ioctl(in,MTSETBLK,0);
if(rc!=0) perror("tapecopy: ioctl(in,MTSETBLK,0)");
rc=ioctl(out,MTSETBLK,0);
if(rc!=0) perror("tapecopy: ioctl(out,MTSETBLK,0)");

filesize=0;
nfiles=0;
totalsize=0;
blocknum=0;

lasteof = 0;
while(1) {
    rc=read(in, buffer, sizeof(buffer));
    if(verbose) {
        fprintf(stderr,"Block %d, size=%d\n",blocknum,rc);
    }
    if(rc<0) {
        perror("tapecopy: read error");
        blocknum++;
    } else if(rc==0) {
      /* end of file marker read */
      if(lasteof) {
         /* end of tape */
         if(verbose) fprintf(stderr,"**EOT**\n");
         write(out, buffer, 0);
         break;
      } else {
         if(verbose) {
            fprintf(stderr,"**EOF**, filesize=%d\n",filesize);
         }
         /* some Un*x systems require closing and opening   */
         /* file to get past end of file marker */
         close(in);
         in=open(argv[1],O_RDONLY);
         /* write file marker */
         write(out, buffer, 0);
```

continues

LISTING 9.5   CONTINUED

```
            nfiles++;
            filesize=0;
            lasteof=1;
            blocknum=0;
        }
    } else {
        size = rc;
        rc = write(out, buffer, size);
        if(rc!=size) {
            perror("tapecopy: write error");
        }
        filesize+=size;
        totalsize+=size;
        blocknum++;

        lasteof=0;
    }
}

if(verbose) fprintf(stderr,"Number of files: %d\n",nfiles);
if(verbose) fprintf(stderr,"Total size: %d\n",totalsize);

close(in);
close(out);

}
```

Serial Port I/O

Using the serial ports is fairly easy. Just open the port O_RDWR and use ioctls or termios to set the communications parameters. See Chapter 26, "Terminal Control the Hard Way," for more information on termios. You may also want to use file pointer I/O instead.

Note that serial ports frequently have two instances: a call in device and a call out device. This is so the getty program can have the connection open to receive incoming sessions, but modem applications can still open it for outgoing connections as long as there is no active incoming session.

Printer Port

The parallel printer driver creates three character special devices: /dev/lp0, /dev/lp1, and /dev/lp2. To talk to the printer directly, you simply open write data to the appropriate device (assuming no other program already has them open). This is usually not what you want to do from an application, however. Instead, you should use the spooling mechanism provided by the `lpd` daemon. You should pipe the data through a user specified queuing program, which will usually be `lpr` or `mpage` with assorted options. It will usually be more convenient to use file pointer I/O for this purpose; the `popen()` function can be used for this purpose (as long as the program is not privileged).

Sound Card

The sound driver creates a number of character special devices for the various subdevices on a typical soundcard. To play back digitized sound samples, you simply open `/dev/audio` (or `/dev/dsp` or `/dsp1`), use `ioctls()` to set the sample rate, number of channels, number of bits per sample, and other parameters and then start writing your audio samples to the open file descriptor (or file pointer). If you are trying to do synchronized sound, you will need to balance the amount of data you write ahead; too little and you will have dropouts due to buffer overflow, but too much will cause noticeable delays. Recording is similar. To use the FM synthesizer, you must first know how to produce a valid MIDI data stream that you then send to the `/dev/midi` device. In some cases, you may find it simpler to invoke an external program such as play, rec, or playmidi to handle your audio.

More information on the programming interface is available at `http://www.opensound.com/pguide/`.

Summary

File descriptor I/O provides low level file I/O functions in a way that is somewhat UNIX specific. For higher level I/O operations, see file pointer I/O in Chapter 10, "File Manipulation." In some cases, you will still need to use some of the functions in this chapter in conjunction with file pointer I/O.

9

I/O ROUTINES

File Manipulation

by Mark Whitis

IN THIS CHAPTER

This chapter describes file manipulation through the file pointer (FILE *) mechanism provided by the stdio library. This library is common to all C implementations for general-purpose computers (but not some embedded systems); therefore, most C programmers should already be reasonably familiar with it. This chapter provides a quick overview of the basics, and gives more attention to various subtleties and Linux/UNIX-specific calls. The functions described in this section are library functions and not system calls.

The stdio library offers several enhancements over file descriptor I/O; in some circumstances, these can be disadvantages as well. The stdio library buffers I/O, reducing the system call overhead. This can sometimes cause problems with output not being delivered when expected and can be a problem if you are concerned about block boundaries, such as with magnetic tapes or some network protocols. The buffering can be disabled. The very popular printf() family of functions work with file pointer I/O, not file descriptor I/O, and there are a variety of other line oriented functions. These functions may also resume system calls that were interrupted by a signal. The portability of the library is also a major advantage.

The File Functions

The description of each function starts with a function prototype definition, borrowed from the man page and/or header file. In the function descriptions that follow, FILE * identifies a file pointer. Most functions described in this section will take a file pointer argument to indicate what stream to operate on; this will not be repeated in each description. Three standard file pointers are normally open when each program starts— stdin, stdout, and stderr. These three file pointers point to streams that normally are connected to the user's terminal unless redirected to a file or pipe.

> **NOTE**
>
> Some functions are actually implemented as macros. Beware of expressions in the arguments that have side effects; these functions may be called more than once.

Opening and Closing Files

The `fopen()`, `freopen()`, and `fclose()` calls are part of the ANSI standard library; `fdopen()` is not. Prototype definitions for these functions are as follows:

```
#include <stdio.h>

FILE *fopen(const char *path, const char *mode);
FILE *fdopen(int fildes, const char *mode);
FILE  *freopen (const  char *path, const char *mode,
   FILE *stream);
int fclose(FILE * stream);
```

The function `fopen()` opens the file named `path` in mode `mode`. The modes are described in Table 10.1. There is no difference between text and binary modes; this distinction is important on non-UNIX operating systems that handle line ends differently (DOS, MS-Windows, MacOS) and translate to and from the UNIX paradigm in text mode. `fopen()` returns a file pointer that is passed to other `stdio` functions to identify the stream; this pointer points to a structure that describes the state of the stream. In the event of an error, it will return NULL and set `errno`.

TABLE 10.1 FILE OPEN MODES

Mode	Read	Write	Position	Truncate	Create	Binary
r	Yes	No	Beginning	No	No	Text
r+	Yes	Yes	Beginning	No	No	Text
w	No	Yes	Beginning	Yes	Yes	Text
w+	Yes	Yes	Beginning	Yes	Yes	Text
a	No	Yes	End	No	Yes	Text
a+	Yes	Yes	End	No	Yes	Text
rb	Yes	No	Beginning	No	No	Binary
r+b or rb+	Yes	Yes	Beginning	No	No	Binary
wb	No	Yes	Beginning	Yes	Yes	Binary
w+b or wb+	Yes	Yes	Beginning	Yes	Yes	Binary
ab	No	Yes	End	No	Yes	Binary
a+b or ab+	Yes	Yes	End	No	Yes	Binary

The `freopen()` function takes a third argument, which is an existing file pointer. This will close and reopen the file pointer so that it points to the new file. It should use the same file descriptor for the underlying file descriptor I/O as well. `freopen()` is typically used to redirect the streams `stdout`, `stdin`, and `stdout`.

10

FILE MANIPULATION

The fdopen() function is used to create a file pointer stream on top of an underlying file descriptor stream created using open(), pipe(), or accept(). The fopen() and freopen() calls are vulnerable security attacks based on race conditions and/or symbolic links; Chapter 35, "Secure Programming," presents a safer, but more restricted, implementation of fopen(). The fclose() system call closes a file. Return values are 0 for success and EOF (-1) for failure (check errno).

Basic Reading and Writing

The functions fread() and fwrite() are used to read data from and write data to streams (files).

```
#include <stdio.h>

size_t  fread(  void *ptr, size_t size, size_t nmemb, FILE
        *stream);
size_t fwrite( const void *ptr, size_t size, size_t nmemb,
        FILE *stream);
```

The first argument is a pointer to a buffer. The next two arguments are the size of a record and the number of records to be written. The return value is the number of records written (not bytes); this value may be less than the number requested. In the event of an error, the return value will normally be less than the number requested; it is possible it might even be negative. You will need to use feof() and ferror() to check why the operation was not completed.

Status Functions

The feof() and ferror() functions return the current status of the stream.

```
#include <stdio.h>

void clearerr( FILE *stream);
int feof( FILE *stream);
int ferror( FILE *stream);
int fileno( FILE *stream);
```

The feof() function returns non-zero if the end of file has been reached; note, however, that the end of file flag will not usually be set until you actually try to read past the end of file. Looping using while(!feof(stream)) will likely result in one extra pass through the loop. The ferror() function returns a non-zero value if the error flag is set on the stream. This function does not set errno, but the previous function call that actually encountered the error did set errno. The end of file and error flags are reset with clearerr().

The `fileno()` function returns the file descriptor number associated with a stream. This allows you to perform file descriptor I/O operations (see Chapter 9, "I/O Routines") on that stream. For example, you might need to issue an `ioctl()` of `fstat()` system call. Be careful going over `stdio`'s head; in particular, be sure to flush your buffers before doing so.

Formatted Output

The `printf()` function should be familiar to anyone with the slightest C programming experience. It prints formatted output, including optional arguments, to a stream under the control of a control string `format`.

```
#include <stdio.h>

int printf(const char *format, ...);
int fprintf(FILE *stream, const char *format, ...);
int sprintf(char *str, const char *format, ...);
int snprintf(char *str, size_t size, const  char  *format, ...);

#include <stdarg.h>

int vprintf(const char *format, va_list ap);
int  vfprintf(FILE  *stream,  const  char *format,
   va_list ap);
int vsprintf(char *str, const char *format, va_list ap);
int vsnprintf(char *str, size_t size, const char  *format,
   va_list ap);
```

There are a number of interesting variations on `printf()`. The functions with an "s" in the name print to a string instead of a stream. The plain "s" variants are inherently broken and should not be used; they are vulnerable to buffer overflow problems. The functions that have "sn" in the name fix the buffer overflow problem. These functions are not implemented on many other operating systems but you should use them anyway. If you need to port your program to an OS that has not fixed this problem, you can at least implement the `snprintf()` calling convention using a wrapper function around `vsprintf()` even if you don't check for overflows. Your code will still be broken on systems that are broken, but it will work properly on systems that have been fixed. A canary value (see Chapter 35) in your wrapper function would also help.

The versions of the function that start with "v" are very handy. These are the varargs versions; actually, they use `stdargs`, which is the same but different. These are very handy if you need to write your own `printf()` function that does something different to the output. I remember years ago when I was forced to work on a Pascal program.

This was during the Pascal fad; based on my own measurements at the time, around 90 percent of programming projects that were started were using Pascal—yet 90 percent of the programming projects which were actually finished were written in C. Management decided they wanted the program to optionally output its responses to a file and/or a printer—a pretty reasonable request. It approximately doubled the size of the program; every write statement had to be replaced with three write statements and two conditionals. And inconsistencies would creep in between the different outputs when the program was changed. Since printf() is a user-defined function and not a statement, you don't have that problem in C. The code fragment in Listing 10.1 shows how you would handle duplicate output to multiple destinations using vprintf() and friends; just use a search and replace operation to change all calls to printf() to your own xprintf(). The listing also shows how we used to accomplish the same thing before the vprintf() family came along. It wasn't guaranteed to work but it did anyway; it effectively copied 32 bytes of the stack (or a bunch of registers on RISC CPUs). You can use a similar tick to divert output to a dialog box. Note that on a Linux system, simply redirecting the output of an unmodified program through the "tee" program would suffice to log the output of the program.

The stdarg macros provide a way to pass a variable number and/or type of parameters to a function. The function must have at least one fixed argument. The argument list in the function prototype must have "..." where the variable arguments begin. This tells the compiler not to generate error messages when you pass additional, and seemingly inconsistent, parameters to this function. It may also tell the compiler to use a stdarg friendly calling convention. The printf() function has always used a variable number and type of arguments, using trickery which eventually led to portability problems (implementations on some processors, particularly RISC processors, pass some or all of the arguments to a function in registers instead of on the stack). printf() itself is the most common application for stdargs. stdargs also provides a way to pass the variable arguments of one function to another function safely and portably. One of the most common uses of this is to write your own printf() style function which, in turn, makes use of the existing ones. A stdargs function declares a variable of type va_list. It then calls a function va_start() with the va_list variable just declared and the last fixed variable; va_start() is a macro so neither parameter needs to be preceded by an "&" (address of) operator. When you are finished, va_end() will free any resources used by va_start(). The va_list variable, often named "ap" for "argument pointer", may now be used to sequence through each variable using the va_arg() macro. The function itself, not the stdargs macros, needs to know the number and type of the arguments; in the case of the printf() functions, this information is determined from the format string. va_arg() takes two parameters: the va_list variable, ap, and the type argument, which is a C language type expression (such as char *); the macro casts its result to the specified type and as a side effect modifies the ap variable to point to the next variable argument (using the size of the specified type as an offset on traditional systems where arguments are passed on the stack). A simple example of a stdargs function that implements a trivial printf() like function can be found on the stdarg man page; for more information on the use of va_arg() and stdargs, please refer to that document. Unlike functions with fixed arguments, functions with variable arguments cannot easily be encapsulated in another wrapper function. The trick here is to make the real function take a va_list argument (instead of the variable argument list to which it refers) and then make a simple wrapper function that does nothing more than initialize the va_list and call the other function. Now programmers can write their own wrapper function by simply calling your real function instead of your wrapper. The xprintf() function in Listing 10.1 is an example of a replacement wrapper function. The ANSI standard essentially requires that the printf() family of functions be implemented as a va_list function and variable argument wrapper, or at least appear to be. Since vsprintf() and vfprint() do the same thing but do different things with the results, a given implementation's efforts to combine the two variations may add confusion here for those who choose to look at the code for the printf() family of functions. Those who want to peruse the stdarg.h file to see how the magic of stdarg is done may find more magic than they expected: the file has disappeared. Although it is possible to implement stdargs in C macros on a traditional machine, gcc handles these macros internally since it has to deal with many different architectures.

LISTING 10.1   vprintf() AND FRIENDS

```c
#include <stdlib.h>
#include <stdio.h>
#include <stdarg.h>

FILE *printer;
FILE *logfile;

int xprintf(const char *format, ...)
{
   va_list ap;

   va_start(ap,format);

   vprintf(format, ap);
   if(printer) vfprintf(printer, format, ap);
   if(logfile) vfprintf(logfile, format, ap);

   va_end(ap);

}
```

10

FILE
MANIPULATION

continues

LISTING **10.1** CONTINUED

```
int old_xprintf(const char *format,
    long a1, long a2, long a3, long a4,
    long a5, long a6, long a7, long a8)
{
    printf(format, a1, a2, a3, a4, a5, a6, a7, a8);
    if(printer)
        fprintf(printer,format, a1, a2, a3, a4, a5, a6, a7, a8);
    if(logfile)
        fprintf(logfile,format, a1, a2, a3, a4, a5, a6, a7, a8);

}
```

Formatted Input

The fscanf() function is used to read formatted input from stdin under the control of a control string format. Many variations exist that read from any arbitrary stream ("f" versions) or from a string ("s" versions). The "v" versions use stdargs. These variations are similar to the variations described for the printf() family.

```
#include <stdio.h>
int scanf( const char *format, ...);
int fscanf( FILE *stream, const char *format, ...);
int sscanf( const char *str, const char *format, ...);

#include <stdarg.h>
int vscanf( const char *format, va_list ap);
int vsscanf( const char *str, const char *format, va_list ap);
int vfscanf( FILE *stream, const char *format, va_list ap);
```

One of the most common mistakes people make using these functions is to pass the value of a variable instead of its address (a pointer); don't forget the "&" operator where necessary. Generally, strings will not need an ampersand but other variables will.

Failure to include a size in the control string for string arguments will permit buffer overflows that can have serious security consequences. If you do include a size, any extra input in a particular field is likely to end up in the wrong field.

Note that the versions of scanf() that read directly from a stream are vulnerable to extra data at the end of the line being read by the next scanf(). For this reason, it is better to read a line into a string buffer and then use sscanf() on it; this also lets you use multiple scanf() calls with different formats to handle different possible input formats.

The return value from all of these functions is the number of fields successfully read. In the event of an error, the function will return EOF (-1) or a number less than the number of fields requested.

Character and Line Based Input and Output

Many functions are available for line-based input and output. These functions generally have two flavors, one that deals with characters and one that works on strings. The function prototypes are listed below.

```
#include <stdio.h>

int fgetc(FILE *stream);
char *fgets(char *s, int size, FILE *stream);
int getc(FILE *stream);
int getchar(void);
char *gets(char *s);
int ungetc(int c, FILE *stream);
int fputc(int c, FILE *stream);
int fputs(const char *s, FILE *stream);
int putc(int c, FILE *stream);
int putchar(int c);
int puts(const char *s);
int ungetc(int c, FILE *stream);
```

Table 10.2 gives a brief summary of these functions. Those that return `int` will return a negative value (EOF) on error (check `errno`). The functions that return a character pointer return either a pointer to the string read (a pointer to the buffer you passed in) or NULL if an error occurred.

TABLE 10.2   CHARACTER AND LINE I/O FUNCTIONS

Function	Direction	Size	Stream	Overflow	Newline
fgetc	Input	Character	Any	No	
fgets	Input	line	Any	No	Kept
getc	Input	Character	Any	No	
getchar	Input	Character	stdin	No	
gets	Input	Line	stdin	Yes	Removed
ungetc	Input	Character	Any	No	
fputc	Output	Character	Any	No	
fputs	Output	Line	Any	No	Not added
putc	Output	Character	Any	No	
putchar	Output	Character	stdout	No	
puts	Output	Line	stdout	No	Added

10

FILE
MANIPULATION

The line-oriented functions are inconsistent in their handling of newlines. The gets() function is vulnerable to buffer overflows and should not be used; use fgets() instead but note the difference in newline handling.

File Positioning

The file positioning functions set the current position of a file; they may not work on streams that do not point to normal files. The prototypes for these functions are listed below.

```
#include <stdio.h>

int fseek( FILE *stream, long offset, int whence);
long ftell( FILE *stream);
void rewind( FILE *stream);
int fgetpos( FILE *stream, fpos_t *pos);
int fsetpos( FILE *stream, fpos_t *pos);
```

The fseek() function sets the position to offset. The whence parameter is SEEK_SET, SEEK_CUR, or SEEK_END; these values determine whether the offset is relative to the beginning, current position, or the end of file. It returns the current position relative to the beginning, or a value of -1 in the event of error (check errno). The ftell() function simply returns the current position. The rewind() function sets the position to zero. The fgetpos() and fsetpos() functions are implemented as variations of ftell() and fseek(); on other operating systems that do not treat all files as a simple stream of data bytes, the fpos_t may be a structure instead of an integer.

Buffer Control

The prototypes for the buffer control functions are as follows. These functions provide for the three main types of stream buffering, unbuffered, line buffered, and block buffered, as well as the ability to flush any buffered but unwritten data out.

```
#include <stdio.h>

int fflush(FILE *stream);
int setbuf(FILE *stream, char *buf);
int setbuffer(FILE *stream, char *buf, size_tsize);
int setlinebuf(FILE *stream);
int setvbuf(FILE *stream, char *buf, int mode , size_t size);
```

The fflush() function flushes the buffers on output stream stream.

The setvbuf() function sets the buffer used by a stream. The arguments are the file pointer for the stream, the address of the buffer to use, the mode, and the size of the buffer. The mode can be one of _IONBF for unbuffered operation, _IOLBF for line buffered, or _IOFBF for fully buffered. If the buffer address is NULL, the buffer will be left alone but the mode will still be changed. The other functions basically are variations of the more versatile setvbuf() function. Use setvbuf() immediately after opening a stream or after fflush(); do not use it if there is any buffered data.

> **TIP**
>
> The code fragment setbuf(stream, NULL); is frequently used to unbuffer a stream, although setvbuf() can also be used.

Deletion and Renaming

The remove() function deletes a file by name and the rename() function renames a file.

```
#include <stdio.h>

int remove(const char *pathname);
int rename(const char *oldpath, const char *newpath);
```

The first argument to each function is the pathname to an existing file. The second argument to rename() is a pathname that describes where the file should be renamed to. Both return a value of zero on success and –1 on error; the specific error code will be found, as usual, in the variable errno. These functions can be vulnerable to symbolic links and race conditions, which are discussed in Chapter 35 "Secure Programming."

Temporary Files

The tmpfile() and tmpnam() functions are part of the ANSI standard C stdio library; the other two (mkstemp() and mktemp()) are peculiar to UNIX systems.

```
#include <stdio.h>

FILE *tmpfile (void);
char *tmpnam(char *s);

#include <unistd.h>
int mkstemp(char *template);
char *mktemp(char *template);
```

The tmpfile() function opens a temporary file. The tmpnam() function generates a filename that may be used to generate a temporary file; if "s" is not NULL the filename is written into the supplied buffer (which could be overflowed since there is no size argument), otherwise it returns a pointer to an internal buffer that will be overwritten the next time the function is used. Neither of these functions allows you to specify where the file will be stored, and they are likely to create a file (or pathname) in a vulnerable shared directory such as /tmp or /var/tmp. These functions should not be used.

10

FILE
MANIPULATION

A simple example of how to use `tmpnam()` to create and open a temporary function is as follows:

```
FILE *tmpfile=NULL;
Char FILENAME[L_tmpnam];
Tempfile=fopen(tmpnam(FILENAME), "rb+");
```

The `mktemp()` function also generates a unique filename for a temporary file, but it uses a template that allows you to specify the path prefix that will be used; the last six characters of the template must be "XXXXXX". The `mkstemp()` function makes a filename using `mktemp()` and then issues an `open()` system call to open it for file descriptor I/O; you can use `fdopen()` to open a `stdio` stream on top of that descriptor.

Temporary files should only be created in safe directories that are not writable by other users (such as ~/tmp or /tmp/$(username)); otherwise, they are vulnerable to race conditions and symlink attacks (see Chapter 35). The filenames generated by these functions are easily guessable.

Summary

The file pointer functions included in the `stdio` library, which is part of the standard C library, provide a more convenient and portable interface to files, particularly for text files.

The primary limitation of the `stdio` library is that it can only manipulate streams that are handled by the underlying file descriptor system calls. My universal streams library does not have this limitation; user supplied functions can be used to handle input and output. You might want to check my Web site to see if this library has been released.

Process Control

by Mark Whitis

In This Chapter

This chapter introduces the basics of process control. In the traditional UNIX model, there are basically two operations to create or alter a process. You can `fork()` to create another process that is an exact copy of the existing process, and you can use `execve()` to replace the program running in a process with another program. Running another program usually involves both operations, possibly altering the environment in between. Newer, lightweight processes (threads) provide separate threads of execution and stacks but shared data segments. The Linux specific `__clone()` call was created to support threads; it allows more flexibility by specifying which attributes are shared. The use of shared memory (see Chapter 17, "Shared Memory") allows additional control over resource sharing between processes.

Attributes

Table 11.1 attempts to summarize how process attributes are shared, copied, replaced, or separate for the four major ways to change a process. Instead of actually copying memory, a feature known as "copy-on-write" is frequently used in modern OSes like Linux. The mappings between virtual and physical memory are duplicated for the new process, but the new mappings are marked as read-only. When the process tries to write to these memory blocks, the exception handler allocates a new block of memory, copies the data to the new block, changes the mapping to point to the new block with write access, and then resumes the execution of the program. This feature reduces the overhead of forking a new process.

TABLE 11.1 PROCESS ATTRIBUTE INHERITANCE

Attribute	`fork()`	*thread*	`__clone()`	`execve()`
		Virtual Memory (VM)		
Code Segment	copy	shared	CLONE_VM	replaced
Const Data Segment	don't care	shared	CLONE_VM	replaced
Variable Data Segment	copy	shared	CLONE_VM	replaced
stack	copy	separate	CLONE_VM	replaced
`mmap()`	copy	shared	CLONE_VM	replaced
`brk()`	copy	shared	CLONE_VM	replaced
command line	copy	shared	CLONE_VM	replaced
environment	copy	shared	CLONE_VM	replaced

Attribute	fork()	*thread*	__clone()	execve()
		Files		
chroot(), chdir(), umask()	copy	shared	CLONE_FS	copy
File descriptor table	copy	shared	CLONE_ FILES	copy[1]
file locks	separate	separate	CLONE_PID	same
		Signals		
Signal Handlers	copy	shared	CLONE_SIGHAND	reset
Pending Signals	separate	separate	separate	reset
Signal masks	separate	separate	separate	reset
Process Id (PID)	different	different	CLONE_PID	same
timeslice	separate	shared	CLONE_PID	same

Footnote[1]: Except file descriptors with the close on exec bit set

System Calls and Library Functions

The calls in this section are a mixture of system calls and library functions. The function prototype at the beginning of each section is borrowed from the man pages and/or header files.

The fork() System Call

The fork() system call creates an almost exact copy of the current process. Both the parent and the child will execute the code following the fork(). An "if" conditional normally follows the fork to allow different behavior in the parent and child processes.

```
#include <unistd.h>

pid_t fork(void);
pid_t vfork(void);
```

If the return value is positive, you are executing in the parent process and the value is the PID of the child. If the return value is 0, you are in the child. If the value is negative, something went wrong and you need to check errno.

Under Linux, vfork() is the same as fork(). Under some operating systems, vfork() is used when the fork will be immediately followed by an execve(), to eliminate unneeded duplication of resources that will be discarded; in order to do this, the parent is suspended until the child calls execve().

The exec() Family

The execve() system call replaces the current process with the program specified by filename, using the argument list argv and the environment envp. If the call to execve() returns, an error obviously occurred and errno will have the cause.

```
#include <unistd.h>

int  execve  (const  char  *filename, char *const argv [],
    char *const envp[]);

extern char **environ;

int execl( const char *path, const char *arg, ..., NULL);
int execlp( const char *file, const char *arg, ..., NULL);
int  execle( const char *path, const char *arg , ...,
    NULL,  char * const envp[]);
int execv( const char *path, char *const argv[]);
int execvp( const char *file, char *const argv[]);
```

The library functions execl(), execlp(), execle(), execv(), and execvp() are simply convenience functions that allow specifying the arguments in a different way, use the current environment instead of a new environment, and/or search the current path for the executable. The versions of the function with an "l" in the name take a variable number of arguments, which are used to build argv[]; the function prototypes in the preceding code have been edited to show the NULL terminator required at the end of the list. Those functions that lack an "e" in the name copy the environment from the current process. Those functions that have a "p" in the name will search the current path for the executable named by file; the rest require that an explicit path to the executable file be specified in path.

With the exception of execle() and execve(), all these functions have serious security vulnerabilities due to their use of the current environment (including path) and should never be used in setuid programs. All these functions and the execve() must be used with a safe path to the executable. There is no exec() function; this is often used, however, as a generic identifier for this family of functions. Only rarely will you want to use these routines by themselves. Normally, you will want to execute a fork() first to exec() the program in a child process.

The `system()` and `popen()` Functions

For lazy programmers, the `system()` and `popen()` functions exist. These functions must not be used in any security sensitive program (see Chapter 35, "Secure Programming").

```
#include <stdlib.h>
int system (const char * string);

#include <stdio.h>
FILE *popen(const char *command, const char *type);
int pclose(FILE *stream);
```

These functions `fork()` and then `exec()` the user's login shell that locates the command and parses its arguments. They use one of the `wait()` family of functions to wait for the child process to terminate.

The `popen()` function is similar to `system()`, except it also calls `pipe()` and creates a pipe to the standard input or from the standard output of the program, but not both. The second argument, `type`, is "r" to read piped `stdout` or "w" to write to `stdin`.

The `clone()` Function Call

The Linux specific function call, `__clone()`, is an alternative to `fork()` that provides more control over which process resources are shared between the parent and child processes.

```
#include <sched.h>

int  __clone(int (*fn) (void *arg), void *child_stack,
   int flags, void *arg)
```

This function exists to facilitate the implementation of `pthreads`. It is generally recommended that you use the portable `pthreads_create()` to create a thread instead, although `__clone()` provides more flexibility.

The first argument is a pointer to the function to be executed. The second argument is a pointer to a stack that you have allocated for the child process. The third argument, `flags`, is created by OR-ing together various `CLONE_*` flags (shown in Table 11.1). The fourth argument, `arg`, is passed to the child function; its function is entirely up to the user. The call returns the process ID of the child process created. In the event of an error, the value -1 will be returned and `errno` will be set.

The `wait()`, `waitpid()`, `wait3()`, and `wait4()` System Calls

These system calls are used to wait for a change of state in a particular process, any member of a process group, or any child process.

```
#include <sys/types.h>
#include <sys/wait.h>

pid_t wait(int *status)
pid_t waitpid(pid_t pid, int *status, int options);

#define _USE_BSD
#include <sys/types.h>
#include <sys/resource.h>
#include <sys/wait.h>

pid_t wait3(int *status, int options,
        struct rusage *rusage)

pid_t wait4(pid_t pid, int *status, int options,
        struct rusage *rusage)
```

The `wait()` call waits for any child process. The `waitdpid()` call waits for a specific process. The BSD-style `wait3()` and `wait4()` calls are equivalent to `wait()` and `waitpid()`, respectively, but also return the resource usage of the child process into the struct pointed to by the argument `rusage`. Where the functions take a `pid` argument, this may be positive, in which case it specifies a specific `pid`; negative, in which case the absolute value specifies a process group; -1, for any process; or 0, for any member of the same process group as the current process. If the call takes an argument `options`, this will be 0, or the result of OR-ing either or both of the options `WNOHANG` (don't block if no child has exited yet) or `WUNTRACED` (return for children that have stopped).

Until a parent process collects the return value of a child process, a child process that has exited will exist in a zombie state. A stopped process is one whose execution has been suspended, not one that has exited.

`select()`

The `select()` call was described in detail in Chapter 9, "I/O Routines." It is mentioned here because it provides a very lightweight alternative to threads and forking processes.

Signals

Signals are events that may be delivered to a process by the same or a different process. Signals are normally used to notify a process of an exceptional event.

```
#include <signal.h>
struct sigaction {
    void (*sa_handler)(int);
    sigset_t sa_mask;
    int sa_flags;
    void (*sa_restorer)(void);
}

void (*signal(int signum, void (*handler)(int)))(int);
int raise (int sig);
int killpg(int pgrp, int sig);
int sigaction(int signum, const struct sigaction *act,
    struct sigaction *oldact);
int sigprocmask(int how, const sigset_t *set,
    sigset_t *oldset);
int sigpending(sigset_t *set);
int sigsuspend(const sigset_t *mask);
void psignal(int sig, const char *s);

#include <sys/types.h>
#include <signal.h>
int kill(pid_t pid, int sig);

#include <unistd.h>
int pause(void);


#include <string.h>
char *strsignal(int sig);
extern const char * const sys_siglist[];
```

The signal() function registers the handler, handler, for the signal signum. The handler may be one of the predefined macro values SIG_IGN (to ignore the signal), SIG_DFL (to restore the default handler), or a user defined signal handler function. The handler is reset to the default behavior when the signal handler is called; it may call signal() again to catch future signals.

The function raise() sends a signal, sig, to the current process. The system call kill() sends a signal, sig, to another process specified by process id pid. The system call killpg() is similar, except it sends the signal to every process in the process group specified by pgrp or the current process's process group if pgrp is zero. For both calls, the current process must have permission to send a signal to the recipient, which generally means they must belong to the same user or the sender must be root. If the signal for kill() is zero, no signal is actually sent, but the usual error checking is performed; this may be used to test for the continued existence of a particular process.

The various signals that may be delivered are defined in the man page signal in section 7 (use the command man 7 signal). The pause() system call suspends the current process until a signal is received. The `sigaction()` system call is an elaborate version of the more common `signal()` call. It sets the new action for signal `signum` to the action pointed to by `act` (if not NULL) and saves the current action into `oldact` (if not NULL).

The `sigaction` structure has four members. The member `sa_handler` is a pointer to the signal handler function; it might also have the value `SIG_DFL` or `SIG_IGN`. The member `sa_mask` indicates which other signals should be blocked while handling this one. The member `sa_flags` is the result of bitwise OR-ing together of the flags `SA_NOCLDSTOP` (disable `SOGCHLD` notification if the child merely stops), `SA_ONESHOT` or `SA_RESETHAND` (which both cause the signal handler to be reset after the first invocation), `SA_RESTART` (which allows some system calls to be restarted after a signal), or either `SA_NOMASK` or `SA_NODEFER` (which allow the same signal to be delivered again while the signal handler is executing). The `sa_restorer` member is obsolete.

The `sigprocmask()` function is used to set the current mask of blocked signals. The argument `how` can be `SIG_BLOCK` (add members of `set` to the set of blocked signals), `SIG_UNBLOCK` (remove members of `set` from the set of blocked signals), or `SIG_SETMASK` (assign the set of blocked signals from `set`). If the pointer `oldset` has a value other than NULL, the previous contents of the mask are saved to the referenced object.

The system call `sigpending()` may be used to determine which signals are currently pending but blocked. The set of pending signals is stored into the object pointed to by `set`. The system call `sigsuspend()` temporarily suspends the current process but first sets the signal mask according to `mask`. These functions return zero for success and -1 for an error (check `errno`).

The function `strsignal()` returns a pointer to a string that describes the signal `sig`. The descriptive strings may be accessed directly in the array `sys_siglist[]`. The `psignal()` function is similar except it prints the description, along with the prefix message "s", to `stderr`.

The function `sigreturn()` should not be called directly; when the kernel invokes a signal handler it inserts a return into this cleanup function on the stack frame. The function `sigpause()` is obsolete; use `sigsuspend()`. The `sigvec()` function has similarly been obsoleted by `sigaction()`.

There can be problems with `setuid()` processes receiving signals from an ordinary user who invokes the process while the process is in a privileged state. Chapter 35 has more details on the security implications of signals.

Many system calls and library functions can be interrupted by signals. Depending on the `SA_RESTART` value set with `sigaction()`, some system calls may be restarted automatically. Otherwise, if a system call is interrupted by a signal (`errno=EINTR`), you may need to reissue the system call with the arguments adjusted to resume where it left off.

Program Termination

The exit() function terminates execution of the current program, closes any open file descriptors, and returns the lower eight bits of the value status to the parent process to retrieve using the wait() family of functions.

```
#include <unistd.h>
void _exit(int status);

#include <stdlib.h>
void exit(int status);
int atexit(void (*function)(void));
int on_exit(void (*function)(int , void *), void *arg);
void abort(void);

#include <assert.h>
void assert (int expression);
```

The parent process will receive a SIGCHLD signal. Any child processes' parent process id will be changed to 1 (init). Any exit handlers registered with atexit() or on_exit() will be called (most recently registered first) before the program ends. The exit() function will call the system call _exit(), which may be called directly to bypass the exit handlers.

The function atexit() registers a function with no arguments and no return value to be called when the program exits normally. The on_exit() function is similar, except that the exit handler function will be called with the exit status and the value of arg as arguments. The atexit() and on_exit() functions return a value of 0 on success and return -1 and set errno if they do not succeed.

The abort() function also terminates the current program. Open files are closed and core may be dumped. If you have registered a signal handler for SIGABRT using signal(), or a similar function, this signal handler will be called first. The parent process will be notified that the child died due to SIGABRT.

The assert() macro evaluates the provided expression. If the expression evaluates to 0 (false) then it will call abort(). The assert() macro can be disabled by defining the macro NDEBUG. assert() is normally used to check your assumptions and make your code more robust, causing it to abort instead of malfunction. It is good practice to check function arguments using assert() at the beginning of each function for situations that otherwise would not be handled properly. assert() can be used to check return values from functions if you don't feel like handling them more gracefully. You can also use assert() to check word sizes and other aspects of the compilation and execution environment. The following code fragments show some calls to assert():

```
assert(result_p);          /* check for NULL pointer */
   assert(result_p!=NULL);   /* ditto */
```

```
assert(sizeof(int)==4);    /* Check word size */
rc=open("foo",O_RDONLY);
assert(rc>=0);             /* check return value from open */
```

Alarms and Timers

The system call setitimer() sets one of three interval timers associated with each
process.

```
#include <sys/time.h>
struct itimerval {
   struct timeval it_interval; /* next value */
   struct timeval it_value;    /* current value */
};
struct timeval {
   long tv_sec;                      /* seconds */
   long tv_usec;                     /* microseconds */
};
int getitimer(int which, struct itimerval *value);
int setitimer(int which, const  struct  itimerval  *value,
      struct itimerval *ovalue);

#include <unistd.h>
unsigned int alarm(unsigned int seconds);
unsigned int sleep(unsigned int seconds);
void usleep(unsigned long usec);
```

The argument may have the value ITIMER_REAL (decrements in real time), ITIMER_VIR-
TUAL (decrements when the process is executing), or ITIMER_PROF (decrements when the
process is executing or when the kernel is executing on the process's behalf). The timers
deliver the signals SIGALRM, SIGVTALRM, and SIGPROF, respectively. The interval timers
may have up to microsecond resolution. The getitimer() system call retrieves the current value into the object pointed to by value. The setitimer() call sets the timer to the
value pointed to by value and stores the old value into the object pointed to by ovalue,
if not NULL. These system calls return zero for success or a value of -1 (check errno)
for an error.

The alarm() function schedules a SIGALRM signal to be delivered in the number of seconds of real time indicated by seconds. The sleep() and usleep() functions suspend
the process for at least the number of seconds or microseconds, respectively, specified by
their single argument. The actual delay may be significantly longer due to clock granu-
larity or multitasking.

All these functions share the same set of timers. Thus alarm(), sleep(), and usleep()
can conflict with each other and with an ITIMER_REAL used with getitimer(). The timeout used by the select() system call might also conflict. If you need to make simultaneous use of more than one function that uses ITIMER_REAL(), you will need to write a

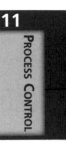

function library that maintains multiple timers and calls setitimer() only with the next one to expire.

Scheduling Parameters

These calls manipulate parameters that set the scheduling algorithm and priorities associated with a process.

```
#include <sched.h>
int sched_setscheduler(pid_t pid, int policy,
    const struct sched_param *p);
int sched_getscheduler(pid_t pid);
struct sched_param {
    ...
    int sched_priority;
    ...
};

#include <unistd.h>
int nice(int inc);

#include <sys/time.h>
#include <sys/resource.h>
int getpriority(int which, int who);
int setpriority(int which, int who, int prio);

#include <sched.h>
int sched_get_priority_max(int policy);
int sched_get_priority_min(int policy);
```

A process with a higher static priority will always preempt a process with a lower static priority. For the traditional scheduling algorithm, processes within static priority 0 will be allocated time based on their dynamic priority (nice() value).

The system calls sched_setscheduler() and sched_getscheduler() are used to set or get, respectively, the scheduling policy and parameters (set only) associated with a particular process. These functions take a process id, pid, to identify the process on which to operate; the current process must have permission to act on the specified process. The scheduling policy, policy, is one of SCHED_OTHER (the default policy), SCHED_FIFO, or SCHED_RR; the latter two specify special policies for time critical applications and will preempt processes using SCHED_OTHER. A SCHED_FIFO process can only be preempted by a higher priority process, but a SCHED_RR process will be preempted if necessary to share time with other processes at the same priority. These two system calls will return -1 in the event of an error (check errno); on success, sched_setscheduler() returns 0 and sched_getscheduler() returns a non-negative result. The system calls sched_get_priority_max() and sched_get_priority_min() return the maximum and minimum priority values, respectively, which are valid for the policy specified by policy). The static priority of SCHED_OTHER processes is always 0; use nice() or setpriority() to set the dynamic priority.

The system call nice() adds inc to the dynamic priority for the calling process, lowering its priority. The superuser may specify a negative value, which will raise the priority. Returns 0 for success or -1 for error (check errno).

The system call setpriority() sets the dynamic priority of a process (which = PRIO_PROCESS), process group (which = PRIO_PGRP), or user (which = PRIO_USER). The priority is set to the value prio, which will have a value between -20 and 20 with lower numbers giving more priority in scheduling. It will return 0 on success and -1 if there is an error (check errno). The system call getpriority() takes the same first two arguments and returns the lowest value (highest priority) of all matching processes. It will return -1 for either an error or if that is the actual result; you must clear errno before using this function and check it afterwards to determine which was the case.

Threads

POSIX threads (pthreads) provide a relatively portable implementation of lightweight processes. Many operating systems do not support threads. The Linux implementation differs from many. In particular, each thread under Linux has its own process id because thread scheduling is handled by the kernel scheduler. Threads offer lower consumption of system resources and easier communication between processes.

There are many potential pitfalls to using threads or any other environment where the same memory space is shared by multiple processes. You must be careful about more than one process using the same variables at the same time. Many functions are not re-entrant; that is, there cannot be more than one copy of that function running at the same time (unless they are using separate data segments). Static variables declared inside functions are often a problem. Parameter passing and return value conventions for function calls and returns that are used on various platforms can be problematic, as can the specific conventions used by certain functions. Returning strings, large structs, and arrays are particularly problematic. Returning a pointer to statically allocated storage inside the function is no good; another thread may execute that function and overwrite the return value before the first one is through using it. Unfortunately, many functions and, worse yet, compilers, use just such a calling convention. GCC may use different calling conventions on different platforms because it needs to maintain compatibility with the native compiler on a given platform; fortunately, GCC favors using a non-broken return convention for structures even if it could mean incompatibility with other compilers on the same platform. Structs up to 8 bytes long are returned in registers, and functions that return larger structures are treated as if the address of the return value (storage space allocated in the calling function) was passed as an argument. Variables that are shared between processes should be declared using the `volatile` keyword to keep the optimizer from changing the way they are used and to encourage the compiler to use atomic operations to modify these variables where possible. Semaphores, mutexes, disabling interrupts, or similar means should be used to protect variables, particularly aggregate variables, against simultaneous access.

Setting or using global variables may create problems in threads. It is worth noting that the variable `errno` may not, in fact, be a variable; it may be an expression that evaluates to a different value in each thread. In Linux, it appears to be an ordinary integer variable; presumably, it is the responsibility of the thread context switching code to save and restore `errno` when changing between threads.

The `pthread_create()` Function

The `pthread_create()` function creates a new thread storing an identifier to the new thread in the argument pointed to by `thread`.

```
#include <pthread.h>

int  pthread_create(pthread_t *thread,
   pthread_attr_t * attr,
   void * (*start_routine)(void *), void * arg);
```

The second argument, `attr`, determines which thread attributes are applied to the thread; thread attributes are manipulated using `pthread_attr_init()`. The third argument is the address of the function that will be executed in the new thread. The fourth argument is a void pointer that will be passed to that function; its significance, if any, is defined by the user.

The `pthread_exit()` Function

This function calls any cleanup handlers that have been registered for the thread using `pthread_cleanup_push()` and then terminates the current thread, returning `retval`, which may be retrieved by the parent or another thread using `pthread_join()`. A thread may also terminate simply by returning from the initial function.

```
#include <pthread.h>

void pthread_exit(void *retval);
```

The `pthread_join()` Function

The function `pthread_join()` is used to suspend the current thread until the thread specified by `th` terminates.

```
#include <pthread.h>

int pthread_join(pthread_t th, void **thread_return);
int pthread_detach(pthread_t th);
```

The other thread's return value will be stored into the address pointed to by `thread_return` if this value is not NULL. The memory resources used by a thread are not deallocated until `pthread_join()` is used on it; this function must be called once for each joinable thread. The thread must be in the joinable, rather than detached, state and no other thread may be attempting to use `pthread_join()` on the same thread. The thread may be put in the detached state by using an appropriate `attr` argument to `pthread_create()` or by calling `pthread_detach()`.

Note that there seems to be a deficiency here. Unlike with the `wait()` family of calls for regular processes, there does not seem to be a way to wait for the exiting of any one out of multiple threads.

Attribute Manipulation

These functions manipulate thread attribute objects. They do not manipulate the attributes associated with threads directly. The resulting object is normally passed to `pthread_create()`. The function `pthread_attr_init()` initializes a new object and the function `pthread_attr_destroy()` erases it. The user must allocate space for the `attr` object before calling these functions. These functions could allocate additional space that will be deallocated by `thread_attr_destroy()`, but in the Linux implementation this is not the case.

```
#include <pthread.h>

int pthread_attr_init(pthread_attr_t *attr);
int pthread_attr_destroy(pthread_attr_t *attr);
int pthread_attr_setdetachstate(pthread_attr_t *attr,
    int detachstate);
int pthread_attr_getdetachstate(const pthread_attr_t *attr,
    int *detachstate);
int  pthread_attr_setschedpolicy(pthread_attr_t *attr,
    int policy);
int pthread_attr_getschedpolicy(const pthread_attr_t *attr,
    int *policy);
int pthread_attr_setschedparam(pthread_attr_t *attr,
    const struct sched_param *param);
```

```
int pthread_attr_getschedparam(const pthread_attr_t *attr,
    struct sched_param *param);
int pthread_attr_setinheritsched(pthread_attr_t *attr,
    int inherit);
int pthread_attr_getinheritsched(const pthread_attr_t *attr,
    int *inherit);
int pthread_attr_setscope(pthread_attr_t   *attr,
    int scope);
int pthread_attr_getscope(const pthread_attr_t *attr,
    int *scope);
int  pthread_setschedparam(pthread_t  target_thread,
    int policy, const struct sched_param *param);
int pthread_getschedparam(pthread_t  target_thread,
    int *policy, struct sched_param *param);
```

The `pthread_setschedparam()` and `pthread_getschedparam()` functions are used to set or get, respectively, the scheduling policy and parameters associated with a running thread. The first argument identifies the thread to be manipulated, the second is the policy, and the third is a pointer to the scheduling parameters.

The remaining functions take one argument that is a pointer to the attribute object, `attr`, to be manipulated, and either set or retrieve the value of a specific attribute that will be obvious from the name. Table 11.2 shows the thread attributes; the default values are marked with an asterisk. High priority real-time processes may want to lock their pages into memory using `mlock()`. `mlock()` is also used by security sensitive software to protect passwords and keys from getting swapped to disk, where the values may persist after they have been erased from memory.

TABLE 11.2   THREAD ATTRIBUTES

Attribute	Value	Meaning
detachstate	PTHREAD_CREATE_JOINABLE*	Joinable state
	PTHREAD_CREATE_DETACHED	Detached state
schedpolicy	SCHED_OTHER*	Normal, non-realtime
	SCHED_RR	Realtime, round-robin
	SCHED_FIFO	Realtime, first in first out
schedparam	policy specific	
inheritsched	PTHREAD_EXPLICIT_SCHED*	Set by schedpolicy and schedparam
	PTHREAD_INHERIT_SCHED	Inherited from parent process

continues

TABLE 11.2 CONTINUED

Attribute	Value	Meaning
scope	PTHREAD_SCOPE_SYSTEM*	One system timeslice
	PTHREAD_SCOPE_PROCESS	for each thread
		Threads share same
		system timeslice
		(not supported
		under Linux)

All the attribute manipulation functions return 0 on success. In the event of an error, these functions return the error value rather than setting errno.

The pthread_atfork() Function

This function registers three separate handlers, which will be invoked when a new process is created.

```
#include <pthread.h>

int  pthread_atfork(void  (*prepare)(void),
   void (*parent)(void), void (*child)(void));
```

The prepare() function will be called in the parent process before the new process is created, and the parent() process will be called afterwards in the parent. The child() function will be called in the child process as soon as it is created. The man page for these functions refers to the fork() process; this seems to be an anachronism since presumably __clone() is now used instead. Any of the three function pointers may be NULL; in that case, the corresponding function will not be called. More than one set of handlers may be registered by calling pthread_atfork() multiple times. Among other things, these functions are used to clean up mutexes that are duplicated in the child process. Return values are 0 for success or an error code.

Thread Cancellation

The pthread_cancel function allows the current thread to cancel another thread, identified by thread.

```
#include <pthread.h>

int pthread_cancel(pthread_t thread);
int pthread_setcancelstate(int state, int *oldstate);
int pthread_setcanceltype(int type, int *oldtype);
void pthread_testcancel(void);
```

A thread may set its cancellation state using setcancelstate(), which takes two arguments. The argument state is the new state and the argument oldstate is a pointer to a variable in which to save the oldstate (if not NULL). The function pthread_setcanceltype changes the type of response to cancellation requests; if type is PTHREAD_CANCEL_ASYNCHRONOUS, the thread will be cancelled immediately or PTHREAD_CANCEL_DEFERRED to delay cancellation until a cancellation point is reached. Cancellation points are established by calls to pthread_testcancel(), which will cancel the current thread if any deferred cancellation requests are pending. The first three functions return 0 for success and an error code otherwise.

The pthread_cleanup_push() Macro

The pthread_cleanup_push() macro registers a handler, routine, which will be called with the void pointer argument specified by arg when a thread terminates by calling pthread_exit(), or honors a cancellation request.

```
#include <pthread.h>
void pthread_cleanup_push(void (*routine) (void   *),
   void *arg);
void pthread_cleanup_pop(int execute);
void  pthread_cleanup_push_defer_np(
   void  (*routine) (void *), void *arg);
void pthread_cleanup_pop_restore_np(int execute);
```

The macro pthread_cleanup_pop() unregisters the most recently pushed cleanup handler; if the value of execute is non-zero, the handler will be executed as well. These two macros must be called from within the same calling function.

The macro pthread_cleanup_push_defer_np() is a Linux-specific extension that calls pthread_cleanup_push() and also pthread_setcanceltype() to defer cancellation. The macro pthread_clanup_pop_restore_np() pops the most recent handler registered by pthread_cleanup_push_defer_np() and restores the cancellation type.

pthread_cond_init()

These functions are used to suspend the current thread until a condition is satisfied. A *condition* is an object that may be sent signals.

```
#include <pthread.h>
pthread_cond_t cond = PTHREAD_COND_INITIALIZER;
int  pthread_cond_init(pthread_cond_t *cond,
   pthread_condattr_t *cond_attr);
int pthread_cond_signal(pthread_cond_t *cond);
int pthread_cond_broadcast(pthread_cond_t *cond);
```

```
int pthread_cond_wait(pthread_cond_t *cond,
   pthread_mutex_t *mutex);
int  pthread_cond_timedwait(pthread_cond_t *cond,
   pthread_mutex_t *mutex, const struct timespec *abstime);
int pthread_cond_destroy(pthread_cond_t *cond);
```

The function `pthread_cond_int()` initializes an object, cond, of type cond_t. The second parameter is ignored under Linux. You can also just copy PTHREAD_COND_INITIALIZER to the variable. The function `pthread_cond_destroy()` is the destructor for objects of type cond_t; it doesn't do anything except check that there are no threads waiting on the condition.

The function `pthread_cond_signal()` is used to restart one, and only one, of the threads waiting on a condition. The function `pthread_cond_broadcast()` is similar, except that it restarts all threads. Both take a condition, of type cond_t, to identify the condition.

The function `pthread_cond_wait()` unlocks a mutex, specified by mutex, and waits for a signal on the condition variable cond. The function `pthread_cond_timedwait()` is similar but it only waits until the time specified by abstime. The time is usually measured in seconds since 1/1/1970 and is compatible with the value returned by the system call time(). These functions are also possible cancellation points and they return 0 for success or an error code in the event of failure.

The `pthread_equal()` Function

The function `pthread_equal()` returns a non-zero value if the threads referred to by thread1 and thread2 are actually the same; otherwise it returns zero.

```
#include <pthread.h>

int pthread_equal(pthread_t thread1, pthread_t thread2);
```

Mutexes

Mutexes are mutual exclusion locks, a form of semaphore. Mutexes are objects of type mutex_t such that only one thread may hold a lock on a given mutex simultaneously. Like any form of semaphore, they are normally used to prevent two processes or threads from using a shared resource at the same time. A thread that tries to lock a mutex that is already locked will be suspended until the lock is released by the thread that has it locked.

```
#include <pthread.h>
pthread_mutex_t fastmutex = PTHREAD_MUTEX_INITIALIZER;
pthread_mutex_t recmutex = PTHREAD_RECURSIVE_MUTEX_INITIALIZER_NP;
pthread_mutex_t errchkmutex
   = PTHREAD_ERRORCHECK_MUTEX_INITIALIZER_NP;
```

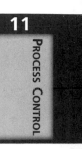

```
int pthread_mutex_init(pthread_mutex_t *mutex,
    const pthread_mutexattr_t *mutexattr);
int pthread_mutex_lock(pthread_mutex_t *mutex));
int pthread_mutex_trylock(pthread_mutex_t *mutex);
int pthread_mutex_unlock(pthread_mutex_t *mutex);
int pthread_mutex_destroy(pthread_mutex_t *mutex);
```

The functions `pthread_mutex_init()` and `pthread_mutex_destroy()` are the constructor and destructor functions, respectively, for mutex objects. The functions `pthread_mutex_lock()` and `pthread_mutex_unlock()` are used to lock and unlock a mutex, respectively. The function `pthread_mutex_trylock()` is similar to `pthread_mutex_lock()` except that it will not block (suspend the thread) if the mutex is already locked. These functions return 0 for success or an error code otherwise; `pthread_mutex_init()` never fails.

Sample Programs

This section presents a library I wrote that demonstrates a number of process control features and some sample programs that use that library.

Child Library

Listing 11.1 shows the header file, `child.h`, and Listing 11.2 shows the actual implementation, `child.c`, of the library. The library contains functions to spawn a set number of child processes, to replace these processes when they die, and to send signals to these processes. It also includes a function that implements a safer and more flexible replacement for the `system()` and `popen()` standard library functions.

The type `child_fp_t` defines a pointer to a function that will be executed in the child process. The two arguments are a pointer to the `child_info_t` structure that describes the child and an arbitrary (user defined) void pointer.

The data structure `child_info_t` has information about a particular child process, including its process id (`pid`), its parent process id (`ppid`), its process number (zero through the number of child processes in a given group), and a pointer to the function to be executed.

The data structure `child_group_info_t` contains information about a group of child processes. The member `nchildren` defines how many processes are listed in the `child` array. The members `minchildren`, `maxchildren`, and `activechildren` define the minimum and maximum numbers of children to maintain and the number currently being maintained; currently, these three values should all be the same. The array `child` contains multiple instances of type `child_info_t`. This data structure maintains information on a group of child processes all running the same function.

The data structure `child_groups_t` defines multiple groups; each group may be running a different function. Member `ngroups` indicates how many groups are defined in the array group of type `child_group_info_t`. This allows functions that wait for or manipulate dissimilar child processes.

The function `child_create()` creates an individual child process. The third argument, `private_p`, is a user defined void pointer that is passed to the created child function. The function `child_group_create()` creates between "min" and "max" copies of a child process (currently the number created will equal "min"). The function `child_groups_keepalive()` replaces children from one or more groups of children when they terminate for any reason. The function `child_group_signal()` sends a signal to all children in a single group. The function `child_groups_signal()` sends a signal to the children in multiple groups. The function `child_groups_kill()` counts the number of children by sending them signal 0, sends each of them `SIGTERM`, and waits until they all die or a couple minutes have elapsed, at which time it aborts them using `SIGKILL`.

The function `child_pipeve()` is a replacement for `system()` and `popen()`. The first three arguments are similar to the arguments for the `execve()` system call and define the program to be executed, its command line arguments, and its environment. The remaining three arguments are pointers to file descriptors for `stdin`, `stdout`, and `stderr`; if these pointers are not NULL, a pipe will be created for the corresponding stream, and a file descriptor for the appropriate end of the pipe will be returned into the referenced objects.

LISTING 11.1   child.h

```
#ifndef _CHILD_H
#define _CHILD_H

#ifdef __cplusplus
extern "C" {
#endif


#define MAX_CHILDREN 32
#define MAX_CHILD_GROUPS 4


extern int child_debug;
```

```c
/* we have a circular reference here */
struct child_info_t;

typedef void (*child_fp_t)(struct child_info_t *, void *);

typedef struct child_info_t {
   int pid;
   int ppid;
   int number;
   child_fp_t child_fp;
} child_info_t;

/* The following should really be kept in shared memory */
typedef struct {
   int nchildren;    /* number in table, not number running */
   int minchildren;
   int maxchildren;
   int activechildren;
   child_info_t child[MAX_CHILDREN];
} child_group_info_t;

typedef struct {
   int ngroups;
   child_group_info_t *group[MAX_CHILD_GROUPS];
} child_groups_t;

void child_create(
   child_info_t *child_info_p,
   child_fp_t child_fp,
   void *private_p
);


child_info_t *child_lookup_by_pid(
   const child_groups_t *child_groups_p,
   int pid
);

int child_group_create(
   child_group_info_t *children_info_p,
   const int min,
   const int max,
   const child_fp_t child_fp,
   void *private_p
);

extern int child_restart_children;
```

continues

LISTING 11.1   CONTINUED

```c
extern void child_groups_keepalive(
   const child_groups_t *child_groups_p
);

extern int child_group_signal(
   child_group_info_t *children_info_p,
   int signal
);

extern int child_groups_signal(
   const child_groups_t *child_groups_p,
   int signal
);

extern int child_groups_kill(
   const child_groups_t *child_groups_p
);

extern int child_pipeve(
   const char *cmdpath,  /* full path to command */
   char * const argv[],   /* Array of pointers to arguments */
   char * const envp[],/* Array of pointers to environment vars*/
   int *stdin_fd_p,      /* Output: fd for stdin pipe */
   int *stdout_fd_p,     /* Output: fd for stdout pipe */
   int *stderr_fd_p      /* Output: fd for stderr pipe */
);

extern void child_print_arg_array(char *name, char * const array[]);


extern void child_init();
extern void child_term();

#ifdef __cplusplus
}
#endif

#endif  /* _CHILD_H */
```

LISTING 11.2   child.c

```c
#include <sys/time.h>
#include <unistd.h>
#include <stdlib.h>
#include <stdio.h>
#include <assert.h>
#include <sys/types.h>
#include <sys/types.h>
```

```c
#include <sys/wait.h>
#include <fcntl.h>
#include <signal.h>
#include <errno.h>



#include "child.h"

/* Linux doesn't even bother to declare DST_NONE */
#ifndef DST_NONE
    #define DST_NONE 0
#endif

int child_debug=0;

void child_create(
    child_info_t *child_info_p,
    child_fp_t child_fp,
    void *private_p
) {
    int rc;
    int fd;
    int seed;
    struct timeval tv;
    struct timezone tz;

    assert(child_info_p);
    assert(child_fp);

    /* struct timezone is obsolete and not really used */
    /* under Linux */
    tz.tz_minuteswest = 0;
    tz.tz_dsttime = DST_NONE;

    rc=fork();
    if(rc == (pid_t) -1) {
        /* error */
        perror("fork failed");
    } else if (rc>0) {
        /* parent */
        child_info_p->pid = rc;
    } else {
        #ifndef USING_SHARED_MEM
            child_info_p->pid = getpid();
            child_info_p->ppid = getppid();
        #endif

        /* reseed random number generator */
        /* if you don't do this in each child, they are */
```

continues

LISTING 11.2   CONTINUED

```c
        /* likely to all use the same random number stream */
        fd=open("/dev/random",O_RDONLY);
        assert(fd>=0);
        rc=read(fd, &seed, sizeof(seed));
        assert(rc == sizeof(seed));
        close(fd);
        srandom(seed);

        gettimeofday(&tv, NULL);
        fprintf(stderr,
            "%010d.%06d: Starting child process #%d, pid=%d, "
            "parent=%d\n",
            tv.tv_sec,
            tv.tv_usec,
            child_info_p->number,
            child_info_p->pid,
            child_info_p->ppid
        );

        child_info_p->child_fp = child_fp;

        child_fp(child_info_p, private_p);

        gettimeofday(&tv, NULL);
        fprintf(stderr,
            "%010d.%06d: child process #%d finishing, pid=%d, "
            "parent=%d\n",
            tv.tv_sec,
            tv.tv_usec,
            child_info_p->number,
             child_info_p->pid,
            child_info_p->ppid
        );

        /* child process ceases to exist here */
        exit(0);
    }
}


child_info_t *child_lookup_by_pid(
    const child_groups_t *child_groups_p,
    int pid
) {
    int i;
    int j;

    assert(child_groups_p);
```

```
    for(i=0; i<child_groups_p->ngroups; i++) {
        for(j=0; j<child_groups_p->group[i]->nchildren; j++) {
            if( child_groups_p->group[i]->child[j].pid == pid ) {
                return(&child_groups_p->group[i]->child[j]);
            }
        }
    }
    return(NULL);

}

int child_group_create(
    child_group_info_t *children_info_p,
    const int min,
    const int max,
    const child_fp_t child_fp,
    void *private_p
) {
    int i;

    children_info_p->nchildren = min;
    children_info_p->maxchildren = max;
    children_info_p->minchildren = min;

    for(i=0; i<min; i++) {
        children_info_p->child[i].number = i;
        children_info_p->child[i].child_fp = child_fp;

        child_create(&children_info_p->child[i],child_fp,
            private_p);
    }

    children_info_p->activechildren = min;

    return(0);
}


int child_restart_children = 1;

/* This function currently does not change the number of */
/* children.  In the future, it could be extended to change */
/* the number of children based on load.  Each time a child */
/* exited, it could restart 0, 1, or 2 children instead of 1 */

void child_groups_keepalive(
    const child_groups_t *child_groups_p
) {
    int rc;
    int child_status;
```

continues

LISTING 11.2   CONTINUED

```c
    int pid;
    child_info_t *child_p;

    while(1) {
        rc=wait(&child_status);
        if(child_restart_children==0) {
            fprintf(stderr,"child_groups_keepalive(): exiting\n");
            return;
        }
        if(rc>0) {
            fprintf(stderr,"wait() returned %d\n",rc);
            pid = rc;
            if(WIFEXITED(child_status)) {
                fprintf(stderr, "child exited normally\n");
            }
            if(WIFSIGNALED(child_status)) {
                fprintf(stderr, "child exited due to signal %d\n",
                    WTERMSIG(child_status));
            }
            if(WIFSTOPPED(child_status)) {
                fprintf(stderr, "child suspended due to signal %d\n",
                    WSTOPSIG(child_status));
            }

            /* Use kill with an argument of zero to see if */
            /* child still exists.  We could also use */
            /* results of WIFEXITED() and WIFSIGNALED */
            if(kill(pid,0)) {

                child_p = child_lookup_by_pid(child_groups_p, pid);
                assert(child_p);
                fprintf(stderr,
                    "Child %d, pid %d, died, restarting\n",
                     child_p->pid, pid);

                child_create( child_p, child_p->child_fp, NULL );
            } else {
                fprintf(stderr,"Child pid %d still exists\n");
            }
        }
    }
}

int child_group_signal(
    child_group_info_t *children_info_p,
    int signal
) {
    int i;
    int count;
```

```
    int rc;
    child_info_t *child_p;

    assert(children_info_p);
    assert(signal>=0);

    count=0;

    for(i=0; i<children_info_p->nchildren; i++) {
        child_p = &children_info_p->child[i];
        fprintf(stderr,"sending signal %d to pid %d\n",
            signal, child_p->pid);
        rc=kill(child_p->pid,signal);
        if(rc==0) count++;
    }
    return(count);
}

int child_groups_signal(
    const child_groups_t *child_groups_p,
    int signal
) {
    int i;
    int pid;
    int count;

    assert(child_groups_p);
    assert(signal>=0);
    count=0;
    for(i=0; i<child_groups_p->ngroups; i++) {
        count += child_group_signal(child_groups_p->group[i],
                    signal);
    }
    return(count);
}

int child_groups_kill(
    const child_groups_t *child_groups_p
) {
    int child_count;
    int rc;
    int i;

    assert(child_groups_p);

    child_count=child_groups_signal(child_groups_p, 0);
    fprintf(stderr, "total children=%d\n", child_count);

    fprintf(stderr, "sending SIGTERM\n");
    child_groups_signal(child_groups_p, SIGTERM);
```

continues

LISTING 11.2   CONTINUED

```c
    /* wait up to 4 minutes for children to die */
    /* wait() may hang if children are already gone */
    for(i=0; i<24; i++) {
        rc=child_groups_signal(child_groups_p, 0);
        if(rc==child_count) return(child_count);
        sleep(5);
    }

    fprintf(stderr, "some children did not die\n");
    fprintf(stderr, "sending SIGKILL\n");
    child_groups_signal(child_groups_p, SIGKILL);
}

/* debugging function for argv and envp */
void child_print_arg_array(char *name, char * const array[])
{
    int i;

    i=0;
    while(1) {
        if(array[i]) {
            fprintf(stderr,"%s[%d]=\"%s\"\n",name,i,array[i]);
        } else {
            fprintf(stderr,"%s[%d]=NULL\n",name,i,array[i]);
            break;
        }

        i++;
    }
}



extern char **environ;

/* This function is intended as a replacement for */
/* system() and popen() which is more flexible and */
/* more secure.  The path to the executable must still */
/* be safe against write access by untrusted users. */

/* argv[] and envp[] must end with a NULL pointer */
/* stdin_fd_p, stdout_fd_p, or stderr_fd_p may be NULL, in */
/* which case, that stream will not be piped.  stdout_fd_p */
/* and stderr_fd_p may be equal */
```

```
/* you may want to use fd_open() on the pipes to use stdio */
/* argv[0] should equal cmdpath */

int child_pipeve(
   const char *cmdpath,   /* full path to command */
   char * const argv[],    /* Array of pointers to arguments */
   char * const envp[],    /* Array of pointers to env. vars*/
   int *stdin_fd_p,        /* Output: fd for stdin pipe */
   int *stdout_fd_p,       /* Output: fd for stdout pipe */
   int *stderr_fd_p        /* Output: fd for stderr pipe */
) {
   int rc;
   int pid;
   int status;
   int stdin_pipe[2];
   int stdout_pipe[2];
   int stderr_pipe[2];
   char *dummy_argv[8];
   char *dummy_envp[8];


   stdin_pipe[0] = -1;
   stdin_pipe[1] = -1;
   stdout_pipe[0] = -1;
   stdout_pipe[1] = -1;
   stderr_pipe[0] = -1;
   stderr_pipe[1] = -1;

   if(stdin_fd_p) {
      rc=pipe(stdin_pipe);
      if(rc!=0) return(-1);
      *stdin_fd_p = stdin_pipe[1];
   }

   if(stdout_fd_p) {
      rc=pipe(stdout_pipe);
      if(rc!=0) {
         if(stdin_pipe[0]>=0) close(stdin_pipe[0]);
         if(stdin_pipe[0]>=0) close(stdin_pipe[1]);
         return(-1);
      }
      *stdout_fd_p = stdout_pipe[0];
   }

   if(stderr_fd_p && (stderr_fd_p!=stdout_fd_p) ) {
      rc=pipe(stderr_pipe);
      if(rc!=0) {
         if(stdin_pipe[0]>=0) close(stdin_pipe[0]);
         if(stdin_pipe[0]>=0) close(stdin_pipe[1]);
```

continues

LISTING 11.2   CONTINUED

```
        if(stdin_pipe[0]>=0) close(stdout_pipe[0]);
        if(stdin_pipe[0]>=0) close(stdout_pipe[1]);
        return(-1);
    }
    *stderr_fd_p = stderr_pipe[0];
}


rc=fork();
if(rc<0) {
  /* error */
  return(-1);
} else if(rc==0) {
  /* child */

  if(stdin_fd_p) {
      /* redirect stdin */
      rc=dup2(stdin_pipe[0],0);
  }

  if(stdout_fd_p) {
      /* redirect stdout */
      rc=dup2(stdout_pipe[1],1);
  }

  if(stderr_fd_p) {
      /* redirect stderr */
      if(stderr_fd_p == stdout_fd_p) {
         rc=dup2(stdout_pipe[1],2);
      } else {
         rc=dup2(stderr_pipe[1],2);
      }
  }

  /* clean up file descriptors */
  #if 0
     for(i=3;i<OPEN_MAX;i++) {
         close(i);
     }
  #endif

  if(envp == NULL) envp = environ;


  if(child_debug>=5) {
     child_print_arg_array("argv",argv);
     child_print_arg_array("envp",envp);
```

```
        fprintf(stderr,"cmdpath=\"%s\"\n",cmdpath);
    }

    fprintf(stderr,"about to execve()\n");

#if 1
    execve(cmdpath, argv, envp);
#else
    dummy_argv[0] = "./child_demo4";
    dummy_argv[1] = "one";
    dummy_argv[2] = "two";
    dummy_argv[3] = "three";
    dummy_argv[4] = NULL;
    dummy_envp[0] = "PATH=/bin:/usr/bin";
    dummy_envp[1] = NULL;

    execve("./child_demo4",dummy_argv,dummy_envp);
#endif
    /* we should never get here unless error */

    fprintf(stderr, "execve() failed\n");
    perror("execve()");
    /* we will be lazy and let process termination */
    /* clean up open file descriptors */
    exit(255);

} else {
    /* parent */
    pid=rc;

#if 0
    rc=wait4(pid, &status, 0, NULL);
#else
    rc=waitpid(pid, &status, 0);
#endif

    if(rc<0) {
        /* wait4() set errno */
        return(-1);
    }
    if(WIFEXITED(status)) {
        fprintf(stderr,"child_pipve(): child exited normally\n");
        return( (int) (signed char) WEXITSTATUS(status));
    } else if(WIFSIGNALED(status)) {
        fprintf(stderr,"child_pipve(): child caught signal\n");
        errno = EINTR;
        return(-1);
    } else {
```

continues

LISTING 11.2   CONTINUED

```
            fprintf(stderr,"child_pipve(): unkown child status\n");
            /* we should handle stopped processes better */
            errno = EINTR;
            return(-1);
        }
    }


}


void child_init()
{
    ;
}

void child_term()
{
    ;
}
```

The `child_demo1.c` Program

The program `child_demo1.c`, shown in listing 11.3, demonstrates the child library by invoking four child processes that do little other than announce their existence, sleep a random amount of time, and then die. Processes that die are automatically restarted. For no especially good reason, it installs signal handlers for several common signals and responds to those signals by doing a `longjmp()` and then killing the children. The use of `longjmp()` here is slightly risky because the local variables in the function have not been declared volatile, so any variables the compiler might have stored in registers will have random values after the `longjmp()`. A future version may fix this oversight.

LISTING 11.3   child_demo1.c

```
#include <sys/time.h>
#include <unistd.h>
#include <stdlib.h>
#include <stdio.h>
#include <assert.h>
#include <sys/types.h>
#include <sys/types.h>
#include <sys/wait.h>
#include <fcntl.h>
```

```c
#include <signal.h>
#include <setjmp.h>

#include "child.h"


void child_process_1(
    child_info_t *child_info_p,
    void *private_p
) {
    int rc;
    int sleep_time;

    assert(child_info_p);

    /* undo signal settings from parent */
    signal(SIGTERM, SIG_DFL);
    signal(SIGINT, SIG_DFL);
    signal(SIGQUIT, SIG_DFL);

    /* This is child process */
    fprintf(stderr,
        "Child process #%d starting, pid=%d, parent=%d\n",
        child_info_p->number,
        child_info_p->pid,
        child_info_p->ppid
    );

    /* Here is where we should do some useful work */
    /* instead, we will sleep for a while and then die */
    sleep_time = random() & 0x7F;
    fprintf(stderr,
        "Child process #%d sleeping for %d seconds\n",
        child_info_p->number,
        sleep_time
    );
    sleep(sleep_time);


    fprintf(stderr,
        "Child process #%d exiting, pid=%d, parent=%d\n",
        child_info_p->number,
        child_info_p->pid,
        child_info_p->ppid
    );
}

child_group_info_t child_group_1;
jmp_buf jump_env;
```

continues

LISTING 11.3 CONTINUED

```c
void sig_handler(int signal)
{
    fprintf(stderr, "pid %d received signal %d\n",
        getpid(), signal);
    child_restart_children = 0;

    #if 0
        /* wake up the wait() */
        /* doesn't work */
        raise(SIGCHLD);
    #endif

    longjmp(jump_env,1);

    /* We opt not to call signal() again here */
    /* next signal may kill us */
}

main()
{
    int i;
    int child;
    child_group_info_t child_group_1;
    child_groups_t child_groups;
    int rc;

    #if 0
        setvbuf(stderr, NULL, _IOLBF, 0);
    #else
        setbuf(stderr, NULL);
    #endif

    /* Note: children inherit this */
    signal(SIGTERM, sig_handler);
    signal(SIGINT, sig_handler);
    signal(SIGQUIT, sig_handler);

    child_group_create(&child_group_1, 4, 4, child_process_1, NULL );

    child_groups.ngroups = 1;
    child_groups.group[0]=&child_group_1;


    rc=setjmp(jump_env);
    if(rc==0) {
      /* normal program execution */
```

```
        child_groups_keepalive(&child_groups);
    } else {
        /* exception handler */
        /* we got here via setjmp() */

        /* restore signal handlers to defaults */
        signal(SIGTERM, SIG_DFL);
        signal(SIGINT, SIG_DFL);
        signal(SIGQUIT, SIG_DFL);

        child_groups_kill(&child_groups);
        exit(0);
    }

}
```

The `child_demo2.c` Program

The program `child_demo2.c`, shown in Listing 11.4, is an extension of `child_demo1.c`.
It implements a very primitive Web server, which preforks 4 processes, each of which
responds to any request by reporting the status of the child process that handled the
request. Each child will terminate after it has handled 10 requests. In a preforked server
situation, you may want to guard against memory leaks and other problems by giving
each child a limited lifetime. It would also be good to set an alarm using `alarm()` at the
beginning of each request so the child will die if the request is not handled in a reasonable length of time for any reason.

LISTING 11.4   `child_demo2.c`

```
#include <sys/time.h>
#include <unistd.h>
#include <stdlib.h>
#include <stdio.h>
#include <assert.h>
#include <sys/types.h>
#include <sys/wait.h>
#include <fcntl.h>
#include <signal.h>
#include <setjmp.h>
#include <sys/socket.h>
#include <netdb.h>
#include <netinet/in.h>
#include <arpa/inet.h>
```

continues

LISTING 11.4 CONTINUED

```c
#include <string.h>
#include <limits.h>

#include "child.h"

int debug=1;


int listen_sock;


void child_process_1(
    child_info_t *child_p,
    void *private_p
) {
    int rc;
    int sleep_time;
    int connection;
    struct sockaddr_in remote_addr;
    int addr_size;
    struct hostent *remote_host;
    char buf[1024];
    char *p;
    int requests_remaining = 10;
    int read_fd;
    int write_fd;
    FILE *in;
    FILE *out;
    char s[128];
    assert(child_p);

    requests_remaining = 10;

    /* undo signal settings from parent */
    signal(SIGTERM, SIG_DFL);
    signal(SIGINT, SIG_DFL);
    signal(SIGQUIT, SIG_DFL);

    /* This is child process */
    fprintf(stderr,
        "Child process #%d starting, pid=%d, parent=%d\n",
        child_p->number,
        child_p->pid,
        child_p->ppid
    );

    while(requests_remaining--) {

        addr_size=sizeof(remote_addr);
```

```
connection = accept(listen_sock,
    (struct sockaddr *) &remote_addr,
    &addr_size);
fprintf(stderr, "accepted connection\n");

remote_host = gethostbyaddr(
    (void *) &remote_addr.sin_addr,
    addr_size, AF_INET);
/* we never bother to free the remote_host strings */
/* The man page for gethostbyaddr() fails to mention */
/* allocation/deallocation or reuse issues */

/* return values from DNS can be hostile */


if(remote_host) {
    assert(strlen(remote_host->h_name)<128);
    assert(remote_host->h_length==4);   /* no IPv6 */

  if(debug) {
      fprintf(stderr, "from: %s\n", remote_host->h_name);
  }
  strncpy(s,remote_host->h_name,sizeof(s));
} else {
  if(debug) {
    fprintf(stderr,
      "from: [%s]\n",inet_ntoa(remote_addr.sin_addr) );
  }
  strncpy(s,inet_ntoa(remote_addr.sin_addr),sizeof(s));
}


read_fd = dup(connection);
write_fd = dup(connection);
assert(read_fd>=0);
assert(write_fd>=0);
in = fdopen(read_fd, "r");
out = fdopen(write_fd, "w");
assert(in);
assert(out);

/* do some work */

while(1) {
    buf[0]=0;
    p=fgets(buf, sizeof(buf), in);
    if(!p) break;  /* connection probably died */
    buf[sizeof(buf)-1]=0;
    p=strrchr(buf,'\n');
    if(p) *p=0;   /* zap newline */
```

continues

LISTING 11.4   CONTINUED

```
            p=strrchr(buf,'\r');
            if(p) *p=0;   /* zap return */

            fprintf(stderr,"buf=<%s>\n",buf);
            p=strchr(buf,':');
            if(p) {
                /* we never actually get here because we start */
                /* spewing out a response as soon as we rx GET */
                /* probably an http: header */
                /* ignore it */
                ;
            } else if(strstr(buf,"GET")) {
                fprintf(stderr,"GET\n");
                fprintf(out,"HTTP/1.0 200 OK");
                fprintf(out,"Content-type: text/html\n");
                fprintf(out,"\n");
                fprintf(out,"<HTML>\n");
                fprintf(out," <HEAD>\n");
                fprintf(out,"  <TITLE>\n");
                fprintf(out,"  Status Page\n");
                fprintf(out,"  </TITLE>\n");
                fprintf(out," </HEAD>\n");
                fprintf(out," <BODY>\n");
                fprintf(out,"  <H1>\n");
                fprintf(out,"  Status Page\n");
                fprintf(out,"  </H1>\n");
                fprintf(out,"  <BR>number=%d\n",child_p->number);
                fprintf(out,"  <BR>pid=%d\n",child_p->pid);
                fprintf(out,"  <BR>ppid=%d\n",child_p->ppid);
                fprintf(out,"  <BR>requests remaining=%d\n",
                    requests_remaining);
                fprintf(out," </BODY>\n");
                fprintf(out,"</HTML>\n");
                break;
            } else {
                /* ??? */
            }

        }

        fprintf(stderr,"closing connection\n");
        /* wrap things up */
        fclose(in);
        fclose(out);
        close(read_fd);
        close(write_fd);
```

```
         close(connection);
      } /* while */


      fprintf(stderr,
         "Child process #%d exiting, pid=%d, parent=%d\n",
         child_p->number,
         child_p->pid,
         child_p->ppid
      );
}

child_group_info_t child_group_1;
jmp_buf jump_env;


void sig_handler(int signal)
{
   fprintf(stderr, "pid %d recieved signal %d\n",
      getpid(), signal);
   child_restart_children = 0;

   #if 0
      /* wake up the wait() */
      /* doesn't work */
      raise(SIGCHLD);
   #endif

   longjmp(jump_env,1);

   /* We opt not to call signal() again here */
   /* next signal may kill us */
}

int port = 1236;

main()
{
   int i;
   int child;
   child_group_info_t child_group_1;
   child_groups_t child_groups;
   int rc;
   struct sockaddr_in tcpaddr;

   tcpaddr.sin_family = AF_INET;
   tcpaddr.sin_addr.s_addr = INADDR_ANY;
   tcpaddr.sin_port = htons( port );
```

continues

LISTING 11.4   CONTINUED

```c
listen_sock = socket(AF_INET, SOCK_STREAM, IPPROTO_IP);
if(listen_sock<0) perror("socket");
assert(listen_sock>=0);

fprintf(stderr, "listening on port %d\n",port);

#if 1
    rc=bind(listen_sock, (struct sockaddr *) &tcpaddr,
        sizeof(tcpaddr));
#else
    rc=bind(listen_sock, (struct sockaddr *) &tcpaddr, 4);
#endif
if(rc!=0) perror("bind");
assert(rc==0);
rc=listen(listen_sock,10);
if(rc!=0) perror("listen");
assert(rc==0);

#if 0
    setvbuf(stderr, NULL, _IOLBF, 0);
#else
    setbuf(stderr, NULL);
#endif

/* Note: children inherit this */
signal(SIGTERM, sig_handler);
signal(SIGINT, sig_handler);
signal(SIGQUIT, sig_handler);

child_group_create(&child_group_1, 4, 4, child_process_1,
    NULL );

child_groups.ngroups = 1;
child_groups.group[0]=&child_group_1;


rc=setjmp(jump_env);
if(rc==0) {
  /* normal program execution */

    child_groups_keepalive(&child_groups);
} else {
  /* exception handler */
  /* we got here via setjmp() */

    /* restore signal handlers to defaults */
    signal(SIGTERM, SIG_DFL);
```

```
        signal(SIGINT, SIG_DFL);
        signal(SIGQUIT, SIG_DFL);

        child_groups_kill(&child_groups);
        exit(0);
    }

}
```

The `child_demo3.c` Program

The program `child_demo3.c`, shown in Listing 11.5, illustrates the use of the `child_pipeve()` function. It will invoke the program named by `argv[1]` and give it the arguments found in the remaining command-line arguments. It merely copies its environment for the child's environment.

Another program, `child_demo4.c`, which is included on the CD-ROM but not as a listing, dumps its arguments and environment and is useful for testing `child_demo3.c`.

LISTING 11.5   `child_demo3.c`

```
#include <sys/time.h>
#include <unistd.h>
#include <stdlib.h>
#include <stdio.h>
#include <assert.h>
#include <sys/types.h>
#include <sys/wait.h>
#include <fcntl.h>
#include <signal.h>
#include <setjmp.h>
#include <sys/socket.h>
#include <netdb.h>
#include <netinet/in.h>
#include <arpa/inet.h>
#include <string.h>
#include <limits.h>

#include "child.h"

int debug=5;

extern char **environ;


main(int argc, char *argv[])
{
    int count;
```

continues

LISTING 11.5   CONTINUED

```c
    int i;
    char **newargv;
    int rc;

#if 1
    /* very primitive example, borrows everything from the */
    /* current process  */
    if(debug>=5) child_print_arg_array("argv",argv);


    fprintf(stderr,"argc=%d\n",argc);
    assert(argc >= 2);
    /* make a new argv[] from argv[] */
    count=0;
    while(1) {
       count++;
       if(argv[count]==NULL) break;
    }
    printf("count=%d\n",count);
    newargv = malloc(sizeof(void *)*(count+2));
    newargv[0] = argv[1];
    for(i=1; i<count; i++) {
       newargv[i] = argv[i+1];
    }
    newargv[i] = NULL;
    printf("argv[1]=%s\n",argv[1]);

    if(debug>=5) child_print_arg_array("newargv",newargv);
    if(debug>=5) child_print_arg_array("environ",environ);

    fprintf(stderr,"invoking program\n");
    rc=child_pipeve(argv[1], newargv, environ,
       NULL, NULL, NULL);
    fprintf(stderr,"program invocation over\n");

    fprintf(stderr,"rc=%d\n",rc);
    if(rc<0) {
       perror("child_pipeve()");
    }

#endif
}
```

Summary

The Linux operating system provides a variety of functions that can be used to manipulate processes. Most of these are shared by some or even all other UNIX and compatible operating systems.

Accessing System Information

by Mark Whitis

IN THIS CHAPTER

In the old days, certain UNIX programs, such as `ps` and `uptime`, accessed kernel data structures directly to retrieve system information. This required knowledge of kernel externals and required care to ensure that the values were not modified as they were being accessed. The programs needed to be setuid root in order to access the kernel data structures; this meant they were vulnerable to security exploits if they were not carefully written. These programs also frequently had to be rebuilt when the kernel was changed because the positions and layouts of the data structures may have changed.

Some more modern systems implement a `/proc` filesystem that contains special files that can be read to access system status information. These files are usually plain text files. Linux makes more information available through the `/proc` filesystem than many other systems.

Entries in the `/proc` filesystem can be created by any kernel module. The code that implements the `/proc` filesystem and some of its entries can be found in `/usr/src/linux/fs/proc`. Portions of the proc namespace are registered using the kernel function `proc_register()`.

The `/proc` files described in this chapter are based on a system running a 2.2.5 kernel. If you have a different kernel version or have drivers installed that create `/proc` entries, you may have a somewhat different selection of files. Many of the files listed here are not mentioned in documentation so I had to rely on my own knowledge, the kernel sources, comparisons with the output of various utilities, and the occasional guess to generate the descriptions. The manual page for `proc` in section 5 (`man 5 proc`) gives more info on many of these files.

I will caution you in advance that this chapter does not contain meticulous documentation for every bit of information available through the `proc` filesystem. The documentation in this chapter is largely based on exploring the contents of the files, the output of certain programs that use the files, kernel sources, and sources to some of the utility programs. You can, and should, do much of this yourself, but focus your efforts on the specific information you need for your current application. This section is intended as a general overview of what information is available from the system and where. If you need a specific piece of information, you will have the motivation to explore that particular portion of the `/proc` filesystem more thoroughly and the code you are writing will be the means to test your statements. Perhaps someone will decide to write an entire book on the `/proc` filesystem or get a bunch of people to do so as part of the Linux Documentation Project; until then, programmers should expect to have to get their feet wet.

I will walk you to the library and show you how to use the card catalog—reading the books is left as an exercise for you.

Process Info

There is a directory under /proc for each user level process running on the system at any given time; the name of this directory is the decimal representation of the process number. In addition, /proc/self is a symbolic link to the current process's directory (this link looks different for each process). Within these directories, there are a number of files.

In the following sections, $pid should be replaced with the process id of the process of interest. Most of these special files can be viewed with more, cat, or strings, or searched with fgrep. The -f option on strings will print the filename, which is handy with wildcards.

> **NOTE**
>
> The source file /usr/src/linux/fs/proc/array.c seems to have most of the routines that actually generate /proc output for the per process entries.

The `cmdline` File

Reading the file /proc/$pid/cmdline returns a single line that is the command line of the process, including the name of the program and all arguments. The command line may be blank for zombie processes and the arguments might not be available if the process is swapped out.

> **TIP**
>
> You can take a quick look at what is running on your system by issuing the following command:
>
> ```
> strings -f /proc/[0-9]*/cmdline
> ```

The `environ` File

Reading the file /proc/$pid/environ returns the process environment. Individual environment strings are separated by null bytes and the end of the environment is marked by an end of file condition. The strings utility displays this in a more readable form than the cat utility.

The `fd` Directory

The directory `/proc/$pid/fd` has an entry for each open file descriptor as a symbolic link to the actual file's inode. An inode contains information about a file. Each inode has the device where the inode resides, locking information, mode and filetype of the file, links to the file, user and group ids of the owner, bytes in the file, and addresses of the file's blocks on the disk.

Opening the file descriptor entry (for example, `/proc/self/fd/1`) opens the file itself; if the file is a terminal or other special device, it may interfere with the process itself by stealing data. You can also use the `fstat()` or `lstat()` system calls to get information about the file. The permissions shown for the file have access for the owner only and the owner read and owner write bits indicate the mode in which the file is open.

There is a utility program that runs on many UNIX systems, with and without `/proc` filesystems, called `lsof`. On a Red Hat system, it is installed in `/usr/sbin/lsof`. This can be handy when you want to get information on what a process is doing, want to know why you can't unmount a particular filesystem because it is busy, or want to investigate suspicious activity. The `fuser` command is similar but searches for specific files. If you have an old distribution or did not do a full install, you may be missing these utilities.

> **TIP**
>
> Programmers especially need to do a full installation of everything included with a Linux distribution CD.

The `mem` File

The file `/proc/self/mem` can be used to access the memory image of a particular process. Ordinary utilities like `strings` cannot be used, but the `mmap()` call should work if you have adequate permission.

`stat`

The file `/proc/$pid/stat` has most of the information usually displayed by `ps` about a process, and then some. Table 12.1 lists the various fields along with their position, the name used to identify the field in the `ps` program, and a description. Cumulative values include the current process and any children that have been reaped (using the `wait()`

family). Many of the time-related fields appear to be measured in jiffies (1/100 sec). There seems to be some discrepancy about whether the counter field is included.

TABLE 12.1 stat FIELDS

#	*Name*	*Description*
1	pid	Process id
2	cmd	Simple name Basename of command line in parentheses (will be used by ps if cmdline is blank)
3	state	R=runnable, S=sleeping, D=uninterruptible sleep, T=traced or stopped, Z=zombie, W=not resident, N=nice
4	ppid	Parent process id
5	pgrp	Process group id
6	session	Session id of process
7	tty	Controlling tty (major, minor)?
8	tpgid	Process id for controlling tty
9	flags	Process flags
10	min_flt	Minor page faults
11	cmin_flt	Minor page faults (cumulative)
12	maj_flt	Major page faults
13	cmaj_flt	Major page faults (cumulative)
14	utime	User time
15	stime	System time
16	cutime	User time (cumulative)
17	cstime	System time (cumulative)
18	counter	Size of processes next timeslice
19	priority	Static scheduling priority
20	nice	Normal scheduling algorithm nice value (dynamic priority)
21	timeout	Timeout value in jiffies
22	it_real_value	Next interval timer expiration in jiffies
23	start_time	When process was started
24	vsize	VM size in bytes (total)
25	rss	Resident Set Size
26	rss_rlim	RSS rlimit

continues

12

ACCESSING SYSTEM INFORMATION

TABLE 12.1   CONTINUED

#	Name	Description
27	start_code	Start of code segment
28	end_code	End of code segment
29	start_stack	Start of stack segment
30	kstk_esp	Current stack frame
31	kstk_eip	Current stack frame
32	signal	Pending signals
33	blocked	Blocked signals
34	sigignore	Ignored signals
35	sigcatch	Caught signals—signals with handlers
36	wchan	Kernel function name process is sleeping in

The status File

The file /proc/$pid/status contains less information but in a more readable format than /proc/$pid/stat. It includes the name, state, process id, parent process id, uids and group ids (including real, effective, and saved ids), virtual memory statistics, and signal masks.

The cwd Symbolic Link

The symbolic link /proc/$pid/cwd points to the inode for the current working directory of the process.

The exe Symbolic Link

The symbolic link /proc/$pid/exe contains a symbolic link to the file being executed. This usually points to a binary file. This could also point to a script that is being executed or the executable processing it, depending on the nature of the script.

The maps File

The file /proc/$pid/maps contains information on the mapped memory regions for the processes. It contains address ranges, permissions, offset (into mapped file), and the major and minor device numbers and inodes for mapped files.

The `root` Symbolic Link

The symbolic link `/proc/$pid/root` is a link to the root directory (set with the `chroot()` system call) for the process.

The `statm` File

The special file `/proc/$pid/statm` lists memory usage by a process. The variable names, in order, used in `array.c` are `size`, `resident`, `share`, `trs`, `lrs`, `drs`, and `dt`. These give the total size (including code, data, and stack), resident set size, shared pages, text pages, stack pages, and dirty pages. Note that "text" often means executable code when you are talking about memory usage. The `top` program displays this information.

General System Info

There are a variety of files in the `/proc` filesystem that give system information that is not specific to a given process. The available files may vary with your system configuration. The `procinfo` command can display a lot of system information based on some of these files.

The `/proc/cmdline` File

This gives the kernel boot command line.

The `/proc/cpuinfo` File

This file gives various information about the system CPU(s). This information is derived from the CPU detection code in the kernel. It lists the generic model (386, 486, 586, and so on) of the CPU and more specific information (vendor, model, and version) where available. It includes the speed of the processor in bogomips, and flags that indicate if various features or bugs were detected. The format of this file is multiple lines with a fieldname, a colon, and a value.

The `/proc/devices` File

This file lists the major character and block device numbers and the name the driver gave when allocating those numbers.

The `/proc/dma` File

This file lists which DMA channels have been reserved by drivers and the name the driver gave when reserving them. The `cascade` entry is for the DMA line that is used to cascade the secondary DMA controller off of the primary controller; this line is not available for other use.

The `/proc/filesystems` File

This file lists the available filesystem types, one per line. This is generally the filesystems that were compiled into the kernel, although it might include others that were added by loadable kernel modules.

The `/proc/interrupts` File

This file has one line per reserved interrupt. The fields are the interrupt number, the number of interrupts received on that line, a field that may have a plus sign (SA INTERRUPT flag set) and the name a driver used when registering that interrupt. The function `get_irq_list()` in `/usr/src/linux/arch/i386/kernel/irq.c` (assuming Intel platform) generates this data.

This is a very handy file to manually "cat" before installing new hardware, as are `/proc/dma` and `/proc/ioports`. They list the resources that are currently in use (but not those used by hardware for which no driver is loaded).

The `/proc/ioports` File

This file lists the various I/O port ranges registered by various device drivers such as your disk drives, ethernet, and sound devices.

The `/proc/kcore` File

This is the physical memory of the system in core file format. It is used with GDB to examine kernel data structures. This file is not in a text format that is viewable using your favorite text viewer (such as less).

The `/proc/kmsg` File

Only one process, which must have root privileges, can read this file at any given time. This is used to retrieve kernel messages generated using `printk()`. The `syslog()` system call (not to be confused with the `syslog()` library function) can be used to retrieve these messages instead. The `dmesg` utility or the `klogd` daemon is normally used to retrieve these messages.

The /proc/ksyms File

This file lists the kernel symbols that have been registered; these symbols give the address of a variable or function. Each line gives the address of a symbol, the name of the symbol, and the module that registered the symbol. The ksyms, insmod, and kmod programs probably use this file. It also lists the number of running tasks, the total number of tasks, and the last pid assigned.

The /proc/loadavg File

This file gives the system load average over several different time intervals as displayed by the uptime command. The important data in this file is the three load values and the process id that it was last run with.

The /proc/locks File

This file contains information on locks that are held on open files. It is generated by the get_locks_status() function in /usr/src/linux/fs/locks.c. Each line represents lock information for a specific file, and documents the type of lock applied to the file. The functions fcntl() and flock() are used to apply locks to files. The kernel may also apply mandatory locks to files when needed. This information appears in the /proc/locks file. The documents locks.txt and mandatory.txt in the /usr/src/linux/Documentation subdirectory discuss file locking in Linux.

The /proc/mdstat File

This contains information on raid devices controlled by the md device driver.

The /proc/meminfo File

This file gives information on memory status and is used by the free program. Its format is similar to that displayed by free. This displays the total amount of free and used physical and swap memory in the system. This also shows the shared memory and buffers used by the kernel.

The /proc/misc File

This reports device drivers that register using the kernel function misc_register(). On my system it reports rtc at 135. 135 is the minor device number used by the real-time clock driver for /dev/rtc. None of the other devices that share major number 10 are listed; perhaps they forget to call misc_register().

This information may have different results from system to system and setup to setup.

The /proc/modules File

This gives information on loadable kernel modules. This information is used by the lsmod program to display the information on the name, size, usecount, and referring modules.

The /proc/mounts File

This gives information on currently mounted filesystems in the format you would normally expect in /etc/mtab. This is the file that would also reflect any currently manually mounted file-systems that may not be included in your /etc/mtab file.

The /proc/pci File

This gives information on PCI devices. It is handy for diagnosing PCI problems. Some of the information that you can retrieve from this file is the device, such as the IDE interface or USB controller, the bus, device, and function numbers, device latency, and IRQ numbers.

The /proc/rtc File

This gives information on the hardware real-time clock including the current date and time, alarm setting, battery status, and various features supported. The /sbin/hwclock command is normally used to manipulate the real-time clock. The format is similar to /proc/cpuinfo.

The /proc/stat File

This has various information on CPU utilization, disk, paging, swapping, total interrupts, contact switches, and the time of last boot (in seconds since 1/1/70). This information is reported by the procinfo program.

The /proc/uptime File

This gives the number of seconds since the system booted and how many of those seconds were spent idle. These are used by the uptime program, among others. Comparing these two numbers gives you a long term measure of what percentage of CPU cycles go to waste.

The `/proc/version` File

This returns one line identifying the version of the running kernel. This information is used by the `uname` program. An example of this would be:

```
Linux version 2.2.5-15 (root@porky.devel.redhat.com)
(gcc version egcs-2.91.66 19990314/Linux (egcs-1.1.2 release))
#1 Mon Apr 19 22:21:09 EDT 1999
```

The output from `/proc/version` appears as a single text string, and can be parsed using standard programming methods to obtain system information as needed.

The `uname` program will access this file for some of its information.

The `/proc/net` Subdirectory

The `/proc/net` subdirectory contains files that describe and/or modify the behavior of the networking code. Many of these special files are set or queried through the use of the `arp`, `netstat`, `route`, and `ipfwadm` commands. The various files and their functions are listed in Table 12.2.

TABLE 12.2   `/proc/net/` FILES

File	Description
arp	Dumps the arp table dev packet statistics for each network interface
dev	Statistics from network devices
dev_stat	Status of network devices
igmp	IGMP multicast groups joined
ip_masq_app	Info on masquerading
ip_masquerade	Info on masqueraded connections
raw	Socket table for raw sockets
route	Static routing rules
rt_cache	Routing cache
snmp	`ip`/`icmp`/`tcp`/`udp` protocol statistics for `snmp` agent; alternate lines give field names and values
sockstat	Lists number of `tcp`/`udp`/`raw`/`pac`/`syn_cookies` in use
tcp	Socket table for TCP connections
udp	Socket table for UDP connections
unix	Socket table for UNIX domain sockets

The /proc/scsi Subdirectory

The /proc/scsi directory contains one file that lists all detected SCSI devices and one directory for each controller driver, with a further subdirectory for each separate instance of that controller installed. Table 12.3 lists the files and subdirectories in /proc/scsi.

TABLE 12.3 /proc/scsi/ FILES

File	Description
/proc/scsi/$driver/$n	One file for each controller where $driver is the name of the SCSI controller driver and $n is a number such as 0,1,2, and so on
/proc/scsi/scsi	Lists all detected SCSI devices; special commands can be written to probe a specific target address, such as "scsi singledevice 1 0 5 0" to probe device ID 5 on channel 0

The /proc/sys Subdirectory

There are many subdirectories within the /proc/sys directory. Table 12.4 contains descriptions of the various files within this directory.

TABLE 12.4 /proc/sys/ FILES

File	Description
kernel/domainname	Domain name
kernel/hostname	Host name
kernel/acct	Process accounting control values
kernel/ctrl-alt-del	Ctrl-Alt-Delete key behavior on keyboard
kernel/osrelease	Kernel version number
kernel/ostype	"Linux"
kernel/panic	Get/set panic timeout; kernel will reboot after this number of seconds following a panic if >0
/kernel/printk	Kernel message logging levels
kernel/real-root-dev	The number (major*256+minor) of the root device
kernel/version	Date of compilation
net/core	General networking parameters
net/core/rmem_default	Socket read buffer default size
net/core/rmem_max	Socket read buffer maximum size
net/core/wmem_default	Socket write buffer default size

File	Description
net/core/wmem_max	Socket write buffer maximum size
net/ipv4	Standard IP networking parameters
net/ipv4/ip_autoconfig	IP configuration -1 if IP address obtained automatically (BOOTP, DHCP, or RARP)
net/ipv4/ip_dynaddr	sysctl_ip_dynaddr: Allow dynamic rewriting of packet address; bitfields - ip_output.c
net/ipv4/ip_forward	Writing a 0 or 1 disables/enables ip_forwarding
vm/bdflush	Disk buffer flushing parameters
vm/freepages	set/get min_freepages ("man stm")
vm/kswapd	/usr/include/linux/swapctl.h
vm/swapctl	/usr/include/linux/swapctl.h

12

ACCESSING
SYSTEM
INFORMATION

Libraries and Utilities

I have compiled a listing of /proc filesystem usage that I have been able to detect in libraries or programs. This is included in the listings for this chapter on the CD-ROM and my Web site but is not printed here. It can be used to find examples on the handling of particular files in the /proc filesystem. Some are simply listed as /proc/ or /proc/$pid/; in these cases the particular files used could not be quickly determined. The list was generated from manual inspection of the results of searching manual pages, libraries, and executable files for the string /proc on a Red Hat system with Powertools and Gnome installed. Some cases where the filename is built up piecemeal were undoubtedly missed. If a program only accesses the /proc filesystem through libraries, it may not be listed at all.

The library libproc contains the /proc filesystem handling code from the ps program.

Summary

The /proc filesystem contains a large amount of information about the current system state. Interpretation of the files in /proc is often fairly obvious from looking at the file or will be documented in the proc man page. Comparing the file with the output of utilities that parse the file can shed light on the subject. In other cases, you will want to examine the kernel sources and/or the source code of programs or libraries that use the /proc filesystem for information on the interpretation of various fields.

Handling Errors

by Kurt Wall

IN THIS CHAPTER

CHAPTER 13

No matter how fast your algorithms run or how good your code is, you, or rather your program, eventually must deal with unanticipated error conditions. The goal of this chapter is to acquaint you with the error handling facilities available and to show you how to use them.

Please Pause for a Brief Editorial

Robust, flexible error handling is crucial for production or release quality code. The better your programs catch and respond to error conditions, the more reliable your programs will be. So, if a library function call sets or returns an error value, test it and respond appropriately. Similarly, write your own functions to return meaningful, testable error codes. Whenever possible, try to resolve the error in code and continue. If continuing execution is not possible, provide useful diagnostic information to the user (or write it in a log file) before aborting. Finally, if you must end your program abnormally, do so as gracefully as possible: closing any open files, updating persistent data (such as configuration information), and making the termination appear as orderly as possible to the user. It is very frustrating when a program simply dies for no apparent reason without issuing any warning or error messages.

C-Language Facilities

Several features of ANSI C (also known, these days, as ISO9899 C) support error handling. The following sections look at the `assert()` routine, usually implemented as a macro but designed to be called like a function, a few handy macros you can use to build your own `assert()`-style function, and some standard library functions specifically designed for detecting and responding to errors.

assert() Yourself

The `assert()` call, prototyped in `<assert.h>`, terminates program execution if the condition it tests returns false (that is, tests equal to zero). The prototype is

```
#include <assert.h>
void assert(int expression);
```

`assert()` prints an error message to `stderr` and terminates the program by calling `abort(3)` if `expression` is false (compares equal to 0). `expression` can be any valid C statement that evaluates to an integer, such as `fputs("some string", somefile)`. So, for example, the program in Listing 13.1 will terminate abruptly at line 17 because the `fopen()` call on line 16 will fail (unless, of course, you happen to have a file named `bar_baz` in the current directory).

LISTING 13.1   `badptr.c`—USING `assert()`

```
1   /*
2    * Listing 13.1
3    * badptr.c - Testing assert()
4    */
5   #include <assert.h>
6   #include <stdio.h>
7
8   int main(void)
9   {
10      FILE *fp;
11
12      fp = fopen("foo_bar", "w");     /* This should work */
13      assert(fp);
14      fclose(fp);
15
16      fp = fopen("bar_baz", "r");     /* This should fail */
17      assert(fp);
18      fclose(fp);                     /* Should never get here */
19      return 0;
}
```

A sample run looks like the following:

```
$ badptr
badptr: badptr.c:17: main: Assertion `fp' failed.
IOT trap/Abort
```

The output shows the program in which the error occurred, `badptr`, the source file in which the assertion failed, `badptr.c`, the line number where the assertion failed, 17 (note that this is not where the actual error occurs), the function in which the error occurred, and the assertion that failed. If you have configured your system to dump core, the directory from which you executed the program will also contain a core file.

The drawback to using `assert()` is that, when called frequently, it can dramatically affect program execution speed. Occasional calls, however, are probably acceptable. Because of the performance hit, many programmers use `assert()` during the development process for testing and debugging, but, in the release version, disable all of the `assert()` calls by inserting #define NDEBUG before the inclusion of <assert.h>, as illustrated in the following code snippet:

```
#include <stdio.h>
#define NDEBUG
#include <assert.h>
```

If NDEBUG is defined, the `assert()` macro will not be called.

13

HANDLING
ERRORS

NDEBUG's value does not matter and can even be 0. The mere existence of NDEBUG is sufficient to disable assert() calls. However, as usual, there's a catch! NDEBUG also makes it
important not to use expressions in the assert() statement that you will need later. In
fact, do not use any expression in assert(), even a function call, that has side effects.
Consider the statement

```
assert((p = malloc(sizeof(char)*100) == NULL));
```

Because NDEBUG prevents the call to assert() if it is defined, p will never be properly
initialized, so future use of it is guaranteed to cause problems. The correct way to write
this statement, if you are using assert(), is

```
p = malloc(sizeof(char) * 100);
assert(p);
```

Even after the assert() statement is disabled, you will still need to test p, but at least
your code will attempt to allocate memory for it. If you embed the malloc() call in an
assert() statement, it will never get called.

As you can see, assert() is useful, but abrupt program termination is not what you want
your users to deal with. The real goal should be "graceful degradation," so that you only
need to terminate the program if a hierarchy of error handling calls all fail and you have
no alternative. The more errors you can successfully resolve behind the scenes without
having to involve or inform the user, the more robust your program will appear to be to
your users.

Using the Preprocessor

In addition to the assert() function, the C standard also defines two macros, __LINE__
and __FILE__, that are useful in a wide variety of situations involving errors in program
execution. You can use them, for example, in conjunction with assert() to more accurately pinpoint the location of the error that causes assert() to fail. In fact, assert()
uses both __LINE__ and __FILE__ to do its work. Listings 13.2–13.4 declare, define, and
use a more robust function for opening files, open_file().

LISTING 13.2   filefcn.h

```
1   /*
2    * Listing 13.2
3    * filefcn.h - Declare a new function to open files
4    */
5   #ifndef FILEFCN_H_
6   #define FILEFCN_H_
7
```

```
8 int open_file(FILE *fp, char *fname, char *mode,
➥int line, char *file);
9
10  #endif /* FILEFCN_H_ */
```

Nothing extraordinary here.

LISTING 13.3   filefcn.c

```
1   /*
2    * Listing 13.3
3    * filefcn.c - Using __LINE__ and __FILE__
4    */
5   #include <stdio.h>
6   #include "filefcn.h"
7
8   int open_file(FILE *fp, char *fname, char *mode, int line,
➥char *file)
9   {
10      if((fp = fopen(fname, mode)) == NULL) {
11          fprintf(stderr, "[%s:%d] open_file() failed\n", file, line);
12          return 1;
13      }
14      return 0;
15  }
```

We merely define our function here. Again, nothing unusual.

LISTING 13.4   testmacs.c

```
1   /*
2    * Listing 13.4
3    * testmacs.c - Exercise the function defined in filefcn.c
4    */
5   #include <stdio.h>
6   #include <stdlib.h>
7   #include "filefcn.h"
8
9   int main(void)
10  {
11      FILE *fp;
12      int ret;
13
14      if(open_file(fp, "foo_bar", "w", __LINE__, __FILE__))
15          exit(EXIT_FAILURE);
16      if(fp)
17          fclose(fp);
18
```

13

HANDLING
ERRORS

continues

LISTING 13.4   CONTINUED

```
19      ret = open_file(fp, "bar_baz", "r", __LINE__, __FILE__);
20      if(ret)
21          exit(EXIT_FAILURE);
22      if(fp)
23          fclose(fp);
24
25      return 0;
}
```

Before compilation, the preprocessor substitutes the __LINE__ symbols with 14 and 19, and replaces __FILE__ with testmacs.c, the name of the source file. If a call to open_file() succeeds, it returns 0 to the caller, otherwise it prints a diagnostic indicating the filename and line number (in the caller) where it failed and returns 1. If we had used __LINE__ and __FILE__ in the definition of open_file(), the line number and filename would not be very useful. As we have defined it, you know exactly where the function call failed.

Executing the program,

```
$ ./testmacs
[testmacs.c:19] open_file() failed
```

we see that it failed at line 19 of testmacs.c, which is the result we expected. __LINE__ and __FILE__ can be very helpful in tracking down bugs. Learn to use them.

Standard Library Facilities

In this context, "standard library" refers to the variables, macros, and functions mandated to be part of the C environment supporting the standard. This section will take an in-depth look at five functions and a variable (gee, that sounds like a movie about programming, "Five Functions and a Variable") that are an important part of any error handling. Their prototypes (and header files) are as follows:

- stdlib.hvoid abort(void);
- stdlib.hvoid exit(int status);
- stdlib.hint atexit(void (*fcn)(void));
- studio.hvoid perror(const char *s);
- string.hvoid *strerror(int errnum);
- errno.hint errno;

The following three functions are also essential components of an error handling toolkit. They are all declared in <stdio.h>.

```
void clearerr(FILE *stream);
```

> Clears the end-of-file (EOF) and error indicators for stream.

```
int feof(FILE *stream);
```

> Returns a non-zero value if the EOF indicator for stream is set.

```
int ferror(FILE *stream);
```

> Returns a non-zero value if the error indicator for stream is set

Understanding errno

Many, but not all, library functions set the global variable errno to a non-zero value when errors occur (most of these functions are in the math library). However, no library function ever clears errno (sets errno = 0), so to avoid spurious errors, clear errno before calling a library function that may set, as the code snippet in Listing 13.5 illustrates.

LISTING 13.5   THE errno VARIABLE

```
1  #include <errno.h>
2  /* more stuff here */
3
4  errno = 0;
5  y = sqrt(x);
6  if(errno != 0) {
7      fprintf(stderr, "sqrt() error"!  Goodbye!\n");
8      exit(EXIT_FAILURE);
9}
```

Functions in the math library often set errno to EDOM and ERANGE. EDOM errors occur when a value passed to a function is outside of its domain. sqrt(-1), for example, generates a domain error. ERANGE errors occur when a value returned from a function in the math library is too large to be represented by a double. log(0) generates a range error since log(0) is undefined. Some functions can set both EDOM and ERANGE errors, so compare errno to EDOM and ERANGE to find out which one occurred and how to proceed.

Using the abort() Function

This is a harsh call. When called, it causes abnormal program termination, so the usual clean-up tasks, such as closing files, and any functions registered with atexit() do not execute (atexit() is discussed later in this chapter). abort() does, however, return an implementation defined value to the operating system indicating an unsuccessful termination. If not restricted by ulimit, abort() also dumps out a core file to aid postmortem debugging. To facilitate debugging, always compile your code with debugging symbols (using -g or -ggdb options with gcc) and don't strip your executables. The assert() call we discussed in a previous section of this chapter calls abort().

> **NOTE**
>
> Stripping binaries means using the strip command to remove symbols, usually debugging symbols, from compiled programs. Doing so reduces their disk and memory footprint, but has the unfortunate side effect of making debugging virtually impossible. Let the foolhardy user strip them.

Using the exit() Function

exit() is abort()'s civilized cousin. Like abort(), it terminates a program and returns a value to the OS, but, unlike abort(), it does so only after doing any clean up and, if you have additional clean up performed by functions registered with atexit(), it calls them as well. status returns the exit value to the operating system. Any integer value is legal, but only EXIT_SUCCESS and EXIT_FAILURE, defined in <stdlib.h>, and 0 are portable return values. Many, if not most, of the programs you have already seen in this book use it. See line 8 of Listing 13.5, for example.

Using the atexit() Function

The atexit() function registers fcn to be called upon normal program termination. Pass atexit() a function that accepts no arguments and returns void. You can use atexit() to guarantee that certain code is executed before your program shuts down completely. As noted in the discussion of abort(), functions registered with atexit() will not be called if abort() executes. If fcn registers successfully, atexit() returns 0, otherwise it returns 1. Listing 13.6 demonstrates how atexit() works.

LISTING 13.6 THE atexit() FUNCTION

```
1   /*
2    * Listing 13.6
3    * chkexit.c - Fun with atexit()
4    */
5   #include <stdio.h>
6   #include <stdlib.h>
```

```
7
8   void f_atexit(void)
9   {
10      fprintf(stdout, "Here we are in f_atexit()\n");
11  }
12
13  int main(int argc, char *argv[])
14  {
15      fprintf(stdout, "Here we are in main()\n");
16      if(atexit(f_atexit) != 0)
17          fprintf(stderr, "Failed to register f_atexit()\n");
18      fprintf(stdout, "Exiting...\n");
19
20      if(atoi(argv[1]))
21          abort();
22
23      return 0;
24}
```

Line 16 is the key line. We pass f_atexit() by feeding the bare function name, f_atexit, to atexit(), testing the return value to make sure the function registered successfully. To run chkexit, pass it a 1 or a 0. If you pass chkexit a 0, it will terminate normally, but a non-zero argument will cause abnormal termination. When we run the program, it confirms that atexit() was called after main() returned:

```
$ ./chkexit 0
Here we are in main()
Exiting...
Here we are in f_atext()
$ ./chkexit 1
Here we are in main()
Exiting...
IOT trap/Abort
```

In the second invocation, f_atext() registers successfully, but the abort() call sidesteps the call. On systems configured to allow core dumps, the abort() call will also produce a message similar to "Aborted (core dumped)" and generate a core file in the current directory.

Using the strerror() Function

If an error occurs, it would probably be helpful to your users (or to you, for that matter) to know what the operating system thinks went wrong. Enter strerror(). It returns a pointer to a string that describes the error code associated with errnum. So, if you pass errno to strerror(), you will get a human readable explanation of what happened, rather than a cold, uninformative number.

Using the `perror()` Function

This handy function prints a system error message. If your code makes a system call that fails, the call returns -1 and sets the variable errno to a value describing the last error, just as many library functions do. perror() uses this value, printing the string argument s, a colon, a space, the error message corresponding to errno, and a newline. So, calling

```
perror("Oops");
```

is the same as calling

```
printf("Oops: %s\n", strerror(errno));
```

Listing 13.7 illustrates both strerror() and perror().

LISTING 13.7 errs.c

```
 1  /*
 2   * Listing 13.7
 3   * errs.c - Demonstrate perror() and strerror()
 4   */
 5  #include <stdio.h>
 6  #include <string.h>
 7  #include <stdlib.h>
 8  #include <math.h>
 9  #include <errno.h>
10
11  int main()
12  {
13      double d;
14
15      errno = 0;
16      d = sqrt(-1);
17      if(errno)
18          fprintf(stderr, "sqrt: %s\n", strerror(errno));
19
20      errno = 0;
21      d = sqrt(-2);
22      if(errno)
23          perror("sqrt");
24
25      exit(EXIT_SUCCESS);
26  }
```

When executed, you can't tell the difference between perror()'s output and the output using strerror().

The System Logging Facility

Writing log messages has been mentioned several times. The good news is that you do not have to write this functionality yourself. Linux provides centralized system logging facilities using two daemons, klogd and syslogd. We will concern ourselves with syslogd, because it controls the generation of messages from user space programs. If your application needs logging abilities, the tool to use is the syslog facility, borrowed from BSD. On most Linux systems, the log files live under /var/log. Depending on the Linux distribution you use, these log files include messages, debug, mail, and news. The standard console logging daemon, syslogd, maintains these files. The header file <syslog.h> defines the interface to syslogd. System administrators set the behavior of syslogd in /etc/syslog.conf. To create a log message, use the syslog() function, prototyped as

```
#include <syslog.h>
void syslog(int priority, char *format, ...);
```

priority is a bitwise OR combination of a *level*, which indicates the severity of the message, and a *facility*, which tells syslogd who sent the message and how to respond to it. format specifies the message to write to the log and any printf()-like format specifiers. The special format specifier %m will be replaced by the error message that strerror() assigns to errno, as if strerror(errno) had been called. Table 13.1 lists the possible values for levels in descending order.

TABLE 13.1 syslog LOGGING LEVELS

Level	Severity
LOG_EMERG	System is unusable
LOG_ALERT	Immediate action required
LOG_CRIT	Critical error, such as hardware failure
LOG_ERR	Error conditions
LOG_WARNING	Warning conditions
LOG_NOTICE	Normal, but significant, message
LOG_INFO	Purely informational message
LOG_DEBUG	Debug or trace output

Table 13.2 lists the facilities' values.

13

HANDLING ERRORS

TABLE 13.2   syslog FACILITY NAMES

Facility	Source of Message
LOG_AUTHPRIV	Private security and authorization messages
LOG_CRON	Clock daemons (crond and atd)
LOG_DAEMON	Other system daemons
LOG_KERN	Kernel messages
LOG_LOCAL[0-7]	Reserved for local/site use
LOG-LPR	Printer subsystem
LOG_MAIL	Mail subsystem
LOG_NEWS	News subsystem
LOG_SYSLOG	Internal messages generated by sylogd
LOG_USER	(DEFAULT) general user level messages
LOG_UUCP	The uucp subsystem

In most cases, it's best to use a facility value of LOG_USER, the default value. Unless, of course, you are writing a mail or news client. However, if the system administrator at your site has set up the local facility levels, LOG_LOCAL[0-7], you could use one of those if they apply. Choosing the correct level is a little trickier. Generally, use one of the levels between LOG_ERR and LOG_INFO, but, if you do send a LOG_ERR message, it will usually get displayed to all users and the system console, and may well send a page to the machine's administrator—hopefully the implication is clear: choose a level value appropriate the your message's contents. My own personal recommendation for user-level programs is LOG_ERR for errors and LOG_INFO for regular, boring log messages.

So, putting it all together, suppose you encounter an error while opening a file. Your syslog() call might look like this:

```
syslog(LOG_ERR ¦ LOG_USER, "unable to open file %s *** %m\n", fname);
```

where fname is the filename you tried unsuccessfully to open. This call generated the following message in /var/log/messages:

```
Mar 26 19:36:25 hoser syslog: unable to open file foo
*** No such file or directory
```

The %m format specifier appended the string "No such file or directory", as if strerror(errno) had been called. Because LOG_USER is the default facility, the previous code snippet could have been written:

```
syslog(LOG_ERR, "unable to open file %s *** %m\n", fname);
```

Similarly, if you simply want to scribble a non-critical log entry, try

```
syslog(LOG_INFO, "this is a normal message\n");
```

The message it wrote to /var/log/messages:

```
Mar 26 19:29:03 hoser syslog: this is a normal message
```

One of the problems with the previous examples is that the log messages generated are not sufficiently unique to locate in a log file that can easily grow to seven or eight megabytes. openlog() comes to the rescue:

```
void openlog(const char *ident, int option, int facility);
```

facility is one of the values from Table 13.2. ident specifies a string to prepend to the message being logged. option is a bitwise OR of zero or more of the options listed in Table 13.3.

TABLE 13.3   THE openlog() OPTIONS

Option	Description
LOG_PID	Include PID in each message
LOG_CONS	Write the message to the console if it can't be logged
LOG_NDELAY	Opens the connection immediately (the default is to wait until syslog() the first time)
LOG_PERROR	Print the message to stderr, in addition to the log

NOTE

<syslog.h> also defines LOG_ODELAY, which means delay opening the connection until syslog()'s first call. Under Linux, the value has no effect, since LOG_ODELAY is the default behavior.

openlog() works by allocating and opening a (hidden) file descriptor syslog(). We describe the descriptor hidden because nothing in the syslog facility's public interface gives you direct access to it. You simply have to trust that it exists.

openlog()'s purpose is to customize logging behavior. However, openlog() is optional—if you do not call it yourself, syslog() calls it automatically the first time your program calls syslog(). A companion function, closelog(), also optional, merely closes the file descriptor `openlog()` opened. To illustrate `openlog()`'s usage, consider the following two code snippets:

```
openlog("my_program", LOG_PID, LOG_USER);
syslog(LOG_NOTICE, "Pay attention to me!\n");
```

This snippet produces

```
Mar 26 20:11:58 hoser my_program[1354]: Pay attention to me!
```

in /var/log/messages, while the next one

```
openlog("your_program", LOG_PID, LOG_USER);
syslog(LOG_INFO, "No, ignore that other program!\n")
```

generates this:

```
Mar 26 20:14:28 hoser your_program[1363]: No, ignore that other program!
```

Note how the `ident` string and the PID replaced the facility string. This makes it very clear what program owns what log messages. In effect, `openlog()` sets the default facility name to `facility` for all future calls of `syslog()` from your program. As you might have guessed, a similar call, `setlogmask()`, sets the default priority:

```
int setlogmask(int priority);
```

The `priority` argument, in this context, is either a single priority or an inclusive range of priorities.

Calling `setlogmask()` sets a default mask for priorities; `syslog()` rejects any message with priorities not set in the mask. `<syslog.h>` also defines two helper macros that help set the mask:

```
int LOG_MASK(int priority)
```

and

```
LOG_UPTO(int priority)
```

`LOG_MASK()` creates a mask consisting of only one priority, the `priority` passed as its argument. `LOG_UPTO()` on the other hand, creates a mask made of a range or priorities. For example, `LOG_UPTO(LOG_NOTICE)` creates a mask that consists of any message of level `LOG_EMERG` through `LOG_NOTICE`. A message with a level of `LOG_INFO` or `LOG_DEBUG` won't get through. Behold, Listing 13.8.

LISTING 13.8   `mask_log.c`

```
1   /*
2    * Listing 13.8
3    * mask_log.c - demonstrate openlog() and family
```

```
4    */
5    #include <syslog.h>
6    #include <stdio.h>
7    #include <unistd.h>
8    #include <stdlib.h>
9
10   int main(void)
11   {
12       int ret;
13
14       openlog("mask_log", LOG_PID, LOG_USER);
15       syslog(LOG_INFO, "This message courtesy of UID #%d\n",
         ➥getuid());
16       syslog(LOG_NOTICE, "Hopefully, you see this\n");
17
18       /* Don't want to see DEBUG and INFO messages */
19       ret = setlogmask(LOG_UPTO(LOG_NOTICE));
20       syslog(LOG_INFO, "You should not be seeing this\n");
21       syslog(LOG_DEBUG, "I hope you don't see this\n");
22       syslog(LOG_NOTICE, "This should still appear\n");
23
24       closelog();
25       exit(EXIT_SUCCESS);
24   }
```

Compiled and executed, /var/log/messages says

```
Mar 26 22:42:06 hoser mask_log[1718]: This message courtesy of UID #100
Mar 26 22:42:06 hoser mask_log[1718]: Hopefully, you see this
Mar 26 22:42:06 hoser mask_log[1718]: This should still appear
```

Success! After we change the priority mask, the messages with LOG_INFO and LOG_DEBUG did not pass through, but messages with higher priority, like LOG_NOTICE get through just fine.

NOTE

A simple way to track /var/log/messages is to open a separate xterm and tail the file, using tail -f /var/log/messages. Each time a new messages is written to the log, it will pop up on your screen.

User Programs

For you shell programmers out there, you have not been forgotten. There exists a user level program, logger(1), that offers a shell interface to the syslog facility. As mentioned, logger is a shell and command-line interface to syslog. Its complete syntax is

```
logger [-is] [-f file] [-p pri] [-t tag] [message ...]
```

The option -i tells logger to add the PID to the log message. Use -t to get the name of the script calling logger into the log message. Listing 13.9 demonstrates how you might use logger in a shell script:

LISTING 13.9   logger.sh

```
#!/bin/sh
# Listing 13.9
# logger.sh - Demonstrate logger(1) interface to syslog
# ####################################################

echo "type the log message and press ENTER"
read _msg
logger -i -t logger.sh $_msg
```

Don't trouble yourself with understanding the syntax, it will be covered in Chapter 34, "Shell Programming with GNU bash." After prompting for a log message, the script reads in the log message, then calls logger to insert it in the log file. A sample run might look like the following:

```
[kwall@hoser 13]$ logger.sh
type the log message and press ENTER
This is a long log message.  I'm making it as long as I possibly can,
➥even to the point of wrapping, to show that log file entries have a
➥fixed length.
```

Here's how the message came out in /var/log/messages:

```
Mar 26 23:26:49 hoser logger.sh[1888]: This is a long log message. I'm
➥making it as long as I possibly
```

As you can see, syslog truncated the message at eighty characters (the shell name, the PID, and the message itself total eighty characters), and prepended the script name and the PID to the message.

Summary

Hopefully, after reading this chapter, you will get some sense of the value of error handling. Unfortunately, there is no single error handling API, just some tools scattered around the system that you have to collect and use together to create robust, error tolerant software. You learned about the rich set of functions the C language provides, including `assert()`, the exit functions `abort()`, `exit()`, and `atexit()`, and the error-handling routines `perror()` and `strerror()`. You were also introduced to the system logging facility and shown how to use it.

Memory Management

by Kurt Wall

In many respects, memory management under Linux is comparable to memory management for any modern PC operating system. This chapter reviews basic C memory management and then looks at some additional capabilities Linux provides. In particular, I will discuss memory mapped files, a very fast way to perform input and output, and memory locking, which is a method that keeps critical data in active memory rather than allowing it be swapped out to disk. I will also cover some special tools for debugging memory problems and LCLint, a free implementation of the classic code analysis program `lint`.

Reviewing C Memory Management

The C programming language supports dynamic memory allocation in the `malloc(3)`, `calloc(3)`, `realloc(3)`, and `free(3)` functions. These functions enable you to obtain, manipulate, and return memory from the operating system on an as-needed basis. Dynamic memory management is essential to efficient programming. Besides more efficient use of memory, a critical system resource, dynamic memory management frees you from coding arbitrary limits in your code. Instead of hitting an artificial size constraint in an array of, say, strings, you can simply request more and avoid unnecessary hard-coded limits. The following sections discuss each of these functions.

Using the `malloc()` Function

The `malloc()` function allocates an uninitialized memory block. It allocates a specified number of bytes of memory, as shown in the following prototype, returning a pointer to the newly allocated memory or NULL on failure:

```
void *malloc(size_t size);
```

Always check `malloc()`'s return value. It is not necessary to cast the pointer `malloc()` returns because it is automatically converted to the correct type on assignment, but you may encounter these casts in older, pre-ANSI code. The memory block you receive is not initialized, so don't use it until you've initialized it. Memory obtained with `malloc()` must be returned to the operating system with a call to `free()` in order to prevent memory leaks.

> **Note**
>
> In general, you can assign a void pointer to a variable of any pointer type, and vice versa, without any loss of information.

Using the `calloc()` Function

The `calloc()` function allocates and initializes a memory block. It uses the following prototype:

```
void *calloc(size_t nmemb, size_t size);
```

This function acts very much like `malloc()`, returning a pointer to enough space to hold an array of `nmemb` objects of size `size`. The difference is that `calloc()` initializes the allocated memory, setting each bit to 0, returning a pointer to the memory or NULL on failure.

Using the `realloc()` Function

The `realloc()` function resizes a previously allocated memory block. Use `realloc()` to resize memory previously obtained with a `malloc()` or `calloc()` call. This function uses the following prototype:

```
void *realloc(void *ptr, size_t size);
```

The `ptr` argument must be a pointer returned by `malloc()` or `calloc()`. The `size` argument may be larger or smaller than the size of the original pointer. Increases or decreases should occur in place. If this is not possible, `realloc()` will copy the old data to the new location, but the programmer must update any pointer references to the new block. The following also apply to `realloc()`'s behavior:

- `realloc()` does not initialize the memory added to the block.
- `realloc()` returns NULL if it can't enlarge the block, leaving the original data untouched.
- `realloc()` called with a NULL pointer as the first argument behaves exactly like `malloc()`.
- `realloc()` called with 0 as the second argument frees the block.

14

MEMORY MANAGEMENT

Using the `free()` Function

The `free()` function frees a block of memory. This function uses the following prototype:

```
void free(void *ptr);
```

The `ptr` argument must be a pointer returned from a previous call to `malloc()` or `calloc()`. It is an error to attempt to access memory that has been freed.

Memory allocation functions obtain memory from a storage pool known as the *heap*. Memory, a finite resource, can be exhausted, so be sure to return memory as you finish using it. Beware, too, of dangling pointers. A memory leak occurs when allocated memory is never returned to the operating system. *Dangling pointers* are the uninitialized pointers left behind after memory is freed. Ordinarily, dangling pointers are not a problem. Trouble only arises when you try to access a freed pointer without reinitializing the memory to which it points, as this code snippet illustrates:

```
char *str;
str = malloc(sizeof(char) * 4)
free(str);
strcpy(str, "abc");
```

KABLOOIE! You will get a segmentation fault (`SIGSEGV`) on the last line.

Using the `alloca()` Function

The `alloca()` function allocates an uninitialized block of memory. This function uses the following prototype:

```
void *alloca(size_t size);
```

The dynamic memory allocation functions covered so far, `malloc()`, `calloc()`, and `realloc()`, all obtain their memory from the heap. `alloca()` behaves like these, except that it obtains memory from the process's stack rather than the heap and, when the function that invoked `alloca()` returns, the allocated memory is automatically freed. Listing 14.1 illustrates the standard library's memory management functions.

LISTING 14.1   USING DYNAMIC MEMORY MANAGEMENT FUNCTIONS

```
1   /*
2    * Listing 14.1
3  * mem.c - Demonstrate malloc(), calloc(), realloc(),
➥alloca(), and free() usage
4    */
5  #include <stdio.h>
6  #include <stdlib.h>
```

```
7
8   void err_quit(char *);
9   void prn(char *, char *, int);
10
11  int main(void)
12  {
13      char *c, *d, *e;
14
15      if((c = malloc(10)) == NULL)
16          err_quit("malloc() failed");
17      prn("malloc", c, 10);
18      free(c);
19
20      if((d = calloc(10, 1)) == NULL)
21          err_quit("calloc() failed");
22      prn("calloc", d, 10);
23
24      strcpy(d, "foobar");
25      fprintf(stdout, "d = %s\n", d);
26      if((d = realloc(d, 20)) == NULL)
27          err_quit("realloc() failed");
28      fprintf(stdout, "d = %s\n", d);
29      prn("realloc", d, 20);
30
31      if((e = alloca(10)) == NULL)
32          err_quit("alloca() failed");
33      prn("alloca", e, 10);
34
35      exit(0);
36  }
37
38  void err_quit(char *msg)
39  {
40      fprintf(stderr, "%s\n", msg);
41      exit(EXIT_FAILURE);
42  }
43
44  void prn(char *memop, char *str, int len)
45  {
46      int i;
47      fprintf(stdout, "%8s : ", memop);
48      for(i = 0; i < len; ++i)
49          fprintf(stdout, "%d ", str[i]);
50      fprintf(stdout, "\n");
51}
```

Lines 15–18 illustrate malloc() usage. We attempt to allocate ten bytes of memory, check malloc()'s return value, display the contents of the uninitialized memory, and then return the memory to the heap. Lines 20–22 repeat this procedure for calloc().

Rather than freeing d, however, we attempt to extend it on lines 26–28. Whether realloc() succeeds or fails, it should still point to the string "foobar". The pointer, e, as shown on lines 31–33, is allocated off the stack and, when main() returns (that is, when the program exits), its memory is automatically freed.

Memory Mapping Files

Although memory mapped files do not, strictly speaking, fall under the "memory management" rubric, the topic is covered here because it is an example of how Linux manages memory. Linux allows any process to map a disk file into memory, creating a byte-for-byte correspondence between the disk file and its image in memory.

Memory mapped files have two chief advantages. The first is faster file I/O. Ordinary I/O calls, such as the read() and write() system calls or the fputs() and fgets() library calls, copy the read or written data through kernel buffers. While Linux has a fast and sophisticated disk-caching algorithm, the fastest disk access will always be slower than the slowest memory access. I/O operations on a memory-mapped file bypass the kernel buffers and, as a result, are much faster. They are also simpler because you can access the mapped file using pointers rather than the usual file manipulation functions.

The second advantage of memory mapped files is data sharing. If multiple processes need to access the same data, the data can be stored in a memory mapped file. Effectively a shared memory model, this makes the data independent of any single process and stores the region's contents in a disk file.

Linux provides a family of function calls to manage memory mapping. These functions, defined in <sys/mman.h>, include mmap(), munmap(), msync(), mprotect(), mlock(), munlock(), mlockall(), and munlockall(). Subsequent sections discuss each of these functions in detail.

Using the mmap() Function

The mmap() function maps a disk file into memory. It uses the following prototype:

```
void *mmap(void *start, size_t length, int prot,
➡int flags, int fd, off_t offset);
```

Map the file open on file descriptor fd, beginning at offset offset in the file, into memory beginning at start. length specifies the amount of the file to map. The memory region will have protections protection, a logical OR of the values in Table 14.1, and attributes specified in flags, a logical OR of the values in Table 14.2. This function returns a pointer to the memory region or -1 on failure.

TABLE 14.1 VALUES FOR PROTECTION

Protection	Access Allowed
PROT_NONE	No access is allowed
PROT_READ	Mapped region may be read
PROT_WRITE	Mapped region may be written
PROT_EXEC	Mapped region may be executed

NOTE

On the x86 architecture, PROT_EXEC implies PROT_READ, so PROT_EXEC is the same as specifying PROT_EXEC ¦ PROT_READ.

TABLE 14.2 VALUES FOR FLAGS

Flag	POSIX Compliant	Description
MAP_ANONYMOUS	no	Create an anonymous mapping, ignoring fd
MAP_FIXED	yes	Fail if address is invalid or already in use
MAP_PRIVATE	yes	Writes to region are process private
MAP_SHARED	yes	Writes to region are copied to file
MAP_DENYWRITE	no	Disallow normal writes to file
MAP_GROWSDOWN	no	Grow the memory downward
MAP_LOCKED	no	Lock pages into memory

A *file descriptor* is a handle to a file opened using the open() system call (file descriptors are discussed in more detail in Chapter 10, "File Manipulation"). offset is usually zero, indicating that the entire file should be mapped into memory.

A memory region must be marked either private, with MAP_PRIVATE, or shared, with MAP_SHARED; the other values are optional. A *private* mapping makes any modifications to the region process private, so they are not reflected in the underlying file or available to other processes. *Shared* maps, on the other hand, cause any updates to the memory region to be immediately visible to other processes that have mapped the same file.

To prevent writes to the underlying disk file, specify MAP_DENYWRITE (but note that this is not a POSIX value and as such is not portable). Anonymous maps, created with MAP_ANONYMOUS, involve no physical file and simply allocate memory for the process's

14

**MEMORY
MANAGEMENT**

private use, such as a custom `malloc()` implementation. `MAP_FIXED` causes the kernel to place the map at a specific address. If the address is already in use or otherwise unavailable, `mmap()` fails. If `MAP_FIXED` is not specified and `address` is unavailable, the kernel will attempt to place the region elsewhere in memory. `MAP_LOCKED` allows processes with root privilege to lock the region into memory so it will never be swapped to disk. User space programs cannot use `MAP_LOCKED`, a security feature that prevents unauthorized processes from locking all available memory, which would essentially bring the system to a standstill.

Using the `munmap()` Function

When you have finished using a memory mapped file, call `munmap()` to unmap the region and return the memory to the operating system. This function uses the following prototype:

```
int munmap(void *start, size_t length);
```

The `start` argument points to the beginning of the region to unmap, and `length` indicates how much of the region to unmap. After a memory block has been unmapped, further attempts to access `start` will cause a segmentation fault (generate a `SIGSEGV`). When a process terminates, all memory maps are unmapped. The `munmap()` function returns 0 on success or, on failure, -1 and sets `errno`.

Using the `msync()` Function

The `msync()` function writes a mapped file to disk. It uses the following prototype:

```
int msync(const void *start, size_t length, int flags);
```

Call `msync()` to update the disk file with changes made to the in-core map. The region to flush to disk begins at the `start` address; length bytes will be flushed. The `flags` argument is a bitwise OR of one or more of the following:

`MS_ASYNC`	Schedules a write and returns
`MS_SYNC`	Data are written before `msync()` returns
`MS_INVALIDATE`	Invalidate other maps of the same file so they will be updated with new data

Using the `mprotect()` Function

The `mprotect()` function modifies the protection on a memory map. This function uses the following prototype:

```
int protect(const void *addr, size_t len, int prot);
```

This function call modifies the protections on the memory region that begins at addr to the protections specified in prot, a bitwise OR of one or more of the flags listed in Table 14.1. It returns zero on success or, on failure, -1 and sets errno.

Locking Memory

Without going into the nitty-gritty details of how it works, memory locking means preventing a memory area from being swapped to disk. In a multitasking, multiuser system such as Linux, areas of system memory (RAM) not in active use may be temporarily written to disk (swapped out) in order for that memory to be put to other uses. Locking the memory sets a flag that prevents it from being swapped out.

There are four functions for locking and unlocking memory: mlock(), mlockall(), munlock(), and munlockall(). Their prototypes are listed below.

```
int mlock(const void *addr, size_t len);
int munlock(void *addr, size_t len);
int mlockall(int flags);
int munlockall(void);
```

The memory region to be locked or unlocked is specified in addr and len indicates how much of the region to lock or unlock. Values for flags may be one or both of MCL_CUR-RENT, which requests that all pages are locked before the call returns, or MCL_FUTURE, indicating that all pages added to the process' address space should be locked. As noted in the discussion of mmap(), only processes with root privilege may lock or unlock memory regions.

Using the mremap() Function

Use the mremap() function to change the size of a mapped file. This function uses the following prototype:

```
void *mremap(void *old_addr, size_t old_len,
➥size_t new_len, unsigned long flags);
```

You will occasionally need to resize a memory region, which is the reason for this function. An analogue of the realloc() call discussed earlier, mremap() resizes the memory region beginning at old_addr, originally with size old_len, to new_len. flags indicates whether the region can be moved in memory if necessary. MREMAP_MAYMOVE permits the address to change; if not specified, the resize operation fails. mremap() returns the address of the resized region or NULL on failure.

Implementing `cat(1)` Using Memory Maps

Listing 14.2 illustrates using memory mapped files. Although it is a naive `cat(1)` implementation, it clearly demonstrates using memory mapped files.

LISTING 14.2   A `cat(1)` IMPLEMENTATION USING MEMORY MAPS

```
 1   /*
 2    * Listing 14.2
 3    * mmcat.c - Implement the cat(1) command using mmap() and family
 4    */
 5   #include <sys/types.h>
 6   #include <sys/mman.h>
 7   #include <sys/stat.h>
 8   #include <unistd.h>
 9   #include <fcntl.h>
10   #include <stdlib.h>
11   #include <stdio.h>
12
13   void err_quit(char *msg);
14
15   int main(int argc, char *argv[])
16   {
17       int fdin;
18       char *src;
19       struct stat statbuf;
20       off_t len;
21
22       /* open the input file and stdout */
23       if(argc != 2)
24           err_quit("usage: mmcat <file>");
25
26       if((fdin = open(argv[1], O_RDONLY)) < 0)
27           err_quit("open failed");
28
29       /* need the size of the input file for mmap() call */
30       if((fstat(fdin, &statbuf)) < 0)
31           err_quit("fstat failed");
32       len = statbuf.st_size;
33
34       /* map the input file */
35       if((src = mmap(0, len, PROT_READ, MAP_SHARED,
         ➥fdin, 0)) == (void *)-1)
36           err_quit("mmap failed");
37
38       /* write it out */
39       fprintf(stdout, "%s", src);
40
41       /* clean up */
42       close(fdin);
```

```
43        munmap(src, len);
44
45        exit(0);
46  }
47
48  void err_quit(char *msg)
49  {
50        perror(msg);
51        exit(EXIT_FAILURE);
52}
```

The interesting pieces of code in this program are lines 30–39. As the comment indicates, we need the input file's size for the mmap() call, hence the call to fstat() on line 30 (fstat() and open() (line 26) are discussed in Chapter 9, "I/O Routines," and Chapter 10, "File Manipulation," respectively). Once we have the file mapped into memory (line 35), we can use the pointer, src, exactly as if we had populated it with an fread() or fgets() call, as we do in the fprintf() statement on line 39. We return to the memory region to the kernel on line 43 by calling munmap(). perror(), used in the utility function err_quit(), was introduced in Chapter 13, "Handling Errors."

From a practical point of view, using a memory mapped file in this example was overkill because it buys us little in terms of performance or code length. In situations where performance is crucial or when you are dealing with time-sensitive operations, however, memory mapped files can be a definite plus. Memory mapping can also be valuable in high security situations. Because processes running with root privilege can lock memory mapped files into memory, preventing them from being swapped to disk by Linux's memory manager, sensitive data such as password files will be less susceptible to scanner programs. Of course, in such a situation, the memory region would have to be set to PROT_NONE so that other process cannot read the region.

Now that you know more about memory maps, the next section examines a few tools to help you debug memory problems.

Finding and Fixing Memory Problems

This section covers a few tools that help you locate memory management problems in your code. Because C assumes you know what you are doing, most C compilers ignore uses of uninitialized memory, buffer overruns, and buffer underruns. Nor do most compilers catch memory leaks or dangling pointers. The tools discussed in this section make up for these compiler shortcomings.

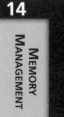

> NOTE
>
> Actually, most compilers accept various switches and options that enable them to catch some subset of the errors just mentioned. gcc, for example, has the -Wall option (discussed in Chapter 3, "GNU cc"). In general, however, compilers do not detect all memory problems, making the tools covered in this section quite valuable.

A Problem Child

Listing 14.3 is beset with bugs, including the following:

- A memory leak (line 18)
- Overruns the end of dynamically allocated heap memory (lines 22 and 28)
- Underruns a memory buffer (line 32)
- Frees the same buffer twice (lines 36 and37)
- Accesses freed memory (lines 40 and41)
- Clobbers statically allocated stack and global memory (lines 48 and 44, respectively)

LISTING 14.3 A PROGRAM WITH MEMORY BUGS

```
1   /*
2    * Listing 14.3
3    * badmem.c - Demonstrate usage of memory debugging tools
4    */
5   #include <stdlib.h>
6   #include <stdio.h>
7   #include <string.h>
8
9   char g_buf[5];
10
11  int main(void)
12  {
13      char *buf;
14      char *leak;
15      char l_buf[5];
16
17      /* Won't free this */
18      leak = malloc(10);
19
```

```
20      /* Overrun buf a little bit */
21      buf = malloc(5);
22      strcpy(buf, "abcde");
23      fprintf(stdout, "LITTLE  : %s\n", buf);
24      free(buf);
25
26      /* Overrun buf a lot */
27      buf = malloc(5);
28      strcpy(buf, "abcdefgh");
29      fprintf(stdout, "BIG : %s\n", buf);
30
31      /* Underrun buf */
32      *(buf - 2) = '\0';
33      fprintf(stdout, "UNDERRUN: %s\n", buf);
34
35      /* free buf twice */
36      free(buf);
37      free(buf);
38
39      /* access free()ed memory */
40      strcpy(buf, "This will blow up");
41      fprintf(stdout, "FREED   : %s\n", buf);
42
43      /* Trash the global variable */
44      strcpy(g_buf, "global boom");
45      fprintf(stdout, "GLOBAL  : %s\n", g_buf);
46
47      /* Trash the local variable */
48      strcpy(l_buf, "local boom");
49      fprintf(stdout, "LOCAL   : %s\n", l_buf);
50
51      exit(0);
52}
```

14

MEMORY
MANAGEMENT

None of these bugs, however, prevent the program from executing, but leaks and clobbered memory usually show up as unpredictable behavior elsewhere in the program. On my system, the program's output was:

```
$ ./badmem
LITTLE  : abcde
BIG     : abcdefgh
UNDERRUN: abcdefgh
FREED   : This will blow up
GLOBAL  : global boom
LOCAL   : local boom
```

On other systems, especially those configured to allow core dumps, the sample program may dump core on the second call to free() (line 37).

Using `mpr` and `check` to Locate Memory Problems

The first tool covered here is Taj Khattra's `mpr` package, available from your favorite Metalab mirror (`ftp://metalab.unc.edu/pub/Linux/devel/lang/c/mpr-1.9.tar.gz`). It can be used to find memory leaks, but it does not find memory corruption errors. In addition, `mpr` also generates allocation statistics and patterns, but those features will not be covered in this section. `mpr`'s method uses simple brute force: it logs all allocation and free requests to an external log file that is later processed using `mpr`'s utilities.

To use `mpr`, download and compile it. The package includes several utility programs and a static library, `libmpr.a`, that you link your program against. To compile Listing 14.3, the command line was:

```
$ gcc -g badmem.c -o badmem -lmpr -L $HOME/lib
```

Be sure to use the `-g` switch to generate debugging symbols because some of `mpr`'s programs require them. Recall from Chapter 3, "GNU cc," that `-lmpr` links `badmem` against `libmpr.a`, and `-L $HOME/lib` prepends `$HOME/lib` to the library search path. Once the program is compiled and linked, set the environment variables `$MPRPC` and `$MPRFI`. `mpr` uses `$MPRPC` to traverse and display the call chain for each allocation and free request, while `$MPRFI` defines a pipeline command for logging (and, optionally, filtering) `mpr`'s output.

```
$ export MPRPC=`mprpc badmem`
$ export MPRFI="cat > badmem.log"
```

With these preliminary steps out of the way, execute the program. If all goes as planned, you should wind up with a file named `badmem.log` in the current directory. It will look something like the following:

```
m:134522506:134516229:134514813:10:134561792
m:134522506:134516229:134514826:5:134565888
f:134522614:134520869:134514880:134565888
m:134522506:134516229:134514890:5:134565888
f:134522614:134520869:134514975:134565888
f:134522614:134520869:134514987:134565888
```

This isn't very informative as is, but the `mpr` documentation explains the format. The log file provides the raw material for `mpr`'s utility programs, which parse, slice, dice, and julienne the log to create meaningful information.

To view memory leaks, use `mprlk`:

```
$ mprlk < badmem.log ¦ mpr -f -l badmem
```

or

```
$ mpr -f -l badmem < badmem.log ¦ mprlk
```

The `-f` and `-l` options report the filename and line number where `mpr` detects the leak. In either case, the output is

```
mprlk: f:main(badmem.c,37):134565888 (NR=6)
m:main(badmem.c,18):10:134561792
```

The output indicates that on line 18 of `badmem.c`, in the `main()` function, we `malloc()` 10 bytes of memory that we never free (the long decimal number is the call chain counter, which `mpr` and its utilities use precisely to track each allocation and free request). Looking back at Listing 14.3, this is exactly correct.

I mentioned a moment ago that `mpr` cannot detect memory corruption errors. While this is true, `mpr` includes the `mcheck()` function from GNU's `malloc()` library, which enables you to detect buffer overruns, buffer underruns, and multiple `free()`s of the same block. In fact, `mpr` compiles `mcheck()` into `libmpr.a` by default. So, the good news is that the buffer overruns and underruns in Listing 14.3 will cause it to abort unless you specifically instruct `mpr` not to use `mcheck()`. The bad news is that `mcheck()` is not terribly informative—it merely complains about a problem and leaves the programmer to determine where the problem occurs. Compiled with `mcheck()`, the sample program aborts each time we clobber memory:

```
$ ./badmem
LITTLE  : abcde
mcheck: memory clobbered past end of allocated block
IOT trap/Abort
```

After fixing the first overrun, the program gets a little farther:

```
$ ./badmem
LITTLE  : abcde
BIG     : abcdefgh
UNDERRUN: abcdefgh
mcheck: memory clobbered before allocated block
IOT trap/Abort
```

Interestingly, mcheck() ignores the larger overrun on line 28, but dies, as you would expect, when the program underruns the buffer on line 32. After fixing these two errors, mcheck() complains about freeing memory twice, as shown in the following code:

```
$ ./badmem
LITTLE  : abcde
BIG     : abcdefgh
UNDERRUN:
mcheck: block freed twice
IOT trap/Abort
```

Fixing the other errors is left as an exercise for you.

Electric Fence

The next tool covered is Electric Fence, written by Bruce Perens. Electric Fence does not catch memory leaks, but it does an excellent job of detecting buffer overruns. You can obtain it from ftp://metalab.unc.edu/pub/Linux/devel/lang/c, although many Linux distributions also ship with it.

Electric Fence uses a system's virtual memory hardware to detect illegal memory accesses, stopping a program on the first instruction that causes a boundary violation. It accomplishes this by replacing the normal malloc() with its own malloc(), and allocating a small section of memory after the requested allocation that the process is not permitted to access. As a result, buffer overruns cause a memory access violation, which aborts the program with a SIGSEGV (segmentation violation). If your system is configured to allow core files (execute ulimit -c to get and set the size of core files allowed), you can then use a debugger to isolate the location of the overrun. Like mpr, to use Electric Fence you have to link your program against a special library, libefence.a:

```
$ gcc -ggdb badmem.c -o badmem -lefence
```

The compile command used the -ggdb option to generate extra gdb-compatible debugging symbols. When executed, the program aborts and dumps core:

```
$ ./badmem

 Electric Fence 2.0.5 Copyright © 1987-1995 Bruce Perens.
LITTLE : abcde
Segmentation fault (core dumped)
```

Next, using the core file, run badmem from the gdb debugger (just follow the example for the time being, because gdb is covered in detail in Chapter 36, "Debugging: GNU gdb").

```
$ gdb badmem
GNU gdb 4.17
```

```
Copyright 1998 Free Software Foundation, Inc.
GDB is free software, covered by the GNU General Public License,
and you are welcome to change it and/or distribute copies of it
under certain conditions
.
Type "show copying" to see the conditions.
There is absolutely no warranty for GDB.  Type "show warranty" for
details.
This GDB was configured as "i386-COL-linux"...
(gdb) run
Starting program: /home/kwall/projects/unleashed/src/14/badmem

  Electric Fence 2.0.5 Copyright (C) 1987-1995 Bruce Perens.
LITTLE  : abcde

Program received signal SIGSEGV, Segmentation fault.
strcpy (dest=0x40003ff8 "abcdefgh", src=0x8055e0c "abcdefgh") at
strcpy.c:35
strcpy.c:35: No such file or directory.
(gdb) where
#0  strcpy (dest=0x40003ff8 "abcdefgh", src=0x8055e0c "abcdefgh")
    at strcpy.c:35
#1  0x80481be in main () at badmem.c:28
#2  0x80480ee in ___crt_dummy__ ()
(gdb)
```

The second line from the bottom of the listing makes it crystal clear that there is a problem at line 28 in badmem.c in the main() function. Once you fix this problem, you would then recompile and rerun the program, and, if it aborts again, repeat the debug/fix/recompile sequence. Once you've thoroughly debugged all of your code, recompile without linking against Electric Fence, and you should be set.

But wait, Electric Fence caught the big overrun on line 28, but it missed the little overrun on line 22. How could this be? This peculiar behavior results from the way the CPU aligns allocated memory. Most modern CPUs require that memory blocks be aligned on their natural word size. Intel x86 CPUs, for example, require that memory regions begin at addresses evenly divisible by four, so malloc() calls ordinarily return pieces of memory aligned accordingly. Electric Fence does the same. So, a request for five bytes actually results in eight bytes being allocated in order to meet the memory alignment requirements! As a result, the small buffer overrun on line 22 slips through the fence.

Fortunately, Electric Fence allows you to control its alignment behavior using the environment variable $EF_ALIGNMENT. Its default value is sizeof(int), but if you set it to zero (0), Electric Fence will detect smaller overruns. After setting $EF_ALIGNMENT to 0, recompiling, and rerunning the program, Electric Fence catches the small overrun at line 22:

14

MEMORY
MANAGEMENT

```
...
Program received signal SIGSEGV, Segmentation fault.
strcpy (dest=0x40003ffb "abcde", src=0x8055df8 "abcde") at strcpy.c:35
strcpy.c:35: No such file or directory.
(gdb) where
#0  strcpy (dest=0x40003ffb "abcde", src=0x8055df8 "abcde") at
➥strcpy.c:35
#1  0x804817e in main () at badmem.c:22
#2  0x80480ee in ___crt_dumhttp://www.sds.lcs.mit.edu/lclint/my__ ()
(gdb)
```

Electric Fence recognizes three other environment variables that control its behavior: `EF_PROTECT_BELOW=1` for detecting buffer underruns; `EF_PROTECT_FREE=1` for detecting access to `free()`ed memory; and `EF_ALLOW_MALLOC_0=1`, which allows programs to `malloc()` zero bytes of memory.

Use a Lint Brush

The traditional tool for detecting code problems is `lint`. Although `lint` is a proprietary program, an open source (possibly better) version of it, LCLint, by David Evans, released under an MIT-style license (see Chapter 39, "Licensing") can be obtained from `http://www.sds.lcs.mit.edu/lclint/` and most free software repositories on the Internet. LCLint is a hugely capable program that accomplishes far more than merely finding memory problems. Unfortunately, there is only time and space to highlight its abilities with respect to memory irregularities. You are strongly encouraged to visit the Web site, download the package, and invest some time and effort in learning to use LCLint—you will be glad you did.

Using LCLint is simple: just execute it (`lclint` is the command name, while LCLint is the formal name), providing the name of one or more source files as arguments:

```
$ lclint badmem.c
LCLint 2.4b — - 18 Apr 98

badmem.c: (in function main)
badmem.c:22:9: Possibly null storage buf passed as non-null param:
                 strcpy (buf, ...)
  A possibly null pointer is passed as a parameter corresponding  to a
  ➥formal  parameter with no /*@null@*/ annotation. If NULL may
  ➥be used for this parameter, add a /*@null@*/ annotation to the
  ➥function parameter declaration. (-nullpass will  suppress message)
  badmem.c:21:8: Storage buf may become null
```

The first line names the function in which the error is found. The second line identifies the filename, the line and column number, and the error message. In this case, `lclint` detected that the program may be passing a NULL argument, `buf`, to `strcpy()`, which requires a non-NULL argument. The third line provides a hint of more information about the error, and the last line provides additional location information, where appropriate.

```
...
badmem.c:37:7: Dead storage buf passed as out parameter: buf
  Memory is used after it has been released (either by passing as an only
param or assigning to and only global. (-usereleased will suppress
message)
    badmem.c:36:7: Storage buf is released
```

This message indicates that badmem.c uses the buf variable on line 37 after buf was released on line 36.

```
badmem.c:41:36: Variable buf used after being released
    badmem.c:37:7: Storage buf released
...
```

This error resembles the previous one, except that on line 41 the code attempts to copy a string into buf after it has already been freed.

In each case, the solution is to go back to the source code file, fix the errors, and pass the corrected code back through lclint. Besides flagging actual and potential errors, however, lclint supports stylized comments, annotations, and control comments. Stylized comments give lclint additional information about a type, a variable, or a function interface that enhances lclint's checks. Annotations are stylized comments that follow a specific syntax defined by lclint that allows you explicitly to express any assumptions about variables, parameters, return values, structure fields, and type definitions. This chapter will not go into any more detail about lclint due to space restrictions, but you are strongly encouraged to invest the time and energy into learning to use it—the benefits will amply repay the effort.

Summary

This chapter covered a potpourri of memory management tools and techniques. It reviewed the standard C functions for obtaining and manipulating memory regions and also looked at using memory mapped files using the mmap() family of system calls. Finally, you were introduced to three tools for locating and correcting memory bugs: mpr, Electric Fence, and LCLint.

14

MEMORY
MANAGEMENT

Interprocess Communication and Network Programming

PART

III

IN THIS PART

CHAPTER 15

Introduction to IPC: Using Pipes

by Mark Watson

IN THIS CHAPTER

This chapter starts the discussion of building distributed applications using Interprocess Communication (IPC). Linux provides a powerful platform for building distributed applications. The World Wide Web (WWW) could be considered the ultimate distributed application, and more Web servers run on Linux than any other operating system. Even if you are building applications to run on a single computer, it still often makes sense to use IPC to break up a program into modules, with well-defined interfaces defined across IPC boundaries. Chapters 16–23 cover "classic" methods of IPC, including the following:

- Message queues
- Shared memory
- Semaphores
- TCP socket programming
- UDP socket programming
- Multicast IP
- Non-blocking socket I/O
- A C++ class library for IPC

This chapter, as well as Chapters 16 through 22, uses the C language for all program examples. Chapter 23 uses the C++ language. All programs for these chapters are located on the CD-ROM in the IPC directory, which contains the following subdirectories:

```
C++
MULTICAST
PIPES
SHARED
UDP
MESSAGEQ
NOBLOCK
SEMAPHORES
SOCKETS
```

You should copy the entire directory tree under the IPC directory to a convenient working directory on your local disk. The text of the chapters in this Part refers to the example source code in the subdirectories of the IPC directory. The chapter text also contains small "snippets" of the example programs for use in explaining how the example programs work. You might find it useful to print out the complete listings of the sample programs to augment reading of the text.

This Part will not cover other useful (and higher level) techniques for building distributed applications like CORBA, Remote Procedure Calls (RPC), Distributed Computing Environment (DCE), and Java's Remote Method Invocation (RMI).

Updates to the examples in this Part and corrected errors will be posted to http://www.markwatson.com/books/linux_prog.html.

Introduction to Using Pipes

Pipes are a one-way communication channel and are accessed through a socket descriptor. Operations on pipes look like operations on local files. Two short examples will be used to illustrate both unnamed and named pipes. Typically, unnamed pipes are used for communication between a parent process and a child (or forked) process. Named pipes are most useful for communication between different programs that share the same file system. Pipes are easy to use, but lack the generality of sockets (which are covered in Chapter 19, "TCP/IP and Socket Programming").

Unnamed Pipes

Unnamed pipes are used when a Linux program forks off a separate process after using the pipe library call to create two file descriptors (one for each end of the pipe). The file unnamed_pipe.c implements both ends of a pipe reader/writer by creating two input/ output file descriptors:

```
int file_descriptors[2];
pipe(file_descriptors);
```

and then forking off a new process using the fork library call:

```
pid_t spawned_process_pid = fork();
```

After the call to fork, there are two copies of the program executing, so we need to check which process is the original (spawning or parent) process, and which process is the copied (spawned or child) process:

```
if(spawned_process_pid == 0) {
  printf("in the spawned (child) process...\n");
} else {
  printf("in the spawning (parent) process...\n");
}
```

In this snippet of code, we simply printed out whether the current process was the parent or child process. In a real application, the functionality of parent and child processes is usually quite different. In this example, the spawned (child) process closes the input file descriptor and writes some data to the output file descriptor:

```
#define INPUT 0
#define OUTPUT 1
    close(file_descriptors[INPUT]);
    write(file_descriptors[OUTPUT],
          "test data", strlen("test data"));
```

The original (spawning or parent) process closes the output file descriptor and reads data from the input file descriptor:

```
    close(file_descriptors[OUTPUT]);
    // wait for data sent by the spawned (child) process:
    returned_count = read(file_descriptors[INPUT],
                          buf,
                          sizeof(buf));
```

Unnamed pipes are the standard method for communication between parent and child processes. In Chapter 19, you will learn how to write socket- based client and server programs. As you will see, sockets are often the right technology for communication between programs in the general case that one program does not spawn another, and when programs are running on different computer systems.

A very common use of unnamed pipes is in server applications that spawn off one or more processes to handle long-running computational tasks. Figure 15.1 shows an example of a server program that uses a child (or spawned) process to handle service requests.

FIGURE 15.1

A server process spawns off a child process to handle long-running tasks.

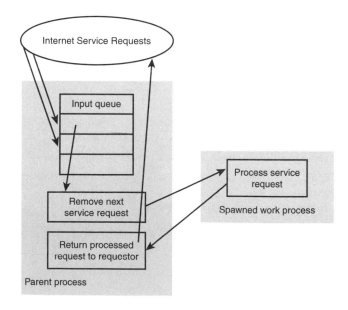

Named Pipes

Named pipes (also referred to as FIFOs) can only be used for communication between two processes that share a common file system. One advantage of named pipes over unnamed pipes is the ability to communicate between two processes that are started independently—where one process does not fork off a new process). The following man pages will be useful when writing applications that use named pipes:

- `man 2 open`—Opens a named pipe created with `mknod`
- `man 2 read`—Reads from a pipe
- `man 2 write`—Writes to a pipe

The directory `src/IPC/PIPES` on the CD-ROM contains two example programs, `read_pipe.c` and `write_pipe.c`, and a "read me" file explaining how to set up a named pipe using the UNIX `mknod` utility. Although it is also possible to create unnamed pipes using the UNIX `pipe` system call, I find named pipes to be more convenient. Named pipes are used in the following example. I assume that you have copied the entire `src` directory from the CD-ROM; change directory to `src/IPC/PIPES` and execute the following:

```
mknod a_pipe p
make
```

The `mknod` utility is used to create special files. `mknod` takes both an argument that appears before the filename, and a file type that appears after the filename on the command line. The argument p indicates that the special file `a_pipe` is a FIFO file. When `mknod` is used to create a FIFO file, no arguments are allowed before the filename.

You can then run the `read_pipe` and `write_pipe` example programs in two separate terminal windows. As you can see in the `read_pipe.c` source file, opening and reading from a named pipe is exactly like reading from a "normal" file:

```
FILE * in_file;
char buf[80];
in_file = fopen("a_pipe", "r");
if (in_file == NULL) {
   perror("Error in fopen");
   exit(1);
}
fread(buf, 1, 80, in_file);
printf("received from pipe: %s\n", buf);
fclose(in_file);
```

The system utility function `perror` is useful for both printing a string message argument (in this example, this is "Error in fopen") and the last system error. Because named pipes can be used with the standard file I/O functions `fopen`, `fread`, and `fwrite`, named pipes are simple to use. Also, in the `write_pipe.c` source file, we see that writing to a named pipe is the same as writing to a "normal" file:

```
FILE * out_file;
char buf[80];
out_file = fopen("a_pipe", "w");
if (out_file == NULL){
    perror("Error opening pipe");
    exit(1);
}
sprintf(buf,"this is test data for the named pipe example\n");
fwrite(buf, 1, 80, out_file);
fclose(out_file);
```

Using named pipes is a simple way to pass data between two programs that have access to the same file system. When reading the source to the example programs, you can look at the man pages for `fopen`, `fread`, `fwrite`, and `fclose` for documentation on these system calls. These example programs simply pass a C-style string as data. You may also want to pass binary data like a `struct` of a C++ object (if the struct or object contains no pointers or references to other objects) through a pipe. If you are passing binary data between computers with a different CPU type, you may have to worry about incompatible data types for primitive types like int, long, float, and packing of structs and C++ objects. If you are programming distributed applications for heterogeneous computer environments, then you may want to use RPC or CORBA.

Summary

Pipes provide a simple method for IPC between a parent process and a child using unnamed pipes and between any two processes running on the same machine using named pipes. The next seven chapters will cover alternative methods of IPC. Even though the use of sockets (covered in Chapter 19) is the most general method for implementing IPC, you should know how to program using pipes because many older UNIX utilities were written using them.

CHAPTER 16

Message Queues

by Mark Watson

IN THIS CHAPTER

Message queues are similar to using pipes but have the advantage of allowing messages to be tagged with specific message types. A message recipient can ask for the next available message ignoring message type (by specifying a desired message type of zero), or the next message of a specific type by specifying a positive non-zero message type. Message queues are used for communication between processes that are running on the same computer. In Chapter 19, "TCP/IP and Socket Programming," socket programming is used to provide a solution for communication between programs running on different computers. Any corrections and updates for this chapter can be found at
http://www.markwatson.com/books/linux_prog.html.

Like pipes, message queues are largely interesting for historical reasons. Many older UNIX programs use message queues.

Creating a Sample Message Queue Program

This section uses a sample program, message_q.c, to show how to set up a message queue, and then uses it to send and receive a message. This single sample program writes to and reads from a message queue. In real applications, one program typically writes to a message queue and another program reads from the message queue. When reading the source to the sample program message_q.c, you will want to check the man pages for msgget, msgsnd, msgrcv, and msgctl. In the example in the following chapter, "Semaphores," the ftok system function is used to get a unique key based on the current directory name; ftok is also used here:

```
key_t unique_key = ftok(".", 'a'); // 'a' can be any character
```

The ftok system call provides a convenient way to calculate a key based on the current directory where a program is running. If we start multiple programs from the same directory and use the preceding call to ftok to calculate a unique key, then they can access a common message queue. The msgget system function gets a queue identifier based on the unique key:

```
int id = msgget(unique_key, IPC_CREAT | 0666);
```

The first argument to msgget is a unique key that we calculated by calling ftok. The second argument specifies the file permissions for the message queue. In this example, the same program reads and writes from the message queue, so the call to msgget uses the IPC_CREAT flag. If you send data through a message queue between two separate programs (obviously, the normal way to use message queues), only one program should create the message queue using the IPC_CREAT flag. The sample program message_q.c deletes the message queue before terminating, but it is also possible to create a message queue and to reuse it with many programs. The value of the variable id (the return value from the call to msgget) will be passed to all calls to msgsnd, msgrcv, and msgctl to identify the message queue. The structure data type msgbuf is defined in the file /usr/include/linux/msg.h:

```
 /* message buffer for msgsnd and msgrcv calls */
struct msgbuf {
    long mtype;           /* type of message */
    char mtext[1];        /* message text */
};
```

In applications using message queues, we need to define our own data structure like msg-buf because the msgbuf struct contains only one character. In the sample program, we allocate 80 bytes for message data. In message_q.c, we define:

```
struct amsgbuf {
  long mtype;
  char mtext[80];
}  mq_test_buf;
```

Before sending a message in message_q.c, we fill in values in the variable mq_test_buf:

```
mq_test_buf.mtype = 123;
sprintf(mq_test_buf.mtext,"test message");
```

We can then use the msgsnd system call to add the message to the message queue:

```
msgsnd(id, (struct msgbuf *)&mq_test_buf,
        sizeof("test message") + 1, 0);
```

When calling msgsnd, the second argument is the address of a struct like msgbuf; the third argument is the length of the data in the msgbuf struct (in this case the field mtext). Passing a zero value for the fourth (last) argument to msgsnd effectively turns off error checking. The data copied into mq_test_buf.mtext is a null terminated string, so I added one to the size of the string to allow for the null termination character. When receiving messages, I usually use the flag IPC_NOWAIT so that the msgrcv system call returns immediately, even if no message is available:

```
int status = msgrcv(id, (struct msgbuf *)&mq_test_buf,
                    80, 123, IPC_NOWAIT);
```

Here, the return value, saved in the variable status, equals -1 if no message is available. The third argument (80 in this example) specifies the size of the mtext field in the message buffer. The fourth argument (123 in this example) specifies the message type to be returned. Only messages with the field mtype equaling 123 will be returned in this example call to msgrcv. If the fourth argument is zero, then the next available message will be returned, regardless of the value of the mtext field in the message buffer. The fifth argument (IPC_NOWAIT in this example) specifies whether the call to msgrcv should wait for a message if none is currently available. Using IPC_NOWAIT causes the call to msgrcv to immediately return if no messages are available. Using `IPC_NOWAIT` effectively turns off error checking. You can use the value zero instead of `IPC_NOWAIT` if you want the call to `msgrvc` to block, waiting for a message.

When you are done using a message queue, you can close it using the `msgctl` system call:

```
msgctl(id, IPC_RMID, 0);
```

The second argument to `msgctl` (`IPC_RMID` in this example) specifies a command. The `IPC_RMID` command indicates that the message queue identified by the value of the variable `id` should be removed; any current blocking (or waiting) calls to `msgrcv` for this queue will immediately return without a message; the system `errno` variable will be set to `EIDRM`.

Message queues are a great technique for reliably passing data between two programs running on the same computer. Another technique, socket programming, will be used in Chapter 19. Sockets are useful for solving the general communications problem—IPC between programs running on different computers.

Running the Sample Message Queue Program

Assuming that you have copied the `IPC` directory contents from the CD-ROM to your local file system, open a new command window, change the directory to `IPC/MESSAGEQ`, make the test program, and run it by typing the following commands:

```
make
message_q
```

You should see the following output:

```
markw@colossus:/home/markw/MyDocs/LinuxBook/src/IPC/MESSAGEQ > make
cc -o message_q message_q.c
markw@colossus:/home/markw/MyDocs/LinuxBook/src/IPC/MESSAGEQ > message_q
unique key=1627570461
message queue id=129
Sending message...
message of type 123 received with data: test message
markw@colossus:/home/markw/MyDocs/LinuxBook/src/IPC/MESSAGEQ >
```

The sample program prints out a unique key that is calculated from the program's directory pathname. The test message is sent and received on message queue with id equal to 129. You will probably get different message queue id numbers when you rerun the sample program.

There are two very useful UNIX utility programs that you should use when you are developing and running programs using shared memory, semaphores, and/or message queues: `ipcs` and `ipcrm`. The `ipcs` utility prints out information on currently allocated shared memory, semaphores, and message queues. The `ipcrm` utility is useful for freeing system resources that were not freed because a program crashed or was not written correctly.

Summary

Message queues are used mostly in older UNIX programs. Usually, it is preferable to use sockets. Message queues are probably most useful when you want to send several types of messages and the message recipient wants to filter messages by type.

Shared Memory

by Mark Watson

Shared memory is the fastest method of IPC for processes that are running on the same computer. One process can create a shared memory area and other processes can access it. You can use shared memory when you need very high performance IPC between processes running on the same machine. There are two ways that shared memory is often used: mapping the /dev/mem device and memory mapping a file. It is much safer to memory map files, rather than /dev/mem (which can crash a system), but memory mapped files have the overhead of using the file system. This chapter looks at a single example that memory maps /dev/mem.

> **CAUTION**
>
> When you write programs and test programs that use shared memory, do not use a computer that is critical to your business. It is best to test shared memory programs on a personal development system.

You will see in this chapter that you need to configure your Linux system to dedicate some real memory for shared memory allocations. This dedicated memory cannot be used by Linux or application programs.

Configuring Linux to Use Shared Memory

You will have to allocate a small block of memory when you boot up Linux by modifying your /etc/lilo.config file and rebooting your system. Here are the changes that I made to my /etc/lilo.config file to allow using shared memory:

```
# Linux bootable  (use 1 megabyte for shared memory)
image = /vmlinuz
append="mem=63m"
root = /dev/hda2
label = linux
# Linux bootable partition config ends
```

I added the append statement to my lilo.config file to indicate that my system only has 63 megabytes of physical memory. My system actually has 64 megabytes of physical memory, so this effectively reserves 1 megabyte of physical memory as shared memory.

> **CAUTION**
>
> You have to run the `lilo` program as root and then reboot your system before changes to `lilo.config` take effect. Make sure that you test shared memory programs, and share memory configuration (using `lilo`) on non-critical computers.

Sample Program Using Shared Memory

The source file `shared_mem.c` shows a very simple example of reading and writing shared memory. We will use the library functions `mmap` and `munmap` in this example; I recommend that you read the man pages for both `mmap` and `munmap`. The following C code sets up shared memory to use (assuming that it starts at the 63 megabyte address):

```c
#define ADDRESS (63*0x100000)
void main() {
  char *mem_pointer;
  int f;
  if ((f=open("/dev/mem", O_RDWR)) < 0) {
    printf("Error opening /dev/mem\n");
    exit(1);
  }
  mem_pointer = (char *)mmap(0, 8192,
                            PROT_READ | PROT_WRITE,
                            MAP_FILE | MAP_SHARED,
                            f, ADDRESS);
```

In this code example, we use the `open` function to open the shared memory device, just as we would open a disk file for reading and writing. The first argument to `mmap` (zero in this example) specifies the starting location for a block of shared memory. A value of zero specifies that `mmap` should allocate the requested block of shared memory at the beginning of the space that is available for shared memory. The second argument specifies the allocation size block of shared memory. In this call to `mmap`, we are only declaring the use of 8192 bytes of shared memory (we allocated a whole megabyte when booting Linux; see the file `/etc/lilo.conf`). The third argument is used to specify protections for the block of shared memory; in this example we have specified that shared memory pages can be read and written to. The fourth argument specifies flags for shared memory; in this example the shared memory pages are mapped as a file and sharable between processes. The fifth argument to `mmap` is a file handle; in this case, the value of the variable `f` was set as the returned value for calling `open` on the shared memory device (`/dev/mem`). The sixth argument to `mmap` is the physical address of the shared memory block; in this example, the expression (`63*0x100000`) evaluates to 63 megabytes, the start of the shared memory area reserved at Linux boot up time (remember our changes to `/etc/lilo.conf`).

Figure 17.1 shows two programs accessing the same block of shared (physical) memory.

FIGURE 17.1

Two programs reading and writing into a shared memory segment.

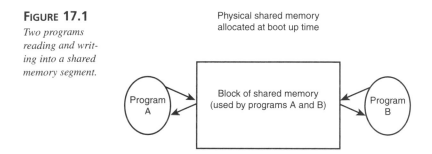

Physical shared memory allocated at boot up time

The following code reads and writes the first two bytes of shared memory every two seconds:

```
for (i=0; i<10; i++) {
  printf("Test iteration %d\n", i);
  printf("first two bytes: %d %d\n",
        mem_pointer[0], mem_pointer[1]);
  mem_pointer[0] = 2*i; // write into shared memory
  mem_pointer[1] = 3*i; // write into shared memory
  printf("first two bytes: %d %d\n",
        mem_pointer[0], mem_pointer[1]); // read from shared memory
  sleep(2);  // wait 2 seconds
}
```

This example uses the system call `sleep` to pause the program's execution for two seconds without wasting CPU cycles. When you are finished using shared memory, use the `munmap` function to free the block:

```
munmap(mem_pointer, 8192);
```

This example (built from the source file `shared_mem.c`) must be run as `root` or using an account with superuser privileges. If you run this demo program in two separate xterm windows (and start them a few seconds apart), you will see the effects of two programs reading and writing the same two bytes of shared memory. Shared memory is a great way to efficiently share data between programs. However, the simple example in the source file `shared_mem.c` ignores the problem of simultaneous access of shared memory by different executing programs.

The best way to insure atomic read/writes to shared memory is to use a semaphore (see Chapter 18, "Semaphores") to prevent more than one program from accessing shared memory for either reading or writing at one time. The problem is that a process writing to shared memory might be interrupted by the kernel, and another program reading the shared memory might be executed and read partially written data. For some applications, it might be safe to simply use a single byte of shared memory for a flag that indicates that some process is using shared memory. If a process writing to shared memory sets this flag byte to a non-zero value and then is interrupted before updating (writing) data in shared memory, any other process that is run can check the single flag byte and see that shared memory is in use. Then, it can sleep for a while before attempting to re-access shared memory.

Running the Shared Memory Program Example

You must have followed the shared memory configuration instructions in the first section of this chapter before running the shared_mem.c example program. Change directories to IPC/SHARED and type the following command to build the example program:

make

Then, do a "su root" to get root privileges and run the shared_mem example program; you should see the following output:

```
markw@colossus:/home/markw/MyDocs/LinuxBook/src/IPC/SHARED > make
cc -o shared_mem shared_mem.c
markw@colossus:/home/markw/MyDocs/LinuxBook/src/IPC/SHARED > su
Password:
colossus:/home/markw/MyDocs/LinuxBook/src/IPC/SHARED # ./shared_mem
Test iteration 0
first two bytes: 0 0
first two bytes: 0 0
Test iteration 1
first two bytes: 0 0
first two bytes: 2 3
Test iteration 2
first two bytes: 2 3
first two bytes: 4 6
Test iteration 3
first two bytes: 4 6
first two bytes: 6 9
Test iteration 4
first two bytes: 6 9
first two bytes: 8 12
Test iteration 5
first two bytes: 8 12
```

```
first two bytes: 10 15
Test iteration 6
first two bytes: 10 15
first two bytes: 12 18
Test iteration 7
first two bytes: 12 18
first two bytes: 14 21
Test iteration 8
first two bytes: 14 21
first two bytes: 16 24
Test iteration 9
first two bytes: 16 24
first two bytes: 18 27
colossus:/home/markw/MyDocs/LinuxBook/src/IPC/SHARED #
```

There are two very useful UNIX utility programs that you should use when you are developing and running programs using shared memory: ipcs and ipcrm. The ipcs utility prints out information on currently allocated shared memory, semaphores, and message queues. The ipcrm utility is useful for freeing system resources that were not freed because a program crashed or was not written correctly.

Summary

Using shared memory is a great technique when you need the fastest possible performance for sharing large amounts of data. The example in this chapter ignored the problems caused by two or more programs writing to shared memory at the same time on multi-processor computers. In the next chapter, you will see how to use semaphores to coordinate access to shared resources.

CHAPTER 18

Semaphores

by Mark Watson

Semaphores are data objects that are used to coordinate actions between separate processes. Semaphores are frequently used to share resources that can only be used by one process at a time. In Chapter 17, "Shared Memory," you saw a simple example of using shared memory between two processes; in this shared memory example, the possible problems of both processes simultaneously accessing the same shared memory are ignored. You can avoid these potential problems by using semaphores to coordinate write access to shared memory and access to other system resources.

The kernel Linux operating system needs to maintain the state of semaphores, rather than user processes. If you have the Linux kernel source code installed on your system, you can examine the include file sem.h to see the definition of the semid_ds data structure that is used by the kernel for maintaining semaphore state information. A semaphore is really a set of data; you can individually use each element of the set. In this chapter, you will use the following three system calls to create, use, and release semaphores:

- semget—Returns an integer semaphore index that is assigned by the kernel
- semop—Performs operations on the semaphore set
- semctl—Performs control operations on the semaphore set

Using semaphores is fairly easy, as you will see in the example program in the next section. However, even though the technique of using semaphores is simple, there are a two problems to be aware of: deadlock and freeing semaphore resources. Deadlock can occur if there is more than one resource whose access is controlled by semaphores. For example, if two processes require access to two non-sharable resources, one process may obtain a semaphore lock on one resource and wait forever for the other because the other process has the second resource locked, waiting for the first resource. When using semaphores it is very important to free semaphores before terminating a program.

An Example Program Using Semaphores

The example program in the file IPC/SEMAPHORE/semaphore.c shows how to create a semaphore set and how to access the elements of that set. When using semaphores and reading through the example program semaphore.c, I encourage you to read the man pages for semget, semop, and semctl. We will use a simple example in this section for two processes coordinating access to a single resource. The resource is identified using an arbitrary integer value. The example program both reads and sets semaphores. In an actual application, two or more programs would access the same semaphore set, so they must all use the same resource value. This simple example can be reused for simple semaphore requirements in your applications without your having to dig too deeply into the full API available for using semaphores.

The example program `semaphore.c` does the following:

- Creates a unique key and creates a semaphore
- Checks to make sure that the semaphore is created OK
- Prints out the value of the semaphore at index 0 (should be 1)
- Sets the semaphore (decrements the value of semaphore at index 0 to 0)
- Prints out the value of the semaphore at index 0 (should be 0)
- Un-sets the semaphore (increments the value of semaphore at index 0 back to 1)
- Prints out the value of the semaphore at index 0 (should be 1)
- Removes the semaphore

Setting the values for semaphores seems counter-intuitive. An element of a semaphore set is considered to be set (that is, indicating that some process is using the associated resource) if the counter value is zero. You free a semaphore (un-set it) by incrementing its value to a value of one.

Figure 18.1 shows the example program's relationship to the Linux kernel and internal data. An application program has no direct access to the data used to maintain semaphore sets; rather, an application program uses the `semget`, `semop`, and `semctl` system calls to create and use semaphore sets.

18

SEMAPHORES

FIGURE 18.1

The Linux kernel is responsible for maintaining data for semaphore sets.

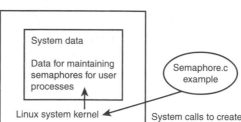

Use a Semaphore Set to coordinate access to a system resource

System data

Data for maintaining semaphores for user processes

Semaphore.c example

Linux system kernel

System calls to create a semaphore set, read a value of elements of semaphore set, and increment and decrement the integer values of members of the semaphore set.

The Linux kernel maintains semaphore data. All use of semaphores is through system calls, and not by direct access to system data.

The following code fragment creates a semaphore:

```
// Start by creating a semaphore:
unique_key = ftok(".", 's');
id = semget(unique_key, 1, IPC_CREAT | IPC_EXCL | 0666);
printf("semaphore id=%d\n", id);
```

The function `ftok` creates a key value based on both a directory path and a seed character. The first argument to `semget` is the unique key returned from `ftok`. The second argument is the number of semaphores in the set to create; just one semaphore is needed for this example. The third argument specifies that the semaphore is created and that the creation should fail if the semaphore already exists. The flags (third argument) are analogous to the flags used in calls to `open` to open a file, but substituting "IPC_" for "O_".

The following code shows how to set a specified member of a semaphore set:

```
union semun options;
options.val = 1;  // specify the value
semctl(id, 0, SETVAL, options);  // operate on semaphore at index 0

// make sure that everything is set up OK:
if (semctl(id, 0, GETVAL, 0) == 0) {
  printf("can not lock semaphore.\n");
  exit(1);
}
```

The `union semun` is defined in the include file `sys/sem.h` (or in another include file included in `sys/sem.h`, such as `linux/sem.h`) and has the following value:

```
/* arg for semctl system calls. */
union semun {
  int val;                    /* value for SETVAL */
  struct semid_ds *buf;       /* buffer for IPC_STAT & IPC_SET */
  ushort *array;              /* array for GETALL & SETALL */
  struct seminfo *__buf;      /* buffer for IPC_INFO */
  void *__pad;
};
```

In this example, we used a call to `semctl` to get the current value of the semaphore at index zero (second argument). The first argument to this call to `semctl` is the semaphore ID that was returned from the call to `semget`. The second argument is the integer index of the member of the semaphore set that we want to access. The third argument to `semctl` is the constant flag `SETVAL` (check the man page documentation using `man semctl` to see other options) used to specify that we want to increment the value of the member of the semaphore set at index zero. The constant `SETVAL` is defined in the include file `sys.sem.h`. The fourth argument to `semctl` is used to provide the data for the set operation. The following code fragment prints out the value of the semaphore at index zero:

```
// Print out the value of the semaphore:
i = semctl(id, 0, GETVAL, 0);
printf("value of semaphore at index 0 is %d\n", i);
```

Again, we have used a call to semctl to get the value of the semaphore at index zero (second argument to semctl). The third value, GETVAL, specifies that we want to get the value of the semaphore set member at index zero. The following code sets the semaphore (decrements its value) by calling semop:

```
// Set the semaphore:
struct sembuf lock_it;
lock_it.sem_num = 0; // semaphore index
lock_it.sem_op  = -1; // operation
lock_it.sem_flg = IPC_NOWAIT; // operation flags
if (semop(id, &lock_it, 1) == -1) {
  printf("can not lock semaphore.\n");
  exit(1);
}
```

The struct sembuf is defined in sys/sem.h, and has the following definition:

```
/* semop system calls takes an array of these. */
struct sembuf {
  ushort  sem_num;       /* semaphore index in array */
  short   sem_op;        /* semaphore operation */
  short   sem_flg;       /* operation flags */
};
```

The second argument to semop is an array of sembuf structures; here we only want to perform one operation, so we created a single sembuf structure, and passed a value of 1 for the third argument that is used to specify the number of commands to execute. The following code un-sets the semaphore (increments its value):

```
// Un-set the semaphore:
lock_it.sem_num = 0;
lock_it.sem_op  = 1;
lock_it.sem_flg = IPC_NOWAIT;
if (semop(id, &lock_it, 1) == -1) {
  printf("could not unlock semaphore.\n");
  exit(1);
}
```

The following code removes a semaphore set. Note that if you do not delete a semaphore, then you will not be able to rerun the example program without either rebooting your Linux system, or by running it from a different directory (which creates a different key).

```
// Remove the semaphore:
semctl(id, 0, IPC_RMID, 0);
```

The constant IPC_RMID is defined in the include file sys/ipc.h (which includes the file linux/ipc.h). Listing 18.1 shows the entire example semaphore program.

18

SEMAPHORES

LISTING 18.1   EXAMPLE SEMAPHORE PROGRAM

```c
/* semaphore.c
   Copyright Mark Watson, 1988.  Open Source Software License
*/

#include <stdio.h>
#include <sys/types.h>
#include <sys/sem.h>
#include <sys/ipc.h>

#if defined(__GNU_LIBRARY__) && !defined(_SEM_SEMUN_UNDEFINED)
        /* union semun is defined by including <sys/sem.h> */
#else
        /* according to X/OPEN we have to define it ourselves */
union semun {
  int val;                        /* value for SETVAL */
  struct semid_ds *buf;           /* buffer for IPC_STAT, IPC_SET */
  unsigned short int *array;      /* array for GETALL, SETALL */
  struct seminfo *__buf;          /* buffer for IPC_INFO */
};
#endif

void main() {
  key_t unique_key;
  int id;
  struct sembuf lock_it;
  union semun options;
  int i;

  // Start by creating a semaphore:
  unique_key = ftok(".", 'a'); // 'a' can be any character
  // Create a new semaphore with 1 member of the set; Note that
  // if you want to use a semaphore created by another program
  // then use 0 instead of 1 for the second argument:
  id = semget(unique_key, 1, IPC_CREAT | IPC_EXCL | 0666);
  printf("semaphore id=%d\n", id);
  options.val = 1;
  semctl(id, 0, SETVAL, options);

  // make sure that everything is set up OK:
  if (semctl(id, 0, GETVAL, 0) == 0) {
    printf("can not lock semaphore.\n");
    exit(1);
  }

  // Now print out the value of the semaphore:
  i = semctl(id, 0, GETVAL, 0);
  printf("value of semaphore at index 0 is %d\n", i);
```

```
// Now set the semaphore:
lock_it.sem_num = 0; // semaphore index
lock_it.sem_op  = -1; // operation
lock_it.sem_flg = IPC_NOWAIT; // operation flags
if (semop(id, &lock_it, 1) == -1) {
  printf("can not lock semaphore.\n");
  exit(1);
}

// Now print out the value of the semaphore:
i = semctl(id, 0, GETVAL, 0);
printf("value of semaphore at index 0 is %d\n", i);

// now un-set the semaphore:
lock_it.sem_num = 0;
lock_it.sem_op  = 1;
lock_it.sem_flg = IPC_NOWAIT;
if (semop(id, &lock_it, 1) == -1) {
  printf("could not unlock semaphore.\n");
  exit(1);
}

// Now print out the value of the semaphore:
i = semctl(id, 0, GETVAL, 0);
printf("value of semaphore at index 0 is %d\n", i);

// Now remove the semaphore:
semctl(id, 0, IPC_RMID, 0);
}
```

Running the Semaphore Example Program

The example program for this chapter is the file semaphore.c in the directory IPC/
SEMAPHORE. Change directory to IPC/SEMAPHORE on your system, use make to build the
example program, and type **semaphore** to run it. You should see the following output:

```
markw@:/home/markw/MyDocs/LinuxBook/src/IPC/SEMAPHORES > make
cc -o semaphore semaphore.c
markwcolossus:/home/markw/MyDocs/LinuxBook/src/IPC/SEMAPHORES > semaphore
semaphore id=0
value of semaphore at index 0 is 1
value of semaphore at index 0 is 0
value of semaphore at index 0 is 1
markw:/home/markw/MyDocs/LinuxBook/src/IPC/SEMAPHORES >
```

As you saw in the discussion in the preceding section, the example program creates a semaphore set and operates on the first element (at index zero) of this semaphore set. The initial value of the element at index zero is 1, it is decremented to 0, then incremented back to 1. The use of semaphores is important to prevent simultaneous access to system resources by separate processes or separate threads inside the same process.

There are two very useful UNIX utility programs that you should use when you are developing and running programs using semaphores: ipcs and ipcrm. The ipcs utility prints out information on currently allocated shared memory, semaphores, and message queues. The ipcrm utility is useful for freeing system resources that were not freed because a program crashed or was not written correctly.

Summary

The use of semaphores is often crucial when more than one program wants to modify a shared resource. Usually it is fine for multiple programs to have read-only access to shared resources. The important idea here is that the Linux operating system maintains the state of semaphores, guaranteeing that only one process at a time gets to set an element of a semaphore set.

TCP/IP and Socket Programming

by Mark Watson

IN THIS CHAPTER

TCP and UDP are transfer layer protocols. TCP is a connection-oriented protocol with guaranteed delivery, whereas UDP is a connectionless protocol without guaranteed message delivery. This chapter covers TCP and socket programming; UDP and socket programming are covered in Chapter 20, "UDP: The User Data Protocol." Socket programming using either TCP or UDP is low-level, "pedal to the metal" technology. Alternatives such as RPC and CORBA provide automatic translation of primitive data types between different types of computers and other high-level functionality, but presently, although there are RPC and CORBA implementations available for Linux, they are not yet part of standard Linux installations. The spirit of Linux and the Internet is to use common, standard protocols and tools, and I have to admit a personal bias toward building distributed systems with simple socket-based interfaces. In this chapter and the next, you will see several examples of socket programming that should be useful for your programming projects. Since all of the examples in this book are Open Source software, you should feel free to reuse the example code in any way that is helpful to you.

Historically, TCP and socket programming started on early UNIX systems. You may see references to UNIX Domain sockets and Berkeley sockets. UNIX Domain sockets were developed for communication between UNIX programs, whereas the more modern Berkeley sockets formed the basis for socket support in modern UNIX systems, Windows, OS/2, Macintosh, and other computer systems. At the risk of slighting historically important UNIX Domain sockets, the examples in this chapter will all use Berkeley style sockets. We will develop two useful examples in this chapter:

- A peer to peer client/server (`client.c` and `server.c`)
- A simple, extensible Web server that also supports XML (Extended Markup Language) (`web_client.c` and `web_server.c`)

System Calls to Support Socket Programming

You will be using the system functions `socket`, `bind`, `listen`, `connect`, `accept`, `recv`, and `send` to build several sample programs in this chapter. The arguments for these system calls are briefly discussed in the following sections before moving on to the sample programs.

socket

A socket is a data communication channel. Once two processes are connected through a socket, they use a socket descriptor to read and write data to the socket. The `socket` system call takes the following arguments:

> int domain
>
> int type
>
> int protocol

There are several possible domain types for sockets. They are defined in `/usr/include/sys/socket.h`. You can find them either directly in `/usr/include/sys/socket.h`, or, in later versions of the C library you can find them in the OS specific `/usr/include/bits/socket.h` (which is included in `/usr/include/sys/socket.h`).

> AF_UNIX—UNIX internal protocols
>
> AF_INET—ARPA Internet protocols (most frequently used option)
>
> AF_ISO—International Standards Organization protocols
>
> AF_NS—Xerox Network System protocols

You will almost always use the AF_INET protocol. There are several types of sockets:

> SOCK_STREAM—Provides a reliable, sequenced, two-way connection (most frequently used option)
>
> SOCK_DGRAM—Connectionless and unreliable connection
>
> SOCK_RAW—Used for internal network protocols (superuser only)
>
> SOCK_SEQPACKET—Only used in AF_NS protocol
>
> SOCK_RDM—Not implemented

You will almost always use SOCK_STREAM type sockets. The third argument to the socket function is the protocol number; a zero value is used for all of the sample programs and other socket programs.

bind

The `bind` function associates a process with a socket. `bind` is usually used in server processes to set up a socket for incoming client connections. The arguments to the `bind` system function are:

> int socket
>
> struct sockaddr * my_addr
>
> int my_addr_length

The first argument to `bind` is the socket value returned from a previous call to the function `socket`. The second argument is the address of a `sockaddr` structure that has the following definition in `/usr/include/linux/socket.h`:

```
struct sockaddr {
    unsigned short  sa_family; // address family, AF_xxx
    char sa_data[14]; // 14 bytes of protocol address
};
```

A `sockaddr` struct must be allocated and passed as the second argument to the function `bind`, but is not directly accessed in the sample program except for initializing its data. For instance, in the `server.c` example, we initialize a `sockaddr` struct:

```
struct sockaddr_in sin;
bzero(&sin, sizeof(sin));
sin.sin_family = AF_INET;
sin.sin_addr.s_addr = INADDR_ANY;
sin.sin_port = htons(port);
bind(sock_descriptor, (struct sockaddr *)&sin, sizeof(sin);
```

The `sockaddr_in` struct is equivalent to the `sockaddr` struct except that it names the individual data sub-elements for setting the protocol address.

listen

After a socket is created and associated to a process with `bind`, a server-type process can call the `listen` function to listen for incoming socket connections. The arguments to the `listen` system call are:

> int socket
>
> int input_queue_size

The first argument to `listen` is the integer socket value returned by a previous call to the function `socket` (and after `bind` is called). The second argument sets the incoming queue size. Often server processes use the `fork` system call to create a duplicate of themselves to handle incoming socket calls; this approach makes a lot of sense if you expect many simultaneous client connections. For most programs, however, it is usually adequate—and simpler—to process incoming connections one at a time and set the incoming queue size to a fairly large value.

connect

The `connect` system call is used to connect a local socket to a remote service. A typical use, as you will see in the socket client example later in this chapter, is to specify the host computer information for a server process running on a remote computer. The arguments to connect are:

> int socket
>
> struct sockaddr * server_address
>
> int server_address_length

The socket argument is defined by the return value from calling the system socket function. The use of the data structure sockaddr is discussed in the socket client example later in this chapter. The first data field in sockaddr (family) allows the specification of the connection type, or family, before calling connect (not all families are listed; see man connect for a full list):

> AF_UNIX—Unix domain sockets (useful for high performance socket interfaces for processes running on the same computer)
>
> AF_INET—Internet IP Protocol (this is the most commonly used family since it allows processes to communicate using general Internet IP addresses)
>
> AF_IPX—Novel IPX (also frequently used in Windows networks)
>
> AF_APPLETALK—Appletalk protocol

The second data element in the sockaddr data structure is a 14 8-bit block of data used to specify the protocol address. You will see in the "Server Example" section later in the chapter how to set up the protocol address for the AF_INET family. In the description of the bind function, you have seen that an equivalent struct sockaddr_in is used that specifies data sub-elements for the protocol address.

recv

The recv function is used to receive messages from a connected socket—a socket that has been connected to a socket using a call to connect. Two other calls that are not used in the examples, recvfrom and recvmsg, are used to receive messages from sockets that are not connection oriented. recvfrom is used in Chapter 20 for UDP socket programming.

The arguments to recv are:

> int socket
>
> void * buf
>
> int buf_len
>
> unsigned int flags

The socket defined by the first argument must have already been connected to a port using connect. The second argument is a pointer to a block or memory where a received message will be stored. The third argument specifies the size (in 8-bit bytes) of the reserved memory block. The fourth argument indicates operation flags; the following values can be combined with the Boolean and (|) operator for the fourth argument (a zero value is always used for the flags in the examples in this chapter):

MSG_OOB—Process out-of-band data (useful for handling high priority control messages), usually zero is used for normal (not out of band) behavior

MSG_PEEK—Peek at an incoming message without reading it

MSG_WAITALL—Wait for the receiving data buffer to be completely full before returning

send

The send system call is used to pass data using a socket to another program. Both client and server applications use the send function; client applications use send to send service requests to remote server processes, and server processes use send to return data to clients. You will see many examples of the use of send in the example programs. The send function takes the following arguments:

int socket

const void * message_data

int message_data_length

unsigned int flags

The first argument is just the socket value returned from a call to the socket function. The second argument contains any data to be transferred. The third argument specifies the size in 8-bit bytes of the message data. The fourth argument is always zero in the example programs developed in this chapter, but the following constants can be used (although they rarely are):

MSG_OOB—Process out of band data (out of band send calls are useful for high priority control messages), usually zero is used for normal (not out of band) behavior

MSG_DONTROUTE—Do not use routing

Client/Server Examples Using Sockets

The source files client.c and server.c on the CD-ROM contain the simple client and server examples that we will develop in this section. The sample server listens on a socket (port 8000) for incoming requests. Any program, like the client.c example, can connect to this server and pass up to 16,384 bytes of data to the server. The server treats the data as ASCII data and converts it to uppercase before returning it to the client program. These two simple programs can be easily reused when writing socket-based client/server programs. The server example does not use fork (use man fork to view documentation) to create new copies of itself; it does set up an input queue for a backlog of 20 service requests. Servers that might potentially receive many simultaneous requests should use fork to create a separate process for handling computationally expensive service requests.

Server Example

The server.c example creates one permanent socket for listening for service requests; when a client connects with the server, a temporary socket is created. Each time a client connects to a server, a new temporary socket is opened between the client and the server. The following data support creating both the permanent socket and the temporary sockets that are created for client connections:

```
struct sockaddr_in sin;
struct sockaddr_in pin;
int sock_descriptor;
int temp_sock_descriptor;
int address_size;
```

We must first define the socket descriptor:

```
sock_descriptor = socket(AF_INET, SOCK_STREAM, 0);
```

We must then fill in the required fields of the struct sockaddr_in sin:

```
bzero(&sin, sizeof(sin));
sin.sin_family = AF_INET;
sin.sin_addr.s_addr = INADDR_ANY;
sin.sin_port = htons(8000); // we will use port 8000
```

Now we are ready to bind the new socket to port 8000:

```
bind(sock_descriptor, (struct sockaddr *)&sin,
     sizeof(sin));
```

19

TCP/IP AND
SOCKET
PROGRAMMING

Finally, we need to start listening on the new socket to port 8000:

```
listen(sock_descriptor,20); //queue up to 20 connections
```

At this point, the example in `server.c` goes into an infinite loop waiting for socket connections from clients:

```
while(1) {
    // get a temporary socket to handle client request:
    temp_sock_descriptor =
        accept(sock_descriptor, (struct sockaddr *)&pin,
               &address_size);
    // receive data from client:
    recv(temp_sock_descriptor, buf, 16384, 0);

    // ... here we can process the client request ...

    // return data to the client:
    send(temp_sock_descriptor, buf, len, 0);
    // close the temporary socket (we are done with it)
    close(temp_sock_descriptor);
}
```

In the `server.c` sample program, the server listens forever for incoming client socket connections. If the program is killed, the permanent socket used for the initial connection with clients is closed automatically by the operating system. Under Linux, this automatic closing occurs very quickly; under Windows NT it may take five or ten seconds.

Client Example

The `client.c` example creates a temporary socket for listening for sending a service request to the example server defined in `server.c`. The following data is used to make the temporary socket connection to the server:

```
int socket_descriptor;
struct sockaddr_in pin;
struct hostent *server_host_name;
```

A client program must know the host IP address. Typically, this might look like `www.a_company.com` or on a local network with names like `colossus` and `carol` (the names of my and my wife's computers on our local area network at home). The sample programs can be run on your Linux computer by referring to the standard IP address for the local computer, 127.0.0.1, which is usually aliased to localhost. Try substituting localhost for 127.0.0.1 in the example `client.c`. The following gets the host computer information:

```
server_host_name = gethostbyname("127.0.0.1");
```

Now that we have the host computer information, we can fill in the struct sockaddr_in pin data:

```
bzero(&pin, sizeof(pin));
pin.sin_family = AF_INET;
pin.sin_addr.s_addr = htonl(INADDR_ANY);
pin.sin_addr.s_addr =
  ((struct in_addr *)(server_host_name->h_addr))->s_addr;
pin.sin_port = htons(port);
```

We are ready to construct a socket connection to the host:

```
socket_descriptor = socket(AF_INET, SOCK_STREAM, 0);
```

Finally, we can connect to the host using this socket:

```
connect(socket_descriptor, (void *)&pin, sizeof(pin));
```

If the server is busy, this call might block (wait) for a while. When the call to connect returns, then we can send data to the server:

```
send(socket_descriptor, "test data",
    strlen("test data") + 1, 0);
```

The following call to recv waits for a response from the server (the variable buf is an array of bytes of length 8192):

```
recv(socket_descriptor, buf, 8192, 0);
```

The data in the variable buf contains data returned from the server. The client can now close the temporary socket connection to the server:

```
close(socket_descriptor);
```

Running the Client and Server Examples

You can open two xterm windows, one for the server and one for the client. Go to the directory that contains the files client.c and server.c (ignore the other files in this directory for now) and type

make

to build the example programs. The server can be started by typing

server

The client (in the other xterm, after changing to the correct directory) can be run by typing

client "This is test data to send to the server."

19

TCP/IP AND
SOCKET
PROGRAMMING

You can stop the server by pressing Control-C in the xterm window where the server is running. You should see the following output from the server sample program:

```
markw@colossus:/home/markw/MyDocs/LinuxBook/src/IPC/SOCKETS > server
Accepting connections ...
received from client:This is test data to send to the server.
```

You should see the following output from the client sample program:

```
markw > client "This is test data to send to the server."
Sending message This is test data to send to the server. to server...
..sent message.. wait for response...

Response from server:

THIS IS TEST DATA TO SEND TO THE SERVER.
```

Running the Server Example Using a Web Browser as a Client

Instead of testing the server.c sample program with the client.c example, we can also use a Web browser. Try opening the Netscape Web browser and entering the following URL:

http://127.0.0.1:8000

Here, 127.0.0.1 is the IP address of the local computer and 8000 is the port number to send to. The Netscape browser will send a request to the server.c program, thinking that it is a Web server. The server.c program will take this request, convert all characters to uppercase, and return this data to the Web browser. The following should show up on your browser:

```
GET / HTTP/1.0 CONNECTION: KEEP-ALIVE USER-AGENT: MOZILLA/4.5 [EN]
(X11; I; LINUX 2.0.35 I686)
HOST:127.0.0.1:8000 ACCEPT: IMAGE/GIF, IMAGE/X-XBITMAP, IMAGE/JPEG,
IMAGE/PJPEG, IMAGE/PNG,
*/* ACCEPT-ENCODING: GZIP ACCEPT-LANGUAGE: EN
ACCEPT-CHARSET: ISO-8859-1,*,UTF-8
```

That was fun, right?

A Simple Web Server and Sample Web Client

In this section, you will implement a simple Web server and a text-based client Web application. You will test the Web server both with the client and by using Netscape Navigator. The source files used in this example are web_server.c and web_client.c.

Implementing a Simple Web Server

The sample program web_server.c uses a utility function read_file to read a local file and return the contents of the file as one large character buffer (variable ret_buf). The variable error_return has the value of an HTML formatted error message.

The following code implements the read_file function for reading the contents of a local file into a buffer:

```
char ret_buf[32768];
char * error_return = "<HTML>\n<BODY>File not found\n</BODY>\n</HTML>";

char * read_file(char * buf, int num_buf) {
  int i;
  char *cp, *cp2;
  FILE *f;
  cp = buf + 5;
  cp2 = strstr(cp, " HTTP");
  if (cp2 != NULL) *cp2 = '\0';
  if (DEBUG) printf("file: ¦%s¦\n", cp);
  // fetch file:
  f = fopen(cp, "r");
  if (f == NULL) return error_return;
  i = fread(ret_buf, 1, 32768, f);
  if (DEBUG) printf("%d bytes read from file %s\n", i, cp);
  if (i == 0)  { fclose(f);  return error_return; }
  ret_buf[i] = '\0';
  fclose(s);
  return ret_buf;
}
```

In the web_server.c example, the function main opens up a socket for listening for service requests in the usual way. web_server.c checks the error codes for all system calls; these checks are left out in the following short description of how the Web server works. The following code is similar to the server socket setup code in the example server.c:

```
int sock;
int serverSocket;
struct sockaddr_in serverAddr;
struct sockaddr_in clientAddr;
int clientAddrSize;
struct hostent* entity;
serverSocket = socket(AF_INET, SOCK_STREAM, 0);
serverAddr.sin_family     = AF_INET;
serverAddr.sin_port       = htons(port);
serverAddr.sin_addr.s_addr = htonl(INADDR_ANY);
memset(&(serverAddr.sin_zero), 0, 8);
```

The following call to bind associates this socket with the desired port number (from the variable port):

```
bind(serverSocket, (struct sockaddr*) &serverAddr,
     sizeof(struct sockaddr));
```

The following call to listen sets a limit of 10 queued requests, and indicates that the program is now ready to accept incoming service requests:

```
listen(serverSocket, 10); // allow 10 queued requests
```

The example in web_server.c is now ready to loop, waiting for incoming connections. A new socket is opened for each incoming service request; the data for a service request is read, the request is processed with data returned to the client, and finally the temporary socket (variable sock)is closed.

The following code fragment from the web_server.c example implements a processing loop that waits for incoming client request:

```
while (1) {
  clientAddrSize = sizeof(struct sockaddr_in);
  do
    sock = accept(serverSocket,
                  (struct sockaddr*) &clientAddr,
                  &clientAddrSize);
  while ((sock == -1) && (errno == EINTR));
  if (sock == -1) {
    printf("Bad accept\n");
    exit(1);
  }

  entity = gethostbyaddr((char*) &clientAddr.sin_addr,
                         sizeof(struct in_addr), AF_INET);
  if (DEBUG) printf("Connection from %d\n",
                    inet_ntoa((struct in_addr) clientAddr.sin_addr));

  i = recv(sock, recvBuffer, 4000, 0);

  if (i == -1)  break;
  if (recvBuffer[i - 1] != '\n') break;
  recvBuffer[i] = '\0';
  if (DEBUG) {
    printf("Received from client: %s\n", recvBuffer);
  }

  // call a separate work function to process request:
  cbuf = read_file(recvBuffer, totalReceived);
  size = strlen(cbuf);
  totalSent = 0;
  do {
```

```
        bytesSent = send(sock, cbuf + totalSent,
                         strlen(cbuf + totalSent), 0);
        if (bytesSent == -1) break;
        totalSent += bytesSent;
    } while (totalSent < size);
    if (DEBUG) printf("Connection closed by client.\n");
    close(sock);
}
```

This code is very similar to the example server.c except here, data received from the
client is interpreted as a request for a local file. The requested local file is read into a
buffer, and the buffer is sent back to the client.

Implementing a Simple Web Client

The short example program web_client.c shows how you might want to interact with a
Web server in a program, rather than using a Web browser. This sample program checks
all error return values from system calls, but these error checks are left out of the following discussion to make the code listings shorter. As always, an error return less than zero
indicates a problem.

The variables host_name and port are used to specify the host computer name and the
port. In the example file web_server.c, the host name is specified as an absolute IP
address (127.0.0.1) specifying the local machine, but any value such as www.lycos.com
or www.markwatson.com would work. Web servers, by default, listen on port 80; port
8000 is used to run the web_server.c example so as to not conflict with the apache Web
server that is installed and run by default in most Linux distributions:

```
char * host_name = "127.0.0.1"; // local host
int port = 8000;
```

The following code (this should look familiar to you by now) gets the Web server host
information and opens a socket connection to the Web server (the file web_server.c contains code for error checking that is not shown here for the sake of brevity):

```
int sd;
struct sockaddr_in pin;
struct hostent *nlp_host;
nlp_host = gethostbyname(host_name);
bzero(&pin, sizeof(pin));
pin.sin_family = AF_INET;
pin.sin_addr.s_addr = htonl(INADDR_ANY);
pin.sin_addr.s_addr = ((struct in_addr *)(nlp_host->h_addr))->s_addr;
pin.sin_port = htons(port);

sd = socket(AF_INET, SOCK_STREAM, 0);
connect(sd, (void *)&pin, sizeof(pin));
```

19

**TCP/IP AND
SOCKET
PROGRAMMING**

```
// NOTE: must send a carriage return at end of message:
sprintf(message,"GET /index.html HTTP/1.1\n");
send(sd, message, strlen(message), 0);
printf("..sent message.. wait for response...\n");
recv(sd, buf, 8192, 0);  // buf is 8192 bytes long
printf("\nResponse from NLPserver:\n\n%s\n", buf);
close(sd); //we are done, close the socket and quit
```

Testing the Web Server and Web Client

Open two xterm windows, and change directory to the IPC/SOCKETS directory in both windows. In the first window, type

make
web_server

In the second window, type

web_client

You should now see the following output in the window where the web_server sample program is running:

```
markw@colossus:/home/markw/MyDocs/LinuxBook/src/IPC/SOCKETS > web_server
Binding server socket to port 8000
Accepting connections ...
Connection from 1074380876
Received from client: GET /index.html HTTP/1.1

file: ¦index.html¦
473 bytes read from file index.html
Connection closed by client.
```

You should see the following output in the window where the web_client sample program is running:

```
markw@colossus:/home/markw/MyDocs/LinuxBook/src/IPC/SOCKETS > web_client
Sending message GET /index.html HTTP/1.1
 to web_server...
..sent message.. wait for response...

Response from NLPserver:

<HTML>
 <HEAD>
   <TITLE>Mark's test page for the web_server</TITLE>
 </HEAD>
 <BODY>
   <H2>This is a test page for the web_server</H2>
   <p>In order to test with another local file, please
   <a href="test.html">click here</a> to load a local
```

```
   file (local to web_server).<p>
   In order to test the web server with a remote link,
   here is a link to Mark Watson's home page on the net.<p>
   Please <a href="http://www.markwatson.com">click here</a>.
 </BODY>
</HTML>
```

Running the Simple Web Server Using Netscape Navigator as a Client

You can easily try the sample Web server using a Web browser like Netscape Navigator. Open a Web browser and enter the following URL:

http://127.0.0.1:8000/index.html

Note that you must specify a filename in the URL because the example Web server does not try default values like index.html or index.htm.

The UNIX netstat utility is very useful to see open socket connections on your computer. Use the following option to see all connections:

```
netstat -a
```

Summary

In this chapter, you learned how to program using TCP sockets with both client and server examples. Socket programming is the basis for most distributed systems. Other, higher level techniques such as CORBA and Java's RMI are also popular, but most existing systems are written using sockets. Even if you use CORBA and RMI, sockets are more efficient, so socket programming is a good technique to know.

UDP: The User Data Protocol

by Mark Watson

IN THIS CHAPTER

CHAPTER 20

The User Data Protocol (UDP) is a lower level protocol than TCP. Specifically, UDP does not provide either guaranteed message delivery or guaranteed notice of delivery failure. Also, UDP messages are not guaranteed to be delivered in the order that they were sent. It is a common opinion that using TCP sockets rather than UDP is a better approach for almost all applications. To be fair, there are several advantages to using TCP, including the following:

- TCP sockets provide either guaranteed delivery or an error condition.
- If large blocks of data must be transferred, using TCP and keeping a socket open can be more efficient than breaking data into small pieces (the physical block size limit for UDP packets is 8192 bytes, but the space available for user data is about 5200 bytes per packet).
- Software is more complex when lost packets need to be detected and re-sent.

I have, however, used UDP on several projects (the NMRD monitoring system for DARPA, the Sleuth real-time fraud detection expert system for PacBell, and a PC-based networked hovercraft racing game for Angel Studios). Using UDP can be far more efficient than using TCP, but I only recommend using it if the following conditions apply:

- The data that needs to be sent fits in one physical UDP packet. UDP packets are 8192 bytes in length, but because of the data for headers I only assume that I can put 5000 bytes of data in one UDP packet.
- Some transmitted data can be lost without destroying the integrity of the system.
- Any lost data does not have to be re-sent.

An ideal candidate for using UDP is a computer game that runs on a local area network. UDP packets are rarely lost on local area networks. Also, if you use UDP packets to send updated game information, then it is reasonable to expect a network game to function adequately if a very small fraction of transmitted data packets are lost.

You will see in the next two sections that using UDP sockets is very similar to the examples using TCP sockets in Chapter 19. If you studied and ran the example programs in Chapter 19, you (almost) already know how to use UDP. You need only change a single argument when calling the function socket to select UDP. The following two short example programs are used in this chapter:

- send.c—Sends 20 text messages to a receiver
- receive.c—Receives text messages from the sender and prints them

Using UDP is a powerful technique for the right type of applications. The overhead for using UDP is much less than using TCP.

An Example Program for Sending Data with UDP

The following example (file send.c in the src/IPC/UDP directory) looks like the earlier socket examples, except that we use SOCK_DGRAM instead of SOCK_STREAM for the second argument when calling socket. We specify AF_INET for the address family so that our example will work with general Internet IP addresses (for example, we could specify something like "markwatson.com" for a host name; a Domain Name Server (DNS) would resolve "markwatson.com" into an absolute IP address like 209.238.119.186). The sockaddr in_address variable is filled exactly the same as the socket example program client.c in the SOCKETS directory on the CD-ROM. The IP address used is 127.0.0.1, which refers to the local machine, so the send.c and receive.c example programs will only work when run on the same computer. This restriction can be easily removed by changing the IP address set in send.c.

```c
#include <stdio.h>
#include <sys/socket.h>
#include <netinet/in.h>
#include <arpa/inet.h>
#include <netdb.h>

int port = 6789;

void main() {
  int socket_descriptor;  int iter = 0;
  int process;
  char buf[80]; // for sending messages
  struct sockaddr_in address;
  // Here, we use SOCK_DGRAM (for UDP) instead of SOCK_STREAM (TCP):
  socket_descriptor = socket(AF_INET, SOCK_DGRAM, 0);
  memset(&address, 0, sizeof(address));
  address.sin_family = AF_INET;
  address.sin_addr.s_addr = inet_addr("127.0.0.1"); // local computer
  address.sin_port = htons(port);
  process = 1;  // flag for breaking out the do-while loop
  do {
    sprintf(buf,"data packet with ID %d\n", iter);
    if (iter >20) {
      sprintf(buf, "stop\n");
      process = 0;
    }
    sendto(socket_descriptor,
           buf, sizeof(buf),
           0, (struct sockaddr *)&address, sizeof(address));
    iter++;
  } while (process);
}
```

20

UDP: THE USER
DATA PROTOCOL

The do-while loop sends 20 messages using UDP. The message simply contains text with the message number for reference (this will be printed by the receive.c program in the UDP directory).

An Example Program for Receiving UDP Data

This example program (receive.c in the UDP directory) is similar to the server.c example program in the SOCKETS directory, except that we use SOCK_DGRAM instead of SOCK_STREAM for the second argument when calling socket. For both TCP and UDP, we use gethostbyname to resolve either a computer name or absolute IP address into a hostent struct. The setup of the struct sockaddr in_sin data and the call to bind is identical to the TCP socket example.

```c
#include <stdio.h>
#include <sys/socket.h>
#include <netinet/in.h>
#include <arpa/inet.h>
#include <netdb.h>

char * host_name = "127.0.0.1"; // local host

void main() {
  int sin_len;
  int port = 8080;
  char message[256];
  int socket_descriptor;
  struct sockaddr_in sin;
  struct hostent *server_host_name;
  server_host_name = gethostbyname("127.0.0.1");
  bzero(&sin, sizeof(sin));
  sin.sin_family = AF_INET;
  sin.sin_addr.s_addr = htonl(INADDR_ANY);
  sin.sin_port = htons(port);
  // set socket using SOCK_DGRAM for UDP:
  socket_descriptor = socket(PF_INET, SOCK_DGRAM, 0);
  bind(socket_descriptor, (struct sockaddr *)&sin, sizeof(sin));
  while (1) {
    sin_len = sizeof(sin);
    recvfrom(socket_descriptor, message, 256, 0,
             (struct sockaddr *)&sin, &sin_len);
    printf("\nResponse from server:\n\n%s\n", message);
    if (strncmp(message, "stop", 4) == 0) break;
  }
  close(socket_descriptor);
}
```

In this example, the `while` loop runs forever, until a message is received from the `send.c` example program that starts with the characters `stop`. In the TCP socket examples, we used `recv`, whereas here we use `recvfrom`. We use `recvfrom` when we want to receive data from a connectionless socket (like UDP). The fifth argument to `recvfrom` is the address of a `struct sockaddr_in sin` data object. The source address of this `sockaddr_in` object is filled in when receiving UDP messages, but the source address is not used in the example program.

Running the UDP Example Programs

To run the UDP example programs, change directory to the UDP directory that you have copied from the CD-ROM, and type the following:

```
make
receive
```

This will build both the `send` and `receive` example programs and start the `receive` program. You should see the following output:

```
markw@colossus:/home/markw/MyDocs/LinuxBook/src/IPC/UDP > make
cc -o receive receive.c
cc -o send send.c
markw@colossus:/home/markw/MyDocs/LinuxBook/src/IPC/UDP > receive
```

In another window, change directory to the UDP directory and run the `send` program; you should see:

```
markw@colossus:/home/markw/MyDocs/LinuxBook/src/IPC/UDP > send
markw@colossus:/home/markw/MyDocs/LinuxBook/src/IPC/UDP >
```

In the first window, where you ran `receive`, you should see many lines of output, beginning with:

```
Response from server:

data packet with ID 0


Response from server:

data packet with ID 1


Response from server:

data packet with ID 2
```

20

**UDP: THE USER
DATA PROTOCOL**

The `receive` program terminates when it receives a message starting with `stop`:

Response from server:

stop

Summary

These UDP example programs show that using UDP is simple, if we do not have to worry about lost messages. Remember that on local area networks, losing UDP message packets is not likely, so a minimal amount of "handshaking" will often suffice to make sure that both sending and receiving programs are running correctly. Even though you will usually use TCP sockets, using UDP is a powerful technique for increasing performance of distributed systems. In Chapter 21, "Using Multicast Sockets," you will see how to use multicast broadcasts from one sender to many receivers. We will use UDP, rather than TCP, for multicast broadcasts. You will see that the code for sending multicast broadcasts is almost identical to using UDP, but you have to do extra work to receive multicast IP broadcasts.

Using Multicast Sockets

by Mark Watson

IN THIS CHAPTER

CHAPTER 21

Multicast broadcasting is a great technology for building distributed systems such as chat tools, community blackboard drawing tools, and video teleconferencing systems. Programs that use multicast broadcasting are very similar to programs that send messages using UDP to a single receiver. The principle change is that you use a special multicast IP address. For example, the IP address of the local computer is 127.0.0.1, whereas the multicast IP address of the local computer is 224.0.0.1. You will see that programs that receive multicast broadcasts are very different from programs that receive normal UDP messages.

Not all computer systems are configured for IP multicast. In the next section, you learn how to configure Linux to support IP multicast. If you use a heterogeneous computer network, then you should know that Windows NT supports multicast IP, but Windows 95 requires a free patch. Most modern network cards support IP multicast. Even if your network card does not support IP multicast, which is unlikely, the examples in this chapter are set up to run on a single computer so you can still experiment with multicast IP programming.

Configuring Linux to Support Multicast IP

Most Linux systems have multicast IP capability turned off by default. In order to use multicast sockets on my Linux system, I had to reconfigure and build my kernel, and then run the following command as `root` after re-booting:

```
route add -net 224.0.0.0 netmask 240.0.0.0 dev lo
```

Make sure that this route has been added by typing

route -e

You should see output like this:

```
markw@colossus:/home/markw > su
Password:
markw # route add -net 224.0.0.0 netmask 240.0.0.0 dev lo
colossus:/home/markw # route -e
Kernel IP routing table
Destination   Gateway   Genmask      Flags   MSS Windowirtt Iface
loopback      *         255.0.0.0    U       3584 0          0 lo
224.0.0.0     *         240.0.0.0    U       3584 0          0 lo
markw #
```

Please note that I ran the `route` commands as `root`. I don't permanently add this route for multicasting to my Linux development system; rather, I manually add the route (as `root`) when I need to use multicast IP. Re-configuring and building the kernel is also fairly simple. On my Linux system, I use the following steps to configure and build a new kernel with multicast IP support:

1. `cd /usr/src/linux`

2. `make menuconfig`

   select networking options

   check the box labeled "enable multicast IP"

   save and exit from `menuconfig`

3. `make dep; make clean; make zImage`

4. `cp /vmlinux /vmlinux_good`

5. `cp arch/i386/boot/zImage /vmlinux`

6. `cd /etc`

7. edit `lilo.conf`, adding a new entry for the `/vmlinux_good` kernel

8. lilo

TIP

Please read the available documentation for building and installing a new Linux kernel. Linux comes with great online documentation in the form of HOWTO documents. Please read the HOWTO documents for building a new kernel and for configuring for multicast IP before you get started.

I already had a multicast IP application written in Java, and it took me about one hour to read the HOWTO documents, rebuild the kernel, and get my existing application running.

Sample Programs for Multicast IP Broadcast

There are no new system API calls to support multicast IP; rather, the existing functions `getsockopt` and `setsockopt` have been extended with options to support multicast IP. These functions have the following signatures:

```
int getsockopt(int socket, int level, int optname,
            void *optval, int *optlen);
int setsockopt(int socket, int level, int optname,
            const void *optval, int optlen);
```

Complete documentation for both functions can be seen by using man getsockopt; the following discussion addresses the use of getsockopt and setsockopt for setting up a socket for use with multicast IP. The second argument, level, sets the protocol level that the selected operation should affect. We will always specify the level as IPPROTO_IP in our examples. The third argument, optname, is an integer value for possible options. The options used for multicast IP are:

SO_REUSEADDR—Enables a given address to be used by more than one process at the same time on the same computer.

SO_BROADCAST—Enables multicast broadcast

IP_ADD_MEMBERSHIP—Notifies the Linux kernel that this socket will be used for multicast

IP_DROP_MEMBERSHIP—Notifies the Linux kernel that this socket will no longer be participating in multicast IP

IP_MULTICAST_TTL—Specifies the time-to-live value for broadcast messages

IP_MULTICAST_LOOP—Specifies whether messages also get broadcast to the sending computer; the default is true, so when a program on your Linux computer broadcasts a message, other programs running on the same computer can receive the message

You will see examples of setting some of these values in the two sample programs broadcast.c and listen.c. The error return values of these functions should always be checked. An error return is a value less than zero. It is usually sufficient to check for a less than zero error condition, and to call the system perror function to print out the last system error. However, you might want to detect the exact error in your program; you can use the following defined constants for specific error codes:

EBADF—Bad socket descriptor (first argument)

ENOTSOCK—Socket (first argument) is a file, not a socket

ENOPROTOOPT—The option is unknown at the specified protocol level

EFAULT—The address referenced by optval (fourth argument) is not in the current process's address space

Sample Program to Broadcast Data with Multicast IP

Broadcasting using multicast IP will look similar to sending data using UDP (see Chapter 20). The sample program source code for this section is the file broadcast.c in the directory IPC/MULTICAST. You first have to set up the socket, as usual:

```
int socket_descriptor;
struct sockaddr_in address;
```

```
socket_descriptor = socket(AF_INET, SOCK_DGRAM, 0);
if (socket_descriptor == -1) {
  perror("Opening socket");
  exit(1);
}
```

Notice that like the UDP examples in the previous chapter, the second argument to the socket call is SOCK_DGRAM, which specifies a connectionless socket. Set up the data used to send the data, as usual, for a socket using UDP:

```
memset(&address, 0, sizeof(address));
address.sin_family = AF_INET;
address.sin_addr.s_addr = inet_addr("224.0.0.1");
address.sin_port = htons(6789); // we are using port 6789
```

Here, one thing out of the ordinary is the IP address 224.0.0.1 that is the multicast equivalent of the localhost IP address 127.0.0.1. In a loop, we will broadcast data every two seconds:

```
while (1) {
  if (sendto(socket_descriptor,
              "test from broadcast", sizeof("test from broadcast"),
              0, (struct sockaddr *)&address, sizeof(address))
       < 0) {
    perror("Trying to broadcast with sendto");
    exit(1);
  }
  sleep(2);
}
```

Except for the multicast IP address 224.0.0.1, this is identical to the example for sending data using UDP (source file send.c in the IPC/UDP directory).

Sample Program to Listen for Multicast IP Broadcasts

The sample program for listening to multicast IP broadcast messages (listen.c in the directory IPC/MULTICAST) is very different than the UDP example. You must do several new things in this example:

- Notify the Linux kernel that a specified socket will participate in a multicast IP broadcast group.

- Enable a socket for multiple use by different processes running on the same computer.

- Set the socket so that broadcast messages are sent to the same machine (this is actually the default) so that we can test multiple copies of the broadcast and listen programs on one test machine.

In the sample program `listen.c`, we first need to set up the socket (in the usual way):

```
int socket_descriptor;
struct sockaddr_in sin;
struct hostent *server_host_name;

  if ((server_host_name = gethostbyname(host_name)) == 0) {
   perror("Error resolving local host\n");
   exit(1);
}


  if ((socket_descriptor = socket(PF_INET, SOCK_DGRAM, 0)) == -1) {
   perror("Error opening socket\n");
   exit(1);
}
```

Before we actually call `bind`, we will set options on the socket for multicast IP. The first thing that we need to do is to allow multiple processes to share the same port:

```
u_char share = 1; // we will need to pass the address of this value
if (setsockopt(socket_descriptor, SOL_SOCKET, SO_REUSEADDR,
               &share, sizeof(share)) < 0) {
   perror("setsockopt(allow multiple socket use");
}
```

Now that we have set up the socket for shared use, it is OK to bind it to a port (the usual bind setup and call):

```
bzero(&sin, sizeof(sin));
sin.sin_family = AF_INET;
sin.sin_addr.s_addr = htonl(INADDR_ANY);
sin.sin_port = htons(port);
if (bind(socket_descriptor,
         (struct sockaddr *)&sin, sizeof(sin)) < 0) {
   perror("call to bind");
}
```

After the call to `bind`, we can set the socket for broadcasting to the same machine; this makes it convenient to test multicast IP broadcasting on a single development computer:

```
u_char loop = 1;
if (setsockopt(socket_descriptor, IPPROTO_IP, IP_MULTICAST_LOOP,
               &loop, sizeof(loop)) < 0) {
   perror("setsockopt(multicast loop on)");
}
```

We have to join a broadcast group. This informs the Linux kernel that incoming data to the specified socket is broadcast data:

```
command.imr_multiaddr.s_addr = inet_addr("224.0.0.1");
command.imr_interface.s_addr = htonl(INADDR_ANY);
```

```
// check to make sure that we are using a legal broadcast IP address:
if (command.imr_multiaddr.s_addr == -1) {
  printf("Error: group of 224.0.0.1 not a legal multicast address\n");
}

// We have a legal broadcast IP address, so join the broadcast group:
if (setsockopt(socket_descriptor, IPPROTO_IP, IP_ADD_MEMBERSHIP,
               &command, sizeof(command)) < 0) {
  perror("Error in setsocket(add membership)");
}
```

Now that the socket is configured for multicast IP broadcast, we loop, listening for broadcasts:

```
while (iter++ < 10) {
  sin_len = sizeof(sin);
  if (recvfrom(socket_descriptor, message, 256, 0,
               (struct sockaddr *)&sin, &sin_len) == -1) {
    perror("Error in receiving response from server\n");
  }

  printf("\nResponse from server:\n\n%s\n", message);
  sleep(2);
}
```

We only loop ten times. Then, the listen.c sample program leaves the broadcast group and closes down the socket:

```
if (setsockopt(socket_descriptor, IPPROTO_IP, IP_DROP_MEMBERSHIP,
               &command, sizeof(command)) < 0) {
  perror("Error in setsocket(drop membership)");
}
close(socket_descriptor);
```

Running the Sample Multicast IP Programs

You should open two command windows, and in each change directory to the src/IPC/MULTICAST directory that you have copied from the CD-ROM. In either of these two windows, type **make** to build the broadcast and listen executables. In the first window, type **listen** and type **broadcast** in the second window. Here is what you should see in the first window (only the first few lines of output are shown since the broadcast program sends the same message ten times):

```
markw@colossus:/home/markw/MyDocs/LinuxBook/src/IPC/MULTICAST > listen

Response from server:

test from broadcast
```

```
Response from server:
```

```
test from broadcast
```

Here is what you should see in the second window:

```
markw@colossus:/home/markw/MyDocs/LinuxBook/src/IPC/MULTICAST > broadcast
```

Notice that both programs were run from a normal user account, not `root`. It is only necessary to run as `root` while building a new kernel and executing the `route` commands.

Summary

Multicast IP is a great technique for efficiently broadcasting information to several programs simultaneously. In this chapter, you learned that broadcasting multicast IP is almost identical to sending data over a socket using UDP, but you have to do some extra work to receive multicast IP broadcasts. Possible applications for multicast IP are networked games and broadcasting audio and video data.

Non-blocking Socket I/O

by Mark Watson

CHAPTER 22

In all of the examples that you have seen so far, the sample programs block (or wait) when calling accept, recv, and recvfrom (recvfrom was used for connectionless sockets for UDP and multicast IP, and recv for the earlier examples using TCP protocol sockets). This blocking behavior may be the default, but it is not strictly necessary. You can use fcntl (with some care to preserve file attributes) to change sockets to non-blocking. What you do not want to do, however, is set a socket to non-blocking and have your program continually check (or poll) the socket to see if data is available; this wastes CPU time! One example of a good use of non-blocking I/O is a distributed game running on a local area network using UDP and multicast IP.

For a simple example, suppose that the game only supports a small number of players. At initialization, the game program reads a local configuration file containing the host name (or absolute IP address) of everyone on the local network who likes to play the game. This file also contains the standard port number for playing the game. The same port number is used for transmitting and receiving data. Most of the CPU time for the game is spent in calculating 3D geometries for solid figures, applying textures, and performing rendering. After each rendering cycle for a display frame, the program could quickly check non-blocking sockets for incoming messages. The sample program in the next section is much simpler: a single program broadcasts messages and checks for new messages using non-blocking sockets.

Sample Program for Non-blocking IO

Listing 22.1 shows an example for both sending and receiving data using multicast IP, UDP, and non-blocking sockets. While this sample program contains error checks on all system calls, these error checks are left out of the following discussion for brevity; as usual, any system call that returns a value less than zero indicates an error condition. The discussion in this section uses code fragments from the file broadcast_and_listen.c. The following statements declare the variables required for this sample program:

Listing 22.1   nb_broadcast_and_listen.c

```
// for setting up for broadcast:
int out_socket_descriptor;
struct sockaddr_in address;
// for setting up for listening for broadcasts
struct ip_mreq command;
u_char loop = 1;   // we want broadcast to also
                   // loop back to this computer
int i, iter = 0;
```

```
int sin_len;
char message[256];
int in_socket_descriptor;
struct sockaddr_in sin;
struct hostent *server_host_name;
long save_file_flags;
```

Most of these statements have been seen repeatedly in earlier examples, with a few additions:

1. We define both a socket descriptor (variable name is out_socket_descriptor) for broadcasting and data (struct sockaddr_in address and struct sockaddr_in sin) for a listening socket.

2. We define the struct ip_mreq command data object for setting group membership using the setsocket system call.

In the following code (from the broadcast_and_listen.c example), we call the socket function to create the output (or broadcast) socket with SOCK_DGRAM as the second argument so that the socket will be connectionless:

```
// For broadcasting, this socket can be treated like a UDP socket:
out_socket_descriptor = socket(AF_INET, SOCK_DGRAM, 0);
```

We want multiple processes on the same computer to have access to the same port, so we must use setsockopt to make the socket shareable:

```
// allow multiple processes to use this same port:
loop = 1;
setsockopt(out_socket_descriptor, SOL_SOCKET, SO_REUSEADDR,
          &loop, sizeof(loop));
```

We want to set the input socket in the normal way, except we specify a multicast IP address 224.0.0.1:

```
memset(&address, 0, sizeof(address));
address.sin_family = AF_INET;
address.sin_addr.s_addr = inet_addr("224.0.0.1");
address.sin_port = htons(port);
// Set up for listening:
server_host_name = gethostbyname(host_name);
bzero(&sin, sizeof(sin));
sin.sin_family = AF_INET;
sin.sin_addr.s_addr = htonl(INADDR_ANY);
sin.sin_port = htons(port);

in_socket_descriptor = socket(PF_INET, SOCK_DGRAM, 0);
```

It is often convenient to test on a single computer, so we set up the input socket so that multiple processes can share a port:

```
// allow multiple processes to use this same port:
loop = 1;
setsockopt(in_socket_descriptor, SOL_SOCKET, SO_REUSEADDR,
           &loop, sizeof(loop));
```

If you don't use this code to enable multiple listeners on a single port, you will need to test using two computers on the same network. We can now bind the input (or listening) socket to the shared port:

```
bind(in_socket_descriptor, (struct sockaddr *)&sin,
     sizeof(sin));
```

For testing on a single computer, we will specify that the input socket also listens for broadcasts from other processes running on the local machine:

```
// allow broadcast to this machine"
loop = 1;
setsockopt(in_socket_descriptor, IPPROTO_IP, IP_MULTICAST_LOOP,
           &loop, sizeof(loop));
```

We want to join a multicast broadcast group, as we did in the `listen.c` program in the directory `IPC/MULTICAST` that we saw in the last chapter.

```
// join the broadcast group:
command.imr_multiaddr.s_addr = inet_addr("224.0.0.1");
command.imr_interface.s_addr = htonl(INADDR_ANY);
if (command.imr_multiaddr.s_addr == -1) {
  printf("Error: group of 224.0.0.1 not a legal multicast address\n");
}
setsockopt(in_socket_descriptor, IPPROTO_IP, IP_ADD_MEMBERSHIP,
           &command, sizeof(command));
```

Finally, we must set the input socket as non-blocking. We first get the "file permissions" of the input socket descriptor, then add the NONBLOCK flag, then save the permissions back to the input socket descriptor using the `fcntl` system function:

```
// set socket to non-blocking:
save_file_flags = fcntl(in_socket_descriptor, F_GETFL);
save_file_flags |= O_NONBLOCK;
fcntl(in_socket_descriptor, F_SETFL, save_file_flags);
```

The main loop of the sample program both broadcasts over the output socket, and listens for messages on the non-blocking input socket. Notice that we broadcast a new message only every seven times through the `while` loop, but we check the non-blocking input socket every time through the loop:

```
// main loop that both broadcasts and listens:
while (iter++ < 20) {
  printf("%d iteration\n", iter);
```

```
    if ((iter % 7) == 0) { // do a broadcast every 7 times through loop
      printf("sending data...\n");
      sendto(out_socket_descriptor,
             "test from broadcast", sizeof("test from broadcast"),
             0, (struct sockaddr *)&address, sizeof(address));
    }
    sleep(1); // wait a second
    // see if there is any data to read on the non-blocking socket:
    sin_len = sizeof(sin);
    i = recvfrom(in_socket_descriptor, message, 256, 0,
                 (struct sockaddr *)&sin, &sin_len);
    if (i > 0) {
      printf("Response from server:\n\n%s\n", message);
    } else {
      printf("No data available to read\n");
    }
  }
}
```

Running the Non-blocking Sample Program

To test the non-blocking sample program in file nb_broadcast_and_listen.c, you should open two or more xterm windows and run nb_broadcast_and_listen in each window. I created three windows, and ran nb_broadcast_and_listen in all three (starting them as close together in time as possible). Here is example output from one of the windows:

```
~/test/IPC/NOBLOCK > nb_broadcast_and_listen
file flags=2
file flags after setting non-blocking=2050
Starting main loop to broadcast and listen...
1 iteration
Response from server:

test from broadcast
2 iteration
No data available to read
3 iteration
No data available to read
4 iteration
No data available to read
5 iteration
No data available to read
6 iteration
Response from server:

test from broadcast
7 iteration
```

```
sending data...
Response from server:

test from broadcast
8 iteration
Response from server:

test from broadcast
9 iteration
No data available to read
10 iteration
No data available to read
```

There were two other copies of the test program running in other windows. You will notice that in most of the iterations through the test loop, there was no data available on the non-blocking input socket.

Summary

The sample program in this chapter was fairly simple to implement. We did have to take special care to allow multiple socket listeners on a single computer and change the file permissions on the socket to non-blocking mode. There are many applications for non-blocking broadcast sockets such as networked games, local broadcast of audio and video data, and some distributed server applications. The best applications for non-blocking broadcast sockets usually require high performance and can tolerate occasional missed data packets.

A C++ Class Library for TCP Sockets

by Mark Watson

In This Chapter

CHAPTER 23

This chapter presents two simple C++ classes that you can use to add client/server socket communication between two programs by simply creating two objects: a client object and a server object. The actual code to perform the socket communications is copied directly from the `client.c` and `server.c` examples used in Chapter 19, "TCP/IP and Socket Programming."

Even though most of the examples in this book are written in the C language, I encourage you to consider C++ as the programming language of choice for Linux (in addition to Java, and special purpose languages like Perl, LISP, Prolog, and so on that are included with your Linux distribution). In fact, even if you prefer the non–object-oriented programming style of C, I still encourage you to build your C programs as C++ programs because the C++ compiler detects more errors at compilation time and C++ uses "type safe" linkages when calling functions and methods. "Type safe" linkages make it more difficult to call a function or method with an incorrect number of arguments, or arguments of the wrong data type. I have found C++ to be more effective on very large projects that I have worked on (with many developers) than C, including PC and Nintendo video games and a realtime fraud detection expert system. The "type safe" linkages in C++ make it easier to integrate code written by large programming teams.

Unfortunately, there is not space in this chapter to accommodate a tutorial on the use of C++, but you can open your favorite Web search engine and search for "C++ programming tutorial". I will also try to keep a few current links to C++ tutorials on my Web page, which supports my contributions to this book:

```
http://www.markwatson.com/books/linux_prog.html
```

Design of C++ Client/Server Classes

The primary requirement for the C++ `Client` and `Server` classes that we will develop in this chapter is ease of use when using these classes in your own programs. This is one of the major benefits of object-oriented programming: the "dirty details" of an object's behavior (the code that does the real work) are hidden in private code, working on private data. You should try to design your classes in any object-oriented language (for example, Java, C++, Smalltalk) with a small and clean public interface, hiding implementation details as private data and code.

Understanding Client Design

The public interface to the `Client` class is very simple: you construct a new client object with the name of the machine that the server object is running on, and the port number that the server object is listening to. The method signature for the constructor for the `Client` class looks like the following:

```
Client(char * host = "127.0.0.1", int port = 8080);
```

If you are just beginning to use C++, you may not have seen default values for arguments used before. With default values for both arguments, you can use a single constructor in many ways to build a new client object, as in the following examples:

```
Client client_1; // host="127.0.0.1", port=8080
Client client_2("buster.acomputercompany.com"); // port=8080
Client * p_client_3 = new Client("buster", 9020);
```

You want to make it easy for programs using the `Client` class to call a server object. The public method `getResponseFromServer` provides a simple interface to a remote server object. This method has the following method signature:

```
char * getResponseFromServer(char *command);
```

This method either blocks or waits for a response from a remote server object, or terminates on an error condition. Figure 23.1 shows the Unified Modeling Language (UML) class diagram for the `Client` class. If you can run Java on your system, you can get a free UML modeling tool at `www.togetherj.com`. This Web site also contains good tutorial information on using UML.

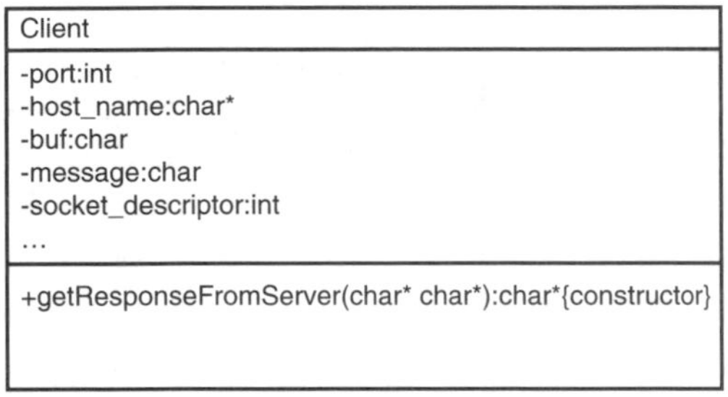

FIGURE 23.1
UML class diagram for the C++ `Client` class.

```
Client
-------------------------------------------
-port:int
-host_name:char*
-buf:char
-message:char
-socket_descriptor:int
...
-------------------------------------------
+getResponseFromServer(char* char*):char*{constructor}
```

Listing 23.1 shows the public and private interface for the `Client` class:

Listing 23.1   `Client.hxx`

```
class Client {
public:
  Client(char * host = "127.0.0.1", int port = 8080);
  char * getResponseFromServer(char * command);
private:
  int port;
  char * host_name;
```

continues

Listing 23.1   CONTINUED

```
char buf[8192];
char message[256];
int socket_descriptor;
struct sockaddr_in pin;
struct hostent *server_host_name;
};
```

The class definition for Client has only two public methods: the class constructor and the method getResponseFromServer. The class definition for Client does not contain any public data.

Understanding Server Design

The Server class will not be quite as easy to use as the Client class because in a real application, each server object typically performs unique tasks. The Server class contains only one public method: a class constructor. The first (and required) argument for the class constructor is a pointer to a function that will be called by the server object to process client requests. After this work function calculates the results for the client, the server object returns the data prepared by the work function to the client. The public method signatures for the constructor is:

```
Server(void (*do_work)(char *, char *, int), int port=8080);
```

The Server class allocates a protected memory buffer temp_buf that is used to hold data that will eventually be returned to the client object. Before calling the Server class constructor, your program must create a function with the following function signature:

```
void my_work_func(char *command,
                  char *return_buffer,
                  int return_buffer_size);
```

This function is passed as the first argument to the Server class constructor and is called to process each service request. You will see an example server application in the next section. Figure 23.2 shows the UML class diagram for the Server class.

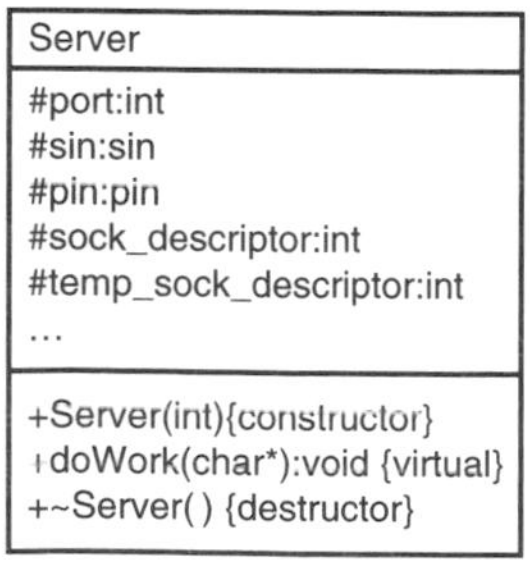

FIGURE 23.2

UML class diagram for the C++ Server class.

```
Server
────────────────────────────
#port:int
#sin:sin
#pin:pin
#sock_descriptor:int
#temp_sock_descriptor:int
...
────────────────────────────
+Server(int){constructor}
ı doWork(char*):void {virtual}
+~Server() {destructor}
```

Listing 23.2 shows the public and protected methods and data for the class `Server`.

Listing 23.2 `Server.hxx`

```
class Server {
public:
  Server(void (*a_work_func)(char *, char *, int), int port = 8080);
  ~Server(); // closes socket, etc.
private:
  void (*work_func)(char *, char *, int);
  int port;
  struct sockaddr_in sin;
  struct sockaddr_in pin;
  int sock_descriptor;
  int temp_sock_descriptor;
  char * temp_buf;
};
```

Implementation of C++ Client/Server Classes

The source files `Client.cxx` and `Server.cxx` in the IPC/C++ directory implement the `Client` and `Server` classes. These classes were simple to implement: mainly pasting in code from the files `client.c` and `server.c` in the directory IPC/SOCKETS. Since the actual implementation code was described in Chapter 19 (the socket programming examples `server.c` and `client.c`), this section will gloss over the socket programming code, and concentrate on the differences between the C and C++ code.

We have already performed the most important task in implementing the `Client` and `Server` classes in the preceding section: writing down the class requirements and designing the public interface for the classes. In large development teams using C++, the most senior developers usually design the classes and interfaces, and more junior team members "turn the crank" and implement the private class behavior. In the `Client` and `Server` classes, implementing the private behavior is as easy as cutting and pasting the example C code into the structure imposed by your simple design.

Implementing the Client

In implementing the `Client` class, you want to be able to reuse a single client object many times to make service requests to a specified server object. Here is the implementation of the `Client` class constructor:

```
Client::Client(char * my_host_name, int my_port) {
  port = my_port;
  host_name = my_host_name;

  if ((server_host_name = gethostbyname(host_name)) == 0) {
    perror("Error resolving local host\n");
    exit(1);
  }

  bzero(&pin, sizeof(pin));
  pin.sin_family = AF_INET;
  pin.sin_addr.s_addr=htonl(INADDR_ANY);
  pin.sin_addr.s_addr =
    ((struct in_addr*)(server_host_name->h_addr))->s_addr;
  pin.sin_port = htons(port);
}
```

You resolve the host computer name and set up the data required to open a socket connection in the `Client` constructor, but you do not actually create a socket interface. The rationale for this is simple: a client object might be created, used for a service request, then not reused for hours, or days. You do not want to tie up a socket connection with the server. Instead, you put the behavior of creating the socket connection in the method `getResponseFromServer`:

```
char * Client::getResponseFromServer(char * str) {

  if ((socket_descriptor = socket(AF_INET, SOCK_STREAM, 0)) == -1)
  {
    perror("Error opening socket\n");
    exit(1);
  }

  if (connect(socket_descriptor,
              (const sockaddr *)&pin, sizeof(pin)) == -1) {
    perror("Error connecting to socket\n");
    exit(1);
  }
  cout << "Sending message '" << str << "' to server...\n";

  if (send(socket_descriptor, str, strlen(str), 0) == -1) {
    perror("Error in send\n");
```

```
      exit(1);
   }

   cout << "..sent message.. wait for response...\n";

   if (recv(socket_descriptor, buf, 8192, 0) == -1) {
     perror("Error in receiving response from server\n");
     exit(1);
   }

   close(socket_descriptor);

   cout << "\nResponse from server:\n" << buf << "\n";
   return buf;
}
```

The system calls for `socket`, `connect`, `send`, `recv`, and `close` were described in Chapter 19.

Implementing the Server

The constructor for the `Server` class is unusual in the sense that the constructor does not return to the calling program. The constructor sets up a processing loop and runs forever. The implementation of the `Server` class constructor is similar to the `server.c` sample program seen in Chapter 19:

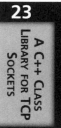

```
Server::Server(void (*a_work_func)(char *,
                                   char *,
                                   int),
               int my_port) {
  work_func = a_work_func;
  port = my_port;
  int address_size;
  int i, len;
  char buf[4000]; // for receiving data from clients

  temp_buf = new char[16384]; // space for return data

  sock_descriptor = socket(AF_INET, SOCK_STREAM, 0);
  if (sock_descriptor == -1) {
    perror("call to socket");
    exit(1);
  }

  bzero(&sin, sizeof(sin));
  sin.sin_family = AF_INET;
```

```
sin.sin_addr.s_addr = INADDR_ANY;
sin.sin_port = htons(port);

if (bind(sock_descriptor, (struct sockaddr *)&sin,
        sizeof(sin)) == -1) {
  perror("call to bind");
  exit(1);
}

if (listen(sock_descriptor, 20) == -1) {
  perror("call to listen");
  exit(1);
}
while(1) {
  temp_sock_descriptor =
    accept(sock_descriptor, (struct sockaddr *)&pin,
          &address_size);
  if (temp_sock_descriptor == -1) {
    perror("call to accept");
    exit(1);
  }

  if (recv(temp_sock_descriptor, buf, 4000, 0) == -1) {
    perror("call to recv");
    exit(1);
  }

  // this calls the work function passed
  // to the class constructor:
  work_func(buf, temp_buf, 16384);

  // the virtual function doWork has filled in the
  // data to be returned to the client in 'temp_buf':

  len = strlen(temp_buf);

  if (send(temp_sock_descriptor,
          temp_buf, len, 0) == -1) {
    perror("call to send");
    exit(1);
  }

  close(temp_sock_descriptor);

  }
}
```

The Server class constructor uses calls to socket, bind, listen, accept, and recv to set up socket connections to remote client objects. The main processing loop in the constructor calls the my_work function with each new service request, waits for my_work to place return data in the `temp_buf` buffer, then returns data to the client object. The following section contains an example of writing a work function, creating a server object, and handling client requests.

Testing the C++ Client/Server Classes

The Server class contains as private data a pointer to a work function that is called to process each client request. The following simple test program defines a simple work function that returns a message to the client, and then creates a server object to handle remote client requests.

```cpp
#include <iostream.h>
#include "Server.hxx"

void my_work_func(char *command, char *return_buffer,
                  int return_buffer_size) {
  cout << "entering my_work_func(" << command << ",...)\n";
  sprintf(return_buffer,"overriden my_work_func.  %s", command);
}

void main() {
  Server * server = new Server(my_work_func); // default to port=8080
}
```

In this example, you could also have created a server object directly instead of using the new operator:

```cpp
Server server(my_work_func);
```

The following short program can be used to test the Client class:

```cpp
#include <iostream.h>
#include "Client.hxx"

void main() {
  // default to host="127.0.0.1", port=8080
  // in the CLient constructor call:

  Client * client = new Client();char * s;
  char buf[100];
  sprintf(buf,"This is a test");
  s = client->getResponseFromServer(buf);
  cout << "Server response: " << s << "\n";
  sprintf(buf,"This is a another test");
  s = client->getResponseFromServer(buf);
  cout << "Server response: " << s << "\n";
  delete client; // closes the socket connection
}
```

The following output is seen when running the `test_client.cpp` sample program:

```
markw@colossus:/home/markw/MyDocs/LinuxBook/src/IPC/C++ > make
g++ -c Client.cpp
g++ -o test_client test_client.cpp Client.o
g++ -c Server.cpp
g++ -o test_server test_server.cpp Server.o
markw@colossus:/home/markw/MyDocs/LinuxBook/src/IPC/C++ > test_client
Sending message 'This is a test' to server...
..sent message.. wait for response...

Response from server:
overriden my_work_func.  This is a test
Server response: overriden my_work_func.  This is a test
Sending message 'This is a another test' to server...
..sent message.. wait for response...

Response from server:
overriden my_work_func.  This is a another test
Server response: overriden my_work_func.  This is a another test
markw@colossus:/home/markw/MyDocs/LinuxBook/src/IPC/C++ >
```

The following output is seen when running the `test_server.cpp` sample program:

```
markw@colossus:/home/markw/MyDocs/LinuxBook/src/IPC/C++ > test_server
entering my_work_func(This is a test,...)
entering my_work_func(This is a another test,...)
```

Summary

This chapter hopefully serves two purposes: introducing some readers to C++ and providing an example of wrapping socket programs in C++ classes to make using sockets easier. This chapter was not a tutorial on C++; interested readers should search the Internet for "C++ programming tutorial" and invest some time in learning the language. C is a great language for writing small programs with a small number of programmers, but C++ is a much better language for large projects.

Using Libraries

by Kurt Wall

IN THIS CHAPTER

CHAPTER 24

This chapter looks at creating and using programming libraries, collections of code that can be used (and reused) across multiple software projects. First, though, we'll examine some of the issues surrounding the two versions of the Linux C library (yes, there are two fundamentally incompatible versions out there).

Libraries are a classic example of software development's Holy Grail, code reuse. They collect commonly used programming routines into a single location. The system C library is an example. It contains hundreds of frequently used routines, such as the output function `printf()` and the input function `getchar()` that would be tedious to rewrite each time you create a new program. Beyond code reuse and programmer convenience, however, libraries provide a great deal of utility code, such as functions for network programming, graphics handling, data manipulation, and, most importantly, system calls.

Comparing `libc5` and `libc6`

Before delving into library usage proper, you need to know about the two competing C libraries, `libc5` and `libc6`, also known as `glibc2`. `libc5` and `libc6` do not actually compete, but the Linux world is moving from the old, very Linux-specific `libc5` (some systems use `glibc1` as a synonym) to the more general, faster, and much more standards-compliant and extensible `libc6`.

`libc5` evolved in parallel with Linux—as Linux matured, the original GNU C library was modified to coincide with kernel changes. While this made for the C library tightly integrated with Linux, it also made the basic library difficult to maintain for other operating systems using GNU's C library. In addition, `libc5`'s heavy reliance on Linux's kernel headers created an unwise set of dependencies. As Linus made changes to kernel headers, these changes had to be regressed into the C library, creating maintenance problems for Linus, the kernel development team, and the C library maintainer. It also slowed kernel development. Conversely, as the C library changed, these changes had to be incorporated into the kernel. In fact, some parts of the kernel relied on undocumented, and thus subject to change, features of the C library and, in some cases, outright bugs.

This situation changed dramatically in 1997 with the first release of `libc6/glibc2`. Almost all of its dependencies on the Linux kernel headers were eliminated, in addition to the following changes:

- The new library was made thread-safe.
- An easily extensible scheme for handling name databases was added.

- The math library was corrected and in many cases speeded up.

- Standards compliance, such as with POSIX.1, POSIX.2, ISO/ANSI C, and XPG4.2 became a reality, or much closer to it.

The price for these enhancements and improvements, however, was introducing fundamental incompatibilities between libc5 and libc6. Until all Linux distributions move to libc6, Linux users have to be aware of and deal with this incompatibility. Distribution builders, such as Caldera and Red Hat, have to provide compatibility libraries to enable users to run programs that depend on one or the other of the library versions while simultaneously basing their distributions on the other library. Worse still, because the C library is so pervasive and fundamental on any Linux (or UNIX) system, upgrading from libc5 to libc6 is a difficult undertaking and, if done incorrectly or carelessly, can render a system unusable.

"What's your point?" I hear you asking. There are several. First, if you are in the market for a new Linux distribution, you can finesse the whole upgrade issue by using a libc6-based distribution. Secondly, if you are a developer, you have to decide whether you will support libc5, libc6, or both. Finally, the entire discussion provides an excellent object lesson in software development, highlighting in international orange the importance of good design and the far-reaching impact of interface changes in core software components. The lesson is simply that thoughtful software design will at least attempt to provide a general, extensible public interface and minimize the necessity for changes that will introduce core incompatibilities.

Library Tools

Before jumping into library creation and usage, this section takes a quick tour of the tools you will need to create, maintain, and manage programming libraries. More detailed information can be found in the manual pages and info documents for each of the commands and programs discussed in the following sections.

Understanding the nm Command

The nm command lists all of the symbols encoded in an object or binary file. One use would be to see what function calls a program makes. Another might be to see if a library or object files provides a needed function. nm uses the following syntax:

```
nm [options] file
```

nm lists the symbols stored in file. Table 24.1 describes useful options for nm.

Table 24.1 nm OPTIONS

Option	Description
-C¦-demangle	Convert symbol names into user-level names, especially useful for making C++ function names readable.
-s¦-print-armap	When used on archive (.a) files, also print the index that maps symbol names to the modules or member names in which the symbol is defined.
-u¦-undefined-only	Only display undefined symbols, symbols defined externally to the file being examined.
-l¦-line-numbers	Use debugging information to print the line number where each symbol is defined, or the relocation entry if the symbol is undefined.

Understanding the ar Command

The ar command uses the following syntax:

```
ar {dmpqrtx} [member] archive files...
```

ar creates, modifies, or extracts archives. It is most commonly used to create static libraries—files that contain one or more object files, called members, of subroutines in precompiled format. ar also creates and maintains a table that cross-references symbol names to the members in which they are defined. Table 24.2 describes the most commonly used ar options.

Table 24.2 ar OPTIONS

Option	Description
-c	Create archive if it doesn't exist from files, suppressing the warning ar would emit if archive doesn't exist.
-s	Create or update the map linking symbols to the member in which they are defined.
-r	Insert files into the archive, replacing any existing members whose name matches that being added. New members are added at the end of the archive.
-q	Add files to the end of archive without checking for replacements.

> **TIP**
>
> Given an archive created with the `ar` command, you can speed up access to the archive by creating an index to the archive. Ranlib does precisely this, storing the index in the archive file itself. `ranlib`'s syntax is:
>
> ```
> ranlib [-v¦-V] file
> ```
>
> This generates a symbol map in `file`. It is equivalent to `ar -s file`.

Understanding the `ldd` Command

The `nm` command lists the symbols defined in an object file, but unless you know what library defines which functions, `ldd` is much more useful. `ldd` lists the shared libraries that a program requires in order to run. Its syntax is:

```
ldd [options] file
```

`ldd` prints the names of the shared libraries required by `file`. For example, on my system, the mail client `mutt` requires five shared libraries, as illustrated below:

```
$ ldd /usr/bin/mutt
        libnsl.so.1 => /lib/libnsl.so.1 (0x40019000)
        libslang.so.1 => /usr/lib/libslang.so.1 (0x4002e000)
        libm.so.6 => /lib/libm.so.6 (0x40072000)
        libc.so.6 => /lib/libc.so.6 (0x4008f000)
        /lib/ld-linux.so.2 => /lib/ld-linux.so.2 (0x40000000)
```

Table 24.3 describes some of `ldd`'s useful options.

Table 24.3   `ldd` OPTIONS

Option	Description
-d	Perform relocations and report any missing functions
-r	Perform relocations for both function and data objects and report any missing functions or data objects

Understanding `ldconfig`

The `ldconfig` command uses the following syntax:

```
ldconfig [options] [libs]
```

`ldconfig` determines the runtime links required by shared libraries that are located in `/usr/lib` and `/lib`, specified in `libs` on the command-line, and stored in `/etc/ld.so.conf`. `ldconfig` works in conjunction with `ld.so`, the dynamic linker/loader, to create and maintain links to the most current versions of shared libraries. Table 24.4 describes typically used options; a bare `ldconfig` updates the cache file.

Table 24.4 `ldconfig` OPTIONS

Option	Description
-p	Merely print the contents of `/etc/ld.so.cache`, the current list of shared libraries about which ld.so knows.
-v	Verbosely update `/etc/ld.so.cache`, listing each library's version number, the directory scanned, and any links that are created or updated.

Environment Variables and Configuration Files

The dynamic linker/loader `ld.so` uses two environment variables. The first is `$LD_LIBRARY_PATH`, a colon-separated list of directories in which to search for shared libraries at runtime. It is similar to the `$PATH` environment variable. The second variable is `$LD_PRELOAD`, a whitespace-separated list of additional, user-specified, shared libraries to be loaded before all others. This can be used to selectively override functions in other shared libraries.

`ld.so` also uses two configuration files whose purposes parallel the environment variables mentioned in the preceding paragraph. `/etc/ld.so.conf` is a list of directories that the linker/loader should search for shared libraries in addition to the standard directories, `/usr/lib` and `/lib`. `/etc/ld.so.preload` is a disk-based version of the `$LD_PRELOAD` environment variable: it contains a whitespace-separated list of shared libraries to be loaded prior to executing a program.

Writing and Using Static Libraries

Static libraries (and shared libraries, for that matter) are files that contain object files, called modules or members, of reusable, precompiled code. They are stored in a special format along with a table or map linking symbol names to the members in which the symbols are defined. The map speeds up compilation and linking. Static libraries are typically named with a .a (for archive) extension.

To use library code, include its header file in your source code and link against the library. For example, consider Listing 24.1, a header file for a simple error-handling library, and Listing 24.2, the corresponding source code.

Listing 24.1   liberr.h

```
1   /*
2    * liberr.h
3    * Declarations for simple error-handling library
4    * Listing 24.1
5    */
6   #ifndef _LIBERR_H
7   #define _LIBERR_H
8
9   #include <stdarg.h>
10
11  #define MAXLINELEN 4096
12
13  /*
14   * Print an error message to stderr and return to caller
15   */
16  void err_ret(const char *fmt, ...);
17
18  /*
19   * Print an error message to stderr and exit
20   */
21  void err_quit(const char *fmt, ...);
22
23  /*
24   * Print an error message to logfile and return to caller
25   */
26  void log_ret(char *logfile, const char *fmt, ...);
27
28  /*
29   * Print a error message to logfile and exit
30   */
31  void log_quit(char *logfile, const char *fmt, ...);
32
33  /*
34   * Print an error message and return to caller
35   */
36  void err_prn(const char *fmt, va_list ap, char *logfile);
37
38  #endif _LIBERR_H
```

24

USING LIBRARIES

Listing 24.2 `liberr.c`

```
1   /*
2    * liberr.c
3    * Implementation of error-handling library
4    * Listing 24.2
5    */
6   #include      <errno.h> /* for definition of errno */
7   #include      <stdarg.h>
8   #include      <stdlib.h>
9   #include      <stdio.h>
10  #include      ?liberr.h"
11
12  void err_ret(const char *fmt, ...)
13  {
14      va_list ap;
15
16      va_start(ap, fmt);
17      err_prn(fmt, ap, NULL);
18      va_end(ap);
19      return;
20  }
21
22  void err_quit(const char *fmt, ...)
23  {
24      va_list ap;
25
26      va_start(ap, fmt);
27      err_prn(fmt, ap, NULL);
28      va_end(ap);
29      exit(1);
30  }
31
32  void log_ret(char *logfile, const char *fmt, ...)
33  {
34      va_list ap;
35
36      va_start(ap, fmt);
37      err_prn(fmt, ap, logfile);
38      va_end(ap);
39      return;
40  }
41
42  void log_quit(char *logfile, const char *fmt, ...)
43  {
44      va_list ap;
45
46      va_start(ap, fmt);
47      err_prn(fmt, ap, logfile);
48      va_end(ap);
49      exit(1);
```

```
50  }
51
52  extern void err_prn(const char *fmt, va_list ap, char *logfile)
53  {
54      int     save_err;
55      char buf[MAXLINELEN];
56      FILE *plf;
57
58      save_err = errno; /* value caller might want printed */
59      vsprintf(buf, fmt, ap);
60      sprintf(buf + strlen(buf), ?: %s", strerror(save_err));
61      strcat(buf, ?\n");
62      fflush(stdout); /* in case stdout and stderr are the same */
63      if(logfile != NULL)
64          if((plf = fopen(logfile, ?a")) != NULL) {
65              fputs(buf, plf);
66              fclose(plf);
67          } else
68              fputs(?failed to open log file\n, stderr);
69      else
70          fputs(buf, stderr);
71      fflush(NULL); /* flush everything */
72      return;
73  }
```

Note

Readers of Richard Stevens' *Advanced Programming in the UNIX Environment* will recognize much of this code. I have used this code for many years because it neatly met my needs for basic error-handling routines. I am indebted to Stevens' generosity in allowing me to reproduce this code here.

24

USING LIBRARIES

A few remarks about the code may be helpful. We include <stdarg.h> in Listing 24.1 because we use ANSI C's variable length argument list facility (If you are unfamiliar with variable length argument lists, consult your favorite C reference manual). To protect against multiple inclusion of the header file, we wrap the header in a preprocessor macro, _LIBERR_H. Do not use these error logging functions log_ret() and log_quit() in production code; the system logging facility defined in <syslog.h> is more appropriate. Finally, this library should not be used in a program that runs as a daemon because it writes to stderr. Such output makes no sense for a daemon because daemons usually do not have a controlling terminal.

To create a static library, the first step is compiling your code to object form:

```
$ gcc -H -c liberr.c -o liberr.o
```

Next, use the `ar` utility to create an archive:

```
$ ar rcs liberr.a liberr.o
```

If all went well, the static library `liberr.a` was created. The output of `nm liberr.a` should prove instructive:

```
 1
 2  liberr.o:
 3            U _IO_stderr_
 4            U _IO_stdout_
 5  000000f0 T err_prn
 6  00000030 T err_quit
 7  00000000 T err_ret
 8            U errno
 9            U exit
10            U fclose
11            U fflush
12            U fopen
13            U fputs
14  000000b0 T log_quit
15  00000070 T log_ret
16            U sprintf
17            U strcat
18            U strerror
19            U strlen
20            U vsprintf
```

Line 2 is the member name. Lines 3–20 list the symbols defined in this archive. The default output format is a three-column list consisting of the symbol value, the symbol type, and the symbol name. A symbol type of U means that the symbol, for example, `fopen` (line 12), is undefined in this member; a T means the symbol exists in the text or code area of the object file. See the `binutils` info page (`info binutils nm`) for a complete description of `nm`'s output.

With the archive created, we need a driver program to test it. Listing 24.3 shows the results of our test. We attempt to open a non-existent file four times, once for each of the four error-handling functions in the library.

Listing 24.3 `errtest.c`

```
1  /*
2   * errtest.c
```

```
3    * Test program for error-handling library
4    * Listing 24.3
5    */
6
7    #include <stdio.h>
8    #include <stdlib.h>
9    #include "liberr.h"
10
11   #define ERR_QUIT_SKIP 1
12   #define LOG_QUIT_SKIP 1
13
14   int main(void)
15   {
16       FILE *pf;
17
18       fputs("Testing err_ret()...\n", stdout);
19       if((pf = fopen("foo", "r")) == NULL)
20           err_ret("%s %s", "err_ret()", "failed to open foo");
21
22       fputs("Testing log_ret()...\n", stdout);
23       if((pf = fopen("foo", "r")) == NULL);
24           log_ret("errtest.log", "%s %s", "log_ret()",
25           "failed to open foo");
26
27       #ifndef ERR_QUIT_SKIP
28       fputs("Testing err_quit()...\n", stdout);
29       if((pf = fopen("foo", "r")) == NULL)
30           err_ret("%s %s", "err_quit()", "failed to open foo");
31       #endif /* ERR_QUIT_SKIP */
32
33       #ifndef LOG_QUIT_SKIP
34       fputs("Testing log_quit()...\n", stdout);
35       if((pf = fopen("foo", "r")) == NULL)
36           log_ret("errtest.log", "%s %s", "log_quit()",
37            "failed to open foo");
38       #endif /* LOG_QUIT_SKIP */
39
40       return EXIT_SUCCESS;
41   }
```

24

The macros on lines 11 and 12 prevent execution of the *_quit() functions on lines
26–30 and 32–36, respectively. To test them, comment out one of the macros and recompile, and then comment out the other and recompile.

Compile the test program using this command line:

```
$ gcc -g errtest.c -o errtest -L. -lerr
```

As discussed in Chapter 3, "GNU cc," -L. tells the linker to look in the current directory for additional libraries, and -lerr specifies the library against which we want to link. Running the program gives the following results:

```
$ ./errtest
Testing err_ret()...
err_ret() failed to open foo: No such file or directory
Testing log_ret()...
```

The function log_ret() writes its output to errtest.log. Using the cat command on errtest.log yields the following:

```
$ cat errtest.log
log_ret() failed to open foo: No such file or directory
```

The testing of the *_quit() functions are left as exercises for you.

Writing and Using Shared Libraries

Shared libraries have several advantages over static libraries. First, shared libraries consume fewer system resources. They use less disk space because shared library code is not compiled into each binary but linked and loaded dynamically at runtime. They use less system memory because the kernel shares the memory the library occupies among all the programs that use the library. Second, shared libraries are marginally faster because they only need to be loaded into memory once. Finally, shared libraries simplify code maintenance. As bugs are fixed or features added, users need only obtain the updated library and install it. With static libraries, each program that uses the library must be recompiled.

The dynamic linker/loader, ld.so, links symbol names to the appropriate shared library at runtime. Shared libraries have a special name, the soname, that consists of the library name and the major version number. The full name of the C library on one of my systems, for example, is libc.so.5.4.46. The library name is libc.so; the major version number is 5; the minor version number is 4; 46 is the release or patch level. So, the C library's soname is libc.so.5. The new C library, libc6 (discussed at the beginning of this chapter) has an soname of libc.so.6—the change in major version numbers indicates a significant library change, to the extent that the two libraries are incompatible. Minor version numbers and patch level numbers change as bugs are fixed, but the soname remains the same and newer versions are usually compatible with older versions.

Applications link against the soname. The ldconfig utility creates a symbolic link from the actual library, libc.so.5.4.46, to the soname, libc.so.5, and stores this information in the /etc/ld.so.cache. At runtime, ld.so reads the cache, finds the required soname and, because of the symbolic link, loads the actual library into memory and links application function calls to the appropriate symbols in the loaded library.

Library versions become incompatible under the following conditions:

- Exported function interfaces change
- New function interfaces are added
- Function behavior changes from the original specification
- Exported data structures change
- Exported data structures are added

To maintain library compatibility, follow these guidelines:

- Add functions to your library with new names instead of changing existing functions or changing their behavior
- Only add items to the end of existing data structures, and either make them optional or initialize them inside the library
- Don't expand data structures used in arrays

Building shared libraries differs slightly from building static libraries. The process of building shared libraries is outlined in the list below:

1. When compiling the object file, use gcc's `-fPIC` option, which generates Position Independent Code that can link and load at any address.
2. Don't strip (remove debugging symbols from) the object file and don't use gcc's `-fomit-frame-pointer` option—doing so could possibly make debugging impossible.
3. Use gcc's `-shared` and `-soname` options.
4. Use gcc's `-Wl` option to pass arguments to the linker, `ld`.
5. Explicitly link against the C library, using gcc's `-l` option.

Returning to the error-handling library, to create a shared library, first build the object file:

```
$ gcc -fPIC -g -c liberr.c -o liberr.o
```

Next, link the library:

```
$ gcc -g -shared -Wl,-soname,liberr.so -o liberr.so.1.0.0 liberr.o -lc
```

Because we will not install this library as a system library in /usr or /usr/lib, we need to create two links, one for the soname:

```
$ ln -s liberr.so.1.0.0 liberr.so.1
```

24

USING LIBRARIES

and one for the linker to use when linking against `liberr`, using `-lerr`:

```
$ ln -s liberr.so.1.0.0 liberr.so
```

Now, to use the new shared library, we revisit the test program introduced in the last section in Listing 24.3. We need to tell the linker what library to use and where to find it, so we will use the `-l` and `-L` options:

```
$ gcc -g errtest.c -o errtest -L. -lerr
```

Finally, to execute the program, we need to tell `ld.so`, the dynamic linker/loader, where to find the shared library:

```
$ LD_LIBRARY_PATH=$(pwd) ./errtest
```

As pointed out earlier, the environment variable `$LD_LIBRARY_PATH` adds the path it contains to the trusted library directories `/lib` and `/usr/lib`. `ld.so` will search the path specified in the environment variable first, ensuring that it finds your library. An alternative to the awkward command linc is to add thc path to your library to `/etc/ld.so.conf` and update the cache (`/etc/ld.so.cache`) by running (as root) `ldconfig`. Yet another alternative is to place your library in `/usr/lib`, create a symbolic link to the soname, and run (as root) `ldconfig` to update the cache file. The advantage of the last method is that you do not have to add the library search path using gcc's `-L` option.

Using Dynamically Loaded Shared Objects

One more way to use shared libraries is to load them dynamically at runtime, not as libraries linked and loaded automatically, but as entirely separate modules you explicitly load using the `dlopen` interface. You might want to use the `dl` (dynamic loading) interface because it provides greater flexibility for both the programmer and end user, and because the `dl` interface is a more general solution.

Suppose, for example, you are writing the next killer graphics manipulation and creation program. Within your application, you handle graphical data in a proprietary but easy-to-use way. However, you want to be able to import and export from and to any of the literally hundreds of available graphics file formats. One way to achieve this would be to write one or more libraries, of the sort discussed in this chapter, to handle importing and exporting from and to the various formats. Although it is a modular approach, each library change would require recompilation, as would the addition of new formats.

The dl interface enables a different approach: designing a generic, format-neutral interface for reading, writing, and manipulating graphics files of any format. To add a new or modified graphics format to your application, you simply write a new module to deal with that format and make your application aware that it exists, perhaps by modifying a configuration file or placing the new module in a predefined directory (the plug-ins that augment the Netscape Web browser's capabilities use a variation of this approach). To extend your application's capabilities, users simply need to obtain new modules (or plug-ins); they (or you) do not need to recompile your application, only to edit a configuration file or copy the module to a preset directory. Existing code in your application loads the new modules and, voilá, you can import and export a new graphic format.

The dl interface (which is itself implemented as a library, `libdl`), contains functions to load, search, and unload shared objects. To use these functions, include `<dlfcn.h>` in your source code and link against `libdl` using `-ldl` in your compilation command or `make` file. Notice that you don't have to link against the library you want to use. Even though you use a standard shared library, you do not use it the normal way. The linker never knows about shared objects and, in fact, the modules do not even need to exist when you build the application.

Understanding the dl Interface

The dl interface provides four functions to handle all of the tasks necessary to load, use, and unload shared objects.

Loading Shared Objects

To load a shared object, use the `dlopen()` function, which is prototyped below:

```
void *dlopen(const char *filename, int flag);
```

`dlopen()` loads the shared object specified in `filename` in the mode specified by `flag`. `filename` can be an absolute pathname, a bare filename, or NULL. If it is NULL, `dlopen` opens the currently executing program, that is, your program. If `filename` is an absolute pathname, `dlopen` opens that file. If it is a bare filename, `dlopen` looks in the following locations, in the order given, to find the file: `$LD_ELF_LIBRARY_PATH`, `$LD_LIBRARY_PATH`, `/etc/ld.so.cache`, `/usr/lib`, and `/lib`.

`flag` can be `RTLD_LAZY`, meaning that symbols from the loaded object will be resolved as they are called, or `RTLD_NOW`, which means that that all symbols from the loaded object will be resolved before `dlopen()` returns. Either flag, if logically OR-ed with `RTLD_GLOBAL`, will cause all symbols to be exported, just as if they had been directly linked.

`dlopen()` returns a handle to the loaded object if it finds `filename`, or returns NULL otherwise.

Using Shared Objects

Before you can use any code in a demand-loaded library, you have to know what you are looking for and be able to access it somehow. The `dlsym()` function meets both needs. It is prototyped as:

```
void *dlsym(void *handle, char *symbol);
```

`dlsym()` searches for the symbol or function named in `symbol` in the loaded object to which `handle` refers. `handle` must be a handle returned by `dlopen()`; `symbol` is a standard, C-style string.

`dlsym()` returns a void pointer to the symbol or NULL on failure.

Checking for Errors

As I wrote in Chapter 13, "Handling Errors," robust code checks for and handles as many errors as possible. The `dlerror()` function allows you to find out more about an error that occurs when using dynamically loaded objects.

```
const char *dlerror(void);
```

If any of the other functions fails, `dlerror()` returns a string describing the error and resets the error string to NULL. As a result, a second immediate call to `dlerror()` will return NULL.

`Dlerror()` returns a string describing the most recent error, or returns NULL otherwise.

Unloading Shared Objects

In order to conserve system resources, particularly memory, when you are through using the code in a shared object, unload it. However, because of the time overhead involved in loading and unloading shared objects, be certain you will not need it at all, or soon, before unloading it. `Dlclose()`, prototyped below, closes a shared object.

```
int dlclose(void *handle);
```

dlclose() unloads the shared object to which `handle` refers. The call also invalidates `handle`. Because the `dl` library maintains link counts for dynamic libraries, they are not deallocated and their resources returned to the operating system until `dlclose()` has been called on a dynamic library as many times as `dlopen()` was successfully called on it.

Using the dl Interface

To illustrate the usage of the dl interface, we revisit our trusty error-handling library one last time, providing a new driver program, shown in Listing 24.4.

Listing 24.4   dltest.c

```
 1  /*
 2   * dltest.c
 3   * Dynamically load liberr.so and call err_ret()
 4   * Listing 24.4
 5   */
 6  #include <stdio.h>
 7  #include <stdlib.h>
 8  #include <dlfcn.h>
 9
10  int main(void)
11  {
12      void *handle;
13      void (*errfcn)();
14      const char *errmsg;
15      FILE *pf;
16
17      handle = dlopen("liberr.so", RTLD_NOW);
18      if(handle == NULL) {
19          fprintf(stderr, "Failed to load liberr.so: %s\n", dlerror());
20          exit(EXIT_FAILURE);
21      }
22
23      dlerror();
24      errfcn = dlsym(handle, "err_ret");
25      if((errmsg = dlerror()) != NULL) {
26          fprintf(stderr, "Didn't find err_ret(): %s\n", errmsg);
27          exit(EXIT_FAILURE);
28      }
29      if((pf = fopen("foobar", "r")) == NULL)
30          errfcn("couldn't open foobar");
31
32      dlclose(handle);
33      return EXIT_SUCCESS;
34  }
```

24

USING LIBRARIES

The command line used to compile Listing 24.4 was:

```
$ gcc -g -Wall dltest.c -o dltest -ldl
```

As you can see, we neither link against `liberr` nor include `liberr.h` in the source code. All access to `liberr.so` comes through the `dl` interface. With the possible exception of the use of a function pointer, Listing 24.4 is straightforward. Lines 23–27 illustrate the correct way to use the `dlerror()` function. We call `dlerror()` once to reset the error string to NULL (line 23), call `dlsym()`, then call `dlerror()` again, saving its return value in another variable so we can use the string later. On line 30, we call `errfcn()` as we normally would. Finally, we unload the shared object and exit. If all has gone well, a sample session of `dltest` will resemble the following:

```
$ LD_LIBRARY_PATH=$(pwd) ./dltest
couldn't open foobar: No such file or directory
```

This is the output we expected. Compare it to the output of Listing 24.2.

> **NOTE**
>
> If you are not familiar with function pointers (see lines 13, 24, and 30 of Listing 24.4), quickly review them in the reference manual of you choice. Briefly, however, line 13 says that `errfcn` is a pointer to a function that has no arguments and that returns nothing (void).

> **NOTE**
>
> Appendix A introduces a symbol table library developed by Mark Whitis. It illustrates the design issues involved in creating a programming library as well as the nuts and bolts of building and maintaining library code. The library itself is also intrinsically useful. I encourage you to check it out.

Summary

This chapter examined a variety of ways to reuse code, using static and shared libraries and dynamically loading shared objects at runtime. The most common usage under Linux is shared libraries.

Device Drivers

by Mark Whitis

CHAPTER 25

This chapter shows how to write a kernel level device driver, specifically in the form of a loadable kernel module. I will present a real world device driver for a stepper motor controller.

Three levels of experimentation are possible with this driver. You can actually build the circuit from the included schematic (see Figure 25.1 in "The Demonstration Hardware" section later in the chapter). You can run the driver on an unused parallel printer port without the circuit attached and optionally view the signals with a logic probe, oscilloscope, or similar device. Or, you can run the driver with the port I/O operations disabled, which will allow you to experiment with the driver without a free parallel port.

The stepper motor driver was chosen both because I need such a driver for my own use and because it is one of the simplest drivers I could think of that would illustrate the use of most of the programming needed to implement a real driver; many other drivers would either be too simple or too complex. It was also selected because I can provide documentation for the hardware along with the driver.

Types of Drivers

Kernel level device drivers are not necessary for many devices. However, there are a variety of types for when they are. This section introduces the different types of drivers and how they are used with the kernel.

Statically Linked Kernel Device Drivers

Device drivers can be compiled and linked directly into the kernel. Statically linked modules once compiled into the kernel remain attached to the kernel until it is rebuilt. Now that loadable kernel modules (LKM) exist, they are preferable. These modules can be loaded and removed without having to relink your kernel. This allows for dynamic configuration of your system. Writing a statically linked driver is almost the same as writing a loadable kernel module. The statically linked and loadable kernel modules are very similar in nature, but the LKM is now the more accepted method.

Loadable Kernel Modules

Loadable Kernel Modules can be loaded and unloaded while the system is running, hence the name. This is a great improvement over having to modify, recompile, and reinstall a new kernel and then reboot every time you want to test a new version. Because it is optional and loaded at runtime, the GPL license on the kernel should not taint your driver code. LKMs do not use up kernel memory when they are not being used and can easily be distributed separately from the kernel.

Shared Libraries

In some cases, the driver can be implemented as a shared library. This is not appropriate if the driver needs special privileges or has special timing needs. Typically, these will be used for higher level drivers that communicate with the hardware using a standard low-level driver (such as the generic SCSI driver).

The SANE scanner library, mentioned in Chapter 2, "Setting Up a Development System," is an example of a shared-library based driver system. The generic SANE scanner shared library selects the appropriate model-specific shared library and dynamically loads it. The model-specific shared library communicates with the scanner over the SCSI bus through the generic SCSI kernel driver.

If you want to write a driver for a scanner or similar imaging device, write a SANE driver. While you are debugging, you might find it easier to structure your program as a plain, unprivileged usermode program and add the SANE interface later.

Unprivileged Usermode Program

Code executes in either kernel mode or user mode. The preceding types run in kernel mode but the others run in user mode (or user space). Code running in kernel mode has unlimited low-level access to the hardware, but access to higher level things such as files and TCP network connections is not that easy to get.

Many devices connect to the computer through a standard communications channel such as SCSI, IDE, serial ports, parallel ports (if they use standard parallel port protocols—many don't), USB, IRDA, and so on. The higher level drivers for these devices frequently do not need any special privileges except for write access on the appropriate /dev file, which can often have its privileges relaxed.

Printer drivers are a good example of drivers of this type. To write a driver for a printer, you write a driver module for the ghostscript postscript interpreter. You can also implement it as a simple standalone program that takes a PBM (Portable BitMap) file (or stream) as input. Ghostscript can be configured to output in PBM files and you can then modify the print queue to pipe the output of ghostscript into your standalone program.

Most RS-232 devices fit in this category. The kernel RS-232 drivers provide the low-level interface to ordinary dumb serial ports as well as to smart multiport serial cards. Some examples of devices that may fit into this category are PDAs, weather stations, GPS receivers, some voice/fax/data modems, some EPROM programmers, and serial printers (including label printers). I use this type of driver for my digital camera although a SANE driver would be more appropriate. The X10 and Slink-e devices, mentioned in

25

DEVICE DRIVERS

Chapter 2, which are RS-232 devices that control lights, coffee pots, CD changers, VCRs, receivers, and other appliances found around the home or office, also fit in this category.

Privileged Usermode Programs

If you need special privileges, such as raw port I/O, an ordinary usermode program running as root may be the way to go, particularly during the early experimentation stage. If you make this program suid or otherwise allow ordinary users (or worse yet remote users) to control or communicate with the program, there can be serious security implications. Chapter 35, "Secure Programming," will discuss the security issues in more detail.

Daemons

Privileged or unprivileged usermode driver programs can be extended into a daemon. In some cases, the daemon will pretty much run by itself. In other cases, you will allow local or remote users to communicate with the daemon; in that case, again, you need to exercise security precautions.

Character Devices Versus Block Devices

Most Linux kernel drivers are likely to implement character special devices. Applications communicate with these devices by reading and writing streams of data to character special files created in /dev using the mknod command.

Block mode drivers are used for disk and CD-ROM I/O and similar operations. These are typically used for devices you would mount a filesystem on. This chapter will not cover block mode drivers; support for new devices will, in most cases, simply require modifications to the existing drivers.

Drivers for SCSI host adapters implement both block (for disk I/O) and character devices (for the generic device interface). They do this through the existing SCSI infrastructure. Network interface drivers are yet another type that does not use the normal character or block mode interface. Drivers for sound cards use character device interfaces. Drivers for the PCI bus, PCMCIA cards, and SBUS (on Sparc systems) have their own peculiar interface and provide infrastructure for other drivers.

Device drivers can also be written that do not actually interact with any hardware device. The null device, /dev/null, is a simple example. Device drivers can be used to add general-purpose kernel code. A device driver can add new system calls or replace existing ones.

The Demonstration Hardware

To demonstrate writing a device driver, I will use a very simple piece of hardware: a three axis stepper motor driver. Stepper motors are a type of motor that lend themselves to simple computer control. The name comes from the fact that these motors move in discrete steps. By energizing different combinations of windings, the computer can command the motor to move a single step clockwise or counterclockwise.

Stepper motors are used in a variety of computer peripherals. Table 25.1 shows how steppers are commonly used.

Table 25.1   STEPPER MOTOR FUNCTIONS IN COMPUTER PERIPHERALS

Peripheral	*Function(s)*
Printer	Paper advance, carriage movement
Pen plotters	Movement of pen and/or paper in X and Y axis
Scanners	Move scanner carriage, filter wheel (3 pass scanners)
Some tape drives	Move head relative to tape
Floppy drives	Head positioning
Old hard drives	Head positioning

Many computer peripherals have an onboard processor that controls the stepper motors, among other things, so you won't need to drive the motor directly in that case. Other devices have no onboard intelligence (no microprocessor); in this case, you will need to control the motor directly in order to write a driver for the device.

Stepper motors are also widely used in robotics and industrial systems. I wrote this driver to control my computerized vertical milling machine. This machine can be used to cut (machine) metal, plastics, circuit boards, and other materials into desired shapes. The X and Y axes move the work and the Z axis moves the spinning cutter bit up and down.

Understanding the Workings of a Stepper Motor

A simple stepper motor has two electromagnet coils, oriented ninety degrees from one another. Each coil can be off or on and it can have two different polarities. To simplify the drive electronics, at the expense of performance, most stepper motors have center tapped windings. By connecting the center to the positive supply voltage and grounding one or the other end of the winding, you can effectively magnetize the winding in either

25

DEVICE DRIVERS

positive or negative polarity (thus reversing the polarity of the magnetic field). These types of motors are called *unipolar* stepper motors. Unipolar stepper motors have 5, 6, or 8 wires. Four of the wires will connect directly to the driver transistors. All of the remaining wires will connect to the positive supply voltage.

You can make a crude stepper motor from a couple scraps of iron, some wire, and a compass; actually, you can dispense with the iron. If you try this, be sure to use a current limiting resistor to prevent burning out the coil, damaging the driver circuit or power supply, or re-magnetizing the compass in a different orientation. Imagine yourself holding the compass so the axis of rotation faces you. Now wind copper wire around the top and bottom edges of the compass to make one coil. Make the second coil by winding around the left and right sides.

Figure 25.1 shows my no-frills stepper motor driver circuit. This circuit can also be used to drive relays, lights, solenoids, and many other devices. More sophisticated circuits will provide higher performance (more torque and/or faster speeds) and greater safety, but this circuit is inexpensive, has a low parts count, and is easy to build and understand with only four transistors and four resistors per motor. This circuit can be built from parts costing less than $25.

Whether or not you intend to build a stepper motor driver, this circuit provides a simple device that can be used to illustrate how to develop Linux device drivers.

There is an insert on the schematic that shows a motor being driven through eight half steps. The B and B* phases are drawn reversed (so I wouldn't have to draw wires crossing) so the driver will actually rotate the motor in the opposite direction from the illustration in the insert. You can change the direction of rotation in the driver by changing the step tables.

There are basically three ways to drive a four phase (bifillar) wound stepper motor. You can think of the four (half) coils as pulling the motor's rotor in the north, east, south, and west directions (not to be confused with north and south magnetic poles). Single phase drive energizes one winding at a time in the sequence North (A), East (B), South (A*), and West (B*); the phase names in parentheses correspond to those on the schematic. Double phase drive uses more power and delivers more torque and faster operation by using the sequence North East (A+B), South East (A*+B), South West (A*+B*), and North West (A+B*). Half stepping provides high torque, high speed, and twice the resolution using the sequence North (A), North East (A+B), East (B), South East (A*+B), South (A*), South West (A*+B*), West (B*), and North West (A+B*). Half stepping will be used for this driver. When you get to the end of the sequence, you simply repeat it in the same order. To reverse the direction of rotation, simply reverse the sequence. To hold the motor still, simply pause the sequence at the desired position, keeping the winding(s) energized.

FIGURE 25.1

A stepper motor driver circuit.

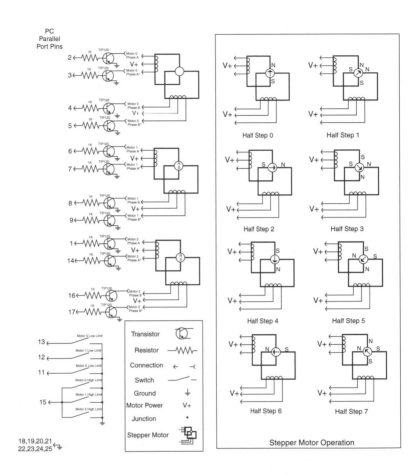

The example motor used in the preceding descriptions has one electrical revolution per mechanical revolution. Most real motors have multiple electrical revolutions per mechanical revolution, which increases torque and resolution at the expense of speed. The most common motors have 24 steps (48 half steps) or 200 steps (400 half steps) per inch. When I built my milling machine, I used 400 half step per revolution motors in combination with a 20 turns per inch screw drive; this gives 8000 steps per inch of movement.

WARNING

Misapplication of this circuit can damage the computer, circuit, motor, or even cause a fire.

Use a power supply that has voltage and current ratings compatible with your stepper motor. This driver circuit has no protection against energizing all four windings simultaneously, which in some cases will damage the motor and/or power supply and could even cause a fire due to overheating. Reduce the supply voltage to 70 percent of the motor's rating to protect against this at the expense of performance; some motors' specifications are already derated for this reason. Make sure the current draw of the motor windings does not exceed the current ratings and power dissipation of the transistors; heat sink the transistors. The stepper motor will generate voltage spikes on the windings during operation. Instead of clamping these spikes, this simple circuit uses a transistor that can withstand the expected voltage spikes; check to make sure the motor you use does not generate spikes large enough to damage the transistor or the motor's insulation. Substituting a TIP122, or other suitable transistor with a higher voltage rating, or adding transient suppression may be required. These transients may cause a painful electric shock if you touch the stepper motor connections while in operation. The transistors used in this circuit have a very high gain (greater than 1000); do not substitute low gain transistors. Some wimpy parallel ports may not be able to supply enough current to drive the transistors, resulting in damage to either the parallel port or transistors. Use of a separate parallel printer card, easily and inexpensively replaced in case of damage, is recommended; built-in parallel ports on laptop computers will be particularly expensive to replace. Do not disconnect the parallel port cable unless both the computer and motor power supply are turned off. Improper ground wiring may result in ground loops. The circuit should be assembled by a qualified electronics technician or at least a proficient hobbyist.

Heat sinks are required on the transistors in most cases. I actually built my circuit on a piece of quarter inch thick aluminum plate and mounted the transistors directly to the plate using mica insulators, insulating shoulder washers used for transistor mounting (you don't want the bolt to short out the transistor), nuts, and bolts. I then soldered the resistors directly to the transistor leads and mounted some terminal strips on standoffs above the transistors for connection to the motors. This construction provides heat sinking through the aluminum plate and does not require a breadboard or printed circuit board.

The four output lines on the control port tend to have 4.7K pullup resistors to 5V. You may want to add smaller pullup resistors to +5V to provide more drive current for the transistors; I did not need to do that. Power for the motor can be supplied by a laboratory power supply, a large battery, or even, for small motors, the PC's 12V supply (available on the disk drive power connectors).

An external clock (pulse generator) can be connected to the parallel port Ack line to provide timing for the stepper motor. This provides a timing source for running the motor at a speed faster than 100 pulses per second (the speed of the Linux jiffy clock). The Linux Real Time extensions could also be used for this purpose.

Standard or Bidirectional Parallel Port

This circuit uses raw output to the PC's parallel printer port. We cannot use the normal printer driver because we are using these signals in a non-standard way. You cannot daisy chain other devices off the same parallel port with this circuit so don't try to use a printer, Zip drive, CD-ROM, or other device on the same port.

I will describe the normal operation of a PC parallel port in standard or bidirectional mode. EPP or ECP modes, available on some ports, function somewhat differently. You may need to configure the port into standard or bidirectional mode via jumper settings or in your machine's BIOS setup for proper operation.

Bidirectional mode allows the eight data lines to be used as either eight inputs or eight outputs instead of just eight outputs. Bit C5 in the control register sets the direction. Some of the chips that are used to provide a parallel port disable the C5 bit unless they are programmed into bidirectional mode using a special setup specific to that chip; this is done to prevent old, poorly written programs from accidentally switching the port direction.

The PC's parallel ports are normally located starting at IO port address of 0x3BC (lp0), 0x378 (lp1), or 0x278 (lp2). Note that these may not directly correspond to the LPTx numbering used in DOS and Windows since these remap lp1 to lp0 and lp2 to lp1 if lp0 is not present. The 0x3BC address was traditionally used for the parallel port on some video cards. The parallel port is programmed using three registers located at three consecutive IO port addresses.

Table 25.2 shows the names given to the individual bits in these three registers. Table 25.3 shows the functions of each bit.

Table 25.2 PARALLEL PORT PROGRAMMING INTERFACE

Register	Address	D7	D6	D5	D4	D3	D2	D1	D0	Read	Write
Data	base+0	D7	D6	D5	D4	D3	D2	D1	D0	Yes	Yes
Status	base+1	S7	S6	S5	S4	S3	S2	S1	S0	Yes	No
Control	base+2	C7	C6	C5	C4	C3	C2	C1	C0	Yes	Yes

Table 25.3   PARALLEL PORT HARDWARE INTERFACE

Bit	Signal	Pin
D0	Data bit 0	2
D1	Data bit 1	3
D2	Data bit 2	4
D3	Data bit 3	5
D4	Data bit 4	6
D5	Data bit 5	7
D6	Data bit 6	8
D7	Data bit 7	9
S0		
S1		
S2		
S3+	-Error	15
S4+	+Select	13
S5+	+PaperOut	12
S6+	-Ack	10
S7-	+Busy	11
C0-	-Strobe	1
C1-	-AutoFeed	14
C2+	-Init	16
C3-	+SelectIn	17
C4	IRQ Enable	none
C5	Output Enable	none
C6		
C7		
None	Ground	18,19,20,21,22,23,24,25

A negative sign in the first column indicates that there is an inverter between the computer and the port. A negative sign in the second column means that this line is considered active low when interfacing to a printer.

Table 25.4 shows the stepper motor connections to parallel port signals.

Table 25.4 STEPPER MOTOR DRIVER CONNECTIONS

Function	Name	Bit	Pin
Motor 0, Phase A	D0	D0	2
Motor 0, Phase A*	D1	D1	3
Motor 0, Phase B	D2	D2	4
Motor 0, Phase B*	D3	D3	5
Motor 1, Phase A	D4	D4	6
Motor 1, Phase A*	D5	D5	7
Motor 1, Phase B	D6	D6	8
Motor 1, Phase B*	D7	D7	9
Motor 2, Phase A	Strobe	C0*	1
Motor 2, Phase A*	AutoLF	C1*	14
Motor 2, Phase B	Init	C2	16
Motor 2, Phase B*	SelectIn	C3*	17
Motor 0, Low limit	Select	S4	13
Motor 1, Low limit	PaperEnd	S5	12
Motor 2, Low limit	Busy	S7*	11
All motors, high limit	Error*	S3	15
External Timer	Ack*	S6	10
Grounds			18,19, 20,21, 22,23, 24,25

Development Configuration

For developing kernel device drivers, two separate computers running the same version of Linux and a way to transfer files between them are recommended. It is very easy to crash a system while doing driver testing with the possibility of corrupting the filesystem as a result. An infinite loop is no big deal in a usermode program but in the bottom half of a device driver it will hang the system. The target system does not need to be very powerful (unless your driver needs lots of CPU cycles); that old junker system you might have lying around may be sufficient. This driver was tested on a 386DX25 with 4MB memory. While this was sufficient to run the driver, loading emacs took over 30 seconds

25

DEVICE DRIVERS

and compiling took almost 4 minutes; memory was the limiting factor. If you are not running the same kernel version on both systems, you may have to recompile on the target system. You can use a floppy, a network connection, or any other suitable means to transfer files to the target system.

> **TIP**
>
> You can reduce the possibility of filesystem damage on the target system in the event of a crash by issuing the sync command before loading the module; sometimes, I even run while /bin/true; do sync; sleep 1; done & to repeatedly sync the filesystem.

Low Level Port I/O

Many systems, including Intel processors, have separate address spaces for memory and I/O ports. I/O ports look something like memory locations, but they may not read back the same value that was written. This causes problems for some drivers on crude operating systems (such as DOS) that would like to do a read/modify/write operation to change one or more bits while leaving the rest unchanged, since they don't know what state another program might have set them to. Under Linux, all I/O to a particular device is normally done by a single device driver, so this is not generally a problem. I/O port locations normally map to data, control, or status registers in peripheral chips on the system. Sometimes reading or writing certain I/O port locations can hang the system. Some NE2000 Ethernet adapters will hang the processor forever if you read from certain I/O ports; these cards are designed to insert wait states until the requested data is available (which it will never be if you read an undefined register). Reads and writes may have side effects. Reading the data register on a serial port UART chip will return the next character in the receive queue and have the side effect of removing the data from the queue. Writing to the same register has the side effect of queuing up a character for transmission.

To enable low-level port I/O in usermode programs running as root, issue the call iopl(3). This grants unlimited access to I/O ports. If you only need access to ports below 0x3FF, you can, for example, use ioperm(0x378, 4, 1) to turn on ports 0x378-0x37B. The second form is more restrictive and will prevent you from accidentally writing to unintended ports.

The outb() function outputs a byte value to an I/O port. The function call outb(0x378,0x01) will output the value 0x01 to port 0x378. Note that the order of these two parameters is opposite what DOS programmers are used to. The function call inb(0x378) will return a byte read from port 0x378. The functions outb_p() and inb_p() are the same as outb() and inb() except that they add a brief delay afterwards; many peripheral chips cannot handle port reads and writes at full bus speeds. The functions outw(), outw_p(), inw(), and inw_p() are similar but for 16-bit values; the "w" stands for word. The functions outl(), outl_p(), inl(), and inl_p() are also similar but for 32-bit values; the "l" stands for long. The size of the I/O port operations should be matched to the size(s) supported by the device.

Programs, whether usermode or kernel mode, which use these input and output functions must be compiled with optimization (-O option to gcc) due to idiosyncrasies in how these functions are implemented in gcc. You need to #include <asm/io.h> to use these functions.

The functions insb(port, addr, count) and outs(port, addr, count) move count bytes between port port and the memory at location addr using efficient repeat string I/O instructions on Intel compatible processors. No paused versions of these functions exist; the point of these instructions is to move data as fast as the bus will allow. Word and long versions also exist. Using the long versions insl() and outsl()should allow you to transfer data at about 66MB/s on a 33MHz PCI bus (the processor will alternate I/O and memory operations).

Beware of reading more data than is available from a data port; depending on the device in question, you will either get garbage or the device will insert wait states until data is available (which might be next week). Check the flags in an appropriate status register to determine if a byte is available. If you know that a certain number of bytes are available, you can read them using a fast string read.

There are similar instructions for memory mapped I/O devices: readb(), readw(), readl(), writeb(), writew(), writel(), memset_io(), memcpy_fromio(), and memcpy_toio(). On Intel compatible processors, these don't actually do anything special, but their use will ease porting to other processors. Memory mapped I/O operations may need special handling to insure they are not mangled by the cache. Memory addresses may need to be mapped between bus addresses, virtual memory addresses, and physical memory addresses (on versions of Linux that don't use a 1:1:1 mapping) using the functions bus_to_virt(), virt_to_bus(), virt_to_phys(), and phys_to_virt().

Many ethernet devices require that a checksum be calculated for each packet. On modern processors, this can typically be done while copying the data at full bus speed. The

25

DEVICE DRIVERS

functions `eth_io_copy_and_sum()` and `eth_copy_and_sum()` are used. Look through the existing ethernet drivers to see how to use these. Modern processors are frequently limited by memory and I/O bandwidth; it is often more efficient to process data as it is moved using processor cycles that would otherwise be wasted.

Initiating Interrupts to Utilize Device Drivers

When a hardware device needs attention from the device driver, it does so by initiating an interrupt. The processor responds to an interrupt by saving its state and jumping to the previously registered interrupt handler. When the interrupt handler returns, the processor restores its state and continues where it left off. Interrupts may be masked (disabled) during the processing of higher priority interrupts or in critical code sections.

A serial port UART, for example, causes an interrupt when the receive buffer is near full or the transmit buffer is near empty. The processor responds to the interrupt by transferring data.

Interrupts are not available to usermode programs; if your device driver requires an interrupt handler, it must be implemented as a kernel device driver. An interrupt handler function is declared using the following syntax:

```
#include <linux/interrupt.h>
#include <linux/sched.h>
void handler(int irq, void *dev_id, struct pt_regs *regs);
```

In most cases, you will ignore the actual value of the arguments but your handler must be declared in this fashion (you can change the function name) or you will get compilation errors. The first parameter is used to allow one handler to handle multiple interrupts and tell which one it responded to. The second is a copy of whatever value you passed when you registered the interrupt (see code below). This value will typically be NULL or a pointer to a structure you defined to pass information to an interrupt handler that can modify its operation. Again, this is helpful for using one handler for multiple interrupts and it also helps you avoid using global variables to communicate with the driver if you want a cleaner program structure. These features will be most likely to be used where one device driver controls multiple instances of a device. The `pt_regs` are the saved processor registers in case you need to inspect or modify the state of the machine at the time it was interrupted; you will not need to use these in a normal device driver.

We register an interrupt handler with the kernel using the call

```
request_irq(irq, handler,  flags, device, dev_id);
```

which returns an integer that will be 0 if the operation succeeded. The first parameter is the number of the interrupt being requested. These are the hardware IRQ numbers, not the software interrupt numbers they are mapped to; note that IRQs 2 and 9 are weird because of the way the PC hardware is designed. The second parameter is a pointer to your handler function. The third parameter contains flags. The SA_SHIRQ flag tells the kernel you are willing to share this interrupt with other device drivers, assuming that your driver, the other driver(s), and the hardware support this option. SA_INTERRUPT is used to affect whether the scheduler ran after the interrupt handler returned. The fourth parameter gives the name of the driver as a text string, which will show up in /proc/interrupts. The last parameter is not used by the kernel at all but will be passed to the handler each time it is invoked. The free_irq() function takes one argument, the interrupt number, which is used to unregister your handler.

The function cli() disables interrupts (CLear Interrupt enable) and sti() (SeT Interrupt enable) re-enables them. These are used to protect access to critical data structures. These will normally be used to protect the top half and the bottom half from each other or protect one interrupt handler from others, but can be used to protect other important operations. It is not polite to keep interrupts disabled for very long. Calls to sti() and cli() can be nested; you must call cli() as many times as you call sti(). In the example device driver, I do not need to use these functions directly but they are called by some of the kernel functions that I use to protect the data structures manipulated by those functions.

Accessing Memory Using DMA

Direct Memory Access (DMA) allows internal peripherals to access memory without the processor needing to execute instructions for each transfer. There are two types of DMA; one uses the DMA controller on the motherboard and the other uses a busmaster controller on the peripheral card.

I suggest you avoid using the motherboard DMA controller if possible. There are a limited number of DMA channels, which can make it hard to find a free channel. This form of DMA is very slow. And this form still requires short interrupt latencies (the time between when the peripheral asserts the interrupt line and the processor responds); when the DMA controller reaches the end of the buffer, you need to quickly reprogram it to use another buffer. This controller requires multiple bus cycles per transfer; it reads a byte of data from the peripheral and then writes it to memory, or vice versa, in two separate operations and inserts wait states as well. This controller only supports 8- and 16-bit transfers.

25

DEVICE DRIVERS

Busmaster DMA requires more complicated circuitry on the peripheral card, but can transfer data much faster and only needs one bus cycle per byte or word transferred. Busmaster controllers can also execute 32-bit transfers.

The kernel functions `set_dma_mode()`, `set_dma_addr()`, `set_dma_count()` and `enable_dma()`, `disable_dma()`, `request_dma()`, `free_dma()`, and `clear_dma_ff()` are used to set up DMA transfers; a driver that uses DMA must run in kernel mode. The example kernel driver in this chapter does not use DMA.

Simple Usermode Test Driver

Listing 25.1 is a very simple program that just causes the stepper motor to slowly make a number of revolutions. This tests for correct hookup of a single stepper motor (Motor 0) and demonstrates the use of `iopl()` and `outb()`.

Listing 25.1 SIMPLE USERMODE DRIVER

```
/* Must be compiled with -O for outb to be inlined,  */
/* otherwise link error                          /
#include <stdlib.h>
#include <stdio.h>
#include <unistd.h>
#include <asm/io.h>


int base=0x378;

void verbose_outb(int port, int value)
{
    printf("outb(%02X,%04X)\n",port,value);
    outb(port,value);
}

unsigned char steptable[8]={0x01,0x05,0x04,0x06,0x02,0x0A,0x08,0x09};

slow_sweep()
{
    int i;

    for(i=0;i<800;i++) {
        verbose_outb(steptable[i%8],base+0);
```

```
        usleep(100000);
    }
}


main()
{
    int i;
    int inval;
    int outval;

    printf("this program must be run as root\n");

    iopl(3);    /* Enable i/o (if root) */

    slow_sweep();

}
```

Debugging Kernel Level Drivers

It is theoretically possible to use the GNU debugger, gdb, in remote debugging mode
with an RS-232 connection between your development machine and your target machine.
More information on this topic is available at
http://www.isi.edu/~johnh/SOFTWARE/XKDEBUG/xkdebug_README.text.

The printk() function is similar to printf but displays output on the console. Beware
of generating too much output, however, or you may effectively lock up your system. I
suggest you pepper your code with statements like if(debug>=5) printk(...). This
will allow you to easily specify the level of debugging information at module load time.
It may be desirable to leave these compiled in so users of your driver can easily debug
problems.

TIP

If you are worried about the overhead of debugging code in your program,
there is an easy way to compile these out without littering your source with
#ifdef DEBUG statements. Use the if(debug>=1) form instead. Then, simply
change the declaration of debug from int to const int using a single #ifdef
NODEBUG. The optimizer (if enabled, which it will always be for kernel modules)
should realize that this code can never be executed and will eliminate the code
from the generated executable. This setup allows the debugging level to be set
at runtime if desired, or debugging can be compiled out entirely.

25

DEVICE DRIVERS

You can set any global or static variable when the module is loaded using `insmod`. This allows you to set various debugging variables that change the operation of the program without recompiling. If you are trying to narrow down a crash in a section of code, you can enclose various small pieces of code in `if(test1) {`, `if(test2) {`, and so on. Then by insmoding the code and selectively defining these values to 1 until a crash occurs, you can quickly narrow down the problem.

Eventually, I plan to make a loadable kernel module version of my symbol table library, described in Chapter 24, "Using Libraries." This would allow you to interactively set or query various variables using the `/proc` filesystem while the driver was running. It would also provide a way for the user to configure driver features in running drivers. Two separate entries in `/proc` could be created; one would be accessible only to root and have access to more variables and another might be world accessible and access a smaller set.

Bottom Half and Top Half

When system calls are issued, the current task keeps executing but changes its state to privileged kernel mode operation. If the kernel code determines that the call should be handled by our device driver, it invokes the corresponding function in our device driver that we have previously registered. These functions, collectively, are the top half of the device driver. These functions normally read data queued by the bottom half, queue data for reading by the bottom half, change the position of a file, open a file, close a file, or perform other similar operations. The top half does not normally communicate directly with the device. The top half functions normally put themselves (and the current task) to sleep, if necessary, until the bottom half has done the actual work.

The bottom half of a device driver handles actual communication with the hardware device. The bottom half is usually invoked periodically in response to hardware interrupts from the device or the 100Hz system jiffie clock (which is, itself, triggered by a hardware interrupt). Bottom half functions may not sleep and should do their work quickly; if they cannot perform an operation without waiting, they normally return and try again in response to the next interrupt.

Creating a Kernel Driver

This section outlines the creation of a more complete stepper motor driver that runs as a kernel driver. More specifically, it is a loadable kernel module. It can also be compiled as a usermode driver, although performance will be limited.

Reviewing the Source Code

This section will go through the source code for the example driver. Many of the kernel functions used to write drivers will be shown in their native habitats. The source code had to be mangled a bit to fit with the 65 column limits allowed by the publisher. Of particular note, some strings were split into two smaller strings on two adjacent lines; the compiler will automatically concatenate these back into a single string.

Header File

Listing 25.2 shows the header file `stepper.h`, which defines some ioctls supported by the driver.

Listing 25.2   `stepper.h`

```
/* define ioctls */

#define STEPPER_SET_DEBUG        0x1641
#define STEPPER_SET_SKIPTICKS    0x1642
#define STEPPER_SET_VERBOSE_IO   0x1643
#define STEPPER_SET_VERBOSE_MOVE 0x1644
#define STEPPER_START            0x1645
#define STEPPER_STOP             0x1646
#define STEPPER_CLEAR_BUFFERS    0x1647
#define STEPPER_NOAUTO           0x1648
#define STEPPER_AUTO             0x1649
```

Ring Buffer Header File

Listing 25.3 shows the header file for the ring buffer code. Listing 25.4 shows the ring buffer implementation. This module implements a ring buffer or FIFO (First In First Out) buffer. These ring buffers are used to buffer data between the top half and the bottom half. These are overkill for the current driver but will be useful for writing more serious drivers that need more buffering. These functions need to be re-entrant; the bottom half may interrupt execution of the top half.

These two files define the data structure, an initialization function, and two functions to write (queue) and read (dequeue) data. Currently, they only accept reads and writes of one byte at a time although the calling convention will not need to be changed for multibyte transfers.

Listing 25.3   ring.h

```
#define RING_SIGNATURE 0x175DE210

typedef struct {
   long signature;
   unsigned char *head_p;
   unsigned char *tail_p;
   unsigned char *end_p;      /* end + 1 */
   unsigned char *begin_p;
   unsigned char buffer[32768];
} ring_buffer_t;


extern void ring_buffer_init(ring_buffer_t *ring);
extern int ring_buffer_read(ring_buffer_t *ring,
   unsigned char *buf, int count);
extern int ring_buffer_write(ring_buffer_t *ring,

   unsigned char *buf, int count);
```

Listing 25.4   ring.c

```
/* Copyright 1998,1999, Mark Whitis <whitis@dbd.com> */
/* http://www.freelabs.com/~whitis/ */

#include "ring.h"

int ring_debug=1;

#ifdef TEST
#define printk printf
#include <stdlib.h>
#include <stdio.h>
#include <unistd.h>
#endif


void ring_buffer_init(ring_buffer_t *ring)
{
    ring->signature=RING_SIGNATURE;
    ring->head_p=ring->buffer;
    ring->tail_p=ring->buffer;
    ring->begin_p=ring->buffer;
    ring->end_p=&ring->buffer[sizeof(ring->buffer)];
    #if 0
       strcpy(ring->buffer,"This is a test.\n");
       ring->head_p +=16;
    #endif
}
```

```
/*
 * returns number of bytes read.  Will not block (blocking will
 * be handled by the calling routine if necessary).
 * If you request to read more bytes than are currently
 * available, it will return
 * a count less than the value you passed in
 */
int ring_buffer_read(ring_buffer_t *ring, unsigned char *buf,
   int count)
{
  #ifdef PARANOID
     if(ring_debug>5) {
        printk("das1600: ring_buffer_read(%08X,%08X,%d)\n",
           ring,buf,count);
     }
     if(ring->signature != RING_SIGNATURE) {
        printk("ring_buffer_read: signature corrupt\n");
        return(0);
     }
     if(ring->tail_p < ring->begin_p) {
        printk("ring_buffer_read: tail corrupt\n");
        return(0);
     }
     if(ring->tail_p > ring->end_p) {
        printk("ring_buffer_read: tail corrupt\n");
        return(0);
     }
     if(count != 1) {
        printk("ring_buffer_read: count must currently be 1\n");
        return(0);
     }
  #endif;
  if(ring->tail_p == ring->end_p) {
     ring->tail_p = ring->begin_p;
  }
  if(ring->tail_p == ring->head_p) {
     if(ring_debug>5) {
        printk("ring_buffer_read: buffer underflow\n");
     }
     return(0);
  }

  *buf = *ring->tail_p++;
  return(1);
}

/*
 * returns number of bytes written.  Will not block (blocking
 * will  be handled by the calling routine if necessary).
```

continues

25

DEVICE DRIVERS

Listing 25.4 CONTINUED

```
 * If you request to write more bytes than are currently
 * available, it will return
 * a count less than the value you passed in
 */
int ring_buffer_write(ring_buffer_t *ring, unsigned char *buf,
   int count)
{
   unsigned char *tail_p;
  #ifdef PARANOID
     if(ring->signature != RING_SIGNATURE) {
        printk("ring_buffer_write: signature corrupt\n");
        return(0);
     }
     if(ring->head_p < ring->begin_p) {
        printk("ring_buffer_write: head corrupt\n");
        return(0);
     }
     if(ring->head_p > ring->end_p) {
        printk("ring_buffer_write: head corrupt\n");
        return(0);
     }
     if(count != 1) {
        printk("ring_buffer_write: count must currently be 1\n");
        return(0);
     }
  #endif
  /* Copy tail_p to a local variable in case it changes */
  /* between comparisons */
  tail_p = ring->tail_p;


  if( (ring->head_p == (tail_p - 1) )
  || ((ring->head_p == (ring->end_p - 1)) && (tail_p==ring->begin_p)) ) {
     if(ring_debug>5) {
        printk("ring_buffer_write: buffer overflow\n");
     }
     return(0);
  }

  *ring->head_p++ = *buf;

  if(ring->head_p == ring->end_p ) {
     ring->head_p = ring->begin_p;
  }
  return(1);
}


#ifdef TEST
```

```
ring_buffer_t buffer;
main()
{
    char c;
    char c2;
    int child;
    int rc;
    int i;
    int j;
    char lastread;
    int errors;
    int reads;
    int writes;

    ring_buffer_init(&buffer);

    c=0;
    lastread=-1;
    errors=0;
    reads=0;
    writes=0;
    for(j=0; j<50000; j++) {
        for(i=0; i<31; i++) {
            rc=ring_buffer_write(&buffer, &c, 1);
            writes++;
            if(ring_debug>2) {
                printf("ring_buffer_write returned %d, "
                    "was passed %d\n",rc,c);
            if(rc==1) c++;
        }

        for(i=0; i<47; i++) {
            rc=ring_buffer_read(&buffer, &c2, 1);
            reads++;
            if(ring_debug>2) {
                printf("ring_buffer_read returned: rc=%d,c2=%d\n",
                    rc,c2);
            }
            if(rc==1) {
                if(c2!=(char)(lastread+1)) {
                    printf("ERROR: expected %d, got %d\n",
                        (char)(lastread+1),c2);
                    errors++;
                }
                lastread=c2;
            }
        }
    }
    printf("number of errors=%d\n",errors);
    printf("number of reads=%d\n",reads);
```

continues

25

DEVICE DRIVERS

Listing 25.4   CONTINUED

```
    printf("number of writes=%d\n",writes);


}
#endif
```

Prologue

Listing 25.5 shows the prologue. This includes the necessary #include directives and variable declarations. A number of the variables are described in the section "Using the Kernel Driver," later in this chapter. The preprocessor macro __KERNEL__ will be defined if the program is being compiled as a kernel level driver; note that this will affect many of the system include files as well as governing conditional compilation in the driver source.

Listing 25.5   PROLOGUE

```
/* Copyright 1999 by Mark Whitis.  All rights Reserved */

/* Must be compiled with -O for outb to be inlined, otherwise */
/* link error */
/* Usermode: gcc -g -O -o teststep teststep.c */
/* LKM: */
/*   gcc -O -DMODULE -D__KERNEL__ -o stepperout.o -c stepper.c */
/*       ld -r -o stepper.o stepperout.o ring.o */

#include "stepper.h"

#ifdef __KERNEL__
   #include <linux/kernel.h>
   #include <linux/config.h>
   #ifdef MODULE
     #include <linux/module.h>
     #include <linux/version.h>
   #else

/* This code is GNU copylefted and should not be statically */
   /*  linked with the kernel. */
   #error This device driver must be compiled as a LKM
   #define MOD_INC_USE_COUNT
   #define MOD_DEC_USE_COUNT
   #endif
   #include <linux/types.h>
   #include <linux/fs.h>
   #include <linux/mm.h>
```

```
    #include <linux/errno.h>
    #include <asm/segment.h>
    #include <asm/io.h>
    #include <linux/sched.h>
    #include <linux/tqueue.h>
#else
    #include <unistd.h>
    #include <stdlib.h>
    /* including stdio will cause grief */
    #include <stdio.h>
    #include <asm/io.h>
#endif

#if 0
    #include <stdarg.h>
    #include <ctype.h>
#endif
#include <string.h>

#ifdef __KERNEL__
    #include "ring.h"
    ring_buffer_t read_buffer;
    ring_buffer_t write_buffer;
    /* Parallel port interrupt to use for timing */
    /*   0=use Linux 100hz jiffie timer */
    static int irq = 0;
    /* Major device # to request */
    static int major = 31;
    /* The device # we actually got */
    static int stepper_major = 0;

    struct wait_queue *read_wait = NULL ;
        /* used to block user read if buffer underflow occurs */
    struct wait_queue *write_wait = NULL;
        /* used to block user write if buffer overflow occurs */
#endif

static int debug = 1;
static int verbose_io=0;
static int verbose_move=0;
static int base=0x378;
static int power_down_on_exit=1;


/* The following set the delay between steps */
#ifndef __KERNEL__
    static int delay = 50000;      /* for usleep */
    static int fastdelay = 0;    /* delay loop */
#else
```

continues

25

DEVICE DRIVERS

Listing 25.5 CONTINUED

```
   static int skipticks = 0;
#endif

/* the following value can be set to 0 to disable the */
/* actual I/O operations.  This will allow experimenting */
/* on a system which does not have a free parallel port */
static int do_io = 1;

#ifdef __KERNEL__
   static int read_is_sleeping = 0;
   static int write_is_sleeping = 0;
   static int abort_read = 0;
   static int abort_write = 0;
   static int read_is_open = 0;
   static int write_is_open = 0;
   static int interrupts_are_enabled = 0;
   static int autostart=1;
#endif

static int tick_counter=0;

int xdest = 0;
int xuser = 0;
int xpos = 0;

int ydest = 0;
int yuser = 0;
int ypos = 0;

int zdest = 0;
int zuser = 0;
int zpos = 0;

unsigned short word;
```

verbose_outb()

Listing 25.6 shows a wrapper for the outb() function, which provides optional debugging output and the ability to disable the outb() for experimentation without the necessary hardware.

Listing 25.6 verbose_outb()

```
void verbose_outb(int port, int value)
{
   #ifndef __KERNEL__
      if(verbose_io) printf("outb(%02X,%04X)\n",port,value);
```

```
#else
   if(verbose_io) printk("outb(%02X,%04X)\n",port,value);
#endif

   if(do_io) outb(port,value);
}
```

Delay Function

The function do_delay(), shown in Listing 25.7, is used in a usermode driver only and provides a delay between steps. It will use the usleep() library function unless fastdelay is nonzero, in which case it will use a delay loop. These delays only set the minimum delay; in a usermode program, multitasking can cause additional delays.

Listing 25.7 DELAY FUNCTION

```
#ifdef __KERNEL__
   void do_delay()
   {
      ;
   }
#else
   void do_delay()
   {
      int i;

      if(fastdelay>0) {
        for(i=0;i<fastdelay;i++) {
           /* dummy operation so optimizer doesn't */
           /* eliminate loop */
           verbose_outb( (word&0x00FF),base+0);
        }
      } else {
        usleep(delay);
      }
   }
#endif
```

Status Reporting

Listing 25.8 shows a function that reports the positions of the stepper motors on each axis. In a usermode program, it will be printed to stdout; in a kernel driver, the result will be stored in a ring buffer for reading using read(), fgets(), fscanf(), or similar function by a usermode control program. The value of the 16-bit output word is also reported; this is the value that was last output to the parallel port data and status registers.

Listing 25.8 STATUS REPORTING

```
void report_status()
{
    char buf[128];
    int rc;
    int i;
    int len;

    sprintf(buf,"x=%d,y=%d,z=%d,word=%08X\n",xpos,ypos,zpos,word);
#ifdef __KERNEL__

    len=strlen(buf);

    for(i=0;i<len;i++) {
        rc=ring_buffer_write(&read_buffer,&buf[i],1);
    }
    /* we need to wake up read function */
    if(read_is_sleeping) {
        if(debug>=5) printk("stepper: waking up read/n");
        wake_up_interruptible(&read_wait);
    }
#else
    puts(buf);
#endif

}
```

Stepper Control

Listing 25.9 shows the functions that actually drive the stepper motors. The function move_one_step() will move each axis up to a single half step. Since the driver bottom half will be called once each time a step is needed, this needs to be a simple incremental move instead of a full end-to-end move. In the usermode version, move_all() will be used to do a complete move.

The arrays x_steptable, y_steptable, and z_steptable indicate which bits need to be set for each of the eight half steps per electrical revolution. These bits can be changed to accommodate different wiring or to reverse the "forward" direction of rotation. The variable flipbits is used to invert certain bits to compensate for inverters included in the standard parallel port interface. The variable irq_enable_bit will be used later to enable interrupts on the parallel port card.

The function parse_one_char() implements a simple parser for move instructions. It operates in a character at a time mode; the bottom half will not need to reassemble commands into lines to use this.

Listing 25.9 STEPPER CONTROL

```
unsigned short x_steptable[8]=
   {0x0001,0x0005,0x0004,0x0006,0x0002,0x000A,0x0008,0x0009};
unsigned short y_steptable[8]=
   {0x0010,0x0050,0x0040,0x0060,0x0020,0x00A0,0x0080,0x0090};
unsigned short z_steptable[8]=
   {0x0100,0x0500,0x0400,0x0600,0x0200,0x0A00,0x0800,0x0900};
unsigned short flipbits = 0x0B00;
unsigned short irq_enable_bit=0x1000;


void move_one_step()
{

  /* This is a very simple multiaxis move routine */
  /* The axis will not move in a coordinate fashion */
  /* unless the angle is a multiple of 45 degrees */
  if(xdest > xpos) {
     xpos++;
  } else if(xdest < xpos) {
     xpos--;
  }

  if(ydest > ypos) {
     ypos++;
  } else if(ydest < ypos) {
     ypos--;
  }

  if(zdest > zpos) {
     zpos++;
  } else if(zdest < zpos) {
     zpos--;
  }
  word = x_steptable[xpos%8]
       ¦ y_steptable[ypos%8]
       ¦ z_steptable[zpos%8];

#ifdef __KERNEL__
     if(interrupts_are_enabled) word ¦= irq_enable_bit;
#endif

  /* Some of the signals are inverted */
  word ^= flipbits;


  /* output low byte to data register */
  verbose_outb( (word & 0x00FF), base+0);
```

continues

25

DEVICE DRIVERS

Listing 25.9 CONTINUED

```
   /* output high byte to control register */
   verbose_outb( (word >> 8), base+2);

   if(verbose_move) report_status();
}

void move_all()
{
   while( (xpos!=xdest) || (ypos!=ydest) || (zpos!=zdest) ) {
      move_one_step();
      do_delay();
   }
}


void parse_one_char(char c)
{
   static int value;
   static int dest=' ';
   static int negative=0;

   #if 0
      c = toupper(c);
   #else
      if( (c>'a') && (c<'z') ) { c = c - 'a' + 'A'; }
   #endif

   switch(c) {
      case('X'):
      case('Y'):
      case('Z'):
         dest=c;
         break;
      case('='):
         break;
      case('-'):
         negative = !negative;
         break;
      case('+'):
         negative = 0;
      case('0'):
      case('1'):
      case('2'):
      case('3'):
      case('4'):
      case('5'):
      case('6'):
      case('7'):
```

```
        case('8'):
        case('9'):
           value *= 10;
           value += (c-'0');
           break;
        case('?'):
           report_status();
        case('\r'):
        case('\n'):
        case(','):
           if(negative) {
              value = -value;
           }
           if(dest=='X') {
              xuser = value;
           } else if(dest=='Y') {
              yuser = value;
           } else if(dest=='Z') {
              zuser = value;
           }
           value = 0;
           negative = 0;

           if( (c=='\n')||(c=='\r') ){
              xdest = xuser;
              ydest = yuser;
              zdest = zuser;

              #ifdef __KERNEL__
                 if(debug>=3) {
                    printk("xdest=%d ydest=%d zdest=%d\n",
                       xdest,ydest,zdest);
                 }
              #endif
           }
           break;
   }
}
```

Seek Operation

The function `stepper_lseek()`, shown in Listing 25.10, is actually the first function that is specific to a kernel level driver and implements part of the top half interface. This function will be called whenever the `lseek()` call is issued to set the file position. Note that `open()`, `seek()`, `fopen()`, and `fseek()` may also call `lseek()`. In this case, we can't change the file position so we return a value of 0.

The parameters inode and file provide pointers to the kernel's internal data structures defining the file the user has opened and will be passed to all of the top half functions. These are defined in /usr/include/linux/fs.h.

The parameters offset and orig define the amount of offset and the origin (beginning of file, end of file, or current position). These values are used to set the current file position and are documented in more detail in the manual page for lseek.

Listing 25.10 SEEK OPERATION

```
#ifdef __KERNEL__
    static int stepper_lseek(struct inode *inode,
        struct file *file, off_t offset, int orig)
    {
        /* Don't do anything, other than set offset to 0 */
        return(file->f_pos=0);
    }
#endif
```

Read and Write Operations

Listing 25.11 shows the function stepper_read(), which is the top half function that implements the file read operation. In our example, this will be used to read the status responses placed in the read ring buffer by report_status(). This function will be called whenever the read() system call is issued from userspace for a file controlled by this device driver; fread(), fgets(), fscanf(), fgets(), and other library functions issue this call.

The parameters node and file are the same as the first two parameters to stepper_lseek(), described in the preceding section. The remaining two parameters, buf and count, provide the address of a data buffer to fill and the number of bytes to read. The kernel function verify_area() must be called to verify that the buffer is valid.

This function calls ring_buffer_read() to get the data. If the data is not available, it must sleep. It uses the kernel function interruptible_sleep_on() to put itself (and the calling task) to sleep and adds itself to a queue, read_wait, of tasks (only one in this case) to be woken up by the bottom half when more data is available. The queue read_wait was defined in the "Prologue" section earlier in the chapter; we can define any number of queues. If you want to put more than one task in a wait queue, it is probably up to you to allocate more wait_queue entries and link them together using the "next" member. Wait queues are declared in /usr/include/linux/sched.h. The function interruptible_sleep_on() is declared in /usr/include/linux/sched.h and the source code to the actual function is in /usr/src/linux/kernel/sched.c.

As written, the `stepper_read()` and `stepper_write()` functions also wake each other up; this may not be necessary, since the bottom half should do this, but was included to help prevent deadlocks between reading and writing. The variable `read_is_sleeping` is set to tell the bottom half to wake us up when more data is available.

The function `stepper_write()` performs the opposite of `stepper_read()` and looks very similar except that the direction of data transfer has been reversed. This function will be called if the `write()` system call has been issued with a file descriptor that references a file controlled by our device.

Listing 25.11 READ AND WRITE OPERATIONS

```
#ifdef __KERNEL__
   static int stepper_read(struct inode *node,
      struct file *file, char *buf, int count)
   {
      static char message[] = "hello, world\n";
      static char *p = message;
      int i;
      int rc;
      char xferbuf;
      int bytes_transferred;
      int newline_read;

      newline_read=0;

      if(!read_is_open) {
         printk("stepper: ERROR: stepper_read() called while "
            "not open for reading\n");
      }
       bytes_transferred=0;

      if(debug>2) printk("stepper_read(%08X,%08X,%08X,%d)\n",
         node,file,buf,count);
      if(rc=verify_area(VERIFY_WRITE, buf, count) < 0 ) {
         printk("stepper_read(): verify area failed\n");
         return(rc);
      }
      for(i=count; i>0; i--) {
         #if 0
            if(!*p) p=message;
            put_fs_byte(*p++,buf++);
         #else
            while(1) {
               rc=ring_buffer_read(&read_buffer,&xferbuf,1);

               if(debug>3) {
                  printk(
```

continues

25

DEVICE DRIVERS

Listing 25.11 CONTINUED

```
                            "stepper: ring_buffer_read returned %d\n",
                            rc);
            }
            if(rc==1) {
                bytes_transferred++;
                put_fs_byte(xferbuf,buf++);
                if(xferbuf=='\n') {
                    printk("stepper_read(): newline\n");
                    newline_read=1;
                }
                break;  /* read successful */
            }

            read_is_sleeping=1;
            if(debug>=3) printk("stepper: read sleeping\n");
            interruptible_sleep_on(&read_wait);
            read_is_sleeping=0;

            if(abort_read) return(bytes_transferred);
        }

        /* we want read to return at the end */
        /* of each line */
        if(newline_read) break;
    #endif
    }
    if(write_is_sleeping) wake_up_interruptible(&write_wait);

    if(debug>=3) {
        printk("stepper_read(): bytes=%d\n", bytes_transferred);
    }
    return(bytes_transferred);
}


static int stepper_write(struct inode *inode,
    struct file *file, const char *buf, int count)
{
    int i;
    int rc;
    char xferbuf;
    int bytes_transferred;

    if(!write_is_open) {
        printk("stepper: ERROR: stepper_write() called"
```

```
                    " while not open for writing\n");
        }

        bytes_transferred=0;

        if(rc=verify_area(VERIFY_READ, buf, count) < 0 ) {
            return(rc);
        }

        for(i=count; i>0; i--) {
                xferbuf = get_fs_byte(buf++);

                while(1) {
                  rc=ring_buffer_write(&write_buffer,&xferbuf,1);
                  if(rc==1) {
                     bytes_transferred++;
                     break;
                  }
                   if(debug>10) printk("stepper: write sleeping\n");

                   write_is_sleeping=1;
                   interruptible_sleep_on(&write_wait);
                   write_is_sleeping=0;
                   if(abort_write) return(bytes_transferred);

                }
        }
        if(read_is_sleeping) wake_up_interruptible(&read_wait);
        return(bytes_transferred);
    }
#endif
```

Ioctls

The function stepper_ioctl(), shown in Listing 25.12, is called whenever the system
call ioctl() is issued on a file descriptor that references a file controlled by our driver.
According to the man page for ioctl(), ioctls are "a catchall for operations that don't
cleanly fit the Unix stream I/O model". Ioctls are commonly used to set the baud rate
and other communications parameters on serial ports, for example, and to perform many
operations for TCP/IP sockets. The various parameters on ethernet and other network
interfaces that are set by the ifconfig program are manipulated using ioctls as are the
ARP table entries. In our case, we will use them to change the values of debugging variables and to change the speed of motion. They will also be used, in the future, to control
starting and stopping of interrupts (and device motion). I have chosen the numbers
assigned to the various ioctls somewhat randomly, avoiding the values defined in

25

DEVICE DRIVERS

/usr/include/ioctls.h. The driver also receives a TCGETS (see Chapter 26, "Terminal Control the Hard Way") which I have been simply ignoring; clearing the data structure pointed to by arg or returning an error of ENOTTY would probably be more appropriate.

Listing 25.12   IOCTLS

```
void stepper_start()
{
  /* do nothing at the moment */
}

void stepper_stop()
{
  /* do nothing at the moment */
}



static int stepper_ioctl(struct inode *iNode,
   struct file *filePtr, unsigned int cmd, unsigned long arg)
{
  switch(cmd) {
    case(STEPPER_SET_DEBUG):
        /* unfriendly user might crash system */
        /* by setting debug too high.  Only allow */
        /* root to change debug */
        if((current->uid==0) || (current->euid==0)) {
           debug=arg;
        } else {
           return(EPERM);
        }
        break;

    case(STEPPER_SET_SKIPTICKS):
        skipticks=arg;
        break;

    case(STEPPER_SET_VERBOSE_IO):
        verbose_io=arg;
        break;

    case(STEPPER_SET_VERBOSE_MOVE):
        verbose_move=arg;
        break;

    case(TCGETS):
        break;

    #if 0
        /* autostart and start/stop are not implemented */
```

```
            /* these would be used to enable interrupts */
            /* only when the driver is in use and to */
            /* allow a program to turn them on and off */

            case(STEPPER_START):
                if(debug) printk("stepper_ioctl(): start\n");
                stepper_start();
                break;
            case(STEPPER_STOP):
                if(debug) printk("stepper_ioctl(): stop\n");
                stepper_stop();
                break;
            case(STEPPER_CLEAR_BUFFERS):
                if(debug) {
                    printk("stepper_ioctl(): clear buffers\n");
                }
                ring_buffer_init(&read_buffer);
                ring_buffer_init(&write_buffer);
                break;
            case(STEPPER_AUTO):
                if(debug) {
                    printk("stepper_ioctl(): enable autostart\n");
                }
                autostart = 1;
                break;
            case(STEPPER_NOAUTO):
                if(debug) {
                    printk("stepper_ioctl(): disable autostart\n");
                }
                autostart = 0;
                break;
        #endif

        default:
            printk("stepper_ioctl(): Unknown ioctl %d\n",cmd);
            break;
    }

    return(0);
}
#endif
```

Open and Close Operations

Listing 25.13 shows the functions `stepper_open()` and `stepper_release()`, which perform open and close operations. These are called when the `open()` or `close()` system
calls are issued for files that are controlled by our device driver. In this example, we control two character special files: `/dev/stepper` and `/dev/stepper_ioctl` with minor

device numbers 0 and 1, respectively. Since we do not allow an arbitrary number of processes to open and close these devices, we do not need to keep track of which streams are associated with which process. We allow three simultaneous opens: one open for write, one open for read, and one (or more) open for ioctl only.

Listing 25.13 OPEN AND CLOSE OPERATIONS

```
#ifdef __KERNEL__
    static int stepper_open(struct inode *inode,
        struct file *file)
    {
        int rc;
        int minor;

        minor = MINOR(inode->i_rdev);
        printk("stepper: stepper_open() - file->f_mode=%d\n",
            file->f_mode);

        /*
         * As written, only one process can have the device
         * open at once.  For some applications, it might be
         * nice to have multiple processes (one controlling, for
         *  example, X and Y while the other controls Z).
         * I use two separate entries in /dev/, with
         * corresponding minor device numbers, to allow a
         * program to open for ioctl while another program
         * has the data connection open.
         * This would allow a Panic Stop application to be
         * written,
         * for example.
         *    Minor device = 0  - read and write
         *    Minor device = 1  - ioctl() only
         */

        /* if minor!=0, we are just opening for ioctl */
        if(minor!=0) {
            MOD_INC_USE_COUNT;
            return(0);
        }

        if(autostart) stepper_start();

        if(file->f_mode==1) {
            /* read */
          if(read_is_open) {
            printk("stepper: stepper_open() - read busy\n");
            return(-EBUSY);
          } else {
            read_is_open=1;
```

```
      abort_read=0;
      MOD_INC_USE_COUNT;
    }
  } else if(file->f_mode==2) {
    /* write */
    if(write_is_open) {
      printk("stepper: stepper_open() - write busy\n");
      return(-EBUSY);
    } else {
      write_is_open=1;
      abort_write=0;
      MOD_INC_USE_COUNT;
    }
  } else {
    printk("stepper: stepper_open() - unknown mode\n");
    return(-EINVAL);
  }
  if(debug) printk("stepper: stepper_open() - success\n");
  return(0);
}


void stepper_release(struct inode *inode, struct file *file)
{

  int minor;

  minor = MINOR(inode->i_rdev);

  if(minor!=0) {
    MOD_DEC_USE_COUNT;
    return;
  }

  printk("stepper: stepper_release() - file->f_mode=%d\n",
    file->f_mode);
  if(file->f_mode==1) {
    /* read */
    if(read_is_open) {
      abort_read=1;
      if(read_is_sleeping) {
        wake_up_interruptible(&read_wait);
      }
      read_is_open=0;
      MOD_DEC_USE_COUNT;
    } else {
      printk("stepper: ERROR: stepper_release() "
        "called unexpectedly (read)\n");
    }
```

continues

Listing 25.13 CONTINUED

```
    } else if(file->f_mode==2) {
      /* write */
      if(write_is_open) {
        abort_write=1;
        if(write_is_sleeping) {
          wake_up_interruptible(&write_wait);
        }
        write_is_open=0;
        MOD_DEC_USE_COUNT;
      } else {
        printk("stepper: ERROR: stepper_release() called"
          " unexpectedly (write)\n");
      }
    } else {
      printk("stepper: stepper_release() "
        "- invalid file mode\n");
    }

    if(!read_is_open && !write_is_open) {
      stepper_stop();
    }
  }
}
#endif
```

File Operations Structure

This structure, shown in Listing 25.14, has pointers to all of the top half functions we
have previously defined. We could have also defined some other functions but we will
leave them set to NULL and the kernel will use a default handler. It might make sense to
implement a `stepper_fsync()` function so we can call `fflush()` (which calls `fsync()`)
in our user program to keep the user program from getting too far ahead of the driver; we
would then sleep until the `write_buffer` was empty and the stepper motors had completed their last move.

Listing 25.14 FILE OPERATIONS STRUCTURE

```
static struct file_operations stepper_fops = {
  stepper_lseek,   /* lseek */
  stepper_read,    /* read */
  stepper_write,   /* write */
  NULL,            /* readdir */
  NULL,            /* select */
  stepper_ioctl,   /* ioctl */
  NULL,            /* mmap */
  stepper_open,    /* open */
  stepper_release,/* close */
```

```
      NULL,            /* fsync */
      NULL,            /* fasync */
      NULL,            /* check_media_change */
      NULL             /* revalidate */
   };
```

Bottom Half

The functions in Listing 25.15, along with the actual stepper control functions shown previously in Listing 25.9, implement the bottom half of the device driver. Depending on whether we are using interrupts or timer ticks (jiffies), either `timer_tick_handler()` or `interrupt_handler()` will be invoked in response to timer ticks or hardware interrupts. In either case, we want to do the same thing so I simply call another function to do the work, which I have named `bottom_half()`.

If `cleanup_module()` is waiting for us to remove ourselves from the timer tick queue by processing the next tick and then not putting ourselves back on the queue, we simply wake up `cleanup_module()` and do nothing else. If the stepper motors are not still processing the last move, we will read any available characters queued by `stepper_write()` and parse them one at a time until they cause a move to occur. If `write` is sleeping because the ring buffer was full, we will wake it up because it may be able to write more characters now that we may have drained some.

We call `move_one_step()` to do the actual work of interacting with the device. If we are using timer ticks, we must put ourselves back on the timer tick queue each time.

Listing 25.15 BOTTOM HALF

```
static int using_jiffies = 0;

static struct wait_queue *tick_die_wait_queue = NULL;

/* forward declaration to resolve circular reference */
static void timer_tick_handler(void *junk);

static struct tq_struct tick_queue_entry = {
   NULL, 0, timer_tick_handler, NULL
};

static void bottom_half()
{
   int rc;
   char c;

   tick_counter++;
   if(tick_die_wait_queue) {
```

continues

25

DEVICE DRIVERS

Listing 25.15 CONTINUED

```
        /* cleanup_module() is waiting for us */
        /* Don't reschedule interrupt and wake up cleanup */
        using_jiffies = 0;
        wake_up(&tick_die_wait_queue);
    } else {
        if((skipticks==0) || ((tick_counter % skipticks)==0)) {

            /* Don't process any move commands if */
            /* we haven't finished the last one */
            if( (xdest==xpos)
            && (ydest==ypos)
            && (zdest==zpos) ) {
                /* process command characters */
                while(
                    (rc=ring_buffer_read(&write_buffer,&c,1))==1
                ){
                    parse_one_char(c);
                    if((xdest!=xpos)
                    || (ydest!=ypos)
                    || (zdest!=zpos) ) {
                        /* parse_one_char() started a move; */
                        /* stop reading commands so current move*/
                        /* can complete first. */
                        break;
                    }
                }
                if(write_is_sleeping) {
                    wake_up_interruptible(&write_wait);
                }

            }
        }

        move_one_step();

        /* put ourselves back in the queue for the next tick*/
        if(using_jiffies) {
            queue_task(&tick_queue_entry, &tq_timer);
        }

    }
}

static void timer_tick_handler(void *junk)
{
    /* let bottom_half() do the work */
```

```
        bottom_half();
    }

    void interrupt_handler(int irq, void *dev_id,
        struct pt_regs *regs)
    {
        /* let bottom_half() do the work */
        bottom_half();
    }
#endif
```

Module Initialization and Termination

Listing 25.16 shows init_module() and cleanup_module(), which are the initialization and termination functions for the module. These functions must use these names since the insmod program invokes them by name.

The init_module() function first initializes the two ring buffers used to buffer reads and writes and resets the flags that indicate that the read or write functions are sleeping. It then registers the major device number with the system using register_chrdev(). This major device number must not already be used and must match the number we use when we make the device special files /dev/stepper and /dev/stepper_ioctl. The first parameter is the major device number. The second is an identifying string that will be listed along with the major number in /proc/devices. The third parameter is the file operations structure we defined earlier; this is where we tell the kernel how to invoke our top half functions.

We call check_region() to test if the I/O ports are available (not used by another driver) and then register them using request_region(). These calls take a base address and a count of the number of consecutive I/O addresses. The check_region() function returns zero if the region is available. The region will later be released with release_region(), which takes the same arguments.

Next we queue up one of our bottom half functions to receive interrupts or timer ticks, depending on the chosen mode of operation. The request_irq() function was described previously. If we are using timer ticks, we use queue_task() to place ourselves in the appropriate queue to receive timer ticks. If we are using hardware interrupts from the parallel port card, we tell the card to assert the hardware interrupt line so we can receive interrupts from an external hardware clock source.

For testing purposes, I have the driver initiate a move of 400 counts (1 turn on the motors I am using); this should be commented out in a production driver. Finally, we announce

25

DEVICE DRIVERS

to the world that we have successfully loaded and return to the `insmod` or "kmod" program that loaded us.

The `cleanup_module()` function is called to terminate and unload the kernel module. It is initiated by the `rmmod` or `kmod` programs. This function basically reverses the actions of `init_module()`. The kernel function `unregister_chrdev()` will unregister the major device number we registered previously and `free_irq()` will free the interrupt we may have registered.

There is, apparently, no way to remove ourselves from the timer tick queue, so we sleep until the bottom half effectively removes us by receiving a timer tick and not re-registering. Note that I should have used the `sleep_on` trick in the event of `MOD_IN_USE` or a failure of `unregister_chrdev()`. Since we cannot abort the unloading of the module, we could wait forever. We could also have the bottom half wake us up every once in a while to retry the failed operations. If appropriate, we power down the stepper motors (by turning all the transistors off) before we announce our termination and return.

Listing 25.16 INITIALIZATION AND TERMINATION

```
int init_module(void)
{
  int rc;
  ring_buffer_init(&read_buffer);
  ring_buffer_init(&write_buffer);
  read_is_sleeping=0;
  write_is_sleeping=0;

  if ((stepper_major = register_chrdev(major,"step",
  &stepper_fops)) <0 ) {
    printk("stepper: unable to get major device\n");
    return(-EIO);
  }
  /* register_chrdev() does not return the major device */
  /* number,  workaround will not be correct if major=0 */
  stepper_major = major;
  if(debug) printk("stepper:init_module():stepper_major=%d\n",
    stepper_major);


  if(check_region(base,4)) {
    printk("stepper: port in use");
    unregister_chrdev(stepper_major, "step");
    return;
  }
  request_region(base,4);

  if(irq && (!interrupts_are_enabled)) {
    rc=request_irq(irq,interrupt_handler,0,"stepper",NULL);
```

```
         if(rc) {
            printk("stepper: stepper_start()  request_irq() "
               "returned %d\n",rc);
         } else {
            printk("stepper: stepper_start() "
               "- enabled interrupts\n");
            interrupts_are_enabled = 1;

            /* now that we are ready to receive them */
            /* enable interrupts on parallel card */
            word = irq_enable_bit;
            verbose_outb( (word >> 8), base+2);
         }
      }
   if(!irq) {
      using_jiffies = 1;
      queue_task(&tick_queue_entry, &tq_timer);
   }

   /* give ourselves some work to do */
   xdest = ydest = zdest = 400;

   if(debug) printk( "stepper: module loaded\n");
   return(0);
}

void cleanup_module(void)
{
   abort_write=1;
   if(write_is_sleeping) wake_up_interruptible(&write_wait);
   abort_read=1;
   if(read_is_sleeping) wake_up_interruptible(&read_wait);

   #if 1
      /* Delay 1s for read and write to exit */
      current->state = TASK_INTERRUPTIBLE;
      current->timeout = jiffies + 100;
      schedule();
   #endif

   release_region(base,4);

   if(MOD_IN_USE) {
      printk("stepper: device busy, remove delayed\n");
      return;
   }
   printk("unregister_chrdev(%d,%s)\n",stepper_major, "step");
   if( unregister_chrdev(stepper_major, "step") ) {
      printk("stepper: unregister_chrdev() failed.\n");
```

25

DEVICE DRIVERS

continues

Listing 25.16   CONTINUED

```
        printk("stepper: /proc/devices will cause core dumps\n");
        /* Note: if we get here, we have a problem */
        /* There is still a pointer to the name of the device */
        /* which is in the address space of the LKM */
        /* which is about to go away  and we cannot abort */
        /* the unloading of the module */
    }

    /* note: we need to release the interrupt here if */
    /* necessary otherwise, interrupts may cause kernel */
    /* page faults */
    if(interrupts_are_enabled) {
        /* Disable interrupts on card before we unregister */
        word &= ~irq_enable_bit;
        verbose_outb( (word >> 8), base+2);

        free_irq(irq,NULL);
    }

    if(using_jiffies) {
        /* If we unload while we are still in the jiffie */
        /* queue, bad things will happen.  We have to wait */
        /* for the next jiffie interrupt */
        sleep_on(&tick_die_wait_queue);
    }

    if(power_down_on_exit) {
        word=flipbits;
        /* output low byte to data register */
        verbose_outb( (word & 0x00FF), base+0);
        /* output high byte to control register */
        verbose_outb( (word >> 8), base+2);
    }

    if(debug) printk("stepper: module unloaded\n");

  }
#endif
```

Main Function

The main() function, shown in listing 25.17, will not be used at all for a kernel mode
driver. It is used as the main entry point when compiled as a usermode driver.

Listing 25.17 THE main() FUNCTION

```
#ifndef __KERNEL__
main()
{
   char c;

   /* unbuffer output so we can see in real time */
   setbuf(stdout,NULL);

   printf("this program must be run as root\n");
   iopl(3);    /* Enable i/o (if root) */

   printf("Here are some example motion commands:\n");
   printf("    X=100,Y=100,Z=50\n");
   printf("    X=100,Y=100\n");
   printf("    Y=100,Z=50\n");
   printf("    X=+100,Y=-100\n");
   printf("    ?    (reports position)");
   printf("End each command with a newline.\n");
   printf("Begin typing motion commands\n");
   while(!feof(stdin)) {
      c = getc(stdin);
      parse_one_char(c);
      move_all();
   }


   if(power_down_on_exit) {
      word=flipbits;
      /* output low byte to data register */
      verbose_outb( (word & 0x00FF), base+0);
      /* output high byte to control register */
      verbose_outb( (word >> 8), base+2);
   }

}
#endif
```

Compiling the Driver

Listing 25.18 shows the Makefile that is used to compile the driver using the make program.

25

DEVICE DRIVERS

Listing 25.18 MAKEFILE

```
default: all

all: stepper.o stepuser

stepper.o: stepper.c ring.h stepper.h
        gcc -O -DMODULE -D__KERNEL__ -o stepperout.o -c stepper.c
        ld -r -o stepper.o stepperout.o ring.o

stepuser: stepper.c
        gcc -g -O -o stepuser stepper.c

ring.o: ring.c ring.h
        gcc -O -DMODULE -D__KERNEL__ -c ring.c
```

Using the Kernel Driver

Use of the drives will be illustrated by a simple sequence of shell commands in Listing 25.19. There is also a sample C program on the CD-ROM that will execute several moves and then read back the position.

Listing 25.19 DRIVER USE

```
# make the devices (once)
mknod /dev/stepper c 31 0
mknod /dev/stepper_ioctl c 31 1

#load the driver
sync; insmod ./stepper.o port=0x378

#give it something to do
cat "X=100,Y=100,Z=100" >/dev/stepper
cat "X=300,Y=300,Z=300" >/dev/stepper
cat "X=0,Y=0,Z=0" >/dev/stepper

#unload driver
sync; rmmod stepper.o
```

Various variables can be set to modify the operation of the driver. In usermode only, the variable delay sets the number of microseconds to sleep between moves; if fastdelay is set, a delay loop of the specified number of iterations will be used instead. In kernel mode, skipticks can be used to slow movement down by skipping the specified number of timer ticks between moves. The variable debug sets the amount of debugging information printed. The variable verbose_io, if nonzero, will cause a debugging message to be printed each time outb() is called. The variable verbose_move, if nonzero, will cause a debugging message to be printed each time the motor(s) are moved. If either `verbose_io` or `verbose_move` is set for a kernel mode driver, use a value for `skipticks` to reduce the rate at which `printk()` is called. The variable `base` sets the I/O port address of the parallel interface to use; the values 0x3BC, 0x378, and 0x278 are the most common. If `power_down_on_exit` is set to a nonzero value, the motors will be shut down when the usermode program exits or the kernel module is removed. The variable `do_io`, if set to zero, will disable the `outb()` calls, allowing experimentation (with `verbose_io` and/or `verbose_move` set) without a free parallel port. Some of these variables may also be set via ioctls.

> **NOTE**
>
> If the driver is issuing a large number of `printk()`s, you may need to type a `rmmod stepper` command blindly because the kernel messages will cause the shell prompt and input echo to scroll off the screen.

Note that the parallel port must not be in use by another device driver (such as lp0). You may need to unload the printer module or boot the system with the `reserve=0x378,4` option at the boot prompt. If you are trying to use interrupts and are having trouble, check for conflicts with other devices (the interrupts on printer cards are usually not used for printers) and check your bios to make sure it is not allocated to the PCI bus instead of the ISA bus or motherboard.

Future Directions

There are some improvements that I may make to this driver in the future. Proper handling of diagonal 3-dimensional moves is a prime candidate. The ability for more than one process to control the driver simultaneously is a possibility. Autostart and `ioctl()` driven start and stop may be implemented to allow use of interrupts only when needed, synchronizing with other processes, and emergency stops. Adding support for the Linux Real Time Extensions (which requires a custom kernel) would allow operation faster than 100 pulses per second; using the extensions while maintaining the standard character device interface may not be trivial, however. Adding a `stepper_select()` function and modifying `stepper_read()` and `stepper_write()` to return with a smaller count than was passed in instead of sleeping would allow the use of `select()` and non-blocking I/O.

25

DEVICE DRIVERS

Other Sources of Information

There are a number of sources of information on device drivers on the Internet and one comprehensive book on the subject.

Writing Linux Device Drivers:

```
http://www.redhat.com/~johnsonm/devices.html
```

Linux Kernel Module Programming Guide:

```
http://metalab.unc.edu/LDP/LDP/lkmpg/mpg.html
```

The Linux Kernel Hackers' Guide:

```
http://khg.redhat.com/HyperNews/get/khg.html
```

Linux Parallel Port Home Page:

```
http://www.torque.net/linux-pp.html
```

The PC's Parallel Port:

```
http://www.lvr.com/parport.htm
```

Linux Device Drivers:

Alessandro Rubini, *Linux Device Drivers*, O'Reilly and Associates, 1997, ISBN 1-56592-292-1, 448pp.

You may also find the kernel sources very useful. The include files and the source code to the routines mentioned are useful references. There are a large number of existing device drivers included with the kernel that can serve as examples.

Summary

Writing a device driver is one of the most complicated programming tasks in the Linux environment. It requires interaction with the hardware, it is easy to crash your system, and it is difficult to debug. There are no man pages for the various kernel functions you will need to use; however, there is more documentation available online and in printed form.

Getting low-level programming information from the manufacturer is often difficult; you may find it necessary to reverse engineer the hardware or select hardware from a reputable manufacturer instead. Many pieces of hardware also have serious design flaws or idiosyncrasies that will complicate writing a driver. Successfully implementing a driver is rewarding, however, and provides needed device support.

Programming the User Interface

IN THIS PART

CHAPTER 26

Terminal Control the Hard Way

by Kurt Wall

IN THIS CHAPTER

This chapter covers controlling terminals under Linux. It will show you the low-level APIs for controlling terminals and for controlling screen output in Linux applications. The notion of terminal control is a hoary holdover from computing's earliest days, when users interacted with the CPU from dumb terminals. Despite its antiquity, however, the underlying ideas still define the way Linux (and UNIX) communicates with most input and output devices.

The Terminal Interface

The terminal, or tty, interface derives from the days when users sat in front of a glorified typewriter attached to a printer. The tty interface is based on a hardware model that assumes a keyboard and printer combination is connected to a remote computer system using a serial port. This model is a distant relative of the current client-server computing architecture. Figure 26.1 illustrates the hardware model.

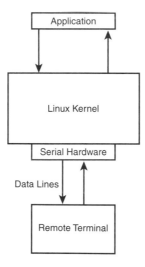

FIGURE 26.1

The terminal hardware model.

Admittedly daunting and complex, the model is sufficiently general that almost every situation in which a program needs to interact with some sort of input or output device, such as a printer, the console, xterms, or network logins, can be described as a subset of the general case. As a result, the model actually simplifies the programmer's task because it provides a consistent programming interface that can be applied in a wide variety of situations.

Why is the terminal interface so complex? Likely there are many reasons, but the two most important are human nature and what the terminal interface must accomplish.

Besides having to manage the interaction between a user and the system, programs and the system, and devices and the system, the terminal interface has to accept input from and send output to a nearly limitless variety of sources. Consider all of the different keyboard models, mice, joysticks, and other devices used to transmit user input. Add to that set all of the different kinds of output devices, such as modems, printers, plotters, serial devices, video cards, and monitors. The terminal interface has to accommodate all of these devices. This plethora of hardware demands a certain amount of complexity.

Complexity also emerges from human nature. Because terminals are interactive, users (people) want to control the interaction and tailor it to their habits, likes, and dislikes. The interface grows in size and feature set, and thus in complexity, as a direct result of this human tendency.

The following section shows you how to manipulate terminal behavior using the POSIX `termios` interface. `termios` provides finely grained control over how Linux receives and processes input. In the section "Using `terminfo`" later in the chapter, you learn how to control the appearance of output on a console or xterm screen.

Controlling Terminals

POSIX.1 defines a standard interface for querying and manipulating terminals. This interface is called `termios` and is defined in the system header file `<termios.h>`. `termios` most closely resembles the System V UNIX termio model, but also incorporates some terminal interface features from Berkeley-derived UNIX systems. From a programmer's perspective, `termios` is a data structure and a set of functions that manipulate it. The `termios` data structure, listed below, contains a complete description of a terminal's characteristics. The associated functions query and change these characteristics.

```
#include <termios.h>

struct termios {
    tcflag_t c_iflag;      /* input mode flags   */
    tcflag_t c_oflag;      /* output mode flags  */
    tcflag_t c_cflag;      /* control mode flags */
    tcflag_t c_lflag;      /* local mode flags   */
    cc_t c_line;     /* line discipline   */
    cc_t c_cc[NCCS];       /* control characters */
};
```

The `c_iflag` member controls input processing options. It affects whether and how the terminal driver processes input before sending it to a program. The `c_oflag` member controls output processing and determines if and how the terminal driver processes program output before sending it to the screen or other output device. Various control flags, which determine the hardware characteristics of the terminal device, are set in the c_cflag member. The local mode flags, stored in c_lflag, manipulate terminal characteristics, such as whether or not input characters are echoed on the screen. The c_cc array contains values for special character sequences, such as ^\ (quit) and ^H (delete), and how they behave. The c_line member indicates the control protocol, such as SLIP, PPP, or X.25—we will not discuss this member because its usage is beyond this book's scope.

Terminals operate in one of two modes, canonical (or cooked) mode, in which the terminal device driver processes special characters and feeds input to a program one line at a time, and non-canonical (or raw) mode, in which most keyboard input is unprocessed and unbuffered. The shell is an example of an application that uses canonical mode. The screen editor vi, on the other hand, uses non-canonical mode; vi receives input as it is typed and processes most special characters itself (^D, for example, moves to the end of a file in vi, but signals EOF to the shell).

Table 26.1 lists commonly used flags for the for terminal control modes.

Table 26.1   POSIX termios FLAGS

Flag	Member	Description
IGNBRK	c_iflag	Ignore BREAK condition on input.
BRKINT	c_iflag	Generate SIGINT on BREAK if IGNBRK is set.
INLCR	c_iflag	Translate NL to CR on input.
IGNCR	c_iflag	Ignore CR on input.
ICRNL	c_iflag	Translate CR to NL on input if IGNCR isn't set.
ONLCR	c_oflag	Map NL to CR-NL on output.
OCRNL	c_oflag	Map CR to NL on output.
ONLRET	c_oflag	Don't output CR.
HUPCL	c_cflag	After last process closes device, close connection.
CLOCAL	c_cflag	Ignore modem control lines.
ISIG	c_lflag	Generate SIGINT, SIGQUIT, SIGSTP when an INTR, QUIT or SUSP character, respectively, is received.
ICANON	c_lflag	Enable canonical mode.
ECHO	c_lflag	Echo input characters to output.
ECHONL	c_lflag	Echo NL characters in canonical mode, even if ECHO is not set.

The array of control characters, c_cc, contains at least eleven special control characters, such as ^D EOF, ^C INTR, and ^U KILL. Of the eleven, nine can be changed. CR is always \r and NL is always \n; neither can be changed.

Attribute Control Functions

The `termios` interface includes functions for controlling terminal characteristics. The basic functions are `tcgetattr()` and `tcsetattr()`. `tcgetattr()` initializes a `termios` data structure, setting values that represent a terminal's characteristics and settings. Querying and changing these settings means manipulating the data structure returned by `tcgetattr()` using the functions discussed in the following sections. Once you are done, use `tcsetattr()` to update the terminal with the new values. `tcgetattr()` and `tcsetattr()` are prototyped and explained below.

```
int tcgetattr(int fd, struct termios *tp);
```

`tcgetattr()` queries the terminal parameters associated with the file descriptor `fd` and stores them in the `termios` struct referenced by `tp`. Returns 0 if OK, -1 on error.

```
int tcsetattr(int fd, int action, struct termios *tp);
```

`tcsetattr()` sets the terminal parameters associated with the file descriptor `fd` using the `termios` struct referenced by `tp`. The `action` parameter controls when the changes take affect, using the following values:

- `TCSANOW`—Change the values immediately.
- `TCSADRAIN`—Change occurs after all output on `fd` has been sent to the terminal. Use this function when changing output settings.
- `TCSAFLUSH`—Change occurs after all output on `fd` has been sent to the terminal but any pending input will be discarded.

Speed Control Functions

The first four functions set the input and output speed of a terminal device. Because the interface is old, it defines speed in terms of baud, although the correct terminology is bits per second (bps). The functions come in pairs, two to get and set the output line speed and two to get and set the input line speed. Their prototypes, declared in the `<termios.h>` header, are listed below, along with short descriptions of their behavior.

```
int cfgetispeed(struct termios *tp);
```

`cfgetispeed()` returns the input line speed stored in the `termios` struct pointed to by `tp`.

```
int cfsetispeed(struct termios *tp, speed_t speed);
```

`cfsetispeed()` sets the input line speed stored in the `termios` struct pointed to by `tp` to `speed`.

```
int cfgetospeed(struct termios *tp);
```

`cfgetospeed()` eturns the output line speed stored in the `termios` struct pointed to by `tp`.

```
int cfsetospeed(struct termios *tp, speed_t speed);
```

`cfsetospeed()` sets the output line speed stored in the `termios` struct point to by `tp` to `speed`.

The `speed` parameter must be one of these constants:

B0 (Closes the connection)	B1800
B50	B2400
B75	B4800
B110	B9600
B134	B19200
B150	B38400
B200	B57600
B300	B115200
B600	B230400

Line Control Functions

The line control functions query and set various properties concerned with how, when, and if data flows to the terminal device. These functions enable you to exercise a fine degree of control over the terminal device's behavior. For example, to force all pending output to complete before proceeding, use `tcdrain()`, prototyped as:

```
int tcdrain(int fd);
```

`tcdrain()` waits until all output has been written to the file descriptor `fd` before returning.

To force output, input, or both to be flushed, use the `tcflush()` function. It is prototyped as follows:

```
int tcflush(int fd, int queue);
```

`tcflush()` flushes input, output (or both) queued to the file descriptor `fd`. The `queue` argument specifies the data to flush, as listed in the following:

- `TCIFLUSH`—Flush input data received but not read.
- `TCOFLUSH`—Flush output data written but not transmitted.
- `TCIOFLUSH`—Flush input data received but not read and output data written but not sent.

Actual flow control, whether it is on or off, is controlled through the `tcflow()` function, prototyped as:

```
int tcflow(int fd, int action);
```

`tcflow()` starts or stops transmission or reception of data on file descriptor `fd`, depending on the value of `action`:

- `TCOON`—Starts output
- `TCOOFF`—Stops output
- `TCION`—Starts input
- `TCIOFF`—Stops input

Process Control Functions

The process control functions the `termios` interface defines enable you to get information about the processes (programs) running on a given terminal. The key to obtaining this information is the process group. For example, to find out the process group identification number on a given terminal, use `tcgetpgrp()`, which is prototyped as follows:

```
pid_t tcgetpgrp(int fd);
```

`tcgetpgrp()` returns the process group ID of the foreground process group `pgrp_id` of the terminal open on file descriptor `fd`, or -1 on error.

If your program has sufficient access privileges (root equivalence), it can change the process group identification number using `tcsetpgrp()`. It is prototyped as follows:

```
int_t tcsetpgrp(int fd, pid_t pgrp_id);
```

`tcsetpgrp()` sets the foreground process group id of the terminal open on file descriptor `fd` to the process group ID `pgrp_id`.

Unless otherwise specified, all functions return 0 on success. On error, they return -1 and set `errno` to indicate the error. Figure 26.2 depicts the relationship between the hardware model illustrated in Figure 26.1 and the `termios` data structures.

The four flags, `c_lflag`, `c_iflag`, `c_oflag`, and `c_cflag`, mediate the input between the terminal device driver and a program's input and output functions. The read and write functions between the kernel and the user program are the interface between user space programs and the kernel. These functions could be simple `fgets()` and `fputs()`, the `read()` and `write()` system calls, or use other I/O functionality, depending on the nature of the program.

FIGURE 26.2

How the hardware model maps to the termios *structure.*

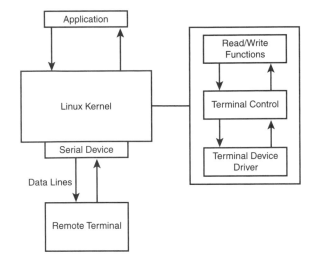

Using the Terminal Interface

Of the functions that manipulate termios structures, tcgetattr() and tcsetattr() are the most frequently used. As their names suggest, tcgetattr() queries a terminal's state and tcsetattr() changes it. Both accept a file descriptor fd that corresponds to the process's controlling terminal and a pointer tp to a termios struct. As noted above, tcgetattr() populates the referenced termios struct and tcsetattr() updates the terminal characteristics using the values stored in the struct.

Listing 26.1 illustrates using termios to turn off character echo when entering a password.

Listing 26.1 noecho.c

```
1   /*
2    * Listing 26-1
3    */
4   #include <stdio.h>
5   #include <stdlib.h>
6   #include <termios.h>
7
8   #define PASS_LEN 8
9
10  void err_quit(char *msg, struct termios flags);
11
12  int main()
13  {
14      struct termios old_flags, new_flags;
```

```
15        char password[PASS_LEN + 1];
16        int retval;
17
18        /* Get the current terminal settings */
19        tcgetattr(fileno(stdin), &old_flags);
20        new_flags = old_flags;
21
22        /* Turn off local echo, but pass the newlines through */
23        new_flags.c_lflag &= ~ECHO;
24        new_flags.c_lflag |= ECHONL;
25
26        /* Did it work?  */
27        retval = tcsetattr(fileno(stdin), TCSAFLUSH, &new_flags);
28        if(retval != 0)
29            err_quit("Failed to set attributes", old_flags);
30
31        /* Did the settings change? */
32        tcgetattr(fileno(stdin), &new_flags);
33        if(new_flags.c_lflag & ECHO)
34            err_quit("Failed to turn off ECHO", old_flags);
35        if(!new_flags.c_lflag & ECHONL)
36            err_quit("Failed to turn on ECHONL", old_flags);
37
38        fprintf(stdout, "Enter password: ");
39        fgets(password, PASS_LEN + 1, stdin);
40        fprintf(stdout, "You typed: %s", password);
41
42        /* Restore the old termios settings */
43        tcsetattr(fileno(stdin), TCSANOW, &old_flags);
44
45        exit(EXIT_SUCCESS);
46    }
47
48    void err_quit(char *msg, struct termios flags)
49    {
50        fprintf(stderr, "%s\n", msg);
51        tcsetattr(fileno(stdin), TCSANOW, &flags);
52        exit(EXIT_FAILURE);
53    }
```

After the variable definitions, line 19 retrieves the termios settings for stdin. Line 20 copies the terminal settings to the new_flags struct, which is the structure the program manipulates. A well-behaved program should restore the original settings before exiting, so, before it exits, the program restores the original termios settings (line 43).

Lines 23 and 24 illustrate the correct syntax for clearing and setting termios flags. Line 23 turns off echo on the local screen and line 24 allows the screen to echo any newlines received in input.

So far, all the program has done is change values in the struct; updating the terminal is the next step. In order to post the changes, use tcsetattr(), as shown on line 27. The TCSAFLUSH option discards any input the user may have typed, ensuring a consistent read. Because not all terminals support all termios settings, however, the POSIX standard permits termios silently to ignore unsupported terminal capabilities. As a result, robust programs should check to make sure that the tcsetattr() call succeeded (lines 28 and 29), and then confirms that ECHO is turned off and ECHONL is turned on in lines 32–36. If the update fails, add appropriate code to handle the error.

With the preliminaries out of the way, the program prompts for a password, retrieves it, then prints out what the user typed. No characters echo to the screen on input, but the call to fprintf() works as expected. As noted above, the last step before exiting is restoring the terminal's original termios state. The err_quit() function displays a diagnostic message and restores the original terminal attributes before exiting.

Changing Terminal Modes

The program in Listing 26.1 did manipulate some terminal attributes, but remained in canonical mode. The program in Listing 26.2 puts the terminal in raw mode and performs its own processing on special characters and signals.

Listing 26.2 RAW MODE

```
1   /*
2    * Listing 26-2
3    */
4   #include <termios.h>
5   #include <unistd.h>
6   #include <signal.h>
7   #include <stdlib.h>
8   #include <stdio.h>
9
10  void err_quit(char *msg);
11  void err_reset(char *msg, struct termios *flags);
12  static void sig_caught(int signum);
13
14  int main(void)
15  {
16      struct termios new_flags, old_flags;
17      int i, fd;
18      char c;
19
20      /* Set up a signal handler */
21      if(signal(SIGINT, sig_caught) == SIG_ERR)
```

```
22                err_quit("Failed to set up SIGINT handler");
23          if(signal(SIGQUIT, sig_caught) == SIG_ERR)
24                err_quit("Failed to set up SIGQUIT handler");
25          if(signal(SIGTERM, sig_caught) == SIG_ERR)
26                err_quit("Failed to set up SIGTERM handler");
27
28          fd = fileno(stdin);
29
30          /* Set up raw/non-canonical mode */
31          tcgetattr(fd, &old_flags);
32          new_flags = old_flags;
33          new_flags.c_lflag &= ~(ECHO | ICANON | ISIG);
34          new_flags.c_iflag &= ~(BRKINT | ICRNL);
35          new_flags.c_oflag &= ~OPOST;
36          new_flags.c_cc[VTIME] = 0;
37          new_flags.c_cc[VMIN] = 1;
38          if(tcsetattr(fd, TCSAFLUSH, &new_flags) < 0)
39                err_reset("Failed to change attributes", &old_flags);
40
41          /* Process keystrokes until DELETE key is pressed */
42          fprintf(stdout, "In RAW mode.  Press DELETE key to exit\n");
43          while((i = read(fd, &c, 1)) == 1)  {
44                if((c &= 255) == 0177)
45                      break;
46                printf("%o\n", c);
47          }
48
49          /* Restore original terminal attributes */
50          tcsetattr(fd, TCSANOW, &old_flags);
51
52          exit(0);
53    }
54
55    void sig_caught(int signum)
56    {
57          fprintf(stdout, "signal caught: %d\n", signum);
58    }
59
60    void err_quit(char *msg)
61    {
62          fprintf(stderr, "%s\n", msg);
63          exit(EXIT_FAILURE);
64    }
65
66    void err_reset(char *msg, struct termios *flags)
67    {
68          fprintf(stderr, "%s\n", msg);
69          tcsetattr(fileno(stdin), TCSANOW, flags);
70          exit(EXIT_FAILURE);
71    }
```

The two error handling functions declared and defined on lines 10–12 and 62–73, respectively, are strictly for convenience. The program creates a signal-handling function to demonstrate that it catches some signals (lines 13, 57–60). The program's real meat appears in lines 31–39. Line 33 turns off canonical mode, local echo, and ignores signals; line 34 turns of the CR to NL translation, and line 35 turns off all output processing. After updating the terminal attributes, the loop on lines 43–46 reads input one character at a time and outputs it to the screen in octal notation. If you press the Delete key, the program exits after restoring the original terminal settings.

A sample run of the program looks like the following:

```
$ ./rawmode
In RAW mode.  Press DELETE key to exit
                        154 Type l
                    151 Type i
                      156 Type n
                        165 Type u
                          170 Type x
                             3 Type Ctrl-C
                            32 Type Ctrl-Z
                             4 Type Ctrl-D
                             $
```

A newline does not perform a carriage return, so input appears on a new line, but at the location of the cursor from the last line. Because the program turned off signals, signals entered at the keyboard, such as ^C (interrupt), ^Z (suspend), and ^D (EOF) get ignored.

Using `terminfo`

Where `termios` gives you very low-level control over input processing, `terminfo` gives you a similar level of control over output processing. `terminfo` provides a portable, low-level interface to operations such as clearing a terminal screen, positioning the cursor, or deleting lines or characters. Due to the wide variety of terminals in existence, UNIX's designers (eventually) learned to standardize descriptions of terminal capabilities in centrally located database files. The word "terminfo" refers both to this database and to the routines that access it.

> **NOTE**
>
> Strictly speaking, the `termcap` database, first used in BSD-derived systems, preceded `terminfo` (the name "termcap" is a contraction of the phrase "TERMinal CAPability). As the `termcap` database grew in size, however, it became too slow for interactive use, and was replaced with `terminfo` in System V-derived UNIX beginning with Release 2.

`terminfo` Capabilities

For each possible terminal type, such as VT100 or xterm, `terminfo` maintains a list of that terminal's capabilities and features, called a *capname*, or CAPability NAME. Capnames fall into one of the following categories:

- boolean
- numeric
- string

Boolean capnames simply indicate whether or not a terminal supports a specific feature, such as cursor addressing or a fast screen-clearing function. Numeric capnames usually define size-related capabilities; for example, how many columns and lines a terminal has. String capnames define either the escape sequence necessary to access a certain feature or the string that would be output if the user pressed a certain key, such as a function key. Table 26.2 lists a small subset of the capabilities about which `terminfo` knows; for a complete list, refer to the `terminfo(5)` man page.

Table 26.2 COMMON TERMINAL CAPABILITIES

capname	Type	Description
am	boolean	Terminal has automatic margins
bce	boolean	Terminal uses background color erase
km	boolean	Terminal has a META key
ul	boolean	Underline character overstrikes
cols	numeric	Number of columns on current terminal
lines	numeric	Number of lines/rows on current terminal
colors	numeric	Number of colors current terminal supports
clear	string	Clear the screen and home the cursor
cl	string	Clear to the end of the line
ed	string	Clear to the end of the screen
smcup	string	Enter cursor address mode
cup	string	Move cursor to (row, column)
rmcup	string	Exit cursor address mode
bel	string	Emit audible bell
flash	string	Emit visual bell (flash screen)
kf[0-63]	string	F[0-63] function key

To use `terminfo`, include `<curses.h>` and `<term.h>`, in that order, in your source file. You also have to link against the curses library, so add `-lcurses` to the compiler invocation.

Using `terminfo`

In pseudo-code, the following is the usual sequence of instructions for using terminfo:

1. Initialize the `terminfo` data structures
2. Retrieve capname(s)
3. Modify capname(s)
4. Output the modified capname(s) to the terminal
5. Other code as necessary
6. Repeat steps 2–5

Initializing the `terminfo` data structures is simple, as shown in the following code:

```
#include <curses.h>
#include <term.h>

int setupterm(const char *term, int filedes, int *errret);
```

`term` specifies the terminal type. If it is null, `setupterm()` reads `$TERM` from the environment; otherwise, `setupterm()` uses the value to which `term` points. All output is sent to the file or device opened on the file descriptor `filedes`. If `errret` is not null, it will either be 1 to indicate success, 0 if the terminal referenced in `term` could not be found in the `terminfo` database, or -1 if the `terminfo` database could not be found. `setupterm()` returns OK to indicate success or ERR on failure. If `errret` is null, `setupterm()` emits a diagnostic message and exits.

Each of the three classes of capabilities (boolean, numeric, and string) has a corresponding function to retrieve a capability, as described in the following:

```
int tigetflag(const char *capname);
```

> Returns TRUE if the terminal specified by term in `setupterm()` supports `capname`, FALSE if it does not, or -1 if `capname` isn't a boolean capability.

```
int tigetnum(const char *capname);
```

> Returns the numeric value of `capname`, ERR if the terminal specified by `term` in `setupterm()` doesn't support `capname`, or -2 if `capname` isn't a numeric capability.

```
char *tigetstr(const char *capname);
```

> Returns a pointer to char containing the escape sequence for `capname`, (char *) null if the terminal specified by `term` in `setupterm()` doesn't support `capname`, or (char *)-1 if `capname` isn't a string capability.

Terminal Control the Hard Way

CHAPTER 26

425

26

TERMINAL
CONTROL THE
HARD WAY

Listing 26.3 uses these functions to query and print a few of the current terminal's capabilities.

Listing 26.3 getcaps.c

```
1   /*
2    * Listing 26-3
3    * getcaps.c
4    * Get and show terminal capabilities using terminfo data structures
5    * and functions
6    */
7   #include <stdlib.h>
8   #include <stdio.h>
9   #include <term.h>
10  #include <curses.h>
11
12  #define NUMCAPS 3
13
14  int main(void)
15  {
16      int i;
17      int retval = 0;
18      char *buf;
19      char *boolcaps[NUMCAPS] = { "am", "bce", "km" };
20      char *numcaps[NUMCAPS] = { "cols", "lines", "colors" };
21      char *strcaps[NUMCAPS] = { "cup", "flash", "hpa" };
22
23      if(setupterm(NULL, fileno(stdin), NULL) != OK) {
24          perror("setupterm()");
25          exit(EXIT_FAILURE);
26      }
27
28      for(i = 0; i < NUMCAPS; ++i) {
29          retval = tigetflag(boolcaps[i]);
30          if(retval == FALSE)
31              printf("`%s' unsupported\n", boolcaps[i]);
32          else
33              printf("`%s' supported\n", boolcaps[i]);
34      }
35      fputc('\n', stdout);
36
37      for(i = 0; i < NUMCAPS; ++i) {
38          retval = tigetnum(numcaps[i]);
39          if(retval == ERR)
40              printf("`%s' unsupported\n", numcaps[i]);
41          else
42              printf("`%s' is %d\n", numcaps[i], retval);
43      }
44      fputc('\n', stdout);
45
```

continues

LISTING 26.3 CONTINUED

```
46      for(i = 0; i < NUMCAPS; ++i) {
47          buf = tigetstr(strcaps[i]);
48          if(buf == NULL)
49              printf("`%s' unsupported\n", strcaps[i]);
50          else
51              printf("`%s' is \\E%s\n", strcaps[i], &buf[1]);
52              /*printf("`%s' is %s\n", strcaps[i], buf);*/
52      }
53
54      exit(0);
55  }
```

The program begins by initializing the `terminfo` data structures and setting up some variables for internal use. Then, it queries and prints three of each of the three classes of terminal capabilities. First, we test for support of the `am` (automatic margin), `bce` (background color erase), and `km` (META key) boolean capabilities (lines 28–34). Then, in lincs 37–43, we query the numeric capabilities `cols` (number of columns the terminal has), `lines` (the number of rows), and `colors` (the number of colors the terminal can display). Lines 46–53 attempt to retrieve three string capabilities, `cup` (the escape sequence to position the cursor), `flash` (the escape sequence to generate a visual bell), and `hpa` (absolute horizontal cursor positioning).

The only tricky part is lines 51 and 52. If the terminal supports a given string capability, `tigetstr()` returns a pointer to char that contains the escape sequence necessary to invoke that feature. If you output that string to the terminal, using `printf()` or `puts()`, in most cases you actually invoke that escape sequence. So, to avoid invoking, for example, the visual bell, the program strips off the first character, `E\` (ESC), and prints out the rest of the string. For our purposes, however, this approach is not optimal because it doesn't display the complete escape sequence. As a result, on line 51 we print static text, `\\E`, to escape the escape sequence.

To see how the program would behave if we did not take this precaution, comment out line 51 and uncomment line 52 before compiling and running the program. If your terminal supports a visual bell (most do), the screen will flash.

> **NOTE**
>
> The `infocmp` command can list all of a terminal type's capabilities. To see `infocmp` in action, issue the command `infocmp -v $TERM`. See `infocmp(1)`'s man page for more information.

Working with `terminfo` Capabilities

Now that you know how to get terminal capabilities, the next step is to update them and put them into effect. `tparm()` modifies a capname; `putp()` and `tputs()` output the change to the screen.

The `putp()` function, prototyped below, assumes that output device is standard output (stdout). As a result, it has a simple calling convention.

```
int putp(const char *str);
```

`putp()` outputs `str` to standard output. It is equivalent to `tputs(str, 1, putchar)`.

`tputs()`, on the other hand, gives you a greater degree of control, and has a correspondingly more complex interface. It is prototyped as:

```
int tputs(const char *str, int affcnt, int (*putc)(int));
```

`tputs()` outputs `str` to the `term` and `filedes` specified in `setupterm()`. `str` must be a `terminfo` string variable or the return value from a `tparm()` or `tigetstr()` call. `affcnt` is the number of lines affected if `str` is a line-related capability or 1 if not applicable. `putc` is a pointer to any `putchar`-style output function that outputs characters one at a time.

Naturally, before you can send a control string, you have to construct it. This is `tparm()`'s job. It is declared as follows:

```
char *tparm(const char *str, long p1, long p2, ..., long p9);
```

`tparm()` constructs a properly formatted parameterized string capname, using `str` and the parameters p1-p9. It returns a pointer to an updated copy of `str` containing the new parameters p1-p9 or NULL on error.

What is a parameterized string? Recall that `tigetstr()` returns the escape sequence used to invoke a terminal string capability. When you executed the program in Listing 26.3, one of the lines printed to standard output should have resembled the following:

```
`cup' is \E[%i%p1%d;%p2%dH
```

This is a parameterized string. This string is called a parameterized string because it defines a generic capability; in this case, moving the cursor to a specific location on the screen, which requires arguments, or parameters. In the case of the `cup` capability, it needs a row number and a column number to know where to place the cursor. To move the cursor on a standard (monochrome) xterm, xterm expects a command that, in semi-comprehensible language, looks like `Escape-[-<row>-;-<column>-H`.

In "terminfo-ese," this translates to \E[%i%p1%d;%p2%dH. The programmer's job is to supply the row and column numbers, which are indicated using %pN, where N is a value between 1 and 9. So, to move to the position (10,15) on the screen, p1 = 10 and p2 = 15. For clarity, Table 26.3 describes the terminfo characters and arguments.

Table 26.3 terminfo CHARACTERS AND ARGUMENTS

Character or Argument	*Description*
\E	Output Escape to the screen
[	Output "[" to the screen
%i	Increment all %p values by 1
%p1	Push the value in %p1 onto an internal terminfo stack
%d	Pop the value in %p1 off the stack and output it to the screen
;	Output ";" to the screen
%p2	Push the value in %p2 onto (the same) internal terminfo stack
%d	Pop the value in %p2 off the stack and output %p2 to the screen
H	Output "H" to the screen

These may seem complicated and obscure, but consider the alternative: hard-coding hundreds of additional lines of terminal-specific code into your program in order to take into account all the possible terminals on which your program will run. Parameterized strings set up a general format for achieving the same effect on all terminals; all the programmer must do is substitute the correct values for the parameters. In my opinion, trading some cryptic-looking strings for hundreds of lines of code is a great trade!

To make all of this more concrete, look at Listing 26.4. It rewrites the last example program, Listing 26.3, using additional terminal capabilities to create a (hopefully) more esthetically pleasing screen.

Listing 26.4 new_getcaps.c

```
1    /*
2     * Listing 26-4
3     * new_getcaps.c
4     * Get and show terminal capabilities using terminfo data structures
5     * and functions
6     */
7    #include <stdlib.h>
8    #include <stdio.h>
9    #include <term.h>
10   #include <curses.h>
```

```
11
12      #define NUMCAPS 3
13
14      void clrscr(void);
15      void mv_cursor(int, int);
16
17      int main(void)
18      {
19          char *boolcaps[NUMCAPS] = { "am", "bce", "km" };
20          char *numcaps[NUMCAPS] = { "cols", "lines", "colors" };
21          char *strcaps[NUMCAPS] = { "cup", "flash", "hpa" };
22          char *buf;
23          int retval, i;
24
25          if(setupterm(NULL, fileno(stdout), NULL) != OK) {
26              perror("setupterm()");
27              exit(EXIT_FAILURE);
28          }
29
30          clrscr();
31          for(i = 0; i < NUMCAPS; ++i) {
32              /* position the cursor */
33              mv_cursor(i, 10);
34              retval = tigetflag(boolcaps[i]);
35              if(retval == FALSE)
36                  printf("`%s' unsupported\n", boolcaps[i]);
37              else
38                  printf("`%s' supported\n", boolcaps[i]);
39          }
40          sleep(3);
41
42          clrscr();
43          for(i = 0; i < NUMCAPS; ++i) {
44              mv_cursor(i, 10);
45              retval = tigetnum(numcaps[i]);
46              if(retval == ERR)
47                  printf("`%s' unsupported\n", numcaps[i]);
48              else
49                  printf("`%s' is %d\n", numcaps[i], retval);
50          }
51          sleep(3);
52
53          clrscr();
54          for(i = 0; i < NUMCAPS; ++i) {
55              mv_cursor(i, 10);
56              buf = tigetstr(strcaps[i]);
57              if(buf == NULL)
58                  printf("`%s' unsupported\n", strcaps[i]);
59              else
60                  printf("`%s' is \\E%s\n", strcaps[i], &buf[1]);
```

continues

LISTING 26.4 CONTINUED

```
61              }
62              sleep(3);
63
64              exit(0);
65      }
66
67      /*
68       * Clear the screen
69       */
70      void clrscr(void)
71      {
72              char *buf = tigetstr("clear");
73              putp(buf);
74      }
75
76      /*
77       * Move the cursor to the specified row row and column col
78       */
79      void mv_cursor(int row, int col)
80      {
81              char *cap = tigetstr("cup");
82              putp(tparm(cap, row, col));
83      }
```

Very little has changed between the two programs. First, I declare two utility functions, clrscr() and mv_cursor(), to clear the screen and position the cursor at a specific location, respectively. Their definitions, lines 70–74 and 79–83, respectively, utilize the putp() function, since we want to update standard output. We save one line of code on line 82 by passing tparm()'s return value directly to putp().

Besides the utility functions, I added a total of nine lines of code to the main program. Before entering the blocks that retrieve and display the terminal capabilities, I want to clear the screen (lines 30, 42, and 53). Inside of each block (lines 32, 44, and 55) the new calls to mv_cursor() position the screen cursor on the i'th row in the tenth column. Finally, after exiting each for loop, a sleep() statement allows you to view the output and see the terminfo function calls do their work.

One final note before ending this chapter. I recognize that the programs used to illustrate termios and terminfo features are neither optimized nor efficient. I eschewed fast, efficient code for didactic clarity. For example, the three for loops in Listings 26.3 and 26.4 could be collapsed into a single for loop by using a function pointer. I preferred to make the illustrations clear and unambiguous without troubling you to decipher C idioms.

Summary

This chapter took a detailed look at two very low-level interfaces for terminal manipulation. It is a large subject, however, so the coverage was not exhaustive. For additional resources, see the man pages for `terminfo(5)`, `termios(3)`, and `term(5)`. The canonical technical reference is the O'Reilly book, *termcap & terminfo,* by John Strang, Linda Mui, and Tim O'Reilly. The next chapter looks at ncurses, a much easier way to use a set of libraries for manipulating terminals.

Screen Manipulation with ncurses

by Kurt Wall

IN THIS CHAPTER

This chapter introduces ncurses, the free implementation of the classic UNIX screen-handling library, curses. ncurses provides a simple, high-level interface for screen control and manipulation. Besides a rich set of functions for controlling the screen's appearance, ncurses also offers powerful routines for handling keyboard and mouse input, creating and managing multiple windows, using forms, and panels.

A Short History of ncurses

ncurses, which stands for "new curses," is a freely redistributable clone of the curses libraries distributed with the System V Release 4.0 (SVR4) UNIX distributed by Bell Labs. The term "curses" derives from the phrase "cursor optimization," succinctly describing how curses behaves. The SVR4 curses package, in turn, was a continued evolution of the curses available with System II UNIX, which itself was based on the original curses implementation shipped with early Berkeley Software Distribution (BSD) UNIX releases.

So, how did curses originate? As you saw in the previous chapter, using termios or, even worse, the tty interface, to manipulate the screen's appearance is code-intensive. In addition, it is also terminal-specific, subject to the idiosyncrasies of the multitude of terminal types and terminal emulators available. Enter the old text-based adventure game, rogue. Ken Arnold, at Berkeley, collected rogue's termcap-based screen-handling and cursor movement routines into a library that was first distributed with BSD UNIX. AT&T's (also known as Bell Labs) System III UNIX included a much improved curses library and the terminfo terminal description database, both written by Mark Horton. Horton's curses implementation included support for color-capable terminals and additional video attributes.

The System V UNIX releases continued curses' march along the feature trail, adding support for forms, menus, and panels. Forms enable the programmer to create easy-to-use data entry and display windows, simplifying what is usually a difficult and application-specific coding task. Panels extend curses' ability to deal with overlapping and stacked windows. Menus provide, well, menus, again with a simpler, generalized interface. Due to space limitations, unfortunately, we will not cover these elements of the ncurses package.

ncurses' immediate ancestor was Pavel Curtis' pcurses package. Zeyd Ben-Halim developed ncurses using Curtis' work as a base. Eric Raymond incorporated many enhancements and continued ncurses' development. Juergen Pfeifer added most of the support for forms and menus to the ncurses package. Thomas Dickey currently maintains ncurses, has done the lion's share of ncurses' configuration for building on multiple systems, and performs most of the testing. A proverbial "cast of thousands" (far more than are currently listed in the NEWS file in the source distribution, which is current back to version 1.9.9e) has contributed fixes and patches over the years.

ncurses' current version is numbered 4.2, although the 5.0 release is currently in beta. In an interesting irony, ncurses is now the approved replacement for the 4.4BSD's "classic" curses, thus having come full circle back to the operating system on which curses originated.

Compiling with ncurses

To compile a program with ncurses, you need its function and variable definitions, so include <curses.h> in your source code:

```
#include <curses.h>
```

Many Linux systems make /usr/include/curses.h a symbolic link to the /usr/include/ncurses.h, so you could conceivably include <ncurses.h>. However, for maximum portability, use <curses.h> because, believe it or not, ncurses is not available on all UNIX and UNIX-like platforms. You will also need to link against the ncurses libraries, so use the -lcurses option when linking, or add -lcurses to the LDFLAGS make variable or the $LDFLAGS environment variable:

```
$ gcc curses_prog.c -o curses_prog -lcurses
```

Debugging ncurses Programs

By default, debug tracing is disabled in ncurses programs. To enable debugging, link against ncurses' debug library, ncurses_g, and either call trace(N) in your code or set the environment variable $NCURSES_TRACE to N, where N is a positive, non-zero integer. Doing so forces debugging output to a file named, appropriately, trace, in the current directory. The larger N's value, the more finely grained and voluminous the debugging output. Useful values for N are documented in <ncurses.h>. For example, the standard trace level, TRACE_ORDINARY, is 31.

> **TIP**
>
> The ncurses package comes with a script, tracemunch, which compresses and summarizes the debug information into a more readable, human-friendly format.

About Windows

This section discusses ncurses' idea of windows, screens, and terminals. Several terms are used repeatedly (and, hopefully, consistently) throughout this chapter, so the following list defines these terms up front to avoid as much confusion as possible.

- *Screen*—Screen refers to the physical terminal screen in character or console mode. Under the X Window system, "screen" means a terminal emulator window.

- *Window*—Window is used to refer to an independent rectangular area displayed on a screen. It may or may not be the same size as the screen.

- stdscr—This is an ncurses data structure, a (WINDOW *), that represents what you currently see on the screen. It might be one window or a set of windows, but it fills the entire screen. You can think of it as a palette on which you paint using ncurses routines.

- curscr—Another pointer to a WINDOW data structure, curscr contains ncurses' idea of what the screen currently looks like. Like stdscr, its size is the width and height of the screen. Differences between curscr and stdscr are the changes that appear on the screen.

- *Refresh*—This word refers both to an ncurses function call and a logical process. The refresh() function compares curscr, ncurses' notion of what the screen currently looks like, to stdscr, updates any changes to curscr, and then displays those changes to the screen. Refresh is also used to denote the process of updating the screen.

- *Cursor*—This term, like refresh, has two similar meanings, but always refers to the location where the next character will be displayed. On a screen (the physical screen), cursor refers to the location of the physical cursor. On a window (an ncurses window), it refers to the logical location where the next character will be displayed. Generally, in this chapter, the second meaning applies. ncurses uses a (y,x) ordered pair to locate the cursor on a window.

ncurses' Window Design

ncurses defines window layout sanely and predictably. Windows are arranged such that the upper-left corner has the coordinates (0,0) and the lower-right corner has the coordinates (LINES, COLUMNS), as Figure 27.1 illustrates.

FIGURE 27.1

An ncurses window.

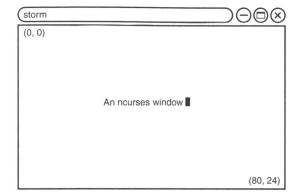

You are perhaps familiar with the $LINES and $COLS environment variables. These variables have ncurses equivalents, LINES and COLS, that contain ncurses' notion of the number of rows and columns, respectively, of the current window's size. Rather than using these global variables, however, use the function call getmaxyx() to get the size of the window with which you are currently working.

One of ncurses' chief advantages, in addition to complete freedom from terminal dependent code, is the ability to create and manage multiple windows in addition to the ncurses provided stdscr. These programmer-defined windows come in two varieties, subwindows and independent windows.

Subwindows are created using the subwin() function call. They are called subwindows because they create a window from an existing window. At the C language level, they are pointers to pointers to some subset of an existing WINDOW data structure. The subset can include the entire window or only part of it. Subwindows, which you could also call child or derived windows, can be managed independently of their parent windows, but changes made to the children will be reflected in the parent.

Create new or independent windows with the newwin() call. This function returns a pointer to a new WINDOW structure that has no connection to other windows. Changes made to an independent window do not show up on the screen unless explicitly requested. The newwin() function adds powerful screen manipulation abilities to your programming repertoire, but, as is often the case with added power, it also entails additional complexity. You are required to keep track of the window and explicitly to display it on the screen, whereas subwindows update on the screen automatically.

ncurses' Function Naming Conventions

While many of ncurses' functions are defined to use stdscr by default, there will be many situations in which you want to operate on a window other than stdscr. ncurses uses a systematic and consistently applied naming convention for routines that can apply to any window. In general, functions that can operate on an arbitrary window are prefixed with the character "w" and take a (WINDOW *) variable as their first argument. Thus, for example, the move(y,x) call, which moves the cursor to the coordinates specified by y and x on stdscr, can be replaced by wmove(win, y, x), which moves the cursor to the specified location in the window win. That is,

```
move(y, x);
```

is equivalent to

```
wmove(stdscr, y, x);
```

> ## NOTE
>
> Actually, most of the functions that apply to stdscr are pseudo-functions. They are #defined preprocessor macros that use stdscr as the default window in calls to the window-specific functions. This is an implementation detail with which you need not trouble yourself, but it may help you better understand the ncurses library. A quick grep '#define' /usr/include/ncurses.h will reveal the extent to which ncurses uses macros and will also serve as good examples of preprocessor usage.

Likewise, many ncurses input and output functions have forms that combine a move and an I/O operation in a single call. These functions prepend mv to the function name and the desired (y, x) coordinates to the argument list. So, for example, you could write

```
move(y, x);
addchstr(str);
```

to move the cursor to specific coordinates and add a string at that location on stdscr, or, you could simply write

```
mvaddchstr(y, x, str);
```

which accomplishes the same thing with a single line of code.

As you might guess at this point, functions also exist that combine an I/O and a move directed to a specific window. So code that looks like

```
wmove(some_win, y, x);
waddchstr(some_win, str);
```

can be replaced with one line that reads

```
mvwaddchstr(some_win, y, x, str);
```

This sort of shorthand permeates ncurses. The convention is simple and easy to pick up.

Initialization and Termination

Before you can use ncurses, you must properly initialize the ncurses subsystem, set up various ncurses data structures, and query the supporting terminal's display capabilities and characteristics. Similarly, before exiting an ncurses-based application, you need to return the memory resources ncurses allocates and reset the terminal to its original, pre-ncurses state.

ncurses Initialization Structures

The initscr() and newterm() functions handle ncurses initialization requirements. initscr() has two tasks, to create and initialize stdscr and curscr, and to find out the terminal's capabilities and characteristics by querying the terminfo or termcap database. If it is unable to complete one of these tasks, or if some other error occurs, initscr() displays useful diagnostic information and terminates the application. Call initscr() before you use any other routines that manipulate stdscr or curscr. Failure to do so will cause your application to abort with a segmentation fault. At the same time, however, only call initscr() when you are certain you need it, such as after other routines that check for program startup errors. Finally, functions that change a terminal's status, such as cbreak() or noecho(), should be called after initscr() returns. The first call to refresh() after initscr() will clear the screen. If it succeeds, initscr() returns a pointer to stdscr, which you can save for later use, if necessary, otherwise it returns NULL and exits the program, printing a useful error message to the display.

If your program will send output to or receive input from more than one terminal, use the newterm() function call instead of initscr(). For each terminal with which you expect to interact, call newterm() once. newterm() returns a pointer to a C data structure of type SCREEN (another ncurses-defined type), to use when referring to that terminal. Before you can send output to or receive input from such a terminal, however, you must make it the current terminal. The set_term() call accomplishes this. Pass as set_term()'s argument the pointer to the SCREEN (returned by a previous newterm() call) that you want to make the current terminal.

ncurses Termination

The initialization functions allocate memory resources and reset the terminal state to an ncurses-friendly mode. Accordingly, you need to free the allocated memory and reset the terminal to its pre-ncurses mode. The termination functions endwin() and delscreen() do this job. When you are through working with a SCREEN, call endwin() before making another terminal the current terminal, then call delscreen() on that terminal to release the SCREEN resources allocated to it, because endwin() does not release memory for screens created by newterm(). If you have not called newterm(), however, and have only used curscr and stdscr, all that is required is a single call to endwin() before you exit your application. endwin() moves the cursor to the lower left-hand corner of the screen, and resets the terminal to its non-visual, pre-ncurses state. The memory allocated to curscr and stdscr is not released because your program can temporarily suspend ncurses by calling endwin(), performing other processing, and then calling refresh().

The following provides a reference for each of the functions discussed so far:

```
WINDOW *initscr(void);
```

Initializes ncurses data structures after determining the current terminal type. Returns a pointer to stdscr on success or NULL on failure.

```
int endwin(void);
```

Restores the previous tty in place before the call to initscr() or newterm(). Returns the integer OK on success or, on failure, ERR, and aborts the application.

```
SCREEN *newterm(const char *type, FILE *outfd, FILE *infd);
```

Analog of initscr() for programs that use multiple terminals. type is a string to be used, if required, in place of the $TERM environment variable; if NULL, $TERM will be used. outfd is a pointer to a file to be used for output to this terminal, and infd is a pointer to a file to be used for input from this terminal. Returns a pointer to the new terminal, which should be saved for future references to the terminal, or NULL on failure.

```
SCREEN *set_term(SCREEN *new);
```

Sets the current terminal to the terminal specified by new, which must be a SCREEN pointer returned from a previous call to newterm(). All subsequent input and output and other ncurses routines operate on the terminal to which new refers. Returns a pointer to the old terminal or NULL on failure.

```
void delscreen(SCREEN *sp);
```

Deallocates memory associated with sp. Must be called after endwin() for the terminal associated with sp.

Illustrating ncurses Initialization and Termination

Listings 27.1 and 27.2 illustrate the usage of the ncurses routines we have looked at so far. The first program, `initcurs`, shows the standard ncurses initialization and termination idioms, using `initscr()` and `endwin()`, while the second one, `newterm`, demonstrates the proper use of `newterm()` and `delscreen()`.

Listing 27.1 `initcurs.c`

```
1   /*
2    * Listing 27.1
3    * initcurs.c - curses initialization and termination
4    */
5   #include <stdlib.h>
6   #include <curses.h>
7   #include <errno.h>
8
9   int main(void)
10  {
11      if((initscr()) == NULL) {
12          perror("initscr");
13          exit(EXIT_FAILURE);
14      }
15
16      printw("This is an curses window\n");
17      refresh();
18      sleep(3);
19
20      printw("Going bye-bye now\n");
21      refresh();
22      sleep(3);
23      endwin();
24
25      exit(0);
26  }
```

We include `<curses.h>` on line 6 for the necessary function declarations and variable definitions. In the absence of any other startup code, we immediately initialize curses with the call to `initscr()` on line 11 (ordinarily, you want to catch the WINDOW * it returns). On lines 16 and 20 we use the `printw()` function (covered in more detail in the next section) to display some output to the window, refreshing the display on lines 17 and 21 so the output will actually appear on the screen. After a three second pause (lines 18 and 22), we terminate the program, calling `endwin()` (line 23) to free the resources `initscr()` allocated.

Listing 27.2   newterm.c

```
 1   /*
 2    * Listing 27.2
 3    * newterm.c -curses initialization and termination
 4    */
 5   #include <stdlib.h>
 6   #include <curses.h>
 7   #include <errno.h>
 8
 9   int main(void)
10   {
11       SCREEN *scr;
12
13       if((scr = newterm(NULL, stdout, stdin)) == NULL) {
14           perror("newterm");
15           exit(EXIT_FAILURE);
16       }
17
18       if(set_term(scr) == NULL) {
19           perror("set_term");
20           endwin();
21           delscreen(scr);
22           exit(EXIT_FAILURE);
23       }
24
25       printw("This curses window created with newterm()\n");
26       refresh();
27       sleep(3);
28
29       printw("Going bye-bye now\n");
30       refresh();
31       sleep(3);
32       endwin();
33       delscreen(scr);
34
35       exit(0);
36   }
```

This program strongly resembles the first one. We use the newterm() call to initialize the curses subsystem (line 13), pretending that we will be interacting with a different terminal. Since we want input and output going to the normal locations, we pass stdout and stdin as the FILE pointers for output and input, respectively. Before we can use scr, however, we have to make it the current terminal, thus the call to set_term() on line 18. If this call fails, we have to make sure to call endwin() and delscreen() to free the memory associated with scr, so we added code to accomplish this in the error checking on lines 20 and 21. After sending some output to our "terminal" (lines 25 and 29), we shut down the curses subsystem, using the required delscreen() call.

Input and Output

ncurses has many functions for sending output to and receiving input from screens and windows. It is important to understand that C's standard input and output routines do not work with ncurses' windows. Fortunately, ncurses' I/O routines behave very similarly to the standard I/O (<stdio.h>) routines, so the learning curve is tolerably shallow.

Output Routines

For the purposes of discussion, we divide ncurses' output routines into character, string, and miscellaneous categories. The following sections discuss each of these in detail.

Character Routines

ncurses' core character output function is addch(), prototyped in <ncurses.h> as

```
int addch(chtype ch);
```

It displays the character ch in the current window (normally stdscr) at the cursor's current position, advancing the cursor to the next position. If this would place the cursor beyond the right margin, the cursor automatically wraps to the beginning of the next line. If scrolling has been enabled on the current window (with the scrollok() call) and the cursor is at the bottom of the scrollable region, the region scrolls up one line. If ch is a tab, newline, or backspace, the cursor moves appropriately. Other control characters display using ^X notation, where X is the character and the caret (^) indicates that it is a control character. If you need to send the literal control character, use the function echochar(chtype ch). Almost all of the other output functions do their work with calls to addch().

> **NOTE**
>
> The ncurses documentation refers to characters typed as chtype as "pseudo-characters." ncurses declares pseudo-characters as unsigned long integers, using the high bits of these characters to carry additional information such as video attributes. This distinction between pseudo-characters and normal C chars implies subtle differences in the behavior of functions that handle each type. These differences are noted in this chapter when and where appropriate.

As mentioned previously, mvaddch() adds a character to a specified window after moving the cursor to the desired location; mvwaddch() combines a move and an output operation on a specific window. waddch() displays a character to a user-specified window.

27

SCREEN
MANIPULATION
WITH NCURSES

The echochar() function, and its window-specific cousin, wechochar(), combine an addch() call with a refresh() or wrefresh() call, which can result in substantial performance enhancements when used with non-control characters.

A particularly useful feature of ncurses routines that use chtype characters and strings (discussed next) is that the character or string to be output can be logically ORed with a variety of video attributes before it is displayed. A partial list of these attributes includes

A_NORMAL	Normal display mode
A_STANDOUT	Use the terminal's best highlighting mode
A_UNDERLINE	Underlining
A_REVERSE	Use reverse video
A_BLINK	Blinking text
A_DIM	Half-intensity display
A_BOLD	Extra-intensity display
A_INVIS	Character will not be visible
A_CHARTEXT	Creates a bitmask to extract a character

Depending on the terminal emulator or hardware capabilities of the screen, not all attributes may be possible, however. See the curs_attr(3) manual page for more details.

Other than control characters and characters enhanced with video attributes, the character output functions also display line graphics characters (characters from the high half of the ASCII character set), such as box-drawing characters and various special symbols. A complete list is available in the curs_addch(3) manual page, but a few of the common ones are listed here:

ACS_ULCORNER	upper-left corner
ACS_LLCORNER	lower-left corner
ACS_URCORNER	upper-right corner
ACS_LRCORNER	lower-right corner
ACS_HLINE	horizontal line
ACS_VLINE	vertical line

The functions described so far effectively "append" characters to a window without disturbing the placement of other characters already present. Another group of routines inserts characters at arbitrary locations in existing window text. These functions include insch(), winsch(), mvinsch(), and mvwinsch(). Following the naming convention discussed earlier in this chapter, each of these functions inserts a character before (in front of) the character under the cursor, shifting the following characters to the right one position; if the right-most character is on the right margin, it will be lost. Note, however, that the cursor position does *not* change after an insert operation. Insertions are completely documented in the curs_insch(3) manual page. The prototypes of the functions we have mentioned so far are in the following list:

```
int addch(chtype ch);
int waddch(WINDOW *win, chtype ch);
int mvaddch(int y, int x, chtype ch);
int mvwaddch(WINDOW *win, int y, int x, chtype ch);
int echochar(chtype ch);
int wechochar(WINDOW *win, chtype ch);
int insch(chtype ch);
int winsch(WINDOW *win, chtype ch);
int mvinsch(int y, int x, chtype ch);
int mvwinsch(WINDOW *win, int y, int x, chtype ch);
```

Unless noted otherwise, *all* functions that return an integer return OK on success or ERR on failure (OK and ERR and a number of other constants are defined in <ncurses.h>). The arguments win, y, x, and ch are, respectively, the window in which the character will be displayed, the y and x coordinates at which to locate the cursor, and the character (including optional attributes) to display. As a reminder, routines prefixed with a "w" take a pointer, win, that specifies the target window; the "mv" prefix combines a move operation to the (y, x) location with an output operation.

String Routines

ncurses' string routines generally behave similarly to the character routines, except that they deal with strings of pseudo-characters or with normal null-terminated strings. Again, ncurses' designers created a standard notation to help programmers distinguish between the two types of functions. Function names containing chstr operate on strings of pseudo-characters, while function names containing only str use standard C-style (null-terminated) strings. A partial list of the functions operating on pseudo-character strings includes

```
int addchstr(const chtype *chstr);
int addchnstr(const chtype *chstr, int n);
int waddchstr(WINDOW *win, const chtype *chstr);
int waddchnstr(WINDOW *win, const chtype *chstr, int n);
int mvaddchstr(int y, int x, const chtype *chstr);
int mvaddchnstr(int y, int x, const chtype *chstr, int n);
int mvwaddchstr(WINDOW *win, int y, int x, const chtype *chstr);
int mvwaddchnstr(WINDOW *win, int y, int x, const chtype *chstr, int n);
```

All the listed functions copy chstr onto the desired window beginning at the cursor's location, but the cursor is *not* advanced (unlike the character output functions). If the string is longer than will fit on the current line, it is truncated at the right margin. The four routines taking an `int n` argument, `addchnstr()`, `waddchnstr()`, `mvaddchnstr()`, and `mvwaddchnstr()`, copy a limit of up to n characters, stopping at the right margin. If n is -1, the entire string will be copied, but truncated at the right margin as necessary.

The next set of string output functions operates on null-terminated strings. Unlike the previous set, these functions advance the cursor. In addition, the string output *will* wrap at the right margin, rather than being truncated. Otherwise, they behave like their similarly named `chtype` counterparts.

```
int addstr(const char *str);
int addnstr(const char *str, int n);
int waddstr(WINDOW *win, const char *str);
int waddnstr(WINDOW *win, const char *str, int n);
int mvaddstr(int y, int x, const char *str tr);
int mvaddnstr(int y, int x, const char *str, int n);
int mvwaddstr(WINDOWS *win, int y, int x, const char *str);
int mvwaddnstr(WINDOWS *win, int y, int x, const char *str, int n);
```

Remember, `str` in these routines is a standard, C-style, null-terminated character array.

The next and last group of output routines we look at are a hodgepodge: calls that draw borders and lines, clear and set the background, control output options, move the cursor, and send formatted output to an ncurses window.

Miscellaneous Output Routines

To set the background property of a window, use `bkgd()`, prototyped as

```
int bkgd(const chtype ch);
```

`ch` is an ORed combination of a character and one or more of the video attributes previously listed. To obtain the current background setting, call `chtype getbkgd(WINDOW *win);` where `win` is the window in question. Complete descriptions of functions setting and getting window backgrounds can be found in the `curs_bkgd(3)` manual page.

At least eleven ncurses functions draw boxes, borders, and lines in ncurses windows. The `box()` call is the simplest, drawing a box around a specified window using one character for vertical lines and another for horizontal lines. Its prototype is as follows:

```
int box(WINDOW *win, chtype verch, chtype horch);
```

`verch` sets the pseudo-character used to draw vertical lines and `horch` for horizontal lines.

The `box()` function:

```
int border(WINDOW *win, chtype ls, chtype rs, chtype ts, chtype bs,
➥chtype tl, chtype tr, chtype bl, chtype br);
```

The arguments are

ls	left side
rs	right side
ts	top side
bs	bottom side
tl	top-left corner
tr	top-right corner
bl	bottom-left corner
br	bottom-right corner

Both the `box()` and the `wborder()` calls draw an outline on the window along its left, right, top, and bottom margins.

Use the `hline()` function to draw a horizontal line of arbitrary length on the current window. `vline()`, similarly, draws a vertical line of arbitrary length.

```
int hline(chtype ch, int n);
int vline(chtype ch, int n);
```

Following ncurses' function naming convention, you can also specify a window in which to draw lines using

```
int whline(WINDOW *win, chtype ch, int n);
int wvline(WINDOW *win, chtype ch, int n);
```

or move the cursor to a particular location using

```
int mvhline(int y, int x, chtype ch, int n);
int mvvline(int y, int x, chtype ch, int n);
```

or even specify a window and request a move operation with

```
int mvwhline(WINDOW *win, int y, int x, chtype ch, int n);
int mvwvline(WINDOW *win, int y, int x, chtype ch, int n);
```

As usual, these routines return OK on success or ERR on failure. `win` indicates the target window; n specifies the maximum line length, up to the maximum window size vertically or horizontally. The line, box, and border drawing functions do not change the cursor position. Subsequent output operations can overwrite the borders, so you must make sure either to include calls to maintain border integrity or to set up your output calls such that they do not overwrite the borders. Functions that do not specifically set the cursor location (`line()`, `vline()`, `whline()`, and `wvline()`) start drawing at the current cursor position. The manual page documenting these routines is `curs_border(3)`. The `curs_outopts(3)` page also contains relevant information.

The final set of miscellaneous functions to consider clears all or part of the screen. As usual, they are available in both plain and window-specific varieties:

```
int erase(void);
int werase(WINDOW *win);
int clear(void);
int wclear(WINDOW *win);
int clrtobot(void);
int wclrtobot(WINDOW *win);
int clrtoeol(void);
int wclrtoeol(WINDOW *win);
```

erase() writes blanks to every position in a window; clrtobot() clears the screen from the current cursor location to the bottom of the window, inclusive; clrtoeol(), finally, erases the current line from the cursor to the right margin, inclusive. If you have used bkgd() or wbkgd() to set background properties on windows that will be cleared or erased, the property set (called a "rendition" in ncurses' documentation) is applied to each of the blanks created. The relevant manual page for these calls is curs_clear(3).

The following listings illustrate how many of the routines discussed in this section might be used. The sample programs only sample ncurses' interface because of the broad similarity in calling conventions for these functions and the large number of routines. To shorten the listings somewhat, we have moved the initialization and termination code into a separate file, utilfcns.c, and #included the header file, utilfcns.h, containing the interface (both files are on the CD-ROM that accompanies this book). Listing, 27.3 illustrates ncurses' character output functions.

Listing 27.3   curschar.c

```
 1 /*
 2  * Listing 27.3
 3  * curschar.c - curses character output functions
 4  */
 5 #include <stdlib.h>
 6 #include <curses.h>
 7 #include <errno.h>
 8 #include "utilfcns.h"
 9
10 int main(void)
11 {
12     app_init();
13
14     addch('X');
15     addch('Y' ¦ A_REVERSE);
16     mvaddch(2, 1, 'Z' ¦ A_BOLD);
17     refresh();
18     sleep(3);
```

```
19
20     clear();
21     waddch(stdscr, 'X');
22     waddch(stdscr, 'Y' | A_REVERSE);
23     mvwaddch(stdscr, 2, 1, 'Z' | A_BOLD);
24     refresh();
25     sleep(3);
26
27     app_exit();
28 }
```

As you can see on lines 14 and 15, the addch() routine outputs the desired character and advances the cursor. Lines 15 and 16 illustrate how to combine video attributes with the character to display. We demonstrate a typical "mv"-prefixed function on line 16, too. After refreshing the screen (line 17), a short pause allows you to view the results. Note that until the refresh call, no changes will be visible on the screen. Lines 21–25 repeat the process using the window-specific routines and stdscr as the target window.

Listing 27.4 briefly demonstrates using the string output functions.

Listing 27.4   cursstr.c

```
 1 /*
 2  * Listing 27.4
 3  * cursstr.c - curses string output functions
 4  */
 5 #include <stdlib.h>
 6 #include <curses.h>
 7 #include <errno.h>
 8 #include "utilfcns.h"
 9
10 int main(void)
11 {
12     int xmax, ymax;
13     WINDOW *tmpwin;
14
15     app_init();
16     getmaxyx(stdscr, ymax, xmax);
17
18     addstr("Using the *str() family\n");
19     hline(ACS_HLINE, xmax);
20     mvaddstr(3, 0, "This string appears in full\n");
21     mvaddnstr(5, 0, "This string is truncated\n", 15);
22     refresh();
23     sleep(3);
24
25     if((tmpwin = newwin(0, 0, 0, 0)) == NULL)
```

continues

LISTING 27.4   CONTINUED

```
26          err_quit("newwin");
27
28      mvwaddstr(tmpwin, 1, 1, "This message should appear in a new
➥window");
29      wborder(tmpwin, 0, 0, 0, 0, 0, 0, 0, 0);
30      touchwin(tmpwin);
31      wrefresh(tmpwin);
32      sleep(3);
33
34      delwin(tmpwin);
35      app_exit();
36 }
```

The getmaxyx() call on line 16 retrieves the number of columns and lines for stdscr—
this routine's syntax does not require that ymax and xmax be pointers. Because we call
mvaddnstr() with a value of n=15, the string we want to print will be truncated before
the letter "t" in "truncated." We create the new window, tmpwin, on line 25 with the same
dimensions as the current screen. Then we scribble a message into the new window (line
28), draw a border around it (line 29), and call refresh() to display it on the screen.
Before exiting, we call delwin() on the window to free its resources (line 34).

Listing 27.5 illustrates using line graphics characters and also the box() and wborder()
calls. Pay particular attention to lines 17–24. Some ncurses output routines move the cursor after output, others do not. Note also that the line drawing family of functions, such
as vline() and hline(), draw top to bottom and left to right, so be aware of cursor
placement when using them.

Listing 27.5   cursbox.c

```
 1 /*
 2  * Listing 27.5
 3  * cursbox.c - curses box drawing functions
 4  */
 5 #include <stdlib.h>
 6 #include <curses.h>
 7 #include <errno.h>
 8 #include "utilfcns.h"
 9
10 int main(void)
11 {
12     int ymax, xmax;
13
14     app_init();
```

```
15      getmaxyx(stdscr, ymax, xmax);
16
17      mvaddch(0, 0, ACS_ULCORNER);
18      hline(ACS_HLINE, xmax - 2);
19      mvaddch(ymax - 1, 0, ACS_LLCORNER);
20      hline(ACS_HLINE, xmax - 2);
21      mvaddch(0, xmax - 1, ACS_URCORNER);
22      vline(ACS_VLINE, ymax - 2);
23      mvvline(1, xmax - 1, ACS_VLINE, ymax - 2);
24      mvaddch(ymax - 1, xmax - 1, ACS_LRCORNER);
25      mvprintw(ymax / 3 - 1, (xmax - 30) / 2, "border drawn the
➥hard way");
26      refresh();
27      sleep(3);
28
29      clear();
30      box(stdscr, ACS_VLINE, ACS_HLINE);
31      mvprintw(ymax / 3 - 1, (xmax - 30) / 2, "border drawn the
➥easy way");
32      refresh();
33      sleep(3);
34
35      clear();
36      wborder(stdscr, ACS_VLINE | A_BOLD, ACS_VLINE | A_BOLD,
37              ACS_HLINE | A_BOLD, ACS_HLINE | A_BOLD,
38              ACS_ULCORNER | A_BOLD, ACS_URCORNER | A_BOLD, \
39              ACS_LLCORNER | A_BOLD, ACS_LRCORNER | A_BOLD);
40      mvprintw(ymax / 3 - 1, (xmax - 25) / 2, "border drawn with
➥wborder");
41      refresh();
42      sleep(3);
43
44      app_exit();
45 }
```

As you might expect, the mvvline() call on line 23 moves the cursor before drawing a vertical line. After all the gyrations to draw a simple border, the box() routine is a breeze (line 30). The wborder() function is more verbose than box() but allows finer control over the characters used to draw the border. The program illustrated the default character for each argument, but any character (and optional video attributes) will do, provided it is supported by the underlying emulator or video hardware.

Output using ncurses requires a few extra steps compared to using C's standard library functions; hopefully we have shown that it is *much* easier than using termios or filling up your code with lots of difficult-to-read newlines, backspaces, and tabs.

Input Routines

ncurses input routines, like its output routines, fall into several groups. This chapter will focus, however, on simple character and string input for two reasons. First and foremost, the routines discussed in this section will meet 90 percent of your needs. Second, ncurses input closely parallels ncurses output, so the material from the previous section should serve as a solid foundation.

The core input functions can be narrowed down to three: getch(), getstr(), and scanw(). getch()'s prototype is

```
int getch(void);
```

It fetches a single character from the keyboard, returning the character or ERR on failure. It may or may not echo the fetched character back to stdscr, depending on whether echoing is enabled or disabled (thus, wgetch() and variants also obtain single characters from the keyboard and may or may not echo them to a program-specified window). For characters to be echoed, first call echo(); to disable echoing, call noecho(). Be aware that with echoing enabled, characters are displayed on a window using waddch() at the current cursor location, which is then advanced one position.

The matter is further complicated by the current input mode, which determines the amount of processing the kernel applies before the program receives the character. In an ncurses program, you will generally want to process most of the keystrokes yourself. Doing so requires either *crmode* or *raw* mode (ncurses begins in *default* mode, meaning that the kernel buffers text normally, waiting for a newline before passing keystrokes to ncurses—you will rarely want this). In raw mode, the kernel does not buffer or otherwise process any input, while in crmode, the kernel process terminal control characters, such as ^S, ^Q, ^C, or ^Y, and passes all others to ncurses unmolested. On some systems, the literal "next character," ^V, may need to be repeated. Depending on your application's needs, crmode should be sufficient. In one of our sample programs, we use crmode, enabling and disabling echoing, to simulate shadowed password retrieval.

The getstr() function, declared as

```
intgetstr(char *str);
```

repeatedly calls getch() until it encounters a newline or carriage return (which will not be part of the returned string). The characters input are stored in str. Because getstr() performs no bounds checking, we strongly recommend using getnstr() instead, which takes an additional argument specifying the maximum number of characters to store. Regardless of whether you use getstr or getnstr(), the receiving buffer str must be large enough to hold the string received plus a terminating null character, which must be added programmatically.

scanw() obtains formatted input from the keyboard in the manner of scanf(3) and family. In fact, ncurses passes the received characters as input to sscanf(3), so input that does not map to available arguments in the format field goes to the bit bucket. As usual, scanw() has variants for movement operations (the "mv" prefix) and that apply to specific windows (the "w" prefix). In addition, the scanw() family of functions includes a member for dealing with variable length argument lists, vwscanw(). The relevant prototypes are:

```
int scanw(char *fmt [, arg] ...);
int vwscanw(WINDOW *win, char *fmt, va_list varglist);
```

The manual pages curs_getch(3), curs_getstr(3), and curs_scanw(3) fully document these routines and their various permutations. Their usage is illustrated in Listings 27.6 and 27.7.

Listing 27.6 cursinch.c

```
 1  /*
 2   * Listing 27.6
 3   * cursinch.c - curses character input functions
 4   */
 5  #include <stdlib.h>
 6  #include <curses.h>
 7  #include <errno.h>
 8  #include "utilfcns.h"
 9
10  int main(void)
11  {
12      int c, i = 0;
13      int xmax, ymax;
14      char str[80];
15      WINDOW *pwin;
16
17      app_init();
18      crmode();
19
20      getmaxyx(stdscr, ymax, xmax);
21      if((pwin = subwin(stdscr, 3, 40, ymax / 3,
➥(xmax - 40) / 2 )) == NULL)
22          err_quit("subwin");
23      box(pwin, ACS_VLINE, ACS_HLINE);
24      mvwaddstr(pwin, 1, 1, "Password: ");
25
26      noecho();
27      while((c = getch()) != '\n' && i < 80) {
28          str[i++] = c;
29          waddch(pwin, '*');
30          wrefresh(pwin);
```

continues

LISTING 27.6 CONTINUED

```
31      }
32      echo();
33      str[i] = '\0';
34      wrefresh(pwin);
35
36      mvwprintw(pwin, 1, 1, "You typed: %s\n", str);
37      box(pwin, ACS_VLINE, ACS_HLINE);
38      wrefresh(pwin);
39      sleep(3);
40
41      delwin(pwin);
42      app_exit();
43 }
```

After we have successfully initialized the ncurses subsystem, we immediately switch to crmode (line 18). Creating a bordered window clearly distinguishes the region in which the user types the password (lines 21–24) from the rest of the screen. For security reasons, we don't want to echo the user's password to the screen, so we disable echoing (line 26) while we read the password. However, to provide visual feedback to the user, we use waddch() to add a "*" to the password window for each character the user types (lines 29 and 30). Upon encountering a newline, we exit the loop, re-enable echoing (line 32), terminate the string containing the password (line 33), and then show the user what she typed (line 36). Note that wprintw() overwrites the box we drew around the password window, so before refreshing the screen, we redraw the window border (line 37).

Listing 27.7 cursgstr.c

```
 1 /*
 2  * Listing 27.7
 3  * cursgstr.c - curses string input functions
 4  */
 5 #include <stdlib.h>
 6 #include <curses.h>
 7 #include <errno.h>
 8 #include <string.h>
 9 #include "utilfcns.h"
10
11 int main(int argc, char *argv[])
12 {
13      int c, i = 0;
14      char str[20];
15      char *pstr;
16
17      app_init();
```

```
18      crmode();
19
20      printw("File to open: ");
21      refresh();
22      getstr(str);
23      printw("You typed: %s\n", str);
24      refresh();
25      sleep(3);
26
27      if((pstr = malloc(sizeof(char) * 20)) == NULL)
28          err_quit("malloc");
29
30      printw("Enter your name: ");
31      refresh();
32      getnstr(pstr, 20);
33      printw("You entered: %s\n", pstr);
34      refresh();
35      sleep(3);
36
37      free(pstr);
38      app_exit();
39 }
```

We leave echoing enabled in this sample because the user likely wants to see what she is typing. We use getstr() first (line 22). In a real program, we would attempt to open the file whose name is typed. On line 32, we use getnstr() so we can illustrate ncurses' behavior when you attempt to enter a string longer than indicated by the length limit n. In this case, ncurses stops accepting and echoing input and issues a beep after you have typed 20 characters.

Color Routines

We have already seen that ncurses supports various highlighting modes. Interestingly, it also supports color in the same fashion; that is, you can logically OR the desired color value onto the character arguments of an addch() call or any other output routine that takes a pseudo-character (chtype) argument. The method is tedious, however, so ncurses also has a set of routines to set display attributes on a per-window basis.

Before you use ncurses' color capabilities, you have to make sure that the current terminal supports color. The has_colors() call returns TRUE or FALSE depending on whether or not the current terminal has color capabilities.

```
bool has_colors(void);
```

ncurses' default colors are:

    COLOR_BLACK

    COLOR_RED

    COLOR_GREEN

    COLOR_YELLOW

    COLOR_BLUE

    COLOR_MAGENTA

    COLOR_CYAN

    COLOR_WHITE

Once you have determined that the terminal supports color, call the start_color() function

```
int start_color(void);
```

which initializes the default colors. Listing 27.8 illustrates basic color usage. It must be run on a terminal emulator that supports color, such as a color xterm.

Listing 27.8   color.c

```
 1 /*
 2  * Listing 27.8
 3  * color.c - curses color management
 4  */
 5 #include <stdlib.h>
 6 #include <curses.h>
 7 #include <errno.h>
 8 #include "utilfcns.h"
 9
10 int main(void)
11 {
12     int n;
13
14     app_init();
15
16     if(has_colors()) {
17         if(start_color() == ERR)
18             err_quit("start_color");
19
20         /* Set up some simple color assignments */
21         init_pair(COLOR_BLACK, COLOR_BLACK, COLOR_BLACK);
22         init_pair(COLOR_GREEN, COLOR_GREEN, COLOR_BLACK);
23         init_pair(COLOR_RED, COLOR_RED, COLOR_BLACK);
24         init_pair(COLOR_CYAN, COLOR_CYAN, COLOR_BLACK);
25         init_pair(COLOR_WHITE, COLOR_WHITE, COLOR_BLACK);
26         init_pair(COLOR_MAGENTA, COLOR_MAGENTA, COLOR_BLACK);
```

```
27          init_pair(COLOR_BLUE, COLOR_BLUE, COLOR_BLACK);
28          init_pair(COLOR_YELLOW, COLOR_YELLOW, COLOR_BLACK);
29
30          for(n = 1; n <= 8; n++) {
31              attron(COLOR_PAIR(n));
32              printw("color pair %d in NORMAL mode\n", n);
33              attron(COLOR_PAIR(n) | A_STANDOUT);
34              printw("color pair %d in STANDOUT mode\n", n);
35              attroff(A_STANDOUT);
36              refresh();
37          }
38          sleep(10);
39      }
40      else {
41          printw("Terminal does not support color\n");
42          refresh();
43          sleep(3);
44      }
45
46      app_exit();
47 }
```

The outer conditional (lines 16, 40–43) ensures that the terminal supports color before continuing, exiting gracefully if it doesn't. After initializing the color system (line 17), we make some simple color assignments using the init_pair() call (lines 21–28), which associates foreground and background colors with a COLOR_PAIR name:

```
int init_pair(short pair, short f, short b);
```

This associates pair with a foreground color f and a background color b, returning OK on success or ERR on failure.

Once the color assignments have been made, we display some text using each pair name in normal text and in standout mode (lines 30–36). Rather than setting the color attributes for each character displayed, we use the attron() call (lines 31 and 33), which sets the current display attributes for the current window, in this case, stdscr. We use attroff() to turn off standout mode before moving to the next color pair (line 35);

```
int attron(int attrs);
int attroff(int attrs);
```

attrs can be one or more logically ORed combinations of colors and video attributes.

As usual, ncurses comes with an extensive set of functions for manipulating window display attributes. They are fully documented in the curs_attr(3) manual page. The curs_color(3) manual pages discuss in considerable detail ncurses' color manipulation interface.

Window Management

We have already mentioned a couple of ncurses' window management functions. In this section, we will discuss them in more detail. All of the window manipulation routines are documented in the curs_window(3) manual page.

```
WINDOW *newwin(int nlines, in ncols, int begin_y, int begin_x);
int delwin(WINDOW *win);
WINDOW *subwin(WINDOW *orig, int nlines, int ncols, int begin_y,
➥int begin_x);
WINDOW *derwin(WINDOW *orig, int nlines, int ncols, int begin_y,
➥int begin_x);
WINDOW *dupwin(WINDOW *win);
```

newwin() creates and returns a pointer to a new window with ncols columns and nlines lines. The new window's upper-left corner is positioned at begin_y, begin_x. subwin() and derwin() creates and returns a pointer to a window with ncols columns and nlines rows, positioned in the center of the parent window orig. The child window's upper-left corner is positioned at begin_y, begin_x relative to the screen, not the parent window. derwin() behaves like subwin() except that the child window will be positioned at begin_y, begin_x relative to the parent window orig, not the screen. dupwin() creates an exact duplicate of the parent window orig. We have already introduced delwin(). Functions that return an integer return OK on success or ERR on failure. Those that return pointers return NULL on failure. Previous listings have illustrated the use of some of these functions, so we eschew further demonstration of their usage.

Miscellaneous Utility Functions

ncurses' utility routines give you a potpourri of ncurses' functionality, including low-level ncurse functions, obtaining environment information, and creating screen dumps.

Screen dumps are interesting. The putwin() and getwin() write and read all data associated with a window to or from a file.

```
int putwin(WINDOW *win, FILE *filep);
WINDOW *getwin(FILE *filep);
```

putwin() copies all of the data for win to the file opened on filep, while getwin() returns a pointer to a WINDOW created from the contents of filep.

The scr_dump() and scr_restore() functions behave similarly, except that they operate on ncurses screens rather than on windows. You cannot, however, mix calls; attempting to read data with scr_restore() that was written with putwin() causes an error.

```
int scr_dump(const char *filename);
```

```
int scr_restore(const char *filename);
```

filename is the name of the file to write or read.

For additional routines to use when reading and writing screen dumps, see the
`curs_scr_dump(3)` and `curs_util(3)` manual pages.

ncurses' `terminfo` and `termcap` routines, documented in `curs_termattrs(3)`,
`curs_termcap(3)`, and `curs_terminfo(3)`, report environment information and give you
direct access to the `termcap` and `terminfo` databases. The following functions obtain
information from the `terminfo` and `termcap` databases.

`int baudrate(void);`	Returns the terminal's output speed in bits per second
`char erasechar(void);`	Returns the user's current erase character
`char killchar(void);`	Returns the user's current kill character
`char *termname(void);`	Returns the value of the environment variable $TERM, truncated to 14 characters
`char *longname(void);`	Returns a long description of the terminal's capabilities, up to 128 characters

Unless you will be programming function keys or have other reasons to access the terminal databases directly, there is no need to access the `termcap` and `terminfo` databases
directly, so we will not discuss those functions here.

In addition to `getmaxyx()` call you have already seen, there are three other routines used
to obtain cursor and window coordinates: `getyx()`, `getparyx()`, and `getbegyx()`.
`getyx()` returns the coordinates of the cursor; `getbegyx()` returns the beginning (upper-
left) coordinates of the window; `getparyx()`, finally, when called on a subwindow,
returns the build window's beginning coordinates, relative to the parent window.

```
void getyx(WINDOW *win, int y, int x);
void getbegyx(WINDOW *win, int y, int x);
void getparyx(WINDOW *win, int y, int x);
```

As with `getmaxyx()`, these three calls are all macros, so y and x do not need to be passed
with &. Our final sample program, Listing 27.9, illustrates using some of these utility
functions.

Listing 27.9 cursutil.c

```
1  /*
2   * Listing 27.9
3   * cursutil.c - curses utility routines
4   */
```

continues

LISTING 27.9   CONTINUED

```
 5 #include <stdlib.h>
 6 #include <curses.h>
 7 #include <errno.h>
 8 #include "utilfcns.h"
 9
10 int main(void)
11 {
12     WINDOW *win;
13     FILE *fdump;
14     int xmax, ymax, n = 0;
15
16     app_init();
17
18     if(!has_colors()) {
19         printw("Terminal does not support color\n");
20         refresh();
21         sleep(3);
22         app_exit();
23     }
24     if(start_color() == ERR)
25         err_quit("start_color");
26
27     init_pair(COLOR_RED, COLOR_RED, COLOR_BLACK);
28     init_pair(COLOR_YELLOW, COLOR_YELLOW, COLOR_BLACK);
29     init_pair(COLOR_WHITE, COLOR_WHITE, COLOR_BLACK);
30
31     bkgd('#' | COLOR_PAIR(COLOR_RED));
32     refresh();
33     sleep(3);
34
35     if((win = subwin(stdscr, 10, 10, 0, 0)) == NULL)
36         err_quit("subwin");
37     wbkgd(win, '@' | COLOR_PAIR(COLOR_YELLOW));
38     wrefresh(win);
39     sleep(1);
40
41     getmaxyx(stdscr, ymax, xmax);
42     while(n < xmax - 10) {
43         mvwin(win, ((ymax - 10) / 2), n);
44         refresh();
45         sleep(1);
46         if(n == ((xmax - 10)/ 2)) {
47             /* Dump the subwindow to a file */
48             fdump = fopen("dump.win", "w");
49             putwin(stdscr, fdump);
50             fclose(fdump);
51         }
52         n += 10;
```

```
53        }
54
55        fdump = fopen("dump.win", "r");
56        win = getwin(fdump);
57        wrefresh(win);
58        sleep(3);
59
60        clear();
61        bkgd(' ' | COLOR_PAIR(COLOR_WHITE));
62        mvprintw(1, 1, "ERASE character: %s\n", unctrl(erasechar()));
63        mvprintw(2, 1, "KILL character : %s\n", uncntrl(killchar()));
64        mvprintw(3, 1, "BAUDRATE (bps) : %d\n", baudrate());
65        mvprintw(4, 1, "TERMINAL type  : %s\n", termname());
66        refresh();
67        sleep(5);
68
69        delwin(win);
70        app_exit();
71   }
```

We packed a lot into this example. Lines 18–25 make sure the terminal can support color, gracefully exiting if they cannot. The next three lines (27–29) set up some colors we use later in the program. After setting the background with red "#"s on a black background (lines 31–33), we create a 10×10 subwindow and set its background to yellow "@"s on a black background. Then we move the child window across its parent in increments of ten (lines 41–53), creating a window dump at n=20. To illustrate how simple it is to redisplay a dumped window, we read in the dump on lines 55–58. Finally, once we clear stdscr, we set the window to white on black and use some of the terminal information routines to display a little bit of information about the current display environment (lines 60–67). The child window deleted, the application exits.

Summary

Hopefully, this chapter has demonstrated enough of ncurses' abilities to make clear that it is both an easier and more powerful interface for manipulating the display than termios. ncurses is a ubiquitous library, used in popular programs such as the mutt mail client, the Midnight Commander file manager, lynx, ncftp, and nvi.

X Window Programming

by Mark Watson

IN THIS CHAPTER

The X Window software was written at MIT as part of the Athena project. X Windows allows a program to use the display of a computer other than the computer the program is running on if the owner of that computer permits it. In 1988, I was helping to build a distributed system where the major components (during development) ran in Norway, Washington D.C., and San Diego. Running programs on a computer in Norway using the display of my Sun workstation in San Diego was "real" telecommuting!

In this chapter, you will learn how to use the primitive X library (Xlib) and the X toolkit (Xt). In the next chapter, you will use the MIT Athena widget set and the Motif Widget set, both of which use the X toolkit. All of the examples can be developed and run on your Linux computer, but keep in mind that you can allow a friend from around the world to run your application if she has an account on your computer and sets the permissions of the X server's display on her computer to allow remote access from the host computer running the application.

> **NOTE**
>
> X Windows is usually thought to be the windowing system for Unix, but X servers are also available for OS/2, Windows, and the Macintosh.

X Concepts

X Windows separates the display and event handling from application programs. Instead, an application program communicates with the X server via a socket interface. The X server handles keyboard input, mouse input, and the display screen. For example, when the user clicks the mouse, the X server detects where the mouse event occurred and sends the mouse event to the appropriate application program. When a window on the display is uncovered, the X server sends the appropriate application a window expose event. Window expose events occur when part or all of a window becomes visible and therefore needs to be redrawn. The application will usually respond by sending back draw operations to the X server to redraw the window contents.

To understand the interaction between X Window application programs and the X server, you need to understand how events are handled and know the draw operations that an application program can request the X server to perform. Figure 28.1 shows the interaction between actual user events, the X server event queue, and application program event queues.

FIGURE 28.1

Interaction between events, the X server, and application programs.

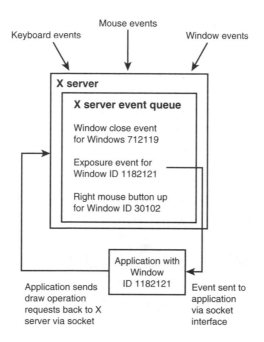

Keyboard events

Mouse events

Window events

X server

X server event queue

Window close event for Windows 712119

Exposure event for Window ID 1182121

Right mouse button up for Window ID 30102

Application with Window ID 1182121

Application sends draw operation requests back to X server via socket

Event sent to application via socket interface

As shown in Figure 28.2, X Window applications can use any combination of the low-level Xlib API, the X toolkit (or the X intrinsics), the Athena Widget set, and the Motif Widget set (Chapter 29). In Chapters 30 and 31, you will also see two higher-level APIs: the GTK and Qt GUI libraries.

FIGURE 28.2

The X Window Programming APIs.

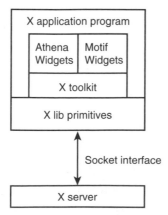

X application program

Athena Widgets

Motif Widgets

X toolkit

X lib primitives

Socket interface

X server

28

X WINDOW PROGRAMMING

The Xlib library provides the interface between application programs and the (possibly remote) X server via a socket interface.

The Xlib API

For most X Window applications that you'll develop, you'll probably use one of the high-level toolkits such as Motif, Athena, GTK, or Qt. However, in addition to providing the software interface between higher-level toolkits and the X server, the Xlib API provides useful graphics operations that you're likely to need in graphics-oriented applications. The sample program `bifurcation.c`, located in the directory `src/X/xlib`, provides a simple example of creating a window, handling events, and performing simple graphics operations using the Xlib API.

> **TIP**
>
> Christophe Tronche maintains an excellent API reference for Xlib at his Web site. I maintain a current link to his site at the URL
> `http://www.markwatson.com/books/linux_prog.html`.

Before looking at the `bifurcation.c` example program, we will first list the Xlib functions for managing displays and windows, list the common event handling functions, and finally look at some commonly used graphics primitives. The most commonly used window and display management functions are covered in the following sections.

XopenDisplay

Xlib functions require a display pointer. We use `XopenDisplay` to connect a program to an X server. The display name has the general form `hostname:display-number:screen-number`. You might want to simply use `localhost` and default the display and screen numbers. The function signature is as follows:

```
Display * XOpenDisplay(char *display_name)
```

XcreateSimpleWindow and XcreateWindow

The function `XcreateWindow` is the general-purpose function for creating new windows on an X display. The simpler `XCreateSimpleWindow` function creates a window using default values inherited from the parent window.

The function signatures are as follows:

```
Window XcreateWindow(Display *display, Window parent,
                     int x, int y,
                     int width, int height,
                     unsigned int border_width,
                     unsigned int depth, int class,
                     Visual * visual,
                     unsigned long valuemask,
                     XSetWindowAttributes * attributes)

Window XCreateSimpleWindow(Display * display,
                           Window parent,
                           int x, int y,
                           unsigned int width,
                           unsigned int height,
                           unsigned int border_width,
                           unsigned long border,
                           unsigned long background)
```

The XSetWindowAttributes structure is defined as follows:

```
typedef struct {
  Pixmap background_pixmap;      // background
  unsigned long background_pixel; // background pixel
  Pixmap border_pixmap;          // border of the window
  unsigned long border_pixel;    // border pixel value
  int bit_gravity;   // one of bit gravity values
  int win_gravity;   // one of the window gravity values
  int backing_store; // NotUseful, WhenMapped, Always
  unsigned long backing_planes; // planes preserved
                                // if possible
  unsigned long backing_pixel;  // value for restoring planes
  Bool save_under;              // should bits under be saved?
  long event_mask;              // set of saved events
  long do_not_propagate_mask;   // set of events that should
                                // not propagate
  Bool override_redirect;   // boolean value for
                            // override_redirect
  Colormap colormap;    // color map to be associated
                        // with window
  Cursor cursor;        // cursor to be displayed (or None)
} XSetWindowAttributes;
```

Mapping and Unmapping Windows

An X Window is made visible by *mapping* and invisible by *unmapping*. The function
signatures for the utility functions that control window visibility are as follows:

```
XMapWindow(Display *display, Window w)
XMapSubwindows(Display * display, Window w)
XUnmapWindow(Display * display, Window w)
```

Mapping a window might not immediately make it visible because a window and all of its parents need to be mapped to become visible. This behavior is convenient because you can make an entire tree of nested (or child) windows invisible by unmapping the top-most window. When you unmap a window, the X server automatically generates a windows expose event for any windows that are uncovered.

Destroying Windows

In order to free system resources, X Windows should be destroyed when they are no longer needed. The XDestroyWindow function destroys a single window, while XDestroySubWindows destroys all child windows. The signatures for these functions are as follows:

```
XDestroyWindow(Display * display, Window w)
XDestroySubwindows(Display * display, Window w)
```

Event Handling

Event handling with the Xlib API is not too difficult. A program must register for the types of events that it is interested in by using XSelectInput, and check for events from the X server by using XNextEvent.

XSelectInput

The function signature for XSelectInput is as follows:

```
XSelectInput(Display * display, Window w, long event_mask)
```

The display variable defines which X server the application is using for display. Events are window-specific and are set by combining the following most commonly used constants for the event mask:

0—No events wanted

KeyPressMask—Keyboard down events wanted

KeyReleaseMask—Keyboard up events wanted

ButtonPressMask—Pointer button down events wanted

ButtonReleaseMask—Pointer button up events wanted

EnterWindowMask—Pointer window entry events wanted

LeaveWindowMask—Pointer window leave events wanted

PointerMotionMask —Pointer motion events wanted

PointerMotionHintMask—Pointer motion hints wanted

Button1MotionMask—Pointer motion while button 1 down

Button2MotionMask—Pointer motion while button 2 down

> Button3MotionMask—Pointer motion while button 3 down
>
> ButtonMotionMask—Pointer motion while any button down
>
> ExposureMask—Any exposure wanted
>
> VisibilityChangeMask—Any change in visibility wanted
>
> ResizeRedirectMask—Redirect resize of this window
>
> FocusChangeMask—Any change in input focus wanted

For more Xlib documentation, check Christophe Tronche's Web site or the X Consortium's Web site at www.x.org.

XNextEvent

An application program can request the next pending event with the function XNextEvent. The function signature for this function is as follows:

```
XNextEvent(Display * display, XEvent * event_return_value)
```

The XEvent structure has a field type that indicates what event occurred. Here you would check the value of event_return_value.type against the following commonly used constant values:

> ButtonPressMask—Any button pressed
>
> Button1PressMask—Button 1 pressed
>
> Button2PressMask—Button 2 pressed
>
> Button3PressMask—Button 3 pressed
>
> ButtonMotionMask—Motion with any button pressed
>
> Button1MotionMask—Motion with button 1 pressed
>
> Button2MotionMask—Motion with button 2 pressed
>
> Button3MotionMask—Motion with button 3 pressed
>
> KeyPress—Any key pressed on the keyboard
>
> KeyRelease—Any key released on the keyboard
>
> Expose—Window is exposed (most applications redrawn)

There are many other possible event types, but these are the most commonly used types.

Initializing Graphics Context and Fonts

An X window has a Graphics Context (GC) that specifies drawing parameters such as foreground and background colors and the current font. An XFontInfo data structure is defined using XLoadQueryFont, which has the following function signature:

```
XFontStruct *XLoadQueryFont(Display * display, char * name)
```

Example font names are 8x10, 9x15, and fixed. A GC is created with XCreateGC that has the following function signature:

```
GC XCreateGC(Display * display, Drawable d,
             unsigned long valuemask,
             XGCValues * values)
```

A Drawable is usually a Window object, but can also be a PixMap. After defining a GC, a program might want to set the font, foreground color, and background color using the following functions:

```
XSetFont(Display *display, GC gc, Font font)
XSetForeground(Display *display, GC gc, unsigned long a_color)
XSetBackground(Display *display, GC gc, unsigned long a_color)
```

A color value can be obtained by using XParseColor or using one of the following macros:

```
BlackPixel(Display * display, Screen screen)
WhitePixel(Display * display, Screen screen)
```

Drawing in an X Window

Usually, drawing in an X Window is performed after a program receives an expose event. The GC can be changed before any drawing command to change the foreground color and other options. The following list of drawing functions shows a sample of the graphics operations available to X Window programmers:

```
XDrawString(Display *display, Drawable d, GC gc,
            int x, int y,
            char * string, int string_length)
```

XDrawString draws a string in the GC's current font and foreground color:

```
XDrawLine(Display *display, Drawable d, GC gc,
          int x1, int y1, int x2, int y2)
```

XDrawLine is used to draw a line between two points, (x1,y2) and (x2,y2):

```
XDrawRectangle(Display *display, Drawable d, GC gc, int x,
               int y, unsigned int width, unsigned int height)
```

XDrawRectangle draws a rectangle using the GC's current foreground color:

```
XDrawArc(Display *display, Drawable d, GC gc, int x, int y,
         unsigned int width, unsigned int height,
         int angle1, int angle2)
```

Here, angle1 specifies the start of the arc relative to the three o'clock position from the center, in units of degrees ×64. The argument angle2 specifics the angle of the arc relative to angle1, also measured in units of degrees ×64. The functions XDrawRectangle and

XDrawArc draw outlines of the requested shapes in the GC's foreground color. The functions XFillRectangle (same arguments as XDrawRectangle) and XFillArc (same arguments as XDrawArc) perform the same operation, except that they fill the requested shape with the foreground color.

A Sample Xlib Program

The source file bifurcation.c in the src/X/xlib directory demonstrates how to create an X Window, trap the button press, expose and resize events, and perform simple graphics operations. The bifurcation.c program plots chaotic population growth using a simple nonlinear equation by biologist Robert Mays. Figure 28.3 shows the bifurcation.c program running.

FIGURE 28.3
The
bifurcation.c
sample Xlib
program.

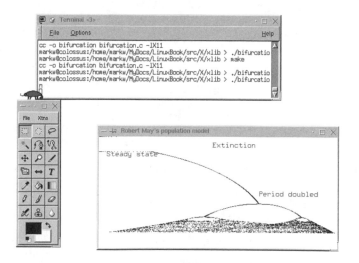

This simple program uses the function draw_bifurcation to draw the window contents. The function prototype (or signature) is as follows:

```
void draw_bifurcation(Window window, GC gc, Display *display,
                      int screen, XColor text_color)
```

The function main defines the following data:

Display *display—For referring to X server's display

int screen—Identifies which screen on the X server you're using

Window win—Identifies the application's window

XColor blue—You want to display text using the color blue

unsigned int width=500—Specifies the initial window width

unsigned int height=231—Specifies the initial window height

XFontStruct *font_info—For using a display font

GC gc—Identifies the windows GC

Colormap cmap—Used to query the X server for the color blue

XEvent x_event—Used to fetch X events

XGCValues values—Used for the GC attributes returned by the X server

The first thing that an X Window program needs to do is to make sure that it can open a display on the desired X server:

```
if ( (display=XOpenDisplay(NULL)) == NULL ) {
    perror("Could not open X display");
    exit(1);
}
```

Here, you exit the program if no X display is available. Specifying NULL as the argument to XOpenDisplay defaults to the the value of the DISPLAY environment variable. You also want to use the default screen on the local X server and to create the window:

```
screen = DefaultScreen(display);
win = XCreateSimpleWindow(display, RootWindow(display, screen),
                         0, 0, width, height, 5,
                         BlackPixel(display, screen),
                         WhitePixel(display, screen));
```

Since you want blue text, you need to ask for it:

```
cmap=DefaultColormap(display,screen);
XParseColor(display,cmap,"blue",&blue);
XAllocColor(display,cmap,&blue);
```

If you ask for a color that is not available, you are likely to get a random color but your program will not crash. As an experiment, try this:

```
XParseColor(display,cmap,"ZZ_NO_SUCH_COLOR",&blue);
```

Unlike color selection, an error in specifying a display font name can cause X programs to crash in fine style. In the following code, you try two fonts that are almost always on an X server:

```
if ((font_info = XLoadQueryFont(display,"9x15")) == NULL) {
    perror("Use fixed font\n");
    font_info = XLoadQueryFont(display,"fixed");
}
```

Here, if you cannot find 9x15 on the server, you try fixed. You are now ready to create a GC for drawing operations inside the window:

```
gc = XCreateGC(display,win,(unsigned long)0,&values);
XSetFont(display, gc, font_info->fid);
XSetForeground(display, gc, BlackPixel(display,screen));
```

Here, you also set the font and foreground color for the GC.

Before mapping the window (making it visible), you need to set the properties for the window manager to use and select which events you want to process:

```
XSetStandardProperties(display, win,
                       "Robert May's population model",
                       "Bifurcation", None,
                       0, 0, NULL);
XSelectInput(display, win, ExposureMask | ButtonPressMask);
```

Here you are using defaults for everything but the window title and the label used by the window manager when this application is iconified. The call to XSelectInput notifies the X server that you want to receive exposure and any button press events. Finally, you are ready to make the window visible and draw the window contents:

```
XMapWindow(display, win);
draw_bifurcation(win,gc,display,screen,blue);
```

The only remaining thing to do in function main is to handle events:

```
while (1) {
XNextEvent(display, &x_event);
    switch (x_event.type) {
    case Expose:
      draw_bifurcation(win,gc,display,screen,blue);
      break;
    case ButtonPressMask:
      XCloseDisplay(display);
      exit(0);
    default:
      break;
    }
}
```

This event loop is simple: you call XNextEvent (which blocks until an event is available) to fill the XEvent x_event variable. The field X_event.type is the integer event type that you compare to the constants Expose and ButtonPressMask. If you get an expose event the window has to be redrawn, so you call draw_bifurcation again. If the user presses any mouse button in the window, you close the connection to the X server with XCloseDisplay and terminate the program.

28

X WINDOW
PROGRAMMING

The function draw_bifurcation is fairly simple:

```
void draw_bifurcation(Window win, GC gc, Display *display,
int screen, XColor font_color) {
  float lambda = 0.1;
  float x = 0.1f;
  float population = 0.0;
  int x_axis, y_axis, iter;
  XSetForeground(display, gc, font_color.pixel);
  XDrawString(display, win, gc, 236,22,
              "Extinction", strlen("Extinction"));
  XDrawString(display, win, gc, 16, 41,
              "Steady state", strlen("Steady state"));
  XDrawString(display, win, gc, 334, 123,
              "Period doubled", strlen("Period doubled"));
  XSetForeground(display, gc, BlackPixel(display,screen));
  for (y_axis=0; y_axis<198; y_axis++) {
    lambda = 4.0f * (0.20f + (y_axis / 250.0f));
    for (iter=0; iter<198; iter++) {
      population = lambda * x * (1.0f - x);
      x_axis = (int)(population * 500.02f);
      if (x_axis > 0.0f && x_axis < 501.0f) {
        XDrawLine(display,win,gc, x_axis, y_axis, x_axis, y_axis);
      }
      x = population;
    }
  }
}
```

For the purposes of this book, the algorithm for deciding where to plot the points in the X Window is not interesting. The following functions are used to draw in the Window's GC:

> XSetForeground—Used to switch the foreground color between black and blue

> XDrawString—Used to draw three text strings in the window using the font set for the GC

> XDrawLine—Used to draw points in the window

You call XSetForeground to change the color for drawing text and plotting lines. Here, you are drawing points by drawing line segments with a length of one pixel. You can run the sample program bifurcation.c by changing the directory to src/X/xlib and typing the following:

```
make
./bifurcation
```

The X Toolkit API

You have seen that the Xlib API is a low-level but very efficient library for writing X Window applications. The X toolkit (or intrinsics) library provides higher-level programming support for writing *widgets*. Widgets are object-oriented display objects, like data entry fields, utilities for plotting data, and so on. They are usually written in the C language, but they're object-oriented in the sense that they support inheritance and maintain private data with a public API for accessing internal widget data. In the next chapter, you will use two popular widget sets: the Athena widgets and the Motif widgets.

Getting Started Using the X Toolkit

Before an application can use the X toolkit, the following function must be called before any other toolkit functions (the type String is defined as char *, and a Cardinal is an int):

```
Widget XtInitialize(String shell_name,
                    String application_class,
                    XrmOptionDescRec *options,
                    Cardinal num_options,
                    int * argc, char **argv)
```

The name and class arguments specify the name and the class of the top-level widget of the application. Typically, you can make up a meaningful name for the application and then create a class name by capitalizing the first letter of the application name. The options argument can usually just be specified as NULL, indicating that there are no special options. If you use NULL to specify options, pass 0 as the value of num_options. The last two arguments are the arguments passed (which are modified by removing any X-specific arguments) to the main function of an application.

The X toolkit uses resources specified as character strings. To make programs more readable, the X toolkit and Xlib include files that define constant names for resource strings:

```
#define XtNwidth "width"
#define XtNheight "height"
#define XtNlabel "label"
```

It is relatively easy to write X applications using widgets, but it is much more difficult to write new widgets. In the next two chapters, we will see how to use Athena and Motif widgets and how to write a new Athena widget.

Setting Widget Arguments Using the X Toolkit

The X toolkit function `XtSetValues` can be used to set values for widget resources. `XtSetValues` can be used for Athena and Motif widgets. Each type of widget (label, text edit, and so on) has different options that can be set using `XtSetValues`. `XtSetValues` starts with the resources core, or base widget classes, and follows a widget's inheritance chain to the widget, setting resources that match the indicated resource name. For example, suppose that you are using an Athena label widget. Inspection of the file `Label.h` (located in `/usr/X11/include/Xaw3D` on my Linux system) shows the following resources for the label widget:

```
Name                   Class                 RepType        Default Value
----                   -----                 -------        -------------
background             Background            Pixel          XtDefaultBackground
bitmap                 Pixmap                Pixmap         None
border                 BorderColor           Pixel          XtDefaultForeground
borderWidth            BorderWidth           Dimension      1
cursor                 Cursor                Cursor         None
cursorName             Cursor                String         NULL
destroyCallback        Callback              XtCallbackList NULL
encoding               Encoding              unsigned char  XawTextEncoding8bit
font                   Font                  XFontStruct*   XtDefaultFont
foreground             Foreground            Pixel          XtDefaultForeground
height                 Height                Dimension      text height
insensitiveBorder      Insensitive           Pixmap         Gray
internalHeight         Height                Dimension      2
internalWidth          Width                 Dimension      4
justify                Justify               XtJustify      XtJustifyCenter
label                  Label                 String         NULL
leftBitmap             LeftBitmap            Pixmap         None
mappedWhenManaged      MappedWhenManaged     Boolean        True
pointerColor           Foreground            Pixel          XtDefaultForeground
pointerColorBackground Background            Pixel          XtDefaultBackground
resize                 Resize                Boolean        True
sensitive              Sensitive             Boolean        True
width                  Width                 Dimension      text width
x                      Position              Position       0
y                      Position              Position       0
```

Here is an example of setting a few resources in a program:

```
Widget label;
Arg args[5];
String app_resources[] =
  { "*Label.Label: Testing Athena Label Widget", NULL };
XtSetValues(args[0], XtNlabel, "The label of a widget");
XtSetValues(args[1], XtNwidth, 100);
XtSetValues(args[2], XtNheight, 90);
```

```
top_level = XtAppInitialize(&application_context, "Test", NULL, 0,
                            &argc, argv,
                            app_resources,
                            NULL, 0);
label = XtCreateManagedWidget("label5", labelWidgetClass,
                              top_level, args, 3);
```

You can also set resource values inside your .Xdefaults file. For example, assume that the program name is test and that you want to set the x-y position of the widget:

```
Test*label5*x:          5
Test*label5*y:          15
```

It is also possible to get a widget's resource values using the X toolkit function XtGetValues.

```
Dimension width, height;
Arg args[2];
Widget label=XtCreateManagedWidget("label", labelWidgetClass,
                                   top_level, NULL, 0);
XtSetArg(args[0], XtNwidth, &width);
XtSetArg(args[1], XtNheight, &height);
XtGetValues(label, args, 2);
printf("Widget width=%d and height=%d\n", width, height);
```

28

X WINDOW
PROGRAMMING

Here, you use the type Dimension for the variables width and height because the resources width and height have the type Dimension. In a similar way, you would use the type Pixel for fetching a widget's background color.

Summary

In this chapter, you have learned the basics of X Window programming using Xlib and the X toolkit. You can also find the source code for many example X Window programs on the Internet. In the next two chapters, you will see higher level toolkits that make it easier to write X Window programs. However, even when you use higher level toolkits such as Athena, Motif, Qt, and GTK, it is important to understand Xlib programming.

Using Athena and Motif Widgets

by Mark Watson

IN THIS CHAPTER

We saw in Chapter 28 how much code is required to write simple programs using the low-level Xlib API. We also reviewed the X toolkit, which is a utility library that is used by Athena, Motif, and most other Top-Level Application widget libraries. In this chapter, we will learn how to do the following:

- Use Athena Widgets
- Use Motif Widgets
- Write our Own Athena Widget
- Use Both Athena and Motif in C++ Programs
- Use a C++ Class Library to Wrap Athena's Paned, Button, Label and Text Widgets

Using Athena Widgets

The Athena widget set was written for the MIT Athena project to provide a distributed computing environment for the students and faculty at MIT. The Athena widgets originally had a "flat" look, but most Linux distributions have an optional package named awt3d that overwrites the libraries for the Athena widgets, substituting the "flat" look with a "3D" look. This chapter is really a tutorial for using Athena widgets. In each section, we will develop one short program that shows how to use labels, command pushbuttons, menus, and text edit-fields.

The Athena Label Widget

The example program for this section, `label.c`, is located in the directory `src/X/Athena` on the CD-ROM. This program requires two `include` files:

```
#include <X11/Intrinsic.h>
#include <X11/Xaw/Label.h>
```

The file `Intrinsic.h` contains the definitions for the X toolkit, and the file `Label.h` defines the Athena `Label` class. Normally, X applications use resource definitions in the `.Xdefaults` file in your home directory for program options that enable you to change both the appearance and behavior of the program. Here, we use an array of character strings to set the resources for the Label widget used in the example. The Label widget has a property `Label` that is defined here:

```
String app_resources[] =
    { "*Label.Label: Testing Athena Label Widget", NULL };
```

In the main function, we must define three variables: a Top Level widget, a Label widget, and an `application context`:

```
  XtAppContext application_context;
  Widget top_level, label;
```

First, we create and save the value of a Top-Level widget for this application and define the value for the variable `application_context`:

```
top_level = XtAppInitialize(&application_context, "test", NULL, 0,
                            &argc, argv,
                            app_resources,
                            NULL, 0);
```

We now create a Child widget to the Top-Level widget. This is our test Label widget:

```
label = XtCreateManagedWidget("label", labelWidgetClass, top_level,
                              NULL, 0);
```

After we call `XtRealizeWidget`, the Top-Level widget and the Label widget are managed.

```
XtRealizeWidget(top_level); // create windows and make visible
```

Finally, we pass the application context to `XtAppMainLoop` to handle all events for this simple application:

```
XtAppMainLoop(application_context); // main event loop
```

As we saw in Chapter 28, the `label.c` example program also contains example code for fetching the `width` and `height` resources of a Label widget:

```
Dimension width, height;
Arg args[2];
XtSetArg(args[0], XtNwidth, &width);
XtSetArg(args[1], XtNheight, &height);
XtGetValues(label, args, 2);
printf("Widget width=%d and height=%d\n", width, height);
```

Figure 29.1 shows an X window containing the `label.c` example program.

FIGURE 29.1

Running the `label.c` *example program in the KDE desktop.*

You can build and run this test program by changing the directory to `src/X/Athena` and typing:

```
make
label
```

The Athena Command Button Widget

The sample program button.c that we will use in this section is very similar to the label.c program from the last section. The source code differs in that it enables you to set up the command button and manage its events.

In the button.c example, we need the following include file:

```
#include <X11/StringDefs.h>
```

in order to get the constant definition for XtNcallback that has a value of callback. The following include file is required in order to define the Athena Command Button widget:

```
#include <X11/Xaw/Command.h>
```

In the last example, label.c, we saw that the Athena Label widget looks for a property Label at runtime in either the local .Xdefaults file or in the default application resources set in the program. In button.c, we also need to set up a default Label property for the widget class Command:

```
String app_resources[] = {
   "*Command.Label: Click left mouse button", NULL,
};
```

We also want the ability to process command-line arguments:

```
XrmOptionDescRec options[] = {
   {"-label", "*Command.label", XrmoptionSepArg, NULL}
};
```

If this sample program is run without arguments, the default label property value "Click left mouse button" is used. If we want the label to read "Click to test", run the sample program like this:

```
button -label "Click to test"
```

Although not necessary, programs should handle Button-Click events in Command Button widgets (otherwise, why use them?). We need to define a Callback function to do any calculations that we want after the button is clicked. Here is our sample Callback function:

```
void do_button_clicked(Widget w,
                       XtPointer client_data,
                       XtPointer call_data) {
   printf("left button clicked\n");
}
```

We will see later how to assign this callback function to the sample Command Button widget. First, we will look at the function main, which has two arguments for processing command-line arguments:

```
void main(int argc, char **argv) {
```

We need to define three variables in the main function: an application context and two widgets (top level, command button):

```
XtAppContext application_context;
Widget top_level, command_button;
```

We call XtAppInitialize to fill in the fields of the application context and to define the Top-Level widget:

```
top_level = XtAppInitialize(&application_context, "Xcommand",
                           options, XtNumber(options),
                           &argc, argv, app_resources,
                           NULL, 0);
```

Unlike the last example (label.c), here we want to save the value of the test widget (the Command Button widget in this case):

```
command_button = XtCreateManagedWidget("command", commandWidgetClass,
                                       top_level, NULL, 0);
```

We defined a Callback function do_button_clicked. Now we will assign this Callback function to the Command Button widget:

```
XtAddCallback(command_button, XtNcallback, do_button_clicked, NULL);
```

Finally, we want to make all the widgets visible and capable of handling events:

```
XtRealizeWidget(top_level);
XtAppMainLoop(application_context);
```

It is important to clearly understand how the events are handled. The Top-Level widget contains the Command Button widget. When the Top-Level widget is realized (made visible), the X server knows to associate events for this sample program with the Top-Level widget. When you click on the command button, the event loop code in XtAppMainLoop is notified via a socket connection from the X server that an event has occurred. The Top-Level widget passes the event down to the command button, and the Callback function is executed.

Assuming that you are running X Windows on your computer, you can see all of the currently open socket connects by typing netstat -a in a terminal window. As an experiment, run netstat twice in a row in a terminal window, but start the sample button.c program after the first time that you run netstat:

```
netstat -a > temp1
button &
netstat -a> temp2
diff temp1 temp2
rm temp1 temp2
```

This will show you the socket connection used to handle this application. The socket I/O is performed between Xlib and the (possibly remote) X server. Figure 29.2 shows a X window containing the button.c example program.

FIGURE 29.2

Running the button.c *example program in the KDE desktop.*

You can build and run this test program by changing the directory to src/X/Athena and typing:

```
make
button
```

The Athena List Widget

The example for this section, list.c, is similar to the two previous examples: label.c and button.c. We will concentrate on handling List widgets and assume that you have read the last two sections. The following include file defines the List widget:

```
#include <X11/Xaw/List.h>
```

We used a Callback function in button.c to handle Button-Click events. The Callback function for a List widget is a little more complex because we want the ability to identify which list item was clicked with the mouse. The third argument for Callback functions is widget-dependent data. For a List widget, the third argument is the address of a XawListReturnStruct object that has two fields in which we are interested here:

Field	Description
int list_index	Index starting at zero of the clicked list item.
char * string	The label of the list item.

The Callback function do_list_item_selected uses the third argument to print out the index and label of the clicked list item:

```
void do_list_item_selected(Widget w, XtPointer unused, XtPointer data) {
  XawListReturnStruct *list_item = (XawListReturnStruct*)data;
  printf("Selected item (%d) text is '%s'\n",
         list_item->list_index, list_item->string );
}
```

The function main defines variables for two widgets and an application context:

```
Widget top_level, list;
XtAppContext application_context;
```

We create a Top-Level widget and fill in the data for the application context:

```
top_level = XtAppInitialize(&application_context, "listexample",
                            NULL, ZERO,
                            &argc, argv, NULL,
                            NULL, 0);
```

When we create a List widget, we supply an array of "char *" string values for the list item labels:

```
String items[] = {
  "1", "2", "3", "4", "5", "six", "seven", "8",
  "9'th list entry", "this is the tenth list entry",
  "11", "12",
  NULL
};
```

For creating a List widget, we use XtVaCreateManagedWidget—an alternative form of XtCreateManagedWidget—that accepts a variable number of options:

```
list= XtVaCreateManagedWidget("list",  listWidgetClass, top_level,
                              XtNlist, items,
                              NULL, 0);
```

We need to associate the Callback function with the List widget in the same way that we saw in the button.c example:

```
XtAddCallback(list, XtNcallback,
              do_list_item_selected, (XtPointer)NULL);
```

As before, we make the widgets visible on the X server and able to handle events:

```
XtRealizeWidget(top_level);
XtAppMainLoop(application_context);
```

Figure 29.3 shows an X window containing the list.c example program.

29

USING ATHENA AND MOTIF WIDGETS

FIGURE 29.3

Running the
list.c *example*
program in the
KDE desktop.

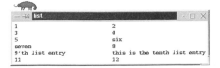

You can build and run this test program by changing the directory to src/X/Athena and typing:

```
make
list
```

The Athena Text Widget

The Athena Text widget has many options that can be set using resource values (either in your .Xdefaults file or defaults defined in the program). The following three include files are defined with Paned, AsciiText, and Command (button) widgets. Paned is a Container widget that is used to hold other widgets. By default, Paned provides small "grabs" that can be used to manually adjust the size of any contained widget.

```
#include <X11/Xaw/Paned.h>
#include <X11/Xaw/AsciiText.h>
#include <X11/Xaw/Command.h>
```

When we define a Text widget, we will want to provide callbacks to display the text in the widget and to erase all of the text in the widget. In order to display the widget's text, we will use the X toolkit XtVaGetValues function that operates on a widget (specified as the first argument). The second argument will be the constant XtNstring that is used to specify that we want to retrieve the value of the string resource. The third argument is an address of a string variable that will be set to point to a block of characters. The storage for this block of characters is managed internally by the Text widget. The fourth argument is NULL to indicate that no further resource values are to be fetched from the Text widget.

The following code listing shows the implementation of the do_display_widget_text callback function. This function is called when there are events in the text widget. For demonstration purposes, we use XtVaGetValues to get the current text in the text widget and then print this text.

```
void do_display_widget_text(Widget w,
                            XtPointer text_ptr,
                            XtPointer unused) {
  Widget text = (Widget) text_ptr;
  String str;
  XtVaGetValues(text,
                XtNstring, &str,
                NULL);
  printf("Widget Text is:\n%s\n", str);
}
```

We also want the ability to erase the text in a Text widget. To do this, we use the X toolkit function XtVaSetValues to set the value of the string resource to the NULL string:

```
void do_erase_text_widget(Widget w,
                          XtPointer text_ptr,
                          XtPointer unused) {
  Widget text = (Widget) text_ptr;
  XtVaSetValues(text,
                XtNstring, "",
                NULL);
}
```

We are adding something new to this example program: a quit button. We could simply call exit, but it is better to clean up any references to shared X resources by first calling XtDestroyApplicationContext. In this example, we declare the application context as a global variable so that the do_quit Callback function has access to application context:

```
XtAppContext application_context;
void do_quit(Widget w, XtPointer unused1, XtPointer unused2) {
  XtDestroyApplicationContext(application_context);
  exit(0);
}
```

As in the previous examples, we define default application resources directly in the program. Here, we are defining resources for the classes Text, erase, and display. Notice that we do not define any default resources for the Quit command button, as we do for the Erase and Display command buttons. The Quit button will default its label with its name—in this case, it's Quit.

The following code listing illustrates how to set up default application resources.

```
String app_resources[] = {
  "*Text*editType: edit",
  "*Text*autoFill: on",
  "*Text*scrollVertical: whenNeeded",
  "*Text*scrollHorizontal: whenNeeded",
  "*erase*label: Erase the Text widget",
  "*display*label: Display the text from the Text widget",
  "*Text*preferredPaneSize: 300",
  NULL,
};
```

The Text widget resource property autoFill is used to control automatic line-wrapping. The Text widget property editType is used to set the text as editable. The preferredPaneSize property sets the desired height in pixels for a widget contained in a Pane widget. The function main defines a Top-Level widget as well as widgets for the text area, the Erase command button, the Display command button, and the Quit command button:

```
Widget top_level, paned, text, erase, display, quit;
```

When we initialize the Text widget, we will use the following for the initial text:

```
char *initial_text= "Try typing\n\nsome text here!\n\n";
```

We initialize the `application context` (here defined using a global variable so that we can access it in the `do_quit` function), define the Top-Level widget in the same way as the previous examples, and create a `paned` window widget:

```
top_level = XtAppInitialize(&application_context,
                            "textexample", NULL, 0,
                            &argc, argv, app_resources,
                            NULL, 0);

paned = XtVaCreateManagedWidget("paned", panedWidgetClass, top_level,
                                NULL);
```

We use the variable number of arguments version of `XtCreateManagedWidget` for creating the Text widget so that we can specify both the widget type `XawAsciiString` and the initial text by setting the `type` and `string` properties:

```
text = XtVaCreateManagedWidget("text", asciiTextWidgetClass, paned,
                               XtNtype, XawAsciiString,
                               XtNstring, initial_text,
                               NULL);
```

Here, we used `paned` as the Parent widget, not the Top-Level widget. Also, for creating a Command widget labeled `"erase"`, we could have used the normal version of `XtCreateManagedWidget` because we are not setting any properties. However, here is an example of calling the version that supports a variable number of arguments (using the `paned` as the parent):

```
erase = XtVaCreateManagedWidget("erase", commandWidgetClass, paned,
                                NULL);
```

In a similar way, we define the `display` and `erase` widgets, then set the Callback functions for all three Command Button widgets. We use `paned` as the parent, not the Top-Level widget:

```
display = XtVaCreateManagedWidget("display", commandWidgetClass, paned,
                                  NULL);

quit = XtVaCreateManagedWidget("quit", commandWidgetClass, paned,
                               NULL);
```

```
XtAddCallback(erase, XtNcallback,
              do_erase_text_widget, (XtPointer) text);
XtAddCallback(display, XtNcallback, do_display_widget_text,
              (XtPointer) text);
XtAddCallback(quit, XtNcallback, do_quit, (XtPointer) text);
```

Finally, as in the previous examples, we make all of the widgets visible on the X server and enter the main event loop:

```
XtRealizeWidget(top_level);
XtAppMainLoop(application_context);
```

Figure 29.4 shows an X window containing the text.c example program.

FIGURE 29.4

Running the text.c example program in the KDE desktop.

You can build and run this test program by changing the directory to src/X/Athena and typing:

```
make
text
```

The Athena Simple Menu Widget

The example program for this section is menu.c, which is located in the src/X/Athena directory. There are three Athena widgets used together to make simple menus:

Widget	Description
MenuButton	Implements a Menu Button widget that manages the simple menu popup shell.
SimpleMenu	Popup shell and container for menu elements.
Sme	Simple menu elements that are added to a simple menu.

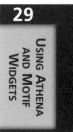

The following `include` files define these widget types:

```
#include <X11/Xaw/MenuButton.h>
#include <X11/Xaw/SimpleMenu.h>
#include <X11/Xaw/Sme.h>
#include <X11/Xaw/SmeBSB.h>
```

Each menu element that is added to a simple menu can have its own unique Callback function to execute the appropriate menu action. In the `menu.c` example, we use a single Callback function `do_menu_selection` that uses the menu element name to determine which menu element was selected by a user. The example program `menu.c` has one menu element labeled `"Exit program"`. Because we want to clean up any X resources and data used before exiting the program, we make the application context a global variable so that it can be used in the Callback function:

```
XtAppContext application_context;

void do_menu_selection(Widget item_selected, XtPointer unused1,
                       XtPointer unused2) {
  char * name = XtName(item_selected);
  printf("Menu item `%s' has been selected.\n", name);
  if (strcmp(name, "Exit program") == 0) {
    XtDestroyApplicationContext(application_context);
    exit(0);
  }
}
```

The `XtName` macro returns the name field from a widget. This name can be used to determine which menu element a user selects while running the example program. Although we usually use our `.Xdefaults` file to customize X application resources, the following data in the `menu.c` example program is used to define default (or "fallback") resources:

```
String fallback_resources[] = {
    "*menuButton.label: This is a menubutton label",
    "*menu.label: Sample menu label",
    NULL,
};
```

This data is allocated as global in the example program; it could also have been defined in the main function. We do define the menu item labels in the main function:

```
    char * menu_item_names[] = {
        "Menu item1", "Menu item2", "Menu item3",
        "Menu item4", "Exit program",
    };
```

It is fine to allocate widget data in the main function. However, you must be careful: if you use a separate "setup" function called from function `main`, make sure you declare any widget setup data as static so its memory allocation does not get lost when the program exits the function. (Remember, non-static data in a function is allocated on a call stack; this storage "goes away" after exiting the function.) We have defined four variables for storing the values of widgets created in the menu.c example program:

```
Widget top_level, menu_button, menu, menu_element;
```

The variable menu_element is reused for each menu element (for example, a Sme widget) created and added to the simple menu. As we have seen in previous examples, we need to create the application's widgets:

```
top_level = XtVaAppInitialize(&application_context,
                        "textmenu", NULL, 0,
                        &argc, argv, fallback_resources,
                        NULL);


menu_button = XtCreateManagedWidget("menuButton",
                                menuButtonWidgetClass,
                                top_level, NULL, 0);

menu = XtCreatePopupShell("menu", simpleMenuWidgetClass, menu_button,
                    NULL, 0);
```

We now loop over each menu element name, creating a new Sme widget and adding it to the simple menu. We also assign our Callback function to each menu element:

```
for (i = 0; i < (int)XtNumber(menu_item_names) ; i++) {
  menu_element = XtCreateManagedWidget(menu_item_names[i],
                                smeBSBObjectClass,
                                menu, NULL, 0);
  XtAddCallback(menu_element, XtNcallback, do_menu_selection, NULL);

}
```

Here, the macro XtNumber provides the number of non-NULL strings defined in the array menu_item_names. The Parent widget of each menu element is set to the variable menu (our simple menu widget). You can run the menu.c example by changing to the src/X/Athena directory and typing:

```
make
menu
```

Using Motif Widgets

I developed and tested the programs in this chapter using the freely available LessTif Motif clone (see www.lesstif.org) and the commercial Metro Link Motif product (see www.metrolink.com). I would like to thank Metro Link for providing me with a copy of their commercial Motif for Linux product. We will use three example programs in this section (they are in the src/X/Motif directory):

29

USING ATHENA
AND MOTIF
WIDGETS

Program	Description
label.c	Introduces Motif.
list.c	Shows how to handle events.
text.c	Combines a panel container with Text and Command Button widgets.

Much of what we learned about using Athena widgets also will be useful for Motif programs. Probably the biggest difference in using Motif lies in using Motif Strings instead of 8-bits-per-character C strings. Another difference lies in the naming and definition of widget resources. Athena widget header files define new resource types for the widget defined in the header file. The names for Motif widget resources are defined in the include file XmStrDefs.h. The following are some example Motif resource names:

```
#define XmNalignment "alignment"
#define XmNallowOverlap "allowOverlap"
#define XmNallowResize "allowResize"
#define XmNclientData "clientData"
#define XmNclipWindow "clipWindow"
#define XmNcolumns "columns"
#define XmNcommand "command"
#define XmNdirListItemCount "dirListItemCount"
#define XmNdirListItems "dirListItems"
#define XmNeditable "editable"
#define XmNlabelString "labelString"
#define XmNoffsetX "offsetX"
#define XmNoffsetY "offsetY"
#define XmNwidth       XtNwidth   // define using X toolkit constant
#define XmNheight      XtNheight  // define using X toolkit constant
```

This is just a sample of the available resources for Motif widgets. This section of Motif programming is quite short, so we will cover only a few of the Motif widgets here.

The Motif Label Widget

The example program for this section is found in the file label.c in the directory src/X/Motif. This example program uses two include files, one for defining the core definitions for all Motif widgets and one for defining the Motif Label widget:

```
#include <Xm/Xm.h>
#include <Xm/Label.h>
```

The function main defines two widgets, one for the Top-Level application widget and one for the Label widget. Note that we use the same Data Type widget as the one used in the

Athena widget examples. The following code shows the definition of a Motif String, and an argument variable for setting the label resource for the string:

```
Widget top_level, label;
XmString motif_string;
Arg arg[1];
```

Here, we define a Top-Level Application widget. This example differs from the Athena widget examples because we do not define an `application context`. We could also have coded the initialization of the Top-Level widget exactly as we did in all of the Athena widget examples.

```
top_level = XtInitialize(argv[0], "test", NULL, 0, &argc, argv);
```

We cannot simply use C strings for Motif String resources. Instead, we must construct a motif string:

```
motif_string =
  XmStringCreateSimple("Yes! we are testing the Motif Label Widget!");
```

Here, we set the `labelString` resource for the Label widget, and then construct the Label widget:

```
XtSetArg(arg[0], XmNlabelString, motif_string);
label = XmCreateLabel(top_level, "label", arg, 1);
XtManageChild(label);
```

As we did in the Athena widget examples, we need to make the Top-Level widget visible and able to manage events:

```
XtRealizeWidget(top_level);
XtMainLoop();
```

Here, we use the `XtMainLoop` X toolkit function to handle events because we did not define an application context when creating the Top-Level Application widget. The Athena widget examples used the function `XtAppMainLoop(XtAppContext applica-tion_context)` to handle X events. If you need the application context of an application, you can use the following function, passing any widget in the application as the argument:

```
XtAppContext XtWidgetToApplicationContext(Widget w)
```

Figure 29.5 shows a screen shot of the `label.c` example program running under the KDE desktop environment.

29

USING ATHENA AND MOTIF WIDGETS

FIGURE 29.5

The Motif Label widget example.

You can build and run this test program by changing the directory to `src/X/Motif` and typing:

```
make
label
```

The Motif List Widget

The example used in this section is in the file `list.c` in the directory `src/X/Motif`. This example shows how to create a Motif List widget and how to handle callbacks. This example uses two `include` files for the core Motif definitions and the definition of the List widget:

```
#include <Xm/Xm.h>
#include <Xm/List.h>
```

We will need a Callback function for handling user selection events in the List widget:

```
void do_list_click(Widget widget, caddr_t data1, XtPointer data2) {
    char *string;
    XmListCallbackStruct *callback = (XmListCallbackStruct *)data2;
    XmStringGetLtoR(callback->item, XmSTRING_OS_CHARSET, &string);
    printf("  You chose item %d : %s\n", callback->item_position, string);
    XtFree(string);
}
```

When this function, `do_list_click`, is called by the event handlers in `XtMainLoop`, the third argument passed is a pointer to a `XmListCallbackStruct` object. In this example, we coerce the third argument to the type `XmListCallbackStruct *` and use the item field that has the type `XmString`. The Motif utility function `XmStringGetLtoR` is used to convert a Motif String to a C string using the default character set. The function `XmStringGetLtoR` allocates storage for the C style string, so we need to use `XtFree` to release this storage when we no longer need to use the string.

The function `main` defines two widgets, an array of three Motif Strings, and an array of four argument variables:

```
    Widget top_level, list;
    XmString motif_strings[3];
    Arg arg[4];
```

We define a Top-Level Application widget with no extra arguments:

```
    top_level = XtInitialize(argv[0], "test", NULL, 0, &argc, argv);
```

Next, we define values for each element of an array of Motif Strings and use this array when creating the Motif List widget:

```
motif_strings[0] = XmStringCreateSimple("list item at index 0");
motif_strings[1] = XmStringCreateSimple("list item at index 1");
motif_strings[2] = XmStringCreateSimple("list item at index 2");

XtSetArg(arg[0], XmNitemCount, 3);
XtSetArg(arg[1], XmNitems, motif_strings);
XtSetArg(arg[2], XmNvisibleItemCount, 3); // all list elements are
➥visible
XtSetArg(arg[3], XmNselectionPolicy, XmSINGLE_SELECT);

list = XmCreateList(top_level, "list", arg, 4);
```

We have specified four arguments for creating the List widget:

- The number of list elements
- The data for the list elements
- The number of list elements that should be visible
- That only one list item can be selected at a time

If we allowed multiple list selections, then we would have to re-write the Callback function do_list_click to handle retrieving multiple selections. After creating the List widget, we specify the Callback function, do_list_click, for the widget, make the List widget and the Top-Level widget visible, and handle X events:

```
XtAddCallback(list, XmNsingleSelectionCallback,
              (XtCallbackProc)do_list_click, NULL);
XtManageChild(list);
XtRealizeWidget(top_level);
XtMainLoop();
```

Figure 29.6 shows the list.c example program running under the KDE desktop environment.

FIGURE 29.6

The Motif List widget example.

You can build and run this test program by changing the directory to src/X/Motif and typing:

```
make
list
```

Using Motif widgets is a little more complex than using Athena widgets, but there are, in general, more options available for Motif widgets. In the last 10 years, I have used

29

USING ATHENA
AND MOTIF
WIDGETS

Athena and Motif widgets equally, choosing which widget set to use based on the application requirements and customer preferences.

The Motif Text Widget

The example program for this section is in the file text.c in the directory src/X/Motif. This example introduces the use of a panel container to hold other widgets. This example uses a Text widget and two Push Button widgets. We need only two include files for this example: one for the core Motif definitions and one to define the Motif Text widget. We use a Motif utility function to create Motif Push Button widgets and a Paned Window widget, so we do not need a separate include file to support these widget types:

```
#include <Xm/Xm.h>
#include <Xm/Text.h>
```

This example uses two Callback functions—one for each Push Button widget. The first Callback function is used to display the text of the Text widget:

```
void do_get_text(Widget widget, caddr_t client_data, caddr_t call_data) {
  Widget text = (Widget)client_data;
  char  *string = XmTextGetString(text);
  printf("The Motif example Text widget contains:\n%s\n", string);
  XtFree(string);
}
```

This is the first Callback function example in which we use the second argument. When we bind this Callback function to the "display text" Push Button widget, we specify that the Text widget should be passed as client data to the Callback function. Looking ahead in the example code:

```
    Widget text = XmCreateText(pane, "text", NULL, 0);
    Widget display_button = XmCreatePushButton(pane, "Display", NULL, 0);
    XtAddCallback(display_button, XmNactivateCallback,
                  (XtCallbackProc)do_get_text, text);
```

Here, the value of the Text widget is specified as the client data for the Callback function.

The second Callback function is simpler; it simply calls the system function exit to terminate the program:

```
void do_quit(Widget widget, caddr_t client_data, caddr_t call_data) {
  exit(0);
}
```

The function main defines five widgets to use:

```
    Widget  top_level, pane, text, display_button, quit_button;
```

The pane widget will be added to the Top-Level Application widget. All of the remaining widgets will be added to pane, which lays out Text and Push Button widgets vertically:

```
top_level = XtInitialize(argv[0], "test", NULL, 0, &argc, argv);
pane = XmCreatePanedWindow(top_level, "pane", NULL, 0);
```

In this example, we set up values for five resources for the Text widget before creating the Text widget:

```
XtSetArg(arg[0], XmNwidth, 400);
XtSetArg(arg[1], XmNheight, 400);
XtSetArg(arg[3], XmNwordWrap, TRUE);
XtSetArg(arg[4], XmNeditMode, XmMULTI_LINE_EDIT);
text = XmCreateText(pane, "text", arg, 5);
```

We want to specify the size of the text-editing area. The Panel widget will automatically adjust its size to the preferred sizes of the widgets that it contains. Setting the width of the Text widget to 400 pixels effectively makes the Panel widget 400 pixels wide because the preferred sizes of the two Push Button widgets will be less than 400 pixels wide unless they are created with very long labels. We specify that the Text widget uses word wrap so long lines are automatically wrapped to the next line of text.

Here, we define the two push buttons as Child widgets to the pane widget and specify their Callback functions:

```
display_button = XmCreatePushButton(pane, "Display", NULL, 0);
quit_button = XmCreatePushButton(pane, "Quit", NULL, 0);

XtAddCallback(display_button, XmNactivateCallback,
              (XtCallbackProc)do_get_text, text);
XtAddCallback(quit_button, XmNactivateCallback,
              (XtCallbackProc)do_quit, NULL);
```

As we noted before, we pass the value of the Text widget as client data to the Callback function for the "display text" Push Button widget. In this example, we individually manage each widget before making the Top-Level widget visible. We then call XtMainLoop to handle events:

```
XtManageChild(text);
XtManageChild(display_button);
XtManageChild(quit_button);
XtManageChild(pane);
XtRealizeWidget(top_level);
XtMainLoop();
```

Figure 29.7 shows a screen shot of the text.c example program running under the KDE desktop environment.

29

USING ATHENA
AND MOTIF
WIDGETS

FIGURE 29.7
*The Motif Text
widget example.*

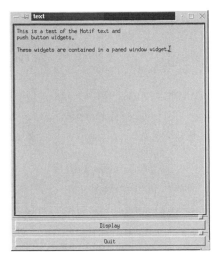

You can build and run this test program by changing the directory to src/X/Motif and typing:

```
make
text
```

This example shows the standard structure for most Motif applications: we create a Pane Window widget that contains all other widgets in the application. This pane widget will handle resizing Child widgets when the user resizes the main application window. An alternative is to place Child widgets directly in the Main Application widget and to specify x-y positions and size of each Child widget.

Writing a Custom Athena Widget

Many X Windows programmers never need to write custom widgets, but the ability to define new widgets is a powerful technique for encapsulating both application data and behavior. In this section, we will create an Athena widget named URLWidget, which displays text from a URL address. Writing new widgets seems like a huge task, but the job can be made easier by finding the source code to a similar widget and modifying it. For this example widget, we will start with the Template example widget from the X Consortium. You will also want to check out their Web site at http://www.x.org.

The source code to the URLWidget and a test program, test.c, is located in the src/X/URLWidget directory. The original template example, which you will likely want to use as a starting point for writing your own Athena widgets, is located in the directory src/X/URLWidget/templates. The URLWidget is a simple widget that fetches the text from a file given a URL Web address, and stores this as a C string in the widget's private data. Whenever the widget has to redraw itself, this string is parsed to pull out the individual lines, and then drawn in the widget's drawable area. There are four files used to implement this widget:

File	Description
fetch_url.c	Some socket code to connect to a Web server and to request a file
URL.h	The public header file that you include in your program when you want to create a URLWidget.
URLP.h	The private, implementation header file
URL.c	The implementation of the URLWidget

I based the files URL.h, URLP.h, and URL.c on the files Template.h, TemplateP.h, and Template.c that carry the copyright:

```
/* XConsortium: Template.c,v 1.2 88/10/25 17:40:25 swick Exp $ */
/* Copyright Massachusetts Institute of Technology 1987, 1988 */
```

The X Consortium, in general, allows free use of their software as long as all copyright notices are left intact.

Using the `fetch_url.c` File

The utility for fetching a remote Web document implemented in the file fetch_url.c, located in the directory src/X/URLWidget, was derived from web_client.c in the directory src/IPC/SOCKETS. This example program was discussed in Chapter 19. The function signature for this utility function is:

```
char * fetch_url(char *url_name);
```

The following are example uses:

```
char * mark_home_page1 = fetch_url("www.markwatson.com");
char * mark_home_page2 = fetch_url("http://www.markwatson.com");
char * mark_home_page3 =
            fetch_url("http://www.markwatson.com/index.html");
```

The following discussion of this utility is brief; you may also want to refer to Chapter 19. Web servers, by default, listen to port 80:

```
int port = 80;
```

The following arrays are used for processing:

Array	Description
`char * buf = (char *)malloc(50000)`	Used for the returned data.
`char message[256]`	Used to build a "GET" message to the Web server.
`char host_name[200]`	Used to construct the proper host name from the URL.
`char file_name[200]`	Used for the optional file name at the end of the URL.
`char *error_string`	Used to construct a proper error message.

This utility function allocates the memory block returned to the caller, but it is the responsibility of the caller to free this memory. The following code determines the correct host name and the optional file name at the end of the URL:

```c
char *sp1, *sp2;
sp1 = strstr(url, "http://");
if (sp1 == NULL) {
  sprintf(host_name, "%s", url);
} else {
  sprintf(host_name, "%s", &(url[7]));
}
printf("1.  host_name=%s\n", host_name);
sp1 = strstr(host_name, "/");
if (sp1 == NULL) {
  // no file name, so use index.html:
  sprintf(file_name, "index.html");
} else {
  sprintf(file_name, "%s", (char *)(sp1 + 1));
  *sp1 = '\0';
}
printf("2.  host_name=%s, file_name=%s\n", host_name, file_name);
```

A connection is now made to the remote Web server:

```c
if ((nlp_host = gethostbyname(host_name)) == 0) {
  error_string = (char *)malloc(128);
  sprintf(error_string, "Error resolving local host\n");
  return error_string;
}
bzero(&pin, sizeof(pin));
pin.sin_family = AF_INET;
pin.sin_addr.s_addr = htonl(INADDR_ANY);
pin.sin_addr.s_addr = ((struct in_addr *)(nlp_host->h_addr))->s_addr;
pin.sin_port = htons(port);
```

```
if ((sd = socket(AF_INET, SOCK_STREAM, 0)) == -1) {
  error_string = (char *)malloc(128);
  sprintf(error_string, "Error opening socket\n");
  return error_string;
}
if (connect(sd, (void *)&pin, sizeof(pin)) == -1) {
  error_string = (char *)malloc(128);
  sprintf(error_string, "Error connecting to socket\n");
  return error_string;
}
```

Then we construct a proper "GET" message for the server and send it:

```
sprintf(message,"GET /%s  HTTP/1.0\n\n", file_name);
if (send(sd, message, strlen(message), 0) == -1) {
  error_string = (char *)malloc(128);
  sprintf(error_string, "Error in send\n");
  return error_string;
}
```

We now wait for a response; the Web server may return data in several separate packets:

```
count = sum = iter = 0;
while (iter++ < 5) {
  count = recv(sd, &(buf[sum]), 50000 - count, 0);
  if (count == -1) {
    break;
  }
  sum += count;
}
```

Finally, we close the socket connection (if the Web server has not already done so) and return the data from the URL:

```
close(sd);
return buf;
```

Using the URL.h File

The file URL.h is the public header file for the URLWidget widget. It is derived from the Template.h file from the X Consortium. This file defines resource names for the widget:

```
#define XtNURLResource          "urlResource"
#define XtCURLResource          "URLResource"
```

For example, we will see later (in the test program test.c) how to set the URLResource property of the URLWidget:

```
XtSetArg(args[2], XtNURLResource, "www.knowledgebooks.com");
```

29

USING ATHENA
AND MOTIF
WIDGETS

The following `struct` definition is used for implementing the `URLWidget` widget:

```
typedef struct _URLRec*        URLWidget;
```

The following declaration is used to define the widget class variable actually used to construct a `URLWidget` widget:

```
extern WidgetClass urlWidgetClass;
```

For example, from the `test.c` program:

```
Widget url = XtCreateManagedWidget("url", urlWidgetClass,
                                    top_level, args, 3);
```

Using the URLP.h File

The `ULRP.h` file serves as the private header file for the `URLWidget` widget. It is derived from the `TemplateP.h` example file from the X Consortium. The private header file requires the definitions from the public header file and the core widget definition header file:

```
#include "URL.h"
#include <X11/CoreP.h>
```

We need to define a unique representation type that is not already in the X11 `StringDefs.h` file:

```
#define XtRURLResource  "URLResource"
```

Every widget has core and class data. Here we must define the class part data structure even though this widget does not require any class data:

```
typedef struct {
  int empty;
} URLClassPart;
```

The following definition defines the class record, comprising the core (default) data and the data for this class:

```
typedef struct _URLClassRec {
  CoreClassPart core_class;
  URLClassPart  URL_class;
} URLClassRec;
```

The following external symbol definition will be defined in the `URL.c` file:

```
extern URLClassRec urlClassRec;
```

The following structure defines the resources specific to this widget type:

```
typedef struct {
  /* resources */
  char* name;
  /* private state */
  char *data;
  GC gc;
} URLPart;
```

The URLPart struct private state data will be initialized in the Initialize function in
URL.c and used in the Redraw function. The resource data name will be set whenever the
XtNURLResource resource is set. The following structure contains the URLPart data:

```
typedef struct _URLRec {
  CorePart     core;
  URLPart            url;
} URLRec;
```

As we will see in the next section, the Initialize and ReDraw functions are passed a
URLWidget object and they refer to the URLPart data through this widget pointer:

```
static void Initialize(URLWidget request, URLWidget new) {
  new->url.data = fetch_url(new->url.name);
}
static void ReDraw(URLWidget w, XEvent *event, Region region) {
    XDrawString(XtDisplay(w), XtWindow(w), w->url.gc, 10, y,
                "test", strlen("test"));
}
```

Using the URL.c File

The file URL.c contains the implementation of the URLWidget widget and is derived from
the example file Template.c from the X Consortium. This implementation requires several header files, most notably the private header file for the URLWidget class:

```
#include <X11/IntrinsicP.h>
#include <X11/StringDefs.h>
#include "URLP.h"
```

As per the Template.c example, we need to define the resource definition so that programs can use the XtNURLResource type:

```
static XtResource resources[] = {
#define offset(field) XtOffset(URLWidget, url.field)
  /* {name, class, type, size, offset, default_type, default_addr}, */
  { XtNURLResource, XtCURLResource, XtRURLResource, sizeof(char*),
    offset(name), XtRString, "default" },
#undef offset
};
```

This definition will allow the implementation of the URLWidget class to correctly modify the XtNURLResource resource. The following definition was copied from the Template.c example, with the fields changed for binding the functions Initialize and ReDraw that are defined in this file:

```
URLClassRec urlClassRec = {
  { /* core fields */
    /* superclass           */ (WidgetClass) &widgetClassRec,
    /* class_name           */ "URL",
    /* widget_size          */ sizeof(URLRec),
    /* class_initialize     */ NULL,
    /* class_part_initialize */     NULL,
    /* class_inited         */ FALSE,
    /* initialize           */ Initialize, // CHANGED
    /* initialize_hook      */ NULL,
    /* realize  */           XtInheritRealize,
    /* actions  */           NULL, // actions,
    /* num_actions          */ 0, // XtNumber(actions),
    /* resources            */ resources,
    /* num_resources        */ XtNumber(resources),
    /* xrm_class            */ NULLQUARK,
    /* compress_motion      */ TRUE,
    /* compress_exposure    */ TRUE,
    /* compress_enterleave  */ TRUE,
    /* visible_interest     */ FALSE,
    /* destroy  */           NULL,
    /* resize   */           NULL,
    /* expose   */           ReDraw,   // CHANGED
    /* set_values           */ NULL,
    /* set_values_hook      */ NULL,
    /* set_values_almost    */ XtInheritSetValuesAlmost,
    /* get_values_hook      */ NULL,
    /* accept_focus         */ NULL,
    /* version  */           XtVersion,
    /* callback_private     */ NULL,
    /* tm_table */           NULL, // translations,
    /* query_geometry       */ XtInheritQueryGeometry,
    /* display_accelerator  */        XtInheritDisplayAccelerator,
    /* extension            */ NULL
  },
  { /* url fields */
    /* empty    */           0
  }
};
```

The function `Initialize` is called after the core widget class `Initialize` function to perform any setup that is specific to this new `URLWidget` class:

```
static void Initialize(URLWidget request, URLWidget new) {
  XtGCMask valueMask;
  XGCValues values;
  printf("name = %s\n", new->url.name);
  // Get the URL data here:
  new->url.data = fetch_url(new->url.name);
  valueMask = GCForeground | GCBackground;
  values.foreground = BlackPixel(XtDisplay(new), 0);
  values.background = WhitePixel(XtDisplay(new), 0);
  new->url.gc = XtGetGC((Widget)new, valueMask, &values);
}
```

The function `Initialize` uses the `fetch_url` function to get data from a remote Web server and sets up the graphics context (GC) for this widget. Note that this data is accessed using the `url` field of the widget. The `clean_text` function is a simple function used to strip control characters out of the text after a line of text is extracted from the original data from the remote Web server:

```
static char buf[50000];
static char buf2[50000];
char * clean_text(char *dirty_text) {
  int i, count = 0;
  int len = strlen(dirty_text);
  for (i=0; i<len; i++) {
    if (dirty_text[i] > 30) buf2[count++] = dirty_text[i];
  }
  buf2[count] = 0;
  return &(buf2[0]);
}
```

The `ReDraw` function is called after widget initialization; it's called again whenever this widget is exposed or resized. `ReDraw` simply takes each line of text that is separated by a new line character, removes any control characters from this text, and uses `XDrawString` to draw the line of text in the correct location in the widget. We also saw the use of `XDrawSTring` in Chapter 28. This example does not use font metrics to determine the height of a line of text; it assumes that a row 12 pixels high is sufficient to hold a line of text.

```
static void ReDraw(URLWidget w, XEvent *event, Region region) {
  //printf("in ReDraw, text is:\n%s\n", w->url.data);
  char *sp1, *sp2, *sp3;
  int len, y = 20;
  sp1 = &(buf[0]);
```

29

USING ATHENA
AND MOTIF
WIDGETS

```
  sprintf(sp1, "%s", w->url.data);
  len = strlen(sp1);
  while (1) {
    sp2 = strstr(sp1, "\n");
    if (sp2 != NULL) {
      // keep going...
      *sp2 = '\0';
      sp3 = clean_text(sp1);
      XDrawString(XtDisplay(w), XtWindow(w), w->url.gc, 10, y,
                  sp3, strlen(sp3));
      y += 12;
      sp1 = sp2 + 1;
    } else {
      // time to stop...
      sp3 = clean_text(sp1);
      XDrawString(XtDisplay(w), XtWindow(w), w->url.gc, 10, y,
                  sp3, strlen(sp3));
      break;
    }
    // check to avoid running past data:
    if (sp1 >= &(buf[0]) + len) break;
  }
}
```

The implementation of the URLWidget is actually very simple. Most of the work lies in following the strict X toolkit protocol for writing widgets. In principle, the URLWidget can be used in any X application, including applications using Motif widgets.

Testing the URLWidget

If you have not already done so, you should compile and run the test.c program by changing the directory to src/X/URLWidget and typing:

make
./test

You must type **./test** instead of **test** to avoid running the system utility "test" that checks file types. This test program is simple. Using a widget should be much easier than writing the code to implement it. We start by including both the standard X11 header files and the public URLWidget header file:

```
#include <X11/StringDefs.h>
#include <X11/Intrinsic.h>
#include "URL.h"
```

The function main defines two widgets (top_level and url)and creates the top_level widget:

```
  Widget top_level, url;
  top_level = XtInitialize(argv[0], "urltest", NULL, 0, &argc, argv);
```

We need to set the `width`, `height`, and `URLResource` resources for the url widget before creating the url widget:

```
Arg args[3];
XtSetArg(args[0], XtNwidth, 520);
XtSetArg(args[1], XtNheight, 580);
XtSetArg(args[2], XtNURLResource, "www.knowledgebooks.com");
url = XtCreateManagedWidget("url", urlWidgetClass, top_level, args, 3);
```

Finally, we realize the Top-Level widget and handle X events:

```
XtRealizeWidget(top_level);
XtMainLoop();
```

Figure 29.8 shows a the `test.c` program running.

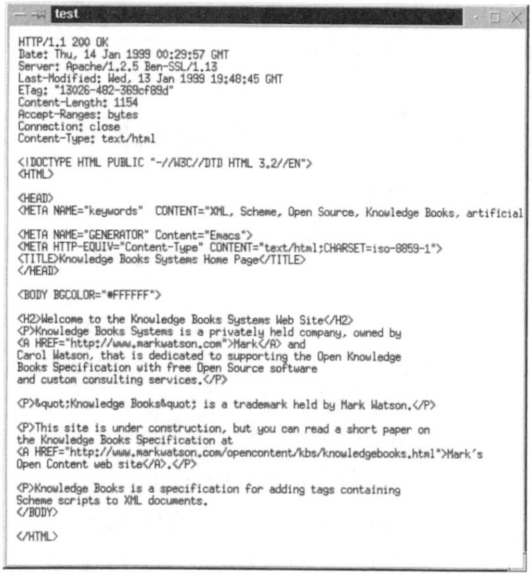

FIGURE 29.8

Testing URLWidget.

Using Both Athena and Motif in C++ Programs

When I first started programming in C++ in the late 1980s, I also learned X Windows programming at roughly the same time. The bad news back then was that the X toolkit and the Athena widgets were not very "C++ friendly," so I spent a great deal of time combining Widgets with C++ programs. Well, the good news now is that the X11 libraries, header files, and so on work effortlessly with the C++ language. If you look in the directory `src/X/list_C++`, you will see two source files:

> `athena.cpp`—this is the `src/X/Athena/list.c` example renamed
>
> `motif.cpp`—this is the `src/X/Motif/list.c` example renamed

Except for one compiler warning about `printf`, these examples compile with the C++ compiler and run fine. Try this yourself; change the directory to `src/X/list_C++` and type:

```
make
athena
motif
```

Because a C++ compiler provides better compile-time error checking than a C compiler, I recommend using C++ instead of C even if you are not using the object-oriented features of C++ (for example, no class definitions).

Using a C++ Class Library for Athena Widgets

In this section, we will learn about a very simple C++ library that encapsulates the following Athena widgets:

Widget	Description
Paned	Wrapped in the C++ class
PanedWindow	(which also generates a Top-Level Application widget).
Label	Wrapped in the C++ class `Label`.
Command Button	Wrapped in the C++ class `Button`.
AsciiText	Wrapped in the C++ class `Text`.

As some motivation for this exercise, I will first show a simple test program that contains absolutely no (obvious) X Windows code. The example program, `test_it.cpp`, is located in the directory `src/X/C++` and is listed below.

`iostream.h` defines standard C++ I/O. The `include` files `PanedWindow.h`, `Label.h`, `Button.h`, and `Text.h` define our C++ classes that wrap the corresponding Athena widgets:

```
#include <iostream.h>
#include "PaneWindow.hxx"
```

```
#include "Label.hxx"
#include "Button.hxx"
#include "Text.hxx"
```

We will create one each of these C++ objects. The button will have a Callback function that prints the content of the text object. We make the `Text` object global so that the `button_cb` Callback function can access it:

```
Text *text;
```

The `button_cb` Callback function uses the public `getText` method of the `Text` class to print whatever text has been typed into the text object:

```
void button_cb() {
  cout << "Text is:\n" << text->getText() << "\n";
}
```

The function `main` is very simple. We construct one instance each of our wrapper classes, use the `PaneWindow` class's public `addComponent` method to add the `Label`, `Button` and `Text` objects to the paned window object, and then call the `PaneWindow` class's public `run` method to handle events. Note that the constructor for the `Button` class takes a C function as the second argument; this function will be called whenever the button is clicked with the mouse pointer.

```
void main() {
  PaneWindow pw;
  Label label("this is a test");
  Button button("Get text", button_cb);
  text = new Text(300, 120);
  pw.addComponent(&label);
  pw.addComponent(&button);
  pw.addComponent(text);
  pw.run();
}
```

Figure 29.9 shows the example program `test_it.cpp` running.

FIGURE 29.9

Testing the C++ class library for wrapping Athena widgets.

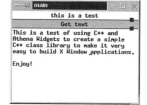

The PaneWindow class does most of the work in this class library. This class is responsible for the behavior of adding sub-components and handling X events. The classes Label, Button, and Text are all derived from a base class Component that has one important virtual method, setup. I designed the class library in this way so that the PaneWindow class can simply keep an array of pointers to instances of classes derived from class Component. The public run method of class PanedWindow creates all of the contained widgets by calling the method setup for each component that has been added to a paned window object. The method run then internally handles all X events.

The implementation of this class library is simple, and you should find it easy to add to this library other widgets for your applications. The only complication involves handling C language Callback functions. We will soon see how this is done in the implementation of the Button class.

The Component Class

The Component class is the base class for the Label, Button, and Text classes. If you want to wrap additional widgets in a C++ class and add them to this library, your new classes should also be derived from the Component class. The header file for this class is fairly simple. As is typical of header files, the entire contents of the Component.hxx file is "wrapped" in a #ifndef statement:

```
#ifndef Component__hxx
#define Component__hxx
```

This #ifdef assures us that this file will not be included twice in any compiled code. We also need the standard X toolkit include file for the definition of the type of Top-Level Application widget:

```
#include <X11/Intrinsic.h>
```

The class definition is simple. The constructor for this class does almost nothing, and the virtual method setup must always be overridden in derived classes because it is a "pure virtual" function—the method is set to zero. The public getWidget method simply returns the values of the private variable my_widget.

```
class Component {
public:
  Component();
  virtual void setup(Widget parent) = 0;
  Widget getWidget() { return my_widget; }
protected:
  Widget my_widget;
};
```

The implementation of the Component class in the file Component.cxx is also simple:

```
// Component.cpp
//

#include <X11/Intrinsic.h>
#include "Component.hxx"

Component::Component() {
   my_widget = (Widget)NULL;
}
```

The class constructor for Component sets the private variable my_widget to a NULL value, which is not strictly necessary.

The PanedWindow Class

It was important to see the definition of the Component class before the PaneWindow class because a pane window object maintains an array of pointers to objects derived from the Component class. The header file for this class is PaneWindow.h, where we need four include file:

```
#include <X11/Intrinsic.h>
#include <X11/StringDefs.h>
#include <X11/Xaw/Paned.h>
#include "Component.hxx"
```

The first three include files are required for X Windows definitions- and the fourth is the header file for the Component class. The PaneWindow class has three public methods:

Method	Description
PaneWindow	Class constructor.
addComponent(Component * comp)	Adds other components to the paned window.
run()	Creates all the contained components and handles events.

The private data for the class PaneWindow contains X Windows-specific data that users of this class library can ignore. There is also private data to store up to 10 pointers to objects belonging to any class derived from the Component class.

```
class PaneWindow {
public:
  PaneWindow();
```

29

USING ATHENA
AND MOTIF
WIDGETS

```
   void addComponent(Component * comp);
   void run();
private:
  Widget top_level;
  Widget pane;
  Component  * components[10];
  int num_components;
  XtAppContext application_context;
};
```

The implementation of the `PaneWindow` class, in the file `PaneWindow.cxx`, requires three include files; the first two are X-related and the third is the class definition header file:

```
#include <X11/Intrinsic.h>
#include <X11/Xaw/Paned.h>
#include "PaneWindow.hxx"
```

The following X resources are defined for the components that might be added to a paned window:

```
static String app_resources[] = {
  "*Text*editType: edit",
  "*Text*autoFill: on",
  "*Text*scrollVertical: whenNeeded",
  "*Text*scrollHorizontal: whenNeeded",
  "*Text*preferredPaneSize: 300",
  NULL,
};
```

If you create new subclasses of `Component` to encapsulate other types of widgets, you might want to add default resources for those widget types to the `app_resources` array. The `PaneWindow` class constructor creates a Top-Level Application widget and an Athena Paned widget:

```
PaneWindow::PaneWindow() {
  int argc = 0;
  char ** argv = NULL;
  top_level = XtAppInitialize(&application_context, "top_level", NULL, 0,
                              &argc, argv, app_resources,
                              NULL, 0);
  num_components = 0;
  pane = XtVaCreateManagedWidget("paned", panedWidgetClass,
                                 top_level, NULL);

}
```

The method run creates components that have been added to the PaneWindow object and then handles X events. The class variable num_components is a counter for the number of components added to this object using the addComponent method:

```
void PaneWindow::run() {
  // Start by adding all registered components:
  for (int i=0; i<num_components; i++) {
    components[i]->setup(pane);
    XtManageChild(components[i]->getWidget());
  }
  XtRealizeWidget(top_level);
  XtAppMainLoop(application_context);
}
```

The method addComponent is used to add components to a PaneWindow object:

```
void PaneWindow::addComponent(Component * comp) {
  components[num_components++] = comp;
}
```

The Label Class

The Label class is derived from the class Component. The class header file Label.hxx requires only one header file, which is the definition file for its base class:

```
#include "Component.hxx"
```

The class definition is simple. The constructor takes three arguments and the class has private data so that the setup method can properly create the label when it is called from the PaneWindow object's run method:

```
class Label : public Component  {
public:
  Label(char * label = "test label", int width=100, int height=20);
  void setup(Widget parent);
private:
  char * my_label;
  int my_width;
  int my_height;
};
```

The implementation for this class is also straight forward. The file Label.cxx requires four include files, three of which are X Windows-specific and one defines the Label class:

```
#include <X11/Intrinsic.h>
#include <X11/StringDefs.h>
#include <X11/Xaw/Label.h>
#include "Label.hxx"
```

The class constructor simply stores its three arguments for later use by the setup method:

```
Label::Label(char *label, int width, int height) {
  my_label = label;
  my_width = width;
  my_height = height;
}
```

The method setup is called by the method run of a PaneWindow object; setup is called with the Athena Paned widget created in the constructor of the PaneWindow object. All component widgets added will therefore have the Athena Paned widget as a common parent:

```
void Label::setup(Widget parent) {
  Arg args[2];
  XtSetArg(args[0], XtNwidth,  my_width);
  XtSetArg(args[1], XtNheight, my_height);
  my_widget = XtCreateManagedWidget(my_label, labelWidgetClass, parent,
                                    args, 2);
}
```

The Button Class

The Button class is much more interesting than the Label class because it has to handle Callback functions. The header file Button.hxx needs two include files: one for the Athena Command widget and one for the definition of the Component C++ class:

```
#include <X11/Xaw/Command.h>
#include "Component.hxx"
```

The header file defines the type of the Callback function as a function pointer to a function with no arguments and that has no return value:

```
typedef void (*button_callback)(void);
```

The class definition is:

```
class Button : public Component {
public:
  Button(char * label = "test label", button_callback cb = 0,
         int width=130, int height=30);
  void setup(Widget parent);
  button_callback my_cb;
private:
  char * my_label;
  int my_width;
  int my_height;
};
```

The class implementation file `Button.cxx` requires four include files: three for X Windows and one that defines the C++ `Button` class:

```
#include <X11/Intrinsic.h>
#include <X11/StringDefs.h>
#include <X11/Xaw/Command.h>
#include "Button.hxx"
```

All instances of the `Button` class use one static C Callback function. This function is passed a pointer to a `Button` object, so that the button object's Callback function can be called. This allows multiple instances of the `Button` class with different Callback functions to function correctly in a single program:

```
static void callback(Widget w, caddr_t data1, caddr_t data2) {
  Button * b = (Button *)data1;
  if (b != 0)  b->my_cb();
}
```

The class constructor stores the values of its four arguments in private data:

```
Button::Button(char *label, button_callback cb,
               int width, int height) {
  my_label = label;
  my_width = width;
  my_height = height;
  my_cb = cb;
}
```

The `setup` method creates the button's widget and sets up the Callback function that is shared by all instances of this class:

```
void Button::setup(Widget parent) {
  Arg args[2];
  XtSetArg(args[0], XtNwidth,  my_width);
  XtSetArg(args[1], XtNheight, my_height);
  my_widget = XtCreateManagedWidget(my_label, commandWidgetClass, parent,
                                    args, 2);
  XtAddCallback(getWidget(), XtNcallback, callback, (XtPointer) this);
}
```

The Text Class

The `Text` class wraps (or encapsulates) the Athena `AsciiText` Top-Level Application widget. The class implementation file `Text.hxx` requires two include files: one for the standard X Windows definitions and one for the C++ `Component` class definition:

```
#include <X11/Intrinsic.h>
#include "Component.hxx"
```

29

USING ATHENA
AND MOTIF
WIDGETS

The class definition defines four public methods:

Method	Description
`Text(int width, int height)`	Class constructor.
`setup(Widget parent)`	Creates the Text widget.
`char *getText()`	Gets the text from the Text widget.
`eraseText()`	Erases all text in the Text widget.

The class defines private data to store the two arguments for the class constructor.

```
class Text : public Component {
public:
  Text(int width=130, int height=30);
  void setup(Widget parent);
  char *getText();
  void eraseText();
private:
  int my_width;
  int my_height;
};
```

The implementation, in file `Text.cxx`, is fairly simple. Four include files are required: three for X Windows and one to define the C++ `Text` class:

```
#include <X11/Intrinsic.h>
#include <X11/StringDefs.h>
#include <X11/Xaw/AsciiText.h>
#include "Text.hxx"
```

The class constructor stores its two arguments in private data for later use by the `setup` method:

```
Text::Text(int width, int height) {
  my_width = width;
  my_height = height;
}
```

The `setup` method creates the Athena `AsciiText` Top-Level Application widget:

```
void Text::setup(Widget parent) {
  Arg args[2];
  XtSetArg(args[0], XtNwidth,  my_width);
  XtSetArg(args[1], XtNheight, my_height);
  my_widget = XtVaCreateManagedWidget("text", asciiTextWidgetClass,
                                      parent,XtNtype,XawAsciiString,
                                      XtNstring, " ",
                                      args, 2, NULL);
}
```

The `getText` method returns the text that the user has typed into the Athena `AsciiText` Top-Level Application widget. The X toolkit function `XtVaGetValues` is used to get the address of the string data for the text that has been typed into the widget:

```
char * Text::getText() {
  Widget w = getWidget();
  String str;
  XtVaGetValues(w,
                XtNstring, &str,
                NULL);
  return str;
}
```

The `eraseText` method removes any text from the Athena `AsciiText` Top-Level Application widget. The `XtVaSetValues` X toolkit function changes the values of one or more resources for a widget. Here, we could have alternatively used the X toolkit function `XtSetValues`.

```
void Text::eraseText() {
  Widget w = getWidget();
  XtVaSetValues(w,
                XtNstring, "",
                NULL);
}
```

The simple C++ class library that we developed in this section should provide you with the techniques required to wrap other widget types in C++ class libraries.

Summary

We have seen how to use both Athena and Motif widgets in this chapter. Both widget sets offer advantages. Athena Widgets are always available for free to X Window programmers, while Motif is a licensed software product. The LessTif libraries are a free implementation of Motif. We also examined the techniques for using the C++ language for writing both Athena and Motif based programs.

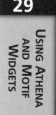

29

USING ATHENA
AND MOTIF
WIDGETS

CHAPTER 30

GUI Programming Using GTK

by Mark Watson

IN THIS CHAPTER

The Gimp Tool Kit (GTK) is widely used for writing X Windows applications on Linux and other versions of Unix. In order to help maintain both portability and software maintenance, GTK is built on top of two other libraries that you may want to use independently of GTK:

Library	Description
GLib	Supplies C libraries for linked lists, hash tables, string utilities, and so on.
GDK	A library that is layered on Xlib. All GTK windowing and graphics calls are made through GDK, not directly to XLib.

GTK has its own Web site (`www.gtk.org`) where you can download the latest version of GTK and read a very good GTK tutorial by Ian Main and Tony Gale. In this chapter, we will introduce GTK and write a short GTK application that displays the tree structure of any XML document. XML, or the Extended Markup Language, is a new standard for storing and transporting data, so this short example program should prove useful. Although the material in this chapter is "self-sufficient," read the GTK tutorial at `www.gtk.org`.

The GTK is an easy-to-use, high-level toolkit for writing GUI applications. GTK was written to support the GIMP graphics-editing program. GTK was originally written by Peter Mattis, Spencer Kimball, and Josh MacDonald.

The GTK toolkit contains a rich set of data types and utility functions. A complete description GTK is beyond the scope of this short introductory chapter. Still, reading this chapter will get you started. For more information, consult the online tutorial and example programs included in the `examples` directory in the standard GTK distribution.

All of the GTK library code and the example code contains the following copyright. In the example programs in this chapter, I copied the style (for example, variable naming conventions) and occasional lines of code, so I consider all of the examples in this chapter to be derivative and therefore also subject to the following copyright notice:

```
/* GTK - The GIMP Toolkit
 * Copyright (C) 1995-1997 Peter Mattis, Spencer Kimball and Josh
MacDonald
 *
 * This library is free software; you can redistribute it and/or
 * modify it under the terms of the GNU Library General Public
 * License as published by the Free Software Foundation; either
 * version 2 of the License, or (at your option) any later version.
 *
 * This library is distributed in the hope that it will be useful,
 * but WITHOUT ANY WARRANTY; without even the implied warranty of
 * MERCHANTABILITY or FITNESS FOR A PARTICULAR PURPOSE.  See the GNU
```

```
* Library General Public License for more details.
*
* You should have received a copy of the GNU Library General Public
* License along with this library; if not, write to the
* Free Software Foundation, Inc., 59 Temple Place - Suite 330,
* Boston, MA 02111-1307, USA.
*/
```

Introduction to GTK

We used the Athena and Motif widgets in Chapter 29. GTK has its own type of widget; the C data structure for this type is called GtkWidget. Windows and any display components created using GTK can all be referenced using a variable of type GtkWidget. Although GTK is written in C, GTK has a strong object-oriented flavor. A GtkWidget object encapsulates data, maintains references to Callback functions, and so on.

The definition (in gtkwidget.h) of the GtkWidget data type is as follows:

```
struct _GtkWidget
{
  GtkObject object; // core GTK object definition
  guint16 private_flags; // private storage
  guint8 state; // one of 5 allowed widget states
  guint8 saved_state; // previous widget state
  gchar *name; // widget's name
  GtkStyle *style; // style definition
  GtkRequisition requisition; // requested widget size
  GtkAllocation allocation; // actual widget size
  GdkWindow *window; // top-level window
  GtkWidget *parent; // parent widget
};
```

GTK widgets "inherit" from GtkWidget by defining a GtkWidget object as the first item in their own structure definition. For example, A GtkLabel widget is defined using a GtkMisc structure, adding data for the label text, width, type, and a flag to indicate if word-wrap is allowed, as shown in the following:

```
struct _GtkLabel {
  GtkMisc misc;
  gchar     *label;
  GdkWChar *label_wc;
  gchar    *pattern;
  GtkLabelWord *words;
  guint   max_width : 16;
  guint    jtype : 2;
  gboolean wrap;
};
```

The `GtkMisc` structure definition starts with a `GtkWidget` structure, adding alignment and padding information, as shown in the following:

```
struct _GtkMisc {
  GtkWidget widget;
  gfloat xalign;
  gfloat yalign;
  guint16 xpad;
  guint16 ypad;
};
```

The important thing to notice here is that although the structure of a `GtkLabel` `GtkWidget` is built with the following nested structures, the `GtkWidget` structure data is at the very beginning of the memory allocated for the `GtkLabel` widget:

```
GtkLabel
  GtkMisc
    GtkWidget
      GtkObject
```

A pointer to any type of `GtkWidget` can be safely coerced to the type (`GtkWidget *`) and the fields in the `GtkWidget` structure can be directly accessed. So, even though GTK is implemented in the C programming language and does not support private data, it has an object-oriented flavor.

Handling Events in GTK

In Chapter 29 you learned that, for Athena and Motif widget programming, the main tasks for writing GUI applications involve creating widgets and writing code to handle events in Callback functions. GTK also uses Callback functions to process events in programs, but in GTK they are referred to as "signal-handlers." The techniques will appear quite similar to the X Windows programming examples in Chapter 28 and Chapter 29. The method signature for GTK Callback functions, or signal-handlers, is defined in the file gtkwidget.h as the following:

```
typedef void (*GtkCallback) (GtkWidget *widget,
                             gpointer   data);
```

We saw the definition of a `GtkWidget` in the last section. A `gpointer` is an abstract pointer that can reference any type of data.

As we will see in the example in the next section, the GTK function `gtk_main()` handles all events that are registered using the `gtk_signal_connect` function to bind events with GTK widgets; the method signature (defined in file gtksignal.h) is as follows:

```
guint  gtk_signal_connect(GtkObject *object,
                          const gchar *name,
                          GtkSignalFunc func,
                          gpointer func_data);
```

There are about 34 separate functions defined in gtksignal.h for registering and unregistering signal-handlers; however, gtk_signal_connect will suffice for the examples in this chapter. The function signature for gtk_signal_connect is as follows:

```
guint  gtk_signal_connect(GtkObject *object,
                          const gchar *name,
                          GtkSignalFunc func,
                          gpointer func_data);
```

The first argument is a pointer to a GtkObject. In practice, however, you pass the address of a GtkWidget object. A GtkWidget contains a GtkObject at the beginning of its structure definition, so it is always safe to coerce a GtkWidget pointer to point to a GtkObject. The second argument to gtk_signal_connect is the name of the event type; here are the most commonly used GTK event-type names:

GTK Event Types	Description
clicked	Used for button widgets.
destroy	Used for window widgets.
value_changed	Used for any type of GtkObject.
toggled	Used for any type of GtkObject.
activate	Used for any type of GtkObject.
button_press_event	Used for any type of widget.
select_row	Used for clist list widgets.
select_child	Used for Tree widgets.
unselect_child	Used for Tree widgets.
select	Used for item widgets (that, for example, might be added to a tree widget).
deselect	Used for item widgets.
expose_event	Occurs when a widget is first created of uncovered.
configure_event	Occurs when a widget is first created or resized.

A Short Sample Program Using GTK

The simple.c file in the src/GTK directory contains a simple GTK application that places a single GTK button widget in a window and connects a Callback function—a signal-handler—to the button to call the local function do_click each time the button is clicked. This file uses a single include file that is required for all GTK applications:

```
#include <gtk/gtk.h>
```

The Callback function do_click is of type GtkCallback and is set to be called whenever the button widget is clicked. We will see in the definition of main function that the

30

GUI
PROGRAMMING
USING GTK

address of an integer-counter variable is passed as program data for this callback (or signal-handler) function. Whenever the GTK event-handling code in `gtk_main` calls this function, it passes the address of this integer variable as the second argument. The first thing that we do in function `do_click` is to coerce this abstract data pointer to the type (`int *`). Now the `do_click` function can change the value of the counter variable that is declared in the `main` function. In your GTK programs, you can specify any type of data for the callback program data.

```
void do_click(GtkWidget *widget, gpointer data)
{
  int * count = (int *) data;
  *count += 1;
  printf("Button clicked %d times (5 to quit)\n", *count);
  if (*count > 4)  gtk_main_quit();
}
```

The `main` function defined in the `simple.c` file is indeed simple. It uses the following eight GTK utility functions:

Function	Description
`gtk_init`	Passes the program's command-line arguments to GTK initialization code. Any arguments processed as GTK options are removed from the argument list. A list of available command-line arguments can be found in the GTK tutorial at www.gtk.org.
`gtk_window_new`	Creates a new window. This function is usually used, as it is in this example, to create a Top Level application window.
`gtk_container_border_width`	This optional function sets the number of pixels to pad around widgets added to a window.
`gtk_button_new_with_label`	Creates a new button label with a specified label.
`gtk_signal_connect`	We saw in the last section how this function assigns a Callback function to a widget for a specified type of event.
`gtk_container_add`	This function is used to add widgets to a window or any type of container widget.
`gtk_widget_show`	This function makes a widget visible. Child widgets are made visible before parent widgets.
`gtk_main`	Finishes initialization and handles events.

Listing 30.1 shows the `main` function, with a discussion of the code appearing after the listing.

Listing 30.1   main FUNCTION FROM simple.c

```c
int main(int argc, char *argv[]){
    // Declare variables to reference both a
    // window widget and a button widget:
    GtkWidget *window, *button;
    // Use for demonstrating encapsulation of data (the address
    // of this variable will be passed to the button's callback
    // function):
    int count = 0;

    // Pass command line arguments to the GTK initialization function:
    gtk_init(&argc, &argv);

    // Create a new top-level window:
    window = gtk_window_new(GTK_WINDOW_TOPLEVEL);

    // Change the default width around widgets from 0 to 5 pixels:
    gtk_container_border_width(GTK_CONTAINER(window), 5);

    button = gtk_button_new_with_label("Click to increment counter");

    // Connect the 'do_click' C callback function to the button widget.
    // We pass in the address of the variable 'count' so that the
    // callback function can access the value of count without having
    // to use global data:
    gtk_signal_connect(GTK_OBJECT(button), "clicked",
                       GTK_SIGNAL_FUNC(do_click), &count);

    // Add the button widget to the window widget:
    gtk_container_add(GTK_CONTAINER(window), button);

    // Make any widgets added to the window visible before
    // making the window itself visible:
    gtk_widget_show(button);
    gtk_widget_show(window);

    // Handle events:
    gtk_main();

}
```

The `main` function creates two `GtkWidget` object pointers: `window` and `button`. These widget pointers are used to reference a top-level window and a button widget. In the call

30

GUI
PROGRAMMING
USING GTK

to gtk_signal_connect, we use macros to coerce arguments to the correct type, as shown in the following:

```
gtk_signal_connect(GTK_OBJECT(button), "clicked",
                   GTK_SIGNAL_FUNC(do_click), &count);
```

For example, in the file gtktypeutils.h, GTK_SIGNAL_FUNC is defined as the following:

```
#define GTK_SIGNAL_FUNC(f)  ((GtkSignalFunc) f)
```

Miscellaneous GTK Widgets

We only use two example programs in this chapter, the simple.c example from the last section, and the XMLviewer.c example developed in the section entitled "A GTK Program for Displaying XML Files." As a result, we will use only a few types of GTK widgets in this chapter, such as the following:

- Window
- Scrolled Window
- Button
- Tree
- Tree Item

All the currently available GTK widgets are documented in the online tutorial at www.gtk.org; we will list briefly in this section some of the commonly used GTK widgets that are not covered fully in this chapter.

Adjustment widgets are controls that can have their value changed by the user, usually by using the mouse pointer. Tooltips widgets are small text areas that appear above other widgets when the mouse hovers over the widget. Dialog widgets are used for both modal and modeless dialog boxes. Text widgets enable the user to enter and edit a line of text. File Selection widgets enable a user to select any file.

The CList widget implements a two-dimensional grid. Menus can be easily created in GTK applications using the menu factory utility functions. Text widgets allow the user to edit multi-line text forms.

You're encouraged to build the examples located in the sub-directories of the examples directory of the GTK distribution. Figure 30.1 shows four of the sample programs: notebook, dial, file selection, and button. You need only about 10 minutes to build and run all of the sample programs included with GTK. This time is well spent because you not only become familiar with the look and feel of the GTK widgets, you can also look at the short source-code files for each sample program.

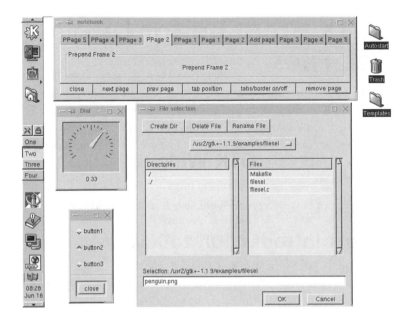

FIGURE 30.1

Four sample programs included with the standard GTK distribution.

GTK Container Widgets

Although there are many types of container widgets in GTK (again, read the online tutorial), we use only one in this chapter: the Scrolled Window widget. A Scrolled Window widget is used inside a Window widget to provide a virtual display area that is potentially larger than the size of the window. As we will see later in the XMLviewer.c sample program, the default action of a Scrolled Window widget is to dynamically create scrollbars as needed (for example, the window might be resized to a smaller size). Other types of container widgets include the following:

Container Widget	Description
Notebook	A set of labeled tabs allows the user to select one of many viewing areas, or pages, in a single widget.
Paned Window	Breaks a window's area into two separate viewing panes. The boundary between the panes can be adjusted by the user.
Tool Bar	Contains a row of buttons used for selecting program options.

If you download and install the current version of GTK from www.gtk.org, you can find sample programs that use all types of container widgets in the examples directory.

A GTK Program for Displaying XML Files

We develop an interesting sample program in this section that reads an XML file from standard input, parses it, and displays its tree structure using a GTK Tree widget. The sample program uses James Clark's XML parser, which is located in the src/GTK/expat directory on the CD-ROM. You might find newer versions on James' Web site (http://www.jclark.com), where you can also find other useful tools for processing XML and SGML documents).

The sample program XMLviewer.c is located in the src/GTK directory on the CD-ROM.

A Short Introduction to XML

If you maintain your own Web site, you are probably familiar with HTML (Hypertext Markup Language)Web. HTML provides tags to indicate the structure of Web documents. An example HTML file might be as follows:

```
<HTML>
 <TITLE>This is a title</TITLE>
 <BODY>
      This is some test text
      for the page. <B>Cool</B>
 </BODY>
</HTML>
```

HTML provides a fixed number of predefined tags, such as the following:

Tag	Description
TITLE	To indicate the title of the page.
BODY	For text that appears on the page.
B	To boldface the text.

From the example, we see that the tag type inside < > characters is the start of the tag and </ > marks the end of a tag. A Web browser knows how to render legal HTML tags. The eXtensible Markup Language (XML) looks similar to HTML, but with the following important differences:

- You can make up new tag types.
- Every opening tag must have a matching closing tag. This is not a requirement in HTML.

Listing 30.2 shows `test.xml`, a short example XML file contained in the `src/GTK` directory for this chapter.

Listing 30.2 THE `test.xml` EXAMPLE XML FILE

```
<?xml version="1.0"?>
<book>
  <title>A test title</title>
  <author>
    <last_name>Watson</last_name>
    <first_name>Mark</first_name>
  </author>
  <scheme>
    (define fff
       (lambda (x) (+ x x)))
    (define factorial
       (lambda (n)
          (if (= n 1)
            1
            (* n (factorial (- n 1)))))))
  </scheme>
</book>
```

Here, we use the tags `book`, `title`, `author`, `last_name`, `first_name`, and `scheme` in this XML document. The first line is a header line to indicate to an XML parser that this file is XML 1.0-compliant. The `test.xml` file is a "well-formed" XML file, but it is not "valid." A valid XML document is both well-formed and has a Document Type Definition (DTD) either included in the file or referenced near the beginning of the file. The discussion of DTDs is outside the scope of our coverage of XML, but you can go to the following Web sites for more information:

> `http://www.w3.org/XML/`
>
> `http://www.software.ibm.com/xml/`

Expat, James Clark's XML Parser

There are freely available XML parsers that are written in many languages (such as, C, C++, Java, Python, and Perl). In this section, we will look at an XML parser written in C by James Clark, whose Web site is `http://www.jclark.com/xml/expat.html`.

You can find this parser on the CD-ROM in the `src/GTK/expat` directory. We will use this parser in the next section to write a GTK program to display both the tree structure and content of XML documents.

30

GUI
PROGRAMMING
USING GTK

The elements.c file in the src/GTK/expat/sample directory shows how the basic parser is used. Applications using the expat parser define Callback functions that are called whenever the parser sees a any of the following three elements:

- A tag
- Data inside of a tag
- An ending tag

The parser performs a depth-first search through the tree structure of an XML file, calling the appropriate callback function when each of these element types is encountered. For example, the elements.c sample program generates the following output on the test.xml file:

```
markw@colossus>cat test.xml ¦ elements
tag name: book
        tag name: title
                     tag data: A test title
        tag name: author
                     tag data:
             tag name: last_name
                         tag data: Watson
                     tag data:
             tag name: first_name
                         tag data: Mark
        tag name: scheme
                     tag data:      (define fff
                     tag data:        (lambda (x) (+ x x)))
                     tag data:      (define factorial
                     tag data:        (lambda (n)
                     tag data:         (if (= n 1)
                     tag data:          1
                     tag data:          (* n (factorial (- n 1))))))
markw@colossus:/home/markw/MyDocs/LinuxBook/src/GTK/expat/sample >
```

Implementing the GTK XML Display Program

Now that we have looked at a short sample XML file (text.xml in the src/GTK directory) and seen screenshots of the XMLviewer application in Figure 30.2, we will look at the implementation of XMLviewer. The XMLviewer.c file is partially derived from James Clark's elements.c sample program located in the src/GTK/expat/sample directory on the CD-ROM. The XMLviewer program requires three include files:

```
#include <stdio.h>
#include <gtk/gtk.h>
#include "xmlparse.h"
```

We require `stdio.h` because we read an XML input file from `stdin`, which is defined in `stdio.h`. All GTK applications need to include `gtk.h`. The `xmlparse.h` header file is the standard header file for using James Clark's `expat` XML parser.

The XMLviewer application creates a GTK Tree widget and adds a GTK Tree Element widget to the tree in the correct place for every XML element (or tag) in the XML file read from standard input. The GTK Tree widget handles the required events for expanding and collapsing sub-trees in the application. We do, however, define the `item_signal_callback` function as an example for handling mouse-selection events in the tree display. The first argument to `item_signal_callback` is a pointer to a GTK Tree Item widgetTree Item widget and the second argument is the name of the signal. Since we place a GTK label widget as the child of each Tree Item widgetTree Item widget that is added to the tree display, the variable `label` can be set to the address of the label widget for this tree item. The GTK utility function `gtk_label_get` is used to get the characters of the label so that they can be printed. The definition of `item_signal_callback` is as follows:

```
static void item_signal_callback(GtkWidget *item, gchar *signame) {
  gchar *name;
  GtkLabel *label;
  label = GTK_LABEL(GTK_BIN(item)->child);
  /* Get the text of the label */
  gtk_label_get(label, &name);
  printf("signal name=%s, selected item name=%s\n", signame, name);
}
```

Next, we define data required to keep track of processing XML elements. This includes a pointer to the current GTK Tree widget and Tree Item widget.

```
GtkWidget  *tree;
GtkWidget *item;
```

As the parse processes sub-trees in the XML document, we use the `subtree[]` array to store widget pointers:

```
#define MAX_DEPTH 10
GtkWidget *subtree[MAX_DEPTH];
```

The following section of code in `XMLviewer.c` defines the three Callback functions for the `expat` parser. We define the following Callback functions:

- `handleElementData`—This is called with the data contained between opening and closing tags. For example, when processing the element "<author>Mark Watson</author>", the data between the tags is "Mark Watson".
- `startElement`—Called with the name of a tag when the tag is first processed.
- `endElement`—Called with the name of the tag after handleElementData is called.

The function `handleElementData` is called by the expat parser to process data inside of tags. The function signature is as follows:

```
void handleElementData(void *userData, const char * data, int len)
```

For the purposes of this chapter on GTK, the mechanics of getting access to this data is not so interesting, but the following code shows how to create new GTK Tree Item widgets:

```
int *depthPtr = userData;
GtkWidget *subitem;
cp = (char *)malloc(len + 1);
for (i=0; i<len; i++) cp[i] = data[i];
cp[len] = '\0';
subitem = gtk_tree_item_new_with_label(cp);
gtk_tree_append(GTK_TREE(subtree[*depthPtr]), subitem);
gtk_signal_connect(GTK_OBJECT(subitem), "select",
                   GTK_SIGNAL_FUNC(item_signal_callback),
                   "tag data select");
gtk_signal_connect(GTK_OBJECT(subitem), "deselect",
                   GTK_SIGNAL_FUNC(item_signal_callback),
                   "tag data deselect");
gtk_widget_show (subitem);
```

Here, the expat parser passes the address of the character data for the tag; it is necessary to make a copy of it and use this copy for creating a GTK item widget. The GTK utility function `gtk_tree_item_new_with_label` creates a new labeled Tree Item widget. This newly created GTK Tree Item widget must be added to the GTK Tree widget in the correct location; this bit of magic is done by the following:

```
gtk_tree_append(GTK_TREE(subtree[*depthPtr]), subitem);
```

The expat parser lets us know the depth in the tree that the item widget should be placed. The array of `GtkWidget` pointers `subtree` is filled in the expat Callback function `startElement`. The GTK Tree Item widget then has two Callback functions (or signal-handlers) set for `"select"` and `"deselect"` events. Both signals are handled by the function `item_signal_callback` that we saw earlier in this section. The last action that the `handleDataElement` function takes is to make the newly created GTK Tree Item widget visible.

The `startElement` function is called by the expat parser to handle beginning XML tags (for example, `"<author>"`). The function signature for `startElement` is as follows:

```
void startElement(void *userData, const char *name, const char **atts)
```

The tag depth is passed in the `userData` argument. We convert this abstract pointer to a pointer to an integer to access the current XML tree tag depth:

```
int *depthPtr = userData;
*depthPtr += 1;
```

The startElement function performs two tasks based on the current depth of the parse tree for the XML document. For the topmost tag in the document, we create a new GTK Tree Item widget and store a pointer to this widget in the item global variable (we will discuss this code fragment after the following listing):

```
if (*depthPtr == 1) {
   item = gtk_tree_item_new_with_label((char *)name);
   gtk_signal_connect(GTK_OBJECT(item), "select",
                      GTK_SIGNAL_FUNC(item_signal_callback),
                                     "top-level item select");
   gtk_signal_connect(GTK_OBJECT(item), "deselect",
                      GTK_SIGNAL_FUNC(item_signal_callback),
                                     "top-level item deselect");
   // a tree item can hold any number of items; add new item here:
   gtk_tree_append(GTK_TREE(tree), item);
   gtk_widget_show(item);
   // Create this item's subtree:
   subtree[*depthPtr] = gtk_tree_new();
   gtk_tree_set_view_mode(GTK_TREE(subtree[*depthPtr]),
GTK_TREE_VIEW_ITEM);
   gtk_tree_item_set_subtree(GTK_TREE_ITEM(item), subtree[*depthPtr]);
}
```

In handling the topmost XML tag, we add the newly created tree item to the GTK tree using the tree global variable to access the GTK Tree widget. As in the handleElementData function, we set signal-handler callbacks for "select" and "deselect" actions. A new GTK Tree widget is created and stored in the subtree array. Note that the subtree array acts as a stack data structure in this program, with the parse depth acting as the stack pointer. This new tree is set as the sub-tree of the newly created GTK Tree Item widget.

If the current parse depth is greater than one (for example, we are not processing the topmost tag in the document), then the processing is simpler than handling the topmost tag in the XML document (we will discuss this code fragment after the following listing):

```
if (*depthPtr > 1) {
   GtkWidget *subitem = gtk_tree_item_new_with_label((char *)name);
   subtree[*depthPtr] = gtk_tree_new();
   gtk_signal_connect(GTK_OBJECT(subitem), "select",
                      GTK_SIGNAL_FUNC(item_signal_callback),
                      "tree item select");
   gtk_signal_connect(GTK_OBJECT(subitem), "deselect",
                      GTK_SIGNAL_FUNC(item_signal_callback),
                      "tree item deselect");
   // Add this sub-tree it to its parent tree:
   gtk_tree_append(GTK_TREE(subtree[*depthPtr - 1]), subitem);
   gtk_widget_show(subitem);
   gtk_tree_item_set_subtree(GTK_TREE_ITEM(subitem),
subtree[*depthPtr]);
}
```

The endElement function is called from the expat parser when an ending tag (for example, "</author>") is processed. The function endElement simply decrements the parse-depth counter, as shown in the following:

```
void endElement(void *userData, const char *name) {
  int *depthPtr = userData;
  *depthPtr -= 1;    // decrement stack pointer
}
```

As an example of the parse depth in an XML document, consider the following XML data, with the parse depth indicated on each line:

```
<book>                                      1
  <title>Kito bit the cat</title>          2
  <author>                                  2
    <name>                                  3
      <last_name>Smith</last_name>         4
      <first_name>Joshua</first_name>      4
    </name>                                 3
  </author>                                 2
</book>                                     1
```

The main function does two things: setting up the XML parser and initializing the GTK widgets. We have already seen the implementation of the XML parser Callback functions for processing opening element tags, element text data, and closing element tags. These Callback (or signal-handler) functions created the GTK tree element widgets, but the main function has the responsibility for creating the topmost GTK Tree widget and the top-level window. The following discussion uses code fragments from the implementation of the main function.

The main function creates a new XML parser object using James Clark's expat library, as shown in the following:

```
XML_Parser parser - XML_ParserCreate(NULL);
```

The XMLviewer application uses a top-level window with a scrolling view area. The following code fragment shows how to set up a scrolling area with scrollbars that are automatically activated when required. We define two variables, window and scrolled_win, as pointers to GtkWidgets and call the standard GTK gtk_init function that we saw in the previous GTK example. The Scrolled Window widget is created with the gtk_scrolled_window function, and this widget is added to the GtkWidget referenced by the window variable. The gtk_scrolled_window_set_policy function can be used to set up automatic handling of scroll bars (as we do here), or it can be used to always make scrollbars visible. The gtk_widget_set_usize function sets the minimum size of the

Scrolled Window widget. The user will not be able to resize the top-level window to make the scrolling window smaller than the size set by `gtk_widget_set_usize`.

```
GtkWidget *window, *scrolled_win;
gtk_init(&argc, &argv);
window = gtk_window_new(GTK_WINDOW_TOPLEVEL);
scrolled_win = gtk_scrolled_window_new(NULL, NULL);
gtk_scrolled_window_set_policy(GTK_SCROLLED_WINDOW(scrolled_win),
                               GTK_POLICY_AUTOMATIC,
                               GTK_POLICY_AUTOMATIC);
gtk_widget_set_usize(scrolled_win, 150, 200);
gtk_container_add(GTK_CONTAINER(window), scrolled_win);
gtk_widget_show(scrolled_win);
```

The GTK library contains a utility callback (or signal-handler) function named `gtk_main_quit`, which can be used to cleanly close down any GTK application. The following line of code sets the `gtk_main_quit` function as the signal-handler for window-delete events for the top-level window. Without the following line of code, the application will not cleanly terminate if the user clicks on the window-close box.

```
gtk_signal_connect(GTK_OBJECT(window), "delete_event",
                   GTK_SIGNAL_FUNC(gtk_main_quit), NULL);
```

In order to leave some space around widget components that are added to any GTK container, you can use the `gtk_container_border_width` function to set the number of pixels between components. By using the following code, the main function sets up a border five pixels wide around the Tree widget:

```
gtk_container_border_width(GTK_CONTAINER(window), 5);
```

The following code uses the `gtk_tree_new` function to create the GTK Tree widget, and the newly created Tree widget is added to the scrolling window:

```
tree = gtk_tree_new();
gtk_scrolled_window_add_with_viewport
(GTK_SCROLLED_WINDOW(scrolled_win),
                                      tree);
```

GTK Tree widgets can be set to either a single tree node selection mode or a multiple selection mode. The following line of code sets the Tree widget to allow only the user to select one tree node at a time:

```
gtk_tree_set_selection_mode(GTK_TREE(tree),
                            GTK_SELECTION_SINGLE);
```

To enable multiple selection, the GTK constant `GTK_SELECTION_SINGLE` that is defined in the `gtkenums.h` file can be replaced by the `GTK_SELECTION_MULTIPLE` constant.

30

GUI
PROGRAMMING
USING GTK

The XML parser, which is referenced with the variable parser, must be configured for the XMLviewer application. The following line of code sets the local variable depth as the user data for the parser:

```
XML_SetUserData(parser, &depth);
```

The following two lines of code configure the XML parser to use the startElement, endElement, and handleElementData Callback functions that we have implemented:

```
XML_SetElementHandler(parser, startElement, endElement);
XML_SetCharacterDataHandler(parser, handleElementData);
```

The XMLviewer program reads the contents of XML from stdin (for example, you run it by typing "**cat test.xml ¦ XMLviewer**"). The following code fragment reads XML data and hands it off to the parser:

```
do {
  size_t len = fread(buf, 1, sizeof(buf), stdin);
  done = len < sizeof(buf);
  if (!XML_Parse(parser, buf, len, done)) {
    printf("%s at line %d\n",
            XML_ErrorString(XML_GetErrorCode(parser)),
            XML_GetCurrentLineNumber(parser));
    return;
  }
} while (!done);
XML_ParserFree(parser);
```

It is important to realize the flow of execution in this code fragment. As the XML_Parse function processes XML data, it calls the startElement, endElement, and handleElementData functions to process start- and ending-element tags and element character data. These functions, in turn, are responsible for constructing new GTK Tree Element widgets and inserting them in the correct position of the tree.

The following two lines of code simply make the top-level window visible and able to handle events:

```
gtk_widget_show(window);
gtk_main();
```

Running the GTK XML Display Program

The XMLviewer application reads XML data from stdin. To compile and execute this example program, change the directory to src/GTK and type the following:

make
cat test.xml ¦ XMLviewer

Figure 30.2 shows two copies of the XMLviewer sample program running side-by-side. On the left side of the figure, the tree is collapsed. The right side of Figure 30.2 shows the XMLviewer application after the user has expanded the sub-tree branches.

FIGURE 30.2

Two copies of the XMLViewer *program running, showing the* test.xml *file.*

A GUI Program Using the Notebook Widget

The last sample program in this chapter shows how to use the GTK Notebook widget. A Notebook widget is a container containing pages with labeled tabs. The example for this section is in the notebook.c and draw_widget.c files in the src/GTK directory. The draw_widget.c file was derived from the scribble-simple.c file in the examples directory in the GTK distribution. The scribble-simple example creates a drawable area and handles mouse events for drawing. We will discuss the implementation of the scribble-simple example (using the draw_widget.c file) after discussing the implementation of the Notebook widget example (using the notebook.c file).

Implementation of the Notebook Widget Sample Program

The notebook.c example is very simple because it is easy to create a GTK Notebook widget and add pages with tabs. The basic technique is simple: create a Notebook widget using the gtk_notebook_new utility function, then add pages to it by following these steps for each page:

1. Create a GTK Frame widget. A Frame widget is a container so you can add anything you want to it (other GTK widgets, custom widgets that you write, and so on.

2. Create a GTK Label widget for the tab. Note that you can use any GTK widget for the tab (Label widget, Pixmap widget, Tree widget—strange, but you could do it—and so on.

3. Use the GTK utility function gtk_notebook_append_page to add the frame (and whatever you have added to the frame) and the tab label to the Notebook widget.

30

GUI PROGRAMMING USING GTK

The following discussion uses code from the notebook.c file. We will skip code that we have discussed in the two previous GTK sample programs (for example, the signal-handler function for "delete_event" that occurs when a user clicks the Close button on the window title bar).

As usual, we create a Top-Level Window widget that is referenced by the window variable. The following code creates a new Notebook widget and adds it to the window:

```
notebook = gtk_notebook_new();
gtk_notebook_set_tab_pos(GTK_NOTEBOOK(notebook), GTK_POS_TOP);
gtk_container_add(GTK_CONTAINER(window), notebook);
gtk_widget_show(notebook);
```

Here, we used the constant GTK_POS_TOP (defined in the gtkenums.h file) to place the notebook page tabs along the top of the widget. The following are other possible values that can be used as the second argument to the gtk_notebook_set_tab_pos function:

```
GTK_POS_LEFT
GTK_POS_RIGHT
GTK_POS_TOP
GTK_POS_BOTTOM
```

The following code from the notebook.c file adds four pages to the Notebook widget (a discussion follows this listing):

```
for (i=0; i < 4; i++) {
  if (i == 0) {
    sprintf(buf1, "Draw something here with the mouse");
    sprintf(buf2, "Draw Tab");
  } else {
    sprintf(buf1, "Frame number %d", i+1);
    sprintf(buf2, "Tab %d", i);
  }
  // Create a frame to hold anything (at all!)
  // that we might want to add to this page
  frame = gtk_frame_new(buf1);
  gtk_container_border_width(GTK_CONTAINER(frame), 10);
  gtk_widget_set_usize(frame, 240, 120);
  gtk_widget_show(frame);
  label = gtk_label_new(buf1);
  if (i == 0) {
    temp_widget = make_draw_widget(240, 120);
    gtk_container_add(GTK_CONTAINER(frame), temp_widget);
  } else {
    gtk_container_add(GTK_CONTAINER(frame), label);
    gtk_widget_show(label);
  }
  label = gtk_label_new(buf2);
  gtk_notebook_append_page(GTK_NOTEBOOK(notebook), frame, label);
}
```

Here, the first page added to the Notebook widget is handled differently from the last three because:

- We want to create a Drawing Area widget to add to the page frame;
- For the first page, we want a different label for the tab (to let users know they can draw on the first page).

The character arrays `buf1` and `buf2` are used, respectively, for labeling the inside frame of the last three pages (but not the first drawing page) and then the page's tab. The `make_draw_widget` function is defined in the `draw_widget.c` file and is discussed in the next section. This function returns a pointer to `GtkWidget` that is simply added to the Frame widget created for the first page of the Notebook widget.

After the four test pages are added to the Notebook widget, the following code sets the first (drawing) page to be the default visible page, makes the Top-Level Window widget visible, and handles events:

```
gtk_notebook_set_page(GTK_NOTEBOOK(notebook), 0);
gtk_widget_show(window);
gtk_main();
```

Implementing the Drawing Widget

The `draw_widget.c` file, which is derived from the `scribble-simple.c` GTK sample program, creates a generic GTK widget with the event-handling behavior and data for allowing the user to draw inside the widget. This generic widget is not a new type of GTK widget. A Draw widget is created by calling the `make_draw_widget` function, which has the following function signature:

```
GtkWidget * make_draw_widget(int width, int height)
```

The `make_draw_widget` function creates a GTK Drawing Area widget and connects signal-handling functions for left-mouse-down and mouse-motion events. In the following discussion, we talk about the `draw_widget.c` file in the `src/GTK` directory, but this file is directly derived from the `scribble-simple.c` GTK sample program, so these comments also apply to `scribble-simple.c`. The signal-handler function `configure_event` is used to create a `pixmap` for off-screen drawing. For "jitter-free" animation, it is usually best to perform drawing operations in an off-screen buffer (or `pixmap`) and copy the pixmap to the window in one operation. This technique is used in video games, word processors, drawing tools, and so on. The following line of code creates a new `pixmap`:

```
pixmap = gdk_pixmap_new(widget->window,
                        widget->allocation.width,
                        widget->allocation.height,
                        -1);
```

The address of the Drawing Area widget is passed to the configure_event function; this pointer to a GtkWidget is used get the required width and height of the pixmap. Notice that if the pixmap already exists, the first thing that configure_event does is to free the memory for the previous pixmap before creating another. The configure_event Function is also called for resize events. The signal-handler function expose_event is called whenever all or part of the Drawing Area widget is exposed; this function simply recopies the pixmap to the visible part of the widget.

The draw_brush function is passed an X-Y position in the Drawing Area widget. The draw_brush function simply paints a small black rectangle in the pixmap and then copies the pixmap to the Drawing Area widget, as shown in the following:

```
void draw_brush (GtkWidget *widget, gdouble x, gdouble y) {
  GdkRectangle update_rect;

  update_rect.x = x - 2;      // 2 was 5 in original GTK example
  update_rect.y = y - 2;      // 2 was 5 in original GTK example
  update_rect.width = 5;      // 5 was 10 in original GTK example
  update_rect.height = 5;     // 5 was 10 in original GTK example
  gdk_draw_rectangle (pixmap,
                      widget->style->black_gc,
                      TRUE,
                      update_rect.x, update_rect.y,
                      update_rect.width, update_rect.height);
  gtk_widget_draw (widget, &update_rect);
}
```

The gtk_widget_draw function causes an Expose event in the specified (by the first argument) widget. In this program, this Expose event causes the expose_event function in the draw_widget.c (and scribble-simple.c) files to be called. The signal-handler function button_press_event is called when any mouse button is pressed, but it only draws in the Drawing Area widget when the button number equals one and the pixmap has already been set in configure_event function:

```
gint button_press_event (GtkWidget *widget, GdkEventButton *event) {
  if (event->button == 1 && pixmap != NULL)
    draw_brush (widget, event->x, event->y);
  return TRUE;
}
```

The signal-handler function motion_notify_event is similar to button_press_event, but handles mouse motion events (listed in abbreviated form):

```
gint motion_notify_event (GtkWidget *widget, GdkEventMotion *event) {
  if (event->state & GDK_BUTTON1_MASK && pixmap != NULL)
    draw_brush (widget, event->x, event->y);
  return TRUE;
}
```

The structures GdkEventButton and GdkEventMotion are defined in the gdktypes.h file. They are shown here in abbreviated form:

```
struct _GdkEventMotion { // partial definition:
  GdkEventType type;
  GdkWindow *window;
  gint8 send_event;
  guint32 time;
  gdouble x;
  gdouble y;
  gdouble pressure;
  guint state;
};

struct _GdkEventButton { // partial definition:
  GdkEventType type;
  GdkWindow *window;
  gint8 send_event;
  guint32 time;
  gdouble x;
  gdouble y;
  guint state;
  guint button;
};
```

The make_draw_widget function is fairly simple, but it does offer an example of setting signal-handlers (or callbacks) for expose, configure, mouse motion and mouse button press events:

```
GtkWidget * make_draw_widget(int width, int height) {
  GtkWidget *drawing_area;
  drawing_area = gtk_drawing_area_new ();
  gtk_drawing_area_size (GTK_DRAWING_AREA (drawing_area), width, height);
  gtk_widget_show (drawing_area);
  /* Signals used to handle backing pixmap */
  gtk_signal_connect (GTK_OBJECT (drawing_area), "expose_event",
                      (GtkSignalFunc) expose_event, NULL);
  gtk_signal_connect (GTK_OBJECT(drawing_area),"configure_event",
                      (GtkSignalFunc) configure_event, NULL);
  /* Event signals */
  gtk_signal_connect (GTK_OBJECT (drawing_area), "motion_notify_event",
                      (GtkSignalFunc) motion_notify_event, NULL);
  gtk_signal_connect (GTK_OBJECT (drawing_area), "button_press_event",
                      (GtkSignalFunc) button_press_event, NULL);
  gtk_widget_set_events (drawing_area, GDK_EXPOSURE_MASK
                        | GDK_LEAVE_NOTIFY_MASK
                        | GDK_BUTTON_PRESS_MASK
                        | GDK_POINTER_MOTION_MASK
                        | GDK_POINTER_MOTION_HINT_MASK);
  return drawing_area;
}
```

30

GUI
PROGRAMMING
USING GTK

The `gtk_drawing_area_size` function sets the preferred size of the Drawing Area widget. The `gtk_widget_set_events` function sets the drawing area to receive signals (or events) from the GTK event-handling code in the GTK utility function `gtk_main`.

Running the GTK Notebook Widget Sample Program

You can compile and run the Notebook widget sample program by changing the directory to `src/GTK` and typing the following:

```
make
notebook
```

Figure 30.3 shows two copies of the Notebook widget sample program running side-by-side. On the left side of the figure, the first page that contains the Drawing Area widget is selected; the Drawing Area widget has a sketch of the author's initials. The right side of Figure 30.3 shows the notebook example with the second page selected.

FIGURE 30.3

Two copies of the Notebook widget program running, showing two different pages in the notebook selected.

The GTK GUI programming library provides a rich set of widgets for building Linux applications. This short chapter was not meant to cover all of GTK; rather, it introduced you to the basics of GTK programming and provided interesting examples using the `XMLviewer.c` and `notebook.c` programs. It's recommended (again) that you visit the official GTK Web site at `www.gtk.org` and read the GTK tutorial. You might also want to install the latest version of GTK and be sure to check out the example programs.

GTK offers a high-level approach to X Windows-based GUI programming. It is a matter of personal taste and style whether you ultimately decide to code in low-level `Xlib`, use either the Athena or Motif widgets, use GTK, or use the C++ library Qt that is covered in the next chapter.

CHAPTER 31

GUI Programming Using Qt

by Mark Watson

IN THIS CHAPTER

The Qt C++ class library for GUI programming was designed and written by Troll Tech. You can check out their Web site at www.troll.no. Qt is a cross-platform library supporting X Windows and Microsoft Windows. At the time of this writing (February 1999), Qt was available for free use on the Linux platform for non-commercial applications. There is a licensing fee for using Qt for commercial use on Linux, as well as any use on Microsoft Windows. Before using Qt, you should check out Troll Tech's Web site and read the license agreement.

The Qt C++ class library is huge, and documenting it fully in this short chapter is not possible. However, if you are a C++ programmer, you might find Qt meets your needs for a very high-level GUI library. Hopefully, the two short examples in this chapter will encourage you to further study the example programs that are provided with the standard Qt distribution. Additionally, you should learn how to use the available Qt C++ classes that provide many ready-to-use user-interface components. You will see at the end of this chapter how easy it is to combine Qt widgets for application-specific purposes using new C++ classes.

You saw in Chapter 30 how to use GTK to easily write X Windows applications in the C language. You will see in this chapter that, for C++ programmers, it is probably even simpler to write X Windows applications for Linux using Qt. If you prefer coding in C rather than C++, then you might want to skip this chapter and use either Athena widgets, Motif widgets, or GTK. Detailed documentation on Qt is available at www.troll.no/qt. In this short chapter, you will see how to use the following techniques:

- Handle events by overriding event methods (for example, mousePressEvent) defined in the base Qt widget class QWidget.

- Handle events by using Qt signals and slots. A C++ pre-processor moc is provided with the Qt distribution to automatically generate C++ code for using signals and slots.

- Write new Qt widget classes by combining existing widget classes.

The examples in this chapter are partially derived from the Troll Tech Qt example programs and tutorial, so the following (representative) copyright applies to the example programs for this chapter:

```
/*******************************************************************
** $Id: connect.cpp,v 2.5 1998/06/16 11:39:32 warwick Exp $
**
** Copyright (C) 1992-1998 Troll Tech AS. All rights reserved.
**
** This file is part of an example program for Qt. This example
** program may be used, distributed and modified without limitation.
**
*******************************************************************/
```

This chapter uses two short examples. The first program shows how to draw graphics in a window and how to handle events by overriding QWidget event methods. The QWidget class is a C++ base class for all other Qt widget classes. This example was derived from the "connect" Qt example program that can be found in the Qt distribution in the `examples` directory. The second example uses the same Qt widget class (QLCDNumber) that is used in the Qt online tutorial example. For the second example in this chapter, we derive a new C++ widget class, StateLCDWidget, that adds two new "slot methods" for increasing and decreasing the value of the number shown in the widget. Other widgets can send signals to either of these slots to change the display value. We will see an example of binding signals (events) from two Push Button widgets to the two slots in StateLCDWidget class.

Event-Handling By Overriding QWidget Class Methods

The example program for this section is located in the `src/Qt/events` directory on the CD-ROM. This example program is very short—only about 50 lines of code—but shows how to create a simple main application window that uses Qt widgets (file `main.cxx`) and how to derive a new widget class, DrawWidget, from the Qt QWidget class (files `draw.hxx` and `draw.cxx`). Before writing the example program for this section, we will look at the most frequently used public interfaces for the C++ QWidget class. Later in this chapter we will look at the alternative event-handling scheme in Qt that uses signals and slots. Both event-handling schemes can be used together in the same program.

Overview of the QWidget Class

The QWidget class is the C++ base class for all other Qt widgets and provides the common API for controlling widgets and setting widget parameters. The QWidget class defines several event-handling methods that can be overridden in derived classes (from the `qwidget.h` file in the Qt distribution), as shown in the following:

```
virtual void mousePressEvent(QMouseEvent *);
virtual void mouseReleaseEvent(QMouseEvent *);
virtual void mouseDoubleClickEvent(QMouseEvent *);
virtual void mouseMoveEvent(QMouseEvent *);
virtual void keyPressEvent(QKeyEvent *);
virtual void keyReleaseEvent(QKeyEvent *);
virtual void focusInEvent(QFocusEvent *);
virtual void focusOutEvent(QFocusEvent *);
virtual void enterEvent(QEvent *);
virtual void leaveEvent(QEvent *);
virtual void paintEvent(QPaintEvent *);
```

```
virtual void moveEvent(QMoveEvent *);
virtual void resizeEvent(QResizeEvent *);
virtual void closeEvent(QCloseEvent *);
```

The purpose of these methods is obvious from the method names, but the event argument types require a short explanation. The QMouseEvent class has the following (partial) public interface:

```
class QMouseEvent : public QEvent { // mouse event
public:
    int x();        // x position in widget
    int y();        // y position in widget
    int globalX(); // x relative to X server
    int globalY(); // y relative to X server
    int button();  // button index (starts at zero)
    int state();   // state flags for mouse
    // constructors, and protected/private interface is not shown
};
```

The example in this section explicitly uses only mouse events. We will capture the mouse's x-y position for mouse press and mouse movement events. We will not directly use the QKeyEvent, QEvent, QFocusEvent, QPaintEvent, QMoveEvent, QResizeEvent, or QCloseEvent classes in this chapter, but you can view their header files in the src/kernel subdirectory in the Qt distribution in the qevent.h file. It is beyond the scope of this short introductory chapter to cover all event types used by Qt, but you can quickly find the class headers in qevent.h for use as a reference.

The QSize class has the following (partial) public interface:

```
class QSize {
public:
    QSize()    { wd = ht = -1; }
    QSize( int w, int h );
    int width() const;
    int height() const;
    void setWidth( int w );
    void setHeight( int h );
    // Most of the class definition not shown.
    // See the file src/kernel/qsize.h in the Qt distribution
};
```

The class interface for QSize is defined in the Qt distribution's src/kernel directory in the qsize.h file. The QWidget class defines several utility methods that can be used to control the state of the widget or query its state (from the qwidget.h file in the Qt distribution), as shown here:

```
int x();
int y();
```

```
QSize size();
int width();
int height();
QSize minimumSize();
QSize maximumSize();
void setMinimumSize(const QSize &);
void setMinimumSize(int minw, int minh);
void setMaximumSize(const QSize &);
void setMaximumSize(int maxw, int maxh);
void setMinimumWidth(int minw);
void setMinimumHeight(int minh);
void setMaximumWidth( int maxw);
void setMaximumHeight(int maxh);
```

These public methods can be used to:

- Get the x-y position of a Qt widget inside a container.

- Get the width and height.

- Get the minimum and maximum preferred size for a widget. (The minimum and maximum size and shape can also be specified.)

Implementing the `DrawWidget` Class

We will implement the example program in two steps. In this section, we will write the `DrawWidget` C++ class. In the next section, we will write a short main program that uses the `DrawWidget`. The `draw.hxx` file in the `src/Qt/events` directory on the CD-ROM contains the C++ class interface for `DrawWidget`. This file was derived from the `con-nect.h` file in the examples directory of the Qt distribution. The class definition requires the definitions of the `QWidget`, `QPainter`, and `QApplication` classes:

```
#include <qwidget.h>
#include <qpainter.h>
#include <qapplication.h>
```

The `QPainter` class encapsulates drawing properties, such as pen and brush styles, background color, foreground color, and clip regions. The `QPainter` class also provides primitive drawing operations, such as drawing points, lines, and shapes. Class `QPainter` also provides high-level drawing operations, such as Bezier curves, text, and images. You can find the C++ class interface for `QPainter` in the Qt distribution's `src/kernel` directory in the `qpainter.h` file.

The `QApplication` class encapsulates the data and provides the behavior for X Windows top-level applications. This class keeps track of all Top Level widgets that have been added to an application. All X Windows events are handled by the `QApplication` class's `exec` method.

Our example `DrawWidget` class is publicly derived from `QWidget` and overrides the three protected methods `paintEvent`, `mousePressEvent`, and `mouseMoveEvent`:

```
class DrawWidget : public QWidget {
public:
  DrawWidget(QWidget *parent=0, const char *name=0);
  ~DrawWidget();
protected:
  void  paintEvent(QPaintEvent *);
  void  mousePressEvent(QMouseEvent *);
  void  mouseMoveEvent(QMouseEvent *);
private:
  QPoint *points;            // point array
  QColor *color;             // color value
  int count;                 // count = number of points
};
```

The array `points` will be used to store the x-y coordinates of mouse events in the widget. The class variable `color` will be used to define a custom drawing color. The variable count will be used to count collected points.

The file `draw.cxx` contains the implementation of the `DrawWidget` class. The include file `draw.hxx` contains the following class header:

```
#include "draw.hxx"
```

We will use an array of 3000 points to record mouse positions inside the widget. The array is initialized in the class constructor and a count of the stored points is set to zero, as shown in the following:

```
const int MAXPOINTS = 3000;  // maximum number of points
DrawWidget::DrawWidget(QWidget *parent, const char *name)
  : QWidget(parent, name)    {
  setBackgroundColor(white);                // white background
  count = 0;
  points = new QPoint[MAXPOINTS];
  color = new QColor(250, 10, 30); // Red, Green, Blue
}
```

The class destructor simply frees the array of points:

```
DrawWidget::~DrawWidget() {
  delete[] points;    // free storage for the collected points
}
```

The method `paintEvent` defined in the example class `DrawWidget` overrides the definition in the base class `QWidget`. A new instance of the class `QPainter` is used to define the graphics environment and to provide the `drawRect` method for drawing a small rectangle centered on the mouse position in the draw widget. The array `points` is filled inside the mouse press and mouse motion event methods.

GUI Programming Using Qt

CHAPTER 31

549

31

GUI
PROGRAMMING
USING QT

```
void DrawWidget::paintEvent(QPaintEvent *) {
  QPainter paint(this);
  paint.drawText(10, 20, "Click the mouse buttons,
  ③or press button and drag");
  paint.setPen(*color);
  for (int i=0; i<count; i++) {          // connect all points
    paint.drawRect(points[i].x()-3, points[i].y()-3, 6, 6);
  }
}
```

The method `mousePressEvent` defined in the class `DrawWidget` overrides the definition in the base class `QWidget`. This method has two functions: to record the current mouse position in the array `points` and to immediately draw a small red (defined by the variable `color`) rectangle centered at the mouse position.

```
void DrawWidget::mousePressEvent(QMouseEvent * e) {
  if (count < MAXPOINTS) {
    QPainter paint(this);
    points[count] = e->pos();          // add point
    paint.setPen(*color);
    paint.drawRect(points[count].x()-3, points[count].y()-3, 6, 6);
    count++;
  }
}
```

The method `mouseMoveEvent` defined in the class `DrawWidget` overrides the definition in the base class `QWidget`. Like the mouse press method, this method has two functions: to record the current mouse position in the array `points` and to immediately draw a small rectangle centered at the mouse position.

```
void DrawWidget::mouseMoveEvent(QMouseEvent *e) {
  if (count < MAXPOINTS) {
    QPainter paint(this);
    points[count] = e->pos();          // add point
    paint.setPen(*color);
    paint.drawRect(points[count].x()-3, points[count].y()-3, 6, 6);
    count++;
  }
}
```

Testing the `DrawWidget`

The example draw widget was simple to implement. The main program to create an application widget, add a draw widget, and handle X Windows events is even simpler. The test file containing the main test function is `main.cxx` and is located in the `src/Qt/events` directory. The only include file that is required is the `draw.hxx` header file because `draw.hxx` includes the required Qt header files:

```
#include "draw.hxx"
```

The function `main` defines an instance of the class `QApplication` and an instance of the example `DrawWidget` class. The `QApplication` method `setMainWidget` specifies that the draw widget is the top level widget in the application. The `show` method is inherited from the class `QWidget` and makes the draw widget visible. The `QApplication` method `exec` handles X Windows events:

```
int main(int argc, char **argv) {
  QApplication app(argc, argv);
  DrawWidget draw;
  app.setMainWidget(&draw);
  draw.show();
  return app.exec();
}
```

This short example program illustrates that the Qt class library really does encapsulate much of the complexity of X Windows programming. If required, you can mix low-level `Xlib` programming with the use of the Qt class library, but this should seldom be required because the Qt library supports drawing primitives.

Figure 31.1 shows the draw program with some scribbling.

FIGURE 31.1

The `main.cxx` *program uses the* `DrawWidget`*.*

Event-Handling Using Qt Slots and Signals

Using Qt slots and signals is a very high-level interface for coordinating events and actions in different Qt widgets. Using slots and signals is a little complex because a C++ preprocessing program (the Qt utility `moc`) is used to automatically generate additional code for this high-level event-handling. The example for this section is located in the `src/Qt/signals_slots` directory. The `Makefile` in this directory is all set up to use the `moc` utility to generate additional source code and then compile and link everything. This `Makefile`, unlike most other `Makefiles` on the CD-ROM, may not run correctly if your system configuration is different than the test machines used for this book. However, this

GUI Programming Using Qt

CHAPTER 31

551

31

GUI
PROGRAMMING
USING QT

`Makefile` was copied and edited from the `Makefile` examples in the programming tutorial that is included in the standard Qt distribution. These tutorial `Makefiles` are built automatically when the Qt distribution is compiled and installed. If the example `Makefile` breaks on your system because of a different location of an X library or header file, compare the first 20 lines of the example `Makefile` with any of the tutorial `Makefiles` in your Qt distribution.

When you install Qt, either from your Linux distribution or by downloading the latest Qt distribution from www.troll.no, the environment `QTDIR` gets set to point to the installed libraries, binary tools, and so on. On my system, `QTDIR` is set to the value `/usr/local/qt`. Qt provides a few simple extensions to the C++ language and uses a preprocessor `moc` (Meta Object Compiler) that is located in the `$QTDIR/bin` directory. Note that the `$QTDIR/bin` directory should be in your search `PATH`. To use the material in this chapter, I assume that you have followed the installation instructions included with the Qt distribution. We will find out how `moc` works later in this chapter, but in the next section we will show a simple example of its use.

Deriving the `StateLCDWidget` Class

The Qt C++ class library contains a wide range of useful widgets. Probably the best way to see all of the different Qt widgets work is to change directory to the examples directory that is included with the Qt distribution, and then build all the example programs and run them. This exercise took me about 20 minutes when I first started using Qt and provided a great introduction to the capabilities of the Qt class library.

We will use the Qt widget class `QLCDNumber` in this section. The `QLCDNumber` widget shows a number in a large font inside the widget. The `QLCDNumber` class has a method for setting the number to be displayed, but for our example program we want to define two slots for increasing and decreasing the displayed number. As we will see later, it is easy to connect signals generated by a user clicking on Qt Push Button widgets to these slots.

To demonstrate event-handling using slots and signals, we will create a new class, `StateLCDWidget`, that contains two slots defined as methods in the class header file:

```
void increaseValue();
void decreaseValue();
```

You will see in the next section how to use a Qt widget's slots; in this section, we will implement the `StateLCDWidget` class and these two slots. The following listing shows the complete header file for the `StateLCDWidget` class, which is located in the `state_lcd.hxx` file in the `src/Qt/signals_slots` directory (discussion follows the code listing):

```
#include <qwidget.h>
#include <qlcdnumber.h>
```

```
class StateLCDWidget : public QWidget {
  Q_OBJECT
public:
  StateLCDWidget(QWidget *parent=0, const char *name=0);
public slots:
  void increaseValue();
  void decreaseValue();
protected:
  void resizeEvent(QResizeEvent *);
private:
  QLCDNumber  *lcd;
  int value;
};
```

The include files qwidget.h and qlcdnumber.h contain the class definitions for the C++ classes QWidget and QLCDNumber in the Qt class library. For real applications, the class StateLCDWidget would normally be derived from the class QLCDNumber, but for a simple example to show how to define slots, it is slightly easier to derive the StateLCDWidget class from the simpler QWidget class and use a containment relationship. Class StateLCDWidget contains an instance of the QLCDNumber class.

In the state_lcd.hxx file, we see some illegal-looking code:

```
Q_OBJECT

public slots:
  void increaseValue();
  void decreaseValue();
```

The Q_OBJECT symbol causes the moc utility to generate so-called "meta object protocol" information that allows examination of an object at runtime to determine some class properties. Support for the meta object protocol is built into some object-oriented programming systems like Common LISP/CLOS. The architects of Qt built on the idea of runtime introspection of objects in order to support the binding of code to slots of a specific object—rather than all instances of a class.

> **NOTE**
>
> The token *slots* is not a reserved word in C++.

When the C++ compiler compiles this code, the token slots are defined to be nothing in the Qt include file qwidget.h. When we build programs using this widget, we must add commands in the Makefile to run the Qt utility program moc that creates a new C++

GUI Programming Using Qt

CHAPTER 31

553

31

GUI
PROGRAMMING
USING QT

source file with extra code for this class. We will take another look at moc after we look at the implementation of the StateLCDWidget class that is in the state_lcd.cxx file. We need two include files to define the StateLCDWidget and QLCDNumber widgets:

```
#include "state_lcd.hxx"
#include <qlcdnumber.h>
```

The class constructor is simple; it calls the super class QWidget constructor and creates an instance of the QLCDNumber class, specifying a maximum of four displayed digits in the instance of QLCDNumber:

```
StateLCDWidget::StateLCDWidget(QWidget *parent, const char *name)
  : QWidget(parent, name)  {
  lcd  = new QLCDNumber(4, this, "lcd");
}
```

The resizeEvent method is required to handle resize events and works by calling the QLCDNumber class method resize:

```
void StateLCDWidget::resizeEvent(QResizeEvent *) {
  lcd->resize(width(), height() - 21);
}
```

Here, the methods width and height are used to calculate the size of the instance of QLCDNumber. The methods width and height refer to the StateLCDWidget; these methods are inherited from the QWidget class. The rest of the class implementation is the definition of the two methods increaseValue and decreaseValue that increment and decrement the private variable value:

```
void StateLCDWidget::increaseValue() {
  value++;
  lcd->display(value);
}
void StateLCDWidget::decreaseValue() {
  value-;
  lcd->display(value);
}
```

Now we will discuss the creation of class slots and the Qt moc utility. We will cover the use of moc for both the StateLCDWidget class defined in this section and the UpDownWidget class developed in the next section. The following rules in the Makefile file specify how the make program should handle source files that use signals and slots:

```
moc_state_lcd.cxx: state_lcd.hxx
        $(MOC) state_lcd.hxx -o moc_state_lcd.cxx

moc_up_down.cxx: up_down.hxx
        $(MOC) up_down.hxx -o moc_up_down.cxx
```

Assume the $(MOC) refers to the absolute path to the moc utility in the Qt distribution's bin directory. If the header file is changed, a new source file (here, moc_state_lcd.cxx and/or moc_up_down.cxx) is automatically generated by moc. The following rules in the Makefile file compile these generated source files:

```
moc_state_lcd.o: moc_state_lcd.cxx state_lcd.hxx
moc_up_down.o: moc_up_down.cxx up_down.hxx
```

Makefile contains rules for building .o files from C or C++ source files. The generated moc files contain code required for a widget to both declare slots and to bind signals to the slots contained in other widgets.

Using Signals and Slots

We developed the StateLCDWidget class in the last section as an example of a simple class that defines slots that other Qt widgets can use. In this section, we will develop another simple widget class—UpDownWidget—that contains one instance of the widget classes StateLCDWidget and two instances of the Qt QPushButton widget class. One push button will have its clicked signal bound to the decreaseValue slot of the instance of class StateLCDWidget and the other push button will have its clicked signal bound to the increaseValue slot of the instance of StateLCDWidget.

The class header file up_down.hxx requires three include files to define the QWidget, QPushButton, and StateLCDWidget classes:

```
#include <qwidget.h>
#include <qpushbutton.h>
#include "state_lcd.hxx"
```

The class definition for UpDownWidget uses two tokens that are "defined away" for the C++ compiler, but that have special meaning for the moc utility: Q_OBJECT and signals. As we saw in the last section, the Q_OBJECT symbol causes the moc utility to generate so-called "meta object protocol information" to support binding code to slots of a specific object, rather than all instances of a class.

The moc utility uses the symbol signals in a class definition to determine which methods can be called for specific instances of the class through slot connections. The important thing to understand here is that just because an object has defined slots, an application program might not bind these slots to signals from another widget object. This binding occurs on an object-to-object basis and not to all instances of a class. The class definition for UpDownWidget shows that three other widget objects are contained in this class: two push-button objects and a StateLCDWidget object:

```
class UpDownWidget : public QWidget {
  Q_OBJECT
```

```
public:
  UpDownWidget(QWidget *parent=0, const char *name=0);
protected:
  void resizeEvent(QResizeEvent *);
private:
  QPushButton *up;
  QPushButton *down;
  StateLCDWidget *lcd;
};
```

The class definition in the up_down.cxx file contains the definition of the class constructor and the resizeEvent method. The constructor definition shows how to bind signals of one widget to the slot of another:

```
UpDownWidget::UpDownWidget( QWidget *parent, const char *name )
  : QWidget( parent, name )
{
  lcd  = new StateLCDWidget(parent, name);
  lcd->move( 0, 0 );
  up = new QPushButton("Up", this);
  down = new QPushButton("Down", this);
  connect(up, SIGNAL(clicked()), lcd, SLOT(increaseValue()) );
  connect(down, SIGNAL(clicked()), lcd, SLOT(decreaseValue()) );
}
```

The connect method is inherited from the QObject which is the base class for QWidget. The method signature, defined in the qobject.h file in Qt distribution's src/kernel directory, is as follows:

```
bool connect(const QObject *sender, const char *signal,
             const char *member );
```

The SIGNAL macro is defined in the qobjectdefs.h file as the following:

```
#define SIGNAL(a)    "2"#a
```

If you add the following line of code to the end of the class constructor:

```
printf("SIGNAL(clicked()) = ¦%s¦\n", SIGNAL(clicked()));
```

you will see the following output from the SIGNAL macro when the constructor executes:

```
SIGNAL(clicked()) = ¦2clicked()¦
```

The code generated by moc will recognize this character string (generated by the SIGNAL macro) and bind the correct signal at runtime. The SLOT macro is defined in the qobjectdefs.h file as follows:

```
#define SLOT(a)  "1"#a
```

If you add the following line of code to the end of the class constructor:

```
printf("SLOT(increaseValue()) = |%s|\n", SLOT(increaseValue()));
```

you will see the following output from the SIGNAL macro:

```
SLOT(increaseValue()) = |1increaseValue()|
```

The code generated by moc will recognize this character string (generated by the SLOT macro) and bind the correct member function at runtime. The resizeEvent method simply re-sizes the StateLCDWidget widget and repositions the two Push Button widgets:

```
void UpDownWidget::resizeEvent(QResizeEvent *) {
  lcd->resize(width(), height() - 59);
  up->setGeometry(0, lcd->height() + 5, width(), 22);
  down->setGeometry(0, lcd->height() +31, width(), 22);
}
```

Here, the width and height of UpDownWidget are used to calculate the position and size of the three widgets contained in UpDownWidget.

Running the Signal/Slot Example Program

We now have developed the StateLCDWidget and UpDownWidget widgets. The main.cxx file contains a simple example program to test these widgets:

```
#include <qapplication.h>
#include "up_down.hxx"

int main(int argc, char **argv) {
  QApplication a(argc, argv);
  QWidget top;
  top.setGeometry(0, 0, 222, 222);
  UpDownWidget w(&top);
  w.setGeometry(0, 0, 220, 220);
  a.setMainWidget(&top);
  top.show();
  return a.exec();
}
```

This example is a little different than the main.cxx file for testing the Drawing Area widget because a separate Top-Level widget is added to the Application widget. Then UpDownWidget is added to this Top-Level widget. The setGeometry method is defined in the qwidget.h file with the method signature:

```
virtual void setGeometry(int x, int y, int width, int height);
```

Only the Top-Level widget must be set visible using the show method. Any widgets contained in the Top-Level widget will also be made visible. Figure 31.2 shows the example program in main.cxx running. Clicking on the Up pushbutton increases the value of the numeric display by one; clicking the Down pushbutton decreases it by one.

FIGURE 31.2

The clicked signals of the two Push Button widgets are connected to slots in the StateLCDWidget *widget.*

Summary

The Qt C++ class library for GUI programming provides a rich set of widgets for building Linux applications using the C++ language. The design and implementation of Qt is very well done and Qt will probably become the GUI library of choice for Linux C++ programmers developing free software applications for Linux. C programmers will probably prefer the GTK library covered in Chapter 30. For a reasonable license fee (see www.troll.no) Qt can be used for commercial Linux applications and Windows applications.

Even if your Linux distribution contains the Qt runtime and development libraries (you might have to install these as separate setup options), you will probably want to visit www.troll.no for the online tutorial, Postscript documentation files, and the latest Qt distribution.

CHAPTER 32

GUI Programming Using Java

by Mark Watson

IN THIS CHAPTER

The purpose of this chapter is to introduce Linux programmers to the Java language and to writing GUI applications using two Java APIs: the Abstract Widget Toolkit (AWT) and the Java Foundation Classes (JFC). There are good tutorials for Java programming and GUI programming at Sun's Java Web site: http://java.sun.com. This chapter starts with a short introduction to Java programming, including short code snippets for reading and writing files, handling multiple threads, and simple socket-based IPC. We will then see an example "chat" program written with the AWT API and then the same program re-written using the JFC API. I used the Linux port of the Java Development Kit (JDK) version 1.1.7 to write this chapter, with JFC version 1.1. The JFC is also referred to as Swing. The examples in this chapter were also tested with the JDK 1.2 (pre-release).

We will cover a lot of material in this chapter by ignoring some deserving topics; we will typically cover only one option of many for many Java programming tasks. For example, there are three common methods for handling events in Java GUI programs. I use only my favorite method (anonymous inner event classes) in the examples in this chapter, completely ignoring (in the text) the other two methods. If the reader runs the example programs in this chapter and reads both the source listings and the text describing the sample code, then she will at least know how to get started with a new Java program of her own. I don't really attempt to teach object-oriented programming in this chapter.

Java is a great programming language, and I hope that it will be widely used by Linux programmers. I work for an artificial-intelligence software company and we do all our programming in Java. I will post any corrections or additions to the material in this chapter on my Web site. I also have several Open Source Java programs that are freely available at my Web site.

A Brief Introduction to Java

Java was originally developed by Sun Microsystems for programming consumer electronic devices. Java became wildly popular as a client-side programming platform when both Netscape and Microsoft offered runtime support for Java applets in their Web browsers. In this chapter, we will not use Java applets; all sample programs run as stand-alone Java programs. The real strength of the Java programming language, however, is when it is used to write multi-threaded server applications. One of the huge advantages of Java over C and C++ is automatic memory management. In C, when you allocate memory with, for example, `malloc`, you must explicitly free the memory when you are done with it. In Java, memory that is no longer accessible by any variables in your program is eventually freed by the Java runtime garbage collector. Another advantage of

Java is the lack of a pointer variable. Although pointers are certainly useful, they are a large source of program bugs. C++ programmers who use exception-handling will be pleased to see that Java has a similar facility for catching virtually any type of runtime error.

Java is an Object-Oriented Language

Java is a strongly typed object-oriented language. Java programs are built by defining classes of objects. New class definitions create new structured data types with "behavior" that is implemented by writing class methods. Methods are similar to functions except that they are associated with either classes or instances of classes. Java is strongly typed in the sense that it is illegal (in the sense that the compiler will generate an error) to call a method with the wrong number or wrong type of arguments. The compiler will also generate an error if, for example, you try to set an integer variable equal to a real variable without explicitly casting the real value to an integer (and vice versa).

It is important to clearly understand the relationship between Java classes and instances of Java classes. In order to show how classes are written and instances of how classes are created, we will look at a simple example program. The source code to this example program is located in the src/Java directory in the Car.java file. Listing 32.1 shows the contents of the Car.java. I assume that the reader knows how to program in the C programming language. If you also know how to program in C++, learning Java will be very easy for you. In Java, anything following the characters // on a line is considered a comment. C style comments (for example, /* this is a comment */) are also supported.

Listing 32.1   THE Car.java FILE

```
// File: Car.java

import java.io.*;

public class Car implements Serializable {
  private String name;
  private float price;
  static private int countCarInstances = 0;

  public Car(String name, float price) {
    // Keep a count of the number of instances of class Car:
    countCarInstances++;
    this.name = name;
    this.price = price;
    System.out.println("Creating Car(" + name + ", " +
                       price + ")");
```

continues

Listing 32.1 CONTINUED

```java
    System.out.println("Number of instances of class Car: " +
                       countCarInstances);
  }

  public String getName() { return name; }
  public float getPrice() { return price; }

  // A static main test method

  static public void main(String [] args) {
    // This program does not use any arguments, but if any
    // command line arguments are supplied, at least
    // print them out:
    if (args.length > 0) {
      for (int i=0; i<args.length; i++) {
        System.out.println("args[" + i + "]=" + args[i]);
      }
    }

    // Create a few instances of class car:

    Car mustang = new Car("Mustang", 15000.0f);
    Car ford = new Car("Thunderbird", 22000.0f);

    String name = ford.getName();
    float price = mustang.getPrice();

    System.out.println("name: " + name + ", price: " + price);
  }
}
```

In Listing 32.1, we start defining a new public class named Car by using the class keyword:

```java
public class Car implements Serializable {
```

Java does not support multiple inheritance, but it does support the implementation of multiple interfaces. Car implements the Serializable interface, which is used for saving objects to files. Later in this chapter, we will write a ChatListener interface and use it in two programs.

In Java, class names, method names, and variable names can be public, protected, or private. Public names are visible anywhere in a program. Private names are visible only inside the class definition. Protected names are visible only inside the class definition or inside any class that is derived from a class using protected declarations. In Listing 32.1, we see that `Car` defines three private class variables: `name`, `price`, and `countCarInstances`. Whenever a new instance `Car` is created, this new instance will have its own `name` and `price` variables. However, since we used the `static` keyword in defining the `countCarInstances` class variable, all instances of `Car` share the same variable. Listing 32.1 shows that a `main` method is also declared static. It is possible, and often a good programming technique, to declare both variables and methods as static in a class definition. The following statement, from Listing 32.1, starts the definition of a class constructor for creating instances of the `Car` class:

```
public Car(String name, float price) {
```

This method requires two arguments, a `String` variable `name` and a `float` variable `price`. Java is an object-oriented language, but it is not a "pure" object-oriented language because, in addition to classes and objects, the Java language also uses primitive data types such as `float`, `int`, `long`, and so on. The body of the class constructor does several things: it copies the arguments to the local call variables with the same names (using the `this` keyword lets the compiler know that an expression like `this.price` refers to the class variable name, and not the argument `price` constructor). The class constructor also increments the `countCarInstances` static variable so that we know how many instances of `Car` are created in any program. Since the class variables `name` and `price` are declared private, we need to provide methods for getting their values so we can reference these values:

```
public String getName() { return name; }
public float getPrice() { return price; }
```

Finally, it is common practice to write test code for a new class in a `static method` called `main`. Any class with a public static method named main that returns void and has an array of `String` values as an argument can also be run as a standalone program.

The notation in the method signature for the static public method `main`:

```
String [] args
```

implies that the argument is an array of `String` variables. In `main`, we see how many elements are in this array with the expression:

```
args.length
```

Here, the variable `length` is a public class variable for the standard Java class `Array`. If the args array has at least two elements, then we can, for example, access the second element in the array with the expression:

```
args[1]
```

The test method `main` does not use the command-line arguments in the `args` array, but they are printed as an example of accessing command-line arguments in a standalone Java program. Any Java class that you want to run as a standalone program must contain a `static public main` method that has one argument: an array of strings for command-line arguments. The `main` test method creates two instances of `Car` using the new operator:

```
Car mustang = new Car("Mustang", 155000.0f);
Car ford = new Car("Ford Thunderbird", 22000.0f);
```

Private data is accessed using the `getName` and `getPrice` methods. The `Car` class implements the Java interface `Serializable`; this means that instances of this class can, as we will see in a later section, be easily written to a file.

Most Linux distributions come with Java. If you have not installed the Java option from your Linux setup program, this is a good time to do it. If you do not have Java version 1.2 or later installed, you will need to download the JFC/Swing package from `http://java.sun.com`. The Web site `http://www.blackdown.org` is a good source of Java tools for Linux.

You can compile Java programs using the `javac` program. Standalone Java applications are executed using the `java` program. The following shows how to compile (using javac) and run (using java) the example program:

```
/home/markw/linuxbook/src/Java: javac Car.java
/home/markw/linuxbook/src/Java: java Car this is a test
args[0]=this
args[1]=is
args[2]=a
args[3]=test
Creating Car(Mustang, 15000.0)
Number of instances of class Car: 1
Creating Car(Ford Thunderbird, 22000.0)
Number of instances of class Car: 2
name: Ford Thunderbird, price: 15000.0
```

The `javac` program compiles files with the extension `.java` into compiled files with the extension `.class`. The program `java` is the JVM (Java Virtual Machine) used to run compiled Java programs.

Using Packages in Java

Java supports packages to separate public class names into separate name spaces. Optionally, any Java source file can begin with a package statement. When referring to any class in a package, the package name precedes the class name, separated by a period.

Here is a simple example of two separate Java source files, each using a different package (p1 and p2).

```java
// File: Hello1.java
package p1;
public class Hello1 {
   public Hello1() {
      System.out.println("Hello1");
   }
}
```

```java
// File: Hello2.java
package p2;
public class Hello2 {
   public Hello2() {
      new p1.Hello1();
   }
}
```

When—in the file Hello2.java (in package p2)—we want to refer to class Hello1 in package p1, we preface the class name with the package name:

```java
new P1.Hello1();
```

Importing other packages is a shorter alternative to specifying a package name before class names in other packages. The second example file Hello2.java could also have been written using an import statement to import all public class names from the p1 package:

```java
// File: Hello2.java
package p2;
import p1.*;  // import all public class names from package p1
public class Hello2 {
   public Hello2() {
      new Hello1();  // now we don't need the package name
   }
}
```

The Java standard class libraries are organized into packages. The following are some of the more commonly used packages:

Package	Definition
java.io	Contains file I/O.
java.net	Contains network utilities.
java.awt	Contains the AWT user interface toolkit.

The java.lang package is a "default" package and is always implicitly included in Java programs, so the following import statement is not required:

```
import java.lang.*;
```

Writing and Reading Files with Java

In this section, we will see simple examples of reading and writing files and saving Java objects to a file using object serialization. Listing 32.2 shows a simple example of writing a text file, and then reading it. Besides file I/O, the example in Listing 32.2 shows the use of Java exceptions. Any code that can cause a runtime error can be placed inside a try and catch code block. The catch statement takes an exception type as an argument. The Java library defines a hierarchy of exception types. For the examples in this chapter, we will always catch the base exception class Exception—catching all runtime errors, including I/O errors, illegal data references, and so on. The statement import java.io.* enables us to use any classes in the java.io package without needing to prepend the package name to any class in this package.

Listing 32.2 THE FileIO.java FILE

```
// File: FileIO.java
//
// Example of writing to a text file, then reading the file
//

import java.io.*;

public class FileIO {

    static public void main(String [] args) {
    // Always wrap file IO in a try/catch statement:
    try {

        // Write a file:

        BufferedWriter bw =
            new BufferedWriter(new FileWriter("temp.txt"));
        bw.write("This is a test\n");
        bw.write("This is a second line of text\n");
        bw.write("Here is the number three: " + 3 + "\n");
        bw.close();

        // Read the file that we just wrote:
```

```
        BufferedReader br =
          new BufferedReader(new FileReader("temp.txt"));
         while (true) {
            String s = br.readLine();
            if (s == null ¦¦ s.length() < 1)  break;
            System.out.println("line from file: " + s);
         }
         br.close();
     } catch (Exception e) {
         System.out.println("Error: " + e);
     }
     }
 }
```

The FileIO class defined in Listing 32.2 contains only a static public main method, so this example is not "object-oriented." The following statement, from Listing 32.2, actually creates instances of two classes (FileWriter and BufferedWriter):

```
BufferedWriter bw =
  new BufferedWriter(new FileWriter("temp.txt"));
```

We have already seen the new operator in Listing 32.1; the new operator is used here to create new instances of a specified class. Here, we are creating an instance of the FileWriter class for the temp.txt file and this object is passed to the constructor for the BufferedWriter class. Use the following syntax to compile and run the code:

```
/home/markw/linuxbook/src/Java: javac FileIO.java
/home/markw/linuxbook/src/Java: java FileIO
```

It is also easy to write the contents of Java objects to a file, and later restore the objects. This is called object serialization. In Listing 32.1, the Car class implements the Java Serializable interface. An interface is a definition of a set of methods that must be defined by a class implementing the interface. The Serializable interface defines two method signatures:

```
private void writeObject(java.io.ObjectOutputStream out)
            throws IOException
private void readObject(java.io.ObjectInputStream in)
            throws IOException, ClassNotFoundException;
```

Although it is possible to write your own default write and read object methods, the examples in Listings 32.3 and 32.4 use the default (inherited) behavior for object serialization.

Listing 32.3 shows how to write instances Car (refer to Listing 32.1) to a file. In addition to using object serialization, we add a "goody" to this example: by using an instance of class GZIPOutputStream to wrap the instance of class FileOutputStream, the output file will be compressed to save disk space. Here, we use the GNU ZIP file format. Regular ZIP formats are also supported. The libraries for handling compression are in the package:

```
import java.util.zip.*;
```

Notice that in Listing 32.3, as usual, we must wrap any file IO inside a `try` and `catch` code block.

Listing 32.3 THE `WriteFile.java` FILE

```java
// File: WriteFile.java
//
// Example of saving Java objects to a compressed data file
//

import java.io.*;
import java.util.zip.*;

public class WriteFile {

    static public void main(String [] args) {
    // Create a few objects to save:
    Car mustang = new Car("Mustang", 15000.0f);
    Car ford - new Car("Thunderbird", 22000.0f);
    // Open a compressed output stream:
    String file_name = "car.data";
    // Always wrap file IO in a try/catch statement:
    try {
        FileOutputStream f = new FileOutputStream(file_name);
        GZIPOutputStream gf = new GZIPOutputStream(f);
        ObjectOutputStream oos = new ObjectOutputStream(gf);
        oos.writeObject(mustang);
        oos.writeObject(ford);
        oos.flush();
        oos.close();
    } catch (Exception e) {
        System.out.println("Error: " + e);
    }
    }
}
```

Listing 32.4 shows how to read instances Car (see Listing 32.1) from a file created with the program in Listing 32.3.

Listing 32.4   THE ReadFile.java FILE

```java
// File: ReadFile.java
//
// Example of saving Java objects to a compressed data file
//

import java.io.*;
import java.util.zip.*;

public class ReadFile {

    static public void main(String [] args) {
    String file_name = "car.data";
    Car c1 = null, c2 = null;
    // Always wrap file IO in a try/catch statement:
    try {
        FileInputStream f = new FileInputStream(file_name);
        GZIPInputStream gf = new GZIPInputStream(f);
        ObjectInputStream ois = new ObjectInputStream(gf);
        c1 = (Car)ois.readObject();
        c2 = (Car)ois.readObject();
        ois.close();

    } catch (Exception e) {
        System.out.println("Error: " + e);
    }
    System.out.println("Cars reads from file: " + c1.getName() +
            " and " + c2.getName());
    }
}
```

Object serialization is useful in itself for saving objects to disk files, and it is the basis for the Java Remote Method Interface (RMI) technology for doing interprocess communication between Java programs. RMI is beyond the scope of this short chapter, but we will see examples of using sockets later in this chapter.

Using Multiple Threads with Java

The Java language makes it particularly easy to do both multi-threaded programming and socket programming. We will see in the next section that using threads is a basic technique for writing robust socket programs in Java. In this section, we will look at a short example program that creates a new thread class MyThread and creates 10 instances of it.

Listing 32.5 contains two Java classes: MyThread and ExampleThreads. When a class, such as MyThread, is derived from the Thread class, it is expected to have a run public method. This method is called when the thread is started by calling the start method.

Listing 32.5 THE ExampleThreads.java FILE

```java
// File: ExampleThreads.java
//
// Example of using Java threads
//

import java.io.*;
import java.util.zip.*;

class MyThread extends Thread {
    public MyThread(String name) {
    super(name);
    this.name = name;
    }
    public MyThread() {
    this("no_name_thread");
    }
    private String name;

    public void run() {
    for (int i=0; i<5; i++) {
        System.out.println(name + " " + i);
        try {
        Thread.sleep(1000); // sleep 1 second
        } catch (Exception e) {
        System.out.println("Thread sleep exception: " + e);
        }
    }
    }
}

public class ExampleThreads {

    static public void main(String [] args) {

    // make an array of MyThread objects:
    MyThread threads[] = new MyThread[10];
    for (int i=0; i<10; i++) {
        threads[i] = new MyThread("my_thread_" + i);
    }
    // now start all the threads:
    for (int i=0; i<10; i++) {
        threads[i].start(); // calls the 'run' method
    }
    }
}
```

The MyThread class was not declared public. Java requires that a file contains only one public class, and the filename must be the name of this public class with the file extension ".java".

Here we see how threads work: you derive a class from Thread and write a run public method that performs the work in the thread. Calling the start method (inherited from the Thread class) starts the thread's run method and immediately returns. In the first loop in ExampleThreads.main, we create 10 threads; in the second loop, we effectively start all 10 threads running simultaneously.

Socket Programming with Java

We saw in the last section how simple it is to use threads in Java programs. Writing programs that use sockets for interprocess communication is also simple if we use separate threads to manage socket connections. Listing 32.6 shows the ExampleSockets class that uses multiple threads to process socket I/O.

Listing 32.6   THE ExampleSockets CLASS

```
import java.net.*;
import java.io.*;

public class ExampleSockets {

    // Default host name and port number:
    final static public String host = "127.0.0.1"; // local host
    final static public int port = 8000;

    protected String my_name = "no_name";

    // inner class to handle socket output:
    class do_output extends Thread {
    private int num_sends;
    PrintStream out;
    public do_output(int num_sends) {
        this.num_sends = num_sends;
        start();
    }
    public do_output() {
        this(10);
    }
    public void run() {
        try {
        Socket s = new Socket(host, port);
```

continues

Listing 32.6 CONTINUED

```java
        DataInputStream in    =
            new DataInputStream(s.getInputStream());
        out = new PrintStream(s.getOutputStream());
        } catch (Exception e) {
        System.out.println("Exception 1: " + e);
        }
        for (int i=0; i<10; i++) {
        out.println(my_name + " sends " + i);
        try { Thread.sleep(500); } catch (Exception e) { }
        }
        try { Thread.sleep(2000); } catch (Exception e) { }
        System.out.println("All done.");
        System.exit(0);
    }
}


// inner class to handle socket input:
class do_input extends Thread {

public do_input() {
    super();
    start();
}
public void run() {
    ServerSocket serverSocket;
    try {
    serverSocket = new ServerSocket(port, 2000);
    } catch (IOException e) {
    System.out.println("Error in socket input: " + e);
    return;
    }

    try {
    while (true) {
        Socket socket = serverSocket.accept();
        new MyServerConnection(socket);
    }
    } catch (IOException e) {
    System.out.println("Error in socket connection: " + e);
    } finally {
    try {
        serverSocket.close();
    } catch (IOException e) {
        System.out.println("I/O exception: " + e);
    }
    }
}
// an inner (inner) class to handle
// incoming socket connections
```

```
public class MyServerConnection extends Thread {
    protected transient Socket client_socket;
    protected transient DataInputStream input_strm;
    protected transient PrintStream output_strm;

    public MyServerConnection(Socket client_socket) {
    this.client_socket = client_socket;
    try {
        input_strm  =
    new DataInputStream(client_socket.getInputStream());
        output_strm =
    new PrintStream(client_socket.getOutputStream());
    }
    catch (IOException io_exception) {
        try { client_socket.close();
      } catch (IOException io_ex2) {  };
        System.err.println("Exception 2: getting" +
                            "socket streams " +
                        io_exception);
        return;
    }
    // Start the thread (i.e., call method 'run'):
    this.start();
    //System.out.println("MyServerConnection is set up.");
    }

    public void run() {
    String input_buf;
    try {
        while (true) {
        input_buf = input_strm.readLine();
        System.out.println("received on socket: "
                            + input_buf);
        }
    }
    catch (Exception exception) { }
    finally {
        try {
        client_socket.close();
        }
        catch (Exception exception) { };
    }
    }
}
}

public ExampleSockets() {
do_input ins   = new do_input();
do_output outs = new do_output();
//ins.start();
```

continues

Listing 32.6 CONTINUED

```
    //try { Thread.sleep(2000); } catch (Exception e) { }
    //outs.start();
    }

  public static void main(String [] args) {
      ExampleSockets ex = new ExampleSockets();
      if (args.length > 0)  ex.my_name = args[0];
  }
}
```

The ExampleSockets.java file contains two inner classes. Instances of an inner class can be created only by the class that contains the inner class definition. Using inner classes has several advantages:

- Inner classes hide the inner class from the rest of your program. Inner classes can only be used by the class that contains them.

- Inner classes have access to any data or methods that are declared public or protected in the outer class.

- Inner classes can be nested (one of the inner classes in this example also contains an inner class of its own).

The class nesting in this example is:

```
ExampleSockets
do_output (derived from Thread)
do_input (derived from Thread)
MyServerConnection (derived from Thread)
```

The inner class do_output has a public run method (this is a thread class) that creates a new socket connection and writes text to this socket. The do_input inner class has its own inner class: MyServerConnection. The do_input inner class is a little more complicated because handling incoming socket connects is a more complex task than opening a socket and writing to it. The method run in the class do_input opens a server socket on a specified port number and enters an "infinite loop" listening for incoming socket connections. An instance of the inner (to do_input) class MyServerConnnection is created to handle each incoming socket connection.

This example program is a little contrived because two threads are created that "talk to" each other over a socket interface. Typically, you would use the code in the do_input inner class when you write a socket-based server class, and you would use the code in do_output when you write a socket client class.

The do_input inner class contains an inner class of its own, MyServerConnection. An instance of the MyServerConnection is constructed with a socket created in the do_input class that connects to the socket created in the do_output class. This socket is used to create both an input stream and an output stream. As you would expect, the text written in do_output.run is received on this input stream and anything written to the output stream is returned to do_output.run (which ignores any input in this example). The MyServerConnection.run method reads from the input stream until an end-of-file or other error condition occurs. Then it exits.

The ExampleSockets constructor appears at the bottom of Listing 32.6 and is fairly simple: we first create an instance of do_input (start the "server") and then create an instance of do_output. This example is fairly simple, but you should be able to copy the code from the do_input as a basis for any Java server programs that you need to write. Similarly, do_output shows how to write client-side code that sends text to a server.

Writing a Chat Engine Using Sockets

We will design and write a simple chat engine in this section that allows two clients to send text messages back and forth using sockets. Later in this chapter, we will introduce both AWT and JFC GUI programming by writing chat clients using both of these GUI APIs. Listing 32.8 shows the ChatEngine class that uses multiple threads to process socket I/O between two chat clients. Two instances of ChatEngine (in different programs) connect to each other and pass text data between them. This class uses an interface definition in the ChatListener.java file that is shown in Listing 32.7. A program that uses an instance of the ChatEngine class must implement the ChatListener interface and register itself with the chat engine object by using the ChatEngine.registerChatListener method.

Listing 32.7 THE ChatListener.java FILE

```
// File: ChatListener.java
//
// Defines the ChatLister interface
//

public interface ChatListener {
    public void receiveText(String s);
}
```

A class implementing the ChatListener interface must define a receiveText method that will be called by a ChatListener object when incoming text is received from its socket. The ChatEngine class contains a registerChatListener method that is used by a class implementing the ChatListener interface to register itself to receive incoming text. We will see examples of defining and using this interface in the sections on writing AWT and JFC chat client programs.

Listing 32.8   THE ChatEngine.java FILE

```java
// File: ChatEngine.java
//
// Defines the non-GUI behavior for both the AWT
// and JFC versions of the chat programs.
//

import java.net.*;
import java.io.*;

public class ChatEngine {
    protected int port=8080;
    protected String host="127.0.0.1";
    private PrintStream out;
    private HandleInputSocket socketThread;

    public ChatEngine() {
    }

    public void startListening(int my_listen_port) {
        System.out.println("ChatEngine.startListening(" +
                            my_listen_port + ")");
        try {
            socketThread = new HandleInputSocket(my_listen_port);
        } catch (Exception e) {
            System.out.println("Exception 0: " + e);
        }
    }

    public void connect(String host, int port) {
        System.out.println("ChatEngine.connect(" + host +
                            ", " + port + ")");
        this.port=port;
        this.host = host;
        try {
            Socket s = new Socket(host, port);
            out = new PrintStream(s.getOutputStream());
        } catch (Exception e) {
            System.out.println("Exception 1: " + e);
        }
    }
```

```java
public void logout() {
    try { out.close(); } catch (Exception e) { }
    socketThread.stop();
    socketThread = null;
}

public void send(String s) {
    try {
        out.println(s);
    } catch (Exception e) { }
}

void registerChatListener(ChatListener cl) {
    this.chatListener = cl;
}
protected ChatListener chatListener = null;

// inner class to handle socket input:
class HandleInputSocket extends Thread {
    int listenPort = 8191;
    public HandleInputSocket(int port) {
        super();
        listenPort = port;
        start();
    }
    public void run() {
        ServerSocket serverSocket;
        try {
            serverSocket =
              new ServerSocket(listenPort, 2000);
        } catch (IOException e) {
            System.out.println("Error in handling socket" +
                                " input: " + e + ", port=" +
                                port);
            return;
        }

        try  {
            while (true) {
                Socket socket = serverSocket.accept();
                new MyServerConnection(socket);
            }
        } catch (IOException e) {
            System.out.println("Error socket connection: " +
                                e);
        } finally {
            try {
                serverSocket.close();
            } catch (IOException e) {
                System.out.println("I/O exception: " + e);
```

continues

Listing 32.8 CONTINUED

```java
                }
            }
        }
        // an inner (inner) class to handle
        // incoming socket connections
        public class MyServerConnection extends Thread {
            protected transient Socket client_socket;
            protected transient DataInputStream input_strm;
            protected transient PrintStream output_strm;

            public MyServerConnection(Socket client_socket) {
                this.client_socket = client_socket;
                try {
                    input_strm  =
    new DataInputStream(client_socket.getInputStream());
                    output_strm =
    new PrintStream(client_socket.getOutputStream());
                }
                catch (IOException io_exception) {
                    try { client_socket.close();
                } catch (IOException io_ex2) {   };
                    System.err.println("Exception 2: getting" +
                                       " socket streams " +
                                       io_exception);
                    return;
                }
                // Start the thread (i.e., call method 'run'):
                this.start();
            }

            public void run() {
                String input_buf;
                try {
                    while (true) {
                        input_buf = input_strm.readLine();
                        if (input_buf == null) {
                            logout();
                            break;
                        }
                        System.out.println("received on socket: "
                                           + input_buf);
                        if (chatListener != null) {
                            chatListener.receiveText(input_buf);
                        }

                    }
                }
                catch (Exception exception) { }
```

```
        finally {
            try {
                client_socket.close();
            }
            catch (Exception exception) { };
        }
    }
}
}
```

This example is very similar to the example for handling socket-based IPC that we saw in the last section. The ChatEngine class uses inner classes to handle reading and writing data from sockets. The two inner classes in ChatEngine are:

HandleInputSocket
    MyServerConnection   (almost identical to the class
                               with the same name in the
                               last section)

In this example, the main class ChatEngine has a send method that writes text to an output stream opened for a socket connection to another instance of ChatEngine. The following are the public methods in the ChatEngine class:

Method	Description
ChatEngine	Class constructor (does nothing).
startListening	Starts the chat engine listening on a specified port.
connect	Connects via a socket to a remote chat engine using a specified host computer name (or absolute IP address) and port number.
logout	Breaks the connection to a remote chat engine.
send	Sends a specified string to the remote chat engine.
registerChatListener	Registers an instance of any class implementing the ChatListener interface to receive incoming text from the remote chat engine.

The HandleInputSocket inner class in Listing 32.8 is similar to the do_input inner class in the last section. This inner class is derived from Thread and the run method listens for incoming socket connections and creates an instance of the MyServerConnection inner class to handle incoming text from the remote chat engine. This example is more general than necessary: the code in the HandleInputSocket class works for any (reasonable) number of socket connections, but in this example we only support two chat engines talking together "peer to peer".

Introduction to AWT

When the Java language was first released by Sun Microsystems, The Abstract Widget Toolkit (AWT) was made available for writing Graphics User Interface (GUI) programs. When the Java language was updated from version 1.0 to 1.1, a new event model and improvements to AWT were included. As this book was written, Sun has released Java version 1.2 (now known as version 2.0), but the API for AWT was not changed. The AWT provides several classes for adding specific components to programs, such as the following:

Class	Description
Button	A command or "push" button.
Label can	For displaying non-editable text (although the text be changed under program control).
TextField	For allowing the user to edit a single line of text.
TextArea	For allowing the user to edit multi-line text.
List	For displaying a list of items.

These graphic components are placed in containers, such as the following:

Container	Description
Panel	The simplest container for holding other Panel objects or graphic components.
Frame	A top-level window with a title bar. A Frame will usually contain one Panel.

The examples in this chapter do not demonstrate drawing lines, shapes, and so on. Figure 32.1 shows the AWTsample.java program running.

FIGURE 32.1

The AWTsample program demonstrates event-handling using anonymous inner classes with the AWT API.

There are several layout managers that can be used to position graphic components inside a Panel. In the GUI examples in this book, we will not use any layout managers; we will use a setBounds method to specify the X-Y position of a graphic component and its width and height. Using a null layout manager is a little unusual for Java programs, but I think that it will make the example programs easier to understand.

The example program in Listing 32.9 implements a AWTSample class. This class is derived from the AWT Frame class, so when we create a new instance of AWTSample, we will get an application window. The class constructor first calls the super class (Frame) constructor by using the super keyword. Then three objects are created using the Panel, Label, and Button classes. We then use the setLayout method to set the layout manager for the panel object to null.

Listing 32.9 THE AWTsample.java FILE

```
// File: AWTsample.java

import java.awt.*;
import java.awt.event.*;

public class AWTsample extends Frame {
    private int count = 0;
    Label countLabel;

    public AWTsample() {
        super("AWT Sample Program");

        Panel panel1 = new Panel();
        countLabel = new Label();
        Button countButton = new Button();
        panel1.setLayout(null);
        setSize(180, 150);
        panel1.setVisible(true);
        countLabel.setText("button clicked " + count + " times");
        countButton.setLabel("click me");
        countButton.addMouseListener(
          new java.awt.event.MouseAdapter() {
            public void mouseClicked(MouseEvent e) {
               countLabel.setText("button clicked " +
                                  ++count + " times");
            }
        });
        panel1.add(countLabel);
        countLabel.setBounds(30, 35, 140, 20);
        panel1.add(countButton);
        countButton.setBounds(40, 65, 100, 30);
        add(panel1);
        setVisible(true);
    }
    static public void main(String [] args) {
        new AWTsample();
    }
}
```

Several useful methods that are defined for most AWT component classes are used in this example, such as the following:

Method	Definition
setVisible	Used here to set a Frame and a Panel to be visible.
setSize	Sets the width and height of a component.
setLabel	Sets the label text for an instance of Label, Button, and so on.
setText	Sets the text of the Label object used to specify how many times the button is clicked.
setBounds	Sets the X an Y position and the width and height of a graphic component.
add	Used to add the label and the button to the panel, and to add the panel to the frame.

The only thing at all complicated about this example is handling the events associated with the user clicking on the button object. However, these events are handled with only a few lines of code:

```
countButton.addMouseListener(
  new java.awt.event.MouseAdapter() {
    public void mouseClicked(MouseEvent e) {
      countLabel.setText("button clicked " +
                        ++count + " times");
    }
});
```

The addMouseListener method is used to associate an instance of the MouseListener with a button (or any other component). Now, it is possible to define a separate class that implements the MouseListener listener interface (which requires defining five methods: mouseClicked, mouseEntered, mouseExited, mousePressed, and mouseReleased). However, there is a MouseAdapter utility class that defines "do nothing" versions of these five methods. In this code example, we are creating an anonymous inner class (for example, it is an inner class with no name associated with it) that overrides mouseClicked. Our mouseClicked method uses the setText method to change the displayed text of a label. In Listing 32.9 we import all classes and interfaces from the ackages java.awt (for the graphic components and containers) and java.awt.event (for the event-handling classes and interfaces).

In Listing 32.9, we define a static public main method that is executed when we compile and run this sample program by typing:

```
javac AWTSample.java
java AWTSample
```

Writing a Chat Program Using AWT

The sample program in Listing 32.10 that implements a chat client using AWT is a little complex because the user interface has several components. Each component is positioned by an X-Y location in a panel and is sized to a specific width and height. The interface to the chat engine class ChatEngine is, however, very simple. The ChatAWT class implements the ChatListener interface and registers itself with an instance of the ChatEngine class. This registration allows the chat engine object to call the receiveText method (required to implement the ChatListener interface) in the class ChatAWT.

Figure 32.2 shows the ChatAWT.java and the ChatJFC.java programs running. We will discuss the ChatJFC program in the section "Writing a Chat Program in JFC." It is virtually identical to the ChatAWT program, except that it uses JFC classes instead of AWT classes.

32

GUI PROGRAMMING USING JAVA

FIGURE 32.2

Both the ChatAWT
(top of the screen)
and ChatJFC *program in the section "Writing a Chat Program in JFC." It is virtually identical to the* ChatAWT *program, except that it uses JFC classes instead of AWT classes.*

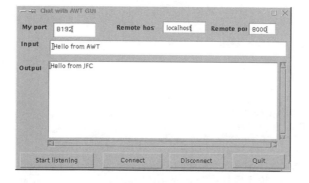

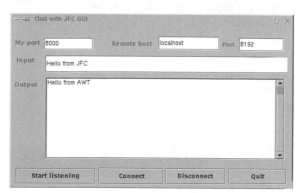

Listing 32.10 THE ChatAWT.java FILE

```java
// File: ChatAWT.java

import java.awt.*;
import java.awt.event.*;

public class ChatAWT extends Frame implements ChatListener{
    Panel panel1 = new Panel();
    Label label1 = new Label();
    TextField myPortField = new TextField();
    Label label2 = new Label();
    TextField hostField = new TextField();
    Label label3 = new Label();
    TextField portField = new TextField();
    Label label4 = new Label();
    TextField inputField = new TextField();
    Label label5 - new Label();
    Button connectButton = new Button();
    Button disconnectButton = new Button();
    Button quitButton = new Button();
    TextArea outputField = new TextArea();

    protected ChatEngine chatEngine;
    Button listenButten = new Button();

    public ChatAWT() {
        super("Chat with AWT GUI");
        chatEngine = new ChatEngine();
        chatEngine.registerChatListener(this);
        Panel p = new Panel();
        quitButton.setBounds(448, 280, 111, 32);
        quitButton.setLabel("Quit");
        quitButton.addMouseListener(
         new java.awt.event.MouseAdapter() {
            public void mouseClicked(MouseEvent e) {
                System.exit(0);
            }
        });
        outputField.setBounds(63, 91, 497, 178);
        listenButton.setBounds(5, 281, 153, 33);
        listenButton.setLabel("Start listening");
        listenButton.addMouseListener(
          new java.awt.event.MouseAdapter() {
            public void mouseClicked(MouseEvent e) {
                chatEngine.startListening(
                   Integer.parseInt(myPortField.getText()));
            }
        });
        panel1.setLayout(null);
        this.setSize(575, 348);
```

```java
label1.setFont(new Font("Dialog", 1, 12));
label1.setBounds(6, 5, 60, 33);
label1.setText("My port");
myPortField.setText("8192");
myPortField.setBounds(72, 11, 90, 33);
label2.setFont(new Font("Dialog", 1, 12));
label2.setBounds(200, 3, 83, 38);
label2.setText("Remote host");
hostField.setBounds(299, 7, 94, 27);
hostField.setText("localhost");
label3.setFont(new Font("Dialog", 1, 12));
label3.setBounds(400, 5, 78, 36);
label3.setText("Remote port");
portField.setBounds(480, 9, 60, 27);
portField.setText("8000");
label4.setFont(new Font("Dialog", 1, 12));
label4.setBounds(4, 43, 50, 28);
label4.setText("Input");
inputField.setBounds(65, 47, 497, 34);
inputField.setText("  ");
inputField.addKeyListener(
  new java.awt.event.KeyAdapter() {
    public void keyPressed(KeyEvent e) {
        if (e.getKeyCode() == '\n') {
            chatEngine.send(inputField.getText());
        }
    }
});
label5.setFont(new Font("Dialog", 1, 12));
label5.setBounds(0, 90, 48, 34);
label5.setText("Output");
connectButton.setBounds(175, 280, 126, 34);
connectButton.setLabel("Connect");
connectButton.addMouseListener(
  new java.awt.event.MouseAdapter() {
    public void mouseClicked(MouseEvent e) {
        chatEngine.connect(hostField.getText(),
            Integer.parseInt(portField.getText()));
    }
});
disconnectButton.setBounds(315, 280, 117, 33);
disconnectButton.setLabel("Disconnect");
disconnectButton.addMouseListener(
  new java.awt.event.MouseAdapter() {
    public void mouseClicked(MouseEvent e) {
        chatEngine.logout();
    }
});
this.add(panel1, null);
panel1.add(label1, null);
```

continues

Listing 32.10 CONTINUED

```
        panel1.add(myPortField, null);
        panel1.add(label2, null);
        panel1.add(hostField, null);
        panel1.add(label3, null);
        panel1.add(portField, null);
        panel1.add(label4, null);
        panel1.add(inputField, null);
        panel1.add(label5, null);
        panel1.add(connectButton, null);
        panel1.add(disconnectButton, null);
        panel1.add(quitButton, null);
        panel1.add(outputField, null);
        panel1.add(listenButten, null);
        setVisible(true);
        panel1.setVisible(true);

    }
    public void receiveText(String s) { // ChatListener interface
        outputField.appendText(s + "\n");
    }

    static public void main(String [] args) {
        new ChatAWT();
    }
}
```

The example in Listing 32.10 is lengthy, but most of the code is simply creating components such as text fields, labels, and buttons, and using `setBounds(int x, int y, int
width, int height)` to position each component inside the panel. When we use the `add`
method to add a component to a panel, the second `null` argument passed to `add` method
indicates that the layout for adding the object is `null`. This example also shows specifying a font:

```
    Label label3.setFont(new Font("Dialog", 1, 12));
```

In addition to `"Dialog"`, you can use other font types such a `"Times"`, `"Helvetica"`, and
so on.

Introduction to JFC

When the Java language was updated from version 1.1 to 1.2 (now known as version
2.0), the Java Foundation Classes (JFC) were added as a standard library in the package
javax.swing. The JFC API is also known as the Swing API. If you are using version 1.1

of the Java development kit, you will need to download the JFC/Swing package from Sun's Java Web site at `http://java.sun.com`. The JFC provides several classes for adding specific components to programs, such as the following:

Class	Description
Jbutton	A command or "push" button.
Jlabel	For displaying non-editable text (although the text can be changed under program control).
JTextPane	For displaying text.
JEditorPane	For allowing the user to edit text.
JTextArea	For allowing the user to edit multi-line text.
Jlist	For displaying a list of items.

These graphic components are placed in containers, such as the following:

Component	Description
JPanel	The simplest container for holding other Panel objects or graphic components.
JFrame	A top-level window with a title bar. A Frame will usually contain one Panel.
JTabbedPane	Creates a multi-tabbed work area. When new JPanel objects are added to a JTabbedPane, you also specify either a text label or an icon that appears in the tab for the JPanel.
JscrollPane	Provides a scrolling viewing area to which other components can be added.

The JFC provides a far richer set of components than AWT. Still, I usually use AWT because programs using JFC tend to take longer to start running and are not quite as responsive. That said, JFC provides many cool features, such as editing styled text, displaying HTML, and so on. The examples in this chapter do not demonstrate drawing lines, shapes, or other graphics.

There are several available layout managers that are used to position graphic components inside a Panel. In the GUI examples in this book, we will not use any layout managers; we will use a setBounds method to specify the X-Y position of a graphic component and its width and height. This is a little unusual for Java programs, but I think that it will make the example programs easier to understand.

The example program in Listing 32.11 implements a JFCSample class. This class is derived from the JFC JFrame class, so when we create a new instance of the JFCSample, we will get an application window. The class constructor first calls the super class (JFrame) constructor by using the super keyword. Then three objects are created using the JPanel, JLabel, and JButton classes.

Listing 32.11 THE JFCsample.java FILE

```java
// File: JFCsample.java

import javax.swing.*;            // swing 1.1
//import com.sun.java.swing.*;   // swing 1.0
import java.awt.*;
import java.awt.event.*;

public class JFCsample extends JFrame {
    private int count = 0;
    JLabel countLabel;

    public JFCsample() {
        super("JFC Sample Program");

        JPanel panel1 = new JPanel();
        countLabel = new JLabel();
        JButton countButton = new JButton();
        panel1.setLayout(null);
        getContentPane().setLayout(null);  // different than AWT
        setBounds(50, 100, 230, 150);
        setVisible(true);
        panel1.setVisible(true);
        countLabel.setText("button clicked " + count + " times");
        countButton.setLabel("click me");
        countButton.addMouseListener(
          new java.awt.event.MouseAdapter() {
            public void mouseClicked(MouseEvent e) {
              countLabel.setText("button clicked " +
                                 ++count + " times");
            }
        });
        getContentPane().add(panel1, null); // add with
                                            // null constraints
        panel1.setBounds(0, 0, 180, 120);
        panel1.add(countLabel, null);       // add with
                                            // null constraints
        countLabel.setBounds(30, 35, 190, 20);
        panel1.add(countButton, null);      // add with
                                            // null constraints
```

```
        countButton.setBounds(40, 65, 100, 30);
    }

    static public void main(String [] args) {
        new JFCsample();
    }
}
```

We then use the `setLayout` method to set the layout manager for the frame object (remember, an instance of `JFCSample` class is also a frame) to `null`. For JFC, we need to use the method `getContentPane` to get the internal container before calling `setLayout`; this is different than the AWT example program in Listing 32.9.

Several useful methods are used in this example:

Method	Description
getContentPane	JFC containers have an internal content pane; this method gets this object, to which we add components.
setVisible	Sets a `Frame` and a `Panel` to be visible.
setSize	Sets the width and height of a component.
setLabel	Sets the label text for an instance of `Label`, `Button`, and so on.
setText	Sets the text of the `Label` object used to specify how many times the button is clicked.
setBounds	Sets the X an Y position and the width and height of a graphic component.
add	Adds the label and the button to the panel, and adds the panel to the frame.

Figure 32.3 shows the `JFCsample.java` program running.

FIGURE 32.3

The JFCsample
program demon-
strates event-
handling using
anonymous inner
classes with the
JFC API.

The only thing at all complicated about this example is handling the events associated with the user clicking on the button object. However, these events are handled with only a few lines of code in the same way that we handled events in the AWT example program in Listing 32.9:

```
countButton.addMouseListener(
  new java.awt.event.MouseAdapter() {
    public void mouseClicked(MouseEvent e) {
      countLabel.setText("button clicked " +
                         ++count + " times");
    }
});
```

The addMouseListener method is used to associate an instance of the MouseListener with a button (or any other component). Now, it is possible to define a separate class that implements the MouseListener listener interface (which requires defining five methods: mouseClicked, mouseEntered, mouseExited, mousePressed, and mouseReleased). However, there is a MouseAdapter utility class that defines "do nothing" versions of these five methods. In this code example, we are creating an anonymous inner class (for example, it is an inner class with no name associated with it) that overrides the mouseClicked. Our mouseClicked method uses the setText method to change the displayed text of a label. In Listing 32.13 we import all classes and interfaces from the packages java.awt (for the graphic components and containers) and java.awt.event (for the event-handling classes and interfaces), and from the package javax.swing to get the Swing (or JFC) classes.

In Listing 32.11, we define a static public main method that is executed when we compile and run this sample program by typing:

```
javac JFCSample.java
java JFCSample
```

The JFCSample program does not handle window closing events, so it must be terminated by typing Ctrl+C in the terminal window where you run the program.

Writing a Chat Program Using JFC

We will develop the ChatJFC program in this section. It is almost identical to the ChatAWT program, only it uses the JFC classes instead of the AWT classes. Both programs were shown in Figure 32.2.

The sample program in Listing 32.12 that implements a chat client using JFC is a little complex because the user interface has several components. Each component is positioned by an X-Y location in a panel and is sized to a specific width and height using the setBounds method. Before looking at the code in Listing 32.12, you should look at the bottom of Figure 32.2, which shows the ChatJFC program running. The ChatJFC program uses the ChatEngine class. The interface to ChatEngine is very simple and was covered in a previous section. The ChatJFC class implements the ChatListener interface and registers itself with an instance of ChatEngine. This registration allows the chat engine object to call the receiveText method (required to implement the ChatListener interface) in the ChatJFC class.

Listing 32.12   THE ChatJFC.java FILE

```java
// File: ChatJFC.java

import javax.swing.*;            // swing 1.1
//import com.sun.java.swing.*;   // swing 1.0
import java.awt.*;
import java.awt.event.*;

public class ChatJFC extends JFrame implements ChatListener{
    JPanel jPanel1 = new JPanel();
    JTextField myPortField = new JTextField();
    JLabel label1 = new JLabel();
    JLabel label2 = new JLabel();
    JTextField hostField = new JTextField();
    JLabel label3 = new JLabel();
    JTextField portField = new JTextField();
    JLabel label4 = new JLabel();
    JTextField inputField = new JTextField();
    JLabel label5 = new JLabel();
    JButton listenButton = new JButton();
    JButton connectButton = new JButton();
    JButton disconnectButton = new JButton();
    JButton quitButton = new JButton();
    JTextArea outputField = new JTextArea();
    JScrollPane jScrollPane1 = new JScrollPane();

    protected ChatEngine chatEngine;

    public ChatJFC() {
        super("Chat with JFC GUI");
        chatEngine = new ChatEngine();
        chatEngine.registerChatListener(this);
        this.setSize(575, 348);
        setVisible(true);
        jPanel1.setLayout(null);
        jPanel1.setBounds(5, 16, 595, 343);
        outputField.setRows(500);
        jScrollPane1.setBounds(66, 92, 498, 168);
        this.getContentPane().setLayout(null);
        quitButton.setBounds(448, 280, 121, 32);
```

continues

32

Listing 32.12   CONTINUED

```
quitButton.addMouseListener(
  new java.awt.event.MouseAdapter() {
    public void mouseClicked(MouseEvent e) {
        System.exit(0);
    }
});
quitButton.setLabel("Quit");
this.setSize(592, 371);
label1.setFont(new Font("Dialog", 1, 12));
label1.setBounds(1, 5, 69, 33);
label1.setText("My port");
myPortField.setBounds(62, 11, 100, 24);
myPortField.setText("8000");
label2.setFont(new Font("Dialog", 1, 12));
label2.setBounds(200, 3, 93, 38);
label2.setText("Remote host");
hostField.setBounds(299, 7, 129, 27);
hostField.setText("localhost");
label3.setFont(new Font("Dialog", 1, 12));
label3.setBounds(433, 5, 45, 36);
label3.setText("Port");
portField.setBounds(469, 9, 93, 27);
portField.setText("8192");
label4.setFont(new Font("Dialog", 1, 12));
label4.setBounds(4, 43, 60, 28);
label4.setText("Input");
inputField.setBounds(65, 47, 507, 34);
inputField.setText("  ");
inputField.addKeyListener(
  new java.awt.event.KeyAdapter() {
    public void keyPressed(KeyEvent e) {
        if (e.getKeyCode()  == '\n') {
            chatEngine.send(inputField.getText());
        }
    }
});
label5.setFont(new Font("Dialog", 1, 12));
label5.setBounds(0, 90, 58, 34);
label5.setText("Output");
listenButton.setBounds(5, 281, 163, 33);
listenButton.setLabel("Start listening");
listenButton.addMouseListener(
  new java.awt.event.MouseAdapter() {
    public void mouseClicked(MouseEvent e) {
        chatEngine.startListening(
          Integer.parseInt(myPortField.getText()));
    }
});
```

```
        connectButton.setBounds(175, 280, 136, 34);
        connectButton.addMouseListener(
          new java.awt.event.MouseAdapter() {
            public void mouseClicked(MouseEvent e) {
                chatEngine.connect(hostField.getText(),
                  Integer.parseInt(portField.getText()));
            }
        });
        connectButton.setLabel("Connect");
        disconnectButton.setBounds(315, 280, 127, 33);
        disconnectButton.addMouseListener(
          new java.awt.event.MouseAdapter() {
            public void mouseClicked(MouseEvent e) {
                chatEngine.connect(hostField.getText(),
                  Integer.parseInt(portField.getText()));
            }
        });
        disconnectButton.setLabel("Disconnect");
        this.getContentPane().add(jPanel1, null);
        jPanel1.add(label1, null);
        jPanel1.add(myPortField, null);
        jPanel1.add(label2, null);
        jPanel1.add(hostField, null);
        jPanel1.add(label3, null);
        jPanel1.add(portField, null);
        jPanel1.add(label4, null);
        jPanel1.add(inputField, null);
        jPanel1.add(label5, null);
        jPanel1.add(listenButton, null);
        jPanel1.add(connectButton, null);
        jPanel1.add(disconnectButton, null);
        jPanel1.add(quitButton, null);
        jPanel1.add(jScrollPane1, null);
        jScrollPane1.getViewport().add(outputField, null);
    }
    private String output_string = "";
    public void receiveText(String s) {
        if (s == null)  return;
        output_string = output_string + s;
        outputField.setText(output_string + "\n");
    }

    static public void main(String [] args) {
        new ChatJFC();
    }
}
```

The ChatJFC program is very similar to the ChatAWT program. I wrote the ChatJFC program by copying the ChatAWT program and doing the following:

- Adding the import swing (JFC) package statement.
- Changing Label to JLabel, Button to JButton, and so on.
- Using the getContentPane method where required to get the internal container for adding components and setting the layout manager to null.

Using Native Java Compilers

There are two native mode Java compilers under development, one by TowerJ (www.towerj.com) and the other by Cygnus (www.cygnus.com). At the time this chapter was written (March 1999), the Cygnus compiler was available only in early test releases, but it looked promising. The TowerJ compiler is a commercial product. I have used it for three programs, and I have seen performance improvements from a factor of four to a factor of 11 over using a JIT (Just In Time compiler). One of the benefits of Java is the portability of its byte code. However, for server-side programs, giving up portability in favor of large performance improvements is often a good option.

Summary

This short chapter has hopefully given you both a quick introduction to the Java language and the motivation to study the language further. There are many sources of information for programming Java on the Internet. Because Web site links change, I will keep current links to my favorite Java resources on the Internet at my Web site (www.markwatson.com/books/linux_prog.html).

Many interesting topics were not covered in this short chapter, such as:

- Drawing graphics
- Writing applets that run inside of Web browsers
- More techniques for handling user interface events

If you are primarily a C or C++ programmer, I urge you to also learn Java. I have been using C for 15 years and C++ for 10 years, but I prefer Java for most of my development work. Yes, it is true that Java programs will run slower than the equivalent C or C++ programs. However, after using Java for about 3 years, I believe that Java enables me to write a large application in about half the time it takes to write the same application in C++. I have talked with other developers who agree that they are approximately twice as productive when programming in Java instead of C or C++.

OpenGL/Mesa Graphics Programming

by Mark Watson

IN THIS CHAPTER

The OpenGL API was developed at Silicon Graphics and has become an industry standard for high-quality 3D graphics. Although there are commercial ports of OpenGL to Linux, a high-quality public domain OpenGL-like implementation called Mesa has been written by Brian Paul. Mesa can not be called OpenGL because it is not licensed from Silicon Graphics, but I have found it to be an effective tool for OpenGL programming on Linux. Mesa might be included with your Linux distribution. Although I assume that you have installed and are using Mesa, I will refer to OpenGL in this chapter. I will keep a current link to the Mesa distribution on my web site.

The OpenGL API is complex. We will use one simple example in this chapter to illustrate how to use the OpenGL auxiliary library to draw simple shapes, placing and rotating the shapes under program control. We will also learn how to use lighting effects and how to change the viewpoint. For most 3D graphics applications (like games), you need a separate modeling program to create 3D shapes, and you also need specialized code to use these shapes in OpenGL programs. The topics of modeling 3D images and using them in OpenGL programs is beyond the scope of this introductory chapter.

Before reading this chapter, please download the latest Mesa distribution and install it in your home directory. The sample program for this chapter is located in the src/OpenGL directory on the CD-ROM. You will have to edit the first line of Makefile to reflect the path in your home directory where you have installed Mesa. The example program uses the OpenGL Utilities Library (GLUT). OpenGL itself is operating system- and device-independent. The GLUT library allows programmers to initialize OpenGL, create windows, and so on in a portable way. There are three example directories in the Mesa installation directory: book, demos, and samples. Please make sure that building Mesa also built executables for the many sample programs in these three directories. Then edit the first line of Makefile for the example program for this chapter and try running it to make sure that Mesa is set up properly on your computer. A few of the example programs in the Mesa distribution may not run with your graphics card; do not worry about this.

OpenGL is a Software Interface to Graphics Hardware

There are OpenGL software interface implementations for most 3D graphics cards, so OpenGL and Mesa will probably run efficiently on your computer unless you have a very old graphics card. Microsoft supports OpenGL on Windows 95, 98, and NT, so the programs that you develop under Linux using Mesa will probably run with few modifications under Windows. I worked at a computer animation company, Angel Studios (www.angel.com), where we used proprietary software for rendering real-time 3D graphics on a wide variety of hardware, including Nintendo Ultra-64, Windows, and SGI workstations. This proprietary software, as an option, used OpenGL to talk with graphics hardware.

The Orbits Sample Program

There are many features of OpenGL that we are not covering in the orbits example program for this chapter (for example, the use of display lists and texture mapping). The sample program in this section does illustrate several OpenGL programming techniques, but it is also simple enough for a tutorial example. The example program orbits.c is located in the src/OpenGL directory.

The sample program uses the GLUT function glutSolidSphere to draw both a large "planet" and a small orbiting satellite. This example demonstrates the following:

- Creating a window for OpenGL graphics and initializing OpenGL
- Creating simple 3D objects using GLUT
- Placing objects anywhere in a three-dimensional space using X-Y-Z coordinates
- Rotating an object about any or all of the x-, y-, and z-axes.
- Enabling the use of material properties so objects can be colored
- Enabling depth tests so that rendered objects close to the viewer correctly cover objects that are obscured
- Handling keyboard events
- Updating OpenGL graphics for animation effects

These operations are performed using both the OpenGL core API and the OpenGL utility library. All OpenGL implementations include the OpenGL utility library, so the simple example in this chapter should be easily portable to other operating systems and OpenGL implementations.

OpenGL uses a modeling coordinate system where the X coordinate moves increasingly toward the right on the screen, the Y coordinate moves increasingly upward, and the z coordinate increases looking into the screen. The origin (for example, at X=Y=Z=0) is located at the center of the screen.

The sample program cycles viewing angle, plus smooth or flat shading, when you hit any key (except for an escape, or q characters, that halt the program) while the program is running.

Figure 33.1 shows the `orbits` sample program running in the default smooth-shaded mode. The background color was changed to white for this figure; the program on the CD-ROM has a black background.

FIGURE 33.1
The orbits *program running with smooth-shading.*

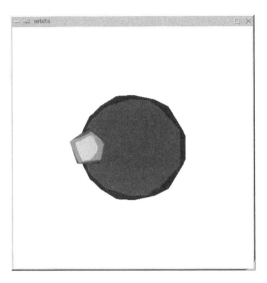

Creating a Window for OpenGL Graphics and Initializing OpenGL

In this chapter, we will use the following OpenGL utility library functions to initialize OpenGL, the GLUT library, and to create a window for drawing:

Function	Description
glutInit	Initializes GLUT and OpenGL.
glutInitDisplayMode	Sets display properties (our example program will set properties allowing for double buffering, depth queuing, and use of RGB colors).
glutInitWindowSize	Sets the size of the main window.
glutInitWindowPosition	Positions the main window on the desktop or X Windows display.
glutCreateWindow	Actually creates the main window.

The initialization code in the sample program looks like the following:

```
glutInit(&argc, argv);
glutInitDisplayMode(GLUT_DOUBLE | GLUT_RGB | GLUT_DEPTH);
glutInitWindowSize(500, 500);
glutInitWindowPosition(100, 100);
glutCreateWindow(argv[0]);
```

In calling `glutInitDisplay`, we use the following constants:

Constant	Description
GLUT_DOUBLE	Enables double buffering for smooth animation.
GLUT_RGB	Specifies the use of RGB color table.
GLUT_DEPTH	Enables the use of a depth buffer to determine when one object is obscuring another in a scene.

Creating Simple 3D Objects Using GLUT

There are several GLUT utility functions for creating both wire frame and solid objects. To create a sphere, use either of the following:

```
void glutSolidSphere(GLdouble radius, GLint slices,
                     GLint stacks);
void glutWireSphere(GLdouble radius, GLint slices, GLint stacks);
```

Here, `radius` is the radius of the sphere. The `slices` argument is the number of flat bands created around the z-axis. The higher the number of slices, the rounder the sphere. The `stacks` argument is the number of flat bands along the z-axis. The higher the `slices` value, the rounder the sphere. Lower `slices` and `stacks` values produce shapes that are drawn quicker. A sphere is drawn (or rendered) centered at the origin in modeling coordinates (for example, when the OpenGL Matrix mode is in modeling mode; more on this later).

To create a cube, use either of the following:

```
void glutSolidCube(GLdouble size);
void glutWireCube(GLdouble size);
```

The `size` argument is the length of any edge of the cube.

To draw a cone, use either of the following:

```
void glutSolidCone(GLdouble base, GLdouble height,
                   GLint slices, GLint stacks);
void glutWireCone(GLdouble base, GLdouble height,
                  GLint slices, GLint stacks);
```

The base argument is the radius of the cone's base. The height argument is the height of the cone. The slices argument is the number of flat bands drawn around the z-axis. The stacks argument is the number of flat bands drawn about the z-axis. The center of the base of the cone is placed at X=Y=Z=0 in the modeling coordinate system. The cone "points" along the z-axis.

If you want to draw a torus, use either of the following GLUT functions:

```
void glutSolidTorus(GLdouble inner_radius,
                    GLdouble outer_radius,
                    GLint nsides, GLint rings);
void glutWireTorus(GLdouble inner_radius,
                   GLdouble outer_radius,
                   GLint nsides, GLint rings);
```

The inner_radius and outer_radius arguments are the inner and outer radii of the torus. The nsides argument is the number of flat bands drawn for each radial section. The rings argument is the number of radial bands.

Placing Objects in 3D Space Using X-Y-Z Coordinates

Before placing objects in a 3D world, we need to make sure that OpenGL is in the model mode. This is accomplished by calling:

```
glMatrixMode(GL_MODELVIEW);
```

We can translate the origin of the model world to coordinates X, Y, and Z by calling:

```
glTranslatef(GLfloat X, GLfloat Y, GLfloat Z);
```

One problem that we have is remembering where we have moved the origin. Fortunately, there are OpenGL utility functions that push the entire state of OpenGL onto a stack, which pulls the state of OpenGL off a stack. These functions are:

```
glPushMatrix();
glPopMatrix();
```

In practice, we usually push the "matrix" (for example, the state of the OpenGL engine), perform drawing operations on one or more objects, then pop the "matrix" back off the stack. The following example shows how to draw a sphere of radius equal to 1.0 at X=10, Y=0.0, and Z=1.0:

```
glPushMatrix();
{
    glColor4f(1.0, 0.0, 0.0, 1.0); // make the sphere red
    glTranslatef(10.0, 0.0, 1.0);  // translate the model
                                   // coordinate system
    glutSolidSphere(1.0, 40, 40);  // Draw a very detailed sphere
} glPopMatrix();
```

As a matter of programming style, I enclose within curly braces any operations between the "push" and the "pop"; this improves the readability of the code. In this example, we also see a call to glColor4f that is used to specify the red, green, and blue drawing colors (values are between 0.0 and 1.0). The fourth argument of glColor4f is the alpha value; an alpha value of 0.0 makes a transparent object—not too useful—and a value of 1.0 makes an entirely opaque object. In the sample program, try changing the alpha value in the calls in display to a value of 0.5 so that you can see through the rendered objects.

Rotating an Object About Any or All of the X-, Y-, and Z- Axes

Rotating objects created with the GLUT utilities for drawing simple shapes is a little more complicated than changing an object's X-Y-Z location. In the example program in display, we draw a central planet that is centered at X=Y=Z=0 and a small satellite that orbits around the central planet. We will start by looking at the code for rotating the central planet about the origin (for example., X=Y=Z=0) of the model coordinate system:

```
// push matrix, draw central planet, then pop matrix:
glPushMatrix();
{
  glRotatef((GLfloat)planet_rotation_period, 0.0, 1.0, 0.0);
  glColor4f(1.0, 0.0, 0.0, 1.0);
  glutSolidSphere(1.0, 10, 8);   // Draw the central planet
} glPopMatrix();
```

Here, we use a planet_rotation variable that is incremented each time the OpenGL scene is drawn. This value ranges between 0.0 and 360.0 because the arguments to glRotatef are in degrees, not radians. The last three arguments of glRotatef specify the rotation axis. The arguments (0.0, 1.0, 0.0) specify that the angle of rotation is about the positive y-axis. By slowly varying the value of planet_rotation_period between 0.0 and 360.0, the central planet slowly rotates.

The placement and rotation of the satellite is more complex because we want to both translate its position and to rotate it. To do this, the code from the example program's display function is as follows:

```
// push matrix, draw satellite, then pop matrix:
  glPushMatrix();
  {
    glRotatef((GLfloat)central_orbit_period, 0.0, 1.0, 0.0);
    glTranslatef(1.9, 0.0, 0.0);
    glRotatef((GLfloat)-satellite_rotation_period,
            0.0, 1.0, 0.0);
    glColor4f(0.0, 1.0, 0.0, 1.0);
    glutSolidSphere(0.2, 5, 4);    // Draw the orbiting satellite
  } glPopMatrix();
```

Initially, we call `glRotatef` to rotate the satellite about the origin—just as we did for the central planet. It is important to realize that the satellite is centered at the origin until we move it. After rotating the coordinate system, we call `glTranslate` to move it to modeling coordinates (1.9, 0.0, 0.0), and finally rotate the coordinate system once again to simulate the satellite's orbit around the planet.

Figure 33.2 shows the `orbits` sample program running in the flat-shaded mode. The background color was changed to white for this screen shot; the program on the CD-ROM has a black background.

FIGURE 33.2
The orbits *program running with flat shading.*

Enabling the Use of `Material` Properties

The example program's `init` function sets up the `OpenGL` environment. The following function call configures the `OpenGL` engine to allow us to later use drawing colors:

```
glEnable(GL_COLOR_MATERIAL);
```

By default, objects are flat-shaded; `init` also configures the `OpenGL` engine to use smooth-shading. When you press the Spacebar, the example program switches between smooth- and flat-shading (and also cycles through one of three viewing positions). The following function call requests a smooth shading drawing model:

```
glShadeModel(GL_SMOOTH);
```

We can also use `glClearColor` to change the default background color for the window. The first three arguments are the red, green, and blue color values for the background;

the last argument specifies the alpha (or transparency) of the background. Here, to make the background almost black, we use low values for the red, green, and blue background-color components. Setting the background alpha to zero makes it totally transparent.

```
glClearColor(0.1, 0.1, 0.1, 0.0);
```

In Figure 33.1 and Figure 33.2, we set the background to white by passing the value 1.0 for the first three arguments of glClearColor. The example orbits.c on the CD-ROM sets a black background, however.

Enabling Depth Tests

The example program's init function sets up the OpenGL environment to use a depth test to hide obscured objects from view. The following function call configures the OpenGL engine to allow us to later use this depth-cueing:

```
glCullFace(GL_BACK);
glEnable(GL_DEPTH_TEST);
```

In addition to making these two calls, we need to add the GLUT_DEPTH option when setting up the GLUT display mode in the main function:

```
glutInitDisplayMode(GLUT_DOUBLE | GLUT_RGB | GLUT_DEPTH);
```

Handling Keyboard Events

It is useful to be able to handle keyboard input in OpenGL graphics programs. Using the GLUT library, this is easily done using a Callback function that is called with the key value whenever any key on the keyboard is pressed. The sample program uses the following Callback function:

```
void key_press_callback(unsigned char key, int x, int y)
```

We will use the first argument key and ignore the last two arguments in the example program. We register this Callback function in the main function by calling:

```
glutKeyboardFunc(key_press_callback);
```

Updating OpenGL Graphics for Animation Effects

In the example program, we use a display Callback function that is called by the GLUT library whenever the window needs to be redrawn. The function signature for display is:

```
void display(void)
```

33

OpenGL/Mesa GRAPHICS PROGRAMMING

We register this Callback function in `main` by calling:

```
glutDisplayFunc(display);
```

The last thing that `display` does before returning is to request an immediate redraw event by calling:

```
glutPostRedisplay();
```

This effectively causes the OpenGL engine and the GLUT event-handler to update the animation continually.

Sample Program Listing

We have seen pieces of most of the example program in the last few sections. In this section, we will list out the entire file with a few additional comments. This example, as seen in Listing 33.1, uses a single `include` file `glut.h` for using both OpenGL/Mesa and the OpenGL utility functions.

Listing 33.1 THE `orbits.c` FILE

```
#include <GL/glut.h>

void init(void)
{
   glClearColor(0.1, 0.1, 0.1, 0.0);
   glEnable(GL_COLOR_MATERIAL);
   glShadeModel(GL_SMOOTH);

   glEnable(GL_LIGHTING);
   glEnable(GL_LIGHT0);
   glEnable(GL_CULL_FACE);
   glCullFace(GL_BACK);
   glEnable(GL_DEPTH_TEST);
}

void display(void) {

   static int central_orbit_period = 0;
   static int planet_rotation_period = 0;
   static int satellite_rotation_period = 0;

   glClear(GL_COLOR_BUFFER_BIT | GL_DEPTH_BUFFER_BIT);

   // push matrix, draw central planet, then pop matrix:
   glPushMatrix();
   {
     glRotatef((GLfloat)planet_rotation_period, 0.0, 1.0, 0.0);
     glColor4f(1.0, 0.0, 0.0, 1.0);
```

```
      glutSolidSphere(1.0, 10, 8);    // Draw the central planet
   } glPopMatrix();

   // push matrix, draw satellite, then pop matrix:
   glPushMatrix();
   {
     glRotatef((GLfloat)central_orbit_period, 0.0, 1.0, 0.0);
     glTranslatef(1.9, 0.0, 0.0);
     glRotatef((GLfloat)-satellite_rotation_period,
               0.0, 1.0, 0.0);
     glColor4f(0.0, 1.0, 0.0, 1.0);
     glutSolidSphere(0.2, 5, 4);      // Draw the orbiting satellite
   } glPopMatrix();

   glutSwapBuffers();
   central_orbit_period = (central_orbit_period + 2) % 360;
   planet_rotation_period = (planet_rotation_period + 1) % 360;
   satellite_rotation_period =
         (satellite_rotation_period + 6) % 360;
   glutPostRedisplay();
}

void reshape(int w, int h) {
   glViewport(0, 0, w, h);
   glMatrixMode(GL_PROJECTION);
   glLoadIdentity();
   gluPerspective(60.0, (GLfloat)w/(GLfloat)h, 1.0, 20.0);
   glMatrixMode(GL_MODELVIEW);
   glLoadIdentity();
   gluLookAt(0.0, 0.0, 4.0, 0.0, 0.0, 0.0, 0.0, 1.0, 0.0);
}

void cycle_view() {
   static int count = 0;
   static int shade_flag = 0;
   if (++count > 2) {
     count = 0;
     shade_flag = 1 - shade_flag;
   }
   glLoadIdentity();
   switch (count)
     {
     case 0:
       gluLookAt(0.0, 0.0, 4.0, 0.0, 0.0, 0.0, 0.0, 1.0, 0.0);
       break;
     case 1:
       gluLookAt(0.0, 5.0, 0.0, 0.0, 0.0, 0.0, 0.0, 0.0, 1.0);
       break;
```

33

OPENGL/MESA
GRAPHICS
PROGRAMMING

continues

Listing 33.1 CONTINUED

```
    case 2:
      gluLookAt(0.0, 0.5, -3.3, 1.0, 0.0, 0.0, -0.7, 0.2, 0.4);
      break;
    }
  if (shade_flag == 0) glShadeModel(GL_SMOOTH);
  else                 glShadeModel(GL_FLAT);

}

void key_press_callback(unsigned char key, int x, int y) {
  switch (key)
    {
    case 27: /* escape character */
    case 'q':
    case 'Q':
      exit(1);
    default:
      cycle_view();
      break;
    }
}

int main(int argc, char *argv[]) {
    glutInit(&argc, argv);
    glutInitDisplayMode(GLUT_DOUBLE | GLUT_RGB | GLUT_DEPTH);
    glutInitWindowSize(500, 500);
    glutInitWindowPosition(100, 100);
    glutCreateWindow(argv[0]);
    init();
    glutKeyboardFunc(key_press_callback);
    glutDisplayFunc(display);
    glutReshapeFunc(reshape);
    glutMainLoop();
    return 0;
}
```

This simple sample program demonstrates how to animate simple geometric objects.
This program can be used as a foundation for writing simple 3D games that use only the
"canned" 3D shapes (such as spheres, cubes, cones, and so on), which are defined in the
OpenGL utility library. More information about OpenGL is available at

http://www.opengl.org/

More information on Mesa can be found at:

http://www.opengl.org/Documentation/Implementations/Mesa.html

Special Programming Techniques

PART
V

IN THIS PART

CHAPTER 34

Shell Programming with GNU bash

by Kurt Wall

IN THIS CHAPTER

Within the first two days of becoming a Linux user in 1993, I wrote my first bash script, a very kludgy effort to automate my backups. This anecdote illustrates how pervasive shell scripting is in Linux. In this chapter, I will give you a firm foundation in the basics of bash shell programming.

Why bash?

GNU's bash (Bourne Again Shell, named in punning homage to the Bourne shell and its author, Steven Bourne) is Linux's default shell. Written by Brian Fox and maintained by Chet Ramey, bash's most popular features are its rich command-line editing facilities and its job control abilities. From the programmer's perspective, bash's chief advantages are its customizability and the complete programming environment it provides, including function definitions, integer math, and a surprisingly complete I/O interface. As you might expect of a Linux utility, bash contains elements of all of the popular shells, Bourne, Korn, and C shell, as well as a few innovations of its own. As of this writing, the current release of bash is 2.0.3. Most Linux distributions, however, use the tried and test-ed 1.14 version. Nevertheless, I will cover bash version 2, pointing out features not available in earlier versions as they arise, because version 2 is much closer to POSIX compliance than version 1.

bash Basics

Throughout this chapter, I assume that you are comfortable using bash, so my discussion focuses on bash's features from the shell programmer's perspective. By way of review, however, I will refresh your memory of bash's wildcard operators and its special characters.

Wilcards

bash's wildcard operators are *, ?, and the set operators, [SET] and [!SET]. * matches any string of characters and ? matches any single character. Suppose you have a directory containing the following files:

```
$ ls
zeisstopnm  zic2xpm   zipgrep    zipsplit   znew
zcmp        zforce    zip        zipinfo    zless
zdiff       zgrep     zipcloak   zipnote    zmore
```

The command ls zi* matches zic2xpm, zip, zipcloak, zipgrep,zipinfo, and zipsplit, but ls zi? only matches zip.

The set operators allow you to use either a range or a disjoint set of characters as wild-cards. To specify an inclusive range of characters, use a hyphen between characters. For example, the set [a-o] includes all of the lowercase characters "a" through "o." Use a comma to indicate a disjoint set, such as the range of characters between "a" and "h" and between "w" and "z". In bash's set notation, this range of characters could be specified with "[a-h,w-z]". If you want to look only for a few individual characters, such as all of the English vowels, the notation "[aeiou]" would do. The "!" prefixing a set means to include everything *not* in the set. So, an easy way to look for all of the consonants is to write [!aeiou].

The following examples illustrate using the set notation and also how you can use the wildcard operators with sets. To list all of the files in the directory above whose second letter is a vowel, you could write:

```
$ ls z[aeiou]*
```

This will match zeisstopnm, zip zipgrep, zipnote, zic2xpm,zipcloak, zipinfo, and zipsplit. On the other hand, to list the files that have only consonants as their second letter, use lsz[!aeiou]*, which matches zcmp, zdiff, zforce, zgrep, zless, zmore, and znew. The command, ls *[0-9]* matches only those filenames containing at least one numeric digit between zero and nine, which is zic2xpm in this case.

Brace Expansion

Brace expansion is a more general case of the filename globbing enabled by wildcard characters. The basic format of an expression using brace expansion follows:

```
[preamble]{str1[,str2[,...]]}[postscript]
```

Each string inside the braces will be matched with the optional preamble and postscript. For example, the following statement

```
$ echo c{ar,at,an,on}s
```

results in

```
cars cats cans cons
```

Because brace expressions can be nested, the preceding statement could be rewritten as follows to obtain the same output:

```
$ echo c{a{r,t,n},on}s
```

Special Characters

The wildcard and set operators are four examples of bash's special characters—characters that have a specific meaning to bash. Table 34.1 lists all of the special characters, with a brief description of each one.

Table 34.1   bash SPECIAL CHARACTERS

Character	Description
<	Redirect input
>	Redirect output
(	Start subshell
)	End subshell
|	Pipe
\	Quote (escape) the next character
&	Execute command in background
{	Start command block
}	End command block
.-	Home directory
`	Command substitution
;	Command separator
#	Comment
'	Strong quote
"	Weak quote
$	Variable expression
*	String wildcard
?	Single character wildcard

Input and output redirection should be familiar to you. Although I will discuss subshells later in this chapter, it is important to note that all the commands between (and) are executed in a subshell. Subshells inherit some of the environment variables, but not all of them. This behavior is different from commands in a block (blocks are delimited by { and }), which are executed in the current shell and thus retain all of the current environment.

The command separator, ;, allows you to execute multiple bash commands on a single line. But more importantly, it is the POSIX-specified command terminator.

The comment character, #, causes bash to ignore everything from the character to the end of the line. The difference between the strong quote and weak quote characters, ' and ", respectively, is that the strong quote forces bash to interpret all special characters literally; the weak quote only protects some of bash's special characters from interpretation as special characters.

Using bash Variables

As you might expect, bash, has variables. Usually they are character strings, but bash also has special facilities for dealing with numeric (integer) values, too. To assign a value to a variable, use the following syntax:

```
varname=value
```

To obtain a variable's value, you can use one of the following two formats:

```
$varname
${varname}
```

The second form, ${varname}, is the more general format and also more difficult to type. However, you must use it to distinguish variables from trailing letters, digits, or underscores. For example, suppose you have a variable named MYNAME and you want to display its value followed by an underscore character. You might be tempted to try the following command:

```
$ echo $MYNAME_
```

but this attempt will fail because bash will attempt to print the value of the variable MYNAME_, not MYNAME. In this situation, you must use the second syntax, as illustrated below:

```
$ echo ${MYNAME}_
```

Listing 34.1 illustrates this subtlety.

Listing 34.1 VARIABLE SYNTAX

```
1  #!/bin/bash
2  # Listing 34.1
3  # varref.sh - Variable syntax
4  #############################
5
6  MYNAME="Kurt Wall"
7  echo '${MYNAME}_ yields: ' ${MYNAME}_
8  echo '$MYNAME_ yields: ' $MYNAME_
```

The strong quotes on lines 7 and 8 prevent bash from expanding the variables. As you can see in the script's output below, $MYNAME_ is empty and prints nothing, but ${MYNAME}_ produces the expected output.

```
$ ./varref.sh
${MYNAME}_ yields:  Kurt Wall_
$MYNAME_ yields:
```

In addition to user-defined variables, bash comes with numerous built-in or predefined variables. Many of these are environment variables, such as $BASH_VERSION or $DIRSTACK. Another subset of predefined variables are the positional parameters that contain the command-line arguments, if any, passed to the script (shell functions, covered later, also accept arguments). The parameter "$0" contains the name of the script; the actual parameters begin at "$1" (if there are more than nine, you must use the ${} syntax—for example, "${10}" to obtain their values). The positional parameters passed to each script or function are local and read-only to those functions. However, other variables declined in a function are global by default, unless you declare them otherwise with the local keyword.

bash also has three special positional parameters, "$#", "$@",and "$#". "$#" evaluates to the number of positional parameters passed to a script or a function (not counting "$0"). "$*" is a list of all the positional parameters, except "$0", formatted as a single string with each parameter separated by the first character the $IFS, the internal field separator (another bash environment variable). "$@", on the other hand, is all of the positional parameters presented as N separate double-quoted strings.

What is the difference between "$*" and "$@"? And why the distinction? The difference allows you to treat command-line arguments in two ways. The first format, "$*", because it is a single string, can be displayed more flexibly without requiring a lot of shell code to do so. "$@", on the other hand, allows you to process each argument individually because its value is N separate arguments. Listing 34.2 illustrates the differences between "$#" and "$@".

Listing 34.2 POSITIONAL PARAMETERS

```
1   #!/bin/bash
2   # Listing 34.2
3   # posparm.sh - Using positional parameters
4   ######################################
5
6   function cntparm
7   {
8       echo -e "inside cntparm $# parms: $*\n"
9   }
```

```
10
11   cntparm "$*"
12   cntparm "$@"
13
14   echo -e "outside cntparm $*\n"
15   echo -e "outside cntparm $#\n"
```

This script's output is as follows:

```
1   $ ./posparm.sh Kurt Roland Wall
2   inside cntparm 1 parms: Kurt Roland Wall
3
4   inside cntparm 3 parms: Kurt Roland Wall
5
6   outside cntparm Kurt Roland Wall
7
8   outside cntparm Kurt Roland Wall
```

Lines 11 and 12 in particular illustrate the practical difference between the positional parameters, $* and $@. For the time being, treat the function definition and calls as a black box. Line 11, using "$*", passes the positional parameters as a single string, so that cntparm reports a single parameter, as show on line 2 of the output list. The second call to cntparm, however, passes the script's command-line arguments as 3 separate strings, so the cntparm reports three parameters (line 4). There is no functional difference in the appearance of the parameters when printed, however, as lines 6 and 8 of the output make clear.

The -e option to the echo command forces it to print the \n sequence as a new line (lines 8, 14, and 15). If you do not use the -e option, do not force a new line with \n because echo automatically adds one to its output.

Using bash Operators

I introduce many of bash's operators in the course of discussing other subjects. In this section, however, I acquaint you with bash's string- and pattern-matching operators. Later sections will use these operators frequently, so covering them now will make the other sections proceed smoothly.

String Operators

The string operators, also called substitution operators in bash documentation, test whether a variable is unset or null. Table 34.2 lists these operators with a brief description of each operator's function.

Table 34.2   bash STRING OPERATORS

Operator	*Function*
`${var:-word}`	If var exists and is not null, returns its value, else returns word.
`${var:=word}`	If var exists and is not null, returns its value, else sets var to word, then returns its value.
`${var:+word}`	If var exists and is not null, returns word, else returns null.
`${var:?message}`	If var exists and is not null, returns its value, else displays "bash: $var:$message" and aborts the current command or script.
`${var:offset[:length]}`	Returns a substring of var beginning at offset of length length. If length is omitted, the entire string from offset will be returned.

To illustrate, consider a shell variable status initialized to defined. Using the first four string operators from Table 34.2 on status results in the following:

```
$ echo ${status:-undefined}
defined
$ echo ${status:=undefined}
defined
$ echo ${status:+undefined}
undefined
$ echo ${status:?Dohhh\! undefined}
defined
```

Now, using the unset command to delete status's definition from the environment, and executing the same commands, the output is as follows:

```
$ unset status
$ echo ${status:-undefined}
undefined
$ echo ${status:=undefined}
undefined
$ echo ${status:+undefined}
undefined
$ unset status
$ echo ${status:?Dohhh\! undefined}
bash: status: Dohhh! undefined
```

It was necessary to unset status a second time because the third command, echo `${status:+undefined}`, reset status to undefined upon executing.

The substring operators listed at the bottom of Table 34.2 are especially useful for, well, obtaining substrings. Consider a variable foo with the value Bilbo_the_Hobbit. The expression ${foo:7} returns he_Hobbit, while ${foo:7:5} returns he_Ho. These two operators are best used when working with data that is in a known, and fixed, format (such as the output of the ls command). Be aware, though, that ls's output format varies widely among the various UNIX-like operating systems, so this sort of shell code would not be portable.

Pattern-Matching Operators

Pattern-matching operators are most useful for working with freely formatted strings or variable-length records delimited by fixed characters. The $PATH environment variable is an example. Although it can be quite long, the individual directories are colon-delimited. Table 34.3 lists bash's pattern-matching operators and their function.

Table 34.2 bash PATTERN-MATCHING OPERATORS

Operator	Function
${var#pattern}	Deletes the shortest match of pattern from the front of var and returns the rest.
${var##pattern}	Deletes the longest match of pattern from the front of var and returns the rest.
${var%pattern}	Deletes the shortest match of pattern from the end of var and returns the rest.
${var%%pattern}	Deletes the longest match of pattern from the end of var and returns the rest.
${var/pattern/string}	Replaces the longest match of pattern in var with string. Replaces only the first match. This operator is only available in bash 2.0 or greater.
${var//pattern/string}	Replaces the longest match of pattern in var with string. Replaces all matches. This operator is only available in bash 2.0 or greater.

The canonical usage of bash's pattern-matching operators is manipulating file and path names. For example, suppose you have a shell variable named myfile that has the value /usr/src/linux/Documentation/ide.txt (which is the documentation for the kernel's IDE disk driver). Using "/*" and "*/" as the pattern, you can emulate the behavior of the dirname and basename commands, as the output from Listing 34.3 illustrates.

34

SHELL PROGRAMMING WITH GNU bash

> **NOTE**
>
> The `dirname` command strips the non-directory suffix from a filename passed to it as an argument and prints the result to standard output. Conversely, `basename` strips directory prefixes from a filename. Part of the GNU shell utilities, `dirname` and `basename` have pathetic man pages, so if you want more information, you will have to read the info pages. To quote their manual pages, "[t]he Texinfo documentation is now the authoritative source."

Listing 34.3 PATTERN-MATCHING OPERATORS

```
1   #!/bin/bash
2   # Listing 34.3
3   # pattern.sh - Demonstrate pattern matching operators
4   ####################################################
5
6   myfile=/usr/src/linux/Documentation/ide.txt
7
8   echo '${myfile##*/}=' ${myfile##*/}
9   echo 'basename $myfile =' $(basename $myfile)
10
11  echo '${myfile%/*}=' ${myfile%/*}
12  echo 'dirname $myfile =' $(dirname $myfile)
```

Line 8 deletes the longest string matching `"*/"` in the filename, starting from the beginning of the variable, which deletes everything through the final `"/"`, returning just the filename. Line 11 matches anything after `"/"`, starting from the end of the variable, which strips off just the filename and returns the path to the file. The output of this script is:

```
$ ./pattern.sh
${myfile##*/}    = ide.txt
basename $myfile = ide.txt
${myfile%/*}     = /usr/src/linux/Documentation
dirname $myfile = /usr/src/linux/Documentation
```

To illustrate the pattern-matching and replacement operators, the following command replaces each colon in the $PATH environment variable with a new line, resulting in a very easy to read path display (this example will fail if you do not have `bash` 2.0 or newer):

```
$ echo -e ${PATH//:/\\n}
/usr/local/bin
/bin
/usr/bin
/usr/X11R6/bin
```

```
/home/kwall/bin
/home/wall/wp/wpbin
```

Of course, your path statement will look somewhat different. The `-e` argument to `echo` tells it to interpret the `\n` as a new line rather than a literal string. Perversely, however, you have to escape the escape (`\\n`) to get the new lines into the variable in order for `echo` to interpret them.

Flow Control

The few shell scripts presented so far have been fall-through scripts, lacking any control structures such as loops and conditionals. Any programming language worth the name must have facilities for repeating certain code blocks multiple times and for conditionally executing, or not executing, other code blocks. In this section, you will meet all of `bash`'s flow-control structures, which include the following:

- `if`—Executes one or more statements if a condition is true or false.
- `for`—Executes one or more statements a fixed number of times.
- `while`—Executes one or more statements while a condition is true or false.
- `until`—Executes one or more statements until a condition becomes true or false.
- `case`—Executes one or more statements depending on the value of a variable.
- `select`—Executes one or more statements based upon an option selected by a user.

Conditional Execution: `if`

`bash` supports conditional execution of code using the `if` statement, although its evaluation of the condition is slightly different from the behavior of the `if` statement of languages like C or Pascal. This peculiarity aside, `bash`'s `if` statement is just as fully featured as C's. Its syntax is summarized below.

```
if condition
then
 statements
[elif condition
 statements]
[else
 statements]
fi
```

First, be sure you understand that `if` checks the exit status of the *last* statement in `condition`. If it is 0 (true), then `statements` will be executed, but if it is non-zero, the else clause, if present, will be executed and control jumps to the first line of code following `fi`. The (optional) `elif` clause(s) (you can have as many as you like) will be executed only if the `if` condition is false. Similarly, the (optional) `else` clause will be executed only if all *else* fails. Generally, Linux programs return 0 on successful or normal completion, and non-zero otherwise, so this limitation is not burdensome.

> **WARNING**
>
> Not all programs follow the same standards for return values, so check the documentation for the programs whose exit codes you test in an `if` condition. The `diff` program, for example, returns 0 if no differences were found, 1 if differences were found, and 2 if there were problems. If a conditional statement fails to behave as expected, check the documented exit code.

Regardless of the way programs define their exit codes, bash takes 0 to mean true or normal and non-zero otherwise. If you need specifically to check or save a command's exit code, use the $? operator immediately after running a command. $? returns the exit code of the command most recently run.

The matter becomes more complex because bash allows you to combine exit codes in `condition` using the && and || operators, which approximately translate to logical AND and logical OR. Suppose that before you enter a code block, you have to change into a directory and copy a file. One way to accomplish this is to use nested `if`s, such as in the following code:

```
if cd /home/kwall/data
then
    if cp datafile datafile.bak
    then
        # more code here
    fi
fi
```

bash, however, allows you to write this much more concisely, as the following code snippet illustrates:

```
if cd /home/kwall/data && cp datafile datafile.bak
then
 # more code here
fi
```

Both code snippets say the same thing, but the second one is much shorter and, in my opinion, much clearer and easier to follow. If, for some reason, the cd command fails, bash will not attempt the copy operation.

Although if only evaluates exit codes, you can use the [...] construct or the bash built-in command, test, to evaluate more complex conditions. [condition] returns a code that indicates whether condition is true or false. test does the same thing, but I find it more difficult to read.

The range of available conditions that bash automatically provides—currently 35—is rich and complete. You can test a wide variety of file attributes and compare strings and integers.

> **NOTE**
>
> The spaces after the opening bracket and before the closing bracket in
> [condition] are required. It is an annoying requirement of bash's shell
> syntax. As a result of this, some people continue to use test. My suggestion is
> to learn to use [condition] because your shell code will be more readable.

Table 34.4 lists the most common file test operators (the complete list can be obtained from bashs excellent manual pages).

Table 34.4   bash FILE TEST OPERATORS

Operator	True Condition
-d file	file exists and is a directory
-e file	file exists
-f file	file exists and is a regular file (not a directory or special file)
-r file	You have read permission on file
-s file	file exists and is not empty
-w file	You have write permission on file
-x file	You have execute permission on file or, if file is a directory, you have search permission on it
-O file	You own file
-G file	file's group ownership matches one of your group memberships
file1 -nt file2	file1 is newer than file2
file1 -ot file2	file1 is older than file2

The sample shell script for the file test operators lists each directory in $PATH followed by some of the attributes for each directory. The code for this script, descpath.sh, is presented in Listing 34.4:

Listing 34.4 FILE TEST OPERATORS

```
 1  #!/bin/bash
 2  # Listing 34.4
 3  # descpath.sh - File test operators
 4  ###################################
 5
 6  IFS=:
 7
 8  for dir in $PATH;
 9  do
10      echo $dir
11      if [ -w $dir ]; then
12          echo -e "\tYou have write permission in $dir"
13      else
14          echo -e "\tYou don't have write permission in $dir"
15      fi
16      if [ -O $dir ]; then
17          echo -e "\tYou own $dir"
18      else
19          echo -e "\tYou don't own $dir"
20      fi
21      if [ -G $dir ]; then
22          echo -e "\tYou are a member of $dir's group"
23      else
24          echo -e "\tYou aren't a member of $dir's group"
25      fi
26  done
```

The for loop, which I discuss in the next section, by default breaks up fields or tokens using whitespace (spaces, newlines, and tabs). Setting IFS (line 6), the field separator, to : causes for to parse its fields on :. For each directory, the script tests whether or not you have write permission (line 11), own it (line 16), and are a member of its group (line 21), printing a nicely formatted display of this information after the name of each directory (lines 12, 14, 17, 19, 22, and 24). On my system, the output of this script is as follows (it will, of course, be different on yours):

```
/usr/local/bin
    You don't have write permission in /usr/local/bin
    You don't own /usr/local/bin
    You aren't a member of /usr/local/bin's group
/bin
    You don't have write permission in /bin
    You don't own /bin
```

```
        You aren't a member of /bin's group
/usr/bin
    You don't have write permission in /usr/bin
    You don't own /usr/bin
    You aren't a member of /usr/bin's group
/usr/X11R6/bin
    You don't have write permission in /usr/X11R6/bin
    You don't own /usr/X11R6/bin
    You aren't a member of /usr/X11R6/bin's group
/home/kwall/bin
    You have write permission in /home/kwall/bin
    You own /home/kwall/bin
    You are a member of /home/kwall/bin's group
/home/kwall/wp/wpbin
    You have write permission in /home/kwall/wp/wpbin
    You own /home/kwall/wp/wpbin
    You are a member of /home/kwall/wp/wpbin's group
```

bash's string tests compare strings based on their lexicographic or dictionary order. This means, for example, that as is less than asd. Table 34.5 lists the string tests.

Table 34.5   bash STRING COMPARISONS

Test	True Condition
str1 = str2	str1 matches str2
str1 != str2	str1 does not match str2
str1 < str2	str1 is less than str2
str1 > str2	str1 is greater than str2
-n str	str has length greater than 0 (is not null)
-z str	str has length 0 (is null)

The integer tests behave as you might expect. Table 34.6 lists these tests.

Table 34.6   bash INTEGER TESTS

Test	True Condition
-eq	equal
-ge	greater than or equal
-gt	greater than
-le	less than or equal
-lt	less than
-ne	not equal

Determinate Loops: `for`

As Listing 34.4 showed, `for` allows you to execute a section of code a fixed number of times. `bash`'s `for` construct, however, only allows you to iterate over a fixed list of values because it does not have a way to automatically increment or decrement a loop counter in the manner of C, Pascal, or Basic. Nevertheless, the `for` loop is a frequently used loop tool because it operates neatly on lists, such as command-line parameters and lists of files in a directory. The complete syntax of `for` is as follows:

```
for value in list
do
    statements using $value
done
```

`list` is a list of values, such as filenames. `value` is a single list item, and `statements` are `bash` expressions that somehow use or manipulate `value`. Linux, interestingly, lacks a convenient way to rename groups of files. Under MS-DOS, if you have 17 files each with a `*.doc` extension, you can use the `COPY` command to copy each `*.doc` file to, say, a `*.txt` file. The DOS command would be as follows:

```
C:\ copy doc\*.doc doc\*.txt
```

Use `bash`'s `for` loop to remedy this shortcoming. The following code can be turned into a shell script—helpfully named `copy`—that does precisely what you want:

```
for docfile in doc/*.doc
do
    cp $docfile ${docfile%.doc}.txt
done
```

Using one of `bash`'s pattern-matching operators, this code snippet makes a copy of each file ending in a `.doc` extension by replacing the `.doc` at the end of the filename with `.txt`.

Indeterminate Loops: `while` And `until`

Where the `for` loop limits how many times a particular section of code will be executed, `bash`'s `while` and `until` constructs cause continued code execution while (as long as) or until a particular condition is met. The only requirement is that either your code or the environment in which it is running must ensure that the condition in question is eventually met, or you will cause an infinite loop. Their syntax is as follows:

```
while condition
do
    statements
done
```

This syntax means that as long as condition remains true, execute statements until condition becomes false (until a program or command returns non-zero):

```
until condition
do
    statements
done
```

In a way, the until syntax means the opposite of while's: until condition becomes true, execute statements (that is, until a command or program returns a non-zero exit code, do something else).

Experienced programmers will recognize that until loops are an invitation to "busy-waiting," which is poor programming practice and often a huge waste of resources, particularly CPU cycles. On the other hand, bash's while construct gives you a way to overcome for's inability automatically to increment or decrement a counter. Imagine, for example, that your pointy-haired boss insists that you make 150 copies of a file. The following sample snippet makes this possible (never mind that PHB is a moron):

```
declare -i idx
idx=1
while [ $idx != 150 ]
do
    cp somefile somefile.$idx
    idx=$idx+1
done
```

In addition to illustrating the use of while, this code snippet also introduces the use of bash's integer arithmetic. The declare statement creates a variable, idx, defined as an integer. Each iteration of the loop increments idx, ensuring that the loop condition eventually tests false and control exits the loop. This script is on the CD-ROM as phb.sh. To delete the files it creates, execute rm somefile*.

Selection Structures: case And select

The next flow-control structure to consider is case, which behaves similarly to the switch statement in C: it allows you to execute blocks of code depending on the value of a variable. The complete syntax for case is as follows:

```
case expr in
 pattern1 )
 statements ;;
 pattern2 )
 statements ;;
 ...
esac
```

34

SHELL
PROGRAMMING
WITH **GNU** BASH

expr is compared to each pattern, and the statements associated with the first match are executed. ;; is the equivalent of a break statement in C, causing control to jump to the first line of code past esac. Unlike C's switch keyword, however, bash's case statement allows you to test the value of expr against patterns that can contain wildcard characters.

The select control structure (not available in bash versions earlier than 1.14) is unique to the Korn and bash shells. Additionally, it does not have an analogue in conventional programming languages. select allows you to easily build simple menus and respond to the user's selection. Its syntax is as follows:

```
select value [in list]
do
 statements that manipulate $value
done
```

Listing 34.5 illustrates how select works.

Listing 34.5   CREATING MENUS WITH select

```
 1   #!/bin/bash
 2   # Listing 34.5
 3   # menu.sh - Creating simple menus with select
 4   #############################################
 5
 6   IFS=:
 7   PS3="choice? "
 8
 9   # clear the screen
10   clear
11
12   select dir in $PATH
13   do
14       if [ $dir ]; then
15           cnt=$(ls -Al $dir | wc -l)
16           echo "$cnt files in $dir"
17       else
18           echo "Dohhh! No such choice!"
19       fi
20       echo -e "\nPress ENTER to continue, CTRL-C to quit"
21       read
22       clear
23   done
```

The script first sets the IFS character to: so that select can properly parse the $PATH environment variable (line 6). Then, it changes the default prompt that select uses, the built-in shell variable PS3, to something more helpful than #? (line 17). After clearing the screen (line 10), it enters a loop, presenting a menu of directories derived from $PATH and prompting the user to make a choice, as illustrated in Figure 34.1.

FIGURE 34.1

select *is an easy way to create simple menus.*

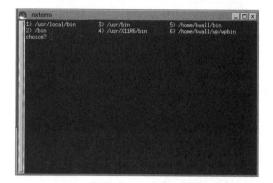

If the user selects a valid choice, the command substitution on line 15 pipes the output of the ls command through the word count command, wc, to count the number of files in the directory and displays the result (lines 14-16). Because ls can be used with no arguments, the script first makes sure the $dir is not null (if it were null, ls would operate on the current directory even if the user selects an invalid menu choice). If the user makes an invalid selection, line 18 displays an error message, followed by the prompt on how to proceed on line 20. The read statement, which I will cover later in the section "Input and Output," allows the user to view the output of line 16 (or 18) and patiently waits for the user to press Enter to iterate through the loop again or to press Ctrl+C to quit.

> **NOTE**
>
> As presented, the script loops infinitely if you do not press Ctrl+C. However, using the break statement is the correct way to proceed after making a valid selection.

As befits a programming language, bash boasts a complete and capable array of flow-control structures. Although they behave in ways slightly different than do their analogues in conventional programming languages, they nevertheless enhance shell scripts with considerable power and flexibility.

34

SHELL PROGRAMMING WITH GNU BASH

Shell Functions

bash's function feature, an expanded version of the function facility available in other shells, has two main advantages:

- Faster execution, because shell functions are already in memory.
- Modularity, because functions help you generalize your shell scripts and allow a better degree of organization.

You can define shell functions using one of the following two forms:

```
function fname
{
    commands
}
```

or

```
fname()
{
    commands
}
```

Either form is acceptable and there is no functional (pun intended) difference between the two. The usual convention is to define all of your functions at the beginning of a script, before they are used, as I did in Listing 34.2. To call a function once it is defined, simply invoke the function name followed by any arguments it needs.

It is worth making clear that, compared to C or Pascal, bash's function interface is very primitive. There is no error-checking and no method to pass arguments by value. However, as with C and Pascal, variables declared inside a function definition can be made local to the function, thus avoiding namespace clashes by preceding the declaration or first use of the variable with the keyword local, as illustrated in the following snippet:

```
function foo
{
    local myvar
    local yourvar=1
}
```

Because Listing 34.2 contains an example of the declaration and use of a shell function, you're referred back to that script. You might try changing the declaration form as an experiment just to persuade yourself that the two forms are equivalent.

> **TIP**
>
> Shell functions make your code vastly easier to read and maintain. Using functions and comments, you can save yourself much weeping, wailing, and gnashing of teeth when you have to go back and enhance that throw-away code you wrote six months ago.

Input and Output

Due to space considerations, I will not cover all of bash's input and output operators and facilities. Many of them deal with the arcana of file descriptors, I/O to- and from-device files, and manipulating standard input and output. The ones I will cover are a few I/O redirectors and string I/O.

I/O Redirectors

You have already seen the basic I/O redirectors, > and <, which redirect output and input, respectively. The output redirector allows you to send the output from a command to a file. For example the command:

```
$ cat $HOME/.bash_profile > out
```

creates a file named out in the current working directory containing the contents of your bash initialization file, .bash_profile, by redirecting cat's output to that file.

Similarly, you can provide the input to a command from a file or command using the input redirector, <. You can rewrite the previous cat command to use input redirection, as shown in the following:

```
$ cat < $HOME/.bash_profile > out
```

The output of this command is the same, and also illustrates that you can redirect input and output simultaneously.

The output redirector, >, will overwrite any existing file. Sometimes this is not what you want, so bash provides the append operator, >>, which adds data to the end of a file. The following command adds the alias cdlpu to the end of my .bashrc initialization file:

```
$ echo "alias cdlpu='cd $HOME/kwall/projects/lpu'"
➥>> $HOME/.bashrc
```

Here-documents are an interesting case of input redirection. They force the input to a command to come from the shell's standard input. A here-document is the way to feed input to a shell script without having to enter it interactively. All of the lines read become input to the script. The syntax follows:

```
command << label
input...
label
```

This syntax says that command should read input until it encounters label on a line by itself. One way to use here-documents is to script programs that do not have a convenient scripting interface. The tried and true ftp program is a fine example. Listing 34.6 illustrates how to script ftp using a here-document:

Listing 34.6   USE A HERE-DOCUMENT TO SCRIPT ftp

```
 1   #!/bin/bash
 2   # Listing 34.6
 3   # ftp.sh - Use a here-document to script ftp
 4   ###########################################
 5
 6   USER=anonymous
 7   PASS=kwall@xmission.com
 8
 9   ftp -i -n << END
10   open ftp.caldera.com
11   user $USER $PASS
12   cd /pub
13   ls
14   close
15   END
```

Line 9 starts ftp in non-interactive mode (-i) and suppresses the auto-login attempt (-n). The script uses END as the label to signal the end of input. Using various ftp commands, the script first opens an ftp session to Caldera Systems' ftp site (line 10). Then it sends the login sequence on line 11 using the $USER and $PASS variables previously defined. Once logged in, it changes to the standard public ftp directory, pub (line 12) and executes an ls command to demonstrate that the script worked. Finally, it closes the session (line 14). Upon encountering the bare END label, the script closes input to ftp and exits both the ftp program and the script. You can also use here-documents to include documentation in scripts.

String I/O

For string output, you have already encountered the echo statement. In addition to its -e options, which enable the interpretation of escaped characters, such as \n (newline) and \t(tab), echo also accepts a -n option that omits appending the final newline to its output. Additional escape sequences that echo understands include those that Table 34.7 lists.

Table 34.7   echo ESCAPE SEQUENCES

Sequence	Description
\a	Alert/Ctrl+G (bell)
\b	Backspace/Ctrl+H
\c	Omit the final newline appended to output
\f	Formfeed/Ctrl+J
\r	Return/Ctrl+M
\v	Vertical Tab
\n	ASCII character with an octal value, where n is one to three digits
\\	A single \

For handling string input, the read operator is what you want. Its syntax is

```
read var1 var2 ...
```

Although ideal for getting input in an interactive mode from a user, read can also be used to process text files one line at a time. In interactive mode, read's use is simple, as the following short code snippet demonstrates:

```
echo -n 'Name: '
read name
echo "Name is $name"
```

Using read to process text files is somewhat more complicated. The easiest way is to create a script and then redirect its input from the file you want to process. Listing 34.7 processes the contents of /etc/passwd.

Listing 34.7   showpass.sh

```
 1   #!/bin/bash
 2   # Listing 34.7
 3   # showpass.sh - Using read to process a text file
 4   ##################################################
 5
 6   IFS=:
 7
 8   while read name pass uid gid gecos home shell
 9   do
10       echo "*********************"
11       echo "name  : $name"
12       echo "pass  : $pass"
13       echo "uid   : $uid"
14       echo "gid   : $gid"
15       echo "gecos : $gecos"
16       echo "home  : $home"
17       echo "shell : $shell"
18   done
```

Setting IFS enables the script to parse the /etc/passwd entries properly (line 6). Line 8 reads the input, assigning each field in turn to the appropriate variable (if the number of input fields exceeds the variables to receive them, the final fields are appended to the last variable in the list, shell in this case). You can execute this script with (at least) one of the following two commands:

```
$ ./showpass.sh < /etc/passwd
```

or

```
$ cat /etc/passwd ¦ ./showpass.sh
```

The output will be the same, regardless of which command you use. An abbreviated form of the output is shown in Figure 34.2, piped through the more command.

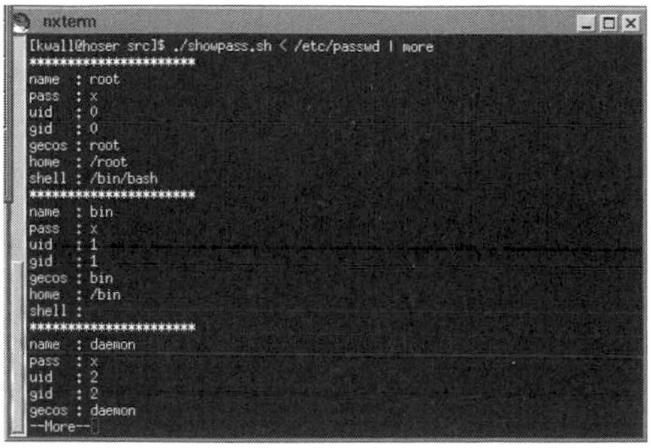

FIGURE 34.2

Using the read
statement to
process text files.

In versions of bash greater than 2.0, read accepts a few options, listed in Table 34.8, that fine-tune its behavior.

Table 34.8   read OPTIONS

Option	Description
-a	Reads values into an array, starting at index 0
-e	Uses the GNU readline library to do the read, enabling use of bash's editing features
-p prompt	Prints prompt before excuting the read

Using read's -p option, instead of writing code such as the following:

```
echo "Enter Name: "
read name
```

you can write

```
read -p "Enter Name: " name
```

Command-line Processing

A polished shell script should process command-line options of the form -option in order to mimic the standard UNIX and Linux command format. The good news is that bash has a built-in command, getopts, that makes processing arbitrary command-line options very easy. Experienced C programmers will recognize that bash's getopts is quite similar to C's standard library routine getopt.

getopts takes two arguments, a string made up of letters and colons, and a variable name. The first argument is a list of valid options; if the option requires an argument, it must be followed by a colon. getopts parses the first argument, picking the options off and assigning each one, in turn (less the leading dash), to the second argument, a user-assigned variable name. As long as options remain to be processed, getopts returns 0, but after it has processed all options and arguments, it returns 1, which makes it ideal for use in a while loop that processes command-line parameters. Listing 34.8 makes the discussion much more concrete.

Listing 34.8   getopts.sh

```
1   #!/bin/bash
2   # Listing 34.8
```

continues

Listing 34.8 CONTINUED

```
 3   # getopts.sh - Using getopts
 4   ############################
 5
 6   while getopts ":xy:z:" opt;
 7   do
 8       case $opt in
 9           x ) xopt='-x set' ;;
10           y ) yopt="-y set and called with $OPTARG" ;;
11           z ) zopt="-z set and called with $OPTARG" ;;
12           \? ) echo 'USAGE: getopts.sh [-x] [-y arg]
➥[-z arg] file ...'
13                   exit 1
14       esac
15   done
16   shift $(($OPTIND - 1))
17
18   echo ${xopt:-'did not use -x'}
19   echo ${yopt:-'did not use -y'}
20   echo ${zopt:-'did not use -z'}
21
22   echo "Remaining command-line arguments are:"
23   for f in "$@"
24   do
25       echo -e "\t$f"
26   done
```

Line 6 states that valid options are x, y, and z, and that y and z must be followed by arguments. As getopts peels the options off, it stores them in opt, which is used as the test value in the case statement (lines 8-15). The case statement handles each of the valid options, including a default case that prints a usage message and exits the script (line 12) if invalid options are used. The arguments passed with the y and z options are stored in the built-in variable $OPTARG. These arguments should be saved in other variables as soon as possible, because $OPTARG will change as getopts iterates through the option list. Lines 18-20 merely print whether or not an option was used and the value of its argument, if applicable.

Lines 16 and 22-25 demonstrate more about how getopts works. $OPTIND is a number equal to the next command-line argument to be processed. The shift built-in moves positional parameters out of the way, that is, shift N moves N positional parameters out of the way. So, $OPTIND-1 equals the number of positional parameters, all of the option arguments, to remove, leaving the non-option arguments in place for normal script processing. Lines 22-25 print the values of each of the remaining positional parameters to demonstrate that they are unmolested. The output of this script, if executed in the source code directory for this chapter, is illustrated in Figure 34.3.

FIGURE 34.3

getopts *simplifies handling command-line options.*

Thanks to the getopts statement, handling long, complex command-lines in a shell script is a breeze. As a result, making your shell scripts behave like other UNIX programs is a breeze, too—at least with respect to calling conventions.

Processes and Job Control

This section continues the focus on building shell scripts that appear polished. This time, I'll talk about using the shell built-in command trap to make your shell scripts more bullet-proof.

Shell Signal-Handling

The primary motivation for using trap is appropriately to handle abnormal events, such as interrupts (Ctrl+C) and suspends (Ctrl+). Although you may not be interested in writing elaborate error-handling code in your throw-away script, even simple code that merely acknowledges the signal gives your code the appearance of robustness. On the other hand, if this chapter has really enthused you for shell-scripting and you get into low-level system programming with bash, trap will be an essential component of your code (yes, Virginia, you *can* do system-programming tasks with shell code).

bash recognizes about 30 signals when running under Linux. To see the complete list, use the command kill -l. In practice, you may need only to take some sort of action for perhaps a dozen signals. In this section I will only concern myself with SIGTERM, SIGINT, and SIGKILL.

Using trap

The syntax of the trap command is:

```
trap command sig1 sig2 ...
```

When any of the signals sig1, sig2, and so forth are received, trap arranges to execute command, which can be a binary, shell script, or shell function. When command completes, the script resumes execution. The signals can be specified by name or by number. Consider listing 34.9. It sets up two signal handlers, one for SIGINT and one for SIGTERM.

Listing 34.9   SIMPLE trap USAGE

```
 1  #!/bin/bash
 2  # Listing 34.9
 3  # trap.sh - Using trap to handle signals
 4  ######################################
 5
 6  trap "echo 'Do not interrupt me!'" INT
 7  trap "echo 'Attempted murder is illegal!'" TERM
 8
 9  echo "$0's PID is $$"
10  while true;
11  do
12      sleep 30
13  done
```

In addition to illustrating trap's usage and behavior, I sneaked in a another bash feature related to job control: the built-in variable $$, which evaluates to the process ID (PID) of the currently executing script (line 9). Line 6 sets up code to execute if the script receives a SIGINT (interrupt or Ctrl+C). Line 7 sets up a handler for SIGTERM that cannot ordinarily be signaled from the keyboard, but must be generated using a command such as kill $(pidof trap.sh. The while loop on lines 10-13 is an infinite loop. true is a bash built-in command that always returns 0; every 30 seconds, the loop repeats itself. We print the shell script's PID so we know which PID to use with the kill command.

If we run this script in the foreground and then attempt to interrupt it using Ctrl+C, the output is as follows:

```
$ ./trap.sh
./trap.sh's PID is 25655
[type CTRL-C]
Do not interrupt me!
```

Your PID will almost certainly be different. Now, put the script into the background and attempt to kill it using kill's default SIGTERM signal:

```
[type CTRL-Z]

[1]+  Stopped                 ./trap.sh
$ bg
[1]+ ./trap.sh &
$ kill %1
Attempted murder is illegal!

$ kill -KILL %1
[1]+  Killed                  ./trap.sh
```

As you can see, you receive the expected output. Because the script has not installed a handler for SIGKILL, you can kill using the kill -KILL syntax.

When evaluating what sort of signals to handle in your code, be sure to have a look at the section 7 manual page, which describes each signal Linux supports in some detail (man 7 signal). By doing so, you can make your shell programs robust and complete.

Summary

This chapter has covered a lot of ground, introducing the fundamentals of programming with the bash shell. After covering basics, such as wildcards, special characters, and brace expansion, I discussed using variables and working with positional parameters. The section on operators showed you how to use bash's string and pattern matching operators. Flow control constructs, such as if, while, and case, enable you to create more flexible, modular shell scripts, as do shell functions. You also learned how to read input and to generate output in shell code. Finally, you learned two ways to make your shell programs appear sophisticated. getopts gives you the ability to process complex command-lines easily and trap allows you to set up signal handlers. For further information about bash programming, see the bash manual page, and the extensive documentation that comes with the source distribution.

34

SHELL PROGRAMMING WITH GNU BASH

CHAPTER 35

Secure Programming

by Mark Whitis

IN THIS CHAPTER

Security is vital for some types of programs and certain types of environments. If you are writing a system that controls a trillion dollars worth of financial assets, security needs to be of the utmost concern.

Security is important, however, for a much wider range of programs and environments than people often realize. From huge corporate offices and banks to your public library to your personal computer, there is a concern for security. Securing personal information is very important, be it credit card information or just your age and email address. Besides securing information, there is also a need for security against malicious attacks from other people on the network. They could break into your system and steal passwords or just simply render your system unusable.

The domino effect is an important issue in computer security. Crackers cover their tracks by breaking into insecure systems and using them to launch attacks against other systems. Crackers regularly install password sniffers on compromised machines and use the intercepted passwords to log in to and compromise other systems, repeating the process ad-infinitum. Anyone who fails to exercise due diligence in keeping their systems secure may face legal liability for damages caused by misuse of those systems.

Types of Applications

The following sections briefly cover some of the many different types of programs that can be exploited. More details on vulnerabilities and defensive coding practices will follow in separate sections; these issues often apply to many different types of programs.

Setuid Programs

The UNIX security model relies heavily on providing access to privileged services through trusted programs that are run by ordinary users but execute with all the privileges of a more powerful user. The files storing these executables have the setuid or setgid bits set, which gives the program all the privileges of the file owner (often root). The untrusted user, however, has control of the arguments, data files, and environment variables used by the program. The user can control the path used by the program to search for other programs it may execute or for shared libraries it may rely on (fortunately many systems, including Linux, will override the shared library path for setuid programs). The user can control when the program runs and when it is prematurely terminated. The user may be able to access the program's internal data by connecting a debugger while the program has temporarily switched to unprivileged operation or by causing the program to dump core. All of these can be used to cause an unwary program to grant unauthorized access.

Network Servers (Daemons)

Servers are good targets for attacks because they are available to do your bidding at any time. A cracker can easily launch a series of attacks against a server until one of them succeeds. The attacker has full control of the data sent to the server and when it is sent. The attacker can cause signals to be sent over a tcp stream.

Network Clients

Although clients are not as easy to attack as servers (because they establish connections at their convenience and not the attacker's), they tend to be very vulnerable. Many clients are very large and complicated programs, and much less attention has been given to security than for a typical server.

Web browsers often permit the server to execute code on the client machine (Java, JavaScript, ActiveX, and so on). It is often not difficult to induce a user to visit a hostile Web site. If an email advertising free money or some similar bait is sent to all the employees of a company, chances are some fool will visit; or users may be targeted individually. Alternatively, instead of targeting a particular site, an attacker can simply prey on whoever comes to visit and will still get some very sensitive sites.

Mail User Agents

Mail User Agents (MUAs) can be targeted directly, particularly with buffer overflow type exploits. And attachments to messages may contain hostile programs or documents that contain macro viruses.

CGI Programs

CGI programs are invoked by the Web server at the request of an HTTP client to handle certain queries, form submissions, or even dynamic generation of entire Web sites. They have most of the vulnerabilities that would be associated with a server. Further, CGI programs are often written in very insecure scripting languages.

Utilities

General utility programs that are not setuid are often thought of as not having security implications. Unfortunately, they may be used in contexts where that is not the case.

Most UNIX compatible systems used to run the find utility periodically to locate old temporary files and core files and delete them. When find executes another program with the files it has located, it passes the command, including a filename, to the shell blindly. Special characters in a filename would be interpreted by the shell, resulting in the ability to execute arbitrary commands. Other programs that are driven by the names of existing files and invoke other programs may have similar vulnerabilities unless precautions are taken.

Many companies may accept zip or tar archives via a Web site or email and then manually or automatically extract and process the file. The filenames themselves may be a problem. Consider what happens when you unpack a tar archive containing a few extra files with names like /etc/passwd or /etc/rhosts. Buffer overflows are theoretically possible in the filename or other header fields.

Simple utilities, such as fgrep, cut, head, and tail, might be called from a CGI program. If these programs were vulnerable to buffer overflows as a result of input patterns, a system using them would be vulnerable to compromise.

Applications

Applications such as word processors and spreadsheets are vulnerable as well. The simple fact of the matter is that people will receive data files from untrustworthy sources. Many of these have macro capabilities and the ability to have a macro automatically execute when a file is loaded; thus the popular "macro virus" was born. Even worse, some systems have mail and Web browsers configured to automatically open the application whenever a data file of that type is received. Far more subtle exploits are possible using buffer overflows, for example.

Specific Code Issues

The following sections discuss issues related to various code features. This discussion emphasizes the C language.

Shell Scripts and system() Calls

Using a shell to process input from untrustworthy users in almost any way is asking for trouble. If you write a shell script to handle CGI requests, chances are very good that you have created a gaping security hole. Likewise if you use the system() function in C, or any similar function in any language, to execute a command that is derived from input from untrustworthy users.

A shell's fundamental purpose is to allow a user to execute any arbitrary system command, and even with various precautions either built in to the shell or the program that uses it, the shell is eager to perform its original function. Any character that has special meaning to the shell can cause problems—spaces, tabs, semicolons, vertical bars, ampersands, and many others can cause grief. Some people who thought they had protected against all the special characters were surprised to find that there were many more in the range of ASCII characters 128–255.

> **Tip**
>
> It is a good idea to write your scripts to only allow the characters or values that you know are acceptable instead of trying to deny all the known bad.

Here is a code fragment, perhaps from a CGI program to look up phone numbers in the company directory.

```
sprintf(command, "fgrep -i %s address.book", name);
system(command)
```

Ignoring the buffer overflow and the use of a utility function of questionable security, this code is extremely vulnerable if `name` comes from an untrustworthy source. Consider what would happen if we search for the employee `; echo intruder.com >>/etc/rhosts;`. Or how about the faithful employee `root /etc/passwd`? Adding quotation marks to our command around the `%s"` will protect us from that rogue space and slow the attacker down for about the amount of time it takes him to type a couple quotation marks.

If you must execute a program with any untrusted user input as arguments, use one of the `exec()` family of calls instead of `system()`:

```
execle("/bin/fgrep", "-i", name, "address.book",
    "PATH=/usr/bin:/bin:/usr/sbin:/sbin\0USER=nobody\0");
```

This leaves the shell out of the picture and closes that particular hole. You should actually use a version that ignores the path and allows you to specify an environment as well. `execle()` and `execve()` are the only ones that meet those criteria.

The `eval` command in many shells is particularly dangerous for shell scripts because it causes a command to be reparsed. Unfortunately, the programming environment offered by most shells is very weak and you are forced to use dangerous commands like `eval` to write non-trivial programs.

One of my all time favorite exploits was in the `mgetty+sendfax` program. It invoked an external program using `system()` or a similar function with the calling station ID as an argument. You didn't even need a computer to use this exploit; you simply programmed an unfriendly string into your fax machine's calling station ID.

35

Secure Programming

Note that some versions of bash drop privileges if they are ever called from a suid or sgid program. This can either help or hurt programs that use the system() call. system() should not be used from these programs anyway because it does not permit control over the environment; use an appropriate member of the exec() family instead. The system() call also executes the user's login shell, which may not interpret a command the way you want.

Input from Untrustworthy Users

Any input that comes from a potentially untrustworthy source must be handled very carefully in any program that executes with privileges the source does not already enjoy. Any program that executes on a different computer from the source of the input inherently has a privilege that the user does not: the right to execute on that machine. This directly applies to all servers, clients, CGI programs, MUAs, and applications that read data files, as well as all setuid programs, and can apply indirectly to common utility programs.

Use of untrusted input, even very indirectly, to generate a system command or a filename is inherently a security issue. Simply copying the input (directly or indirectly) to another variable requires caution (see the following section, "Buffer Overflows"). Logging the data to a file that might be processed by another program or displayed on a user's terminal is a cause for concern as well.

WARNING

Control characters and delimiters such as space, semicolon, colon, ampersand, vertical bar, various quotation marks, and many others can cause problems if they ultimately end up in shell commands, filenames, or even log files.

Buffer Overflows

Buffer overflows are one of the most common vulnerabilities and can affect all types of sensitive programs. In the simplest case, a buffer overflow allows the user supplying input to one untrusted variable to overwrite another variable, which is assumed to be safe from untrusted input. Imagine the trivial program in Listing 35.1 running with stdin/stdout connected to an outside source through some means.

Listing 35.1   A SIMPLE BUFFER OVERFLOW PROGRAM AND ITS EXECUTION

```
#include <stdlib.h>
#include <stdio.h>
main()
```

```
{
    char command[80]="date";
    char name[20];

    printf("Please enter your name: ");
    gets(name);
    printf("Hello, %s, the current date and time is: ",name);
    fflush(stdout);
    system(command);
}

$./a.out
Please enter your name: bob
Hello bob, the current date and time is: Wed Mar 10 11:18:52 EST 1999
$./a.out
Please enter your name: run whoami
Hello, run whoami, the current date and time is: whitis
$
```

Now, what happens if the user says his name is "I would like to run /bin/bash"? Instant shell prompt. The infamous Internet worm created by Robert Morris, Jr. in 1988 used a similar buffer overflow.

It turns out that "command" is stored in memory right above "name". Local variables in most implementations of C and many other languages are stored next to each other on the stack. Of course, crackers trying to repeat this feat with other programs often found the variables they were overwriting were too mundane to be of much use. They could only usefully overwrite those variables declared in the same function before the variable in question. True, the variables for the function that called this function were just a little further along on the stack, as well as the function which called it, and the function before it; but before you overwrote those variables you would overwrite the return address in between and the program would never make it back to those functions.

About eight years later, buffer overflow exploits started becoming much more common. You see, the return address is a very important value. By overwriting its value, you can transfer control of the program to any existing section of code. Of course, you still need an existing section of code that will suit your evil purposes and you need to know exactly where it is located in memory on the target system. Dissatisfied with being limited to the existing code? Well, why not supply your own binary executable code in the string itself? Write it carefully so it does not include any zero bytes that might get lost in a string copy operation. Now you just need to know where it will end up in memory. You can make a lot of guesses. A further improvement is to include a thousand NOP instructions in the string itself so that your aim doesn't have to be exact; this reduces the number of attempts needed a thousand fold. This is explained in much further detail in the article

"Smashing the Stack for Fun and Profit" by Aleph One in Phrack 49. Now you can execute any arbitrary code. Exploiting newly discovered buffer overflows became a cookbook operation.

You might try to protect your program by declaring all your variables as static to keep them off the stack. Besides the coding disadvantages, you now make yourself more vulnerable to the more simplistic buffer overflows.

The solar designer non-executable< stack kernel patch will make the stack non-executable; this provides some protection while causing difficulties for signal handling, trampoline functions, objective C, and Lisp. At the expense of reducing the protection offered, the patch has workarounds for the affected code. You can also get around this by return-into-libc exploits or their procedure linkage table variants.

Canary values are another technique useful for providing protection against buffer overflows. Listing 35.2 shows a trivial program with a buffer overflow that would be exploitable using the stack smashing technique, except that we have added canary values.

Listing 35.2 CANARY VALUES

```
#include <stdlib.h>
#include <stdio.h>
#include <assert.h>

int canary_value = 0x12345678;

void function()
{
   int canary;
   char overflowable[12];

   canary=canary_value;

   printf("type some text: ");
   gets(overflowable);

   assert(canary==canary_value);
   return;
}

main()
{
   function();
}
```

Of course, it is helpful to initialize the canary value to a random number when your program starts up; otherwise, an attacker can simply insert the known canary value at the appropriate place in the overflow. A canary value with a zero byte in the middle can make it easier to guess but harder to overwrite because most overflows will stop at a zero byte, which is interpreted as an end of string.

The stackguard compiler is a version of gcc that has been extended to automatically insert canary values and checks into every function. The non-executable stack patch and the stackguard compiler can help protect against buffer overflows if you have control over the machines the program is compiled and executed on. If you will be distributing a program, manual canary checking is more appropriate. None of these tools are a substitute for eliminating buffer overflows; they simply provide some extra protection.

Potential buffer overflows are usually the result of calling a function and passing it the address of a string to modify without also giving it size information. Frequently, the problem lies in an ancient function in the C standard library. gets(), sprintf(), strcpy(), and strcat() are some of the most common sources of overflows; the vast majority of uses of these functions create a buffer overflow. Table 35.1 lists some vulnerable standard library functions and alternatives. Note that strncpy() and strncat() will still not terminate the string properly. Use of scanf(), and variants, without a maximum width specifier for character strings is vulnerable.

A flexible strncpy() replacement can be found on my Web site. This version allows a variety of different semantics to be selected at compile time. For example, you can select whether or not the remainder of the destination string will be filled with zeros. Not filling is faster and can be used with a virtually infinite size to emulate strcpy() when the buffer size is not known, but such usage is likely to result in unexpected buffer overflows just like strcpy(). Filling with zeros guards against accidental disclosure of sensitive information and will also cause coding errors (specifying the wrong size) to show up early in the debugging process. This version also handles NULL source or destination pointers and zero sizes gracefully.

Table 35.1   VULNERABLE STANDARD LIBRARY FUNCTIONS AND ALTERNATIVES

Bad Syntax	Better Syntax	Notes
gets()	fgets()	Different handling of newlines may leave unread characters in stream
sprintf()	snprintf()	Not available on many other OSes
vsprintf()	vsnprintf()	Not available on many other OSes
strcpy()	strncpy()	Omits trailing null if there is an overflow
strcat()	strncat()	Omits trailing null if there is an overflow
stpcpy()	stpncpy()	Copies exactly the specified size of characters into the target

In addition to these string handling library routines, other library functions or your own functions may be vulnerable if they have a poorly designed calling convention that does not include a size for modifiable strings. Coding errors, such as boundary errors, may cause overflows in routines that do string operations.

Note that even some of the "improved" functions exhibit troublesome behavior in response to an overflow. Some of them will not write past the end of the string but will not terminate it properly either, so other functions that read that string will see a bunch of garbage tacked onto the end or may segfault. Similarly, functions such as `fgets()` or `fscanf()` with a size limit may leave unread data at the end of a long line of text. This data will typically be read later and treated as a separate line of text, which may change its interpretation considerably; it is very likely that the residual text will end up in the wrong variable (or the right one, from the cracker's point of view).

Differential truncation can be a problem. If you truncate a string to one length in one place and a different length in another, you may find that you treat the same value differently. Two condition tests in different parts of the program can result in unusual paths through the program due to differential truncation.

> **NOTE**
>
> Buffer overflows are not confined to strings; other arrays can also be over-flowed.

Environment Variables

Many environment variables can be manipulated to cause inappropriate behavior of programs. The `LD_LIBRARY_PATH` can be used to cause a program to use a trojan version of a library; fortunately, Linux now disables the use of this variable for setuid programs. The related variables `LD_KEEPDIR`, `LD_AOUT_PRELOAD`, and `LD_AOUT_LIBRARY_PATH` are similarly subject to abuse. `PATH` can be used to trick a privileged program into invoking a trojan version of some executable.

The `TZ` variable can cause abnormal behavior, including buffer overflows. Compare the output of the commands `"date"` and `"TZ='this is a long string' date"`. `TZ` can also be used to mislead programs about the current time or date, possibly allowing actions that should be prohibited; try `"TZ=EST600 date"`. The related variable `TZDIR` can probably be misused as well.

The termcap variables TERM and TERMCAP can be abused. The iP (initialization program) or iprog capability can be used to trick any curses based program into executing an arbitrary program.

Locale variables can influence many standard library functions. LANG, LC_ALL, LC_COL-LATE, LC_CTYPE, LC_MONETARY, LC_NUMERIC, and LC_TIME can affect many characters and their placement, such as the currency symbol, decimal point character, thousands separator, grouping character, positive sign, and negative sign. They can also influence formatting, such as the number of fractional digits, whether a currency symbol precedes a value and whether there is a space after it, whether parentheses are used to surround negative numbers, and whether to use 12 hour or 24 hour time. Under the influence of these variables, programs may generate strings of unexpected length or will be parsed improperly, and existing strings may be parsed incorrectly as well. The setlocale() function can be used to override these settings.

ENV can be used to make a shell invoke other programs even in some situations where the user would not normally be able to issue commands to a shell. This affects any user whose login shell is actually a script (such as one that tells the user that they aren't allowed to log in), as well as other users. Some system administrators use a login shell of /bin/true or /bin/false to disable users; these are actually shell scripts. This has been exploited in the past in conjunction with Telnet's ability to set environment variables. system() and related calls might be affected, such as the following:

- SHELL might affect use of system() and related calls.
- DISPLAY and HOSTDISPLAY can cause X Windows–capable programs to open a window on the attacker's machine.
- HOSTTYPE and OSTYPPE might trick some programs into running a trojan binary instead of a system utility.
- USER, HOSTNAME, and HOME will affect programs that rely on them instead of getting the information from a more reliable source.
- MAIL might trick a shell into telling you when a file you cannot see has been updated.

A quick look at the standard library shared object file reveals the following suspicious strings, many of which are probably environment variables that will affect the operation of some functions:

NLSPATH	MALLOC_CHECK
MALLOC_TRACE	LANGUAGE
RES_OPTIONS	LC_MESSAGES
LOCALDOMAIN	LC_XXX

```
POSIXLY_CORRECT              POSIX
JMALLOC_TRIM_THRESHOLD_      LOCPATH
MALLOC_TOP_PAD_              DYNAMIC
MALLOC_MMAP_THRESHOLD_       GLOBAL_OFFSET_TABLE_
MALLOC_MMAP_MAX_
```

It is possible that functions in the standard library, or other libraries, may respond to some of these values or save them for future reference before you get a chance to clobber them. In some cases, you might even need to use a separate wrapper program to clobber these before your program starts up. A program can probably also act as a wrapper for itself by `fork()`ing and `exec()`ing itself, altering the execution environment as needed. If the parent process is allowed to die afterwards, it may not receive signals aimed at the original process. The parent may also have to forward signals it receives to the child.

Some versions of `telnetd` allow remote users to set the DISPLAY, TERM, and USER environment variables and/or arbitrary variables including ENV.

Programs that run with privilege under the influence of untrustworthy users should take steps to negate the effect of the environment variables on their own operation, and also be sure to replace the environment with a safe environment when invoking other programs. Such programs should also call `setlocale()` to override any inherited settings.

The `gethostbyname()` Function

The values returned by `gethostbyname()` should not be trusted. Anyone who controls a portion of the IN-ADDR.ARPA reverse mapping domain space can cause just about any value to show up here. A bogus response may offer the name of a trusted host. Always do a forward lookup on the returned value and compare the results with the original IP address. The `tcp wrappers` package made the mistake of calling `gethostbyaddr()` twice instead of buffering the result, once to check the consistency of the forward and reverse mappings and again to get the host name to compare against trusted host names. A hostile DNS server can return one value that matches its real identity, thus satisfying the consistency test, and then return the name of a trusted machine to gain access. DNS replies can also be spoofed, which could cause a false positive match for the consistency check. The name that is returned might be longer than some buffer you will eventually copy it to.

Signals

Signals may cause programs to behave in unexpected ways, often with security consequences. The user who invokes a setuid program can send signals to it.

Some signals may also be delivered over the network to a program that has any open TCP/IP connection by the program at the other end. SIGPIPE may be delivered if a TCP/IP connection is closed by the other end. SIGURG can be delivered if out of band signaling is used. Wuftp v2.4, the FTP daemon used on many Linux and other systems, had an interesting remote root exploit. Wuftpd caught those two signals and tried to handle them in a reasonable manner. It turned out that some client programs would abort a file transfer by not only sending an ABOR command, with out-of-band signaling, but also closing the data connection. The SIGURG signal may arrive while the SIGPIPE signal is being handled. The SIGPIPE handler sets the euid back to 0 before doing some other stuff. While this might seem safe since the handler is about to call _exit() to terminate the entire process, the SIGURG signal may arrive in the interim. The SIGURG program uses a longjmp() to terminate the current execution sequence (which also aborts the SIGPIPE handler) and revert back to the main command handler. Now you have a wuftpd process that is running as root but is still accepting commands from the remote user. It also turns out that a side effect of this peculiar combination of signals is to record the user as logged out and close the logfile, so no further activity is logged. The remote user can now, for example, download a password file, add a user with root privileges and a known password, and then upload the modified file over the original. This exploit actually can occur by accident under normal conditions, which was apparently how it was discovered. There are other parts of the wuftpd code that were vulnerable to signals, and many other programs are vulnerable as well.

Any program that relies on switching the euid (or egid) back and forth between a privileged user and an unprivileged one must be very careful about signals that occur while in the privileged state. Any signals that occur while in the privileged state must be handled very carefully; temporarily suspending signal delivery during these critical blocks of code is advisable. Ironically, for other programs you may want to look out for signals in the unprivileged state; daemons that were started by root may be immune to signals from unprivileged users except when they drop permissions to emulate that user.

You should also be aware that many system calls and library functions may return before completing their task if a signal is received; this is so the program can resume execution along a different path if desired. For example, the read() and write() system calls may return before reading or writing the specified number of bytes of data if a signal occurs; in this case, errno will be set to EINTR. The POSIX standard allows these functions to return either -1 or the number of bytes actually transferred; if it returns -1, it may not be possible to resume the connection reliably since you do not know how many bytes were transferred (unless the implementation undoes the partial transfer). When using these functions, you should check if the number of bytes read equals the number requested.

I believe that the higher level fread() and fwrite() functions normally resume an interrupted transfer after a signal (as long as the handler permits it) but this might not be true in all cases (unbuffered streams come to mind).

Some system calls that can probably be interrupted by signals include the following:

accept()	write()	chdir()	chmod()	chown()	chroot()
close()	connect()	dup()	execve()	fcntl()	fsync()
fwrite()	ioctl()	link()	lseek()	mkfifo()	mknod()
msgop()	nanosleep()	open()	pause()	poll()	read()
readlink()	readv()	recv()	rename()	select()	semop()
send()	sigaction()	sigpause()	stat()	statfs()	truncate()
unlink()	ustat()	utime()	wait()	wait4()	

The siginterrupt() function can be used to specify, to a degree, whether system calls will resume after a particular signal.

Some library functions that are probably affected include getch(), wgetch(), mvgetch(), mvwgetch(), ungetch(), has_key(), errno(), pthread_cond_timedwait(), readv(), writev(), and system(). Users of pthreads will want to consult the documentation for additional considerations regarding signals and interrupted signal calls.

Incorrect handling of an interrupted system call or function could result in some serious breaches of security. If one imagines a program that reads a text file or data stream using an interruptible function and does not handle interruption properly, delivering a signal at the right time might have the same effect as sneaking in a newline. Similarly, interrupted writes can cause the omission of newlines or other text. Many exploits are possible just by adding additional delimiters or removing existing ones. A line break is usually the most powerful delimiter.

> **TIP**
>
> The order in which variables are declared, read, or written may affect the degree of vulnerability due to interrupted system calls, buffer overflows, special characters, and other types of exploits.

Signals will cause premature timeouts from various functions. The ping program is setuid but prevents users other than root from using its flood ping feature, which could clog networks. It was discovered that invoking ping and sending it a bunch of signals could allow an unprivileged user to effectively flood ping.

Userid and Groupid

A process under Linux has a uid associated with it, which is the numeric identifier used by the kernel to identify the user. It also has a gid, which identifies the primary group membership of the user.

Linux also supports an euid and egid, which are the effective user and group identifier. For a setuid and/or setgid program, the euid and/or egid values initially indicate the privilege user and group ids inherited from the file ownership and setuid and/or setgid permissions of the executable file. The uid and gid are initially set to the uid and gid of the invoking process or user.

Programs may change the uid, euid, gid, and egid values within certain constraints. If the program is not running as root, it can only set the real value to the effective value, set the effective value to the real value, or swap the two. If the program is running as root, it can set any of these values to any other value.

The getuid(), geteuid(), getgid(), and getegid() system calls can retrieve the corresponding values. The setuid(), setgid(), seteuid(), and setegid() calls can set the corresponding values, although the first two calls may have the side effect of modifying the effective and saved values as well if the caller is root. The setreuid() and setregid() calls set both the real and effective values simultaneously, which is particularly useful to swap the values (two separate calls to set the individual functions might have the side effect of losing the privilege to perform the second operation).

Linux behaves as if the POSIX _POSIX_SAVED_IDS feature is enabled with some other semantics that provide compatibility with BSD. Kernel versions prior to 1.1.38 were broken and saved ids did not work properly.

More recent versions of the Linux kernel prohibit setuid or setgid programs from dumping core; programs that are likely to be ported to other operating systems or older Linux systems should use the setrlimit() system call to prevent core dumps by setting the maximum size to zero. Core dumps can be triggered and inspected to obtain privileged information. Symbolic links may also be used to trick a privilege program dumping core into clobbering an important file. Similarly, a debugger may be connected to a running setuid/setgid program while it is running in the unprivileged state. This may allow inspection of sensitive data obtained while in the privileged state or perhaps even modifying data that will affect the operation of the program when it reverts to the privileged state. Removing read permission on the executable file prevents this. Core dumps and debugger connections have been used to dump the contents of the normally unreadable shadow password file.

35

SECURE PROGRAMMING

Beware of zero and negative one. Uninitialized variables, default values, values returned by running `atoi()` on a non-string value, and a variety of other events can result in a variable having the value zero, and zero is also often used to unset a value. If that variable is later used to set any of the uid or gid values, a program may run in the privileged state when it intended to run in the unprivileged state. The value -1 passed to any of these functions has the effect of leaving the original value unchanged, which can also cause an unintended retention of privileges or may set the value to the saved value. On many systems the user `nobody` had a value of 65535, which if stored in a signed 16-bit value also means -1. Anytime you set the real values or set the effective values to a value other than the real value, the saved uid is set to the new effective id.

In addition to the primary group, any process has supplementary groups inherited from the user. The `getgroups()` and `setgroups()` are used to access this information. Many programmers have forgotten to clear the supplementary groups when lowering privileges; on many systems this can result in the process having unintended privileges from, for example, the root, bin, daemon, and adm groups.

The `setfsuid()` and `setfsgid()` calls allow separate control of the userid and group used for filesystem operations. Using these can allow a privilege program to access files with the kernel, enforcing the restrictions appropriate to the supplied user without the process running as that user and exposing itself to signals from that user. To maintain compatibility with BSD, use just `setreuid()` and `setregid()`. To maintain compatibility with `_POSIX_SAVED_IDS`, use just `setuid()` and `setgid()`.

There are problems with writing portable code that will work on any platform as any privileged user and be able to temporarily drop privileges and reraise them, and also be able to permanently drop them. The POSIX semantics seem to be particularly broken. BSD is more flexible. Linux tries to emulate both at the same time with extensions. Mixing BSD, POSIX, and Linux specific semantics in the same program may not work as expected. Privileged programs that are not run as root should be able to use the POSIX semantics to temporarily drop privileges by calling `setuid()` and `setgid()` with the appropriate values before and after. Similarly, privileged programs that are not run root should be able use `setreuid()` and `setregid()` to swap real and effective user ids. To temporarily drop root privileges on Linux, only use `setuid()` and `setegid()`. Calling `setuid()`, `setgid()`, `seteuid()`, and `setegid()` with unprivileged values should permanently drop privileges. It would be best to abstract these operations by writing higher level functions that can be modified to suit the idiosyncrasies of a particular platform.

Library Vulnerabilities

The standard library, and other libraries used by your program, may have various vulnerabilities. Many library functions have been found which were vulnerable to buffer overflows. You may want to wrap calls to library functions in a function of your own that insures string values are not longer than the library is known to handle. The process of loading shared libraries can be affected by environment variables on some systems; although recent Linux versions ignore them for setuid programs, care may still be needed when loading another program from any privileged program. Many library functions themselves are susceptible to environment variables.

Executing Other Programs

The system(), popen(), execl(), execlp(), execv(), and execvp() calls are all vulnerable to shell special characters, PATH, LD_*, or other environment variables; use execve() or execle() instead.

When you run another program, it will inherit your execution context, which may include environment, copies of file descriptors, uid, gid, euid, egid, and supplementary groups. Special memory mappings performed by munmap() or mmap() might be inherited.

Before running execve() or execle() you will probably want to run fork(); otherwise the new program will replace the current one. After you run fork(), you should be sure to drop uid, euid, gid, egid, and supplemental groups as appropriate. Close any open files you do not want the subprocess to have access to. If you need to build a pipe for input or output, do so and then modify any file descriptors for redirection.

There is a Linux specific function called __clone() that works something like fork() but allows you finer control over the execution environment.

/tmp Races

Programs that use publicly writable directories are vulnerable to /tmp races or similar exploits. The program files in /tmp can be modified to gain unauthorized access. Symbolic links to existing files from the filename a program is about to use in a world-writable directory can cause a privileged program to clobber a file on behalf of the user. The attacker may even be able to get arbitrary text inserted into the file, although there may be garbage before or after it; often, the text will still serve the nefarious purpose of the attacker.

35

SECURE PROGRAMMING

Instead of using /tmp, use a subdirectory specific to each user such as /tmp/username or /tmp/uid. For best protection, these directories should be created at account creation time rather than when the program runs. The user-specific directory should have permissions to prevent access by other users.

/tmp race conditions often depend on modifying the contents, location, or permissions between two consecutive operations of a file. Race conditions can depend on exact timing and can be hit or miss, but there are techniques that often may be employed which will insure that the race is won on the first try.

Denial of Service Attacks

Denial of Service (DOS) attacks are those that do not allow the intruder unauthorized access but allow them to interfere with normal operation of the system or access by normal users. Some DOS attacks can cause the machine to crash, which can damage data and may help an intruder gain access since some exploits need the machine to reboot.

While you can reduce vulnerability to DOS attacks, it is generally not possible to make a system immune to them. They come in so many flavors and are often indistinguishable from normal activities except by observing patterns of behavior. Many DOS attacks are also aimed at the TCP/IP stack itself.

One of the simplest forms of a DOS attack is to send large numbers of requests or to start a number of requests but not finish them. Large numbers of requests can monopolize CPU cycles, network bandwidth, or consume other resources. A smaller number of requests that are started but not finished can use up the maximum number of simultaneous TCP connections for a particular process, preventing legitimate connections. If there is not an upper limit on the maximum number of incoming connections and subprocesses, a daemon can be induced to start hundreds of suprocesses, which will slow down the machine and may even fill up the process table to the point where other programs cannot spawn their own subprocesses.

If a program temporarily locks some resource, it can often be tricked into keeping it locked so other programs, or other instances of the same program, have to wait for the resource.

Often network-based attacks use third-party machines to conceal their identity or amplify their ferocity. For some types of attacks, they can forge bogus source addresses. Fortunately, the Linux TCP stack's SYN flood protection will help shield you from random addresses.

Some of the countermeasures will be in the program itself while others may be in the TCP/IP stack, the local firewall, or a firewall that is located at the upstream end of your network connection (a local firewall cannot protect a link from flooding). Some counter-measures will be automatic, whereas others will be manual.

Some techniques for reducing the impact of DOS attacks include taking actions that may adversely affect some legitimate users but allow others through. These countermeasures are normally enabled only when the system perceives it is under attack. Degraded operation is better than no operation. Timeouts may be decreased to small values that allow resources to be freed faster but could prevent users with slow machines or connections from using the system. Access attempts from large network blocks may be disabled. Some services, or portions thereof, may be disabled. Packets associated with connections from users who have already authenticated may be given priority over questionable ones. Packets associated with IP addresses that have been used by legitimate users in the past may be given priority over those from unfamiliar addresses. Users with valid accounts may be permitted to use the service while all anonymous users are denied. Bandwidth may be increased or decreased. You may secretly bring up the server or a backup on one or more different IP address or networks and notify legitimate users of the alternate (not necessarily giving them all the same information so if there is a turncoat a smaller group will be affected). You may set up some sort of front end that has a much lower resource consumption per session, which validates incoming connections in some way and only forwards or redirects reasonable ones to your main server.

You may use cryptographically encoded tokens, which can be validated without keeping a list of different sessions or ip addresses and distinguish valid connections or at least allow you to send packets back to that host. The Linux TCP stack deals with SYN flood attacks by returning a cryptographically encoded sequence number with the SYN-ACK packet. It keeps no record of the SYN but it can tell when it gets the ACK packet that it must have sent a SYN-ACK to that host and considers the three-way handshake complete.

Often, you have to rely on your upstream provider and other ISPs to trace the traffic back toward the source. In some cases you can launch counterattacks, although there are legal and ethical considerations. If the attacker is not using a half-open connection on you, you may be able to use those techniques to slow down the attacking machine. Some mail servers, when they recognize spam, suddenly become slow (reading or writing, say, one character per second) tying up the mail relay used by the spammers.

Random Numbers

Random number generators should be cryptographically secure. The rand() library function is not remotely suitable for a secure program. If you use all 32 bits of the result from rand(), you disclose the internal state of the random number generator and an attacker can guess what other past and recent values are. There are also only four billion possible values that need to be tried. While the `rand()` function is guaranteed not to repeat until it has used all four billion values, if you only use a smaller number of bits from each word they will be much less random and will even repeat frequently.

I have seen a couple random password generators that used `rand()`. These took only minutes to break and it was even observed that of a sample of two passwords assigned by one such generator, both were identical. The `random()` function might not be truly cryptographically secure, but it is much better than `rand()`. It has up to 2048 bits of internal state and returns much more random data.

A good random number generator would maintain a very large internal state, include cryptographic hashes in its algorithm, and allow mixing in more entropy over time. Seeding a random number generator must be done carefully. People often seed the random number generator with the current time at one-second precision. If you can guess roughly when the program started, you need try only 86,400 possible seed values per day of ambiguity. Linux provides /dev/random, which may be used as a source of some entropy to use as part of the seed. The script /etc/rc.d/init.d/random on a Red Hat system is used to save the state of /dev/random across reboots, thereby increasing the amount of entropy available immediately after a reboot.

> ### TIP
>
> If you fork multiple subprocesses, be sure to reseed the random number generator or take other steps to insure that each process does not return the same stream of numbers.

Tokens

Tokens are often used by, for example, a Web application to identify individual sessions. They are typically passed in the URL, hidden form fields, or as cookies. A cryptographic random number generator, hash, or other cryptographic technique should be used to generate these. Otherwise, an attacker may find it easy to guess their values.

Be careful with a session token stored in a URL. It may end up being submitted to another Web site in the referrer field or in the logfiles for a caching Web proxy.

Passwords

Passwords should be sufficiently long and be chosen from a large number of values. Mixing uppercase, lowercase, digits, and symbols is recommended. It should not be a word in any dictionary or a predictable modification of one.

Random passwords generated by programs are often actually very weak and are also written down by users who can't remember them. Theoretically, you could write a strong password generator but in actual practice the ones I have normally encountered were trivial to break. You might think that a random password eight characters long from a set of 96 characters would require seven quadrillion guesses for a complete brute force attack. If you only used a 16bit random number generator, the attacker need only try 65,536 possibilities if they can guess your algorithm. A good 32-bit generator would need about four billion. A typical `rand()` based generator, although supposedly 32-bit, would only generate around 4000. And a brute force attack needs to try half the possibilities on average before it finds a match. If the seed is weak, you may need to search far fewer possibilities.

Passwords should be stored and matched using a one-way encryption algorithm. Passwords should be changed periodically; otherwise, even good passwords can be broken with a brute force attack running over an extended period of time against the encrypted password. Multiple failed password attempts should automatically lock out an account to minimize guessing and brute force attacks. This does create a possible DOS attack, however.

Passwords are vulnerable to snooping over network connections if encryption is not used and to keystroke grabbers on insecure client machines. Even if a user has already authenticated, you may want to require reauthentication before performing sensitive operations such as dispersing funds. The user may have stepped away from their computer momentarily and been replaced by someone else.

> **WARNING**
>
> Default passwords for accounts and trapdoor passwords create security holes.

Filenames

Filenames specified by the user or derived from untrustworthy user input are risky. If they are used, they should be very carefully vetted. If possible, use a more restrictive naming convention than UNIX allows.

For example, check the length. Allow only characters A–Z, a–z, 0–9, underscore, dash, dot, and slash. Do not allow them to start or end with a dash, dot, or slash. Do not allow any two or more consecutive characters from the set of dots and slashes. Do not allow the slashes at all if subdirectories are not needed. Prepend a fixed directory name to the file or pathname.

35

SECURE PROGRAMMING

Some of these rules may seem weird but they make for a relatively simple function that can weed out dangerous filenames without stopping too many useful names. The pathname "../../../.././/.///////etc/./password" contains multiple tricks that can cause many programs to do bad things even if a fixed string is added onto the front. It also illustrates the folly of the deny known bad approach. A comparison against the name "/etc/password" will fail but that is exactly the file that path will open in most contexts.

In many applications, the resulting pathnames should be parsed into their separate directory components. Each in turn should be further checked against Linux file permissions, additional rules imposed by your application (including separating users who do not have an identity with the kernel from each other), and symbolic links at each step of the path. If you are working in a directory that is world-writable or accessible to even a single untrustworthy user, your checking code should be insensitive to race conditions.

In some applications it is appropriate to rely on the underlying Linux file permissions as enforced by the kernel with the program running, at least temporarily, as a specific user known to the system. In other applications, typically where the remote user does not have a unique identity on the local system, it is appropriate to roll your own access checks. In other situations you may need a combination of the two.

Guessing the names of backup files can be used to access documents that would otherwise be off limits. This trick has been employed to read the source code to CGI programs instead of executing them. Where possible, it is better to use sequential filenames generated by the program itself in a directory tree that is not accessible by untrustworthy users.

Symbolic Links

Many of the most common operations are vulnerable to symbolic links and similar attacks. While tedious workarounds are possible for many calls, many other common operations cannot be done safely in a variety of common situations. Worse, these problems can affect even mundane programs in fairly common real-world situations. The vulnerabilities listed here were evaluated against the 2.0.x kernels; it appears that there has not been any improvement in the 2.2.x kernels. Dropping privilege to the level of the user initiating an operation is not sufficient, either. A workaround will be described, and illustrated in code listings, which solves some of these problems for reading and writing files, changing ownership, and permissions.

Operations such as creating or deleting a new file or directory cannot be done safely even with the illustrated workaround, although it reduces the vulnerability. Fortunately, it appears there may be a ray of hope in the `rename()` call. If this call is used, restricted to moving to the current working directory (which you will need to change using the usual workaround described in Listing 35.3), you can create or modify a file in a known safe place and rename it into its proper location. Use of this is quite cumbersome. Each user on the system will need to have a safe directory on each and every partition where they could possibly create or modify a file (this could be particularly annoying on a small removable device) in a directory that anyone else has write access to, and a program will need to be able to locate that directory. A less general solution, confined to a particular application, is somewhat less daunting.

A symbolic link created by a local user on a system from their Web directory to the root directory might allow remote users access to every single file on the system, depending on server configuration and the access checks it performs.

Symbolic links are often used in combination with race conditions to overwrite or delete otherwise inaccessible files. These race conditions may occur in publicly writable directories (such as the /tmp races mentioned previously) or may be used to change what file is being referred to between the access checks and the file access itself.

Any program, including suid program servers and any program that is run as root or another privileged user, which opens, creates, unlinks, or changes permissions on a file where any directory (including, but not limited to, shared directories such as /tmp or a user's home directory tree) is inherently dangerous. Symbolic links, hard links, or rename() calls can be used to trick the program into providing unauthorized access. To guard against such problems, it is often necessary to parse each component of a path-name and test the accessibility of each directory in turn, checking for symbolic links and race conditions. I think Linux and most other operating systems still lack a combination of system calls that allow this to be done with complete safety. Unfortunately, there is no flstat() function that would allow you to check directory information associated with a file descriptor (instead of just a pathname) and also return information on symbolic links instead of silently following. It is, therefore, necessary to use both fstat() and lstat() together with open() and fchdir() as well as backtracking after opening the next stage in the path to see if any changes have occurred. I will refer to this as the usual workaround in the following discussion. This workaround has the undesirable side effect of changing the current working directory and will not work if any component of the path has execute-only permission.

If there is a possibility that an open() call could create a file in a directory in which an ordinary user has permissions, you must drop permissions to the least common denominator of all users who have write access to that directory (often not possible) or use the rename() trick. Even if a file will not be created, if an existing file will be modified (flags contains O_WRONLY or O_RDWR) you must at least stat() the file before opening and fstat() it afterwards (before writing any data) and compare the results to guard against symlink attacks. These precautions must be taken in privileged programs and may also be necessary in ordinary programs as well if anyone other than the user running the program has write access to the directory. Basically, all shared directories are dangerous, not just those that are writable by everyone. One ordinary user who can anticipate that another user with write access to a directory they share will create or modify a file of a given name can induce the victim to clobber a file. Even if you `fchdir()` down each component of the path using `lstat()`, `open()`, and `fstat()`, you are still vulnerable to symlinks in the last component. The `truncate()` call to truncate a file is vulnerable, but fortunately the usual workaround can be used with `ftruncate()`.

Root, due to its unlimited privileges (at least on local filesystems) effectively shares every directory owned by another user, making root exploits possible if root takes any action in those directories.

Similar precautions may apply to changing the permissions of a file or ownership. `chown()` should never be used; use `fchown()` or `lchown()` instead. `chmod()` should also never be used, use `fchmod` instead with `lstat()`, `chdir()`, and `fstat()`. When using `fchmod()` or `fchown()`, always check that `chmod` (or at least the program) does follow links, although it does have dereferencing calls so perhaps the system call is okay. `chown` does follow links—use `lchown`.

The `access()` call, used to check if the real uid/gid has access to a particular directory, is vulnerable. The normal use of this function before calling `open()` is also vulnerable to race conditions because the attacker can change things between the two operations.

Many calls primarily used by root are vulnerable but typical use of them is safe because they are normally used in a safe environment. The `acct()` call is vulnerable, but since it is normally issued only by root with a trusted pathname, there should not be a problem. The `chroot()` call is vulnerable; do not `chroot()` to a directory unless the path to that directory is not writable by any untrusted users. The `mknod()` call is vulnerable; confine use of this call to /dev/.

The `execve()` call (and all other members of the `exec()` family) is vulnerable. Do not invoke any programs if the path to them is not well guarded (this wouldn't be a good idea anyway in many applications); the standard directories /bin/, /sbin/, /usr/bin/, /usr/sbin/, and, hopefully, /usr/local/bin and /usr/local/sbin should be okay on most systems. Invoking programs in a user's /home/$USER/bin directory, where otherwise appropriate, should be okay if the program is running as that user and no one else has write access to /home/$USER or /home/$USER/bin. Shared directories, such as a common development directory, are risky due to symbolic links as well as trojan programs. All developers in a shared development project must be trusted.

Creating, deleting, or renaming either directories or files is not safe. open() and creat() have already been covered. The mkdir(), rmdir(), and unlink() commands are all vulnerable with no alternatives or workaround. The utime() call, which changes the access time of files, is vulnerable and there is no alternative or workaround.

The system calls specifically for dealing with links are vulnerable to various degrees. The link() call is vulnerable. There are no alternatives and the usual workaround does not apply. symlink() is vulnerable unless there is no leading path component (the link is being created in the current directory). Use the usual workaround to traverse to the proper directory and then create the link. The target of a symlink must also be checked at the time the link is followed. The readlink() is vulnerable if there are any directory components in the path. When used within the confines of the current directory, it should be okay since it reads the contents of the link rather than following it.

The stat() call is vulnerable. fstat() may be used with the usual workaround. lstat() will not follow a symbolic link; you must use it only in the current working directory, however. fstat() and lstat() are used together with open() and fchdir() to implement the usual workaround; these are safe when used in this particular way, traversing each component of a pathname. But they still cannot protect system calls against links in the final pathname component unless an fxxx() version, which uses file descriptors instead of names, or an lxxx() call, which ignores links, is available or the call itself inherently does not follow links.

The statfs() call, which reports the disk usage on a mounted partition, can be fooled by symbolic links. The consequences of this are minor compared to most of the others and, fortunately, filesystems are rarely mounted in places where ordinary users could tamper with the path.

The rename() call is potentially vulnerable to symbolic links at any stage of either path except the last component of the target path. If you are moving from a safe path to another path and you use the usual workaround to traverse all components of the target directory, you should be safe.

Many standard library functions use the vulnerable system calls. One of the most obvious and frequently used examples is fopen(). In this case, you can use open() with the usual workaround and then use fdopen() on the already open file descriptor. As long as you are not creating a file, you should be safe this way.

The realpath() standard library function is handy for translating names into their canonical form (stripped of all symbolic links, consecutive slashes, ".", and ".."). It is not safe against race conditions. Even if it were safe itself, there would be the same problem as with the access() call; the interval between calling realpath() and performing any operations on the file would allow for race conditions.

35

SECURE
PROGRAMMING

It would not be a good idea to rely on getcwd() to safely return the current working directory or to assume you could get back here safely with the path even if the returned value is correct. Use open() to open the current directory (".") and save the file descriptor; that way, you should be able to get back even if some clown moves or deletes it.

It will be necessary to decide how you want to follow symbolic links. One option is to not follow them at all. Another is to always follow them. An intermediate approach is to follow symlinks if the object pointed to is owned by the same user that owns the link or if the link is owned by root. If you follow any links, you need to exercise caution. Be aware that on many systems, each user's home directory may be a link from /home/$USER to some other location; not following links at all will deny access to the user's home directory. On other systems, "directories" such as /usr, /tmp, and /var may be symbolic links from the root filesystem to a larger file system.

Hard links may also create some of the same problems as symbolic links. In more detail, the standard workaround, illustrated in Listing 35.3, is to break the path into individual directory components at each "/". Traverse each component in the following manner. lstat() the component you are about to open. If the link count is greater than 1 you may have a hard link exploit. You can check the Linux specific symlink flag and stop if it is set, but you cannot rely on it because of race conditions; we will catch both in a subsequent step anyway. Now open() the directory component for reading. Then fstat() the open file descriptor and compare it to the results returned earlier by lstat(); any discrepancy indicates that a symbolic link was crossed or the directory entry has been changed in the interim. Now use fchmod() to change to the already open directory and then close() the file descriptor.

Listing 35.3 illustrates a safer replacement for the chroot() and open() system calls and the fopen() standard library function. This illustrates the usual workaround, and wrappers for other system calls can be patterned after these functions.

Listing 35.3 SOME SAFER I/O FUNCTIONS

```
/* Copyright 1999 by Mark Whitis.  All rights reserved. */
/* See the following URL for license terms: */
/* http://www.freelabs.com/~whitis/software/license.html */

#include <stdlib.h>
#include <sys/types.h>
#include <sys/stat.h>
#include <fcntl.h>
#include <stdio.h>
#include <errno.h>
#include <string.h>
#include <assert.h>
```

```
#include <limits.h>
#include <unistd.h>

int debug=5;

/*
 * These functions have the unpleasant side effect of
 * changing the working directory (although they try to
 * restore it).  This can be bad if you need re-entrant
 * code.  Also, be careful in signal handlers - you might
 * find yourself in a very unfriendly place.  Strange
 * things might also happen on strange remote filesystems
 * which do not obey UN*X semantics.
 */


int one_chdir_step(char *name)
{
   int fd;
   int rc;
   struct stat lstats;
   struct stat fstats;

   if(debug>=5) {
      fprintf(stderr,
         "one_chdir_step(): attempting to chdir to %s\n", name);
   }

   rc = lstat(name, &lstats);
   if(rc<0) {
      if(debug) perror( "one_chdir_step(): lstat()");
      return(-1);
   }

   #if 0
      if(lstats.st_nlink>1) {
         /* hard link detected; this might be legit but we */
         /* are paranoid */
         if(debug) {
            fprintf(stderr,
               "one_chdir_step(): lstats.st_nlink=%d\n",
               lstats.st_nlink);
         }
         errno = EXDEV;
         return(-1);
      }
   #endif

   /* this will fail if directory is execute only */
   fd = open(name, O_RDONLY, 0);
```

continues

35

SECURE PROGRAMMING

Listing 35.3   CONTINUED

```c
    if(fd<0) {
        if(debug) perror( "one_chdir_step(): open()");
        return(-1);
    }

    rc = fchdir(fd);
    if(rc<0) {
        if(debug) perror( "one_chdir_step(): fchdir()");
        close(fd);
        return(-1);
    }

    rc = fstat(fd,&fstats);
    if(rc<0) {
        if(debug) perror( "one_chdir_step(): fstat()");
        close(fd);
        return(-1);
    }

    /* perhaps we should check some other fields here as well */
    if( (fstats.st_dev != lstats.st_dev )
    ¦¦  (fstats.st_ino != lstats.st_ino )
    ) {
        /* we have probably traversed a symbolic link or the */
        /* directory has changed both may be normal or a sign */
        /* of hostility */
        if(debug) {
            fprintf(stderr,
                "one_chdir_step(): stat comparison failed\n");
        }
        close(fd);
        return(-1);
    }

    if(debug>=5) {
        fprintf(stderr, "one_chdir_step(): successful\n");
    }

    close(fd);
    return(0);
}

/* note this can leave us in a weird, and possibly hostile, */
/* place if it fails although it tries to resore the current */
/*  working directory */

int safer_chdir(char *pathname)
{
    char pathtokens[PATH_MAX];
```

```
        char *current;
        int saved_cwd;
        int saved_errno;
        int rc;

        saved_cwd = open(".", O_RDONLY, 0);
        if(saved_cwd<0) {
            if(debug) perror( "safer_chdir(): could not open current dir");
            return(-1);
        }
        strncpy(pathtokens, pathname, sizeof(pathtokens));
        pathtokens[sizeof(pathtokens)-1]=0;

        if(pathname[0]=='/') {
            /* leading delimeter confuses strtok() */
            one_chdir_step("/");
        }

        /* strtok() is ugly and really shouldn't be used */
        /* Not reentrant */
        current = strtok(pathtokens,"/");

        while(current) {
            rc=one_chdir_step(current);
            if(rc<0) {
                /* something went wrong, attempt to restore current */
                /* directory and return.  We might even want to call */
                /* abort if the fchdir() fails */
                saved_errno=errno;
                fchdir(saved_cwd);
                close(saved_cwd);
                errno=saved_errno;
                return(-1);
            }

            current = strtok(NULL,"/");

        }

        close(saved_cwd);
        return(0);

}


int safer_open(const char *pathname, int flags, mode_t mode)
{
    char pathtokens[PATH_MAX];
    char *p;
```

continues

Listing 35.3 CONTINUED

```c
char *prefix;
char *basename;
int saved_cwd;
int saved_errno;
int fd;
int rc;

if(flags & O_CREAT) {
    /* we cannot safely create a file.  Use the  */
    /* rename() trick instead.  But this function */
    /* still does it more safely than the normal open() */

    if(debug) {
        fprintf(stderr, "safer_open(): O_CREAT is risky\n");
    }
}

saved_cwd = open(".", O_RDONLY, 0);
if(saved_cwd<0) {
    if(debug) {
        perror( "safer_open(): could not open current dir");
    }
    return(-1);
}

strncpy(pathtokens, pathname, sizeof(pathtokens));
pathtokens[sizeof(pathtokens)-1]=0;
p = strrchr(pathtokens,'/');
if(p) {
    *p = 0;
    prefix = &pathtokens[0];
    basename = p+1;
} else {
    prefix = "";
    basename = &pathtokens[0];
}

if(*prefix) {
    rc=safer_chdir(prefix);
    if(rc<0) {
        if(debug) {
            perror("safer_open(): could not safer_chdir()");
        }
        saved_errno=errno;
        fchdir(saved_cwd);
        close(saved_cwd);
        errno=saved_errno;
        return(-1);
    }
```

```
   }
   fd = open(basename, flags, mode);
   if(fd<0) {
      if(debug) perror("safer_open(): could not open()");
      saved_errno=errno;
      fchdir(saved_cwd);
      close(saved_cwd);
      errno=saved_errno;
      return(-1);
   }

   /* success */
   fchdir(saved_cwd);
   close(saved_cwd);
   return(fd);
}

/* for symetry.  No special handling */
int safer_close(int fd)
{
   return(close(fd));
}


/* Note that fopen() and lseek() are an exception to
 * the usual naming pattern.  "l" has nothing to do
 * with links and "f" has nothing to do with file
 * descriptors.  fdopen() is what you would
 * expect to be called fopen.
 *
 * It is still not a good idea to create a file with
 * safer_fopen() unless it is in a directory no one else
 * has write access to.
 *
 * The trick here is we use safer_open() and fdopen() to
 * replace fopen()
 */

FILE *safer_fopen(const char *path, const char *mode)
{
   int open_flags;
   int append;
   int fd;
   off_t offset;
   int saved_errno;
   FILE *file;

   append=0;
   if(strcmp(mode,"r")==0) {
      open_flags = O_RDONLY;
```

continues

Listing 35.3 CONTINUED

```c
    } else if(strcmp(mode,"r+")==0) {
       open_flags = O_RDWR;
    } else if(strcmp(mode,"w")==0) {
       open_flags = O_WRONLY;
    } else if(strcmp(mode,"w+")==0) {
       open_flags = O_RDWR | O_CREAT;
    } else if(strcmp(mode,"a")==0) {
       open_flags = O_WRONLY;
       append=1;
    } else if(strcmp(mode,"a+")==0) {
       open_flags = (O_RDWR | O_CREAT);
       append=1;
    } else {
       errno=EINVAL;
       return(NULL);
    }

    fd=safer_open(path, open_flags, 0666);
    if(fd<0) {
       return(NULL);
    }
    if(append) {
       offset=lseek(fd, 0, SEEK_END);
    }

    if(offset == (off_t) -1 ) {
       saved_errno=errno;
       close(fd);
       errno=saved_errno;
       return(NULL);
    }

    file=fdopen(fd, mode);

    if(!file) {
       saved_errno=errno;
       close(fd);
       errno=saved_errno;
       return(NULL);
    }
    if(debug>=5) {
       fprintf(stderr, "safer_fopen(): open successful\n");
    }
    return(file);
}

int safer_fclose(FILE *stream)
{
```

```
    int fd;

    fd=fileno(stream);
    fclose(stream);
    close(fd);
}


/* Invoke the program with a pathname as an argument. */
/* It will try to open the path as a file and print */
/* the files contents */
main(argc,argv)
int argc;
char *argv[];
{
    int i;
    char buf[4096];
    int fd;
    FILE *file;
    int rc;

    /* these two tests depend on printing out the CWD below */
    /* you cannot affect parent process CWD */

    #if 0    /* one_chdir_step() test */
       for(i=1; i<argc; i++) {
          one_chdir_step(argv[i]);
       }
    #endif

    #if 0    /* safer_chdir() test */
       assert(argc==2);
       safer_chdir(argv[1]);
    #endif

    #if 0    /* safer_open() test */
       assert(argc==2);
       fd=safer_open(argv[1],O_RDONLY,0);
       if(fd<0) {
          perror("error opening file");
          exit(1);
       } else {
          printf("open succesful\n");
       }
       rc=read(fd, buf, sizeof(buf));
       if(debug>=5) printf("rc=%d\n",rc);


       close(fd);
    #endif
```

35

SECURE
PROGRAMMING

continues

Listing 35.3 CONTINUED

```
#if 1  /* safer_fopen() test */
   assert(argc==2);
   file = safer_fopen(argv[1],"r");
   if(!file) {
      perror("Opening file");
      exit(1);
   }
   buf[0]=0;   /* clear buffer */
   while(fgets(buf,sizeof(buf),file)) {
      buf[sizeof(buf)-1]=0; /* terminate string */
      fputs(buf,stdout);
   }
   safer_fclose(file);
#endif

   getcwd(buf, sizeof(buf));
   printf("CWD=%s\n",buf);
}
```

chroot() Environments

Where possible, a server should operate in a chroot()ed environment. This will limit all file accesses to the chroot()ed directory tree, even those that result from execution of arbitrary code from a buffer overflow. Please note, however, that it is impossible to prevent such arbitrary binary code running as root from escaping from a chroot() jail.

> **NOTE**
>
> It is a good idea to explicitly set the current working directory for setuid programs or after executing chroot() to a relatively safe directory.

Splitting Programs

It is often a good idea to split privileged programs into smaller pieces that communicate with each other, with each program running with the minimum privileges needed to accomplish its duties. This minimizes the damage that can be caused by buffer overflows and many other exploits and allows you to focus your auditing on the critical programs. Be careful that the communications between programs is not itself vulnerable to attack. The qmail program, a replacement for sendmail, is one of the most aggressive examples of this approach. No one has come up with a way to exploit flaws in qmail itself to gain unauthorized access, although there have been minor DOS attacks.

Interprocess Communication

Virtually any method of interprocess communication can create weaknesses if you are not careful. Even if there were no vulnerabilities in the mechanism itself, you must be careful about the data that is passed. In general, DOS attacks are possible on all forms.

A pipe between a parent and a child is fairly safe. However, since the parent is often invoked by an untrusted user and the child performs privileged services, you need to be careful that the child was not started in a hostile execution environment, that data validation occurs in the child, and that the parent is who you think it is. The parent-child relationship can be cumbersome in many applications.

TCP/IP connections have the advantage of being usable over the network, but that can be a disadvantage as well since TCP/IP sockets are more accessible to the outside world. Peer information can be obtained if a trusted `identd` is running. It is possible for a peer to generate a couple types of signals.

UNIX domain sockets are not accessible to remote machines, which is a security advantage, but it also can be a disadvantage in many other respects. However, UNIX domain sockets rely on world-writable directories to create the socket unless both processes are running as the same user. This can be easily exploited using /tmp races. Various UNIX domain socket implementations have various serious problems. The file permissions are not checked for UNIX domain sockets on Solaris, BSD 4.3, or SunOS, so all sockets are world readable and writable; creating the socket in a protected directory may be safe. Linux and BSD 4.4 do check the permissions. Some older but still widely used Linux kernels will panic if you open too many sockets. There is no portable way to identify the peer on such a socket either; even the unportable ways are unpleasant. `SIGPIPE` and possibly other signals may be delivered.

Linux 2.1.x and probably 2.2.x have the ability to query the peer uid on sockets using socket options on one or maybe both types of sockets.

SYS V IPC messages, shared memory, and semaphores implement permission checks similar to file permission checks; I don't know of a reliable way to get the uid of a connected process, and more than two processes can share these resources. Semaphores are vulnerable to deadlocks. Since shared memory may be used to share access to internal program data structures, programs may be lazy about validating the information, or it may be changed between validation and use (copying to regular memory and then validating the data would be safer). It is also easy to insert executable code into shared memory and then use a buffer overflow to invoke it. A limited number of shared memory segments or semaphores can exist at one time and the table tends to fill up, particularly when processes are aborted, which can even lead to accidental denial of service. With the DIPC extensions (which are not installed by default) these resources may be shared across multiple machines, which has both advantages and disadvantages. DIPC is not available on other platforms (kernel mods are required). Programs that use DIPC may also have to deal with byte ordering problems.

Named pipes rely on the existence of a separate fifo object in the filesystem for each possible simultaneous connection, and probably do not queue connection requests; it appears that they honor file permissions.

Psuedottys can probably be used as an IPC mechanism. A variety of signals may be delivered. Filesystem permissions are checked but the filesystem objects are shared with other programs like telnetd, and so permissions need to be set at runtime by a process running as root. You need a way to tell the other process which psuedotty pair to use.

TLI allows access to uids/gids but apparently it isn't very well documented. TLI is not that widely available and may not even be available on Linux.

The `identd` Daemon

The identd daemon runs on computers and may be polled to determine the name of the user who owns a particular open TCP/IP connection using the RFC 1413 protocol. The data returned by identd is not necessarily trustworthy but is still useful. Only trust the data from an identd server for authentication purposes if you trust the security of the machine and the integrity of anyone who has root access.

identd is typically used to identify users and log that information. If there is trouble, that information may help narrow down the blame. Of course, anyone can run a bogus identd server on any machine they control. That is actually not the weakness it appears to be because after an attack your action will be to deny access to the smallest group possible, which includes the attacker. If you can narrow it down to a particular user you deny access to that user; otherwise, you deny access to the entire machine or even an entire network.

If you accept connections from the localhost or other secure machines on your local network, identd on those machines can usually be trusted to the same degree the machines themselves are and may be used to help authenticate users. identd queries may be vulnerable to various "man in the middle" and TCP hijacking attacks, which should be taken into account. Use of identd in this manner also helps validate that local TCP connections have not been spoofed; if that is the case, your identd daemon on the other side is likely to return an error that the connection in question does not exist on that machine. The attacker will have to work harder to spoof the original connection and the identd one as well. Your firewall should be configured to prevent outsiders from spoofing or hijacking TCP connections between internal hosts.

Beware, however, of ssh port forwarding or IP masquerading and `identd`. And take pre-cautions to insure that the response you received actually originated on the local host. A secret token of some sort is advisable to further verify the local origin and identity of a TCP/IP connection. This token may be stored, for example, in a file accessible only by a particular user.

TCP Versus UDP

This may ruffle a few feathers, but I don't recommend using UDP for anything because of its serious security drawbacks. TCP is vulnerable to DOS via open connections in which the data transfer is never completed, but in almost every other security aspect it is superior to UDP. UDP has some performance advantages that make it popular for applications such as remote filesystem access and real-time video and audio. Yet even those applications tend to have TCP versions. As a programmer, if you implement a UDP version you will probably have to supplement it with a TCP version to get through firewalls. You might as well start with the TCP version; there likely won't be a compelling reason to implement UDP.

TCP is much less vulnerable to source address spoofing than UDP due to the three-way handshake. TCP is vulnerable to hijacking but with UDP you don't even need to hijack.

TCP sessions can be authenticated once per session at the application level. A firewall only needs to validate a TCP connection when it is first opened and can tell what direction the connection is being made from, which is vital information to a firewall. There is no direction information for UDP; a firewall can't tell if an arbitrary UDP packet is an inbound request (which should usually be blocked) or an inbound reply (which may need to be allowed). Most firewalls block almost all UDP traffic and that which they don't block is very vulnerable to misuse.

Any application that does use UDP should probably reject any packets that originate from certain well known ports, particularly the one used by DNS; those packets are probably attacks that snuck through a firewall.

The popularity of UDP for real-time audio and video is primarily due to the fact that if a packet doesn't arrive there is no point in transmitting it. TCP connections may be used to for these applications with appropriate throttling algorithms, which limit the amount of data transmitted to what the link can sustainably handle. UDP applications also should throttle the data or quality will suffer. The only real difference is that a few extra retrans-mitted TCP packets may use up bandwidth when the throttling is not perfect. Multicast applications are stuck with UDP; these applications will be completely unusable across most firewalls.

Dynamic Versus Static Memory Allocation

Allocation of fixed size buffers can cause some inconvenience by imposing hard limits, but those limits are likely to be well known and clients can try to avoid them in advance. Differential truncation or residual data on a line after reaching a hard limit can cause problems as mentioned previously.

Programs that use dynamic memory are prone to memory leaks and fragmentation. Memory leaks are often not a big problem in short lived utility programs but they can cause problems in preforked server processes, which may normally live for days. As a guard against memory leaks, I normally make the process check the number of requests it has serviced and its total memory usage between requests, then have the process die and be replaced by a fresh process if either limit has been exceeded. The first check keeps minor leaks from consuming more memory than needed and the second stops fast leaks quickly.

Programs that use dynamic memory can also be the targets of DOS attacks that exhaust available system memory. Setting process limits with setrlimit() can help prevent total exhaustion of system resources but it may result in the process being terminated without warning; this could occur in an unexpected and inconvenient place, which could leave unfinished business. Having the process monitor its own usage can give it the opportunity to die more gracefully, but it may not always catch the problem in time unless the checks permeate all code that reads or copies data.

Buffer overflows in dynamically allocated memory can corrupt the memory pool itself; creative use of this might even permit an attacker to write to any arbitrary section of memory. Programmers who make heavy use of dynamic memory often allocate a new memory block after measuring the length of a string that will be copied; this is resistant to buffer overflows on copies but other techniques need to be used when reading from a data stream.

Use of stale pointers is a common problem in programs that use dynamic memory and can result in crashes, unpredictable behavior, and other buffer overflows or values mysteriously appearing in the wrong variable. It is helpful in programs that use either type of memory allocation scheme to include a distinctive signature field in each type of data structure. This will make it easier to detect many cases where a pointer points at the wrong data.

Programs that use dynamic memory, with or without using setrlimit() or other limiting techniques, still have hard limits, despite the rhetoric to the contrary; the limits are just larger and often less predictable. I prefer to avoid dynamic allocation in most cases and to exercise care when I do use it. Both schemes require careful usage.

Security Levels

The security level features implemented in newer kernels allow you to designate certain files as immutable or append only. While you cannot really use those from your own programs, they can be used to restrict access to important files, which may help reduce the damage caused by some exploits.

POSIX.1e Capabilities

POSIX.1e style capabilities being developed (Linux-Privs Project) will allow much finer control of the privileges a program has. Instead of very course controls, such as being root and not being root, this will allow fine tuning of exactly which privileged system calls a program can execute. By giving up all privileges that are not needed, a program can minimize the effects of many exploits.

A program that only needs the ability to bind to a restricted socket, for example, can give up others. Unfortunately, many daemons require the setuid() family of calls and I don't know of any plans to separate the ability to switch between various ordinary uids (normal users) and switching to privileged ones (root, bin, etc.). This would be very handy for the many daemons that access a user's files on their behalf. If you have write access to root's files, you can easily gain root privileges.

Erasing Buffers

If you use some form of binary communications with other processes you should be careful to erase buffers, particularly the portion of strings after the terminating null, to insure that you do not accidentally divulge sensitive information. Many years ago, I wrote a program that allowed me to obtain the plaintext of passwords from a NetWare server immediately after they had been accessed by someone else in another building. The server did not clear its buffers and always sent a reply of a certain minimum length; my program simply issued a system call that would fail and all but the first couple bytes of the previous request's response were returned unmodified.

HTML Form Submissions Past Firewalls

Web browsers on machines inside your firewall can be tricked by outside Web sites into transmitting arbitrary text to internal TCP based services (by specifying the target service in the ACTION attribute of the FORM tag). Some encodings permit more flexibility in attacks than others. Many browsers will block a few well-known services from being the target of form submissions. This deny known bad approach is problematic. All text-based (and possibly some binary encoded) TCP services other than HTTP should look for strings typically sent by Web browsers such as GET, PUT, POST, Content-Type:, Content-Length:, Referrer:, and Accept:. If any line received begins with one of these strings, log an attempted security violation (preferably along with the Referrer: field) and terminate processing of data and commands on that connection.

Snooping, Hijacking, and Man in the Middle Attacks

When writing servers and clients, you should keep in mind that it is possible for an attacker to modify or take over an existing TCP connection. UDP services are much more vulnerable. A "man in middle" attack can take over a TCP connection or even modify it in transit. This is easier if the attacker controls a machine between the two systems, or is at least attached to a network segment that the packets travel over. Hijacking attacks can be done remotely without control over the intervening network. Hijacking attacks normally involve guessing the sequence numbers on packets and interjecting packets with the right sequence number. A vulnerability recently reported in the Linux TCP/IP stack allows hijacking without needing to guess the sequence number; this will probably be fixed fairly quickly but many systems will still be running older kernels.

Snooping (a.k.a. sniffing or eavesdropping) on packets in transit is common. This is particularly common on ethernet segments where a compromised machine is used to snoop some or all packets on the ethernet segment. Every machine on a typical ethernet can intercept packets travelling between any two machines on that ethernet segment, including packets that are transiting the local network on their journey between two other networks. An attacker who has broken into your ISP's Web server may be able to see every packet that travels in and out of your Internet connection. Hubs do nothing to protect against this. Switches, bridges, routers, and firewalls reduce the vulnerability to snooping and spoofing by reducing the network into smaller segments. Many of these devices are not designed with security in mind, however, and can be tricked to allow sniffing or spoofing; choose and configure your network hardware carefully.

Particularly sensitive communications should require periodic re-validation, particularly before critical transactions such as those that would cause funds to be dispersed. Encryption is strongly recommended for sensitive communications.

Any security sensitive internal communications should be behind a firewall. Among other checks, the firewall should make sure that no outside host can spoof (masquerade as) any internal host, including localhost (127.0.0.1). This will make spoofing or hijacking of internal connections considerably more difficult but cannot protect connections where one party is outside.

HTML Server Includes

If your Web server has the server include feature enabled, there are a number of security implications, depending on your server version and configuration. An ordinary user on the system (or anyone who can install Web pages) may be able to use server includes to read an otherwise restricted file. Even worse, they may be able to execute arbitrary programs on the machine. Many CGI programs can be tricked into including server include tags in their output, which may be parsed by the server, allowing any remote user to do the same things. The server include tags may be included in form input, cookies, or the URL and may inadvertently be echoed by a CGI script.

Preforked Server Issues

Preforked servers, where a server spawns a fixed number (or limited range depending on load) of child processes in advance to handle incoming connections, are very efficient but have some special considerations. The code that manages the number of child processes often actually gives the server some protection against DOS attacks, which would cause the spawning of large numbers of processes. Remote users will have as much or more trouble getting through but the operation of the local machine is less likely to be disrupted.

Since preforked server processes often handle many different transactions, care must be taken to ensure that an attacker cannot influence the internal state in a way that could affect the processing of subsequent transactions. You must also ensure that an attacker cannot obtain information still stored in internal data structures about past transactions. Erasing data structures and the stack (use a recursive function that calls itself many times and initializes a large automatic variable with zeros) will help. Memory leaks will be more of a problem in preforked servers and other long-lived processes.

Timeouts

Any network client or server should have configurable timeouts with defaults appropriate to the application. In server processes, I normally set a timer using `alarm()` or `setitimer()` at the beginning of each transaction. The signal, if it arrives, must be handled appropriately. In the event that a DOS attack is detected, it may be appropriate to dramatically reduce the timeouts for the duration of the attack; this will adversely affect some users but will probably improve service for most.

35

SECURE PROGRAMMING

Three Factor Authentication

Authentication of users is normally based on one or more of the following three factors: biometric, knowledge, or possessions. Biometric factors are things such as signatures, fingerprints, retina scans, and voice prints. The second factor is based on something you know, usually a secret password, key, or token. The third is based on something you have in your possession, such as a smart card, a ring, a credit card sized one time password or time-based password generator, or a pregenerated list of challenge responses. For high security applications, it is advisable to use all three.

There is an interesting device called the Biomouse, which is a small fingerprint reader. A newer version also includes a smart card reader in the same unit. Linux drivers are available.

Many of these newfangled gadgets can be useful but they all have their limitations. Ignore all the sales hype that says they are invulnerable. Smart cards should have onboard encryption processors, not merely be memory based devices. Even then there is an impressive array of technology available to attack smart cards (or any other integrated circuit-based security device). Biometrics can be faked or recorded. You leave thousands of copies of your fingerprints every day that could be used to reconstruct your finger. The Biomouse senses pores as well as ridges, so a latent print may not be sufficient to reconstruct the necessary image but there can be other sources of that data, particularly from the biometric devices themselves. The fingerprint scanner used by a merchant down the street when one of your employees cashed a check or the elevator button that is really a clandestine scanner may be the key to fooling your fingerprint scanners. Voice prints can be recorded. The most common time-based token generator cards are based on old undocumented algorithms that would not be likely to withstand a serious reverse engineering attack. In extreme cases, biometric devices may be defeated by forcing an authorized user to allow access, or by very sophisticated mimicking devices. The data from these gadgets may be vulnerable to interception on a compromised workstation or network. These vulnerabilities are also a good reason to use two or three factor authentication. Gadgets can help to improve security, but beware of a false sense of security.

Pluggable Authentication Modules

Linux has borrowed the Pluggable Authentication Module (PAM) concept from Sun Microsystems. These separate out the authentication code from the application and put it in some shared library modules, which may be configured as needed for various sites. PAM can be configured to use /etc/passwd, shadow passwords, one-time passwords, zero knowledge systems such as SRP, remote authentication servers, and biometric systems such as the Biomouse. Other PAM modules check whether a user is on a local console or a remote terminal. Configuration files edited by the system manager instruct PAM on which modules to use for which applications and under which circumstances.

Applications that use PAM need to be modified to use the PAM API and should to be prepared to act as the middleman for a more complicated dialog than simply asking for a username and password. The PAM guides are available online at `http://www.sics.se/~pelin/pam/` and include a sample program.

Changing passwords is supported by PAM but changing other fields in `/etc/passwd` and `/etc/shadow` is not. Use the `putpwent()` function or see the sample program in Appendix A, "A Symbol Table Library," for an example of how to access the file directly.

If you want your program to be portable to systems that do not have PAM, I suggest writing a dummy PAM library that calls `getpw()` or `getpwent()` and `crypt()`, or try porting `libpwdb` to the target system. If you are not using PAM or `libpwdb`, you may need to deal with shadow passwords and NIS.

General Program Robustness

It is important to write security sensitive programs to be as robust as possible. Many security exploits depend on the fact that programs behave in unexpected ways in response to unexpected circumstances.

Check return values from functions. Check `errno` after using functions that set `errno` (such as some math functions). Make extensive use of `assert()` to verify assumptions. Functions that take pointers should do something sensible with NULL values. Functions that take a size parameter, giving the size of a string parameter which will be modified, should handle a size of zero or even a negative size.

Cryptography

This section will be brief and skimpy on the technical details due to export laws that make export of cryptographic hardware, software, or technical advice illegal, although a book is probably the safest way to export technical information on cryptography.

Encryption is vital to safeguarding sensitive information, particularly in transit. Cryptography is used to ensure the privacy of information in transit or storage, authenticate users and messages, and prevent repudiation (denying that you originated a message later when it proves inconvenient).

35

SECURE
PROGRAMMING

Small or large licenses for use of RSA's encryption software, RSAref, in commercial software (including the underlying algorithms) in clients and servers are obtained from Consensus (`http://www.consensus.com`); there are some inconvenient terms regarding reverse engineering. The cost per copy is significantly higher than the high volume licenses available to large software companies, but this is probably the most viable option for small software companies. SSLeay (see the following section, "Encryption Systems") can be compiled to use RSAref. If you want to use the various free applications in a commercial environment, it is possible to obtain licenses to the RSA algorithm for all free software on a given machine for price per machine; `Information` on this can be found at `http://www.rsa.com`.

Types of Cryptographic Algorithms

Beware of any encryption system that relies on an unpublished algorithm. These are usually extremely weak and might not even keep your kid sister out.

Hash functions provide one way (irreversible) encryption. These are commonly used for password storage, to generate one time passwords, and as file signatures used to determine whether a file has been altered. Although you cannot decrypt a hashed password, you can encrypt passwords supplied by the user and compare the hash values. Examples of hash algorithms are MD5, MD2, MD4, SHA, Tiger, and RIPE-MD-160. Hash functions can also be turned into symmetric ciphers.

Symmetric cipher algorithms use the same key to both encrypt and decrypt information. DES, 3DES, Blowfish, Twofish, RC4, and SAFER are examples of symmetric algorithms. Some of these algorithms are limited to fixed key lengths; others allow variable key lengths.

One problem with symmetric algorithms is key distribution. Both the sender and recipient need to have the same secret key. Asymmetric cipher algorithms use two separate keys, one public and one private. The public key can be made readily available. A document encrypted with the public key can only be decrypted with the private key and vice versa. Because these algorithms are normally much less efficient than symmetric systems, asymmetric systems are normally used to exchange a unique secret session key, which is then used to encrypt the actual data stream using a symmetric algorithm. Asymmetric systems normally require much longer key lengths to achieve the same level of security. 1024 bits is commonly used for a symmetric system. RSA, ElGamal, and LUC are public key (asymmetric) systems. Elliptic curves are also used.

Digital signatures use public key encryption and/or hashes to permit verifying the originator and/or content of a message and prevent repudiation of a message. X.509 certificates are essentially specially formatted and digitally signed binary documents that attest to the identity of a person, company, or Web server. The PGP encrypted mail system relies on key signatures, which are similar to certificates, to validate the association of a particular public key with a particular person or organization. Although certificates are usually issued by a central authority, key signatures are usually issued by specific individuals and each user of PGP decides whose signatures to trust; this forms what is referred to as a "web of trust".

Cryptographically secure pseudo-random number generator algorithms are an important part of many encryption systems, particularly public key systems. These are used for many purposes, including generating the unique session key, initially generating the private and public key pairs, and generating unique tokens for use a tokens for Web sites. RFC 1750 has recommendations for random number generators (`ftp://ftp.isi.edu/in-notes/rfc1750.txt`).

Zero knowledge systems can provide more security for user authentication without using algorithms that could encrypt data, and thus be subject to export controls. Stanford's SRP (Secure Remote Password) provides zero knowledge based password verification, which is not vulnerable to eavesdropping. Optionally, exchange of a session key for session encryption and a PAM module, and modified telnet and ftp programs are available. More information is available at `http://srp.stanford.edu/srp/`.

A more detailed overview of the different algorithms can be found on the Internet at `http://www.ssh.fi/tech/crypto/algorithms.html`. Bruce Schneier's book *Applied Cryptography* (2nd Edition, John Wiley & Sons, 1995) is the standard text in the field. This book is actually exportable but the floppy containing the software included as listings in the book is not. The cryptography FAQ, at `http://www.cis.ohio-state.edu/hypertext/faq/usenet/cryptography-faq/`, has more additional information, and most of the Web sites mentioned in this section will have links to other sites of interest.

Most ciphers are block oriented; they encrypt a block of some number of bits at a time and the operation is repeated until the whole stream is encrypted. Block chaining is frequently used so that the results of one block affect the operation of the next block. The block length is often equal to the key length.

Encryption Systems

The SSL algorithm is a public key based system introduced by Netscape and used to encrypt arbitrary TCP/IP data streams, and is widely used for encryption of Web pages. SSLeay is a very popular implementation of SSL. It can be downloaded from `ftp://ftp.psy.uq.oz.au/pub/Crypto/` and `ftp://www.replay.com`. These Web sites also have some other cryptography software. If you want to add encrypted TCP/IP communications to an application, check out SSLeay.

PGP, RIPEM, and GnuPG, CTC, S/MIME, and MOSS are public key based systems for secure email. Visit `http://www.gnupg.org/` for more information on GNU Privacy Guard and `http://www.bifroest.demon.co.uk/ctc/`.

SSH is a public key based replacement for the UNIX `rsh` program. SSH provides secure remote command execution, remote login, and remote copy. Personal use and even some commercial uses are free but a paid license is needed for many commercial uses. Other implementations are available; see `http://www.net.lut.ac.uk/psst/`. If you are writing a program that needs to invoke another program on another machine, SSH may suit your needs.

IPSEC refers to a set of interoperable standards for packet encryption at the router level. SWAN (`http://www.cygnus.com/~gnu/swan.html`), NIST Cerberus (`http://www.antd.nist.gov/cerberus/`), and the University of Arizona's Linux IPSEC implementation (`http://www.cs.arizona.edu/security/hpcc-blue/`) are various implementations available for Linux.

Encryption Vulnerabilities

Many algorithms are vulnerable to known plaintext and chosen plaintext attacks. Fortunately, most of the strong systems used today are resistant to these attacks.

Even if the underlying cryptographic algorithm is impenetrable, various flaws in the application of that algorithm can introduce vulnerabilities. The use of weak keys or weak random number sources (poor algorithm or poor seed) can cause problems. Do not trust public key cryptography too much on systems that do not have a source of hardware entropy for the random number generator. Linux has `/dev/random`, to provide a source of hardware entropy, derived from the timing of keyboard, mouse, interrupt, and disk access events. When you disable unnecessary services on a Linux system, do not disable `/etc/rc.d/init.d/random`, which saves state between reboots. FreeBSD and OpenBSD also have random devices but most other operating systems do not. Accidentally giving away the state of your random number generator by using it in other ways may simplify attack, particularly with weaker random number generators.

Breaking up data into small blocks encrypted separately can increase vulnerability in several ways. This often interrupts the block chaining. Padding may need to be used if data blocks are not an even multiple of the encryption block size. It may be possible for an attacker to insert blocks in the encrypted data stream. The SSH version 1 protocol included a cryptographically weak CRC-32 hash (designed to protect against line noise, not sneaky people) to verify the integrity of each data block.

A buffer overflow in critical portions of the network handling code could provide a way to compromise both the encrypted data streams and the computer system itself.

Reusing the same key more than once is a problem on many commonly used symmetric ciphers. This is one reason that most public key systems exchange a unique session key each session for the faster symmetric algorithm used to encrypt the actual data, instead of saving the session key for future communications between the two parties. Although many public key systems will allow you to bypass the asymmetric algorithm and use the symmetric algorithm using only a fixed secret key (which you have installed on both systems), this should probably be avoided since many of the symmetric algorithms these systems use can be compromised by key reuse.

Public key systems can be vulnerable to diverted connections, "man in the middle" and, to a lesser extent, tcp hijacking attacks. Since many public key systems exchange public keys when they initiate a connection, there can be problems if you are talking to the wrong host or if an attacker is intercepting and modifying the data stream as it crosses the Net; in these cases, the attacker can supply the wrong public key. Using certificates issued by a trusted authority for the machines at both ends of the connection or keeping a permanent record of known public keys between sessions can help.

These are just some of the ways in which cryptosystems can be compromised. Rather than attempt to provide an exhaustive list of vulnerabilities or detailed technical information, this section is intended to prompt the reader to think defensively and to conduct further research.

Summary

Writing secure programs requires careful attention to detail and thinking defensively. You should also imagine yourself as an attacker and look for potentially exploitable vulnerabilities. Using the information discussed in this chapter can help you spot the areas of your code that can provide the holes that people could exploit. An independent code review is recommended, as well as extensive testing in a non-mission critical environment.

Debugging: GNU gdb

by Kurt Wall

CHAPTER

36

As much as we all hate to admit it, software will have bugs. This chapter describes one of the Free Software Foundation's premier tools, gdb, the GNU DeBugger. While debugging sessions will never be aggravation free, gdb's advanced features lighten the load and enable you to be more productive. Time and effort invested in learning gdb is time well spent if you can track down and fix a serious bug in just a few minutes. gdb can make this happen.

Compiling for gdb

As you learned in Chapter 3, "GNU cc," debugging requires that your source code be compiled with -g in order to create an enhanced symbol table. So, the following command:

```
$ gcc -g file1.c file2.c -o prog
```

will cause prog to be created with debugging symbols in its symbol table. If you want, you can use gcc's -ggdb option to generate still more (gdb-specific) debugging information. However, to work most effectively, this option requires that you have access to the source code for every library against which you link. While this can be very useful in certain situations, it can also be expensive in terms of disk space. In most cases, however, you should be able to get by with the plain -g option.

As also noted in Chapter 3, it is possible to use both the -g and -O (optimization) options. However, because optimization changes the resulting program, the relationship you expect to exist between the code you wrote and the executing binary may not exist. Variables or lines of code may have disappeared or variable assignments may occur at times when you do not expect it. My recommendation is that you wait until you have debugged your code as completely as possible before starting to optimize it. In the long run, it will make your life, especially the parts of it you spend debugging, much simpler and less stressful.

WARNING

Do not strip your binaries if you distribute programs in binary form. It is a matter of courtesy to your users and may even help you. If you get a bug report from a user who obtained a binary-only version, she will be unable to provide helpful information if you used strip to discard all symbols from the binary in order to make the binary smaller. Although she *might* be willing to download a source distribution in order to recompile with debugging enabled, it would be presumptuous of you to ask.

Using Basic gdb Commands

Most of what you will need to accomplish with gdb can be done with a surprisingly small set of commands. This section shows you just enough gdb commands to get you going. A later section, "Advanced gdb Concepts and Commands," will cover a few advanced features that will come in handy.

Starting gdb

To start a debugging session, simply type **gdb progname [corefile]**, replacing prog-name with the name of the program you want to debug. Using a core file is optional, but will enhance gdb's debugging capabilities. For this chapter, we will use Listing 36.1 to work through examples.

Listing 36.1   A PROGRAM WITH BUGS

```
1   /*
2    * Listing 36.1
3    * debugme.c - Poorly written program to debug
4    */
5   #include <stdio.h>
6   #include <stdlib.h>
7
8   #define BIGNUM 5000
9
10  void index_to_the_moon(int ary[]);
11
12  int main(void)
13  {
14      int intary[10];
15
16      index_to_the_moon(intary);
17
18      exit(EXIT_SUCCESS);
19  }
20
21  void index_to_the_moon(int ary[])
22  {
23      int i;
24      for(i = 0; i < BIGNUM; ++i)
25          ary[i] = i;
26  }
```

I compiled this program using the following command:

```
$ gcc -g debugme.c -o debugme
```

I tried to run it by typing `./debugme`, and it immediately caused a segmentation fault and dumped core (on Red Hat 5.2).

The first step is to start `gdb`, using the program name, `debugme`, and the core file, `core`, as arguments:

```
$ gdb debugme core
```

The screen should resemble Figure 36.1 after `gdb` initializes.

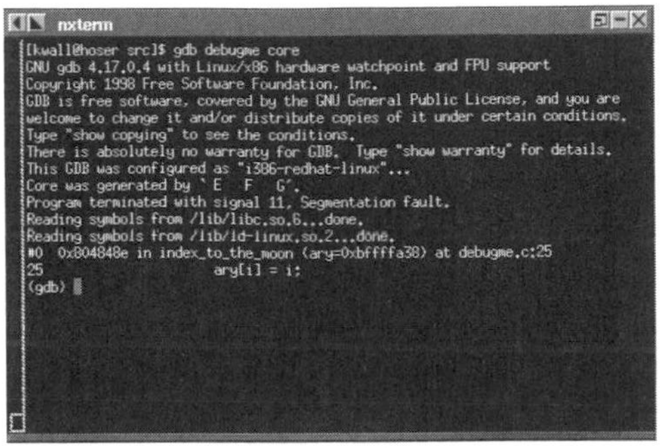

FIGURE 36.1

The `gdb` start-up screen.

If you don't like the licensing messages (they annoy me), use the `-q` (or `—quiet`) option to suppress them. Another useful command-line option is `-d dirname`, where `dirname` is the name of a directory, to tell `gdb` where to find source code (it looks in the current working directory by default). As you can see from the figure, `gdb` reports the executable that created the core file and why the program terminated. In this case, the program caused a signal 11, which is a segmentation fault. It also helpfully displays the function it was executing and the line it believes caused the fault (line 25).

The first thing you would want to do is run the program in the debugger. The command to do this is `run`. You can pass any arguments to the `run` command that your program would ordinarily accept. In addition, the program will receive a properly set up shell environment as determined by the value of the environment variable `$SHELL`. If you want, however, you can use `gdb` commands to set or unset arguments and environment variables after you have started a debugging session. To do so, type **set args arg1 arg2** to set command-line arguments and **set environment env1 env2** to set environment variables.

> **TIP**
>
> If you forget a gdb command or are not sure of its exact syntax, gdb has a rich help system. A bare `help` command typed at the gdb prompt will give a short listing of available command categories, while `help <topic>` will print help information for `<topic>`. As always, gdb has a complete help system, TeXinfo documentation, and an excellent manual, *Debugging With GDB*, which is available online and by mail order from the FSF.

Attempting to run the program in the debugger, it stops after receiving the SIGSEGV signal:

```
(gdb) run
Starting program: /home/kwall/projects/lpu/36/src/debugme

Program received signal SIGSEGV, Segmentation fault.
0x804848e in index_to_the_moon (ary=0xbffffa08) at debugme.c:25
25                      ary[i] = i;
(gdb)
```

Inspecting Code in the Debugger

The question, though, is what was happening in the function `index_to_the_moon`? You can execute the `backtrace` command to generate the function tree that led to the seg fault. The function trace looks like the following:

```
(gdb) backtrace
#0  0x804848e in index_to_the_moon (ary=0xbffffa08) at debugme.c:25
#1  0x804844f in main () at debugme.c:16
#2  0xb in ?? ()
(gdb)
```

> **TIP**
>
> It is not necessary to type complete command names while using gdb. Any abbreviation that is unique will do. For example, `back` will suffice for `backtrace`.

So, the problem was, indeed, in `index_to_the_moon()`, which was called from the `main()` function. It would be helpful, however, to have some idea of the context in which the offending line(s) of code exist. For this purpose, use the `list` command, which takes the general form, `list [m,n]`. `m` and `n` are the starting and ending line numbers you want displayed. Just a bare `list` command will display ten lines of surrounding code, as illustrated in the following:

```
(gdb) list
20
21  void index_to_the_moon(int ary[])
22  {
23      int i;
24      for(i = 0; i < BIGNUM; ++i)
25          ary[i] = i;
26  }
(gdb)
```

With a clear picture of what is happening in the code, you can then decide what has gone wrong.

Examining Data

One of `gdb`'s most useful features is the capability to display both the type and the value of almost any expression, variable, or array in a program being debugged. It will print the value of any expression legal in the language in which your program is written. The command is, predictably enough, `print`. The following are some `print` commands and their results:

```
(gdb) print i
$1 = 382
(gdb) print ary[i]
Cannot access memory at address 0xc0000000.
(gdb) print ary[i-1]
$2 = 381
```

Although in this example, the program crashed at `i=382`, where it crashes on your system will depend on its memory layout.

The second command, `print ary[i]`, makes it pretty clear that the program does not have access to the memory location specified, although it does have legal access to the preceding one. The $1 and $2 refer to entries in the value history. If you want to access these values in the future, use these aliases rather than retyping the command. For example, the command $1-1 produces:

```
(gdb) print $1-1
$4 = 381
```

You are not limited to using discrete values, because gdb can display the values of an arbitrary region of memory. To print the first memory locations associated with ary, use the following command:

```
(gdb) print ary@10
$5 = {0xbfffffa08, 0x0, 0x1, 0x2, 0x3, 0x4, 0x5, 0x6, 0x7, 0x8
```

The notation @10 means to print the 10 values that begin at ary. Say, on the other hand, that you want to print the five values stored in ary beginning with the 71st element. The command for this would be the following:

```
(gdb) print ary[71]@5
$6 = {71, 72, 73, 74, 75}
```

Because each print command creates an entry in gdb's value history, you can use the aggregate array values later on.

You might be wondering why the first print command displayed hexadecimal values and the second one displayed decimal values. First, remember that arrays in C are zero-based. Remember also that the bare array name is a pointer to the base of the array. So, gdb looked at ary, saw that it was the address of the array's base, and displayed it and the following nine values as memory addresses. Memory addresses are customarily displayed in hexadecimal. If you want to display the first ten values stored in ary, use the indexing operator, [], with the index of the first value, 0, as illustrated:

```
(gdb) print ary[0]@10
$9 = {0, 1, 2, 3, 4, 5, 6, 7, 8, 9}
```

> **NOTE**
>
> gdb is usually compiled with support for the GNU readline library, which means that it supports the command-line editing and history features of the bash shell. For example, to recall a previous command, use the up arrow key to scroll back through the command history. See the readline manual page for more details about command-line editing.

gdb also can tell you the types of variables using the whatis command:

```
(gdb) whatis i
type = int
(gdb) whatis ary
type = int *
(gdb) whatis index_to_the_moon
type = void (int *)
```

This feature may seem rather useless because, of course, you know the types of all the variables in your program (yeah, right!). But, you will change your mind the first time you have to debug someone else's code or have to fix a multi-file project and have not looked at one of the source files for a couple of months.

Setting Breakpoints

As you debug problematic code, it is often useful to halt execution at some point. gdb allows you to set breakpoints on several different kinds of code constructs, including line numbers and function names, and also enables you to set conditional breakpoints, where the code only stops if a certain condition is met.

To set a breakpoint on a line number, use the following syntax:

```
(gdb) break <linenum>
```

and, to set a breakpoint on a function name, use:

```
(gdb) break <funcname>
```

In either case, gdb will halt execution before executing the specified line number or entering the specified function. You can then use print to display variable values, for example, or use list to review the code that is about to be executed. If you have a multi-file project and want to halt exccution on a line of code or in a function that is not in the current source file, use the following forms:

```
(gdb) break <filename:linenum>
(gdb) break <filename:funcname>
```

Conditional breakpoints are usually more useful. They allow you temporarily to halt program execution if a particular condition is met. The correct syntax for setting conditional breakpoints is:

```
(gdb) break <linenum or funcname> if <expr>
```

expr can be any expression that evaluates to true (non-zero). For example, the following break command stops execution at line 25 of debugme when the variable i equals 15:

```
(gdb) break 25 if i == 15
Breakpoint 1 at 0x804847c: file debugme.c, line 24.
(gdb) run
Starting program: /home/kwall/projects/lpu/36/src/debugme

Breakpoint 1, index_to_the_moon (ary=0xbffffa08) at debugme.c:25
25                          ary[i] = i;
(gdb)
```

As you can see, gdb stopped on line 25. A quick print command confirms that it stopped at the value of i we requested:

```
(gdb) print i
$14 = 15
```

If the program is already running when you enter the run command, gdb will say that the program has already started and ask if you want to restart it from the beginning. Say yes.

To resume executing after hitting a breakpoint, simply type continue. If you have set many breakpoints and have lost track of what has been set and which ones have been triggered, you can use the info breakpoints command to refresh your memory. The delete command allows you to delete breakpoints, or you can merely disable them. Figure 36.2 illustrates the output of the following commands:

```
(gdb) info breakpoints
(gdb) delete 3
(gdb) disable 4
(gdb) info breakpoints
```

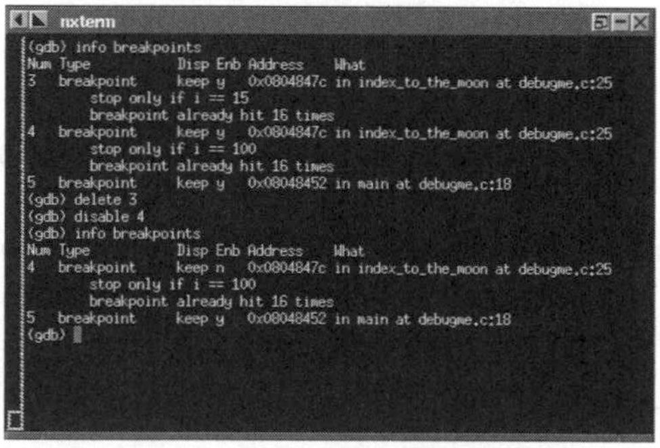

FIGURE 36.2

gdb *has sophisticated facilities for managing breakpoints.*

In Figure 36.2, I used the info command to obtain a list of available breakpoints, deleted the third breakpoint, disabled the fourth, and then redisplayed breakpoint information. It probably will not surprise you that the command to re-enable a disabled breakpoint is enable N, where N is the breakpoint number.

Examining and Changing Running Code

You have already seen the print and whatis commands, so we will not rehash them here, except to point out that if you use the print command to display the value of an expression, and that expression modifies variables the program uses, you are changing values in a running program. This is not necessarily a bad thing, but you do need to understand that what you are doing has side effects.

One of the whatis command's shortcomings is that it only gives you the type of a variable or function. If you have a structure, such as the following:

```
struct s {
    int index;
    char *name;
} *S;
```

and type

```
(gdb) whatis S
```

gdb reports only the name of the structure

```
type = struct s *
```

If you want the structure's definition, use the ptype command as follows:

```
(gdb) ptype S
type = struct s {
    int index;
    char *name;
} *
```

If you want to change the value of a variable (keeping in mind that this change will affect the running code), the gdb command is:

```
(gdb) set variable varname = value
```

where varname is the variable you want to change and value is varname's new value. Returning to Listing 36.1, use the delete command to delete all the breakpoints and watchpoints you may have set, and then set the following breakpoint:

```
(gdb) break 25 if i == 15
```

and run the program. It will temporarily halt execution when the variable i equals 15. After the break, issue this command to gdb:

```
(gdb) set variable i = 10
```

This resets i to 10. Execute a print i command to confirm that variable's value has been reset, and then issue the step command three times, followed by another print i. You will see that i's value has incremented by one after one iteration through the for loop. Besides demonstrating that you can alter a running program, these steps also illustrate how to single-step through a program. The step command executes a program one statement at a time.

> **NOTE**
>
> It is not necessary to type "step" three times. gdb remembers the last command executed, so you can simply press the Enter key to re-execute the last command, a real finger saver. This works for most gdb commands. See the documentation for more details.

The next command, on the other hand, executes an entire function when it encounters one, while the step command would only "step" into the function and continue execution one statement at a time.

The final method for examining a running program I will discuss is calling functions, using the call, finish, and return commands. Table 36.1 lists the syntax and function of these commands.

Table 36.1 COMMANDS FOR WORKING WITH FUNCTIONS

Command	Description
call name(args)	Call and execute the function named name with the arguments args
finish	Finish running the current function and print its return value, if applicable
return value	Stop executing the current function and return value to the caller

Use the call command in exactly the same way you would call the named function. For example, the command

```
(gdb) call index_to_the_moon(intary)
```

executes the function index_to_the_moon with intary as the argument. You can set breakpoints and use gdb features as you normally would when you call a function this way. If you do set a breakpoint inside the function, you can use continue to resume execution, finish to complete the function call and stop execution when the function returns, or use the return command to abort the function and return a specified value to the caller.

Advanced gdb Concepts and Commands

This section discusses a few complicated concepts and some sophisticated commands that will make your gdb usage more productive and less frustrating. The concepts include gdb's notions of variable scope and variable context. The commands include traversing the call stack, working with source files, the shell command, and attaching to an existing process.

Variable Scope and Context

At any given time, gdb considers a variable either active or inactive, which affects the variables to which you have access and can examine and manipulate. You cannot access variables that are not "in context" or are inactive. There are a few rules that define what constitutes an active or in context variable.

- Local variables in any function are active if that function is running or if control has passed to a function called by the controlling function. Say the function foo() calls the function bar(); as long as bar() is executing, all variables local to foo() and bar() are active. Once bar() has returned, only local variables in foo() are active, and thus accessible.

- Global variables are always active, regardless of whether the program is running.

- Nonglobal variables are inactive unless the program is running.

So much for variable context. What is gdb's notion of variable context? The complication arises from the use of static variables, which are file local, that is, you can have identically named static variables in several files, and they will not conflict because they are not visible outside the file in which they are defined. Fortunately, gdb has a way to identify to which variable you are referring. It resembles C++'s scope resolution operator. The syntax is

```
file_or_funcname::varname
```

where varname is the name of the variable to which you want to refer and file_or_funcname is the name of the file or the function in which it appears. So, for example, given two source code files, foo.c and bar.c, each containing a variable named baz, that is declared static, to refer to the one in foo.c you might write the following:

```
(gdb) print `foo.c'::baz
```

The single quotes around the filename are required so that gdb knows you are referring to a filename. Similarly, given two functions, blat() and splat(), each with an integer variable named idx, the following commands would print the addresses of idx in each function:

```
(gdb) print &blat::idx
(gdb) print &splat::idx
```

Traversing the Call Stack

gdb provides two commands for moving up and down the call stack, which is the chain of function calls that got you to the current location in the code. Imagine a program in which the main() function calls the function make_key(), which in turn calls the function get_key_num(). The function get_key_num() in turn calls number(). Listing 36.2 shows a dummy program illustrating this.

Listing 36.2 A CALL CHAIN THREE FUNCTIONS DEEP

```
1    /*
2     * Listing 36.2
3     * callstk.c - A complicated calling chain to illustrate
4     * traversing the call stack with gdb
5     */
6    #include <stdio.h>
7    #include <stdlib.h>
8
9    int make_key(void);
10   int get_key_num(void);
11   int number(void);
12
13   int main(void)
14   {
15       int ret = make_key();
16       fprintf(stdout, "make_key returns %d\n", ret);
17       exit(EXIT_SUCCESS);
18   }
19
20   int make_key(void)
21   {
22       int ret = get_key_num();
23       return ret;
24   }
25
26   int get_key_num(void)
27   {
28       int ret = number();
29       return ret;
```

continues

Listing 36.2   CONTINUED

```
30  }
31
32  int number(void)
33  {
34      return 10;
35  }
```

Using the break command, set a breakpoint at line 32:

```
(gdb) break 32
Breakpoint 1 at 0x80484fc: file callstk.c, line 32.
```

and then run the program with the run command. It stops at line 32. Next, type the command where, which prints the following (the hexadecimal addresses will almost certainly be different):

```
(gdb) where
#0  number () at callstk.c:33
#1  0x80484cf in make_key () at callstk.c:22
#2  0x804849b in main () at callstk.c:15
(gdb)
```

The display shows the call chain in reverse order; that is, that number() (#0) was called by make_key()(#1), which in turn had been called by the main() function. The up command moves up the call stack one function call, placing you on line 22. The down command moves control back the number() function. Executing the step command three times moves you back or up the get_key_num() function, at which point you could print the value of the variable ret to see its value. Figure 36.3 illustrates the results of the command sequence just described.

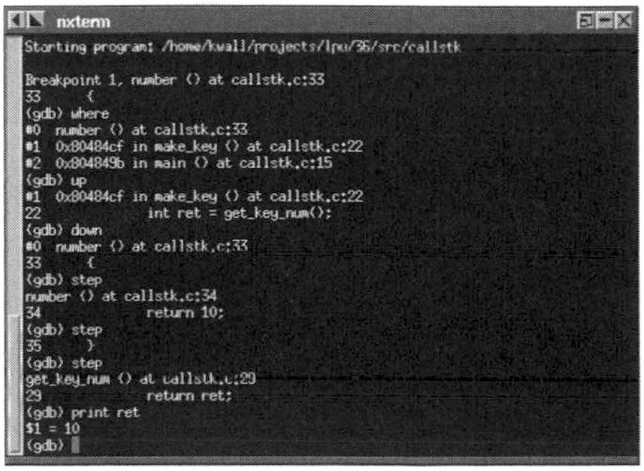

FIGURE 36.3

Traversing
callstk's *call*
chain.

The commands for traversing the call chain, combined with those for examining variable values, give you low-level insight into the innards of a running program. This level of control will prove invaluable to you as you hone your debugging skills and track down intractable bugs buried deep inside a chain of function calls.

Working with Source Files

Locating a specific function in a multi-file project is a breeze with gdb, provided you use the -d switch, mentioned in the section "Starting gdb", to tell it where to find additional source code files. This is a particularly helpful option when all of your source code is not located in your current working directory or in the program's compilation directory (which is recorded in its symbol table). To specify one or more additional directories, start gdb using one or more -d <dirname> options, as illustrated in the following:

```
$ gdb -d /source/project1 -d /oldsource/project1 -d
➥/home/gomer/src killerapp
```

To locate the next occurrence of a particular string in the current file, use the search <string> command. Use reverse-search <string> to find the previous occurrence. Returning to Listing 36.2 for a moment, suppose the program has stopped at the breakpoint you set in the previous example, line 32. If you want to find the previous occurrence of the word "return," use the following command:

```
(gdb) reverse-search return
```

gdb obliges and displays the text listed below:

```
(gdb) reverse-search return
29              return ret;
```

Using the search and reverse-search commands is especially helpful in large source files that have dozens or hundreds of lines.

Communicating with the Shell

While running a debugging session, you will often need to execute commands at the shell's command prompt. gdb provides the shell command to enable you to do so without leaving gdb. The syntax for this command is

```
(gdb) shell <command>
```

where command is the shell command you want to execute. Suppose you have forgotten what your current working directory is. Simply execute the following command :

```
(gdb) shell pwd
```

and gdb will pass the command pwd to the shell, executing it with /bin/sh:

```
/home/kwall/projects/lpu/36/src
```

Attaching to a Running Program

The final advanced procedure I will discuss is how to use gdb to attach to a running process, such as a system daemon. The procedure to accomplish this is very similar to starting gdb, except that the second argument to gdb is the PID (process ID) of the executable to which you want to attach, rather than the name of the core file. gdb will complain that it cannot find a file named PID, but you can safely ignore this because gdb always checks for a file first to see if there is a core file available. Figure 36.4 is a truncated display of U's attempt to attach to the httpd server daemon running on my system.

FIGURE 36.4

Attaching to the httpd *server daemon.*

Attaching to a running process automatically halts it so you can inspect its status using the normal gdb commands. When you are done, simply type quit, which will detach from the running process and allow it to continue. If gdb is already running, you can use the attach and file commands to obtain access to the program. First, use the file command to specify the program running in the process and to load its symbol table, as in the following:

```
(gdb) file httpd
Reading symbols from httpd...(no debugging
➥symbols found)...done.
(gdb) attach 386
Attaching to program `/usr/sbin/httpd', Pid 386
Reading symbols from /lib/libm.so.6...done.
Reading symbols from /lib/libcrypt.so.1...done.
Reading symbols from /lib/libdb.so.2...done.
Reading symbols from /lib/libdl.so.2...done.
Reading symbols from /lib/libc.so.6...done.
Reading symbols from /lib/ld-linux.so.2...done.
...
```

As you can see from this example, `attach` expects a process ID as its argument, then proceeds to load symbols from the various libraries against which the attached program has been linked. Again, when you have completed examining the attached process, issue the `detach` command to allow it to continue executing.

Summary

This chapter has only scratched the surface of gdb's capabilities. A full exposition of what it can do would require several hundred pages. As stated at the beginning of this chapter, the more time you invest in learning gdb, the more benefit you will derive from your debugging sessions. In this chapter, you have learned how to start gdb, have seen the basic commands required for the simplest usage, and have used some of its more advanced features. gdb is your friend—learn to exploit it.

Finishing Touches

PART
VI

IN THIS PART

CHAPTER 37

Package Management

by Kurt Wall

IN THIS CHAPTER

The topic of package management, which is the creation, distribution, installation, and upgrade of software, particularly source code, usually gets no attention in programming survey books such as this one. This unfortunate oversight is remedied in this chapter, which looks at the GNU project's `tar` and `install` utilities and Red Hat's Red Hat Package Manager, RPM.

The previous thirty-six chapters focused on hacking code and on tools and utilities that ease the hacker's endeavor. However, the fastest, coolest code in the world will become shelfware if it is extraordinarily difficult to install or renders a user's system useless after she installs it. The same applies to upgrading existing software. For many years, the Free Software Foundation's `tar` and `install` utilities were the *de facto* standard for distributing software, either in source or binary form. They worked (and still work) well, if you understood their limitations, particularly with respect to version and dependency checking. Red Hat's RPM system addresses these and other warts of `tar` and `install`, and, properly used by hacker and end user alike, make software distribution a breeze.

Understanding tar Files

`tar`, which stands for Tape ARchiver, creates, manages, and extracts multi-file archives, known as "tarfiles," or, more affectionately and idiomatically, "tarballs." `tar` is the traditional utility used to create archives, along with `cpio`, which is not covered. A complete description of `tar` reaches well beyond this book's scope, so this chapter focuses on typical and simple usage as related to the creation and management of software distribution. It is also assumed that the user downloading your code knows how to unpack a tarball and view a README file that explains the idiosyncrasies of installing your software. Table 37.1 discusses `tar`'s command-line options, which the following sections discuss in more detail.

Table 37.1 `tar` COMMAND-LINE OPTIONS

Option	Description
c	Create an archive
f archive_name	Name the archive archive_name
r	Append files to the archive
u	Update existing files in the archive
t	List the contents of the archive
v	Generate verbose output
z	Create or work with a compressed archive (gzip is the default compression utility)

Creating tar Files

In its simplest form, the command to create a tarball is

```
$ tar cf {archive_name} {file_Spec}
```

c says to "create" a tarball from the file(s) indicated by `file_spec`. f says to name the
tarball `archive_name`. You will generally want to compress the tarball to save disk space
and download time. The easiest way to do so, using GNU's `tar`, is to add z to the option
list, which causes `tar` to invoke another GNU utility, `gzip`, on the tarball to compress it,
as in the following:

```
$ tar czf {archive_name} {file_spec}
```

To illustrate, the CD-ROM that accompanies this book contains the source files used to
build the `tar` utility itself (version 1.12, to be precise). First, create a tarball (you will
need to copy the contents of the file from the source code directory on the CD-ROM,
`/source/37`, to your hard disk):

```
$ tar cf tar.tar *
```

We use the standard wildcard (*) to request that all files and directories in the current
directory be stored in the tarball. A quick `ls` command shows that none of the source
files were removed, but that a new file, named, as requested, `tar.tar`, was created:

```
total 3683
-rw-r--r--   1 kwall     users        11451 Apr 19  1997 ABOUT-NLS
-rw-r--r--   1 kwall     users         1040 Apr 19  1997 AC-PATCHES
-rw-r--r--   1 kwall     users         9656 Apr 23  1997 AM-PATCHES
-rw-r--r--   1 kwall     users          732 Apr 18  1997 AUTHORS
...
drwxr-xr-x   2 kwall     users         1024 Apr 25  1997 src
-rw-r--r--   1 kwall     users           10 Apr 25  1997 stamp-h.in
-rw-r--r--   1 kwall     users      3256320 May  3 22:54 tar.tar
drwxr-xr-x   2 kwall     users         1024 Apr 25  1997 tests
```

As you can see, the tarball is quite large. You can either run `gzip` on the file separately,
or use `tar`'s z option to reduce the file size and, thus, the download time:

```
$ tar czf tar.tar.gz *
$ ls -l tar.tar.gz
-rw-r--r--   1 kwall     users      2590545 May  3 23:42 tar.tar.gz
$ gzip tar.tar
$ ls -l tar.tar.gz
-rw-r--r--   1 kwall     users      1712020 May  3 23:41 tar.tar.gz
```

The compression option slows down `tar`'s operation somewhat, but saves typing. On the
other hand, calling `gzip` directly results in much better compression, but you have to
type an additional command to prepare your package for distribution. Hackers being lazy
critters, `Makefiles` usually include a target such as `dist` that creates a gzipped tarball.

37

PACKAGE
MANAGEMENT

This reduces the amount of typing you'll have to do and is also a convenience: simply type **make dist** and your package is ready to upload for the rest of the world to download.

Updating tar Files

So, now you have a nicely packaged and compressed tarball. But, suddenly, you realize you neglected to include the documentation. You *did* write documentation, didn't you? Never fear, you can easily add new files to (or update existing files in) the tarball using tar's append or update options.

To append your newly written documentation to the compressed tarball we created a few sentences ago, execute

```
$ tar rfz tar.tar.gz *.doc
```

(which assumes that the files you want to append all have a .doc extension). The r instructs tar to append the specified files to the end of the tarball. If, similarly, you modified some files already present in the archive and want to update the tarball with the modified files, use tar's update option (u):

```
$ tar uzf tar.tar.gz {updated_file_spec}
```

where updated_file_spec indicates the files that have changed.

Listing the Contents of tar Files

Finally, if you lose track of what files your tarball contains, or their dates, you can list the files in an archive using, predictably, the list option (t):

```
$ tar tzvf tar.tar.gz
```

We have added GNU's standard option for verbose output, v. Executing this command produces the following listing (truncated for brevity's sake):

```
-rw-r--r-- kwall/users 3246080 1999-05-03 23:48 ABOUT-NLS
-rw-r--r-- kwall/users    1040 1997-04-19 13:35 AC-PATCHES
-rw-r--r-- kwall/users    9656 1997-04-23 07:15 AM-PATCHES
-rw-r--r-- kwall/users     732 1997-04-18 13:32 AUTHORS
-rw-r--r-- kwall/users   85570 1997-04-25 18:21 BACKLOG
-rw-r--r-- kwall/users    2545 1997-04-24 06:16 BI-PATCHES
-rw-r--r-- kwall/users   17996 1996-03-24 11:49 COPYING
...
-rw-r--r-- kwall/users      63 1997-04-25 14:05 doc/version.texi
-rw-r--r-- kwall/users  354244 1997-04-24 07:19 doc/tar.texi
-rwxr-xr-x kwall/users    1961 1997-03-18 13:14 doc/convtexi.pl
-rw-r--r-- kwall/users   18106 1997-02-02 09:55 doc/getdate.texi
-rw-r--r-- kwall/users    9241 1997-04-15 16:28 doc/header.texi
...
```

Understanding the `install` Command

Consider `install` a `cp` command on steroids. In addition to copying files, it sets their permissions and, if possible, their owner and group. It can also create destination directories if they do not already exist. `install` is usually used in `Makefiles` as part of a rule for a target named (something like) "install." It can also be used in shell scripts.

`install`'s general syntax is

```
$ install [option[...]] source[...] dest
```

where `source` is one or more files to copy and `dest` is either the name of the target file or, if multiple files are specified in `source`, a directory. `option` can be one or more values listed in Table 37.2.

Table 37.2   `install` COMMAND-LINE OPTIONS

Option	Argument	Description
-g	group	Set the group ownership on file(s) to the GID or group name specified in `group`. The default GID is that of the parent process calling `install`.
-o	owner	Set the ownership of file(s) to the UID or user name specified in `owner`. The default `owner` is root.
-m	mode	Set the file mode (permissions) to the octal or symbolic value specified in `mode`. The default file mode is 755, or read/write/execute for owner and read/execute for group and other.

To specify `dest` as a directory, use the following syntax:

```
$ install -d [option [...]] dir[...]
```

The `-d` switch instructs `install` to create the directory `dir`, including any parent directories necessary, using any of the attributes listed in Table 37.2 or the default attributes.

In our first example, taken from the `Makefile` for gdbm, the GNU database library, after expanding some of the `make` variables, the "install" target is:

```
1   install: libgdbm.a gdbm.h gdbm.info
2       install -c -m 644 libgdbm.a $(libdir)/libgdbm.a
3       install -c -m 644 gdbm.h $(includedir)/gdbm.h
4       install -c -m 644 $(srcdir)/gdbm.info $(infodir)/gdbm.info
```

The make variables libdir, includedir, srcdir, and infodir are, respectively, /usr/lib, /usr/include, /usr/src/build/info, and /usr/info. So, libgdbm.a and gdbm.h will be read/write for the root user and read-only for everyone else. The file libgdbm.a gets copied to /usr/lib; gdbm.h, the header, winds up in /usr/include. The Texinfo file, gdbm.info, gets copied from /usr/src/build/info to /usr/info/gdbm.info. install overwrites existing files of the same name. The -c option is included for compatibility with older versions of install on other UNIX versions. You should include this, but, in most cases, it will be ignored.

> **NOTE**
>
> Under Linux, install silently ignores -c; it has no effect.

Our second and final example, Listing 37.1, creates a sct of directories under /tmp and sets some odd file modes on the files installed to demonstrate install features the first example did not cover. It is available as a shell script on the CD-ROM. Unless you have peculiar permissions on /tmp, it should execute without incident. The script uses some of the files from the tar source distribution on the CD-ROM. Feel free to delete the entire /tmp/lpu-install directory after it completes and you have inspected its contents.

Listing 37.1   lpu-install.sh

```
 1 #!/bin/sh
 2 # Listing 38.1
 3 # lpu-install.sh - Demonstrate (perverse) `install' usage
 4 # #####################################################
 5
 6 INSTALL=$(which install)
 7 LPU=/tmp/lpu-install
 8 SRC=./src
 9
10 for DIR in 10 20 30
11 do
12     $INSTALL -c -d -o $USER $LPU/$DIR
13     $INSTALL -c -m 111 -o $USER $SRC/*.c $LPU/$DIR
14 done
15
16 if [ $USER = root ]; then
17     for GRP in $(cut -f1 -d: /etc/group)
18     do
19         $INSTALL -c -d -o $USER -g $GRP $LPU/$GRP
20         $INSTALL -c -m 400 -g $GRP *.el $LPU/$GRP
21     done
22 fi
```

If the syntax of the shell script confuses you, re-read Chapter 34, "Shell Programming with GNU `bash`." Or, skip it, since our interest here is `install`'s behavior (lines 12 and 13 and 19 and 20). Note, however, that the second code block (lines 16[nd]21) will fail if not run by the root user. Line 12 creates three directories rooted in `/tmp`: `/tmp/lpu-install/10`, `/tmp/lpu-install/20`, and `/tmp/lpu-install/30`. Line 13 copies all of the C code files from the `./src` subdirectory of the current working directory to each of these three subdirectories. We use the `-o` option to set user ownership, repetitive in this case because the default owner would be that of the user executing the script.

The second code block creates a set of directories named after each of the groups defined on your system. Each directory is owned by the default user, but the group name is the same as the directory name (line 19). Line 20 copies any `elisp` files in the current working directory to the appropriate directory, again setting the group ownership to the directory name and making the files read-only for the owner/user. No other users or groups have any privileges to the file. This usage of `install` is strange, but nevertheless illustrates why we consider `install` "a better `cp`" command.

Understanding the Red Hat Package Manager (RPM)

The Red Hat Package Manager, although it bears Red Hat's name, is a powerful, general, and open software packaging system used in Caldera's OpenLinux, S.u.S.E.'s distribution, and, of course, Red Hat Linux. It is most frequently used for Linux, but versions of it are available for many UNIX versions, including Solaris, SunOS, HP-UX, SCO, AIX, and Digital UNIX. The discussion of RPM in this book focuses on creating source code packages; Ed Bailey's excellent book, *Maximum RPM*, covers mundane issues such as installing, upgrading, and removing RPMs, as well as its uses by package creators and maintainers. Point your browser at `http://www.rpm.org/` for the latest version, complete documentation, FAQs and HOWTOs, and a downloadable version of the book (but, regarding the book, you are strongly encouraged to purchase it and reward both author and publisher for making it freely available).

Minimum Requirements

To create RPMs, you need RPM itself, the source code you want to compile, an `rpmrc` file to set some RPM defaults and control its behavior, and a `spec` file to control the package build process. It is assumed you have an otherwise functional development environment (compilers, tools, editors, cold pizza, Jolt cola, coffee, and such) and that your source code compiles successfully.

Before we proceed, however, it is essential to convey the mindset motivating RPM. RPM always begins with pristine sources. "Pristine," in this context, means original or unpatched code as it came from the developer (in most cases, this is you). RPM allows you, or someone else, to apply one or more patch sets, either to modify the software to build on a particular system, create system specific configuration files, or to apply (or back out) bug fixes before (re)compiling. The emphasis on unmodified sources allows you or your users always to begin a build from a known base and to customize it to fit particular circumstances. As a developer, this gives you considerable flexibility with respect to creating useful and reliable software and also a valuable level of control over how your software gets compiled and installed.

So, to boil it to two simple rules:

1. Always start creating an RPM with unmodified sources.

2. Apply patches as necessary to fit the build environment.

Configuring RPM

The `rpmrc` file controls almost every element of RPM's behavior. Your system administrator may have a global `rpmrc` file in `/etc`. If you would like to override one or more of the global settings, create a `~/.rpmrc` that contains your preferred settings. Before you begin, however, you may want see RPM's current configuration. Use the `--showrc` option to accomplish this, as shown in the following:

```
$rpm --showrc
ARCHITECTURE AND OS:
build arch            : i386
compatible build archs: i686 i586 i486 i386 noarch
build os              : Linux
compatible build os's : Linux
install arch          : i686
install os            : Linux
compatible archs      : i686 i586 i486 i386 noarch
compatible os's       : Linux
RPMRC VALUES:
builddir              : /usr/src/OpenLinux/BUILD
buildroot             : (not set)
buildshell            : /bin/sh
bzip2bin              : /bin/bzip2
dbpath                : /var/lib/rpm
...
```

The values in this abbreviated listing are the defaults on one of the authors' OpenLinux 1.3 systems; your system may have slightly different settings. As you can see, the output is divided into two sections: architecture and operating system settings, which define the build and install environment; and `rpmrc` values, which control RPM's behavior. The global configuration file, /etc/rpmrc, should be used for settings of a system-wide sort, such as vendor, require_vendor, distribution, and require_distribution. The local file, $HOME/.rpmrc, contains values specific to the user building an RPM, such as pgp_name, pgp_path, packager, and signature.

We created a short rpmrc file for the purposes of this chapter:

```
distribution           : Linux Programming Unleashed
require_distribution    : 1
vendor                 : Gomer's Software Hut and Lounge
topdir                 : /usr/src/krw
packager               : Anyone Brave Enough to Claim It
optflags               : -O2 -m486 -fno-strength-reduce
tmppath                : /usr/tmp
```

In most cases, few settings in the rpmrc file require changing.

Controlling the Build: Using a spec File

The spec file, after the source code itself, is the most important element of an RPM, because it defines what to build, how to build it, where to install it, and the files that it contains. Each spec file you create should be named according to the standard naming convention, *pkgname-version-release.spec*, where *pkgname* is the name of the package, *version* is the version number, typically in x.y.z format, and *release* is the release number of the current version. For example, the name xosview-1.4.1-4.spec breaks down to version 1.4.1, release number 4, indicating that this is the fourth "version" (don't get confused by the diction) of version 1.4.1 of xosview. Xearth-1.0-4.spec is release 4 of version 1.0. Each spec file has eight sections, which the following sections describe.

Header

The header section contains information returned by RPM queries, such as a description, version, source location, patch names and locations, and the name of an icon file.

Prep

The prep section consists of whatever preparation must take place before the actual build process can begin. Generally this is limited to unpacking the source and applying any patches.

Build

As you might expect, the build section lists the commands necessary to compile the software. In most cases, this will be a single make command, but it can be as complex and obtuse as you desire.

Install

Again, the name is self-explanatory. The install section is the name of command, such as `make install`, or a shell script that performs the software installation after the build successfully completes.

Install/Uninstall Scripts

These scripts, which are optional, are run on the *user's* system when the package is removed or installed.

Verify Script

Usually, RPM's verification routines are sufficient, but if they fall short of your needs, this section lists any commands or shell scripts to execute that make up for RPM's shortcomings.

Clean

This section handles any post-build clean up, but is rarely necessary since RPM does an excellent job cleaning up after itself.

File List

An essential component (an RPM will not build without it), this section contains a list of files that make up your package, set their file attributes, and identify documentation and configuration files.

Analyzing a spec File

The following spec file is taken from the xearth package shipped with Caldera OpenLinux 1.3, `/usr/src/OpenLinux/SPECS/xearth-1.0.spec`. This section of the chapter analyzes each section. The first part of the spec file is the header:

```
Summary: Displays a lit globe
Name: xearth
Version: 1.0
Release: 4
Group: System/Desktop
Copyright: MIT
Packager: rwp@lst.de (Roger Pook)
Icon: xearth.xpm
URL: http://cag-www.lcs.mit.edu/~tuna/xearth/index.html
Source0: ftp://cag.lcs.mit.edu/pub/tuna/xearth-1.0.tar.gz
Patch0: xearth-1.0-caldera.patch
# Provides: - optional -
# Requires: - optional -
# Conflicts: - optional -
BuildRoot: /tmp/xearth-1.0
```

```
%Description
Xearth sets the X root window to an image of the Earth,
as seen from your favorite vantage point in space,
correctly shaded for the current position of the Sun.
By default, xearth updates the displayed image every
five minutes.  The time between updates can be changed
with the -wait option (see below); updates can be disabled
completely by using the -once option (see below).  Xearth
can also render directly into PPM and GIF files instead
of drawing in the root window.
```

This is the end of the header section. As you can see, there is a ton of information provided, which can be retrieved from RPM's database using RPM's powerful query capabilities. The name, version, and release information bears directly on the build process, but the balance of the information is strictly informational.

The next section of a spec file is the prep section. It defines the steps necessary to prepare the package to be built.

```
%Prep
%setup
%patch0 -p1
```

The prep section is pretty simple: it applies a patch, in this case, /usr/src/OpenLinux/SOURCES/xearth-1.0-caldera.patch, to the pristine sources. That's it. Badda bing, badda boom.

Well, the situation is a bit more complex. The line %setup is an RPM macro. It accomplishes a number of tasks, in this case, cding into the BUILD directory, deleting the remnants of previous build attempts (if any), uncompressing and extracting the source code, a gzipped tarball, /usr/src/OpenLinux/SOURCES/xearth-1.0.tar.gz, cding into the extracted directory, and recursively changing ownership and permission on the extracted directory and its files. This is the simplest way the %setup macro can be used. It takes a variety of arguments that modify its behavior, but in most cases, the default behavior is what you want and all you will need. We refer the curious reader to *Maximum RPM* for all of the details.

After the prep section comes the build section. It details how to build the package.

```
%Build
xmkmf
make CXXDEBUGFLAGS="$RPM_OPT_FLAGS" CDEBUGFLAGS="$RPM_OPT_FLAGS"
```

Again, the build section is straightforward. In effect, the two commands are a script passed to /bin/sh to build the package. RPM checks the return codes for each step, aborting the build with a useful message if an error occurred.

Once the package is built, you will probably want it installed. The install section provides the information required to do so.

```
%Install
DESTDIR=$RPM_BUILD_ROOT; export DESTDIR
[ -n "`echo $DESTDIR ¦ sed -n 's:^/tmp/[^.].*$:OK:p'`" ] &&
➥rm -rf $DESTDIR ¦¦
(echo "Invalid BuildRoot: '$DESTDIR'! Check this .spec ...";
➥exit 1) ¦¦ exit 1

make install
make install.man

# gzip man pages and fix sym-links
MANPATHS=`find $DESTDIR -type d -name "man[1-9n]" -print`
if [ -n "$MANPATHS" ]; then
  chown -Rvc root.root $MANPATHS
  find $MANPATHS -type l -print ¦
    perl -lne '($f=readlink($_))&&unlink($_)&&symlink("$f.gz",
➥"$_.gz")¦¦die;'
  find $MANPATHS -type f -print ¦
    xargs -r gzip -v9nf
fi
```

Just like the prep and build sections, RPM executes lines in the install section as a
`/bin/sh` script. Caldera's xearth package contains both standard `make` targets, `install`
and `install.man`, and custom shell code to fine-tune the installation.

After a package builds and installs successfully, RPM will remove the detritus left over
from the build and install process. The clean section of the spec file manages this.

```
%Clean
DESTDIR=$RPM_BUILD_ROOT; export DESTDIR
[ -n "`echo $DESTDIR ¦ sed -n 's:^/tmp/[^.].*$:OK:p'`" ] && rm -rf
$DESTDIR ¦¦
(echo "Invalid BuildRoot: '$DESTDIR'! Check this .spec ..."; exit 1) ¦¦
exit 1
Caldera's clean section simply makes sure that the xearth build
➥directory is completely removed, unsubtly suggesting a problem with
➥spec file (its commands, actually) if problems arise.  You will
➥usually not require this section, if you stick with RPM's default
➥build tree.
%Files
%doc README BUILT-IN GAMMA-TEST HISTORY
/usr/X11R6/bin/xearth
/usr/X11R6/man/man1/xearth.1x.gz
```

As noted previously, the file section consists of a list of files that make up the package. If
the file does not exist in this list, it will not be included in the package. The `%doc` token
expands to the value of `defaultdocdir` that `rpm --showrc` reported earlier, `/usr/doc`,

plus the standard package name, xearth-1.0-4 (thus, to /usr/doc/xearth-1.0-4). You can also use %doc to mark other files as documentation and cause them to be installed in other directories. Again, in most cases, the default behavior will prove sufficient.

However, you must still create the file list yourself. Despite RPM's power, it cannot read your mind and create the file list. Probably the easiest way to create the list is to use the files your makefile generates and add to that list any documentation or configuration files required.

Building the Package

With the spec file created, we are ready to build the package. If you are confident the spec file is correct, just change to the directory holding the spec file

```
$ cd /usr/src/OpenLinux/SPECS
```

and issue the "build everything in sight" command:

```
$ rpm -ba xearth-1.0-4.spec
```

If everything works correctly, you will wind up with a binary package, /usr/src/OpenLinux/RPMS/i386/xearth-1.0-4.i386.rpm, and a new source rpm, /usr/src/OpenLinux/RPMS/i386/xearth-1.0-4.src.rpm. At this point, arrange to copy the binary package to a new machine, install it, and test it. If it installs and runs properly, upload your source RPM to your favorite software repository, and you are finished.

If, regrettably, you run into problems, RPM's build command accepts a number of options that enable you to step through the build process to identify and, hopefully, fix problems. The following is a brief description of the options:

- -bp—Validate the spec file's prep section
- -bl—Validate the file list in %files
- -bc—Perform a prep and compile
- -bi—Perform a prep, compile, and install
- -bb—Perform a prep, compile, install, and build only a binary package
- --short-circuit—Add this argument to skip straight to the specified build step (p,l,c,I,b)
- --keep-temps—Preserve the temporary files and scripts created during the build process
- --test—A mock build to see what would be done (also performs --keep-temps)

Once you resolve the errors, rebuild using -ba, upload your masterpiece, and wait for the kudos to roll in.

37

PACKAGE
MANAGEMENT

Summary

Compared to tarballs and GNU `install`, from a developer's perspective, RPM can seem like a great deal of work. Indeed, using it requires a few extra steps. Over the long haul, RPM pays dividends in terms of package maintenance and convenience. We are not in a position to dictate which to use. Let the market decide—and the market is clearly heavily in favor of RPM.

Documentation

by Kurt Wall

IN THIS CHAPTER

This chapter shows you how to create documentation for your programs. It initially covers the ubiquitous manual page, or *man page* (the term man page is used throughout this chapter). Then, it examines an SGML-based tool, SGML-tools, which allows you to create documentation in many formats from a single master document.

man Pages

If you've ever worked on any sort of UNIX system, you have doubtless used the man(1) facilities to access online documentation. Although they seem archaic in this day and age, when everything you need to know is a few clicks away on the World Wide Web, man pages are, nevertheless, quintessential UNIX. Linux is no different, and in this section you will learn how to create man pages of your own.

> **Tip**
>
> You will frequently see numbers in parentheses after a command, such as man(1). These numbers refer to the section of the manual where the command is covered. Manual sections are covered later in this chapter.

Components of a man Page

The first thing you need to know is the typical layout of a man page, which Table 38.1 describes.

Table 38.1   MAN PAGE LAYOUT

Section	Description
NAME	The program or command name, the man section number, and the release date
SYNOPSIS	How to invoke the command, with a complete list of all options and arguments
DESCRIPTION	A brief summary of the command and its usage
OPTIONS	An alphabetical list of options and arguments, if any
FILES	A list of the files the command uses or can use
ENVIRONMENT	A list of the environment variables the command uses or can use
DIAGNOSTICS	A list of the error messages the command generates and possible solutions

Section	Description
BUGS	Indicates the known bugs and misfeatures and, optionally, how to contact the program author to correct them
AUTHOR	The name of the command's author and/or maintainer, preferably with an email address or URL
SEE ALSO	Cross-references to related commands and information

You can add other sections if necessary. The layout described in Table 38.1 is only suggested; this is Linux, after all. The only required section is NAME because some of the related documentation commands, such as makewhatis(8) and appropos(1) rely on the NAME section.

Sample man Page and Explanation

Listing 38.1 contains the complete source of a rather whimsical man page documenting the coffee command.

Listing 38.1   Sample man Page

```
.\" Process using
.\" groff -man -Tascii coffee.1
.\" These four lines show you how to insert a comment into a groff source
.\" file.  They will not be visible to the groff processor.
.TH COFFEE 1 "16 January 1999"
.SH NAME
coffee \- Control the networked coffee machine
.SH SYNOPSIS
.B coffee [-s] [-b
.I blend
.B ] [—scorch] [—blend
.I blend
.B ]
.I num_cups
.SH DESCRIPTION
.B coffee
sends a request to the remote coffee machine (usually the device
.B /dev/cfpt0(4)
to initiate a brew cycle to create
.I num_cups
```

continues

Listing 38.1   CONTINUED

```
of coffee.  It assumes the device is turned on and that the water and bean
reservoirs have sufficient stocks actually to complete the brew cycle.For
those who prefer GNU's long options, they are supplied.
.SH OPTIONS
.TP
.B -s, --scorch
Scorch the coffee.  Rather than waiting for the brewed coffee to
age and oxidize on the warming plate, the freshly brewed coffee
is piped through a super-heating device, effectively simulating
the flavor of 6 oz. of liquid coffee that has been left on the
burner for 2 hours.
.TP
.B -b, --blend
Specify the blend of coffee to be brewed.
.I blend
is one of
.I costarican, java,
or
.I decaf.
If
.B -b
.I blend
is not specified, the default
.I regular
(blech) is assumed.
.SH FILES
.TP
.B /dev/cfpt0(4)
The default coffee machine.  Large installations may have multiple coffee
machines, specified as
.B /dev/cfpt[0-15].
.TP
.B /dev/expr0(4)
The espresso machine.  Usually only in the boss's office.
.SH ENVIRONMENT
.TP
.B CF_BLEND
Set this variable to your preferred
.I blend.
Equivalent to
.B coffee -b $CF_BLEND.
.SH DIAGNOSTICS
None.  This section is here for illustration purposes only.
.SH "SEE ALSO"
.BR creamer (1),
.BR grind (1)
.BR sweetener (1),
.SH NOTES
If there were any notes, they would go here.
```

```
.SH AUTHOR
Kurt Wall <kwall@xmission.com>
.SH BUGS
You may have to get up out of your chair if the whole bean repository is
empty.  Multiple successive requests queued to the same device can cause
overflow.
```

To view this as a nicely formatted man page, use the command

```
$ groff -Tascii -man coffee.man ¦ less
```

If everything worked correctly, the output should look like Figure 38.1.

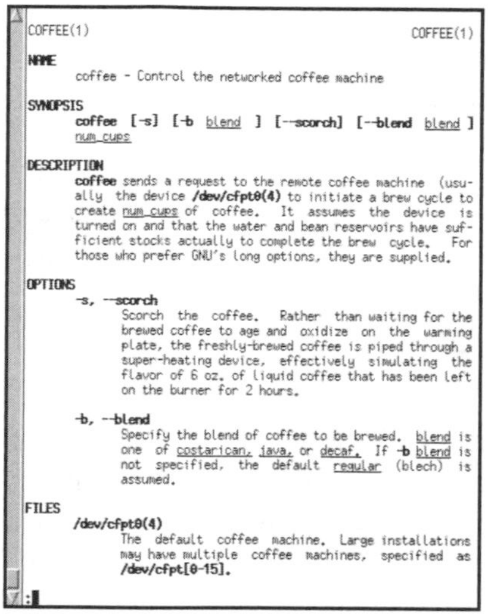

FIGURE 38.1

Viewing a man page.

Using the groff Command

Don't be put off by the apparent obscurity of the raw groff code. It is quite easy to understand. Groff requests are preceded by a "." and are, obviously, quite succinct. .TH, used once per man page, sets the page title, the section number, and the version date. The format shown for the NAME section is very important. Following .SH NAME, place the command name followed by a backslash and dash (\ -)followed by a short (one-line) description of the command's purpose. The \ - is critical because makewhatis(8), apropos(1), and man -k rely on this format when searching for man pages.

Each .SH command introduces a section; introduce subsections with the .SS directive (Listing 38.1 lacks subsections). The .TP directive creates a new paragraph with a hanging tag; that is, indent the second and subsequent lines relative to the first line. The other groff commands specify font types or weights, as Table 38.2 describes.

Table 38.2 groff COMMANDS

Command	Description
.B	Bold
.BI	Bold alternating with italic
.BR	Bold alternating with roman
.I	Italic
.IB	Italic alternating with bold
.IR	Italic alternating with roman
.R	Roman
.RI	Roman alternating with italic
.RB	Roman alternating with bold

Requests for specific fonts affect an entire line, so, if you need to embed bold or italic fonts in an otherwise normal text line, start a new line in your source file, specify the font, type the appropriate text, then, on the next line, continue with the normal text. This technique was used in the SYNOPSIS section of Listing 38.1.

Linux Conventions

Linux man pages use a few conventions; if you follow these, your man pages will be consistent with other man pages. Function names and function arguments always appear in italics. Filenames should appear in italics, too. In the SYNOPSIS section, however, a file that is #included should appear in bold. Special macros (normally in uppercase) and #defined variables should also be bold. Enumerated lists, like the OPTIONS section on our sample page, should be bold and use the .TP command for indentation. References to other man pages, as in the SEE ALSO section, should include the section number in parentheses, and the entire reference should appear in bold with roman type, using the .BR command.

Tip

To insert comments into your groff source, start each comment line with .\" and type your comment. Lines 1–4 of our sample page illustrate this trick.

You can use Listing 38.1 as a template for your own man pages. Once you have completed writing your man page, create a preprocessed version and install it in the appropriate section under /usr/man/manN, where N is 1–9. Table 38.3 lists the "standard" division of UNIX man pages:

Table 38.3   STANDARD LINUX MAN PAGES

Section	Description
1	User commands and programs
2	System calls provided by the kernel
3	Library calls provided by program libraries
4	Devices and special files
5	File formats and conventions
6	Games
7	Macro packages and conventions
8	System administration commands
9	Additional kernel routines (Linux-specific section)

Your installation program should install a preformatted, gzipped man page into the appropriate subdirectory of /usr/man. Hopefully, you will take pains not only to create adequate documentation, but also make sure that your documentation is correct and that it is accessible. The only thing more frustrating than documentation buried seven layers deep in a directory is a man page that fails to accurately describe what the program really does.

See, creating a man page wasn't difficult at all! Should you feel really inspired to learn all about groff and man pages, check out these resources:

- Troff User's Manual, Joseph T. Ossanna and Brian W. Kernighan
- Troff Resources Page at http://www.kohala.com/~rstevens/troff/troff.html
- The Man Page mini-HOWTO
- The man(7) man page

38

DOCUMENTATION

Creating SGML Documents Using SGML-tools

Even though creating a man page is a relatively trivial undertaking, the effort is partially wasted because the man page format does not travel well. SGML, the Standardized General Markup Language, is a much more portable format because, from a single source file, you can output files in multiple formats, such as the following:

- Postscript
- HTML
- Plain text

- DVI
- TeX
- LyX
- man pages

This section will look at the SGML-tools package, a suite of programs used throughout the Linux community to create documentation of all sorts.

SGML-tools

Writing an SGML document is quite similar to creating a Web page using HTML. Tags, SGML directives enclosed in angle brackets (<tag_name>) tell the SGML parser to apply special formatting to the text enclosed between a <tag_name>...</end_tag_name> pair. We will use the coffee man page example re-worked as an SGML document to illustrate the format of an SGML document. The line numbers are an explanatory convenience; they do not appear in the SGML source file. All of the listings in this section examine this document in detail.

Each SGML-tools document contains a "preamble" section that specifies the document type, title information, and the like.

```
1       <!doctype linuxdoc system>
2       <article>
3
4       <title>The Linux Coffee Device-HOWTO
5       <author>Kurt Wall <tt>&lt;kwall&commat;xmisson.com&gt;</tt>
6       <date>v1.0, January 16, 1999
7       <abstract>
8       This document is a whimsical description of the Linux Coffee
➥Device.
9       </abstract>
10
11      <toc>
12
```

The document preamble defines the document type, its title, and other preparatory or identifying information. Line 1 tells the SGML parser to use the linuxdoc document type definition. Line 2 indicates to the parser that this will be an article. Lines 4–6 add identifying information; and lines 7–9 will put a short summary in italics at the top of the article. The <toc> tag on line 11 will be replaced by a table of contents automatically built from <sectN> headings used in the document. The elements in the preamble should follow this order.

```
13      <sect>NAME
14      <p>
15      coffee - Control the networked coffee machine
16
```

Line 13 starts a section, titled NAME, followed by a <p> element, which forces a new paragraph. The <p> is only required after a <sect> tag. The body text begins on line 15. If you need to start a new paragraph in the regular text, simply insert a blank line between the final sentence of one paragraph and the first sentence of the next. Sections can be nested five levels deep:

<sect>   Specifies a top-level section, such as 1, 2, and so forth

<sect1>   Specifies a subsection, such 1.1 or 1.2

<sect2>   Specifies a third-level subsubsection

<sect3>   Specifies a fourth-level subsubsubsection

<sect4>   Specifies a fifth-level subsubsubsubsection

Lines 17–28 illustrate the use of tags that specify certain kinds of formatting, such as bold face, italic, and emphasized text.

```
17      <sect>SYNOPSIS
18      <p>
19      <bf>coffee</bf> [<bf>-s</bf>&verbar;<bf>—scorch</bf>] [<bf>
        ➥b</bf>&verbar;
        ➥<bf>--blend</bf> <em>blend</em>] <em>num_cups</em>
20
21      <sect>DESCRIPTION
22      <p>
23      coffee sends a request to the remote coffee machine (usually the
        ➥device
24      <bf>&sol;dev&sol;cfpt0(4)</bf> to initiate a brew cycle to create
        ➥<em>num_cups</em>
25      of coffee.  It assumes the device is turned on and that the water
26      and bean reservoirs have sufficient stocks actually to complete
27      the brew cycle. For those who prefer GNU's long options,
28      they are supplied.
```

The salient points from these two sections are, first, that items you want in boldface text should be enclosed with <bf>...</bf> tags; italic elements go between ... tags; and special characters, such as "<" or "/", which have special meanings to either the SGML parser or one of the underlying formatters, such as LaTeX, have to be specified using a special notation of the format &symbol;. Because SGML uses < and > to delimit tags, if you want a literal < in your text, you would type <. Use > to obtain a literal >. Other special characters include the following:

&   for the ampersand (&)

$ for a dollar sign ($)

for a hash symbol (#)

%   for a percent sign (%)

˜   for a tilde (~)

The SGML-tools documentation contains a complete list of all the special characters. Lines 29–46 in the following listing show the use of some of the special characters listed above.

```
29      <sect>OPTIONS
30      <p>
31
32      <sect1>-b
33      <p>
34      <bf>-b</bf>, <bf>—blend</bf> <em>blend</em> -
35      Specify the blend of coffee to be brewed.  <em>blend</em> is one
of
36      <em>costarican</em>, <em>java</em>, or <em>decaf</em>.  If
 ➥<em>blend</em>
37      is not specified, the default <em>regular</em> &lpar;blech&rpar; is
 ➥assumed.
38
39      <sect1>-s
40      <p>
41      <bf>-s</bf>, <bf>--scorch</bf> -
42      Scorch the coffee.  Rather than waiting for the brewed coffee to
        age and
43      oxidize on the warming plate, the freshly-brewed coffee is piped
        through
44      a super-heating device, effectively simulating the flavor of
        6 oz. Of liquid
45      coffee that has been left on the burner for 2 hours.
46
```

In this excerpt, we used a couple of <sect1> tags. In the final output, these will create X.1 and X.2 subsections and, since we are using the <toc> tag to create a table of contents, the table of contents will have two subentries for these subsections.

Lines 47–81, finally, complete the SGML source code for the document.

```
47      <sect>FILES
48      <p>
49      <bf>&sol;dev&sol;cfpt0(4)</bf> - The default coffee machine.
        Large installations may have multiple
50      coffee machines, specified as <bf>&sol;dev&sol;cfpt[0-15]
        </bf>.
51
52      <bf>&sol;dev&sol;expr0(4)</bf> - The espresso machine.  Usually
        only in the boss's
53      office.
54
```

```
55    <sect>ENVIRONMENT
56    <p>
57    <bf>&dollar;CF_BLEND</bf>
      Set this variable to your preferred blend.
58    Equivalent to <bf>coffee -b &dollar;CF_BLEND</bf>.
59
60    <sect>DIAGNOSTICS
61    <p>
62    None.  This section is here for illustration purposes only.
63
64    <sect>SEE ALSO
65    <p>
66    <bf>creamer(1)</bf>, <bf>grind(1)</bf>, <bf>sweetener(1)</bf>
67
68    <sect>NOTES
69    <p>
70    If there were any notes, they would go here.
71
72    <sect>AUTHOR
73    <p>
74    Kurt Wall &lt;kwall&commat;xmission.com&gt;
75
76    <sect>BUGS
77    <p>
78    You may have to get up out of your chair if the whole bean
      repository is empty.
79    Multiple successive requests queued to the same device can
80    cause overflow.
81    </article>
```

In the final excerpt, we used the `</article>` tag to tell the SGML parser that this is the end of the document. The CD-ROM contains the complete SGML source file, `coffee.sgml`, and several output versions: HTML, GNU info, LaTeX, LyX, and RTF (Rich Text Format).

SGML-tools Tags

SGML-tools is not limited to the tags shown in the previous example. Internal cross-references, URL references, two types of lists, and index generation are described in this section.

Internal cross-references that refer readers to another section of your document are a breeze to create. Suppose you have a section titled "Frobnication." To create a cross-reference, add a label to that section:

```
<sect1>Frobnication<label id="frobnication">
```

When you need to refer to this section, use the `<ref>`tag:

```
See also <ref id="frobnication" name="Frobnication"> for more information.
```

In documents that support hypertext-style linking (such as HTML), the reader would activate the link to jump to the labeled section. The name element inserts the section name, and exists for document formats that do not support hypertext links.

Naturally, you can also insert URL elements, using the `<url>` tag. This feature is specifically aimed at the World Wide Web and supports normal HTML documents, files obtainable via FTP, mailto: and news: URLs, and so on. The format is

```
You can find out more about frobnication in the
<url url="www.somedomain.com/frobnication.html"
        name="Frobnication HOWTO">
```

The name element in this example would be rendered as an HTML hypertext link to the URL specified on the first line. To support documents that do not speak HTML, use the `<htmlurl>`element because it will suppress generation of the URL in all formats except HTML:

```
You can find out more about frobnication in the
<htmlurl url="www.somedomain.com/frobnication.html"
        name="Frobnication HOWTO">
```

In non-HTML formats, the HTML is replaced by the name element.

To create bulleted or numbered lists, use the `<itemize>...</itemize>` and `<enum>...</enum>`tags, respectively, and tag each list item with an `<item>` tag. For example:

```
<itemize>
<item>This is the first item in a bulleted list
<item>This is the second item in a bulleted list.
</itemize>

<enum>
<item>This is the first item in a numbered (enumerated) list.
<item>This is the second item in a numbered (enumerated) list.
</enum>
```

Finally, enclosing document text between `<idx>...</idx>` or `<cdx>...</cdx>` tags, you can force the generation of index entries. After processing the SGML source file, you will also have a file named with a `.ind` extension that contains the specified index words with page references to the formatted document. Unfortunately, this tag only works for LaTeX. All of the other SGML processors ignore it.

Formatting SGML Documents

Once you have an SGML source document, you are ready to create the output. Suppose your source document is named `colonel_panic.sgml`. If you want to check your syntax, the command is

```
$ sgmlcheck colonel_panic.sgml
```

The only output you should see is a series of "Processing…" messages. Once you've verified the syntax,

```
$ sgml2txt colonel_panic.sgml
```

creates a nicely formatted plain text document, `colonel_panic.txt`. The command lines to create similarly named man pages, LaTeX, DVI, PostScript, and HTML files are

```
$ sgml2txt —man  colonel_panic.sgml
```

```
$ sgml2latex colonel_panic.sgml
```

```
$ sgml2latex —ouput=dvi colonel_panic.sgml
```

```
$ sgml2latex —ouput=ps colonel_panic.sgml
```

```
$ sgml2html colonel_panic.sgml
```

See the man pages for all the possible options and arguments.

Summary

In this chapter, you learned how to create man pages using `groff` and how to use the more powerful and flexible SGML-tools. Because Linux uses a highly decentralized development process, thorough, accurate, and easily accessible documentation is a must. Using the tools discussed in this chapter will make formatting and maintaining documentation simple. Actually writing the documentation, of course, is still up to you.

Licensing

by Kurt Wall

CHAPTER 39

This chapter looks at the thorny, lawyer-infested issue of software licensing. We are not lawyers, of course, so we will not presume to give legal advice on how you should license your applications. The material in this chapter reflects our understanding of the available licenses for free software. If you have questions, we strongly recommend that you consult an attorney specializing in intellectual property law.

You will not long use Linux or write and distribute software for Linux before running directly into licensing and copyright questions. There exists an ever-growing variety of licenses used with "free software." The most common licenses are the MIT license, the BSD license, the Artistic license, the two GNU licenses, and the Open Source Definition. The following sections discuss each of these licenses.

The MIT/X-style License

MIT-style licenses, created at the Massachusetts Institute of Technology, are the least restrictive of free software licenses. Using, obtaining, and distributing software licensed under an MIT-style license allows the licensee to "use, copy, modify, and distribute" software and its documentation for any purpose without fees or royalties. MIT licenses (indeed, all of the licenses we discuss in this chapter) also include a disclaimer that the software is provided "as is" without warranty, so if your use of or modifications to the software ignite global, thermonuclear war, it's your problem.

The only conditions placed on software covered under an MIT-style license are that the copyright notices and disclaimers may not be altered or removed and that they must appear on all copies of the software. Creators of derived works (works based, in part, on another application covered under the MIT license) may not use the name of the original author to promote derived work without the author's prior written permission.

A template form of the MIT/X-style license is reproduced below. To use this template in your own projects, replace <year> and <copyright holders> with appropriate text.

```
                          MIT License

      Copyright (c) <year> <copyright holders>

      Permission is hereby granted, free of charge, to any person
      obtaining a copy of this software and associated documentation
      files(the "Software"), to deal in the Software without,
      restriction, including without limitation the rights to,
      use,copy, modify, merge, publish, distribute, sublicense,
      and/or sell copies of the Software and to permit
      persons to whom the Software is furnished to do so
      subject to the following conditions:
```

The above copyright notice and this permission notice shall be
included in all copies or substantial portions of the Software.

THE SOFTWARE IS PROVIDED "AS IS", WITHOUT WARRANTY OF ANY KIND,
EXPRESS OR IMPLIED, INCLUDING BUT NOT LIMITED TO THE WARRANTIES OF
MERCHANTABILITY, FITNESS FOR A PARTICULAR PURPOSE AND
NONINFRINGEMENT. IN NO EVENT SHALL THE AUTHORS OR COPYRIGHT
HOLDERS BE LIABLE FOR ANY CLAIM, DAMAGES OR OTHER LIABILITY,
WHETHER IN AN ACTION OF CONTRACT, TORT OR OTHERWISE, ARISING
FROM, OUT OF OR IN CONNECTION WITH THE SOFTWARE OR THE USE OR
OTHER DEALINGS IN THE SOFTWARE.

The BSD-style License

BSD-derived licenses are only slightly more restrictive than the MIT class of licenses.
Software, in binary or source form, may be used and redistributed without restriction,
provided that the following conditions are met:

- The original copyright and disclaimer statements are neither modified nor
  removed.
- The original authors' names may not be used to promote derived works without
  prior written permission.
- Any advertising material for derived work must include an acknowledgment of the
  original author.

A copy of the BSD-style license is included below in template form. To generate your
own license from this template, replace <owner>, <organization>, and <year> with
appropriate values.

```
The BSD License

<owner>
<organization>
<year>

Copyright (c) <year>, <owner>
All rights reserved.

Redistribution and use in source and binary forms, with or without
modification, are permitted provided that the following conditions
are met:

* Redistributions of source code must retain the above copyright
  notice, this list of conditions and the following disclaimer.
```

39

LICENSING

```
* Redistributions in binary form must reproduce the above
  copyright notice, this list of conditions and the following
  disclaimer in the documentation and/or other materials provided
  with the distribution.

* All advertising materials mentioning features or use of this
  software must display the following acknowledgement:
  This product includes software developed by <organization>
  and its contributors.

* Neither name of the University nor the names of its
  contributors may be used to endorse or promote products derived
  from this software without specific prior written permission.

THIS SOFTWARE IS PROVIDED BY THE COPYRIGHT HOLDERS AND CONTRIBUTORS
"AS IS" AND ANY EXPRESS OR IMPLIED WARRANTIES, INCLUDING, BUT NOT
LIMITED TO, THE IMPLIED WARRANTIES OF MERCHANTABILITY AND FITNESS
FOR A PARTICULAR PURPOSE ARE DISCLAIMED. IN NO EVENT SHALL THE
REGENTS OR CONTRIBUTORS BE LIABLE FOR ANY DIRECT, INDIRECT,
INCIDENTAL, SPECIAL, EXEMPLARY, OR CONSEQUENTIAL DAMAGES (INCLUDING,
BUT NOT LIMITED TO, PROCUREMENT OF SUBSTITUTE GOODS OR SERVICES;
LOSS OF USE, DATA, OR PROFITS; OR BUSINESS INTERRUPTION) HOWEVER
CAUSED AND ON ANY THEORY OF LIABILITY, WHETHER IN CONTRACT, STRICT
LIABILITY, OR TORT (INCLUDING NEGLIGENCE OR OTHERWISE) ARISING IN
ANY WAY OUT OF THE USE OF THIS SOFTWARE, EVEN IF ADVISED OF THE
POSSIBILITY OF SUCH DAMAGE.
```

The Artistic License

Larry Wall, creator of Perl, also created the Artistic License. This license states the conditions under which software may be copied so that, in the words of the license preamble, "the Copyright Holder maintains some semblance of artistic control over the development of the package, while giving the users of the package the right to use and distribute the Package in a more-or-less customary fashion, plus the right to make reasonable modifications."

Simply stated, the Artistic License permits anyone to use, modify, and redistribute software without restriction, either for free or for a nominal fee. Any original copyright notices and disclaimers must be preserved. Significant modifications to the original software must be prominently noted, and a modified version cannot be masqueraded as the original version. Modifications, like the original software, should also be made "freely available." Finally, the standard disclaimer of no warranty applies, and the name(s) of the original author(s) may not be used to promote derived works without specific written permission.

The GNU General Public Licenses

The Free Software Foundation, founded by Richard M. Stallman, publishes two software licenses: the GNU General Public License (GPL) and the GNU Library General Public License (LGPL). Most of the GNU project's software and documentation is released under the terms of the GPL, but certain libraries are covered under the LGPL. This section discusses both licenses in detail, since most of the free software available is covered under the GPL or similar terms, including the Linux kernel itself.

The GNU General Public License

The GPL is one of the most restrictive free software licenses you will encounter. It is also one of the longest. If using the words "restrictive" and "free" in the same sentences confuses you, consider what the GPL and LGPL have to accomplish: create a legally binding document keeping free software free and protected from proprietary patents. "Free software" in the GPL and LGPL refers to freedom, not money. Or, as Richard Stallman explains, think free speech, not free beer.

This paragraph, from the GPL's preamble, succinctly summarizes what the GPL is and does:

"When we speak of free software, we are referring to freedom, not price. Our General Public Licenses are designed to make sure that you have the freedom to distribute copies of free software (and charge for this service, if you wish); that you receive source code or can get it if you want it; that you can change the software or use pieces of it in new free programs; and that you know you can do these things."

The balance of the GPL is largely devoted to elaborating this paragraph. Additional sections explain that free software comes without warranty and that modifications to free software should be clearly marked. Although burdened by legalese, the GPL and LGPL are much easier to comprehend and much shorter than the licenses one generally encounters with non-free or commercial software. The GPL's salient points are as follows:

- Software covered by the GPL may be distributed verbatim, provided that all copyrights and disclaimers are left intact. The act of distribution may be performed for a fee, but the software itself remains free.

- New software using or derived from software licensed under the GPL is itself licensed under the GPL.

- Modified versions of the software may be distributed under the same terms as item (1) above, provided that modifications are clearly marked and dated and the modified program itself is distributed under the GPL.

- The source code to a modified GPL'd program must be made available and be obtainable without cost beyond the cost of performing a source distribution.

- Modification or distribution of a GPL's program constitutes acceptance of the license.

- If any condition is imposed upon you, with respect to a GPL's program, that contradicts the terms of the GPL and makes adhering to both the GPL and the other obligations impossible, the only alternative is to cease distributing the program entirely.

- No warranty exists for the software, except where and when explicitly stated in writing.

To apply the GPL to a new program you create, apply the standard copyright notice,

```
<one line program name and description of what it does>
Copyright © <ccyy> <name of author>
```

and include the following abbreviated GPL license statement in your source code or other documentation,

```
This program is free software; you can redistribute it and/or modify it
under the terms of the GNU General Public License as published by the
Free Software Foundation; either version 2 of the License, or (at your
option) any later version.

This program is distributed in the hope that it will be useful,
but WITHOUT ANY WARRANTY; without even the implied warranty of
MERCHANTABILITY or FITNESS FOR A PARTICULAR PURPOSE.  See the
GNU General Public License for more details.

You should have received a copy of the GNU General Public License
along with this program; if not, write to the Free Software
Foundation, Inc., 59 Temple Place, Suite 330, Boston, MA  02111-1307   USA
```

Finally, add instructions on how you can be contacted.

The GNU Library General Public License

The GNU LGPL addresses a severe deficiency of the GPL—namely, item (2) in the preceding section, which states that any software that includes GPL'd software itself falls under the GPL. As the LGPL preamble notes:

"Linking a program with a library without changing the library is, in some sense, simply using the library and is analogous to running a utility program or application program. However, in a textural and legal sense, the linked executable is a combined work, a derivative of the original library, and the ordinary General Public License treats it as such."

As a result, many developers would not use GNU libraries because the act of linking a GPL'd library to an application program turned the application into a GPL'd program, a situation many individuals and companies found unacceptable. Concluding that a modified GPL would encourage greater usage of GNU libraries (or, more "effectively promote software sharing," one of the GNU project's primary goals), the GNU project created a special license—the LGPL—to cover a certain number of its own libraries and any other library a developer or company would see fit to release under the LGPL.

Without rehashing the entire license, the LGPL places no restrictions on programs that link against shared library versions of libraries covered by the LGPL. If an application is not linked against a shared library licensed under the LGPL, you must provide object files for your application that enable it to be relinked with new or altered versions of the library. So, you are not required to make your source code available or to make your application freely redistributable.

The Open Source Definition

The Open Source Definition, published by the Open Source Organization, is not a license. Rather, it establishes a set of conditions that software must meet before it can be legitimately labeled "Open Source" software. "Open Source" has been registered as a certification mark, meaning that the Open Source Organization can set conditions for the usage of the phrase. For more information about the Open Source Organization, visit their Web site at `http://www.opensource.org`.

> **NOTE**
>
> Software in the Public Interest (SPI) and the Open Source Organization currently both claim rights to the Open Source certification mark. The dispute is unfortunate, but until it is resolved, it might be best to avoid using the mark; the conditions for its use may change. For more information on the dispute, visit SPI's Web site at `http://www.spi-inc.org`.

39

LICENSING

The Open Source Definition lists 10 conditions that define open source software. The definition begins with the observation that "Open source doesn't just mean access to the source code." The complete text of the Open Source Definition is reproduced below.

```
The Open Source Definition

(Version 1.4)
```

Open source doesn't just mean access to the source code. The distribution terms of an open-source program must comply with the following criteria:

1. Free Redistribution

The license may not restrict any party from selling or giving away the software as a component of an aggregate software distribution containing programs from several different sources. The license may not require a royalty or other fee for such sale. (rationale)

2. Source Code

The program must include source code, and must allow distribution in source code as well as compiled form. Where some form of a product is not distributed with source code, there must be a well-publicized means of obtaining the source code for no more than a reasonable reproduction cost — preferably, downloading via the Internet without charge. The source code must be the preferred form in which a programmer would modify the program. Deliberately obfuscated source code is not allowed. Intermediate forms such as the output of a preprocessor or translator are not allowed. (rationale)

3. Derived Works

The license must allow modifications and derived works, and must allow them to be distributed under the same terms as the license of the original software. (rationale)

4. Integrity of The Author's Source Code.

The license may restrict source-code from being distributed in modified form only if the license allows the distribution of "patch files" with the source code for the purpose of modifying the program at build time. The license must explicitly permit distribution of software built from modified source code. The license may require derived works to carry a different name or version number from the original software. (rationale)

5. No Discrimination Against Persons or Groups.

The license must not discriminate against any person or group of persons. (rationale)

6. No Discrimination Against Fields of Endeavor.

The license must not restrict anyone from making use of the program in a specific field of endeavor. For example, it may not restrict the program from being used in a business, or from being used for genetic research. (rationale)

7. Distribution of License.

The rights attached to the program must apply to all to whom the program is redistributed without the need for execution of an additional license by those parties. (rationale)

8. License Must Not Be Specific to a Product.

The rights attached to the program must not depend on the program's being part of a particular software distribution. If the program is extracted from that distribution and used or distributed within the terms of the program's license, all parties to whom the program is redistributed should have the same rights as those that are granted in conjunction with the original software distribution. (rationale)

9. License Must Not Contaminate Other Software.

The license must not place restrictions on other software that is distributed along with the licensed software. For example, the license must not insist that all other programs distributed on the same medium must be open-source software. (rationale)

10. Conforming Licenses and Certification.

Any software that uses licenses that are certified conformant to the Open Source Definition may use the Open Source trademark, as may source code explicitly placed in the public domain. No other license or software is certified to use the Open Source trademark.

(The following information is not part of the Open Source Definition, and it may change from time to time.)

The GNU GPL, the LGPL, the BSD license, the X Consortium license, the Artistic, the MPL the QPL the libpng license, the zlib license, and the IJG JPEG library license are examples of licenses that we consider conformant to the Open Source Definition.

To have a license reviewed for certification, write certification@opensource.org. We strongly encourage use of already-certified licenses from the above list, since this allows use of the Open Source mark without the need for review. Please report misuse of the Open Source mark to mark-misuse@opensource.org.

To view the complete Open Source Definition and its accompanying rationale, see http://www.opensource.org/osd.html.

39

LICENSING

Choosing the Right License

We stated at the beginning of this chapter that we are not lawyers, so we cannot give legal advice. We merely observe that much of the free software available is licensed under the terms of the GPL. On the other hand, the GPL's license is restrictive and, in general, software derived from GPL-licensed software becomes GPL software, too. Some find this unacceptable and choose one of the license styles, or simply create their own. The choice you make depends on your personal preferences, valid legal advice, and, perhaps, your own philosophical commitments.

A Symbol Table Library

by Mark Whitis

This appendix describes a symbol table library. Symbol tables add a simple but useful object-oriented paradigm to the C language. This library is not currently included in any Linux distribution but might be incorporated in future distributions. The software is included on the CD-ROM accompanying this book and can also be downloaded from the author's Web site (which might have a more recent version) at `http://www.freelabs.com/~whitis/software/symbol/`.

In most programming environments, the compiler or interpreter uses a symbol table to keep track of identifiers and the properties of the objects they refer to, but the environment does not give the programmer much, if any, access to the symbol table from a running program. This library is intended to allow running C programs to use a symbol table to simplify operations such as parsing command-line arguments, reading configuration files, reading and writing data files, and communicating with other processes (running on the same or a diffcrent computer).

The library currently emphasizes reading and writing data in text form using "name=value" pairs, which are both machine- and human-readable. The library is also useful for debugging because it makes it easy to dump internal program data. In the future, GUI interfaces to the symbol table library may make it easy to present data structures to interactive users for modification. Many programs have been written that allow configuration by editing a text file or via a GUI but not both; I think that programs should support both modes of operation and the symbol table, with GUI extensions, will permit that while reducing code size.

The symbol table library has been used in the past to read HTML form data; to provide a remote procedure call mechanism that is very flexible, easy to debug and log, and is insensitive to version differences or differences in byte order; and to access database management systems. The code is not available for distribution, although I expect to incorporate many of these features into future versions.

The symbol tables used by this package are defined at program compile time using a number of macros. Rather than a simple table structure, the table is stored as a list of {token,value} pairs. This allows the library to support more complicated features and for new features to be added without needing to change existing tables.

Available Documentation

In addition to what is provided in this chapter, there are a number of other sources. I have a Web page with general information on the package; a copy of this page, corresponding to a particular version, is included in the tarball on the CD-ROM accompanying this book. The program `sttest.c`, which is used to test the proper operation of the

library, illustrates the use of many of the functions. And the userchange example program, excerpts of which are included in this chapter, provides further illustration.

Programs that use the symbol table library should include the header files

```
#include <symbol.h>
#include <basetype.h>
```

and link with the share library libsymtab.so. You may need to modify the search path used on your system to find include files and shared libraries if it does not already include /usr/local/include and /usr/local/lib.

Sample Program: userchange

The userchange program is a program that can update password (/etc/passwd) file entries on the local or a remote host. It is not really intended for serious system administration use in its current form since it does not support password encryption, shadow passwords, or NIS (Network Information System—once called Yellow Pages but that turned out to cause trademark problems). userchange is capable of updating all of the fields in the /etc/passwd file but it does not update the shadow password file. Like the useradd, userdel, and usermod programs, changepassword is only intended for use by trusted system administrators and does not encrypt passwords for the user. This can be done separately using the passwd program.

userchange illustrates how to use the symbol table library to do a number of things:

- Read a configuration file (./userchange.rc).
- Parse command line parameters. Any parameters specified on the command line will override those in the configuration file.
- Display a collection of variables for information or debugging.
- Communicate data structures between programs.

Almost all of the code for the userchange program, with the exception of the routine that actually modifies the password file, will be included in the various listings for this chapter.

basetypes

A number of predefined types are defined in basetype.h. The unsigned 8-, 16-, and 32-bit integers are defined by integer8u_t_st, integer16u_t_st, and integer32u_t_st, respectively. The signed integers are similarly described by the tables integer8s_t_st, integer16s_t_st, and integer32s_t_st. Integers used to store boolean values are described by cboolean_t_st. Normal null terminated C strings are defined by asciiz_t_st. And there is some support for a list of non-zero length strings separated by null characters and terminated by an additional null that is described in asciizz_t_st (note the extra "z"). Floating point types are not currently defined but can easily be added using the existing types as an example (or check the Web page to see if they have already been added).

Defining a Symbol Table to Describe a Structure Type

I normally try to name all types using an identifier that ends in _t to help avoid confusion. I add _st to the type name to get the name of the symbol table. The symbol table describing the passwd_t type will be named passwd_t_st.

Although the C compiler can handle expressions like sizeof(int), it cannot calculate the size of member b of struct a using sizeof(a.b) or calculate the offset of a within b; we must have an actual variable to perform the calculations. I define a dummy variable with a name that is simply dummy_ prepended to the type name (that is, passwd_t dummy_passwd_t;); the SIZEOF() and OFFSET_OF() helper macros depend on this naming convention at the expense of a little wasted space. Note that the dummy_ variables are variables, not types, even though their names end in _t; this little bit of confusion is necessary because the compiler will let us append two strings to make a new variable name but not trim off the suffix.

A symbol table is usually declared as an initialized array of type st_t; usually the size is left blank for the compiler to fill in. Various macros are used to define the {token, value} pairs. A table should always begin with ST_BEGIN_TABLE() and end with ST_END_TABLE() and may have an optional identifier specified with ST_IDENTIFIER().

Each member of the structure is defined using ST_BEGIN() and ST_END() pairs. A number of variables are used to describe the properties of each member:

- ST_IDENTIFIER()   Defines the identifier used to refer to this member. This is normally the same as the member name used in the C definition, although it can be different if you want to define more user friendly names.

- ST_DESCRIPTION()   Gives a short description that could be used for user interaction or to generate comments in a file.

- ST_OFFSET()   This defines the offset, in bytes, from the beginning of the structure and normally calculated by the compiler, typically with help from the OFFSET helper macro. If you have a structure type named passwd_t that has a member

username, the OFFSET(passwd_t, username) will calculate the offset of
passwd_t.username. It is equivalent to the expression (&dummy_passwd_t.user-
name - &dummy_passwd_t).

- ST_SIZEOF()   This specifies the size of a member in For structures, the helper
  macro SIZEOF is normally used. SIZEOF(passwd_t, username) will return the size
  of passwd_t.username. It is equivalent to the expression
  sizeof(dummy_passwd_t.username).

- ST_TYPE()   This is a reference to the symbol table that describes the type of the
  member.

Listing A.1 shows the definition of the structure passwd_t, the dummy variable
dummy_passwd_t, a real variable passwd, and the corresponding symbol table
passwd_t_st used in the sample program.

LISTING A.1   userchange Password Structure and Symbol Table

```
typedef struct {
    char    username[128]; /* user name */
    char    pwcrypt[128];  /* encrypted password */
    uid_t   uid;           /* numeric user id */
    gid_t   gid;           /* numer group id */
    char    gecos[128];    /* real name */
    char    homedir[128];  /* home directory */
    char    shell[128];    /* shell program */
} passwd_t;

passwd_t dummy_passwd_t;
passwd_t passwd;

st_t passwd_t_st[]= {
  ST_BEGIN_TABLE(),
     ST_IDENTIFIER("passwd_t"),

     ST_BEGIN(),
        ST_IDENTIFIER("username"),
        ST_DESCRIPTION("User name"),
        ST_OFFSET( OFFSET(passwd_t, username)),
        ST_SIZEOF( SIZEOF(passwd_t, username)),
        ST_TYPE(asciiz_t_st),
     ST_END(),

     ST_BEGIN(),
        ST_IDENTIFIER("pwcrypt"),
        ST_DESCRIPTION("Encrypted Password"),
        ST_OFFSET( OFFSET(passwd_t, pwcrypt)),
```

continues

LISTING A.1 continued

```
            ST_SIZEOF( SIZEOF(passwd_t, pwcrypt)),
            ST_TYPE(asciiz_t_st),
        ST_END(),

        ST_BEGIN(),
            ST_IDENTIFIER("uid"),
            ST_DESCRIPTION("Numeric user id"),
            ST_OFFSET( OFFSET(passwd_t, uid)),
            ST_SIZEOF( SIZEOF(passwd_t, uid)),
            ST_TYPE(integer32u_t_st),
        ST_END(),

        ST_BEGIN(),
            ST_IDENTIFIER("gid"),
            ST_DESCRIPTION("Numeric group id"),
            ST_OFFSET( OFFSET(passwd_t, gid)),
            ST_SIZEOF( SIZEOF(passwd_t, gid)),
            ST_TYPE(integer32u_t_st),
        ST_END(),

        ST_BEGIN(),
            ST_IDENTIFIER("gecos"),
            ST_DESCRIPTION("Gecos (real name)"),
            ST_OFFSET( OFFSET(passwd_t, gecos)),
            ST_SIZEOF( SIZEOF(passwd_t, gecos)),
            ST_TYPE(asciiz_t_st),
        ST_END(),

        ST_BEGIN(),
            ST_IDENTIFIER("homedir"),
            ST_DESCRIPTION("Home directory"),
            ST_OFFSET( OFFSET(passwd_t, homedir)),
            ST_SIZEOF( SIZEOF(passwd_t, homedir)),
            ST_TYPE(asciiz_t_st),
        ST_END(),

        ST_BEGIN(),
            ST_IDENTIFIER("shell"),
            ST_DESCRIPTION("user's shell program"),
            ST_OFFSET( OFFSET(passwd_t, shell)),
            ST_SIZEOF( SIZEOF(passwd_t, shell)),
            ST_TYPE(asciiz_t_st),
        ST_END(),

    ST_END_TABLE()
};
++end listing
```

Defining a Random Collection of Variables

Defining a random collection of variables is similar to defining a structure type. The primary difference for scalar variables is that we use the ST_AT() macro to define the absolute address of a variable instead of ST_OFFSET() to define the relative address (offset). Don't forget the usual C idiosyncrasies: & (the "address of" operator) is needed for simple variables and structs but is not required for arrays (including strings); make sure you use & where required. The OFFSET() and SIZEOF() helper macros are not used for random variables.

To include a structure type variable, first define the type in a separate symbol table if that hasn't already been done. Then include a reference to it between ST_BEGIN_STRUCT_REF() and ST_END_STRUCT_REF(). We use the same attribute macros we use with any other variable: ST_IDENTIFIER(), ST_AT(), ST_SIZEOF(), ST_TYPE(), and ST_DESCRIPTION(). The identifier specified will be prepended with a period to the member name to get the full name. If you specify " " (null string, not NULL) as the identifier, it will be treated as an anonymous structure effectively promoting all of the members into the same namespace as the parent structure. This hides the structure representation from the user. The example program will use an anonymous structure to allow users to refer to members of the passwd_t structure by using, for example, "username" instead of "passwd.username". In that case, the structure members are mixed in with various other random variables.

The user accessible options for the userchange program, including an anonymous structure reference, are defined in Listing A.2. These values can be set in either the configuration file for the program or as command-line arguments.

LISTING A.2 Program Options Symbol Table

```
char hostname[128] = "";  /* name of host to operate on */
int read_stdin = 0;
char operation[16] = "view";
char passwd_file[128]="./passwd";
int show_args = 0;
#ifdef USE_SSH
   char remote_command[256] =
      "ssh %s -l root userchange read_stdin=1";
#else
   char remote_command[256] = "./userchange read_stdin=1";
#endif
```

continues

LISTING A.2   continued

```
st_t options_st[]= {
   ST_BEGIN_TABLE(),
      ST_BEGIN_STRUCT_REF(),
         ST_IDENTIFIER(""),
         ST_TYPE(passwd_t_st),
         ST_AT(&passwd),
         ST_SIZEOF(sizeof(passwd)),
         ST_DESCRIPTION("Password structure"),
      ST_END_STRUCT_REF(),

      ST_BEGIN(),
         ST_IDENTIFIER("hostname"),
         ST_AT(hostname),
         ST_SIZEOF(sizeof(hostname)),
         ST_TYPE(asciiz_t_st),
         ST_DESCRIPTION("host to view/modify password on"),
      ST_END(),

      ST_BEGIN(),
         ST_IDENTIFIER("operation"),
         ST_AT(operation),
         ST_SIZEOF(sizeof(operation)),
         ST_TYPE(asciiz_t_st),
         ST_DESCRIPTION("view,add,modify,delete"),
      ST_END(),

      ST_BEGIN(),
         ST_IDENTIFIER("remote_command"),
         ST_AT(remote_command),
         ST_SIZEOF(sizeof(remote_command)),
         ST_TYPE(asciiz_t_st),
         ST_DESCRIPTION("Command for remote updates"),
      ST_END(),

      ST_BEGIN(),
         ST_IDENTIFIER("read_stdin"),
         ST_AT(&read_stdin),
         ST_SIZEOF(sizeof(read_stdin)),
         ST_TYPE(cboolean_t_st),
         ST_DESCRIPTION("nonzero=read args from standard in"),
      ST_END(),

      ST_BEGIN(),
         ST_IDENTIFIER("passwd_file"),
         ST_AT(passwd_file),
         ST_SIZEOF(sizeof(passwd_file)),
         ST_TYPE(asciiz_t_st),
         ST_DESCRIPTION("passwd file to modify"),
      ST_END(),
```

```
    ST_BEGIN(),
        ST_IDENTIFIER("st_debug"),
        ST_AT(&st_debug),
        ST_SIZEOF(sizeof(st_debug)),
        ST_TYPE(cboolean_t_st),
        ST_DESCRIPTION("Debugging level for symtab lib"),
    ST_END(),

    ST_BEGIN(),
        ST_IDENTIFIER("show_args"),
        ST_AT(&show_args),
        ST_SIZEOF(sizeof(show_args)),
        ST_TYPE(cboolean_t_st),
        ST_DESCRIPTION("Show all arguments"),
    ST_END(),

  ST_END_TABLE()
};
++end listing
```

Including Another Symbol Table

One symbol table can be included in another using ST_INCLUDE(). This causes the symbol table parsing routines to recurse into the other symbol table. The results should be similar to cutting and pasting the other table into the current table without ST_BEGIN_TABLE() and ST_END_TABLE().

You can use this to create multiple symbol tables that define different, but overlapping, subsets of the overall namespace. You could define two symbol tables, newbie_options_st and wizard_options_st, and use an include to incorporate all of the newbie options into the wizard options. Then, by simply choosing which of the two tables you refer to, you can control which options a given user can see or modify without duplicating a lot of symbol table entries.

If your program consists of a number of relatively independent modules, you can use the include feature to keep your symbol tables modular as well. Each module can have an options symbol table that describes options used by that module. The main program can then define a symbol table that uses an include to reference all of the individual module option symbol tables.

Includes are different from structure references. A structure reference allows you to specify an identifier that is prepended to each member name, but includes do not. A structure reference allows you to specify the address of the variable described in a structure, but an include does not; normally you include symbol tables that already have ST_AT() definitions for the individual members.

Error Reporting

The userchange program uses a simple structure, error_t, to report errors. In addition to an error number, it includes two text fields—a text error message and a field name. The error number is useful for interpretation by another program. The text is a human-readable message. The fieldname makes it easy for humans or programs to associate the error with the particular variable that caused it. You might, for example, have a generic error number EEXIST (a constant defined in the system include file errno.h), a text message "Already Exists", and a field "username".

The userchange program uses the same error numbers as the standard library, but you could use a different scheme. You might, for example, use the three digit scheme used by SMTP, FTP, and many other protocols. In that scheme, each digit successively refines things. Even if the program does not understand the exact error described by the error number, it can make an intelligent guess about how to handle it. The first digit gives the program an idea of whether the problem response describes success, a permanent error (unknown user), or a temporary error (out of disk space).

This error reporting scheme is specific to the userchange program (and some other programs I have written) and not the symbol table library. Future additions to the library might incorporate a similar approach.

The error_t structure and the symbol table that describes it are shown in Listing A.3.

LISTING A.3 userchange error_t

```
typedef struct {
    int number;         /* error number */
    char text[256];     /* error text */
    char field[256];    /* field, if any, where error occured*/
} error_t;

/* dummy value used to calculate offsets in symtab */
error_t dummy_error_t;

error_t error = {0,"Operation presumed successful",""};

st_t error_t_st[]= {
    ST_BEGIN_TABLE(),
        ST_BEGIN(),
            ST_IDENTIFIER("number"),
            ST_SIZEOF( SIZEOF(error_t,number) ),
            ST_TYPE(integer32s_t_st),
            ST_OFFSET( OFFSET(error_t, number) ),
            ST_DESCRIPTION("Error number"),
        ST_END(),
```

```
ST_BEGIN(),
    ST_IDENTIFIER("text"),
    ST_SIZEOF( SIZEOF(error_t,text)),
    ST_TYPE(asciiz_t_st),
    ST_OFFSET( OFFSET(error_t, text) ),
    ST_DESCRIPTION("Error text"),
ST_END(),

ST_BEGIN(),
    ST_IDENTIFIER("field"),
    ST_SIZEOF( SIZEOF(error_t,field)),
    ST_TYPE(asciiz_t_st),
    ST_OFFSET( OFFSET(error_t, field) ),
    ST_DESCRIPTION("Error field"),
ST_END(),


    ST_END_TABLE()
};
++end listing
```

Smart Pointers

Smart pointers are one of the most important data structures used by the symbol table library. A smart pointer is a struct with two members. The member `table` is a pointer to the symbol table that describes an object. The member `object` is a pointer to the object described by the symbol table. Either may be NULL, if unknown; however, the library will normally expect at least the `table` member to have a value. Smart pointers are declared using the type `smart_pointer_t`. The constructor function `st_smart_pointer()` may be used to make a smart pointer from two arguments; the first is the table pointer and the second is the object pointer. Often, when calling a library function, you can simply use this constructor to build on-the-fly without having to define a smart pointer variable.

Normally, the smart pointer will point to a structure and the symbol table that describes it or the smart pointer may point to NULL and a symbol table describing a random collection of variables scattered throughout memory. Some of the internal functions use more arcane combinations.

Symbol Table Library Functions

The symbol table library includes a number of routines that are used to process symbol tables and the objects they describe. These are declared in `symbol.h` and defined in `symbol.c`.

Many of the functions have one parameter that takes an option structure specific to that function. This structure defines various options which are used to vary the behavior of the function. The options for a couple functions include a member named `prefix`, for example, which will be prepended to each line or variable name; this is frequently used for indentation by assigning a string value with some number of spaces. For each of these option structures, there is a corresponding default structure that is initialized to the default values. Often, simply passing the default structure as an argument is sufficient. If you want different options, declare a variable of the corresponding type and initialize it by copying the default structure to it before setting any of the members. This is good programming practice when dealing with structures in general; this way, your program will be unlikely to break due to uninitialized members when additional members are added to the structure.

Only three functions will be used by a typical program besides the smart pointer constructor described previously; these three are very flexible. The following sections describe these functions. There are some other functions, used less frequently, which will be briefly mentioned.

The `st_show()` Function

```
#include <symbol.h>
extern void st_show(
    FILE *stream,
    smart_pointer_t sp,
    st_show_opt_t *options
);
extern st_show_opt_t st_show_defaults;
```

This function will print out all the variables (or structure members) pointed to by the smart pointer `sp`. Output will be to the stream `stream`, which may be `stdout`, `stderr`, an open file, a pipe, a serial port, a TCP/IP network connection, or just about any valid UNIX stream; `stdout` and `stderr` will typically print to the user's `tty` if they haven't been redirected. If you want to read a file, it is up to you to open the file before calling this function.

Each line of output will be preceded by the contents of the string member `options.prefix`. This will typically be `""` (null string) but can also be a number of spaces (that is, `" "`) for indentation or a value like `errror.` to augment the name. Note that at some point in the future I will probably define two separate prefixes, one for lines and the other for variable names.

Output will be one line per variable or structure member and will look something like this (using the error struct as an example).

```
error.number=10
error.text="The sky is falling"
error.field="chicken.little"
```

The `st_read_stream()` Function

```
#include <symbol.h>
extern int st_read_stream(
    FILE *stream,
    smart_pointer_t sp,
    st_read_stream_opt_t options
);
extern st_read_stream_opt_t st_read_stream_defaults;
```

This function is the opposite of `st_show()`. It reads a number of values from a stream, in the same "name=value" (one per line) format output by `st_show()`.

It is pretty lax about quotation marks; double quotes may be used or in many cases omitted. Lines beginning with "#" or "/" will be treated as comments and ignored and blank lines should also be ignored. Leading whitespace will be ignored at the beginning of each line. Input will continue until an end of file condition is sensed or a line consisting of one of the termination strings defined in the options is read. The default termination strings are END and DATA. You can also define another stream, `options.echo`; this will cause all data read to be copied to that stream. This is helpful for creating a log of all transactions, for example.

The `st_parse_args()` Function

```
#include <symbol.h>
extern void st_parse_args(smart_pointer_t table,
    int argc,
    char **argv);
```

This function is used to parse command-line arguments. The smart pointer will refer to a structure or collection of variables. The parameters `argc` and `argv` are usually just copies of the parameters to the function `main()` in your program. Command-line parameters are expressed in simple name=value form with no leading switch characters:

```
userchange operation=view username=root
```

Other Functions

Some other functions will be used by programs or symbol table extensions that want to add additional forms of interaction (such as a GUI or database access). Table A.1 describes these functions.

TABLE A.1   Other Symbol Table Functions

Function	*Description*
st_set()	This function takes a smart pointer, two strings, a variable name, and a value, and assigns the value to the variable after looking up the variable in the symbol table pointed to by the smart pointer.
st_walk() st_walk_next()	These two functions are used to traverse a symbol table, stopping at each variable or member.
st_lookup()	This function is used to find a given identifier within a symbol table.
st_find_attrib()	This function is used to retrieve the value of an attribute associated with a symbol table or subset.
st_tostring()	These two functions invoke the text st_from_string() conversion methods associated with a basetype.

userchange main()

This section covers the main() function piece-by-piece, starting with the declarations. We need to declare main() in the traditional manner with argc and argv to have access to the command-line parameters.

```
main(argc,argv)
int argc;
char *argv[];     /* or char **argv */
{
    passwd_t options;
    char command[256];
    FILE *pipe;
    FILE *rc_file;
    st_show_opt_t st_show_options;
```

In the first block, we read a configuration file. In this case, the file will be named ./userchange.rc in the current directory. In a typical application, you might want to try reading a couple different files, /etc/userchange.rc and $(HOME)/userchange.rc in succession. We must open the file ourselves; the symbol table library does not do that for us. In the event of failure, we will simply skip the remainder of this block of code.

The options symbol table, `options_st`, was previously defined to include a random assortment of variables, including the hostname for remote operation, the operation to be performed, the debugging level for the symbol table package, the `passwd` structure that contains all the password fields we can change, and others.

A call to `st_read_stream()` does the actual work. We pass in three arguments: The stream we already opened (from the config file); a smart pointer, constructed on the fly, which contains a pointer to the `options_st` symbol table and NULL for the object address, as is appropriate for a random collection of variables; and, lastly, we pass in the default options for the `st_read_stream()` function.

```
/* read rc (configuration) file */
rc_file=fopen("./userchange.rc","r");
if(rc_file) {
   st_read_stream(rc_file,
      st_smart_pointer(options_st, NULL),
      st_read_stream_defaults);
   fclose(rc_file);
}
```

Now we will parse the command-line arguments using the same `options_st` symbol table we used for reading the configuration file. The function `st_parse_args()` does all the work. We pass a smart pointer with a pointer to the table and no additional address information (NULL), just as we did in the preceding code. And we pass `argc` and `argv`, the arguments passed to `main()` by the C runtime initialization module ("crt0" or equivalent). `argc` is a count of how many arguments are being passed and `argv` is an array of pointers to character strings, each of which is a single argument passed on the command line. The name of the program is passed as the first argument, `argv[0]`, so don't be surprised if `argc` is one greater than you expected.

```
/* parse command line arguments */
st_parse_args(   st_smart_pointer(options_st, NULL),
   argc, argv);
```

If you want to see the values of the options after initialization, reading the config file, and parsing arguments, just pass the argument `show_args=1`, which will trigger the next block of code. `st_show()` is one of the most commonly used functions. We do not need any special function options right now, so we just use the defaults

```
/* show all the arguments, if appropriate */
if(show_args) {
   st_show(   stdout,
      st_smart_pointer(options_st, NULL),
      &st_show_defaults);
}
```

If the program was invoked with the option read_stdin=1, that will trigger this next
block of code to read additional options from stdin. This is typically used when a second slave copy of the program is being run on a remote machine. It might also be used if
the program was being driven by a cgi-bin or GUI frontend.

The st_read_stream() function is conceptually the exact opposite of st_show() and
there is a direct correspondence between the arguments.

```
/* read options from stdin, if appropriate */
if(read_stdin) {
   st_read_stream(stdin, st_smart_pointer(options_st, NULL),
      st_read_stream_defaults);
}
```

At this point, we have used all the symbol table library functions we need for this program. We will use them in slightly different ways below as we do application-specific
things. The first test is to see if hostname has been set, and if so, we will invoke a remote
slave.

```
/* Test if local operation is desired or if we should */
/* forward request to another machine*/
if(strlen(hostname)>0) {
```

The remote_command variable should contain a command that will invoke a remote program; the substring %s will be used to substitute the name in using snprintf().
snprintf() is like printf() except it prints to a string and, unlike its more common
cousin sprintf(), allows you to pass in the size to protect against overflows. In this
case, we use remote_command as the format control string.

```
/* remote operation */
fprintf(stderr,"*** REMOTE OPERATION***\n");
snprintf(command, sizeof(command),
   remote_command, hostname);
```

If the remote slave is invoked with a hostname it would attempt to execute another copy
of itself. This would happen again and again. Reliably detecting if the hostname matches
the current host is a bit of a nuisance, since a typical networked host has at least three
names and may have more if it has multiple network interfaces, virtual hosts, or aliases
(DNS CNAME records). If your machine is named "gonzo.muppets.com" then the
names "gonzo.muppets.com," "gonzo," and "localhost" all refer to the local host. Since
we don't need the hostname anymore, we will take the simple expedient of clobbering
the hostname.

```
/* quick kluge to make remote end consider it */
/* to be a local update */
hostname[0]=0;
```

Here will we use the `popen()` command to run the command with the stream `pipe` piped to its standard input. The command itself will probably invoke a remote copy of `changeuser` with the `stdin` and `stdout` streams forwarded across the network connection. In this case, it is sufficient to only have `stdin` connected to a pipe; `stdout` will simply be inherited. If we needed to parse the responses, we would need pipes for both `stdin` and `stdout`, which would be more than `popen()` can handle; in that case, we would need to use `pipe()`, `fork()`, either `system()` or `exec()`, and a bunch of glue code. We would also need to be careful to avoid a deadlock where both programs were waiting for input from each other, or one program could not write more output until the other program read the output from the first, but the second program was waiting for the first program to read its output.

```
pipe=popen(command, "w");
assert(pipe);
```

Now we will use `st_show` to dump the options to the pipe we just created. We will terminate that output using a line which reads END; if we just closed the pipe to produce an end of file condition, the slave program might be terminated before it had a chance to perform the operation and generate a response.

```
st_show(pipe, st_smart_pointer(options_st, NULL),
    &st_show_defaults);
fprintf(pipe,"END\n");

/* we don't process output of child at all here */
/* the childs output will end up on stdout */
```

Now we need to close the pipe, which will have the side effect of waiting for the child process to finish.

```
/* wait for child to exit */
pclose(pipe);
```

The remainder of the program is used for local operation (or the slave in a master-slave relationship).

```
} else {
/* local operation */
```

The function `pw_update()`, which is not included in the listings for this chapter, reads the `passwd` file and, optionally, writes a new copy with modifications. It take four parameters. The first is a pointer to an error structure that will be updated with the results of the operation. The second parameter is a pointer to a `passwd` structure that contains values for all of the fields; this may be modified if we are retrieving information. The third is a string giving the name of the file to operate on. The fourth is a string that specifies the operation to be performed; this may have the values view, add, change, or modify. We invoke the function once with the operation specified by the user and a second time just to read back the data for verification.

```
pw_update(&error, &passwd, passwd_file, operation);

pw_update(&error, &passwd, passwd_file, "view");
```

Now we are going to output a response message for the user or program that invoked userchange. This will begin with the line RESPONSE followed by the error structure, indented 3 spaces and prefixed with the name of the structure. Then we will output a line which reads DATA, followed by the passwd structure, containing the values of all the fields of the passwd file, indented 3 spaces. Finally, we will output a line which reads END to terminate the response.

We set the indentation level or other prefix by changing the value of prefix in the function options we pass to st_show(). As mentioned previously, we will initialize the options properly by copying a default option structure. st_show() will be invoked twice and we will modify and reuse the function options structure, st_show_options, each time.

```
    /* set indentation level */
    st_show_options = st_show_defaults;

    fprintf(stdout, "RESPONSE\n");

    strncpy(st_show_options.prefix,
        "   error.",sizeof(st_show_options));
    st_show(stdout, st_smart_pointer(error_t_st, &error),
        &st_show_options);
    fprintf(stdout, "DATA\n");

    strncpy(st_show_options.prefix,"   ",
        sizeof(st_show_options));
    st_show(stdout, st_smart_pointer(passwd_t_st, &passwd),
        &st_show_options);
    fprintf(stdout, "END\n");

  }

  exit(0);
}
```

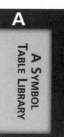

Sample Execution

The code fragment below shows sample commands to test execution of userchange after setting up a suitable environment. First, we create a blank password file (do not do this in the real /etc directory). Then we initialize the configuration file, userchange.rc, to values suitable for testing; the blank dummy password file will be used instead of the real one and the program will just call another copy of itself on the same machine instead of trying to invoke a copy of itself on a remote system. Finally, we use the userchange program to create a user named root with an encrypted password, a user id of 0, a group id of 0, a comment (gecos) field value of root, a home directory of /root, and the shell /bin/bash.

```
rm passwd
touch passwd
echo 'passwd_file="./passwd"' >userchange.rc
echo 'remote_command="./userchange read_stdin=1" >>userchange.rc
./userchange operation=add username=root pwcrypt=WwXxYyZz uid=0 gid=0
➥gecos="root" homedir=/root shell=/bin/bash
```

The symbol table library simplifies certain forms of user interaction, reading and writing configuration and other data files, and communications with other processes. As the library is enhanced, there may be a few changes that break existing programs in minor ways; if you will be distributing your programs you might want to bind to a specific version of the shared library (that is, link to libsymtab.so.0.55 instead of merely libsymtab.so).

GNU GENERAL PUBLIC LICENSE

Version 2, June 1991

Copyright © 1989, 1991 Free Software Foundation, Inc.

675 Mass Ave, Cambridge, MA 02139, USA

Everyone is permitted to copy and distribute verbatim copies of this license document, but changing it is not allowed.

Preamble

The licenses for most software are designed to take away your freedom to share and change it. By contrast, the GNU General Public License is intended to guarantee your freedom to share and change free software—to make sure the software is free for all its users. This General Public License applies to most of the Free Software Foundation's software and to any other program whose authors commit to using it. (Some other Free Software Foundation software is covered by the GNU Library General Public License instead.) You can apply it to your programs, too.

When we speak of free software, we are referring to freedom, not price. Our General Public Licenses are designed to make sure that you have the freedom to distribute copies of free software (and charge for this service if you wish), that you receive source code or can get it if you want it, that you can change the software or use pieces of it in new free programs; and that you know you can do these things.

To protect your rights, we need to make restrictions that forbid anyone to deny you these rights or to ask you to surrender the rights. These restrictions translate to certain responsibilities for you if you distribute copies of the software, or if you modify it.

For example, if you distribute copies of such a program, whether gratis or for a fee, you must give the recipients all the rights that you have. You must make sure that they, too, receive or can get the source code. And you must show them these terms so they know their rights.

We protect your rights with two steps: (1) copyright the software, and (2) offer you this license which gives you legal permission to copy, distribute and/or modify the software.

Also, for each author's protection and ours, we want to make certain that everyone understands that there is no warranty for this free software. If the software is modified by someone else and passed on, we want its recipients to know that what they have is not the original, so that any problems introduced by others will not reflect on the original authors' reputations.

Finally, any free program is threatened constantly by software patents. We wish to avoid the danger that redistributors of a free program will individually obtain patent licenses, in effect making the program proprietary. To prevent this, we have made it clear that any patent must be licensed for everyone's free use or not licensed at all.

The precise terms and conditions for copying, distribution and modification follow.

GNU GENERAL PUBLIC LICENSE

TERMS AND CONDITIONS FOR COPYING, DISTRIBUTION AND MODIFICATION

0. This License applies to any program or other work which contains a notice placed by the copyright holder saying it may be distributed under the terms of this General Public License. The "Program", below, refers to any such program or work, and a "work based on the Program" means either the Program or any derivative work under copyright law: that is to say, a work containing the Program or a portion of it, either verbatim or with modifications and/or translated into another language. (Hereinafter, translation is included without limitation in the term "modification".) Each licensee is addressed as "you".

Activities other than copying, distribution and modification are not covered by this License; they are outside its scope. The act of running the Program is not restricted, and the output from the Program is covered only if its contents constitute a work based on the Program (independent of having been made by running the Program). Whether that is true depends on what the Program does.

1. You may copy and distribute verbatim copies of the Program's source code as you receive it, in any medium, provided that you conspicuously and appropriately publish on each copy an appropriate copyright notice and disclaimer of warranty; keep intact all the notices that refer to this License and to the absence of any warranty; and give any other recipients of the Program a copy of this License along with the Program.

You may charge a fee for the physical act of transferring a copy, and you may at your option offer warranty protection in exchange for a fee.

2. You may modify your copy or copies of the Program or any portion of it, thus forming a work based on the Program, and copy and distribute such modifications or work under the terms of Section 1 above, provided that you also meet all of these conditions:

a) You must cause the modified files to carry prominent notices stating that you changed the files and the date of any change.

b) You must cause any work that you distribute or publish, that in whole or in part contains or is derived from the Program or any part thereof, to be licensed as a whole at no charge to all third parties under the terms of this License.

c) If the modified program normally reads commands interactively when run, you must cause it, when started running for such interactive use in the most ordinary way, to print or display an announcement including an appropriate copyright notice and a notice that there is no warranty (or else, saying that you provide a warranty) and that users may redistribute the program under these conditions, and telling the user how to view a copy of this License. (Exception: if the Program itself is interactive but does not normally print such an announcement, your work based on the Program is not required to print an announcement.)

These requirements apply to the modified work as a whole. If identifiable sections of that work are not derived from the Program, and can be reasonably considered independent and separate works in themselves, then this License, and its terms, do not apply to those sections when you distribute them as separate works. But when you distribute the same sections as part of a whole which is a work based on the Program, the distribution of the whole must be on the terms of this License, whose permissions for other licensees extend to the entire whole, and thus to each and every part regardless of who wrote it.

Thus, it is not the intent of this section to claim rights or contest your rights to work written entirely by you; rather, the intent is to exercise the right to control the distribution of derivative or collective works based on the Program.

In addition, mere aggregation of another work not based on the Program with the Program (or with a work based on the Program) on a volume of a storage or distribution medium does not bring the other work under the scope of this License.

3. You may copy and distribute the Program (or a work based on it, under Section 2) in object code or executable form under the terms of Sections 1 and 2 above provided that you also do one of the following:

a) Accompany it with the complete corresponding machine-readable source code, which must be distributed under the terms of Sections 1 and 2 above on a medium customarily used for software interchange; or,

b) Accompany it with a written offer, valid for at least three years, to give any third party, for a charge no more than your cost of physically performing source distribution, a complete machine-readable copy of the corresponding source code, to be distributed under the terms of Sections 1 and 2 above on a medium customarily used for software interchange; or,

c) Accompany it with the information you received as to the offer to distribute corresponding source code. (This alternative is allowed only for noncommercial distribution and only if you received the program in object code or executable form with such an offer, in accord with Subsection b above.)

The source code for a work means the preferred form of the work for making modifications to it. For an executable work, complete source code means all the source code for all modules it contains, plus any associated interface definition files, plus the scripts used to control compilation and installation of the executable. However, as a special exception, the source code distributed need not include anything that is normally distributed (in either source or binary form) with the major components (compiler, kernel, and so on) of the operating system on which the executable runs, unless that component itself accompanies the executable.

If distribution of executable or object code is made by offering access to copy from a designated place, then offering equivalent access to copy the source code from the same place counts as distribution of the source code, even though third parties are not compelled to copy the source along with the object code.

4. You may not copy, modify, sublicense, or distribute the Program except as expressly provided under this License. Any attempt otherwise to copy, modify, sublicense or distribute the Program is void, and will automatically terminate your rights under this License. However, parties who have received copies, or rights, from you under this License will not have their licenses terminated so long as such parties remain in full compliance.

5. You are not required to accept this License, since you have not signed it. However, nothing else grants you permission to modify or distribute the Program or its derivative works. These actions are prohibited by law if you do not accept this License. Therefore, by modifying or distributing the Program (or any work based on the Program), you indicate your acceptance of this License to do so, and all its terms and conditions for copying, distributing or modifying the Program or works based on it.

6. Each time you redistribute the Program (or any work based on the Program), the recipient automatically receives a license from the original licensor to copy, distribute or modify the Program subject to these terms and conditions. You may not impose any further restrictions on the recipients' exercise of the rights granted herein. You are not responsible for enforcing compliance by third parties to this License.

7. If, as a consequence of a court judgment or allegation of patent infringement or for any other reason (not limited to patent issues), conditions are imposed on you (whether by court order, agreement or otherwise) that contradict the conditions of this License, they do not excuse you from the conditions of this License. If you cannot distribute so as to satisfy simultaneously your obligations under this License and any other pertinent obligations, then as a consequence you may not distribute the Program at all. For example, if a patent license would not permit royalty-free redistribution of the Program by all those who receive copies directly or indirectly through you, then the only way you could satisfy both it and this License would be to refrain entirely from distribution of the Program.

If any portion of this section is held invalid or unenforceable under any particular circumstance, the balance of the section is intended to apply and the section as a whole is intended to apply in other circumstances.

It is not the purpose of this section to induce you to infringe any patents or other property right claims or to contest validity of any such claims; this section has the sole purpose of protecting the integrity of the free software distribution system, which is implemented by public license practices. Many people have made generous contributions to the wide range of software distributed through that system in reliance on consistent application of that system; it is up to the author/donor to decide if he or she is willing to distribute software through any other system and a licensee cannot impose that choice.

This section is intended to make thoroughly clear what is believed to be a consequence of the rest of this License.

8. If the distribution and/or use of the Program is restricted in certain countries either by patents or by copyrighted interfaces, the original copyright holder who places the Program under this License may add an explicit geographical distribution limitation excluding those countries, so that distribution is permitted only in or among countries not thus excluded. In such case, this License incorporates the limitation as if written in the body of this License.

9. The Free Software Foundation may publish revised and/or new versions of the General Public License from time to time. Such new versions will be similar in spirit to the present version, but may differ in detail to address new problems or concerns.

Each version is given a distinguishing version number. If the Program specifies a version number of this License which applies to it and "any later version", you have the option of following the terms and conditions either of that version or of any later version published by the Free Software Foundation. If the Program does not specify a version number of this License, you may choose any version ever published by the Free Software Foundation.

10. If you wish to incorporate parts of the Program into other free programs whose distribution conditions are different, write to the author to ask for permission. For software which is copyrighted by the Free Software Foundation, write to the Free Software Foundation; we sometimes make exceptions for this. Our decision will be guided by the two goals of preserving the free status of all derivatives of our free software and of promoting the sharing and reuse of software generally.

NO WARRANTY

11. BECAUSE THE PROGRAM IS LICENSED FREE OF CHARGE, THERE IS NO WARRANTY FOR THE PROGRAM, TO THE EXTENT PERMITTED BY APPLICABLE LAW. EXCEPT WHEN OTHERWISE STATED IN WRITING THE COPYRIGHT HOLDERS AND/OR OTHER PARTIES PROVIDE THE PROGRAM "AS IS" WITHOUT WARRANTY OF ANY KIND, EITHER EXPRESSED OR IMPLIED,

INCLUDING, BUT NOT LIMITED TO, THE IMPLIED WARRANTIES OF MER-
CHANTABILITY AND FITNESS FOR A PARTICULAR PURPOSE. THE ENTIRE
RISK AS TO THE QUALITY AND PERFORMANCE OF THE PROGRAM IS WITH
YOU. SHOULD THE PROGRAM PROVE DEFECTIVE, YOU ASSUME THE COST
OF ALL NECESSARY SERVICING, REPAIR OR CORRECTION.

12. IN NO EVENT UNLESS REQUIRED BY APPLICABLE LAW OR AGREED TO
IN WRITING WILL ANY COPYRIGHT HOLDER, OR ANY OTHER PARTY WHO
MAY MODIFY AND/OR REDISTRIBUTE THE PROGRAM AS PERMITTED
ABOVE, BE LIABLE TO YOU FOR DAMAGES, INCLUDING ANY GENERAL,
SPECIAL, INCIDENTAL OR CONSEQUENTIAL DAMAGES ARISING OUT OF
THE USE OR INABILITY TO USE THE PROGRAM (INCLUDING BUT NOT LIM-
ITED TO LOSS OF DATA OR DATA BEING RENDERED INACCURATE OR LOSS-
ES SUSTAINED BY YOU OR THIRD PARTIES OR A FAILURE OF THE PROGRAM
TO OPERATE WITH ANY OTHER PROGRAMS), EVEN IF SUCH HOLDER OR
OTHER PARTY HAS BEEN ADVISED OF THE POSSIBILITY OF SUCH DAM-
AGES.

END OF TERMS AND CONDITIONS

Linux and the GNU system

The GNU project started 12 years ago with the goal of developing a complete free
UNIX-like operating system. "Free" refers to freedom, not price; it means you are free to
run, copy, distribute, study, change, and improve the software.

A UNIX-like system consists of many different programs. We found some components
already available as free software—for example, X Windows and TeX. We obtained other
components by helping to convince their developers to make them free—for example, the
Berkeley network utilities. Other components we wrote specifically for GNU—for example, GNU Emacs, the GNU C compiler, the GNU C library, Bash, and Ghostscript. The
components in this last category are "GNU software". The GNU system consists of all
three categories together.

The GNU project is not just about developing and distributing free software. The heart of
the GNU project is an idea: that software should be free, and that the users' freedom is
worth defending. For if people have freedom but do not value it, they will not keep it for
long. In order to make freedom last, we have to teach people to value it.

The GNU project's method is that free software and the idea of users' freedom support
each other. We develop GNU software, and as people encounter GNU programs or the
GNU system and start to use them, they also think about the GNU idea. The software
shows that the idea can work in practice. People who come to agree with the idea are
likely to write additional free software. Thus, the software embodies the idea, spreads the
idea, and grows from the idea.

This method was working well—until someone combined the Linux kernel with the GNU system (which still lacked a kernel), and called the combination a "Linux system."

The Linux kernel is a free UNIX-compatible kernel written by Linus Torvalds. It was not written specifically for the GNU project, but the Linux kernel and the GNU system work together well. In fact, adding Linux to the GNU system brought the system to completion: it made a free UNIX-compatible operating system available for use.

But ironically, the practice of calling it a "Linux system" undermines our method of communicating the GNU idea. At first impression, a "Linux system" sounds like something completely distinct from the "GNU system." And that is what most users think it is.

Most introductions to the "Linux system" acknowledge the role played by the GNU software components. But they don't say that the system as a whole is more or less the same GNU system that the GNU project has been compiling for a decade. They don't say that the idea of a free UNIX-like system originates from the GNU project. So most users don't know these things.

This leads many of those users to identify themselves as a separate community of "Linux users", distinct from the GNU user community. They use all of the GNU software; in fact, they use almost all of the GNU system; but they don't think of themselves as GNU users, and they may not think about the GNU idea.

It leads to other problems as well—even hampering cooperation on software maintenance. Normally when users change a GNU program to make it work better on a particular system, they send the change to the maintainer of that program; then they work with the maintainer, explaining the change, arguing for it and sometimes rewriting it, to get it installed.

But people who think of themselves as "Linux users" are more likely to release a forked "Linux-only" version of the GNU program, and consider the job done. We want each and every GNU program to work "out of the box" on Linux-based systems; but if the users do not help, that goal becomes much harder to achieve.

So how should the GNU project respond? What should we do now to spread the idea that freedom for computer users is important?

We should continue to talk about the freedom to share and change software—and to teach other users to value these freedoms. If we enjoy having a free operating system, it makes sense for us to think about preserving those freedoms for the long term. If we enjoy having a variety of free software, it makes sense to think about encouraging others to write additional free software, instead of additional proprietary software.

We should not accept the splitting of the community in two. Instead we should spread the word that "Linux systems" are variant GNU systems—that users of these systems are GNU users, and that they ought to consider the GNU philosophy which brought these systems into existence.

This article is one way of doing that. Another way is to use the terms "Linux-based GNU system" (or "GNU/Linux system" or "Lignux" for short) to refer to the combination of the Linux kernel and the GNU system.

Copyright 1996 Richard Stallman

(Verbatim copying and redistribution is permitted without royalty as long as this notice is preserved.)

The Linux kernel is Copyright © 1991, 1992, 1993, 1994 Linus Torvalds (others hold copyrights on some of the drivers, file systems, and other parts of the kernel) and and is licensed under the terms of the GNU General Public License.

The FreeBSD Copyright

All of the documentation and software included in the 4.4BSD and 4.4BSD-Lite Releases is copyrighted by The Regents of the University of California.

Copyright 1979, 1980, 1983, 1986, 1988, 1989, 1991, 1992, 1993, 1994 The Regents of the University of California. All rights reserved.

Redistribution and use in source and binary forms, with or without modification, are permitted provided that the following conditions are met:

1. Redistributions of source code must retain the above copyright notice, this list of conditions and the following disclaimer.

2. Redistributions in binary form must reproduce the above copyright notice, this list of conditions and the following disclaimer in the documentation and/or other materials provided with the distribution.

3. All advertising materials mentioning features or use of this software must display the following acknowledgement:

This product includes software developed by the University of California, Berkeley and its contributors.

4. Neither the name of the University nor the names of its contributors may be used to endorse or promote products derived from this software without specific prior written permission.

B

GNU GENERAL
PUBLIC LICENSE

THIS SOFTWARE IS PROVIDED BY THE REGENTS AND CONTRIBUTORS "AS IS" AND ANY EXPRESS OR IMPLIED WARRANTIES, INCLUDING, BUT NOT LIMITED TO, THE IMPLIED WARRANTIES OF MERCHANTABILITY AND FITNESS FOR A PARTICULAR PURPOSE ARE DISCLAIMED. IN NO EVENT SHALL THE REGENTS OR CONTRIBUTORS BE LIABLE FOR ANY DIRECT, INDIRECT, INCIDENTAL, SPECIAL, EXEMPLARY, OR CONSEQUENTIAL DAMAGES (INCLUDING, BUT NOT LIMITED TO, PROCUREMENT OF SUBSTITUTE GOODS OR SERVICES; LOSS OF USE, DATA, OR PROFITS; OR BUSINESS INTERRUPTION) HOWEVER CAUSED AND ON ANY THEORY OF LIABILITY, WHETHER IN CONTRACT, STRICT LIABILITY, OR TORT (INCLUDING NEGLIGENCE OR OTHERWISE) ARISING IN ANY WAY OUT OF THE USE OF THIS SOFTWARE, EVEN IF ADVISED OF THE POSSIBILITY OF SUCH DAMAGE.

The Institute of Electrical and Electronics Engineers and the American National Standards Committee X3, on Information Processing Systems have given us permission to reprint portions of their documentation.

In the following statement, the phrase "this text" refers to portions of the system documentation.

Portions of this text are reprinted and reproduced in electronic form in the second BSD Networking Software Release, from IEEE Std 1003.1-1988, IEEE Standard Portable Operating System Interface for Computer Environments (POSIX), copyright C 1988 by the Institute of Electrical and Electronics Engineers, Inc. In the event of any discrepancy between these versions and the original IEEE Standard, the original IEEE Standard is the referee document.

In the following statement, the phrase "This material" refers to portions of the system documentation.

This material is reproduced with permission from American National Standards Committee X3, on Information Processing Systems. Computer and Business Equipment Manufacturers Association (CBEMA), 311 First St., NW, Suite 500, Washington, DC 20001-2178. The developmental work of Programming Language C was completed by the X3J11 Technical Committee.

The views and conclusions contained in the software and documentation are those of the authors and should not be interpreted as representing official policies, either expressed or implied, of the Regents of the University of California.

www@FreeBSD.ORG

$Date: 1997/07/01 03:52:05 $

INDEX

Other Related Titles

Maximum RPM
Edward Bailey
ISBN: 0-672-31105-4
$39.99 US /$56.95 CAN

Sams Teach Yourself GIMP in 24 Hours
Joshua Pruitt and Ramona Pruitt
ISBN: 0-672-31509-2
$24.99 US /$37.95 CAN

Sams Teach Yourself C in 21 Days, Fourth Edition
Peter Aitken and Bradley L. Jones
ISBN: 0-672-31069-4
$29.99 US /$42.95 CAN

Sams Teach Yourself StarOffice 5 for Linux in 24 Hours
Nicholas Wells
ISBN: 0-672-31412-6
$19.99 US /$29.95 CAN

Sams Teach Yourself C++ in 21 Days, Third Edition
Jesse Liberty
ISBN: 0-672-31515-7
$29.99 US / $42.95 CAN

Sams Teach Yourself TCP/IP Network Administration in 21 Days
Brian Komar
ISBN: 0-672-31250-6
$29.99 US / $42.95 CAN

Bob Lewis's IS Survival Guide
Bob Lewis
ISBN: 0-672-31437-1
$24.99 USA/$37.95 CAN

Maximum Security, Second Edition
Anonymous
ISBN: 0-672-31341-3
$49.99 US / $71.95 CAN

Sams Teach Yourself Java 2 Platform in 21 Days, Professional Reference Edition
Rogers Cadenhead
ISBN: 0-672-31438-X
$49.99 US / $71.95 CAN

Linux Complete Command Reference
Red Hat
ISBN: 0-672-31104-6
$49.99 US /$70.95 CAN

Sams Teach Yourself Samba in 24 Hours
Gerald Carter
ISBN: 0-672-31609-9
$24.99 US /$34.95 CAN

SAMS

www.samspublishing.com

All prices are subject to change.

THE COMPREHENSIVE SOLUTION

Unleashed *takes you beyond the average technology discussions. It's the best resource for practical advice from experts and the most in-depth coverage of the latest information.* **Unleashed**—*the necessary tool for serious users.*

Red Hat Linux 6 Unleashed

David Pitts; Bill Ball
ISBN: 0-672-31689-7
$39.99 USA/$59.95 CAN

Other Unleashed Titles

JAVA 1.2 Class Libraries Unleashed

Krishna Sankar
0-7897-1292-X
$39.99 US/ $57.95 CAN

UNIX Unleashed, System Administrator's Edition

Robin Burk et al
0-672-30952-1
$59.99 US / $84.95 CAN

C++ Unleashed

Jesse Liberty
0-672-31239-5
$39.99 US/$57.95 CAN

JFC Unleashed

Michael Foley
0-7897-1466-3
$39.99 US/ $57.95 CAN

HTML 4 Unleashed, Second Edition

Rick Darnell
0-672-31347-2
$39.99 US/$57.95 CAN

TCP/IP Unleashed

Tim Parker
0-672-30603-4
$55.00 US/ $74.95

COBOL Unleashed

Jon Wessler
0-672-31254-9
49.99 US/$71.95 CAN

Programming Windows 98/NT Unleashed

Viktor Toth
0-672-31353-7
$49.99 US/ $70.95 CAN

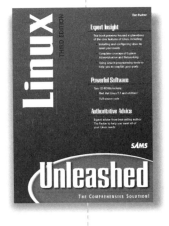

Linux Unleashed, Third Edition

David Pitts and Bill Ball
0-672-31372-3
$39.99 US /$57.95 CAN

UNIX Unleashed, Third Edition

Robin Burk
0-672-31411-8
$49.99 US / $71.95 CAN

SAMS

www.samspublishing.com

All prices are subject to change.